CANADIAN
TAX PAPER

NO.
103

# Canadian Tax Policy

## THIRD EDITION

Robin W. Boadway

Harry M. Kitchen

CANADIAN TAX FOUNDATION

L'ASSOCIATION CANADIENNE

D'ÉTUDES FISCALES

**Canadian Cataloguing in Publication Data**

Boadway, Robin W., 1943-
    Canadian tax policy

3rd ed.
(Canadian tax paper, ISSN 0008-512X; no. 103)
Includes bibliographical references and indx.
ISBN 0-88808-130-8

1. Taxation — Canada. 2. Canada — Economic policy —
1991- I. Kitchen, Harry M. II. Canadian Tax Foundation.
III. Title. IV. Series: Canadian tax papers; no. 103.

KE5669.B62 1999      336.2'00971      C99-931411-4
KF6290.ZA2B62 1999

# Contents

# List of Tables and Figures

---

## Tables

# Figures

# Preface

Traditional textbooks in public finance rarely provide a full account of the institutional details and policy implications of the Canadian tax and transfer system. As a result, instructors, students, tax policy analysts, practitioners, and others who are interested in taxation issues in Canada must consult a wide variety of sources in order to marry the analytical economic arguments with the realities of the tax-transfer system as it exists. This book is intended to simplify that undertaking. It combines a reasonably detailed account of the structure of existing taxes and transfers in Canada with an analysis of their economic effects. Although the economic literature on the subject is becoming ever more sophisticated, we have attempted to explain the economic effects of each tax and transfer in terms that will be comprehensible to the non-specialist. We hope thereby to reduce the communications gap between economists and others who are interested in the processes of tax making, tax interpretation, and tax reform—important processes that need to be widely understood.

In addition to examining the standard efficiency and fairness arguments of the more significant taxes, the book emphasizes the growing importance of international competitiveness, growth, productivity, and innovation to the formulation and analysis of tax policy issues. In particular, it discusses and evaluates several emerging policy issues, including the choice between expenditures and income as a basis for taxation, inflation and indexation, the use of refundable tax credits, the harmonization of federal and provincial taxes and the sharing of tax room by the two levels of government, the tax treatment of the family, business tax reform, and the integration of the personal and corporate income tax. The book also considers issues related to commodity taxes (with specific emphasis on the goods and services tax), payroll taxes, property taxes, and transfers to individuals.

In writing this book, we have benefited from assistance, comments, and advice from a number of individuals. Richard Bird and Roger Smith reviewed the entire manuscript and offered a number of helpful and useful comments. David Perry of the Canadian Tax Foundation willingly and enthusiastically offered suggestions, advice, and general direction throughout the editorial process. We must also thank Alex Scala for editing the manuscript and Robin MacKnight and the Canadian Tax Foundation for their ongoing support and encouragement while the book was in preparation.

Robin Boadway
Queen's University
Kingston, Ontario

Harry Kitchen
Trent University
Peterborough, Ontario

May 1999

# 1

# Canadian Tax Policy Issues at the Millennium

## Introduction: Tax Issues in a Broader Context

The purpose of this book is to survey the various elements of the Canadian tax system, to outline their institutional characteristics and their economic effects, and to assess the current state of the tax system and the suggestions that various observers have advanced for its structural reform. Tax reform is an ongoing policy issue. As time passes, economic circumstances change, technology advances, and our knowledge of the effects of taxes improves. Change has been particularly rapid in recent years. To put into context the problems policy makers face, this introductory chapter will review the factors that influence the setting in which tax policy decisions are taken.

The past two decades have seen a remarkable transformation in the issues of tax policy that Canadian governments at all levels face. This transformation reflects changes in the Canadian economy and in the economic policy-making environment generally. It is useful to begin with a review of some of the more important changes in environment and the constraints they will impose on tax policy in the coming years.

## The Opening Up of the International Economy

The Canadian economy has always been relatively open to the rest of the world. We have relied heavily on international capital to finance our development, and a high proportion of our output is traded. But the challenges facing the country from abroad have increased markedly in recent years. The free trade agreements with the United States and Mexico have exposed the economy to more competition from our neighbours. The rapid economic growth in low-wage countries, especially in Asia, have put competitive pressures on Canadian producers of tradable goods and services, making it imperative that our tax system intrude on economic decisions as little as possible. Not only are goods and services freer to move across international borders, but factors of production are as well. The globalization of world capital markets has been remarkable. International flows of financial capital can respond instantly to changes in a nation's economic circumstances, and firms themselves have become more and more footloose. Even labour is able to move more freely than before among the countries of North America, and workers with skills in high demand essentially form an international market.

The Canadian economy's increased exposure to international competition imposes important constraints on tax policy. It is generally agreed that tax systems should strive to make Canadian producers as competitive as possible. But "competitiveness" is a term that is not free of ambiguity. For example, a general non-discriminatory tax, such as a fully uniform tax on consumption, production, or payrolls, may seem to put all Canadian producers at a disadvantage vis-à-vis foreign producers and hence be "non-competitive." In fact, however, the economic law of comparative advantage implies that not all of the producers in a country can be disadvantaged: the value of the Canadian dollar (the exchange rate) will adjust to account for different levels of uniform taxation, just as it adjusts to account for changes in price levels. A competitive tax system, then, is one that does not put some producers at a disadvantage relative to others, especially foreign producers: it treats different industries uniformly and does not favour foreign producers over domestic ones.[1] As we shall see, a desire to make the tax system more uniform, or non-discriminatory, has been an important principle of tax reform in Canada in recent years. It was a major argument for the replacement in 1991 of the federal manufacturers' sales tax (MST) with the goods and services tax (GST), and for the elimination, as part of the 1987 income tax reforms, of some elements of preferential treatment from the corporate tax system. But although these measures certainly made the tax system less discriminatory, much remains to be done.

The greater international mobility of financial and physical capital also imposes constraints on domestic tax policy. Attempts to impose taxes on capital income originating in Canada—so-called *source-based taxes* on capital income—can be at least partially self-defeating. To the extent that capital flows toward the country with the highest after-tax return, source-based taxes on capital income will reduce the amount of capital in Canada and thereby impose an economic burden on factors of production in Canada that work with capital. This effect will be mitigated to the extent that foreign countries provide tax relief for taxes borne abroad by their own corporations; thus the United States, for example, offers corporate tax credits for taxes that US firms pay abroad. But crediting arrangements of this kind are usually far from perfect. Moreover, firms can often avoid one country's capital taxes by undertaking tax-planning measures. They can, for example, arrange to have their profits flow through affiliated companies in low-tax countries, engage in imaginative financing schemes to take advantage of the deductibility of interest from most corporate tax systems, or set their notional transfer prices on cross-border transactions within the firm so that their corporate income is shifted to low-tax jurisdictions. Some authors have argued that the openness

---

[1] For a discussion of the implications of business taxation for competitiveness, see Neil Bruce, "The Cost of Capital and Competitive Advantage," in Thomas J. Courchene and Douglas D. Purvis, eds., *Productivity, Growth and Canada's International Competitiveness* (Kingston, Ont.: Queen's University, John Deutsch Institute for the Study of Economic Policy, 1993), 77-117.

of capital markets and the increased importance of transnational corporations makes taxing capital income increasingly difficult.[2]

Taxation of the capital income of residents wherever it is earned, or *residence-based taxation* of capital income, does not pose the same problems as source-based taxation. Residents are less mobile than is capital and so are less likely to move to avoid the tax. On the other hand, high capital income tax rates at the personal level might provide a temptation to engage in outright evasion. It is, after all, relatively difficult to detect income earned on assets held abroad.

Similar, though less stark, problems arise from international labour mobility. If highly skilled and hence highly paid professionals are able to relocate abroad, tax systems that impose a high rate of tax at the upper end of the income scale can lead to emigration. Thus Canadian professionals may simply decide to accept employment in the United States. Alternatively, and no less ominously, firms that employ highly skilled people may decide to locate in low-tax jurisdictions. High-income persons may not, in fact, be highly responsive to differences in tax rates, especially if the higher tax rates reflect higher levels of public services,[3] but empirical evidence one way or the other is relatively scarce. So the possibility that high taxes might provoke a "brain drain" is not one that policy makers can lightly discount.

## Tax Reforms in Other Countries

The extent to which the forces of globalization work to Canada's disadvantage depends in part on tax systems abroad, especially those of our major competitors. Many other countries in the Organisation for Economic Co-operation and Development (OECD) have reformed their tax systems in order to make them conform to international realities. Although different countries have proceeded in different ways, all of their reforms have some elements in common.

---

[2] Some examples include Richard M. Bird and Charles E. McLure Jr., "The Personal Income Tax in an Interdependent World," in Sijbren Cnossen and Richard M. Bird, eds., *The Personal Income Tax: Phoenix from the Ashes* (Amsterdam: Elsevier Science Publishers, 1990), 235-55; Roger H. Gordon, "Can Capital Income Taxes Survive in Open Economies?" (July 1992), 47 *The Journal of Finance* 1159-80; and Donald J.S. Brean, "Here or There? The Source and Residence Principles of International Taxation," in Richard M. Bird and Jack M. Mintz, eds., *Taxation to 2000 and Beyond*, Canadian Tax Paper no. 93 (Toronto: Canadian Tax Foundation, 1992), 302-33. For a contrary view, see Jack M. Mintz, "Is There a Future for Capital Income Taxation?" (1994), vol. 42, no. 6 *Canadian Tax Journal* 1469-1503.

[3] Devoretz has argued that the overall impact of high tax rates on the retention of highly skilled persons in Canada is minimized because this emigration tends to be at least partially offset by the immigration of skilled persons from abroad. Of course, the latter might occur whether or not there is tax-induced emigration from Canada. See Don J. Devoretz, ed., *Diminishing Returns: The Economics of Canada's Recent Immigration Policy*, Policy Study 24 (Toronto: C.D. Howe Institute, 1995).

In the realm of commodity taxation, most OECD countries have adopted value-added tax (VAT) systems with broad bases and fairly uniform tax rates. (The major exceptions are the United States, which has no national sales tax, and Australia, where there is currently some impetus for adopting a VAT system.) Under a VAT, producers at all stages of production collect a tax on their sales but are able to claim a credit on the taxes paid on their inputs. Broadly based VAT systems have a number of economic advantages (we shall discuss these advantages more fully in the next chapter). The system of taxing sales and crediting taxes on inputs makes it possible to treat domestically produced goods on a par with foreign products: exports can be purged of domestic taxes, and imports can be taxed as if they were produced at home. This system also ensures that business and capital inputs are not inadvertently taxed, and thus that the tax system does not interfere with businesses' investment decisions. Finally, if the VAT base is defined broadly to include all goods and services, the tax system will treat all goods and services equivalently.

The widespread adoption of the VAT system of commodity taxation has had another important consequence. It has solidified the place of commodity, or indirect, taxes in the tax mix of most OECD countries. Given the efficiency with which commodity taxes can raise revenues, it is not surprising that, once they are enacted, governments rely on them heavily. An implication is that less reliance needs to be placed on direct taxes, including income, payroll, property, and capital or wealth taxes.

Among the direct taxes, the primary targets of reform have been individual and corporate income taxes. Here the emphasis has been on broadening the base, lowering the rates, and flattening the rate structure, all in order to make the tax system more efficient and less discriminatory. The fact that changes of this kind have figured prominently in tax reform in the United States has obvious implications for Canadian policy makers. Any reduction in individual and corporate income tax rates in the United States puts pressure on Canada to conform. The alternative is to risk the loss of businesses and highly skilled persons to the United States. Moreover, the apparent success of the US reforms was bound to influence political debate in Canada. It is no coincidence, therefore, that the Canadian government has in recent years broadened the income tax bases, reduced the preferential treatment of certain activities, and simplified the rate structure, though Canada has not perhaps gone as far in any of these matters as has the United States.

The other main object of tax reform on the international agenda has been to reduce taxes overall—that is, the share of gross national product (GNP) taken as tax revenues. This goal has proved somewhat more difficult to achieve than other reforms, and most countries have been content so far with arresting the growth of average tax rates.

## The Size of Government

Concern over rising tax rates reflects a more general concern about the size of government. For a variety of reasons, government expenditures have grown relentlessly as a proportion of GDP over the post-war period. Specifically, expenditures of all levels of government in Canada rose from 21.3 to 51.7 percent of GDP between 1950 and 1992. They have since declined, falling to 47.9 percent, or roughly the 1990 level, in 1995.[4] Some of the growth in expenditures may be demand-related: for example, the income elasticity of demand for public services may be greater than unity, or demographic factors such as increased longevity may increase the demand for certain types of public services. Some of it may be supply-related: for example, the relative price of providing a given level of public services may have risen because productivity growth has been lower in the public sector than in the private sector.[5] But one explanation for expenditure growth that has a direct bearing on the tax system is the post-war rise of the welfare state.

A relatively high proportion of government expenditures are for transfers rather than for goods and services, and transfers have been among the most rapidly growing components of government expenditures. The rapid growth in transfers is in part a consequence of the fact that the welfare state consolidated in the early post-war period was based on the principle of *universality*. Transfers such as those to the elderly or to children were viewed as entitlements available to all. Likewise, social insurance programs, such as unemployment insurance, were generous and far-reaching. Demographic and economic factors alike have caused programs of this kind to grow more rapidly than other expenditures, and this growth has in turn increased tax burdens.

Naturally, governments have sought ways to achieve the objectives of redistribution and economic security in less costly ways. One alternative is to target transfers more narrowly to those most in need. To the extent that income is a suitable criterion for targeting transfers, the tax system is a natural means to this end. Indeed, economists have long advocated using the income tax system to effect transfers. The so-called *negative income tax* is just such a use of the tax system for this purpose, and as our later discussion of the Canadian individual income tax system makes clear, progress toward a negative income tax has already begun. A system of refundable tax credits has been instituted as a partial substitute for universal transfers.

## Debt Reduction

Some of the impetus for reducing the size of government has come from the need to deal with the large public debts that many OECD countries accumulated during the 1980s and early 1990s. The Canadian government, like many

---

[4] See Karen Treff and David B. Perry, *Finances of the Nation, 1996* (Toronto: Canadian Tax Foundation, 1996), B:11, table B.6.

[5] This argument is from William J. Baumol, "Macroeconomics of Unbalanced Growth: The Anatomy of Urban Crisis" (June 1967), 57 *The American Economic Review* 415-26. For a fuller discussion of the sources and consequences of the relevance of the size of government in the global economy, see Robin Boadway, "The Constraints of Global Forces Are Exaggerated" (July/August 1995), 16 *Policy Options* 11-16. See also William G. Watson, *Globalization and the Meaning of Canadian Life* (Toronto: University of Toronto Press, 1998).

others, has chosen to deal with its debt by reducing government expenditures rather than by implementing discretionary tax increases. This choice, naturally, has compounded the need to find ways in which to reduce the size of the government sector without sacrificing the main objectives of government policy. At the same time, however, it has reduced the freedom available to governments for the purpose of reforming the tax system. In Canada, despite the professed desire of government to attack deficits and debts by reducing expenditures rather than increasing taxes, a rise in tax revenues has contributed more to balancing budgets than expenditure cuts. In part, this outcome has been simply a result of vigorous economic growth, which has caused tax revenues to rise naturally. It has also been a consequence, however, of the incomplete indexing of the income tax system. Bracket creep is the process whereby the increases in nominal taxable incomes that result from inflation push people into higher tax brackets and reduce the value of their credits and exemptions. Between 1988 and 1998, according to one estimate, bracket creep caused 18 percent of tax filers in Canada to become taxable or to rise into higher tax brackets. To put the matter in another way, it increased the federal income tax rate over the period by about 1.5 percentage points.[6] This has happened because the tax system is effectively indexed only for inflation rates that exceed 3 percent. Even modest rates of inflation, however, can have positive revenue effects.

Thus income tax revenues in Canada have proved to be quite elastic in their response to GDP growth. Although the government has eschewed discretionary tax increases as a method of addressing the budget deficit problem, it has been quite content to let automatic tax increases achieve a substantial part of the task. In other words, the government has been reluctant to reduce tax rates despite political pressures to do so.

## Changes in Industrial Structure

A nation's tax system must fit its economic structure. The Canadian economy, like most other industrialized economies, has undergone some fundamental restructuring over the post-war period. To put the matter simply, the service sector's share of GDP has increased significantly, in part at the expense of goods-producing industries, and this trend seems destined to continue. The commodity tax system of the first few decades of the post-war period was designed with goods production in mind; both the federal government and the provinces excluded most services from commodity taxation. As service industries became more and more important, this arrangement proved to be unduly restrictive.

Within the goods industries, the post-war tax system was designed to provide preferential treatment to particular sectors or activities deemed to be

---

[6] See Organisation for Economic Co-operation and Development, *OECD Economic Surveys 1996-1997: Canada* (Paris: OECD, 1997), 93.

important, such as investment in machinery and equipment or the manufacturing and processing of goods. This systematic favouring of certain activities complemented a longstanding policy of protecting Canadian import-competing industries, particularly manufacturing ones. In recent decades, however, bilateral and multilateral trade agreements have whittled away the traditional system of protection based on tariffs. This development, together with the growing importance of service industries, has led to a general perception that the tax structure designed for another era is no longer appropriate. This perception too has bolstered the case for broadening tax bases and making them less discriminatory.

## Increasing Inequality of Earnings

A common feature of the evolution of industrialized economies in recent years has been a tendency for the distribution of earnings (before taxes and transfers) to become more unequal over time.[7] For a variety of reasons, the demand for better-paid, higher-skilled workers has increased relative to supply more rapidly than has demand for lower-paid, less-skilled workers. One likely reason for this development is the introduction of technological improvements that have replaced low-paying jobs with machines. As well, the rapid economic growth of low-wage countries may have enhanced the comparative advantage of goods produced by higher-skilled workers in industrialized countries. In any case, the gap between high- and low-income earners appears to be growing, and this growth makes it increasingly difficult for the tax-transfer system to achieve given societal redistributive objectives. As the number of workers at the bottom end of the earnings distribution increases, so does the cost of achieving a given level of support to low-income workers and the unemployed. This consideration leads policy makers to search for more effective ways of targeting transfers to those who need them most, without making the tax burden too onerous for the most mobile members of the workforce.

## Canada's Decentralized Fiscal System

A feature that distinguishes Canada's economic system from many others, and one that has significant implications for the country's tax system, is the substantial degree of decentralization in our federation. Canadian provinces and their municipalities have considerably more fiscal responsibility than do lower-level jurisdictions in other federations. They raise more revenue than the federal government does, and they spend more as well. In fiscal year 1994-95, for example, the federal government's own-source revenue was less than $140 billion, whereas provincial and local own-source revenues were $166 billion. In the same year, federal expenditures were $174 billion and pro-

---

[7] See, for example, Charles M. Beach and George A. Slotsve, *Are We Becoming Two Societies?: Income Polarization and the Myth of the Declining Middle Class* (Toronto: C.D. Howe Institute, 1996).

vincial and local expenditures were $215 billion. Moreover, the relative impor-
tance of provincial and local expenditures has been increasing. Between 1985
and 1995, federal spending rose by 72 percent, whereas provincial and local
spending rose by 140 percent.[8] These trends reflect both the fact that
provincial and local governments provide some of the most important and
most rapidly growing public services and the fact that they have access to
virtually all of the same broad-based tax sources as the federal government.

Canada's fiscal decentralization has a number of economic advantages.
The provinces have considerable freedom to deliver public services to their
citizens in accordance with local needs and preferences. The fact that they
must raise much of their own revenues, especially those at the margin, suggests
a high degree of accountability. Moreover, the decentralization of responsibilities should lead to more cost-effective and innovative service delivery.

But fiscal decentralization also brings challenges for the tax system. For
one thing, the administrative costs of collection and compliance are likely to
be an issue in a decentralized system. If two levels of government apply taxes
to the same base, taxpayers will have to contend with two tax administrations
and comply with two different sets of rules, unless some arrangements for
harmonization are in place. Since some taxpayers operate in more than one
province, there is also a need to allocate the tax base among the provinces. In
the absence of agreed-upon rules, there is a possibility of double taxation.

In addition to raising these administrative complexities, fiscal decentralization can impair the efficiency and the equity of the tax system. If labour
and capital are mobile, provincial tax policies, intentionally or not, will affect
their allocation across provinces. In the extreme, provinces may engage in
"beggar-thy-neighbour" tax competition, which in the end will work to their
disadvantage. In addition, provincial tax policies have spillover effects on the
federal government. An increase in a province's income tax rates that reduces
its tax base will also reduce the federal tax base in the province and thereby
reduce federal income tax revenues. If provinces do not take this spillover
effect into account, they may set their tax rates too high.[9] Federal-provincial
conflicts may also arise over the extent of redistribution in the tax system. If
the provinces set their taxes independently of federal taxes, the progressivity
of the tax system as a whole may vary from province to province; thus the
provinces can to some degree thwart national redistributive policies. Whether
or not this outcome is desirable is a matter of opinion—some economists take
the view that national standards of redistributive equity should prevail; others

---

[8] These data come from Treff and Perry, supra footnote 4, at appendix A. For a broad over-
view of the evolution of the Canadian federal fiscal system, see David B. Perry, *Financing the
Canadian Federation, 1867 to 1995: Setting the Stage for Change*, Canadian Tax Paper no. 102
(Toronto: Canadian Tax Foundation, 1997).

[9] For a survey of the various fiscal spillovers that can arise among governments in a federation, see Bev Dahlby, "Fiscal Externalities and the Design of Intergovernmental Grants"
(July 1996), 3 *International Tax and Public Finance* 397-412.

argue that individual communities should be allowed to choose the extent of redistribution that best suits their societal norms. In any case, the provinces' power to act independently in matters of taxation can compromise their ability to achieve even their own redistributive objectives. If some provinces were to decide that less generous transfers to the poor and less onerous taxes on the rich would both discourage the poor from residing within their boundaries and attract the rich, the result might be a "race to the bottom"— that is, an episode of tax competition that ended with all of the provinces' implementing less redistribution than their citizens actually wanted.

These considerations suggest that fiscal decentralization is a mixed blessing. Desire to avoid the worst consequences of the decentralization of tax responsibilities can affect the sharing of various tax sources between the federal and provincial levels of government in a federation. For example, taxes on mobile tax bases (such as business income) may be less decentralized than taxes on less mobile bases (such as consumption or real property). Taxes that are especially important for the purposes of redistribution (such as direct taxes and wealth transfer taxes) may also be more centralized than other taxes. Moreover, for taxes that are decentralized, there may be negotiated fiscal arrangements that seek to avoid the worst consequences of decentralization. These arrangements may, for example, harmonize federal and provincial tax bases in order to avoid the administrative complexities that arise when tax bases are not uniform. They may also include fiscal transfers to the provinces in order to avoid the inefficiencies and inequities across the federation that would otherwise arise from interprovincial differences in tax rates.[10] These considerations will play an important part in our examination of the Canadian tax system, given the extent to which that system is decentralized to the provinces.

## An Overview of the Canadian Tax System

The Canadian tax system consists of a mix of taxes levied by both the federal government and the provincial governments. The mix includes both *direct* taxes—taxes that are levied directly on taxpayers, such as income, wealth, and payroll taxes—and *indirect* taxes—taxes that are levied on transactions, such as general sales taxes and specific excise taxes. Since many of these taxes are levied on a relatively broad base, there is considerable overlap among them, with the result that the same base effectively bears several taxes. This state of affairs is common in all countries, and it is typically justified on the ground that compliance problems and adverse incentives may arise if the tax rate on any one base is too large.

To put the relevance of various tax policy issues into perspective, it is useful to begin with a statistical summary of the Canadian tax system. We

---

[10] For a discussion of the role of the fiscal arrangements in a federation, see Robin W. Boadway and Paul A.R. Hobson, *Intergovernmental Fiscal Relations in Canada*, Canadian Tax Paper no. 96 (Toronto: Canadian Tax Foundation, 1993).

shall follow this with a summary of the structure of the main taxes used in Canada. The following tables paint a picture of the relative magnitude of various taxes in Canada, how these taxes are divided among the three levels of government, how they compare with taxes in other countries, and how they have changed over time.

## A Statistical Summary of Canadian Taxation

Table 1.1 shows how tax collections by each level of government evolved over the period 1926 to 1996. Of interest here is the fact that taxes in total increased from 13.4 percent of GDP in 1926 to 21.4 percent in 1950 to 36.6 percent in 1996. The rise has not been even, however. It was fairly rapid up to the end of World War II and then fell off. It rose at a steady pace during the 1950s and 1960s as the post-war welfare state took shape. The rate of increase tailed off in the 1980s but rose dramatically in the 1990s as governments addressed their large budgetary deficits.

Of particular relevance for Canada is the changing distribution of tax collections by level of government. Local government taxation as a share of GDP has remained remarkably stable since the 1920s; if anything, it has fallen slightly. Throughout the post-war period, local taxation has been roughly 4 percent of GDP. Both federal and provincial taxation have grown markedly since 1926, but in the post-war period federal taxation has grown significantly less than has provincial taxation. In 1996, the federal government still collected more revenue than the provinces did, but provincial and local tax revenues combined exceeded federal tax revenues. This state of affairs makes Canada one of the most fiscally decentralized federations in the world—a circumstance that has potentially profound implications for tax policy, as we shall emphasize from time to time in this book.

Table 1.2 indicates the importance of each of the main taxes used by the federal government and by provincial and municipal governments. As the table indicates, the federal government and the provinces jointly occupy four broad tax bases—individual income taxes, corporate income taxes, general sales taxes, and payroll taxes. As well, both levy excise taxes. The provinces have as an additional source of revenue taxes on renewable and non-renewable resources. The municipalities rely heavily on property taxes. The table shows how the mix of taxes used by the federal and provincial/municipal levels of government have changed since 1970. The proportion of total revenues obtained from the personal income tax has risen gradually from 28.4 percent in 1970 to almost 34 percent in 1995, and the federal government and the provinces have shared in this gain. General sales tax revenues rose dramatically in the 1990s, after having fallen in previous decades. The increase is almost entirely attributable to the increase in federal revenues from this source. Corporate taxes have become less important since 1970, as have excise and customs duties. Property taxes, which are in the domain of the provinces and their municipalities, have risen in the 1990s after having declined over the previous two decades. Payroll taxes too have increased in the past few years, mainly at the federal level.

**Table 1.1 Total Taxes by Level of Government and as a Percentage of GDP for Selected Years**

| Year | Federal $ million | Federal Percent of GDP | Provincial $ million | Provincial Percent of GDP | Local $ million | Local Percent of GDP | Total $ million | Total Percent of GDP |
|------|------------------|------------------------|----------------------|---------------------------|-----------------|----------------------|-----------------|----------------------|
| 1926 ... | 355 | 6.6 | 110 | 2.0 | 252 | 4.7 | 717 | 13.4 |
| 1939 ... | 470 | 8.0 | 234 | 4.0 | 284 | 4.8 | 988 | 16.8 |
| 1946 ... | 2,447 | 20.1 | 417 | 3.4 | 332 | 2.7 | 3,196 | 26.3 |
| 1950 ... | 5,313 | 14.7 | 1,160 | 4.0 | 1,024 | 32.6 | 7,497 | 21.4 |
| 1960 ... | 9,896 | 15.4 | 4,647 | 4.3 | 2,477 | 4.0 | 17,020 | 23.7 |
| 1970 ... | 34,398 | 15.8 | 19,250 | 9.1 | 7,186 | 4.1 | 60,834 | 30.1 |
| 1980 ... | 61,414 | 14.6 | 36,824 | 10.5 | 12,233 | 3.3 | 110,471 | 29.5 |
| 1985 ... | 74,249 | 15.5 | 55,158 | 11.5 | 15,433 | 3.2 | 150,536 | 31.5 |
| 1990 ... | 113,213 | 16.9 | 90,666 | 13.6 | 24,274 | 3.6 | 238,271 | 35.6 |
| 1993 ... | 121,766 | 17.1 | 93,629 | 13.1 | 29,163 | 4.1 | 256,274 | 36.0 |
| 1996 ... | 137,176 | 17.2 | 109,614 | 13.8 | 30,362 | 3.8 | 291,913 | 36.6 |

Source: Karin Treff and David B. Perry, *Finances of the Nation, 1997* (Toronto: Canadian Tax Foundation, 1997), B:8-9, table B.5.

Table 1.3 shows how tax revenue as a percentage of GDP in Canada and the other countries in the Group of Seven (G7) changed over the period 1965 to 1994; it also compares the G7 figures with the averages for all members of the OECD. (The G7 consists of the seven largest industrialized economies in the world; the OECD includes all industrialized countries.) In 1994, taxes in Canada were 36.1 percent of GDP, or somewhat less than the OECD average of 38.4 percent. The ratio for Canada was fourth among the ratios for the G7; it was lower than the ratios for the three continental European countries but significantly higher than those for Japan and the United States. Taxes were only 27.6 percent of GDP in the United States, a figure almost one-quarter less than the figure for Canada. With one exception, the G7 countries, including Canada, have seen their tax revenues grow gradually and at much the same rate relative to GDP over the past 30 years. The exception is the United States, where taxes as a percentage of GDP have increased relatively little. Indeed, the Canadian and US ratios have diverged gradually since 1965, when they were roughly the same.

Table 1.4 compares Canada's tax mix with those of the other G7 countries and with the OECD averages for the main tax categories. As the table shows, reliance on individual income taxes is much greater in Canada than in any other G7 country, and the figure for Canada is also greater than the OECD average. Canada also makes greater use of property taxes than do the other G7 countries, and in this case the contrast with the OECD average is especially pronounced. Corporate taxes are everywhere a relatively small revenue source, and their importance in Canada is roughly comparable with their importance in other industrialized nations. Canada uses taxes on commodities less than all other G7 countries except Japan and the United States. Finally, although payroll taxes are becoming more important in Canada, this

Table 1.2   Taxes as a Percentage of Total Revenue by Type
and Level of Government

|  | 1970 | 1975 | 1980 | 1985 | 1995 |
|---|---|---|---|---|---|
| Personal income tax .............. | 28.4 | 28.9 | 28.6 | 30.4 | 33.9 |
| Federal .................... | 20.0 | 19.3 | 17.6 | 18.7 | 20.5 |
| Provincial/municipal ......... | 8.4 | 9.6 | 11.0 | 11.7 | 13.4 |
| Corporate tax ................. | 9.9 | 11.8 | 9.5 | 8.4 | 6.5 |
| Federal .................... | 7.5 | 8.7 | 6.7 | 6.2 | 4.3 |
| Provincial/municipal ......... | 2.4 | 3.1 | 2.8 | 2.2 | 2.1 |
| Property tax .................. | 10.9 | 8.3 | 8.1 | 8.9 | 11.1 |
| Federal .................... | 0.0 | 0.0 | 0.0 | 0.0 | 0.0 |
| Provincial/municipal ......... | 10.9 | 8.3 | 8.1 | 8.9 | 11.1 |
| General sales tax .............. | 12.7 | 10.8 | 9.7 | 10.8 | 14.0 |
| Federal .................... | 7.1 | 5.3 | 4.5 | 4.6 | 6.9 |
| Provincial/municipal ......... | 5.6 | 5.5 | 5.2 | 6.2 | 7.1 |
| Excise/customs tax .............. | 9.3 | 7.9 | 6.4 | 7.3 | 6.4 |
| Federal .................... | 5.3 | 5.5 | 2.2 | 4.1 | 3.7 |
| Provincial/municipal ......... | 4.0 | 2.7 | 4.4 | 3.2 | 2.7 |
| Payroll tax ................... | 8.5 | 8.6 | 8.7 | 8.4 | 9.7 |
| Federal .................... | 4.1 | 5.1 | 4.9 | 4.6 | 6.3 |
| Provincial/municipal ......... | 4.4 | 3.5 | 3.8 | 3.8 | 3.4 |
| Other taxes .................. | 3.0 | 3.8 | 4.5 | 10.3 | na |
| Federal .................... | 1.4 | 2.5 | 1.3 | 4.1 | na |
| Provincial/municipal ......... | 1.6 | 1.3 | 3.2 | 6.2 | na |
| Non-tax revenue ............... | 17.4 | 19.8 | 24.5 | 15.5 | 14.1 |
| Federal .................... | 5.9 | 5.8 | 6.6 | 4.6 | 3.5 |
| Provincial/municipal ......... | 11.5 | 14.0 | 17.9 | 11.0 | 10.6 |
| Total ........................ | 100.0 | 100.0 | 100.0 | 100.0 | 100.0 |
| Federal .................... | 51.3 | 52.0 | 47.7 | 46.9 | 45.3 |
| Provincial/municipal ......... | 48.7 | 48.0 | 52.3 | 53.1 | 54.7 |

na   not available.

Source: Canadian Tax Foundation, *The National Finances* and *Finances of the Nation*,
various years.

Table 1.3   Tax Revenue as a Percentage of GDP:
International Comparisons

|  | 1965 | 1970 | 1975 | 1980 | 1985 | 1994 |
|---|---|---|---|---|---|---|
| Canada ................. | 25.9 | 31.3 | 32.4 | 31.6 | 33.1 | 36.1 |
| France................... | 34.5 | 35.1 | 36.9 | 41.7 | 44.5 | 44.1 |
| Germany................. | 31.6 | 32.9 | 36.0 | 38.2 | 38.1 | 39.3 |
| Italy ................... | 25.5 | 26.1 | 26.2 | 30.2 | 34.5 | 41.7 |
| Japan .................. | 18.3 | 19.7 | 20.9 | 25.4 | 27.5 | 27.8 |
| United Kingdom .......... | 30.4 | 36.9 | 35.5 | 35.3 | 37.9 | 34.1 |
| United States ............ | 25.8 | 29.2 | 29.0 | 29.3 | 28.7 | 27.6 |
| OECD average ........... | 26.5 | 29.7 | 32.7 | 35.0 | 36.9 | 38.4 |

Source: David B. Perry, "International Tax Comparisons," Fiscal Figures feature (1995),
vol. 43, no. 6 *Canadian Tax Journal* 2256-64.

**Table 1.4  Tax Mixes in the Group of Seven Countries, 1994**

| | Individual income taxes | Corporate income taxes | Payroll taxes | Goods and services taxes | Property taxes |
|---|---|---|---|---|---|
| | *percentage of GDP* | | | | |
| Canada .............. | 13.4 | 2.4 | 6.1 | 9.5 | 4.0 |
| France .............. | 6.2 | 1.6 | 19.1 | 12.0 | 2.3 |
| Germany ............. | 10.4 | 1.1 | 15.4 | 11.3 | 1.1 |
| Italy ............... | 10.6 | 3.7 | 13.0 | 11.8 | 2.3 |
| Japan ............... | 5.4 | 4.1 | 9.8 | 4.3 | 3.2 |
| United Kingdom ....... | 9.4 | 2.7 | 6.1 | 12.0 | 3.7 |
| United States ......... | 9.8 | 2.5 | 7.0 | 5.0 | 3.3 |
| OECD average ........ | 10.7 | 2.9 | 10.2 | 12.1 | 1.9 |

Source: Same as table 1.3.

country's use of them is still well below their use in most of the other G7 countries and in the OECD as a whole.

## The Structure of Canadian Taxes

We shall deal separately with all of the main tax types in subsequent chapters, but it is worthwhile to summarize their key features here. The following discussion concentrates on the most general properties of each tax.

### The Personal Income Tax

Canadian residents are obliged to pay tax on their taxable incomes earned worldwide to the federal government and to the provinces in which they reside. Each taxpayer calculates his taxable income (total income less allowable deductions), applies a rate schedule to the resulting figure to determine tax liabilities, and then subtracts various non-refundable credits to yield "basic federal tax." Taxes owing to the federal government are equal to basic federal tax plus, for high-income taxpayers, some temporary surtaxes or minus, for low-income taxpayers, some additional and, in this case, refundable tax credits (if a taxpayer ends up with negative taxes owing, the refundable credits are actually paid out). Provincial taxes are then calculated in one of two ways. In all of the provinces except Quebec, taxpayers currently compute their provincial tax liabilities by applying a provincially determined tax rate to basic federal tax and deducting provincial tax credits from the calculated amount. Revenue Canada acts as the tax-collecting agency for these provinces, a quid pro quo for the provinces' having adopted the federal base and rate structure. Each of the provinces that have accepted this arrangement has negotiated a *tax collection agreement* with the federal government. Quebec chooses not to participate in a tax collection agreement. It legislates its own income tax system, and taxpayers resident in that province must fill out a separate provincial return. In practice, however, the structure of the Quebec income tax is similar to the structure of the other provincial taxes.

The description presented here refers to the income tax system as defined by the federal government.

Taxable income is defined to include most sources of income, including labour income (wages, salaries, and income from self-employment), capital income (interest, dividends, and capital gains), property income, including income from intellectual property (rent, royalties), and transfers (pensions and employment insurance benefits). There are some exceptions. Some types of capital income are *sheltered* from income tax. The main example is capital income on savings for retirement through either an employer-operated scheme—a registered pension plan (RPP)—or a self-operated scheme—a registered retirement savings plan (RRSP). Individual investments in human capital (education, training) are treated in the same manner as retirement savings except that the returns cannot be deferred until retirement—they must be taken when higher incomes are earned. They are therefore partially sheltered. Some types of capital or property income are exempt from tax. The most important type of income in this category is imputed income on owner-occupied housing and other consumer durables. Only three-quarters of capital gains are taxable. Some transfers are exempt, the most important being welfare payments and inheritances. Deductions are allowed for various expenditures deemed to be costs of earning income (such as union dues, moving costs, and child care expenses).

The rate structure that is applied to taxable income consists of three tiers, or brackets. There are non-refundable tax credits for basic living expenses, family size, age, and disability, and temporary surtaxes for high-income persons. Additional non-refundable credits are available for charitable donations, medical expenses, political contributions, tuition fees, and social insurance contributions. Two refundable tax credits are used to deliver assistance to low-income taxpayers—a goods and services tax (GST) credit based on family income and size, and a child tax benefit based on the number of children and family income. These credits are a potentially significant innovation, since they represent a potential for delivering social policy through the tax system. A dividend tax credit is available for dividends received from taxable Canadian corporations. The dividend tax credit is a measure for integrating the personal and corporate income taxes, and it is intended to compensate shareholders for corporate taxes withheld on their behalf. Finally, taxpayers are allowed a credit for foreign taxes paid on their incomes. This credit ensures that taxpayers are not taxed twice on the same income.

The tax system is indexed annually for inflation. The indexation factor is the change in the consumer price index (CPI) less 3 percent, and it is applied to the tax credits and the tax brackets. Indexation has not been triggered since 1992, the last year in which inflation was above 3 percent.

As we have mentioned, all of the provinces except Quebec have signed tax collection agreements with the federal government; the agreements are a means of harmonizing federal and provincial individual income taxes. The provinces abide by the federal base and rate structure and simply apply tax rates of their own choosing to basic federal tax. Provinces are also allowed to apply their own provincial tax credits, provided that the credits are non-discriminatory, easy to administer, and non-distortionary, and that they respect the common base.[11] Revenue Canada collects provincial individual income taxes for the agreeing provinces.

## The Corporate Income Tax

For tax purposes, corporations resident in Canada are treated much like individuals: they are taxed on their income earned anywhere in the world. In addition, non-resident corporations are taxed on the income they earn in Canada. Taxable income of corporations is defined as being the same as business income of unincorporated businesses, which is taxed as the income of the individual owners. Corporate taxable income is meant to reflect the income earned by the shareholders of the corporation—that is, the equity income of the corporation. Income accruing to a corporation's debt holders is taxed in the hands of the owners, which may be either individuals or other corporations. The definition of taxable income basically mirrors the definition used in standard accounting practices. It includes all revenues less current costs less allowable capital costs, where all items are measured on an accrual basis rather than a cash-flow basis.[12] Revenues include both revenues from the sale of goods and services and income received from financial assets, except for dividends from Canadian corporations (which have already been taxed at source). Current costs include payments for current inputs such as labour, materials, business services, promotions, rents, and so on. Capital costs include all interest costs and the costs of using capital inputs—that is, inputs that are used to produce output over a period of time. In the case of depreciable capital (machinery and equipment, and buildings), the allowance is a *capital cost allowance*. In the case of inventories, it is the cost of drawing down the inventory at the time of use (rather than at the time of purchase). Some resource properties are allowed a *depletion allowance*.

The distinction between capital costs and current costs is not always clear. In many instances, costs of a capital nature are treated as if they were current and are deducted when they are incurred. Firms may deduct expenditures for advertising, research and development (R & D), and exploration when they occur despite the fact that they yield benefits in future tax periods. The same principle applies to human capital investment, such as employee training. Firms may also deduct immediately the cost of acquiring certain resource properties. The fact that the corporate tax provisions treat some capital

---

[11] The last requirement is in fact flexible, since three provinces are allowed under their tax collection agreements to levy flat rate taxes on net income. Moreover, the federal government has agreed to let the provinces apply rate structures of their own choosing to the federal base in 2001 and thereafter. We shall discuss this innovation in more detail in chapter 3.

[12] That is, revenues and costs are included when the transaction takes place rather than when payment is consummated. Thus, revenues include accounts receivable and costs include accounts payable.

expenditures as if they were current has important implications for the effect of the corporate tax on different types of business activities, a point that we shall discuss in chapter 4.

The federal government applies a single basic federal rate to corporate taxable income, though with some exceptions. Corporate income earned outside of Canada is taxed at a higher rate, in consequence of the fact that no provincial tax applies. Lower rates apply to manufacturing and processing income earned in Canada, and to the income of small Canadian-controlled private corporations.[13] There is also a temporary surtax in place. The provinces apply their own corporate taxes. As in the case of the individual income tax, however, the provinces can sign a tax collection agreement with the federal government. In this case, the province chooses a tax rate to apply to federal taxable income, and Revenue Canada administers the provincial tax jointly with the federal tax. Alberta, Ontario, and Quebec administer their own corporate income taxes. In practice, their tax bases are quite similar to federal taxable income. All of the provinces, including the three that administer their own taxes, abide by the same *allocation formula* for determining how the income of a corporation that operates in more than one province is to be allocated among provinces. A province's allocation is the average of the province's share of the corporation's sales revenues and its payroll.

Like the individual income tax system, the corporate tax system makes various tax credits available. At the federal level, there is an investment tax credit for new investments in depreciable capital in regions of very high unemployment. Research and development expenditures are eligible for a tax credit, as are charitable donations and gifts, political contributions, and wages and salaries incurred in making films in Canada. Firms may also claim credits against Canadian tax liabilities for corporate taxes paid to foreign governments. The provinces, including those that participate in tax collection agreements, offer their own tax credits for a variety of expenditures; they include credits for particular industrial activities such as R & D, investment, and resource activities.

An important feature of the corporate income tax system is its treatment of businesses with negative taxable income in a given year. Negative tax liabilities can be carried forward and backward for limited periods, but without interest. Thus the treatment of losses is not symmetrical with the treatment of profits, which are always taxed in the same year. Firms that are likely to experience losses, such as small, growing firms and firms in risky businesses, are treated less favourably than firms whose income streams are steady or firms—usually large firms—that are able to offset losses in some areas of operation against profits in others. As it happens, small firms and risky firms are often important sources of employment growth and innovation.

---

[13] A Canadian-controlled private corporation is a private corporation, resident in Canada, that is not controlled by one or more non-resident persons or by any public corporations.

Unlike the individual income tax system, which provides partial indexing of tax brackets and credits for inflation, the corporate income tax system is not indexed. All components of taxable income are measured in nominal terms, with no relief for inflation. This state of affairs has especially important implications for capital costs. In a world of inflation, interest costs tend to increase to compensate lenders for the fact that the real value of loans has eroded: a $10,000 bond will be worth 5 percent less after a year in which the prices of goods and services have risen by 5 percent. If interest rates rise by 5 percent to reflect the reduction in the underlying value of the asset, the interest payment will include that reduction. If borrowing businesses can deduct the full nominal cost of the interest, they are in effect being allowed to deduct a partial repayment of the loan. The result is an understatement of true shareholder profits. On the other hand, the rate at which businesses are able to deduct the use of capital goods, by means of the capital cost allowance and the inventory deduction, will understate the true cost of using the capital. The deductions will be based on the original (historic) cost of acquiring the assets, but meanwhile the assets' replacement cost will have risen. Consequently, the firms' profits will be overstated. Whether, on balance, inflation causes a given firm's profits to be understated or overstated depends upon the importance to the firm of the interest deduction relative to the capital cost and inventory deductions. The less a firm relies on interest financing, the more likely it is that inflation will cause the firm's taxable income to overstate its true profits. In any case, the effect of inflation on taxable profits is likely to vary from business to business, and therefore inflation introduces capricious elements into the tax treatment of different firms.

As we have mentioned, the corporate tax is intended to be a tax on the equity income earned by corporations on behalf of their shareholders. This immediately raises the issue—an important one in later chapters—of the relation of the corporate tax to the personal tax. The most obvious question is, Why do we need a corporate tax as well as the individual tax? Why not just tax shareholders' incomes at the individual level? The simple answer is that if corporate source income were taxed only in the hands of the shareholder, shareholders could postpone paying the tax by retaining the income in the corporation rather than taking it as dividends or capital gains.[14] According to this view, the corporate tax serves as an indispensable *withholding tax* on income earned on behalf of shareholders. It may also be viewed as a withholding tax on foreign shareholders whose incomes might otherwise escape Canadian tax completely. As chapter 4 will suggest, the corporate tax may be more than a withholding tax, but viewing it from a withholding perspective suggests that measures should be taken to ensure that taxes withheld at the corporate level be recognized at the personal level as having been paid. That is, the two systems should be *integrated*. In the Canadian system, the vehicle for integration is the dividend tax credit. As mentioned,

---

[14] If capital gains were taxed as they accrued, rather than as they are realized, this argument would have much less force. But taxing capital gains on accrual is very difficult.

this is a credit paid to individual taxpayers based on the dividends they receive from Canadian corporations. The dividend tax credit is an imperfect integration device, since the amount of the credit bears no direct relation to the amount of corporate tax that had been paid on the earnings from which the dividend results. For example, the credit applies whether the corporation is in a tax-paying position or not, or whether it is engaged in a tax-favoured activity or not.

In addition to corporate income taxes, both the federal government and the provinces impose capital taxes on corporations. The federal government imposes a general capital tax on all of the capital of all large corporations, and a heavier tax on the capital of financial institutions. The base for the general capital tax is the value of shareholders' equity plus most liabilities. For financial institutions, the base is shareholders' equity plus long-term debt. All of the provinces also impose a capital tax on banks and on trust and loan companies. Seven provinces also have a general capital tax.

As we have shown, the corporate tax system provides incentives for certain types of business activity and disincentives for others. Some of this bias is intentional: thus the tax system sets a preferential rate for manufacturing and processing and provides tax credits for new investment and R & D. Some of it is unintentional: thus inflation affects the tax treatment of different firms differently, and firms in risky industries receive adverse tax treatment relative to other firms when they show a loss. In short, the tax system can influence the relative profitability of different types of businesses, and thereby harm the ability of some businesses to compete. Much of the impetus for business tax reform in recent years has been a desire to remove the differential treatment accorded to different types of business activities and put all activities on a "level playing field."

## General Sales Taxation

The income tax is the most broadly based of the taxes typically used in industrialized countries. If the income tax base were used in Canada in its most general form, it would include all of gross national product (GNP), which is the measure of income earned at home and abroad by Canadians, and would also include income earned in Canada by non-residents. Most other tax bases are less broadly defined, though they may nevertheless overlap considerably with the income base. The base for a general sales tax is usually restricted to consumption expenditures and so differs from gross domestic product (GDP), which is the value of all goods and services produced by the national economy, by excluding investment goods, government expenditures, and exports and including imports.

Canada's federal general sales tax, the GST, is of this form. It is a value-added tax on consumption whose base includes almost all consumption goods and services on a destination basis. Investment goods, exports, and government expenditures are not taxed, but imported consumer goods are.

The main exceptions to the GST's comprehensiveness as a consumption-based tax are food, which is not taxed, and sales by very small firms, residential rents, health services, and educational services, all of which are exempt at the point of sale.[15] Rebates are given on inputs purchased by municipalities, universities, schools, and hospitals (the so-called MUSH sector). A preferential tax rate applies to sale of new housing. On balance, the GST is a fairly uniform tax that applies to a very broad base, one that includes most consumption expenditures.

All of the provinces but Alberta also have general sales taxes of their own. In some cases, the tax is harmonized with the GST; in others, it is not. New Brunswick, Newfoundland, and Nova Scotia have all fully harmonized their sales taxes with the federal GST. All of these provinces apply a single value-added tax, referred to as the harmonized sales tax (HST). It is essentially equivalent to the GST except that the rate includes a uniform provincial rate for the three provinces. The HST effectively operates as a revenue-sharing system. The revenues that represent the provincial portion of the HST tax rate are paid to the provinces according to estimated final consumption in each province. Obviously, the provinces must abide by the base and rate structure of the federal GST. Quebec retains its own general sales tax, which is a type of value-added tax and extends to most goods and services, but this tax is partially harmonized with the GST. The unique feature of the harmonization arrangement is that Revenue Québec acts as the tax collector not only for its own tax, but also for the federal GST within Quebec. In all of the other provinces with general sales taxes, the tax is a single-stage retail sales tax (RST) that applies to a base much narrower than the GST base. Most services are exempt, and many goods as well, and the rate structures tend to be much less uniform than the GST rate structure. This is so because the provinces use their retail sales taxes to achieve their own policy goals, including vertical equity and the favouring of certain activities. Thus the provincial RSTs favour goods that are important to low-income families and services. Moreover, because the retail sales tax is a single-stage tax, many business inputs are taxed and exports contain taxes paid at earlier stages of production.

## Specific Commodity Taxes

Both levels of government also levy specific excise taxes or duties on a limited range of goods. The most important are excises on alcoholic beverages, tobacco products, and motor fuels. Since the bases for these taxes appear to be relatively unresponsive to price increases, the taxes have an

---

[15] Goods whose sales are *exempt* escape taxation at the retail stage. The GST, however, has been paid at earlier stages and is not credited at the exempt stage. The result is that only the value added at the exempt stage escapes tax. Goods, such as food, that bear no tax are said to be *zero-rated*. They bear no tax when sold to consumers, but in addition the retailer may claim a tax credit on purchases of the product from the previous stage. The implication is that the full value of the product escapes tax.

obvious usefulness as revenue sources. Otherwise, the usual justification for their use is that they correct for adverse externalities or serve as benefit taxes (user fees) for large-expenditure items such as transportation facilities, hospital services, and police services. The various roles of specific excise taxes are discussed more fully in chapter 5.

## Payroll Taxes

Another set of potentially broadly based taxes are those based on wages and salaries. Like the general sales tax bases, the bases for these taxes include a large proportion of GDP (or GNP). Thus payroll taxes are another source of overlap among tax bases. Unlike income and consumption taxes, however, payroll taxes in Canada have been used in a relatively limited way and earmarked for specific expenditure programs. Both the federal government and the provinces make some use of payroll taxes, mainly to finance social insurance programs. The federal government finances both employment insurance (EI) and the Canada Pension Plan (CPP) by payroll taxes, and in both cases the tax is based on earnings and subject to upper limits. These taxes are paid by both employers and employees. Several provinces levy small payroll taxes, often earmarked for health financing, and Quebec levies a payroll tax to finance the Quebec Pension Plan (QPP). Provincial workers' compensation programs are financed by employer contributions that are based on payrolls. Despite their limited use at present, payroll taxes are potentially an important part of the Canadian tax mix. As table 1.4 has shown, many countries make much heavier use of them than Canada does.

## Natural Resource Revenues

Natural resources are an important source of wealth and economic activity in Canada, and therefore a natural object of taxation. Provinces have the de facto right to raise revenues from renewable and non-renewable resources located within their own borders. Since different provinces are endowed with very different types and quantities of resources, it is not surprising that the nature of resource taxation and the amounts of revenue generated from resources vary considerably across the provinces. Revenues from oil and gas production derive from sales of leases, production taxes, and royalties on production. Mining operations are subject to mining taxes and leases, which typically apply to some measure of profits but differ by type of mineral and by province. Forestry revenues include leases, stumpage fees, and royalties. Fishing generates revenues through licences and permits. Finally, water power revenues come from the profits of provincially owned hydroelectric corporations and from water power rentals. Very few natural resource revenues are based on the true rent of the resource, though provinces are moving increasingly toward net-profit taxation regimes. The existence of resource taxes can have considerable influence on decisions by firms to explore for natural resources, and to exploit natural resources once they have been acquired.

## Property Taxes

Real property represents another potentially large general tax base. Taxes on property are a natural source of local revenues, given the immobility of the tax base and the difficulty of avoiding the tax. They are used to finance local services and varying proportions of education and welfare services. In some provinces, the property tax is a provincial tax, though the municipalities have some ability to impose their own rates. In others, the tax is levied by the municipalities. The tax rate applies to some measure of assessed value for each piece of real property (land and buildings). Assessment practices vary considerably across the provinces and even across municipalities within a province. Some provinces use relatively recent market values and update them frequently. Others use property values from as long ago as the 1950s. Property tax rates differ for residential, commercial, and industrial properties; residential properties typically bear the lowest rate. Municipalities often levy separate business taxes on the users (rather than the owners) of business properties. Altogether, property taxes are often an important part of the costs of doing business, though that importance varies substantially across jurisdictions.

## Federal-Provincial Transfers

Provincial governments obtain only part of their revenues from own sources. A significant proportion comes from the federal government in the form of transfers. Although it is not an important purpose of this book to consider non-tax sources of revenue, it is worthwhile to briefly summarize the relevance of federal-provincial transfers for the tax system.[16]

The transfer system has two main components—the Canada health and social transfer (CHST) and equalization. Roughly speaking, the CHST is primarily a vertical transfer with only a limited intent to redistribute among the provinces, whereas equalization is meant to redistribute horizontally among the provinces. The CHST replaced the established programs financing (EPF) and Canada assistance plan (CAP) transfers in 1996. The EPF transfers were approximately equal per capita, whereas the CAP transfers varied with welfare expenditures across the provinces—though a cap on transfers applied to the three wealthiest provinces. The CHST initially retained the CAP formula for distribution of the transfers, but the transfers themselves were much smaller than they had been under EPF and the CAP.[17] The 1999 federal budget has transformed CHST transfers into an equal per-capita amount for all provinces.

---

[16] A more detailed summary of the system of federal-provincial fiscal arrangements may be found in Perry, supra footnote 8. The implications of the fiscal arrangements for tax policy are addressed in Boadway and Hobson, supra footnote 10.

[17] Federal cash transfers for EPF and CAP were $27.1 billion in 1995-96, and the CHST transfers that replaced them amounted to $21 billion in 1998-99. See "Reforming Federal-Provincial Fiscal Arrangements: Towards a National Consensus," paper prepared for the meeting of Provincial and Territorial Finance Ministers, June 8, 1998.

The size of the CHST helps to determine the amount of tax room that the provinces must occupy in order to finance their expenditure responsibilities. Although this circumstance does not directly affect the overall tax structure, the size of the CHST could have indirect, and longer run, consequences for the tax structure. The smaller is the CHST transfer, the smaller will be the share of tax room occupied by the federal government. A diminution of federal tax room might make it more difficult both to maintain the system of income tax harmonization and to extend tax harmonization to other tax sources, especially sales taxes. The tax collection agreement system has, for historic reasons, relied on the federal government to set the tax base and rate structure. As the provinces obtain a larger and larger share of the available income tax room, they naturally want more and more say in setting tax policy, including the choice of the base and rate structure. Not surprisingly, as income tax room has devolved to the provinces, the tax collection agreements system has come under more and more strain. To the extent that federal-provincial transfers have eroded, so too, perhaps, has the system of tax harmonization. Of course, the effect of federal transfers to the provinces on tax harmonization is not the only factor that determines the optimal size of the transfers. Our purpose here is simply to draw attention to this effect as one potential cause of a reduction in the importance of federal transfers to the provinces.

Equalization payments are made to those provinces whose ability to raise revenues falls below a national norm. According to section 36(2) of the Constitution Act, 1982, their purpose is "to ensure that provincial governments have sufficient revenues to provide reasonably comparable levels of public services at reasonably comparable levels of taxation." To the extent that the equalization system fulfils this principle of the Canadian constitution, it is said to enable citizens to be treated similarly wherever they reside and to prevent mobile resources from moving to wealthier provinces not in order to take advantage of differences in productivity but simply in order to achieve the benefits of lower tax rates.

All of the provinces except Alberta, British Columbia, and Ontario currently qualify for equalization. The calculation of equalization entitlements is, in principle, straightforward. For each of 37 different provincial revenue sources, the federal government defines a standardized base that is representative of the various bases used by the provinces and calculates the size of this tax base for each province. It then calculates a *national average tax rate* for that base by dividing total provincial revenues by the sum of the tax bases of all of the provinces. The next step is to calculate for each province the amount of tax revenues per capita that would be collected by applying the national average tax rate to the province's base. The federal authorities then calculate the amount of revenue that would be obtained by applying the national average tax rate to the per-capita tax base averaged over five representative provinces (British Columbia, Manitoba, Ontario, Quebec, and Saskatchewan). Each province's per-capita equalization entitlement (positive or negative) for the revenue source in question is the difference between the amount calculated for the representative five provinces and the amount calculated for the province itself. This procedure is repeated for each of the 37 revenue sources, and the total per-capita equalization entitlement for each province is the sum of its entitlements for all of the revenue sources. Each of the seven provinces with positive aggregate equalization entitlements receives a transfer equal to the aggregate per-capita entitlement times provincial population. The other three provinces receive no transfers.

The final result of the equalization system is that the provinces can provide public services at tax rates that vary from province to province much less than they would in the absence of the system. This outcome goes some way toward fulfilling the requirement embodied in the constitution. It also reduces the inefficiency and inequity that arise from the fact that the provinces vary widely in their capacities for raising revenue.

## Current Tax Policy Issues

The chapters that follow this one will look in detail at each of the main taxes in the Canadian tax system. Of course, the individual elements of the tax system cannot be considered fully in isolation from the system as a whole, and so the final chapter will discuss some of the issues on the current and ongoing agenda for tax reform. Before we turn to the individual taxes, it will be useful in the balance of this chapter to summarize some of the main policy issues that have arisen in debates about reform of the Canadian tax system. This summary should provide the reader with a context for the discussion of the individual taxes.[18]

## Taxation for the Global Economy

The Canadian economy has always relied on international markets both as a source of foreign products and as an outlet for our own products. It is only relatively recently, however, that the merits of exposing Canadian producers to the full force of international competition have been recognized. International competition benefits consumers by giving them access to the broadest range of products at the lowest prices. It benefits the economy by constraining it to use its resources as efficiently as possible. Moreover, the opportunities available in world markets should provide an incentive to increase productivity and discover new products so that the incomes of Canadians will rise as rapidly as possible.[19] Of course, not all observers agree with the advocates of free trade. Given our purposes here, it is not necessary that we adjudicate that debate. Freer international trade is an objective of the Canadian government, a circumstance reflected in the government's endorsement of the North American free trade agreement and the World Trade Organiza-

---

[18] Some of these issues are also discussed briefly in *OECD Economic Surveys 1996-1997: Canada*, supra footnote 6.

[19] The most forceful case for freer trade was put by the Macdonald royal commission; see Canada, Royal Commission on the Economic Union and Development Prospects for Canada, *Report* (Ottawa: Supply and Services, 1985).

tion. Our producers are therefore destined to be exposed to international competition. The relevant question here is, What implications does that exposure have for the tax system?

Three basic principles might be suggested for the guidance of tax policy in an era of increasing competitiveness. The first is that, subject to an important proviso, taxes should interfere as little as possible with the allocation of resources dictated by the competitive forces of the economy. To use the economist's jargon, the tax system should be as *neutral* as possible: the price mechanism alone should determine which industries thrive and which decline. The proviso is that there may be legitimate instances of market failure that the tax system might be used to address. For example, it might be used to reduce environmental externalities or to provide assistance to persons whose market incomes are unacceptably low or who have been hurt by misfortune. Or it might be used to deal with externalities that arise from the process of economic growth itself—a point that our next principle addresses.

The second principle is that the tax system should be conducive to innovative and productivity-enhancing activities. These activities are often associated with investment, risky ventures, research and development, human capital investment, and entrepreneurial efforts. It may be that it is not enough for the tax system to adopt a neutral stance toward activities of this kind. Recent theories of growth assert that there may be significant externalities involved in the growth process. The benefits of innovative and productivity-enhancing activities may not be captured fully by those who undertake the activities; they may instead spill over to others in the economy. In these circumstances, the tax system may have to actively encourage activities that are likely to lead to innovation and productivity growth.

The third principle is that the tax system must take account of the fact that valuable factors of production may be internationally mobile. Any attempt to impose taxes on these factors must be tempered by the recognition that they might flee the country.

These three principles suggest some broad objectives for the tax system. To achieve the goal of neutrality, taxes imposed on businesses should be as non-discriminatory as possible in their treatment of different types of businesses and different types of decisions taken by businesses. Thus taxes on labour payments, on sales, and on property values should not vary greatly across industries or locations. Taxes on business income should ensure that the profits generated by different types of capital decisions are taxed as uniformly as possible. Deductions for capital costs should represent as closely as possible the true cost of using the capital. Capital cost allowances should reflect the replacement cost of depreciation. Renewable resources, non-renewable resources, and inventories should be costed as they are used. Expenditures for activities such as exploration and development and investments in intangible assets should be treated as capital expenditures. Preferential treatment of specific activities or industries should be avoided unless there is a clear argument based on market failure for doing otherwise. In particular, the tax incentives available to firms should not be used as instruments for avoiding the costs of adjustment that changing market conditions entail.

Our second principle was that the tax system should be conducive to innovation and growth. To this end, it should encourage savings and investment—which suggests that it should avoid punitive tax rates on capital income. In order to induce innovation, entrepreneurship, and human capital formation, the tax system should treat investments in innovation and training favourably. To ensure that risk is not discouraged, taxes should to the extent possible treat losses symmetrically with gains, through appropriate loss-offsetting measures.

Finally, to ensure that mobile businesses and skilled persons will not be discouraged for tax reasons from locating in Canada, average tax rates on businesses and on personal incomes should not be significantly higher in Canada than they are in competing jurisdictions.

As we shall see in later chapters, recent reforms of the Canadian tax system have moved it toward these objectives. The individual and corporate income tax bases have been broadened, corporate income tax rates have been reduced, and a number of special incentives under the corporate income tax have been eliminated. The GST's predecessor, the MST, favoured services over goods, foreign-produced goods over domestic goods, and business inputs that were not subject to retail sales tax over inputs that were subject to tax; the replacement of the MST by the more broadly based GST has largely eliminated these biases. The payroll taxes have maintained broad bases and uniform rates. As well, certain other elements of the tax system have contributed to the objective of productivity growth—in particular, the relatively generous provisions for sheltering retirement savings and the tax incentives for investment in R & D.

Nevertheless, some sources of concern remain. Individual income tax rates are high compared with rates in the United States. This is especially true of the rates that apply to persons with above-average incomes, who tend to be more mobile than other taxpayers. Thus the marginal tax rate for a person who earns twice the average wage is 48 percent in Canada and 43 percent in the United States. For those who earn the average wage, the marginal tax rate is 46 percent in Canada and 30 percent in the United States.[20] And, although the income tax system provides relatively generous shelter for retirement savings, capital income that cannot be sheltered is taxed at relatively high individual rates. This state of affairs provides a disincentive to save and thereby reduces the funds available to capital markets. It also increases the incentive to avoid taxes by holding assets abroad.

---

[20] *OECD Economic Surveys 1996-1997: Canada*, supra footnote 6. Of course, average tax rates are more relevant for location decisions. Given the structure of tax brackets in the two countries, however, one would expect higher Canadian marginal tax rates to translate into higher average tax rates.

Business taxes are far from uniform and, in some cases, relatively onerous. Studies have shown that the corporate income tax system in Canada
imposes a relatively large disincentive effect on investment. Economists
measure the disincentive by using the concept of a *marginal effective tax rate*
(METR); this concept is discussed in more detail in chapter 4. Roughly speaking, the METR measures the share of profits paid as taxes on investments that
are producing a normal rate of return for investors: the higher is the METR,
the greater is the disincentive to invest. It has been calculated that the
METR for manufacturing in 1995 was 25.5 percent in Canada and 21.5 percent in the United States, while for services it was 32.2 percent in Canada
and 20 percent in the United States.[21] In Canada, the disincentive to invest
is much higher in some industries than in others. Resource industries tend to
have relatively low METRs because of the generous deductions that the corporate income tax system allows for the costs of discovering, acquiring, and
exploiting resource properties. The highest METRs are in the construction
and trade industries. Manufacturing industries are in the middle range.

The corporate income tax system also tends to discriminate against firms
that are growing rapidly and firms that are engaged in high-risk investments—precisely the firms that might be expected to be innovative and
highly productive. As we noted earlier, loss-making firms, those with
negative tax liabilities, are not treated symmetrically with profitable firms
because they are not fully credited with the "negative taxes." Large firms,
unlike small ones, can often offset negative taxes in one part of their operations against positive taxes elsewhere. Many newer firms must rely heavily
on new equity financing; those that do are treated less favourably than
established firms with access to internal finance. The result is that METRs for
small firms may be quite high even though small firms enjoy preferentially
low statutory tax rates.

Like the corporate income tax, other taxes imposed on businesses in
Canada are often higher than their counterparts in competing countries.
Canadian firms face capital taxes at both the federal and provincial levels of
government. Taxes on labour usage, including personal income taxes, tend to
be relatively high in Canada, even though payroll taxes are lower here than
they are in most other industrialized countries. In 1994, average taxes
payable on labour earnings were 29 percent in Canada and 23 percent in the
United States. Moreover, Canada's relative position has deteriorated in recent
years: in 1980, average taxes were only 21 percent of labour earnings in both
Canada and the United States.[22] Local property and business taxes too are
higher in Canada than they are in most competing jurisdictions. Thus
property taxes as a share of GDP are higher here than they are in any of the

---

[21] These data come from Duanjie Chen and Kenneth J. McKenzie, "The Impact of Taxation
on Capital Markets: An International Comparison of Effective Tax Rates on Capital," prepared
for Capital Market Issues, a conference sponsored by Industry Canada, where more extensive
international comparisons may be found.

[22] *OECD Economic Surveys 1996-1997: Canada,* supra footnote 6.

other countries in the G7. This situation is unlikely to change soon, given that provincial governments have taken to passing on part of their deficits to municipalities by reducing municipal transfers. The potential consequence of these relatively high tax burdens is that firms will be discouraged from locating in Canada.

Finally, although implementation of the GST has removed the inefficiencies associated with the MST and ensured that most products consumed in Canada are treated comparably, provincial sales taxes continue to be a source of discriminatory treatment. Only four provincial sales tax systems are fully harmonized with the federal GST. All of the other provinces but one retain their own retail sales taxes, all of which have narrow bases, tax some business inputs, and fail to ensure uniform treatment of domestic and foreign-produced goods. In the absence of full harmonization, consumption taxes will continue to be a source of inefficiency.

There is, of course, more to tax policy than the pursuit of competitiveness, innovation, and growth. In practice, tax policy in Canada will be constrained by the need to take account of other objectives of economic policy, some of which we address below. It will also be constrained by the very openness of the Canadian economy to international competition in the markets for goods and services, in labour and capital markets, and in financial markets. International competition has several implications for tax policy. To begin with, tax policy in an open economy is complicated by the fact that the bases on which taxes are imposed may be mobile across international borders. Any attempt to tax either products or factors of production that are highly mobile will be frustrated, at least in part. This is so because the prices of internationally mobile factors are largely determined on world markets; consequently, much of the tax on mobile factors will be shifted back to less mobile factors, an outcome that may distort domestic production patterns in capricious ways. The mobility of factors must be taken into account in designing the tax system. Thus it is better to avoid taxing transactions that are highly mobile in favour of taxing those that are not. For example, capital is highly mobile, so the taxation of business income earned in Canada can be largely frustrated, except to the extent that international crediting arrangements exist—a point we shall discuss below. The mobility of capital implies that the tax will not affect the after-tax rate of return. The taxation of business income will induce an outflow of investment, and a corresponding reduction in the income earned by labour and other factors that are employed by capital. Thus the business income tax effectively becomes a tax on these other, less mobile factors of production.

But is capital, in fact, highly mobile? In many economies, there is a close correlation between aggregate investment and aggregate saving, a circumstance that suggests that domestic investment is financed largely from domestic savings rather than from foreign capital. Even so, financial capital may be mobile enough to ensure that rates of return on capital in Canada must conform with the rates established in world financial markets. There may be, at most, some segmentation of domestic capital markets from international capital markets in the case of smaller, especially private, firms. Moreover, the savings-investment correlation seems to have weakened significantly in recent years.

A further caveat is in order. The taxation of business income in Canada can be accommodated if appropriate foreign-tax crediting arrangements exist. If taxes levied in Canada on foreign firms can be credited against the firms' tax liabilities in their home countries, the tax revenue obtained in Canada is essentially a transfer from foreign treasuries. Thus the tax creates no disincentive for these firms. The argument has particular relevance in the case of US corporations that operate in Canada, given the scale of their presence here. And in fact these corporations are able to obtain a credit against their US tax liabilities for Canadian taxes paid. This arrangement does not, however, prevent the tax from adversely affecting Canadian firms and giving them an incentive to shift capital abroad.

The existence of corporate-tax crediting arrangements in other countries has a bearing on the design of the corporate income tax system in Canada. These arrangements will be fully successful in removing the disincentive effect of the Canadian tax only if the Canadian tax system conforms reasonably closely with the foreign systems. That is, the value that a foreign shareholder receives under his country's system for Canadian taxes paid must be reasonably close to the amount of Canadian taxes paid by the firm. One must, however, set against the advantages of conforming with other countries' corporate tax systems the distortion that a corporate tax system imposes on domestic investment: high corporate tax rates may succeed in transferring large amounts from foreign treasuries, but they also reduce the incentive of Canadian corporations to invest in Canada. There is thus a policy tradeoff involved.[23]

Labour is much less mobile than capital. Workers' mobility is limited not only by the costs of moving, both financial and non-pecuniary, but also by restrictions on immigration. Some types of workers are more mobile than others, especially those whose skills are in high demand internationally. Examples include entrepreneurs, executives, professionals, and high-technology workers, all of whom tend to receive relatively high incomes. Any attempt to achieve redistributive goals by imposing high taxes on these people will be partially frustrated if it induces some of them to flee the country. The implication is that average tax rates in Canada for higher- income persons ought not to be excessive relative to average rates in the United States, the country with which Canada is in closest competition for highly skilled labour

---

[23] These issues are discussed in more detail in Robin W. Boadway, Neil Bruce, and Jack M. Mintz, *Taxes on Capital Income in Canada: Analysis and Policy*, Canadian Tax Paper no. 80 (Toronto: Canadian Tax Foundation, 1987). For a recent discussion of the withholding role of the corporate tax in an open economy, see Richard M. Bird, *Why Tax Corporations?* Working Paper 96-2 (Ottawa: Department of Finance, Technical Committee on Business Taxation, December 1996).

and entrepreneurs. Against this consideration must be set the possibility that the higher taxes may reflect higher public service levels, especially in areas such as health and education—though services in these areas may not be important to persons who are young, healthy, and well educated.

Businesses pay other direct taxes besides the corporate tax, and these taxes too may influence their decisions about investment in Canada. Capital taxes have disincentive effects similar to those of corporate income taxes, and in an open economy such as Canada's they tend as corporate taxes do to be shifted back to labour and other immobile factors. Property taxes too impinge upon business capital, though it is sometimes argued that the services financed by property taxes provide offsetting benefits. This argument does not apply, however, if the local services provided through property taxes mainly benefit residents rather than businesses. Finally, there are the special taxes levied on resource firms. These taxes lack the significant withholding function of the corporate income tax: their primary function is to capture a share of the resource rents for the public sector. Properly designed resource taxes can tax resource rents without providing a disincentive to exploit resources. Successful resource taxation uses a variety of devices, including cash-flow taxation and competitive sales of leases.[24]

So far in the present discussion we have focused on the implications for tax design of the mobility of capital and highly skilled labour. The openness of the international economy to relatively unimpeded trade in goods and services has somewhat different implications. This openness implies that the domestic producer prices of goods and services are largely determined by world prices. Given both the exogeneity of product prices and the relative immobility of the bulk of the labour force, it follows that both general consumption taxes and taxes on labour income are borne mainly by the domestic residents who pay the taxes: they can neither be shifted to foreigners through higher prices nor easily be avoided by migration. In fact, the effects of broadly based taxes on labour income—that is, payroll taxes—and consumption taxes are presumably equivalent. Both reduce real wages (nominal wages deflated by the consumer price index), payroll taxes by reducing after-tax wages, consumption taxes by increasing the price level. As a consequence, both are broad residence-based taxes. Given the general immobility of labour, different countries can levy different average tax rates without affecting their competitiveness, provided that the taxes are broadly based and not excessively progressive relative to competitors' taxes. This presumes, of course, that wages are flexible enough to allow these taxes to be passed back to labour. If there is enough real-wage "stickiness" to keep after-

---

[24] The alternatives are laid out in some detail in Robin Boadway and Frank Flatters, *The Taxation of Natural Resources: Principles and Policy Issues*, Policy Research Working Paper 1210 (Washington, DC: World Bank, 1993). Resource taxation is discussed further in chapter 4.

tax wages from falling in response to the tax, the result may be some involuntary unemployment. If labour markets are flexible, however, broadly based payroll taxes, like broadly based consumption taxes, need not be "taxes on jobs" or detrimental to competitiveness. This analysis suggests that Canada can tax its residents at rates different from the rates in other countries, including the United States, without fear of becoming non-competitive. This is not to say that these taxes will not have effects. If the supply of labour is responsive to after-tax real wages, higher taxes will cause a *voluntary* reduction in labour supplied, but not unemployment.

These conclusions assume, however, that consumption taxes apply systematically to all consumption purchases made by residents. This will be the case if the consumption tax is imposed consistently on a destination basis, so that imports are fully taxed and exports are fully exempted, with the result that domestic producers stand on a level playing field with their foreign competitors. The GST achieves this result: exported goods are credited fully for GST payments at earlier stages; imports are fully subject to the GST. The provincial sales taxes that have been harmonized with the GST operate to the same effect. The other provincial sales tax systems do not: they do not apply consistently to imports, and they do not fully credit exports for taxes levied on purchases of inputs at any previous stage of production.

One further way in which an open economy might constrain tax policy is through its effect on cross-border shopping. If taxes on consumption are higher in one jurisdiction than in another and the border is open, consumers have an incentive to purchase goods and services in the jurisdiction with lower tax rates. The importance of this consideration in an international context is limited. In Canada's case, the requirement to report purchases at the border and have domestic taxes applied to them reduces consumers' ability to take advantage of lower tax rates in the United States or elsewhere—at any rate, to take advantage of them legally. A potentially larger problem arises from the fact that consumption tax rates vary somewhat across provincial boundaries, where no border controls exist. We shall turn shortly to the special problems that arise for tax policy in a federation in which the provinces have significant tax-setting responsibilities.

Finally, although tax auditing is always imperfect and some amount of tax evasion is a fact of life, the opportunities for some forms of evasion (and avoidance) are enhanced in an international environment. As was just mentioned, consumers can avoid commodity taxation by shopping abroad and failing to properly claim purchases, or by outright smuggling. What is perhaps more important, capital income earned abroad can be difficult to monitor, especially if it accrues in a non-treaty country. As well, firms can use methods such as transfer pricing and intrafirm borrowing and lending to shift business income from high-tax to low-tax jurisdictions. These problems impose a severe constraint on governments' ability to levy taxes on capital income and on commodities at rates higher than the rates in neighbouring jurisdictions.

## The Federal-Provincial Dimension

Once again, Canada is a highly decentralized federation. Both the federal government and the provinces have the power to impose a wide range of taxes. In the case of the federal government, there is virtually no constitutional restriction. Section 91(3) of the Constitution Act, 1982 states that the authority of Parliament includes "[t]he raising of money by any mode or system of taxation." The only real restrictions on the federal government's fiscal authority are therefore economic and political ones. In the case of the provinces, the constitution is somewhat less permissive: it limits the provinces to "[d]irect taxation within the province in order to the raising of a revenue for provincial purposes" (section 92(2)). In practice, however, this limitation has not been effective. The provinces have been able to constitute their sales and excise taxes in ways that have led the courts to interpret them as being direct taxes, contrary to standard economic usage. The provinces have accomplished this result by defining their sales and excise taxes as taxes on the consumer rather than the seller: retailers are deemed to be agents of the provincial government who collect the taxes from the intended payers, the consumers. This interpretation would seem to be problematic for provinces that wish to introduce value-added taxes, which involve taxation at stages before the retail stage, but, because the taxes paid at earlier stages are reimbursed, the courts have ruled that the VAT formula does not violate the proscription against provinces' levying indirect taxes.[25]

The fact that the provinces (and their municipalities, which are regarded as being within the jurisdiction of the provinces) have access to virtually the same set of broadly based taxes as the federal government raises an additional set of issues for tax policy, both federal and provincial.[26] Taxes levied by the provinces compound the inefficiencies imposed by federal taxes and can, in addition, induce inefficiencies in the allocation of resources across provinces. These inefficiencies may simply be a result of the fact that different provinces have different agendas and may, accordingly, choose different tax rates and structures, and different services and transfers as well. Businesses and individuals may therefore have a fiscal incentive to locate in one province rather than another, or to invest more in one than in another. Alternatively, provinces may deliberately engage in "beggar-thy-neighbour policies"—that is, policies designed specifically to attract economic activity, presumably at the expense of other provinces. If all of the provinces engage in policies of this kind, the policies will tend to be self-defeating. For example, they may result in all of the provinces' giving unnecessary concessions to taxpayers and forgoing valuable tax revenue as a result. More gen-

---

[25] For a full discussion of the judicial interpretation of the provinces' power to tax, see Peter H. Hogg, *Constitutional Law of Canada*, 4th ed. (Toronto: Carswell, 1997).

[26] Although the territories are under federal jurisdiction, they have essentially the same taxing powers as the provinces, with the exception that they do not have access to resource revenues. In what follows, most of what we say about the provinces also applies to the territories.

erally, to the extent that factors of production are mobile across provinces, provinces will be reluctant to increase tax rates for fear of losing these factors to other provinces. When all of the provinces act in this way, they in effect compete to push tax rates down. In the end, the competition results in tax rates that are too low. If the provinces could coordinate their tax policies, they would all agree to higher tax rates. Since there are 10 provinces, however, any agreement causing them to refrain from engaging in tax competition would be hard to enforce.[27]

Interprovincial competition can also involve instruments other than tax rates. Provinces might use industrial subsidies or public services, especially infrastructure, to attract businesses. A province might also use the progressivity of its taxes as an instrument of competition; that is, it might reduce progressivity in order to attract high-income persons and reduce transfers in order to discourage welfare recipients from locating in the province.

Interprovincial tax competition is not the only source of tax-induced inefficiency in a federal setting. Provincial tax setting may also be inefficient because of the so-called vertical fiscal externalities that arise because of the interdependency between provincial and federal taxation. When provinces increase their tax rates, their tax bases tend to decrease; and the more elastic the tax base is, the more it will decrease. A province might be expected to take the revenue loss from the shrinkage in the base into account when it sets its tax rates. Since the federal government occupies similar tax bases, however, it too will suffer a revenue loss when the provinces increase their tax rates. Since the provinces do not take full account of the revenue losses that their tax increases impose on the federal government, they underestimate the full cost of increasing tax rates on the public sector as a whole. To use the economist's jargon, the provinces tend to underestimate the true marginal cost of public funds. Contrary to the tendency of interprovincial tax competition, this tendency induces the provinces to set tax rates too high on bases that are relatively elastic.[28]

A final source of inefficiency in the Canadian federation is the fact that the provinces vary in their capacities to raise tax revenue. If one province has, say, larger natural resource endowments or a population of higher

---

[27] Bird and Smart have argued that the equalization system severely blunts the effects of tax competition for the have-not provinces. Equalization payments are based on shortfalls of provincial tax bases relative to a national norm: low-income provinces receive a payment determined by the application of the national average tax rate to this shortfall. If a have-not province increases its tax rates on a mobile tax base, it will be effectively reimbursed for the loss in revenues it incurs as a result of any loss of base. Thus any incentive it might have otherwise had to reduce tax rates will be missing. For these provinces at least, the incentive for tax competition is blunted. This may go a long way toward explaining why even the small provinces impose relatively high taxes on business income. See Richard M. Bird and Michael Smart, *Federal Fiscal Arrangements in Canada: An Analysis of Incentives*, Discussion Paper no. 8 (Toronto: University of Toronto, International Centre for Tax Studies, 1996).

[28] For a summary of these fiscal externality effects, see Dahlby, supra footnote 9.

average incomes than another province, it will be able to levy taxes at a lower rate than the other province in order to finance the same level of public services. This advantage will serve to attract factors of production and businesses for purely fiscal reasons: location will be influenced by average tax rates as well as by productivity considerations. The result can be an inefficient allocation of resources across provinces. The literature sometimes refers to this source of inefficiency as *fiscal inefficiency*.[29] But differential tax capacities also give rise to a form of inequity across provinces, referred to as *fiscal inequity*. Persons with a given income will get lower net benefits from the public sector in a province with low tax capacity than they will get in one with high tax capacity. This outcome violates a principle of government policy called horizontal equity, which is dealt with in detail in the next chapter.

In addition to causing inefficiencies and inequities, the overlapping of tax jurisdictions also increases the costs of tax administration and compliance. If a business operates in more than one province, it will incur the extra compliance costs of dealing with more than one tax authority. The provincial tax authorities, for their part, will need to determine what portion of the business's activities take place within its borders. The fact that the federal government and the provinces both occupy the main tax fields implies further duplication of collection and compliance costs.

As the discussion to this point has shown, the decentralization of taxing authority makes for economic inefficiency, fiscal inequity, and administrative complexity. Fortunately, Canada, unlike some other federations (such as the United States), has mechanisms in place that are designed to mitigate these problems. The two most important mechanisms are both major components of Canada's system of federal-provincial fiscal arrangements. They are the equalization system and the tax harmonization arrangements. Let us briefly consider these components in turn.[30]

## Equalization

Section 36(2) of the Constitution Act, 1982, states that "Parliament and the government of Canada are committed to the principle of making equalization payments to ensure that provincial governments have sufficient revenues to provide reasonably comparable levels of public services at reasonably comparable levels of taxation." This section is the basis for the Canadian equalization system, whose purpose is to address the fiscal inefficiencies and inequities that would otherwise exist in a federation composed of provinces of varying degrees of affluence. As we explained earlier, equalization transfers are paid by the federal government to the provinces (currently all

---

[29] For a discussion of the inefficiencies that arise from differences in revenue-raising capacities across provinces, see Boadway and Hobson, supra footnote 10 and Dan Usher, *The Uneasy Case for Equalization Payments* (Vancouver: Fraser Institute, 1995).

[30] See Boadway and Hobson, supra footnote 10, for more discussion of these and other components of the federal-provincial fiscal arrangements.

except Alberta, British Columbia, and Ontario) whose ability to raise revenues from provincial taxes falls below a national norm. It has been calculated that, in recent years, the equalization system has raised the per-capita tax capacities of the low-income provinces to 98 percent of the national average.[31] This program is largely responsible for the fact that average tax rates for most bases diverge relatively little among provinces.

The principle of equalization is now enshrined in the Canadian constitution and appears to have widespread political support. The budget deficit and public debt crisis of the early 1990s, however, put the equalization system under pressure that has not yet abated. Part of the federal approach to deficit reduction has been to decentralize fiscal responsibilities to the provinces. Table 1.5 shows how each province's own-source revenues have changed as a share of its total revenues relative to general purpose and specific purpose transfers between the mid-1970s and the mid-1990s. As the table indicates, all of the provinces have come to rely more and more on own-source revenues. This is so largely because of a decline in the importance of specific purpose transfers, including those for health, welfare, and post-secondary education.

The importance of general purpose transfers, which consist mostly of equalization payments, has remained largely unchanged. It is likely, however, that the pressure on the provinces to become more self-sufficient will continue into the foreseeable future. Even so, it is not out of the question that provincial program expenditures will resume their historical upward trend. Either outcome—increasing provincial self-reliance or increased provincial spending—could well force provincial tax rates to rise.[32] In that case, equalization entitlements too would have to rise to achieve the objectives of the system. Whether this would be politically feasible is an open question. If it were not, tax rates or service levels across provinces would have to diverge even further, and fiscal inefficiencies and inequities would result.

## Tax Harmonization

There are enormous advantages to a decentralized system of revenue raising. If provinces are able to legislate their own taxes, accountability is enhanced and tax structures can take account of local needs and preferences. But decentralization has its downside.[33] In the absence of coordination among the provinces and between the provinces and the federal government, the

---

[31] Ibid., at 124, table 4.7.

[32] Alternatively, provinces may simply pass on reductions in federal transfers to their municipalities in the form of reduced provincial-municipal transfers. In fact, provincial transfers to municipalities have tended lately to be roughly similar in size to the transfers that the provinces have received from the federal government. This scenario suggests that the federal reduction in transfers will give rise to an increase in municipal tax rates.

[33] For an account of the benefits and costs of decentralizing fiscal responsibilities, see Robin Boadway, "The Folly of Decentralizing the Canadian Federation" (Winter 1996), 75 *Dalhousie Review* 313-49.

### Table 1.5 Federal Transfers as Percentages of Provincial Revenues, Fiscal Years 1975-76 and 1996-97

| | General purpose transfers | | Specific purpose transfers | | Own-source revenues | |
|---|---|---|---|---|---|---|
| | 1975-76 | 1996-97 | 1975-76 | 1996-97 | 1975-76 | 1996-97 |
| Newfoundland .......... | 27.6 | 30.3 | 21.7 | 12.7 | 50.7 | 57.0 |
| Prince Edward Island ..... | 27.1 | 23.9 | 17.7 | 12.5 | 45.2 | 53.6 |
| Nova Scotia ............ | 28.3 | 27.5 | 19.4 | 12.8 | 52.3 | 59.7 |
| New Brunswick ......... | 23.8 | 23.9 | 23.6 | 14.4 | 52.6 | 61.7 |
| Quebec ............... | 11.8 | 9.9 | 10.8 | 7.7 | 77.4 | 82.4 |
| Ontario ............... | 2.7 | — | 18.5 | 12.9 | 78.8 | 87.1 |
| Manitoba ............. | 13.6 | 19.8 | 22.9 | 11.9 | 63.5 | 68.3 |
| Saskatchewan .......... | 7.7 | 5.9 | 16.1 | 11.4 | 76.2 | 82.7 |
| Alberta ............... | 1.7 | — | 11.8 | 10.1 | 86.5 | 89.9 |
| British Columbia ........ | 1.4 | — | 17.2 | 9.2 | 81.4 | 90.8 |

Sources: Karin Treff and David B. Perry, *Finances of the Nation, 1996* (Toronto: Canadian Tax Foundation, 1996); and *Provincial and Municipal Finances, 1985* (Toronto: Canadian Tax Foundation, 1986).

overall tax structure could vary considerably across jurisdictions. The result, as we have shown, would be inefficiency in the allocation of resources, inequity across jurisdictions, and a complex tax system for both taxpayers and tax administrators. It is possible to avoid some of these problems without sacrificing the advantages of decentralized taxing responsibility through a system of tax harmonization between governments.

In Canada, harmonization has been achieved in the income tax field through the system of tax collection agreements (TCAs) between the federal government and the participating provinces. Under both the TCAs for personal income taxes and those for corporate taxes, as we noted earlier, the federal government collects the tax for the participating provinces, allows them to set their own tax rates, and administers province-specific tax credits—provided that the credits do not discriminate against non-residents or distort national markets. In return, the provinces agree to abide by the federal tax base and, in the case of the personal income tax, the federal rate structure as well. The TCAs have maintained a single tax administration for the participating provinces and a fairly uniform base and rate structure for the personal and corporate income taxes. Moreover, although some provinces have declined to participate in the TCAs, these provinces' tax systems have not strayed too far from the system maintained by the TCAs. The non-participating provinces have also abided so far by a common formula for allocating tax revenues among provinces. It is unlikely that this would be the case were the other provinces not part of the TCA system.

The TCA system originated when the federal government dominated the income tax fields. It was natural that the provinces would agree to let the federal government become their tax collecting agency, and that they would accept the federal government as the sole authority for determining the income tax bases and, in the case of the personal income tax, the rate structure as well. Not surprisingly, as the provinces become more self-reliant, and as their share of the income tax fields becomes larger and larger, pressures on the TCAs are growing. Provinces are asking for, and being granted, more and more province-specific tax credits, allowances, and other measures. Some of these provisions apply to businesses and may impede efficient resource allocation within the federation. Others change the degree of progressivity of the tax structure across the provinces. Some provinces have openly contemplated leaving the TCAs in order to be able to set their own provincial tax policies with less constraint. The danger is that a breakdown of the TCAs could impair the efficiency and the equity of the internal economic union.

What these developments suggest is that the time has come for some new thinking about the sharing of tax room between levels of government, and about the form of tax harmonization. What is needed is some means of reconciling the decentralization of revenue-raising responsibilities with the laudable objective of harmonizing both the income tax and the sales tax systems. In this context, the key problem is that of determining just how the main tax bases should be shared between the federal government and the provinces—a problem that until recently has not been considered explicitly.[34] Given the growing fiscal importance of the provinces, it is not likely that the federal government can continue to dominate all of the major tax fields. In which tax fields, then, if any, should the federal government be dominant? Basically, this question amounts to asking whether the federal government should be dominant in the income tax fields, the sales tax fields, or neither. If it is to be dominant in neither, the question arises whether tax harmonization of the kind we have now can survive: the federal government probably cannot continue to insist on having sole responsibility for defining the bases, let alone the rate structure as well. Nor is it obvious that a joint decision-making arrangement for determining the base is feasible, especially in a system of parliamentary democracy where legislatures have final say on fiscal matters.

If joint federal-provincial control of the main tax fields is not feasible, the question becomes whether the federal government should dominate the income tax field or the sales tax field. There are two main arguments for not letting the federal share of income tax room diminish further, and in fact for increasing it. The first is that the income tax is the tax that works best as a redistributive device, and that redistribution ought to be mainly a federal responsibility so that common norms apply nationwide and redistribution does not get eroded away by interprovincial tax competition. Because income

---

[34] An exception was the Carter report (Canada, *Report of the Royal Commission on Taxation* (Ottawa: Queen's Printer, 1966), which recommended that the federal government vacate entirely the sales tax fields and concentrate its efforts mainly on income taxes. For a discussion of the principles of assignment of tax responsibilities in a federation, see Irene K. Ip and Jack M. Mintz, *Dividing the Spoils: The Federal-Provincial Allocation of Taxing Powers* (Toronto: C.D. Howe Institute, 1992).

taxation applies to capital and to business income, which are highly mobile across provinces, and because it is naturally more complicated than, say, sales taxation, it is more susceptible to use as an instrument of tax competition than most other taxes. Consequently—and this brings us to the second argument—it is more important to harmonize income taxes than it is to harmonize sales taxes. And, as we have suggested, the harmonization of income taxes, at least through the existing system of TCAs, depends upon the federal government's maintaining its dominance of the personal and corporate income tax fields.

If the federal government is to maintain a dominant share of the income tax fields, then given the existing degree of fiscal decentralization (which is probably not negotiable), it cannot have a majority share in the sales tax field as well. This reality is difficult to reconcile with the desire to harmonize federal and provincial sales taxes and thus capture the advantages of value-added taxation, since it is probably not possible in a federation to harmonize a VAT system in a way that leaves the provinces with any real taxing authority. Consequently, although sales tax harmonization has been carried out to a limited degree, it is unlikely to be achieved nationwide. This being the case, it seems sensible at least to retain the harmonized income tax system—a task that may require the federal government to consolidate or even to enlarge its present share of the income tax room.

As we noted earlier, there has been some harmonization in the general sales tax field. The HST system achieves its objective of complete harmonization in the three participating provinces, but it does so at some cost. The participating provinces must abide not only by the federal base, but also by the common provincial rate. This means that the provinces have in effect no independent taxing authority in the sales tax field. They must adhere completely to the federal base, and any changes in the rate must be agreed to jointly with the other participating provinces. The system is therefore more of a revenue-sharing scheme than a tax harmonization scheme. It is not clear whether other provinces can be enticed to join the HST, given the loss in autonomy that membership involves. As matters stand, the differences between the rate structure in the participating provinces and the rate structures in the other provinces no doubt increase administration costs somewhat. In Quebec, the less-than-complete harmonization of the GST and the QST reflects the province's retention of fundamental autonomy in the matter of general sales taxation.

There has been even less harmonization in tax fields other than the income tax and sales tax fields. Provincial resource taxes are far from harmonized. Property taxes vary widely across the provinces. The same goes for excise taxes, payroll taxes, capital taxes, and so on. What is even more significant, the provincial transfer systems (such as welfare) differ widely from one another. The differences in tax structure across provinces provide plenty of scope for beggar-thy-neighbour policies and other policies that distort the Canadian internal economic union.

## The Tax Mix

The division of tax room between levels of government is one important dimension of the tax structure. Another is the division of the task of raising revenue among different types of taxes, referred to as the *tax mix*. All countries have a variety of taxes, but the most important ones are those that apply to broad bases. The four main broadly based taxes are income taxes, general sales taxes, tax on labour income, and property taxes. Because these taxes are broadly based, their bases overlap to a great extent. Labour income taxes apply to all of the income tax base except capital income. The base for general sales taxes is consumption, which is simply income less savings. General sales taxes and labour income taxes are roughly equivalent in present value terms. Property taxes are much less broadly based than the other major taxes, and overlap much less with other taxes. Like the income tax, however, they do effectively tax part of a taxpayer's capital income.[35] The fact that countries tend to apply a mix of taxes to these overlapping bases raises some fundamental tax policy issues. Why is a tax mix needed if all of the broad tax bases are so similar? It would seem to be simpler to have only one tax and reduce the costs of collection accordingly. Given that all governments do use a mix of broadly based taxes, why are the bases not even more similar?

The economics literature does not have definitive answers to these questions. One likely reason why governments use a mix of taxes is that the tax rate for a single tax would be onerously high—a circumstance that might encourage taxpayer resistance, and tax avoidance or evasion with it. It is also likely that governments use different tax bases in order to achieve different objectives. For example, some taxes are better suited to lower-level jurisdictions and others to higher-level jurisdictions. Thus the property tax is a relatively good tax for financing local governments because its base is immobile. Similarly, the income tax serves a redistributive purpose and so is appropriate for use by the federal government. Sales taxes can differentiate among products in ways that income taxes cannot, and for this reason they too can contribute to redistributive objectives—for example, by applying different rates to necessities than they apply to luxury goods. Different taxes can also have very different effects on the savings rate, a circumstance that may be relevant to economic growth. To put this matter simply, taxes that the taxpayer pays earlier in life reduce savings relative to those that he or she pays later in life. For example, payroll taxes reduce savings more than sales taxes do: the former reduce the disposable income out of which savings are made early in life.[36]

---

[35] The property tax is a tax on asset values. One can demonstrate the equivalence between a tax on asset values and a tax on capital incomes as follows: If $A$ is the value of an asset and $r$ is the going rate of return, capital income in a given year is $rA$. An annual tax on asset values at the rate $t$ yields tax revenues of $tA$. A tax on capital income at the rate $s$ yields $srA$. The two are equivalent if $t = sr$.

[36] For a detailed summary of the effect of various taxes on savings, see Charles M. Beach, Robin W. Boadway, and Neil Bruce, *Taxation and Savings in Canada* (Ottawa: Supply and

(The footnote is continued on the next page.)

Like most other countries, Canada uses a mix of the main broadly based taxes—income taxes, sales taxes, payroll taxes, and property taxes. As table 1.5 shows, our mix differs from those of other OECD countries in some marked ways. We rely relatively more on income taxes and less on payroll and sales taxes than most other OECD countries do, and we rely especially heavily on property taxes. Although there is no imperative reason why Canada's tax mix should mimic the mixes used elsewhere, there is some room for changing the mix if it is felt that the existing one puts some of our businesses at a competitive disadvantage. With this point in mind, let us consider Canada's degree of reliance on each of the main tax bases.

## Property Taxes

The relatively high reliance on property taxes in Canada is a cause for some concern. Much of the revenue from property taxes is used to finance provincial and municipal services that may not directly benefit property-tax payers, especially those in the business sector. To the extent that this is the case, property taxes amount to a tax on doing business, and thus they may well serve to discourage businesses from locating in Canada.

It would not be a simple matter to reduce our present reliance on property taxes. The provinces determine the extent to which financial responsibility is devolved to the local governments, but federal fiscal policies too can influence the level of local taxation. In recent years, for example, the federal government has reduced its transfers to the provinces, which in turn have obliged their local governments to take on larger shares of the burden of financing local services.

## Income Taxes

The corporate income tax's share of the tax mix in Canada is not out of line with its share in other countries. Individual income tax rates, on the other hand, are on average high in Canada compared with rates in the United States. Since Canadians are more likely to move to the United States than to any other country, one can argue that Canada's reliance on personal income taxes should be reduced. Higher-income taxpayers are more likely than lower-income taxpayers to be internationally mobile, and this consideration makes progressivity an issue as well. The Canadian personal income tax has a more progressive rate structure than does its US counterpart, especially given the so-called temporary surtaxes levied at the higher end of the income scale by both the federal government and the provinces.

The federal government would not find it easy to reduce the present reliance on personal income taxes, given that the provinces too occupy the

---

[36] Continued ...

Services, 1988); and James Davies and France St-Hilaire, *Reforming Capital Income Taxation in Canada: Efficiency and Distributive Effects of Alternative Options* (Ottawa: Supply and Services, 1987).

personal tax field. The provinces could easily undo a unilateral federal reduction in income tax rates by raising their own rates—an outcome that would have an adverse effect on the sharing of income tax room without improving the tax mix. In recent years, many provinces have as a matter of policy tried to reduce their income tax rates, so the problem has not arisen, but it is difficult to predict what will happen in the future as the provinces adjust to smaller federal transfers. It is certain, in any case, that any reduction in overall income tax rates would require some cooperation between the two levels of government. Unless both levels agreed to a given change in the tax mix, one level of government could frustrate the intent of the other.

## General Sales Taxes

Sales taxation is less important in Canada than it is in any of the member nations of the European Union, but much more important than it is in the United States, where federal sales taxation is non-existent. Nonetheless, there is no argument based on competitiveness for bringing Canadian sales taxes more in line with sales taxes in the United States. On the contrary, there would seem to be scope for increasing reliance on sales taxation should policy makers choose to do so. A general sales tax on the VAT pattern, such as the GST, is especially suited to an open economy. The VAT form of sales taxation, which allows a full rebate for taxes paid when products are exported and imposes full taxation on imports, treats domestically produced goods comparably with foreign goods. Provincial RSTs do not have this advantage, so any increase in the importance of sales taxation in the tax mix that involved increased provincial reliance on RSTs would lead to further inefficiencies. Thus any increase in the share of sales taxes in the overall tax mix would have to be limited to an increase in the use of the GST.

This solution has an important shortcoming. Greater federal reliance on the GST would in the long run increase the income tax room available to the provinces, an outcome that could further jeopardize the integrity of the income tax harmonization arrangements. The only obvious way to avoid this outcome would be to entice the larger provinces into an HST-style harmonization arrangement as a way of enhancing the sales tax component of the tax mix, and it seems highly unlikely that the larger provinces would fall in with this scheme.

Increased reliance on the GST, or on sales taxation generally, might also make the tax system more regressive and thereby compromise the redistributive objective of government. It would be possible, however, to overcome the adverse consequences for lower-income persons by enhancing the GST credit, a measure that proved to be highly effective when the GST was first introduced. Whether this solution would be acceptable to taxpayers is another matter: it is not clear that the public perceived the introduction of the GST to be distribution-neutral, despite the fact that it was designed to be. Taxpayer resistance to the GST is itself a barrier to increasing its importance. To the extent that the public does not perceive the tax to be a fair one, it might react to an increase in the GST rate by engaging in tax evasion.

## Payroll Taxes

Payroll taxes are by far the least important of the broadly based taxes used by the federal government and the provinces. The federal government has used them not as a source of general revenues, but rather as a source of earmarked funding for social insurance programs. A similar story applies at the provincial level, though the provinces have made some limited use of general payroll taxes. In any case, the level of payroll taxes is lower in Canada than it is in any of the other OECD countries. Yet there is concern, especially within the business community. Payroll taxes have grown relatively rapidly in recent years, and they will grow even more rapidly if the federal government follows through on its recent proposal to refinance the Canada Pension Plan by increasing the contribution rate.

It is not obvious why Canadian governments have not made more use of payroll taxation, given its popularity in many other countries. Payroll taxes satisfy many of the criteria for a good tax, criteria that we discuss in detail in chapter 2.[37] In addition to having a broad base, they impose minimal distortions on economic decisions, apart from the labour-leisure choice. Unlike the income tax, payroll taxes do not discourage savings and investment. The collection of payroll taxes, through payroll deductions, is relatively easy. For provincial governments, payroll taxation has the advantage that its base, labour income, is relatively immobile across provinces. Payroll taxes are not particularly well suited to a redistributive role, especially given the way in which the federal tax system has structured them, with an upper limit to tax payments based on labour income. The regressivity of payroll taxation, however, like that of the GST, could be dealt with by enhancing the system of refundable tax credits under the income tax system. The main drawbacks of payroll taxation seem to be the difficulties it poses for firms that have cash-flow problems and the administrative burden that it imposes on small firms. It also has its detractors in the business community, who tend to perceive it as being a tax on business—or more colourfully, a tax on jobs. As we shall discuss in chapter 6, there is some empirical evidence that payroll taxes increase unemployment in the short run, though this effect seems largely to disappear in the long run as the tax is absorbed in the wages of workers.

## The Tax Treatment of Savings

As we mentioned above, one of the things that distinguishes different forms of broadly based taxation is their treatment of savings—or more precisely the return to savings, capital income. The income tax nominally includes capital income in the tax base, though as we have seen there are many important exceptions to this rule. General sales taxes almost always apply only to consumption expenditures, a limitation that effectively excludes net savings

---

[37] See also the extensive treatment of the economics of payroll taxes and their potential as a major tax source in Jonathan R. Kesselman, *General Payroll Taxes: Economics, Politics, and Design*, Canadian Tax Paper no. 101 (Toronto: Canadian Tax Foundation, 1997).

from the tax base. Savings are ultimately taxed if they are used eventually to finance consumption; in the meantime, capital income on the savings is allowed to accumulate free of sales tax. In effect, therefore, the sales tax system exempts capital income. Similarly, the payroll tax base includes labour income but not capital income. Thus the choice of tax mix affects the extent to which capital income is included in the tax base. This observation raises the more general issue of how savings and capital income *should* be treated by the tax system.

The tax treatment of savings is a concern that goes to the heart of tax policy and tax design, since it addresses the issue of the appropriate base for broadly based taxation. We shall discuss this issue in detail in chapter 2, so it will do here simply to indicate the main arguments for taxing capital income preferentially or even for excluding it from taxation altogether.

The economic arguments for treating capital income preferentially are based on the standard criteria of equity, efficiency, growth, and administrative simplicity.[38] The equity argument is based on the notion that the personal tax base ought to reflect how well-off a person is. Some economists argue that the amount a person consumes is a better indicator of the person's well-being than is his income, since consumption is what generates the goods and services that yield consumer satisfaction. To put the matter differently, consumption is what a taxpayer takes from the economy, whereas income is what the taxpayer contributes. A tax system that exempts savings achieves the objective of taxing consumption alone. It might be argued that savings represent future consumption, so they too should be included in the tax base. There are, however, two problems with this argument. First, the taxpayer may not consume his savings but, instead, pass them on as a bequest or a gift. Second, even if savings will be used for consumption in the future, forcing the consumer to pay a tax in advance of the consumption amounts to discriminating against future consumption relative to present consumption. These equity arguments address the choice of a fair tax base; they do not address the degree of progressivity of the tax system. But progressivity is not really at issue here. In principle, one can achieve any degree of progressivity with any base, since progressivity is a function not of the base but of the rate structure.

The efficiency and growth arguments for excluding capital income from the base arise from the fact that a tax that includes capital income in its base distorts the savings decision. By reducing the after-tax rate of return obtained by savers to a level below the rate of return determined on the capital market, an income-based tax system provides a disincentive to save. The presence of this disincentive reduces not only the efficiency of the capital market but also the amount of savings available to finance investment. Thus it retards job creation and growth. The treatment of savings by the tax system affects the

---

[38] These arguments are all fully documented in Economic Council of Canada, *The Taxation of Savings and Investment* (Ottawa: Supply and Services Canada, 1987).

private savings rate in other ways as well. We noted earlier that the effect of taxes on savings depends in part on the timing of a taxpayer's tax liabilities over his lifetime. The tax bases that fall later in the taxpayer's lifetime will tend to encourage more savings. Thus a tax system that shelters savings should result in more personal savings, and thus more financing for investment (although some of the investment may accrue abroad), than will a system that taxes the income from savings. There is a further advantage to inducing taxpayers to save for future consumption, especially to finance consumption during retirement: the more taxpayers save for their own retirement, the less dependent they will be on public transfers. In fact, many observers argue that the anticipation of public transfer support in retirement causes persons to *reduce* their own savings for retirement. This argument is often invoked to justify not only the encouragement of retirement savings through preferential tax treatment but also the policy of making some saving for retirement mandatory, through schemes such as the Canada and Quebec pension plans.[39]

Taxes that treat savings or capital income preferentially can also enhance administrative simplicity. As we shall discuss in detail in chapter 2, one of the most difficult problems in administering a full-fledged income tax system is how to properly include capital income in the base. Some forms of asset income are very difficult to measure, such as the imputed rent on owner-occupied housing, the return on human capital investment, and the return on unincorporated business investment. Capital gains are difficult to include in the base as they accrue rather than when they are realized. Indexing of capital income is necessary, a point we discuss further below. Finally, the relative ease with which some taxpayers can avoid capital income taxation by holding foreign assets compromises the ability of the authorities to enforce the tax system.

Given the weight of the arguments in support of preferential treatment of savings or capital income, it is not surprising that the Canadian tax system already favours capital income in a number of ways. The tax mix includes general sales taxes and payroll taxes, which effectively do not tax capital income, and also income taxes, which do. Even within the income tax system, some assets are treated on a consumption-tax basis, either by exempting the income from these assets from taxation or by allowing taxpayers to shelter these assets from tax. The return on housing and other consumer durables is tax-exempt. Much personal investment in human capital accumulation is effectively taxed on a cash-flow basis whereby it is exempt from tax when undertaken (given that forgone earnings are the most important costs associated with the accumulation of human capital) but subject to tax later when the investment bears fruit. Finally, savings for

---

[39] For a discussion of this rationale for tax assistance for retirement savings, see Keith G. Banting and Robin Boadway, eds., *Reform of Retirement Income Policy* (Kingston, Ont.: Queen's University, School of Policy Studies, 1997).

retirement that are accumulated through individual registered retirement savings plans (RRSPs) and company registered pension plans (RPPs) are sheltered from capital income tax. These forms of asset accumulation account for a high proportion of savings, and therefore a high proportion of capital income as well. On the other hand, some taxes, such as the corporate income tax and property taxes, only tax capital income, though the effect of the former is muted by the dividend tax credit. Overall, however, it is likely that the tax system significantly favours capital income over labour income. It is possible to argue, in fact, that overall we are much closer to having a consumption tax system than an income tax system.

The policy question is whether the present arrangements go far enough in exempting capital income—or, perhaps, too far. Although many economists favour a move to a full-fledged consumption tax, this change would probably not gain widespread political support. Though a move to a full-fledged consumption income tax may be unlikely, some improvements in the tax sheltering of capital income are probably possible. The three key areas of saving—for retirement, housing, and human capital investment—are all on the reform agenda. Given the pressures on the public pension system,[40] the case for maintaining some form of tax assistance for retirement savings is strong. The current system of sheltering retirement savings by allowing a deduction from taxable income and allowing the savings to accumulate tax-free until they are removed in retirement seems fair and efficient. It is analogous to treating these savings on a consumption tax basis. The main issue is whether the levels of allowable savings are high enough. The higher are the limits to contributions, the closer the system comes to being a true consumption tax system. This is clearly an important policy issue.

Any attempt to change the tax treatment of either housing or human capital investment in a substantial way would be fraught with difficulty. Improving the tax treatment of housing would involve either including imputed rent in the tax base, which would be administratively difficult, or affording mortgage interest deductibility, a step that would provide a significant incentive to home ownership. In the case of human capital investment, one can make an argument for enhancing the incentives available to individuals. Investments in human capital may well have externalities associated with them in the form of enhanced productivity. This type of investment is hampered, however, by liquidity constraints and extreme riskiness of returns. A number of measures designed to address these problems have been advocated recently; they include deductibility of the interest costs incurred in borrowing to finance education and the use of income-contingent loans to insure against the riskiness associated with human capital accumulation.[41]

---

[40] See the discussion in Organisation for Economic Co-operation and Development, *OECD Economic Surveys 1995-1996: Canada* (Paris: OECD, 1996), chapter 4; and Banting and Boadway, supra footnote 39.

[41] See Ontario, *Excellence, Accessibility, Responsibility: Report of the Advisory Panel on Future Directions for Postsecondary Education* (Toronto: Queen's Printer for Ontario, 1996).

## Instruments of Redistribution

The tax system, more precisely the personal income tax system, is one of many policy instruments available to the government for redistributive purposes. The others include transfers delivered to the least well-off through social assistance programs; transfers to the elderly; social insurance programs such as employment insurance, workers' compensation, and health insurance; and the provision of public services such as education, social services, housing, and day care. There is a large literature on the appropriate mix of policy instruments, and their institutional delivery mechanisms, for address-ing redistributive issues. Meanwhile, more and more economists have come to agree that there are significant economic limitations on the optimal degree of progressivity of the income tax system. Study after study of the "optimal income tax," following the path-breaking work of the Nobel Laureate James Mirrlees, has shown that given the adverse incentive consequences of pro-gressive taxation and its effects on taxpayer compliance, the income tax rate structure should be fairly flat.[42]

As we shall discuss in chapter 2, the evidence on the progressivity of the Canadian tax system is consistent with this conclusion. Taken overall, the tax system seems to be roughly proportional to income. This does not imply that government policy considered more generally is not redistributive. Much of what governments do on the expenditure side of the budget appears to be motivated by redistributive objectives, and it seems clear that a substantial amount of redistribution does, in fact, take place through expenditure programs[43]—a consideration that further weakens the case for a highly progressive income tax structure.

Nonetheless, determining the optimal degree of progressivity continues to be an important policy issue, especially given the evidence that market earn-ings are becoming more and more unevenly distributed. Much of the policy concern related to redistribution concentrates on the two ends of the income distribution, the poorest and the richest members of society. Different consider-ations apply in each of these two cases, so it will do to discuss them separately.

### Transfers to the Least Well-Off

In principle, the tax-transfer system ought to be the primary instrument for delivering transfers to the least well-off. Indeed, economists and policy specialists alike have long advocated the adoption of a *negative income tax* as

---

[42] Mirrlees's work is extremely technical. For a summary of his results, see A.B. Atkinson and J.E. Stiglitz, *Lectures on Public Economics* (London: McGraw-Hill, 1980).

[43] For a recent summary of this view, see Dominique van de Walle and Kimberly Nead, eds., *Public Spending and the Poor: Theory and Evidence* (Baltimore: Johns Hopkins University Press, 1995). For Canadian evidence, see G.C. Ruggeri, D. Van Wart, and R. Howard, *The Government as Robin Hood: Exploring the Myth* (Kingston, Ont.: Queen's University, School of Policy Studies, 1996).

an integral part of the progressive tax system.[44] The income tax system, with its self-reporting and auditing enforcement structure, would seem to be suited for the task of providing financial assistance to the poor and needy, including the working poor, the elderly, the disabled, and children. But this capability has never really been exploited with full vigour (though Canada has made more use of it than most other OECD countries).[45]

Most of the job of providing assistance to the poor has been relegated to the provincial welfare systems. Welfare has many advantages as a delivery device for transfers. Social workers, the gatekeepers in a welfare system, are well placed to determine who needs assistance and to respond quickly to changes in their clients' circumstances. But welfare also has its disadvantages. It is costly to administer, since social workers must deal with their caseloads on an individual basis. In addition, it is often charged with blunting the incentives for welfare recipients to seek work, to become trained, or to behave honestly. Nor does it appear to be suitable as a means of assisting the working poor. Finally, the provinces' welfare systems, like their tax systems, are susceptible to interprovincial competition, in this case competition to reduce their welfare rolls at the expense of other provinces.

These considerations suggest that the income tax system could usefully assume a much more important role than it has assumed to this point in the delivery of transfers to the poor. It would be especially appropriate if the federal income tax system were used for this purpose, since the primary responsibility for achieving redistributive equity rests with the federal government. In fact—a point we shall discuss further in chapter 3—the federal income tax system has already acquired some experience in delivering transfers to the poor through its system of selective refundable tax credits—the GST credit and the child tax benefit. These credits are essentially a form of negative income tax, which like the income tax itself is self-reported and, in principle, subject to auditing.[46] Although the refundable tax credits are not as responsive as welfare is to the changing circumstances of recipients, they are nonetheless more responsive than is the tax system itself. Moreover, unlike the tax system as such, they are based on family income, an arrangement that undoubtedly adds some complexity to the system but may be more effective than using individual income would be at targeting transfers to those who need them most.

---

[44] The popularization of the idea goes at least as far back as Milton Friedman, *Capitalism and Freedom* (Chicago: University of Chicago Press, 1962). It has been recommended for Canada by various commissions and government position papers. Examples include Canada, Department of National Health and Welfare, *Income Security for Canadians* (Ottawa: Queen's Printer, 1970); and François Vaillancourt, reserach coordinator, *Income Distribution and Economic Security in Canada*, Collected Research Studies of the Royal Commission on the Economic Union and Development Prospects for Canada, vol. 1 (Toronto: University of Toronto Press, 1985).

[45] See the summary in K.C. Messere, *Tax Policy in OECD Countries: Choices and Conflicts* (Amsterdam: IBFD Publications, 1993).

[46] A recent auditor general's report has noted that, in fact, Revenue Canada has devoted few resources to auditing the refundable tax credits for overpayment and ineligibility.

The advent of refundable tax credits contingent on family income is a major innovation in tax policy with significant potential for future development. The credits could be used to turn the income tax system into a proper tax-transfer system that treated negative tax liabilities symmetrically with positive ones. A system of this kind would rationalize the entire system of redistribution at the lower end by enhancing progressivity in a way that was both administratively inexpensive and efficient in that it would not distort recipients' incentives. Integration of the tax and transfer systems would permit proper income testing of the latter and thereby avoid some of the problems that afflict the provincial welfare systems. The implicit tax-back rates—the rates at which transfers would decline as income rose—would trade off work incentives against program costs: higher tax-back rates ensure that transfers are more closely targeted to those in need but also entail higher work-disincentive effects. Finally, transfers delivered through the tax system could apply to all types of poor persons—the disabled, the working poor, the elderly, and single parents.

Given that Canada is a federation, there is always the issue of jurisdiction. Which level of government should be responsible for assisting the poor? In practice, transfers delivered through the tax system could, and should, exist alongside provincial welfare programs. As we have mentioned, the latter are better than the tax system would be at targeting transfers to those in need and responding quickly to changing circumstances of recipients. But the exact mix of federal and provincial assistance to the poor could be determined jointly by the governments themselves. Whatever the mix, it would certainly be desirable for there to be some harmonization of the transfer programs offered by the two levels of government.

## Progressivity at the Top

The problem of how to identify and achieve the optimal degree of progressivity in the income tax at the top of the income scale is somewhat different. Some inequality of incomes is a matter of differences in lifetime earnings. In principle, an income tax system can reduce that difference. But there are obvious constraints on the extent to which it does so. For one thing, a taxpayer's earnings can vary considerably over his or her lifetime, and a tax system that taxes incomes progressively on an annual basis may be treating unfairly taxpayers who are temporarily at the peak of their earnings profiles. Indeed, it has been estimated that a substantial proportion of the inequality observed in annual income data disappears when one adopts a longer time horizon (we shall return to this subject in chapter 2). A second and perhaps more important point is that persons at the upper end of the income distribution are on average likely to be more mobile internationally than those lower down. Tax systems that are highly progressive can adversely affect the location decisions of such persons and, what may be more important, the location decisions of the businesses that employ them. This circumstance imposes a cost on progressivity that policy makers must assess.

Inherited wealth is another source of inequality of incomes, and there are several ways of redistributing wealth of this kind. One is simply to include capital income in the progressive tax system, since capital income will accrue disproportionately to wealthy persons. An alternative is to implement a tax on the wealth itself, or on the transfer of wealth—at least in the case of significant sums of wealth. Many industrialized countries do impose such taxes, though with varying degrees of success. Canada is an exception: our system of inheritance taxes essentially collapsed when that form of taxation was transferred to the provinces in the early 1970s, a graphic example of tax competition at work! We do, of course, tax capital to a limited extent, and real property as well, through the property tax. Accrued capital gains are taxed on death. But these are hardly effective ways of redistributing from those with large amounts of inherited wealth. That purpose would require some form of wealth transfer tax on large estates. Like any other method of redistribution, a tax of this nature would have adverse efficiency consequences. It might be costly to enforce, and it might adversely affect wealth holdings within Canada.

How redistributive is the Canadian tax system? Is it becoming more or less progressive as time goes by? We shall look at these issues in detail in chapter 2. Here, it is enough to indicate briefly how important income taxes and transfers are to persons at various income levels. Table 1.6 divides the population into five per-capita income groups, or quintiles: the first quintile represents the 20 percent of the population with the lowest incomes, the second quintile the next 20 percent of the population by income, and so on. For each quintile, the table shows the average amount of income taxes, transfers, and both taxes and transfers as a percentage of income for three years—1971, 1986, and 1993. The figures take into account both federal and provincial income taxes and both federal and provincial transfers, such as welfare assistance, unemployment insurance, and public pensions. These data indicate that average tax rates have increased over time, but that they have increased more for higher-income quintiles. So, the tax system has become more progressive. The transfer system has also become more "progressive"— considerably so. Lower-income persons have received substantial increases in transfers as a percentage of income. When taxes and transfers are combined, the net effect too shows an increase in progressivity. For the bottom three quintiles, transfers less taxes as a percentage of income have increased, whereas for the top quintile it has decreased by a modest amount.

This trend to increased progressivity in the tax-transfer system also appears when one uses family income as the basis of comparison. A recent study has calculated how taxes as a proportion of income have changed for various real family income levels between 1954 and 1994 for various sizes of family.[47] The study finds that higher-income families of all sizes had higher average tax rates in 1994 than in 1970, whereas almost all lower-income families had lower average tax rates. This outcome reflects the combination

---

[47] See Roger S. Smith, "The Personal Income Tax: Average and Marginal Tax Rates in the Post-War Period" (1995) vol. 43, no. 5 *Canadian Tax Journal* 1055-76, at 1085, table 7.

### Table 1.6   Average Income Tax and Transfer Rates by Quintile, 1971, 1986, and 1993

|  | Quintile | | | | | |
|---|---|---|---|---|---|---|
|  | Lowest | Second | Third | Fourth | Highest | Total |
|  | *percentage of income* | | | | | |
| Income tax |  |  |  |  |  |  |
| 1971 | 2.1 | 7.5 | 12.1 | 14.8 | 19.7 | 15.2 |
| 1986 | 2.5 | 8.7 | 14.4 | 17.6 | 21.8 | 17.2 |
| 1993 | 2.6 | 8.4 | 15.0 | 19.2 | 24.4 | 18.9 |
| Transfer payments |  |  |  |  |  |  |
| 1971 | 53.4 | 18.2 | 5.7 | 3.4 | 2.0 | 26.7 |
| 1986 | 59.5 | 31.2 | 13.0 | 6.9 | 11.3 | 18.0 |
| 1993 | 67.8 | 40.4 | 18.0 | 9.7 | 14.5 | 16.1 |
| Transfer payments minus income tax |  |  |  |  |  |  |
| 1971 | 51.3 | 10.7 | −6.4 | −11.4 | −17.7 | −8.6 |
| 1986 | 57.0 | 22.5 | −1.4 | −10.7 | −18.5 | −5.9 |
| 1993 | 65.2 | 32.0 | 3.0 | −9.5 | −20.2 | −4.4 |

Source: Roger S. Smith, "The Personal Income Tax: Average and Marginal Tax Rates in the Post-War Period" (1995), vol. 43, no. 5 *Canadian Tax Journal* 1055-76 (data obtained from Statistics Canada, *Income After Tax, Distribution by Size in Canada, 1993*, catalogue no. 13-210).

of flattening out the rate structure, substituting tax credits for many deductions, and introducing refundable tax credits. These policies may well have gained political impetus from the observed tendency for the before-tax income distribution to worsen.

This completes our introductory summary of tax policy issues. Before we turn, in the next chapter, to the principles of taxation, it is worth listing what most observers would identify as being desirable features for Canada's tax system as we enter the third millennium:[48]

• All Canadian businesses should be treated on a par with their competitors at home and abroad.

• The tax system should encourage savings and investment, innovation, risk taking, and human capital formation.

• There should be no undue tax incentive for highly skilled persons or businesses to locate outside of Canada.

• The mix of taxes assigned to the federal government and the provinces and the harmonization of these taxes should avoid the inefficiencies that arise from interprovincial tax competition, without impairing the provinces' ability to exercise their fiscal responsibilities in an accountable way.

---

[48] Some of these features were also stressed in *OECD Economic Surveys 1996-1997: Canada*, supra footnote 6.

• A related point: the system of transfers should enable all of the provinces to use comparable tax rates in meeting their expenditure commitments.

• The overall mix of income, sales, and payroll taxes should achieve the desired degree of progressivity, taxation of capital income, and ease of compliance and enforcement.

• There should be a targeting of transfers to the poor through the tax system that retains work incentives and economizes on costs, and that is coordinated with provincial welfare systems.

• The income tax system should be indexed to the extent that indexation is administratively feasible, so that inflation does not lead to capricious tax effects.

We shall return to these points in the final chapter.

# 2

# The Principles of Taxation

## Introduction

The previous chapter outlined the Canadian tax system, the context in which tax policy decisions must be made, and the main tax policy issues that face policy makers in Canada. Subsequent chapters will consider in more detail each of the main types of taxes used in Canada, but the tax system must also be considered in its entirety. Governments must obtain all of their tax revenues from the same set of taxpayers, and the many tax bases that they use to extract taxes from citizens overlap substantially. Thus there ought to be an overriding set of principles that governs the design of the tax system as a whole. In this chapter, we shall step back and take a general look at the fundamental principles of a good tax system, principles that public finance specialists have developed over many years.

The tax-transfer system has two main functions: to finance public sector expenditures on goods and services, and to transfer purchasing power between individuals and thereby improve the distribution of income and wealth. This chapter outlines the economic principles that governments must consider in choosing taxes and transfers to fulfil these functions. In addition, it discusses several structural problems that have been prominent in the ongoing debate about tax reform. The matters at issue include the choice of a personal tax base, the indexation of the tax system to deal with inflation, and the choice between a personal tax with a progressive rate structure and one with a single rate.

Taxes are not the only means of obtaining revenue for public sector activities. Governments also raise significant amounts of revenue through the issuing of debt, the creation of money, and the sale of goods and services. The scope of this book, however, precludes a consideration of the appropriate balance among the various means of obtaining public funds. Our analysis assumes simply that some given total amount of revenue must be raised by taxes, and our concern will be with the manner in which the existing system accomplishes this end, with the economic impact of that system, and with the question whether a different system could raise the same amount of revenue more fairly and with a lower economic cost. Although we shall ignore the raising of revenue by governments through the sale of goods and services— that is, through voluntary user prices[1]—we do take into account earmarked

---

[1] User prices as a source of government revenue and as a method for rationing the use of government services have been discussed fully in Richard M. Bird, *Charging for Public Services: A New Look at an Old Idea*, Canadian Tax Paper no. 59 (Toronto: Canadian Tax Foundation, 1976).

taxes such as contributions under the Canada and Quebec pension plans and the employment insurance plan. Since these plans are coercive rather than voluntary, the payments made under them are rightfully regarded as tax levies. To be more precise, they are equivalent to payroll taxes.

Besides providing goods and services and redistributing income, governments also perform a stabilization function. That is, they use fiscal and monetary policies to influence both the aggregate level of economic activity and macroeconomic variables such as interest rates, the exchange rate, and the rate of inflation. In addition, they influence the allocation of economic activity in the private sector by undertaking various regulatory activities, such as mandating the purchase or provision of certain types of products (for example, automobile insurance). These roles of government may involve the use of taxes and may affect the way in which taxes impinge on the economy, but we shall not discuss them here. We shall also ignore the use of tariffs as revenue-raising devices, since their primary role in Canada is not to raise revenue but to influence economic activity in particular industries. In any case, tariffs are becoming less and less important as the liberalization of world trade proceeds.

Let us turn, then, to the economic principles of taxation.

## The Principles of a Good Tax System

Economists judge the efficacy of a tax system or of reforms to the tax system according to a number of widely accepted criteria. One criterion is equity: is the burden of the resources transferred to the public sector by the tax system distributed fairly among members of the society? Another is efficiency: does the tax system interfere as little as possible with the use of the competitive price mechanism to allocate the economy's scarce resources? A third criterion is economic growth: is the tax system conducive to a high rate of growth? The final criterion is ease of administration: are the collection costs imposed on the government and the compliance costs imposed on taxpayers suitably low? We shall refer to these criteria again and again in the chapters on individual taxes, so it is important to discuss them carefully here. In practice, the various criteria will conflict with one another, and no one tax will be ideal in terms of all of them. The more equitable a tax is, the less efficient—and the more detrimental to economic growth—it is likely to be. This is the classic equity-efficiency, or equality-output, tradeoff that economists often stress: a more equal division of the economic pie may entail a smaller pie to be divided. Moreover, attempts to improve the equity of the tax system often make the tax system more complicated and more difficult to enforce. Some taxes are more equitable than others, some are more efficient than others, some are easier to administer and enforce than others, and so on. Ultimately, the task of trading off one criterion against another requires a judgment. Each of the criteria is considered below.

### Equity

Taxes ultimately involve the removal of purchasing power from individuals in the economy, and the tax structure will determine how the burden of the reduction in purchasing power is shared by individuals in different circumstances. The impact of taxes may vary with a household's income, its spending patterns, its family structure, the age of its members, and so on. The government can influence the pattern of this variation by its choice of tax bases and rate structures. The principle of equity suggests that the burden of taxation should be shared fairly among individuals according to their circumstances. This principle was stressed by the famous report of the Royal Commission on Taxation (the so-called Carter report), whose proposals found their way into the major income tax reforms of 1971.[2] It also accounted for many of the changes in the individual income tax that were introduced under the last major reform, in 1987.[3]

Any measure of the equity or fairness of the tax system obviously involves weighing the burden borne by one taxpayer against the burden borne by another. That is, it requires what economists refer to as interpersonal comparisons of "well-being" or "welfare." This requirement immediately makes the application of the principle of equity difficult, since no objective measure of well-being is possible. Economists often simply lay out for the policy maker the consequences that different tax policy options would have for the distribution of the tax burden, leaving it to the policy maker to decide which is the most equitable option (and to trade equity off against other policy objectives). Nevertheless, economists generally distinguish between two concepts of equity—horizontal equity and vertical equity. Horizontal equity refers to persons in comparable circumstances; that is, persons who are equally well off. Vertical equity refers to persons in different circumstances; that is, persons who are not equally well off.

## Horizontal Equity

The principle of horizontal equity implies that equals should be treated equally. Thus a tax is said to be horizontally equitable if two persons who have the same level of well-being before the tax is imposed still have the same level of well-being after it is imposed. This concept of equity rests, of course, on a value judgment; nevertheless, the concept is widely accepted by economists and policy makers. As simple as the idea of horizontal equity may seem to be, however, ensuring that a tax system satisfies this idea is a difficult task. If the criterion of horizontal equity is to be satisfied, there must be a basis for comparing the well-being of one person with that of another. One must be able to judge whether person A is better off, worse off, or neither better off nor worse off than person B. Since we cannot measure well-being, however, comparisons of this are inherently subjective.

It is usually argued that some general notion of income—one that encompasses all sources of income—is a satisfactory basis for comparisons of well-being. We shall discuss one such definition of income, *comprehensive*

---

[2] Canada, *Report of the Royal Commission on Taxation* (Ottawa: Queen's Printer, 1966).

[3] Canada, Department of Finance, *Tax Reform 1987: Income Tax Reform* (Ottawa: the department, June 18, 1987).

*income*, in detail below. Roughly speaking, comprehensive income is the flow of new purchasing power to a person over a given period—say, a year. If one person has more comprehensive income than another, then he can purchase more of the things that he prefers than the other person can and therefore is better off than the other person. Although it is often taken for granted that comprehensive income is a reasonably good proxy measure for the actual or potential well-being of an individual, several conceptual problems arise if income is used as the sole measure of equity.

To begin with, income does not measure all sources of economic well-being. As a rule, the earning of income requires the expenditure of time and energy. Suppose that two individuals have the same amount of time in which to earn income, and that one chooses more income and less leisure and the other more leisure and less income. Since the opportunity to earn income is the same for both individuals, they may be said to be equally well off— equally well off, that is, in the absence of taxes. A tax system that taxes income alone will not be horizontally equitable, since it will not take the benefit of leisure into account: it will systematically favour persons who choose leisure over earned income. Leisure is a form of *imputed income*. Other forms of imputed income, such as the value of a homemaker's time or the value of food grown for one's own consumption, contribute to horizontal inequity in the same way. Indeed, all forms of non-market activity are excluded from the income tax base.

A similar problem arises from the fact that some persons are inherently more productive than others. They earn a given amount of income with less effort, in terms of either time spent or intensity of effort, than other persons. A tax based on income will not take differences in effort into account and will therefore be horizontally inequitable. Of course, since the tax authorities cannot observe effort, it is probably impossible to design a tax system that does take effort into account. This means that a fully horizontally equitable tax is not possible: the tax system can only account for observable sources of horizontal inequity. The impossibility of observing individuals' effort is an even more important constraint on vertical equity, as we shall discuss shortly.

Another consideration that limits the usefulness of income as an index of horizontal equity is the fact that income is measured for tax purposes as a flow over a given interval, typically one year. Since a person's income can fluctuate considerably over time, his income in a given year may not represent his average income or standard of living over his lifetime. An income tax system that ignores these fluctuations will lead to horizontal inequities if it is "progressive"—that is, if the percentage of income paid as tax (the *average tax rate*) increases with income. The Canadian income tax system is designed in this way. Under a progressive tax system, if two persons have the same average income over a period of several years but one person's income fluctuates more than the other's, the person with the fluctuating income will pay more income tax.

In principle, there are two ways in which a progressive income tax can deal with fluctuating incomes without creating horizontal inequities. The first is to use as the tax base some notion of "permanent income"—that is, the average level of income that one can expect a person to achieve over his lifetime.[4] This approach, however, is obviously an impractical one. The second method is to average income for tax purposes over a number of years. There are several ways of doing this. Backward averaging allows a taxpayer to treat an abnormally high increase in income as if the increase were spread over several years in the past. This type of averaging is particularly helpful to new entrants to the labour force and to those who experience a large increase in income in a particular year. It does not help those whose incomes fall from one year to the next. The remedy for them would be a system of forward averaging, under which a taxpayer can spread income for tax purposes in a year of high income over a number of future years when his income is lower. This is the method that was previously, but is no longer, used in Canada; as we shall discuss in chapter 3, Canada now has *no* averaging system. Forward averaging does not help those who experience sudden increases in income unless their income falls again in the future. A more general system of averaging would allow taxpayers to average their current year's income with their income in both past and future years. A system of this kind is certainly feasible in administrative terms in this age of computerized information systems. The difficulty would be to determine the number of years over which the averaging should take place. In any period of years, the average level of taxes may change, and it is not clear how one would determine the appropriate tax rate to apply to income that has been averaged over a period in which this happens.[5] It should be noted that although averaging is feasible in the case of taxes levied on individuals, such as an income tax or an expenditure tax (discussed below), it is not feasible in the case of taxes levied anonymously on transactions—so-called in rem taxes such sales taxes and excise taxes. On the other hand, since the latter taxes are relatively non-progressive, the issue is not as important in their case as it is in the case of the income tax.

A final way in which a comprehensive income tax can create horizontal inequities is by failing to take into account differences among individuals in their ability to enjoy the use of income. Two persons with the same opportunities to earn income may have different levels of well-being if they differ in health, age, or other personal circumstances. Most income tax systems attempt to recognize these differences by allowing reductions in tax liabilities for medical and dental expenditures, old age, disability, and dependants. Some systems also allow deductions on the ground of horizontal equity for the cost of earning income or child care. We shall consider further how the tax system does and should account for differences in personal circumstances

---

[4] The idea of permanent income is commonly used by economists. For an early, but complete, analysis of the idea, see Milton Friedman, *Theory of the Consumption Function* (Princeton, NJ: Princeton University Press, 1957).

[5] Some of these issues are discussed in more detail in the classic work by the late Nobel Laureate William S. Vickrey, *Agenda for Progressive Taxation* (New York: Ronald Press, 1947).

later in this chapter and in chapter 3. In rem taxes cannot allow for these differences, just as they cannot allow for fluctuations in income.

Despite all of these difficulties, comprehensive income—suitably defined and with suitable deductions and exemptions—has been widely accepted as an appropriate base for the taxation of individuals. It is not, however, the only possible base. We shall discuss later in this chapter a tax base that is now widely recognized as a suitable alternative to the income tax—namely, the personal expenditure or consumption tax.

## Vertical Equity

The criterion of vertical equity involves the determination of how to treat persons with different levels of well-being. It raises the question of how progressive the tax system should be. The value judgment required here is even more difficult than the one required in the case of horizontal equity. The latter requires only the determination of when individuals in different circumstances are equally well off. Vertical equity involves determining the extent of differences in well-being and deciding how far public policy should go in redressing these differences.

A common argument for progressivity is based on the so-called principle of utilitarianism. According to this principle, the benefit of giving an additional dollar to a person—the person's marginal utility—falls as his income rises. By this reckoning, dollars taken from high-income persons involve less sacrifice than those taken from low-income persons. Alternatively, one might argue that the aim of an equitable tax system should be to reduce the inequalities that exist between different persons' utility levels. This is the basic rationale for progressivity of the tax system: to redistribute from the better-off to the less well-off.

The principle of utilitarianism is really only a principle; implementing it is fraught with difficulties.[6] Three problems, in particular, are worth stressing. The first, once again, is that a person's utility—that is, his well-being—is virtually impossible to measure. The early utilitarians of the 19th century actually believed that it might be possible to measure a person's utility just as we measure his height or weight. This is now recognized to be impractical, if not conceptually impossible.

The second problem is that even if we could have empirical, objective measures of the utility levels of different persons we would still have to decide how far public policy should go to equalizing utility levels. To use the economist's jargon, What should the social welfare function be? To see what is at stake here, consider two people who differ in their ability to convert income into utility. Person A is a much more efficient "utility machine" than

---

[6] The concept of utilitarianism and some of its difficulties are discussed in Amartya K. Sen, *On Economic Inequality* (Oxford: Clarendon Press, 1973).

person B; this is so, let us say, because person B has a disability. If each has an income of $20,000, person A obtains a higher level of utility than person B, and also a higher marginal utility. Now, if the aim of social policy were to maximize the sum of utilities, which was the objective of classical utilitarianism, then income would be redistributed from person B to person A, from the less efficient utility machine to the more efficient. The sum of utilities would rise, but utility levels would become even more unequal. If the aim of social policy were instead to reduce the inequality of utility levels, then redistribution would go the other way, from the high-utility person (person A) to the low-utility person (person B). This example is not farfetched: policy makers must decide how much to redistribute to persons who are disabled and who therefore require relatively large amounts of income if they are to sustain a comfortable life. The example shows that value judgments must be made in deciding redistribution policy, value judgments that ultimately determine the degree of progressivity in the tax system. Societies generally have adopted the view that public policies should be used to redistribute toward the less well-off in society. But the degree of redistribution can vary from country to country, and even from province to province within a country.

In these circumstances, the economist is left with the task of advising policy makers how to implement given societal norms of vertical equity. This brings us to the third problem that governments face. Suppose there is a generally accepted set of norms for transfers from the better-off to the less well-off. The problem then is to identify who is better off and who is less well off. Ultimately, how well off a person is depends upon individual characteristics, such as ability, productivity, health, and so on. Governments cannot observe these characteristics and so cannot base their tax and transfer policies on them. The best that they can do is to use imperfect indicators of well-being, such as income. But incomes are not given: they can be affected by individual behaviour. The more that a government attempts to redistribute to those with low incomes, the greater is the incentive for persons with higher income-earning abilities to earn lower incomes and thereby increase their eligibility for reduced taxes or increased transfers. Thus arises the so-called equity-efficiency tradeoff: given income as the only measure of well-being, governments can increase vertical equity only at the expense of economic efficiency. Economists refer to this consequence of imperfect information as an underlying "limit to redistribution"; that is, they have come to the view that the main impediment to redistributive policy is the inadequacy of the information available to governments.[7]

Simulation studies have shown that, even with highly redistributive norms for vertical equity, the optimal progressivity of income-based tax-transfer

---

[7] This way of looking at the redistribution problem is attributed to the Nobel Laureate James Mirrlees. For a summary of the implications of imperfect information for government policy, see Robin Boadway, "Public Economics and the Theory of Public Policy" (November 1997), 30 *Canadian Journal of Economics* 753-72.

systems is surprisingly limited. The seminal study by James Mirrlees, who used parameter values that allowed his simulation model to represent the stylized features of industrialized economies, found that the optimal re-distributive tax system was not much different from a linear progressive, or flat, income tax system.[8] A flat tax system is one in which there is a fixed exemption level and a constant marginal tax rate. The important thing here is that a system of this kind operates as a negative income tax at the lower end of the income distribution; that is, persons earning the lowest incomes re-ceive transfers instead of paying taxes. Mirrlees notes, moreover, that there are typically persons at the lower end of the income distribution, those with low productivities in the workplace, who have no employment income but do receive transfers. His calculations of progressivity assume that under a flat tax system they would, of course, continue to receive transfers. Simulation studies of this kind are technically very complicated and are conducted under several simplifying assumptions. Even though their results are not im-plementable, however, they may still be useful for policy purposes, since they suggest that it may not be desirable for the individual income tax to be too progressive.

Also useful is the understanding, now shared by most economists, that the main impediment to redistributive policy is the inadequacy of the informa-tion available to governments. This understanding has led to a recognition that income is a rather crude indicator of relative well-being and hence to the further recognition that the pursuit of vertical equity might be enhanced by the use of non-tax instruments that complement the income tax—instruments that attempt to overcome some of the informational disadvantages that constrain governments. Examples include in-kind transfers rather than cash transfers (such as public housing and welfare services); transfers delivered through welfare agencies, whose function is precisely to obtain information on the needs faced by different types of persons; and transfers targeted on the basis of variables other than income.

The upshot of the present discussion is that a government concerned solely with equity might wish to institute a highly progressive tax system in order to transfer income from the better-off to the less well-off. Indeed, if all persons were deemed to be able to convert income into utility equally well, a tax system whose sole purpose is to achieve vertical equity should make incomes equal. This would imply a very progressive tax system indeed, one that involved 100 percent marginal tax rates. There are, obviously, compelling reasons for not equalizing incomes completely through the tax system, rea-sons stressed by the literature on optimal income taxation. The disincentive effects of so high a rate of progression would be very severe. Individuals

---

[8] See J.A. Mirrlees, "An Exploration in the Theory of Optimum Income Taxation" (1971), 38 *Review of Economic Studies* 175-208. Subsequent studies have tended to confirm this finding. For a review, see Gareth D. Myles, *Public Economics* (Cambridge, Eng.: Cambridge University Press, 1995), chapter 5.

would have no incentive to earn income if the tax system were to provide equal incomes in any case. Given a lesser rate of progression, the disincentive effects, or the efficiency costs of taxation, would be correspondingly less. Ultimately, policy makers have to strike some balance between vertical equity and economic efficiency. Judgments must be made, first, about the rate at which the sacrifice involved in giving up a dollar declines as income rises and, second, about the tradeoff between vertical equity and the concomitant increase in disincentives as the tax-transfer system becomes more progressive. Since this tradeoff requires a value judgment, reasonable people can, and obviously do, disagree about the optimal degree of progressivity of the tax system. We shall discuss the disincentive or efficiency effects of taxation in the next subsection of this chapter.

In assessing the vertical equity achieved by the tax system, one ought to have some notion of how the tax burden is, in fact, shared among persons in different income groups. This is called the *incidence* of the tax system. As we have mentioned, the purpose of taxes is to transfer purchasing power from households to governments. Tax incidence studies attempt to determine how the reduction in purchasing power is ultimately shared among income groups. Unfortunately, it is not enough simply to observe who is legally liable to pay the various taxes, referred to as the *legal incidence* of taxes. Those who actually pay the taxes do not necessarily bear the full resource loss represented by the taxes paid, since adjustments in the price system may shift the burden of the tax to other parties. For example, the goods and services tax (GST) is legally incident upon the producers who collect and pay the tax. Yet the imposition of the GST is almost certain to lead to a rise in prices of the taxed consumer products, with the result that some or all of the tax will eventually be shifted to consumers. Similarly, the corporate income tax may be partially shifted forward to consumers, in the form of higher prices, or backward to owners of factors of production hired by the corporation, in the form of reduced factor prices. If by reducing the demand for capital the tax causes rates of return on capital economy-wide to fall, then it may even be shifted to capital owners in the unincorporated sector. Thus the ultimate burden of a tax, or its *effective incidence*, may be shared among consumers, workers, and capital owners. The effective incidence differs from the legal incidence by the amount of shifting that has taken place.

Tax shifting is a reflection of the manner in which market prices respond to a change in taxes, so it can be explained using the economist's notions of supply and demand. Consider the simple case of a specific excise tax on some commodity, say, tobacco products. If the suppliers bear some of the tax, they will reduce the amount of tobacco that they supply, since the effective price that they receive is lower now than it was in the absence of the tax. The reduction in supply, however, will induce a rise in price, since the demanders will bid up the price in attempting to purchase the reduced amount of tobacco available. The extent to which a price rises in response to a fall in market supply will determine how much in the end the supply (and demand) will fall. If the quantity demanded is fairly insensitive to price changes—that is, if demand is inelastic—demanders will be willing to pay a much higher price to consume a slightly lower quantity of tobacco. In this case, the price will rise by a large amount in response to a slight fall in output, and the suppliers will, in effect, have succeeded in shifting a good part of the tax forward to demanders. If demand is more elastic, however, output will fall more, prices will rise less, and suppliers will end up absorbing a larger proportion of the tax in the form of a lower price.

On the other hand, the more responsive supply is to price changes—that is, the more elastic it is—the greater will be the reduction in output, and again the demanders will bear more of the tax in the form of a higher price. In summary, the extent to which a specific excise tax tends to be shifted forward to demanders increases with the inelasticity of demand and the elasticity of supply. In fact, specific excise taxes are often levied on goods for which demand is fairly inelastic (such as alcohol, tobacco, and gasoline); it is usual to assume that these taxes are borne largely by demanders even if their legal incidence is on suppliers.

Figure 2.1 illustrates the shifting of an excise tax geometrically by using the economists' constructs of demand and supply curves. The four panels of the figure contain demand and supply curves for four products, denoted $X$ in each case, that differ in their elasticities. Consider panel A. The demand curve, $D$, indicates the quantities of $X$ that would be demanded at various prices, $p$. The supply curve, $S$, shows the amounts that suppliers would be willing to supply at various prices. In the absence of an excise tax, the market equilibrium is at price $p_0$ and at quantity $X_0$. Suppose now that a tax is imposed of $t$ per unit sold. The tax is collected by the suppliers, so the supply curve shifts vertically by the amount $t$—for each quantity sold, the producers must charge an amount $t$ over and above the price they receive. In the new equilibrium, where demand equals supply, the quantity traded will be $X_1$. The price received by suppliers will now be $p_1$, and the price paid by demanders will be $p_1 + t$. As one can see, even though the suppliers pay the tax, the price they receive has not fallen by the full amount of the tax. Part of the tax is borne by the demanders, whose price has risen. That is, the suppliers have shifted part of the tax to the demanders. In panel A, the demand curve is relatively inelastic—changes in price do not cause much change in demand—and most of the tax is shifted to the demanders. Panel B shows that if demand is very elastic, very little of the tax is shifted to demanders; most of it is borne by the suppliers. Panels C and D indicate the influence of supply elasticities on the incidence of the tax. In panel C, supply is very inelastic, and the suppliers end up bearing most of the tax. In panel D, supply is elastic, and it is the demanders who bear most of the tax. We shall use this form of analysis again in some of the chapters to follow.

The incidence of a specific excise tax is relatively easy to analyze, since it is a tax imposed upon a single good that is a relatively small component of total output. One can safely ignore other markets and study only the response of the market on which the tax is imposed. This is what economists refer to

**Figure 2.1    Incidence of an Excise Tax**

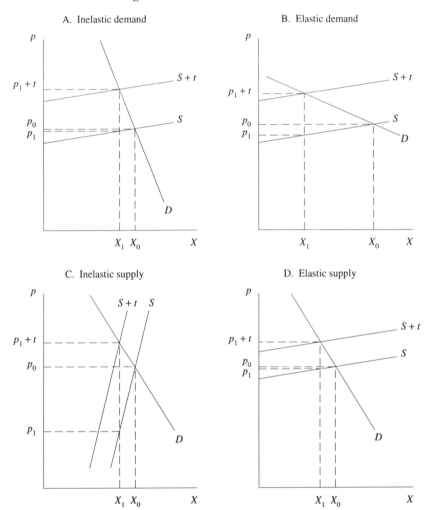

A. Inelastic demand

B. Elastic demand

C. Inelastic supply

D. Elastic supply

as a *partial equilibrium analysis*. Other taxes, however, fall on the markets for several goods or factors, and one cannot ignore the interdependencies that exist among markets. Consider, for example, the imposition of a partial factor tax—a tax that is imposed on one factor of production in some of its uses. An example is the corporate income tax, which one can view as a tax on capital in the corporate sector of the economy. As we shall discuss in chapter 4, this tax is levied on the net income earned by the shareholders of capital in the corporate sector but not in the unincorporated sector of the economy. The analysis of such a tax is considerably more complicated than the specific excise tax case, but we can provide an intuitive description of the forces at work here.[9]

One way in which to understand the incidence of a tax such as the corporate tax is to imagine the chain of events that would occur after the imposition of the tax. The rate of return to capital in the corporate sector would fall, and there would be a gradual reallocation of capital from the corporate sector to the unincorporated sector.[10] This reallocation would continue until the after-tax rate of return was the same in the two sectors. The new economy-wide rate of return to capital would be lower than the rate of return before the imposition of the tax, but not necessarily by the full amount of the tax. Some of the tax might have been shifted in the process.

Thus the corporate tax, to the extent that capital owners bear it, will eventually be borne equally by capital owners in the corporate sector and capital owners in the unincorporated sector. This is so because market forces will equalize the net returns to capital in the two sectors. Again, however, some of the tax may be shifted elsewhere. When the tax is imposed, three distinct things occur that have a bearing on the incidence of the tax. First, the relative costs of production in the corporate sector rise, causing the prices of the products produced there to rise. Consumers respond by reducing their demand for these goods and increasing it for other goods, thereby inducing resources to move out of the corporate sector and into other sectors. The extent of this reallocation will depend on the elasticities of demand for goods produced in the corporate sector. If the elasticities are low, corporate sector prices will rise without there being any great shift of resources, and to a large extent the tax will be shifted forward to consumers of corporate-sector products. The less elastic is the demand, the greater will be the shifting of the tax to consumers of these products and the less will be the reallocation of resources out of the corporate sector and into the unincorporated sector.

Second, the resources that are reallocated are generally used in different proportions in the corporate sector and the unincorporated sector. For example, if the corporate sector is labour-intensive relative to the unincorporated sector—that is, if it employs a higher ratio of labour to capital—then the ratio of the labour released from the corporate sector to the capital released will be higher than the current ratio of labour use to capital use in the unincorporated sector. Consequently, if all of the factors released are to be absorbed into the unincorporated sector, the price of labour (the wage rate) will have to fall relative to the price of capital (its rate of return). Thus labour

---

[9] On the other hand, one can analyze a general factor tax, such as a tax on wages (a payroll tax), by using demand and supply curves for the labour market. For a more detailed and slightly more technical discussion of the incidence of taxes, including the corporate income tax, see Robin W. Boadway and David E. Wildasin, *Public Sector Economics* (Boston: Little Brown, 1984), chapter 12. See also Harvey S. Rosen, Paul Boothe, Bev Dahlby, and Roger S. Smith, *Public Finance in Canada* (Toronto: McGraw-Hill Ryerson, 1998), chapter 17.

[10] In addition to this reallocation of capital, the change in the rate of return to capital might also lead to a change in the quantity of capital accumulated.

will suffer as a result of the tax, and to the extent that it suffers capital owners will have shifted part of the tax to labour. The greater is the difference between the two sectors in the ratio of labour use to capital use, the greater the shift will be.[11]

Finally, within the corporate sector, the tax will make capital relatively more expensive to use and so there will be a tendency to economize by substituting labour for capital. The rise in the labour intensity of production will be accompanied by a fall in the wage rate relative to the rental rate. This outcome constitutes another form of shifting of the tax onto labour.

Any calculation of the overall incidence of the corporate tax will require a determination of the net change in prices from all sources of market interaction—obviously, a difficult task. We shall review what empirical evidence there is on the incidence of the corporate tax in chapter 4.

Similar difficulties arise in estimating the incidence of other broadly based taxes and transfers. For example, a personal income tax on all sources of income is legally incident upon individuals according to their incomes from labour, capital, and land. Taxpayers may respond to the tax by reducing their supplies of these factors to the market. The response is likely to be different, however, for each of the three factors. The result is that the mix of labour, capital, and land available for production will change, and therefore both aggregate output and the relative prices of goods will change as well. Again, the precise analysis of incidence is very complicated. As a result, economists have resorted to simulation studies that use a fully specified "model" of the economy, consisting of many sectors, to compute the effects of tax changes.[12]

Often, studies of tax incidence make more or less arbitrary a priori assumptions about the shifting of taxes and use those assumptions to generate estimates of tax incidence. One widely used method derives from the work of the late Canadian economist, Irwin Gillespie.[13] We shall illustrate this

---

[11] If the corporate sector is capital-intensive, this effect will work in the opposite direction. That is, the return to capital will fall relative to the wage rate.

[12] This technique is referred to as applied general equilibrium analysis. For a summary of its use in tax incidence studies, see John B. Shoven and John Whalley, "Applied General-Equilibrium Models of Taxation and International Trade: An Introduction and Survey" (September 1984), 22 *Journal of Economic Literature* 1007-51.

[13] W. Irwin Gillespie, *The Incidence of Taxes and Public Expenditures in the Canadian Economy*, Studies of the Royal Commission on Taxation no. 2 (Ottawa: Queen's Printer, 1966). More recent studies of a similar kind include James A. Johnson, *The Incidence of Government Revenues and Expenditures*, a study prepared for the Ontario Committee on Taxation (Toronto: Queen's Printer for Ontario, 1968); Allan M. Maslove, *The Pattern of Taxation in Canada* (Ottawa: Economic Council of Canada, 1973); David A. Dodge, "Impact of Tax, Transfer, and Expenditure Policies of Government on the Distribution of Personal Income in Canada" (March 1975), 21 *Review of Income and Wealth* 1-52; W. Irwin Gillespie, *The Redistribution of Income in Canada* (Toronto: Gage, 1980); B.G. Dahlby, "The Incidence of Government Expenditures and Taxes in Canada: A Survey," in François Vaillancourt, research coordinator, *Income Distribution and Economic Security in Canada*, Collected Research Studies of the Royal

(The footnote is continued on the next page.)

procedure by discussing a recent use of it by Vermaeten, Gillespie, and
Vermaeten to estimate the incidence of the Canadian tax system for each of
four years in the period 1951 to 1988. The method proceeds by first clas-
sifying taxpayers according to a fairly inclusive measure of income, called
*broad income.* Broad income encompasses as many sources of income
available for use by individuals as is feasible given the available data. In
Vermaeten, Gillespie, and Vermaeten, broad income includes tax-inclusive
market income (wages and salaries, income from self-employment, and
various forms of capital income), non-reported market income and imputed
income (capital gains and imputed rent on owner-occupied homes, earnings
on sheltered retirement savings plans and pensions, employer benefits, and
gifts and inheritances), transfers received from the government (pensions,
unemployment insurance, welfare, and payments for families), and taxes paid
by others that are borne by individual taxpayers (the portions of commodity
taxes, corporate taxes, payroll taxes, resource taxes, and property taxes
deemed to be shifted to taxpayers).

This array gives a measure of nominal income for taxpayers. Nominal
income, however, does not accurately indicate the true spending power that a
person has at his disposal in periods of inflation, since inflation will erode the
person's holdings of real wealth. As we discuss below, part of the interest
and other capital income that an individual receives on his asset holdings will
reflect compensation for the decline in the real value of the assets resulting
from inflation. The analysis by Vermaeten, Gillespie, and Vermaeten, unlike
previous studies, adjusts broad income for inflation by reducing all interest,
dividends, and capital gains by the rate of inflation. Thus the study's broad
income measure is in real terms. This is important, since capital income as a
proportion of broad income varies by level of income. Incidence measures
would be biased if this correction for inflation were not carried out.

The next step is to attribute tax burdens to individuals with different broad
incomes. As we noted above, the taxpayer who pays a tax is not necessarily
the one who bears its true incidence: the tax can be shifted. The assignment
of taxes to individuals by broad income level involves making an assumption
about how each tax is shifted. Vermaeten, Gillespie, and Vermaeten adopt
three different shifting models but focus mainly on a "standard" case. In their
standard case, which parallels one commonly used in the literature, the incidence of the main taxes is as follows: the individual income tax is borne by the
taxpayer; the corporate income tax is borne by shareholders of corporations;

---

[13] Continued ...

Commission on the Economic Union and Development Prospects for Canada (Toronto:
University of Toronto Press, 1985), 111-51; Frank Vermaeten, W. Irwin Gillespie, and Arndt
Vermaeten, "Tax Incidence in Canada" (1994), vol. 42, no. 2 *Canadian Tax Journal* 348-416;
G.C. Ruggeri, D. Van Wart, and R. Howard, "The Redistributional Impact of Taxation in
Canada" (1994), vol. 42, no. 2 *Canadian Tax Journal* 417-51; and Arndt Vermaeten, W. Irwin
Gillespie, and Frank Vermaeten, "Who Paid the Taxes in Canada, 1951-1988?" (September
1995), 21 *Canadian Public Policy* 317-43. It is the last study that we discuss here.

commodity taxes on consumer goods are borne by consumers of the taxed products; commodity taxes on government purchases are borne by those who pay personal income tax; commodity taxes on exports and capital goods are shared by consumers and labour-income earners; payroll taxes are borne entirely by employees; property taxes on land are borne by property owners; property taxes on structures are borne by users; profit taxes levied on natural resources are borne by the owners; royalties are borne by consumers; and miscellaneous fees and taxes are borne by consumers. Of course, transfer payments received by individuals are assumed to be "borne" by the recipients. Although Vermaeten, Gillespie, and Vermaeten emphasize their standard case, they also present two alternative cases, a "progressive" case and a "regressive" case. In the progressive case, business owners bear commodity taxes paid on capital goods and exports, property taxes, royalties, and the employer share of payroll taxes. In the regressive case, consumers bear all commodity taxes, the employer portion of payroll taxes, and half of corporate taxes.

The procedure classifies individuals by broad-income decile groups: the bottom decile represents the 10 percent of the population with the lowest incomes, the next decile the 10 percent with the next lowest incomes, and so on up to the top decile. Thus each decile contains an equal number of persons. Of course, as time goes by, the income brackets within each decile will change, both because per-capita incomes will be rising and because the distribution of incomes will change. Nevertheless, this procedure allows one to compare patterns of tax incidence across years. One then determines the progressivity of the tax system by calculating the average tax rate for each income decile; that is, the ratio of the tax burden assigned to persons within the decile to real broad income for persons within the decile. Vermaeten, Gillespie, and Vermaeten perform the calculation for each of four years, 1951, 1961, 1969, and 1988.

Given the wealth of information generated by this procedure, Vermaeten, Gillespie, and Vermaeten are able to report a number of interesting indications of how tax burdens have varied over the period of their study. A summary of the main results for their standard case is as follows.

• Measured as a proportion of real broad income, the average tax rate for the entire population was 27 percent in 1951 and 1961. It rose to 34 percent in 1969 and to 37 percent in 1988. These increases were much less than the increases in average tax rates based on money income alone, which rose from 33 percent in 1969 to 47 percent in 1988. The reason for the difference is that components of broad income other than money income have become relatively more important over the period. Vermaeten, Gillespie, and Vermaeten suggest that this finding should allay concerns that tax burdens have risen dramatically over the past two decades.

• One can disaggregate the tax system into federal, provincial, and local taxes. Over the entire period, the average rates of federal and local taxation changed relatively little. Almost all of the growth in rates occurred at the provincial level. Thus the average federal tax rate (based on real broad income) was 18.4 percent in 1951 and 18.8 in 1988. The average local rate rose from 3.0 percent in 1951 to 4.0 percent in 1988. The average provincial rate, however, almost tripled, rising from 5.3 percent in 1951 to 14.5 percent in 1988. This result reflects two developments over the period: provincial expenditure responsibilities were increasing rapidly in areas such as health, education, and welfare, and the provinces were becoming more reliant on own-source revenues and less on transfers from the federal government.

• Table 2.1 shows how overall tax incidence changed between 1951 and 1988. The pattern of tax incidence was U-shaped in 1951: average tax rates were regressive over the bottom four deciles, roughly proportional over the next five, and sharply progressive only in the highest decile. A similar pattern prevailed in 1961 and 1969. In 1988, however, the tax incidence pattern was roughly proportional for the bottom two deciles, slightly progressive for the next three deciles, proportional for the next four, and mildly progressive for the top decile. Generally speaking, then, the top and bottom deciles gained relative to the middle deciles. What stands out overall is the relative absence of progressivity in the tax system. It is really not much different from a proportional tax.[14] This finding accords well with what has become a conventional view of redistributive policy: most redistribution takes place on the expenditure side of the budget rather than on the tax side.

• If one disaggregates the tax incidence patterns by level of government, some interesting differences emerge. Throughout the period 1951 to 1988, the federal tax system was somewhat more progressive than the tax system as a whole. In 1988, it was progressive over the five lowest broad-income deciles, proportional over for the next four deciles, and progressive again in the top decile. Over the period, it became more progressive for the poor and less progressive for the richest. The local tax rate, dominated by the property tax, was regressive throughout the income distribution over the entire period. In 1988, provincial tax rates were roughly proportional, much like the overall rates. Over the period, they became less regressive at the bottom end of the income scale; otherwise, the pattern of incidence changed relatively little. Of course, the substantial increase in provincial average tax rates over the period shifted the entire provincial tax pattern upward.

• Finally, different types of taxes have very different patterns of progressivity. In the Vermaeten, Gillespie, and Vermaeten study, personal income taxes were progressive throughout the income distribution and became increasingly so over the period 1951 to 1988, thanks to various tax reforms that broadened the base and changed the structure of deductions, exemptions, and credits (see chapter 3). In 1988, the corporate tax was roughly proportional

---

[14] The authors also report incidence patterns for the progressive and regressive cases. Not surprisingly, the former is more progressive and the latter more regressive than the standard case. Nevertheless, the extent of redistribution achieved by the tax system is still relatively limited.

**Table 2.1  Effective Tax Rates by Broad Income Percentile Group, 1951, 1961, 1969, and 1988**

| | Percentile group | | | | | | | | | | | |
| | 1-10% | 11-20% | 21-30% | 31-40% | 41-50% | 51-60% | 61-70% | 71-80% | 81-90% | 91-98% | 99-100% | All |
|---|---|---|---|---|---|---|---|---|---|---|---|---|
| | percent | | | | | | | | | | | |
| **1951** | | | | | | | | | | | | |
| Personal income tax | 0.60 | 1.70 | 2.60 | 2.40 | 2.80 | 3.30 | 3.80 | 4.80 | 7.00 | 8.20 | 6.20 | 5.20 |
| Corporate income tax | 1.90 | 1.10 | 0.80 | 0.80 | 0.90 | 0.90 | 1.20 | 1.60 | 4.10 | 28.20 | 5.20 | —a |
| Commodity taxes | 23.50 | 14.60 | 14.00 | 11.60 | 11.10 | 11.60 | 12.00 | 10.80 | 10.30 | 8.50 | 5.10 | 10.20 |
| Payroll taxes | 1.80 | 1.60 | 2.10 | 2.10 | 2.30 | 2.10 | 2.40 | 2.10 | 0.80 | 0.30 | 0.10 | 1.30 |
| Property taxes | 6.20 | 4.70 | 3.90 | 3.60 | 3.20 | 3.20 | 3.10 | 2.90 | 2.70 | 2.40 | 1.90 | 2.90 |
| Estate and other taxes | 4.40 | 2.50 | 2.00 | 1.60 | 1.40 | 1.40 | 1.40 | 1.20 | 1.10 | 1.00 | 4.80 | 1.80 |
| Total | 36.50 | 26.90 | 25.80 | 22.10 | 21.60 | 22.50 | 23.60 | 23.00 | 23.50 | 24.50 | 46.20 | 26.60 |
| **1961** | | | | | | | | | | | | |
| Personal income tax | 0.40 | 1.00 | 1.90 | 2.80 | 3.90 | 5.30 | 6.70 | 7.30 | 8.50 | 8.00 | 7.50 | 6.40 |
| Corporate income tax | 0.60 | 0.60 | 0.40 | 0.40 | 0.40 | 0.50 | 0.50 | 0.70 | 1.00 | 2.50 | 15.40 | 3.10 |
| Commodity taxes | 19.40 | 13.10 | 11.70 | 11.40 | 11.60 | 11.60 | 11.80 | 11.50 | 11.40 | 8.50 | 5.20 | 10.20 |
| Payroll taxes | 5.00 | 3.80 | 4.30 | 4.10 | 4.00 | 2.90 | 1.60 | 1.20 | 0.40 | 0.30 | 0.10 | 1.60 |
| Property taxes | 7.60 | 6.20 | 5.10 | 5.20 | 5.10 | 4.90 | 4.60 | 4.40 | 4.20 | 3.30 | 2.30 | 4.20 |
| Estate and other taxes | 4.50 | 2.40 | 1.70 | 1.40 | 1.30 | 1.20 | 1.10 | 1.10 | 1.00 | 0.90 | 4.90 | 1.80 |
| Total | 37.50 | 27.00 | 25.10 | 25.40 | 26.30 | 26.40 | 26.40 | 26.20 | 26.70 | 23.60 | 35.40 | 27.30 |
| **1969** | | | | | | | | | | | | |
| Personal income tax | 1.20 | 3.20 | 5.30 | 7.30 | 9.30 | 10.30 | 11.20 | 11.90 | 13.00 | 12.30 | 12.20 | 10.80 |
| Corporate income tax | 0.90 | 0.60 | 0.80 | 0.60 | 0.60 | 0.60 | 0.65 | 0.90 | 1.10 | 3.10 | 17.50 | 3.40 |
| Commodity taxes | 20.50 | 14.20 | 13.70 | 12.80 | 12.90 | 12.40 | 11.50 | 11.00 | 10.20 | 8.10 | 5.70 | 10.40 |
| Payroll taxes | 5.20 | 4.80 | 5.10 | 5.50 | 5.30 | 4.70 | 4.40 | 3.50 | 3.10 | 2.00 | 0.90 | 3.40 |
| Property taxes | 8.50 | 5.80 | 5.70 | 5.30 | 4.80 | 4.40 | 4.10 | 4.10 | 3.70 | 3.80 | 2.80 | 4.10 |
| Estate and other taxes | 6.60 | 3.20 | 2.50 | 2.00 | 1.90 | 1.70 | 1.50 | 1.40 | 1.20 | 1.40 | 3.30 | 1.90 |
| Total | 42.90 | 31.90 | 33.00 | 33.50 | 34.70 | 34.10 | 33.40 | 32.80 | 32.30 | 30.60 | 42.40 | 34.10 |

(The table is concluded on the next page.)

**Table 2.1  Concluded**

| | | | | | | Percentile group | | | | | | |
| | 1-10% | 11-20% | 21-30% | 31-40% | 41-50% | 51-60% | 61-70% | 71-80% | 81-90% | 91-98% | 99-100% | All |
|---|---|---|---|---|---|---|---|---|---|---|---|---|
| | | | | | | *percent* | | | | | | |
| 1988 | | | | | | | | | | | | |
| Personal income tax . . . . . . . | 1.00 | 4.30 | 6.90 | 8.90 | 11.10 | 13.30 | 14.40 | 15.30 | 15.90 | 17.50 | 19.00 | 14.60 |
| Corporate income tax . . . . . | 0.40 | 0.70 | 0.80 | 0.90 | 0.80 | 0.90 | 0.90 | 1.20 | 1.30 | 2.10 | 11.60 | 2.50 |
| Commodity taxes . . . . . . . . | 14.00 | 12.20 | 11.90 | 11.90 | 11.30 | 10.90 | 10.20 | 9.40 | 8.50 | 7.50 | 5.90 | 9.10 |
| Payroll taxes . . . . . . . . . . . . | 2.20 | 3.20 | 4.50 | 5.70 | 6.60 | 7.10 | 7.20 | 6.80 | 6.20 | 4.90 | 1.70 | 5.40 |
| Property taxes . . . . . . . . . . . | 8.00 | 6.50 | 5.70 | 5.10 | 4.50 | 4.20 | 3.80 | 3.60 | 3.30 | 3.00 | 3.00 | 3.80 |
| Estate and other taxes . . . . . | 5.25 | 3.50 | 2.80 | 2.50 | 2.20 | 2.00 | 1.80 | 1.60 | 1.50 | 1.30 | 1.40 | 1.80 |
| Total . . . . . . . . . . . . . . . . . | 30.80 | 30.40 | 32.60 | 34.90 | 36.60 | 38.30 | 38.20 | 37.80 | 36.50 | 36.20 | 42.50 | 37.20 |

ᵃ Not available.
Source: Arndt Vermaeten, W. Irwin Gillespie, and Frank Vermaeten, "Who Paid the Taxes in Canada, 1951-1988?" (September 1995), 21 *Canadian Public Policy* 317-43, at table 4.

up to the top two income deciles and became mildly progressive in the ninth decile and sharply progressive in the top decile. This distribution reflects the pattern of ownership of corporate capital. Payroll taxes in 1988 were highly progressive up to the median income and regressive thereafter. This result is not surprising, given that payroll taxes do not increase with income beyond certain limits. In the earlier years of the period, however, payroll taxes tended to be roughly proportional over the first five deciles and slightly regressive thereafter. In 1988, commodity taxes were somewhat regressive throughout the income distribution and property taxes were much more regressive, especially at lower income levels.

One must treat the results of the Vermaeten, Gillespie, and Vermaeten study with caution, since they are based upon particular assumptions about shifting. We know from the work of others that different shifting assumptions give very different results. For example, Browning has argued that sales and excise taxes are borne by factor suppliers rather than by consumers.[15] His argument is that because transfers to households are typically indexed for the price level, the effect of increases in the price level attributable to sales and excise taxes will be offset by accommodating changes in transfers. This consideration is particularly important in the case of low-income persons who rely heavily on transfers, since of course incidence studies conducted under the traditional methodology show that low-income groups bear a disproportionately large share of the burden of commodity taxes. If one allocates sales and excise taxes according to factor incomes, they turn out to be progressive rather than regressive. Thus Ruggeri, Van Wart, and Howard, by following Browning's suggestion, found the Canadian tax system to be much more progressive than previous estimates had indicated it to be.[16]

More generally, Whalley has demonstrated that one can find virtually any incidence pattern for the Canadian tax system, from progressive to regressive, by using various but equally plausible sets of shifting assumptions.[17] Progressivity increases if one assumes that sales taxes apply not only to current consumption but also to future consumption (savings), that savings give rise to future taxes on capital income, that inflation itself constitutes a tax that applies to the fruits of savings, and that payroll taxes are to some extent benefit taxes and so should be omitted from incidence calculations because their burden will be offset by the benefits they finance. Whalley finds that if one adjusts the standard incidence calculations by using all of the above assumptions the result will be a relatively progressive tax system

---

[15] Edgar K. Browning, "The Burden of Taxation" (August 1978), 86 *Journal of Political Economy* 649-71.

[16] Ruggeri, Van Wart, and Howard, supra footnote 13.

[17] John Whalley, "Regression or Progression: The Taxing Question of Tax Incidence" (November 1984), 17 *Canadian Journal of Economics* 654-82. See also France St-Hilaire and John Whalley, "Recent Studies of Efficiency and Distributional Impacts of Taxes: Implications for Canada," in Wayne R. Thirsk and John Whalley, eds., *Tax Policy Options in the 1980s*, Canadian Tax Paper no. 66 (Toronto: Canadian Tax Foundation, 1982), 28-64.

rather than one that is roughly proportional. By the same token, he suggests a number of alternative adjustments that lead to the opposite conclusion. Most of the adjustments in this case have to do with taxes on capital income. Corporations may be able to shift the burden of their taxes backward onto labour payments. Given a highly open economy, in which product prices and returns on capital income are largely set in international markets, this assumption may be a reasonable one. Labour, rather than asset owners, may also bear the burden of taxes on personal capital income, given the ease with which capital may be shifted abroad to avoid taxation, or shifted into untaxed assets (such as housing). It might even be argued that the portion of labour income that is attributable to human capital accumulation will not be borne by the household, given that the accumulation of human capital is a substitute for the accumulation of assets that yield taxable capital income. Whalley shows that by taking these considerations into account, it is possible to make the Canadian tax system appear to be very regressive. One is left with a very agnostic view of all descriptions of the pattern of tax incidence.

Whalley's results indicate just how sensitive tax incidence studies are to the shifting assumptions they use, and one could add other concerns to those expressed by Whalley. Incidence studies ignore the existence of unemployment and the policy responses to it, such as unemployment insurance. They also do not take account of the effects of non-tax instruments such as minimum wage laws, quantity controls in sectors such as agriculture, and industrial subsidies, all of which have distributive effects. Perhaps most important, most studies concentrate on the tax side. As we have mentioned, it is becoming widely recognized that many public expenditures are essentially devices for redistribution. Expenditure programs in the areas of health, education, welfare, and social insurance are ultimately motivated by redistributive goals. The extent to which these programs succeed in redistributing real income is uncertain, but their existence reduces the urgency of relying on the tax system for redistribution.

Another significant problem with standard tax incidence studies is that they rely on annual income data. Annual income distributions, however, can be affected significantly by individuals who are temporarily in extreme income positions. For example, the lower income groups contain persons who are temporarily out of work and retired persons whose incomes may be much lower than their consumption. The higher income groups contain persons who are in their peak earnings period. It has been estimated that up to one-half of inequalities in annual incomes are attributable to variations in income over the course of individuals' lives.[18] This being the case, basing tax incidence on annual income statistics can be misleading. An alternative procedure is to calculate tax incidence on the basis of lifetime incomes rather than annual incomes.

---

[18] James Davies, France St-Hilaire, and John Whalley, "Some Calculations of Lifetime Tax Incidence" (September 1984), 74 *The American Economic Review* 633-49.

Different taxes affect individuals differently in different periods of their lives. Sales and excise taxes are paid throughout a lifetime, whereas payroll taxes and property taxes are not. Income taxes too have an uneven lifetime profile, and this unevenness is aggravated by the taxes' progressive nature. Because transfers received tend to be concentrated in periods of low annual income, they are likely to be much less progressive on a lifetime basis than they are on an annual basis. The treatment of saving must also be reassessed in a lifetime context. If households save largely for future consumption, then sales and excise taxes are paid on both current consumption and savings. In this case, as we mentioned above, they are likely to be less regressive than the standard incidence studies indicate they are. But if a high proportion of household saving is for bequests, as some evidence suggests it is, sales and excise taxes may be regressive even on a lifetime basis. How these considerations would affect tax incidence calculations based on lifetime incomes is not obvious.

Measuring fiscal incidence on a lifetime basis is a very demanding task. One must construct longitudinal lifetime income and tax profiles on the basis of annual cross-sectional data, an undertaking that requires information on patterns of lifetime earnings, savings, inheritances, and bequests. An ambitious lifetime fiscal incidence study for Canada undertaken by Davies, St.-Hilaire, and Whalley[19] applies shifting assumptions to the five major tax types similar to the standard ones used by Vermaeten, Gillespie, and Vermaeten. Much like the studies of annual incidence, it finds that the tax system as a whole is only mildly progressive. Moreover, the extent of progressivity varies relatively little when different shifting assumptions are adopted. These results reflect the fact that tax types that are progressive if one uses annual data (such as personal income taxes and corporate taxes) and those that are regressive if one uses annual data (such as sales and excise taxes and payroll taxes) are less progressive or less regressive, respectively, if one uses lifetime data.

Another major shortcoming of conventional tax incidence studies is their assumption that pre-tax incomes are not affected by the introduction of taxes. Taking account of how the tax system affects market prices and incomes is not a trivial matter. It involves specifying a model of the workings of the economy. Economists have constructed models, referred to as *computable general equilibrium* models, that make the tax system a component of a fully specified model of the market economy and allow incidence to be determined endogenously through the working of the economy.[20] They thus avoid the need for rather arbitrary shifting assumptions.

Of course, this benefit is obtained at a cost. Computable general equilibrium models may not be able to take advantage of the highly disaggregated

---

[19] Ibid.

[20] The use of computable general equilibrium models for policy analysis is outlined and defended in Shoven and Whalley, supra footnote 12.

fiscal data that are used in standard tax incidence studies. Moreover, in place of the arbitrary shifting assumptions, one must select an almost equally arbitrary economic model, not to mention parameters for technologies and tastes. It may be possible to choose the economic parameters in a relatively informed way. Econometric estimates of parameters of the supply and demand sides of the market economy may be available, though in practice their availability is quite limited. In addition, one can choose values for the variables that make it possible to calibrate the model so that it replicates the real world. Nonetheless, it is now well known that the results of computable general equilibrium models can be very model-specific. Harris and Cox illustrated this point in their examinations of the potential effects of free trade on the Canadian economy, work that influenced the Macdonald royal commission to advocate free trade with the United States.[21] The standard computable general equilibrium model assumes fully competitive markets in all industries. Harris and Cox, however, treated the manufacturing industries as being oligopolistic, with economies of scale that arise from fixed costs. As a consequence, they found the gains from free trade to be substantial—in particular the gains attributable to rationalization of the manufacturing sector and to larger production runs; these are results that do not arise in the more conventional models.

The use of general equilibrium analysis to study the incidence of taxes had its genesis in seminal work on the corporate tax by Harberger, which was later synthesized and extended to other taxes by Mieszkowski.[22] The original interest was in the effect of taxes on the *functional distribution of income*, which is essentially the effect of taxes on capital income relative to labour income. Harberger found that although the corporate tax was essentially a tax on the corporate sector of the economy, given the parameter values he used its incidence in general equilibrium fell on capital in general.

The use of computable general equilibrium models to study the incidence of taxes by income class has been quite limited, and virtually non-existent for the Canadian case. Most analyses have had more limited objectives, such as

---

[21] See Richard G. Harris, *Trade, Industrial Policy and Canadian Manufacturing* (Toronto: Ontario Economic Council, 1984); and David Cox and Richard Harris, "Trade Liberalization and Industrial Organization: Some Estimates for Canada" (February 1985), 93 *Journal of Political Economy* 115-45.

[22] Arnold C. Harberger, "The Incidence of the Corporation Income Tax" (June 1962), 70 *Journal of Political Economy* 215-40; Peter M. Mieszkowski, "Tax Incidence Theory: The Effects of Taxes on the Distribution of Income" (December 1969), 7 *Journal of Economic Literature* 1103-24. This work used algebraic rather than computational analysis in studying the general equilibrium effects of small changes in the tax system and used linear approximations to extrapolate discrete changes in the system from the results of this analysis. John B. Shoven and John Whalley, "A General Equilibrium Calculation of the Effects of Differential Taxation of Income from Capital in the U.S." (1972), 1 *Journal of Public Economics* 281-321, used computable general equilibrium techniques to replicate Harberger's work and arrived at virtually identical results.

studying the effects of individual taxes or of particular tax reforms.[23] This is so because of the difficulty of modelling economies to include the vast array of taxes in existence and their complexity of design. One notable exception is a study by Piggott and Whalley that compared the general equilibrium allocation of the tax system in the United Kingdom in 1973 with a benchmark system that raised the same revenues through a proportional sales tax on all goods and services. The study found that the UK tax system was quite progressive, much more so than conventional tax incidence studies typically found it to be.[24] In particular, the benchmark tax system left the top decile of the income distribution 25 percent worse off than it was under the existing system and the bottom decile 20 percent better off.

## Efficiency

Taxes and transfers impede the efficient operation of markets for the allocation of the economy's resources. One of the important properties of competitively operating markets is that in the absence of taxes and other distortions they tend to produce products at least cost and allocate them to their best, or most valued, uses. Markets are said to allocate resources *efficiently*. When the market price equilibrates the supply and demand for a commodity, the price that demanders are willing to pay for the last unit of output sold, which is the monetary value they attach to it (or the so-called *marginal value*), just equals the price or cost that the competitive suppliers incur in producing it (or the *marginal cost*). The imposition of a tax on any market drives a wedge between the amount that the demanders are willing to pay and the amount required to compensate suppliers for producing additional amounts. The value that the economy places on having another unit produced exceeds the cost to society of producing it, but because of the tax no more will be produced. The result is that society's resources are not being used efficiently.[25]

The same principle applies to the markets for factors of production, such as labour and capital. If a tax is imposed on labour income, the price that firms (the demanders of labour) pay is the labour cost including the tax, and the price that workers (the suppliers) receive is that payment less the tax. Firms will demand labour to the point where its marginal value just equals the pre-tax wage. Workers will supply labour until the marginal cost of supplying labour (as opposed to taking leisure) equals the after-tax wage. In a market equilibrium, the marginal value to demanders will exceed the marginal cost to suppliers, so an efficient amount of labour will not be used. In general, too little of any taxed product or factor of production will ultimately be supplied and demanded, or sold.

---

[23] For a summary of several studies, see Shoven and Whalley, supra footnote 12.

[24] John Piggott and John Whalley, *UK Tax Policy and Applied General Equilibrium Analysis* (Cambridge, Eng.: Cambridge University Press, 1985).

[25] Of course, there are other reasons why resources may not be used efficiently, such as the existence of some non-competitive markets. We ignore issues of this kind here.

The severity of the problem depends on how sensitive demands and supplies are to prices. The more responsive demand and supply are to price changes, the greater the reduction in output will be when a tax is imposed on a market, and the more inefficient or distorting will the tax be. This point is illustrated geometrically in figure 2.2. Consider panel A, which depicts the market for a product, $X$, when the demand, $D$, is inelastic. For simplicity, we assume that supply, $S$, is perfectly elastic; for example, $X$ could be a product that is purchased on foreign markets. In the absence of a tax, $X_0$ is sold at a market price of $p_0$. Now a tax at the rate $t$ is imposed. The price rises to $p_1 = p_0 + t$, and the quantity demanded falls to $X_1$. The demand curve, $D$, represents the amount that consumers are willing to pay for various amounts of $X$. Thus the area $X_1abX_0$ indicates the value that consumers place on the amount of $X$ that they no longer consume; that is, it is their willingness to pay for it. It represents a loss to consumers. On the other hand, the savings in resources from no longer having to produce the amount $X_1X_0$ is the area $X_1cbX_0$, since the supply curve, $S$, represents the marginal costs of producing various quantities of $X$. Thus the net loss to society from the tax is the area $cab$; this loss is referred to as the *deadweight loss* or *excess burden* of the tax. The tax revenue raised is $p_1acp_0$. Panel B depicts the outcome when the demand is relatively elastic. The key point is that the deadweight loss per dollar of revenue raised, $cab/p_1acp_0$, is greater the more elastic is the demand curve. Often, of course, it is difficult to know with any degree of certainty how responsive a market has been to the imposition of the tax. Subsequent chapters will discuss what there is in the way of empirical evidence about the responsiveness of markets to particular types of taxes.

Most taxes impose some sort of distortion, sometimes more than one. It is inevitable, therefore, that the tax system as a whole will be distortionary. The efficiency consequences of any one distortion depend upon the nature of the market in question. Generally speaking, the inefficiency associated with a tax increases with the reduction in market output induced by the tax distortion. The more elastic are demand and supply, the greater the change in output will be and the more inefficient the tax. From an efficiency point of view, therefore, it is best to impose taxes on markets that do not respond much to price changes. It is worthwhile summarizing the types of distortions imposed by the major taxes and transfers in the Canadian system.

## The Personal Income Tax

This tax is levied on both labour income and capital income, although as we discussed in chapter 1 the tax exempts some types of capital income (for example, imputed rent on owner-occupied housing) and treats others preferentially (for example, capital gains). In taxing labour income, the income tax distorts the labour market by causing the wage paid by a firm to exceed the net wage eventually received by a worker. Owing to the progressive nature of the tax, the distortion becomes more pronounced as income rises. This distortion introduces an incentive to reduce the supply of labour and increase leisure. Although individuals may, in the short run, have relatively

**Figure 2.2  Deadweight Loss of an Excise Tax**

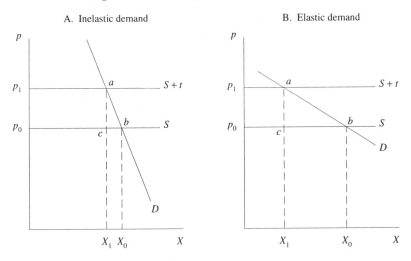

little discretion in choosing the amount of labour they supply, there are various dimensions along which they may respond to taxes in the longer run. Although hours of work are standardized in many occupations, workers can often choose how much overtime to work, or whether to work part time or full time. They can choose how hard to work in order to seek promotion. They can choose when and for how long to participate in the labour force. They can choose how much time and effort to devote to improving their skills (referred to as *human capital investment*). And they can choose what occupation to work at, or whether or not to be self-employed. Some occupations include significant rewards for non-pecuniary costs (climatic conditions, danger, health risks, and so forth). Taxes will discourage persons from choosing occupations that have non-pecuniary costs. By the same token, they will also discourage persons from taking risky occupations, which tend to be accompanied by fluctuating incomes; under a progressive income tax, as we noted earlier, a person whose income fluctuates will pay more tax over a period of years than will a person who receives the same income in each year of the period. Finally, high taxes also provide an incentive for taxpayers to move to localities with lower taxes, including jurisdictions in other countries. All of these factors represent distortions, and hence efficiency costs, that arise from the taxation of labour income.

To the extent that capital income is taxed, the income tax also distorts the market for savings and investment (the capital market), since the after-tax returns received on savings are less than the pre-tax rate of return paid by the demanders of savings, the borrowers. This distortion will discourage saving. The tax may also distort the supply of funds for risky investments, since part of the income from capital that is taxed may reflect a payment for risk taking.

On the other hand, since the income tax does not include imputed income in its base, it favours activities that yield imputed income over other activities. For example, it encourages households to accumulate wealth in the form of housing rather than in the form of assets whose returns are taxable.

High income-tax rates also provide an incentive for avoiding taxes through tax-planning measures or through outright tax evasion. Avoidance might be particularly tempting for recipients of capital income, given the possibility of shifting assets abroad. The taxation of labour income is presumably somewhat harder to evade, especially given that income taxes on the wage and salary income of employees are deducted at source. The self-employed have significantly more ability to evade taxes.

These are the most general types of distortions that the income tax imposes. The income tax system is a very complex one; it includes a myriad of provisions, including special exemptions, deductions, and credits, that impose distortions. We shall discuss them in more detail in chapter 3.

## The Corporate Income Tax

This tax is levied on profits earned in the corporate sector. It is a tax on the returns to the capital owned by corporate shareholders; that is, equity income. The return on the part of corporate capital that is financed by debt does not pay corporate tax, since interest payments on the debt are deductible. The corporate tax can distort the market for investment and savings in at least six ways.

First, the equity income of corporations pays the corporate tax, whereas the equity income of unincorporated business does not. Part of the tax is effectively reimbursed to shareholders through a dividend tax credit—a credit against personal income taxes that is equal to a proportion of the dividends shareholders receive from Canadian corporations. On balance, however, corporate equity capital bears a discriminatory tax. Consequently, there is an incentive for capital to reallocate for tax reasons from the corporate sector to the unincorporated sector and thus a tax-induced distortion in the allocation of capital between the two sectors.

Second, the corporate tax treats different industries differently. For example, preferential tax rates apply to manufacturing and processing activities, and preferential writeoffs are available to the resource industries. These tax preferences give rise to intersectoral misallocations of resources.

Third, the tax also treats different types of investments differently, regardless of the industries in which they are used. Thus investments in intangibles such as advertising and training, whose costs can be written off immediately, are treated preferentially relative to physical assets such as buildings, whose costs can only be written off gradually.

Fourth, the tax treatment of investments varies with the way in which they are financed. Since firms are allowed to deduct the interest paid on debt but not the cost of equity finance, they have an incentive to increase their debt financing; that is, to become more highly *levered*. Firms with high debt-equity ratios will have lower tax burdens than firms with low ratios.

Fifth, the corporate tax system places firms in a loss position at a disadvantage relative to other firms. Firms that have positive tax liabilities must pay them. Those that have negative tax liabilities can carry them forward or backward, in order to set them against future or past positive tax liabilities, only for limited amounts of time. In the absence of past profits, they cannot receive their negative tax liabilities as credits immediately. In the meantime, they forgo the interest that they would have obtained had the negative taxes been refunded. Because the tax system does not treat positive and negative tax liabilities symmetrically, it discriminates against firms that are young and growing and therefore temporarily in a negative income position. This discrimination also extends to firms that engage in risky ventures. Yet both types of firms are valuable because of their potential contribution to employment and productivity growth.

Finally, the taxation of capital income in the corporate sector is likely to reduce the overall amount of capital investment in the economy by driving a wedge between the pre-tax return required on investment and the net return required by corporate savers. In addition, it may serve to discourage foreign firms from investing in Canada, except to the extent that Canadian taxes can be credited abroad. We discuss all of these effects in detail in chapter 4.

## Payroll Taxes

Payroll taxes are effectively taxes on labour income. As such, they impose a distortion on the labour market: the price paid for labour by demanders includes the tax, whereas the price received by suppliers is net of the tax. The fact that most payroll tax receipts are earmarked for social insurance programs such as the Canada Pension Plan (CPP), the Quebec Pension Plan (QPP), or employment insurance (EI) may alleviate the labour-market distortion to some extent. If contributions under these programs are directly related to the benefits received, their disincentive effect on labour supply will be reduced. In Canada, however, payroll taxes are rarely fully related to subsequent benefits received. The distortion in this case is the same as the distortion of the labour market that arises from the income tax. Unlike the latter, however, payroll taxes do not distort capital markets.

There has been considerable concern in recent years about the effect of payroll taxes on the demand side of the labour market. The concern is that taxes on labour income increase the price of labour and thereby reduce the number of jobs offered by the private sector. In theory, the validity of this concern depends on how the labour market responds to payroll taxes. If the supply of labour is completely unresponsive to changes in the wage rate (that is, if it is inelastic), then in a well-functioning labour market a payroll tax will be shifted back fully to labour suppliers; that is, after-tax wages will be reduced by the full amount of the tax. The price that firms pay for labour will not change, nor will the demand for labour. The more responsive labour supply is to the after-tax wage, the less the tax can be shifted backward and the more firms will have to pay for the same supply of labour. The result will be a reduction in the demand for labour but not necessarily an increase in unemployment: the supply of labour will be reduced but it will still equal the demand for labour.

Of course, if there are imperfections in the labour market, reductions in the supply of jobs can lead to increased unemployment. For example, minimum-wage laws tend to reduce the number of jobs available for low-skilled workers. If firms must pay higher payroll taxes on low-wage jobs, they will reduce further the number of low-wage jobs that they offer, thereby exacerbating the unemployment induced by the minimum wage. Similarly, unionized workers may be able to pass a good part of the payroll tax on to their employers, and this too will cause a loss in jobs.

There have been some recent empirical analyses of the effects of payroll taxes on jobs in Canada. Di Matteo and Shannon summarize the literature on the effects of payroll taxation on wages and employment, and they also provide some estimates of their own.[26] Using statistical techniques, they estimate that a 1 percent increase in the payroll tax rate increases wage costs to employers by 0.56 percent, causing a reduction in employment of 0.32 percent, or about 40,600 jobs. (These are long-run effects.) Part of the tax is absorbed by workers: after-tax wages fall by about 0.44 percent. Other authors have found that relatively more of the tax is shifted back to labour, so the literature is far from being definitive.[27]

The effect of payroll taxes on employment should not be viewed in isolation. Payroll taxes are not the only taxes that distort the labour market. We have already shown that the income tax falls in part on labour income, and we shall show below that the federal and provincial sales taxes are also equivalent to a tax on labour. From a broad perspective, therefore, labelling payroll taxes as "taxes on jobs" is not warranted. We discuss payroll taxes in more detail in chapter 6.

## The Goods and Services Tax

The federal GST is a very broadly based tax on consumer expenditures; it taxes at a uniform rate almost all goods and services purchased for consumption in Canada. A proportional consumption tax will discourage activities

---

[26] Livio Di Matteo and Michael Shannon, "Payroll Taxation in Canada: An Overview" (Summer 1995), 3 *Canadian Business Economics* 5-22.

[27] See, for example, Charles Beach, Zhengi Lin, and Garnett Picot, "The Employer Payroll Tax in Canada and Its Effects on the Demand for Labour" (mimeograph, 1995), and Michael G. Abbott and Charles M. Beach, "The Impact of Payroll Taxes on Employment and Wages: Evidence for Canada, 1970-1993," in Michael G. Abbott, Charles M. Beach, and Richard P. Chaykowski, eds., *Transition and Structural Change in the North American Labour Market* (Kingston, Ont.: Industrial Relations Centre Press, 1997), 154-234.

whose purpose is to yield income to spend on consumer goods. A general tax on consumption, therefore, is in effect a tax on earnings.[28] As such, it imposes a distortion on labour supply analogous to the distortion imposed by a payroll tax. To put the matter in another way, a general sales tax will increase the price level for consumer goods relative to the wage rate. Thus real wages will decline and work effort will be discouraged. The GST's effect on work effort, however, is not nearly as important as that of the income tax, which has much higher marginal tax rates. (The marginal income tax rate is the amount of tax paid on the last dollar of income earned; it must not be confused with the average tax rate, which is the ratio of total income taxes paid to total income.)

A tax on consumption further resembles a tax on earnings in having no disincentive effect on savings. Savings are just future consumption, which is taxed under a consumption tax at the same rate as present consumption. This circumstance distinguishes the GST from the income tax, which, as we have seen, includes capital income in its base.

The GST is not fully general, since it excludes some products from its base and treats others preferentially. The main exclusion is food, and housing is preferentially treated. In addition, the system exempts very small producers. Because the GST base is not comprehensive, the tax does to some extent distort the allocation of resources among sectors. But this distortion is minimal compared with the distortion caused by most other taxes—including other forms of general sales taxation such as the retail sales tax, which we shall discuss next. The relative absence of distortion results from the GST's multi-stage nature: taxes are paid on the sales made by producers at each stage of production, but the producers are allowed a credit for taxes paid at earlier stages. Thus producers have an incentive to ensure that all input taxes are fully credited. As a result, business inputs bear no net tax, and taxes can be fully credited when products are exported.

There is one further potential incentive problem with the GST. Producers can evade the tax illegally by failing to submit taxes on their sales, although the opportunities for successful evasion are reduced by the fact that the crediting system leaves a "paper trail." Nevertheless, possibilities for evasion do exist, especially at the final stage of sales to the consumer. In any case, the addition of the GST to other taxes that producers pay, including the income tax and provincial sales taxes, compounds the overall incentive to evade.

---

[28] Given the consumer's budget constraint, lifetime spending will equal lifetime earnings plus any inheritances less bequests. If consumers leave the same value of bequests as they inherited, lifetime consumption will equal lifetime earnings (both properly discounted to a present value). A tax on consumption would be equivalent to a tax on earnings. Of course, if bequests differ from inheritances, the two will not be exactly equivalent. A tax on consumption will not distort the decision how much to leave to one's heirs as a bequest if taxpayers recognize that their heirs too will have to pay the consumption tax on spending out of bequests. Of course, this may be a far-fetched assumption.

## Provincial Retail Sales Taxes

Like the GST, the provinces' retail sales taxes (RSTs) are general taxes on consumption. As such, they too impose a distortion on the labour market: by reducing purchasing power, they drive a wedge between the price paid for labour by firms and the real wage received by labour suppliers. The GST and the RSTs differ, however, in two significant ways. First, RSTs generally have much narrower bases and more instances of preferential treatment. They exclude most services from the base and also some products that are deemed to be important to low-income persons, such as children's clothing. Second, since RSTs are levied on a single-stage basis, they are unable to avoid taxing some business inputs—in particular, inputs purchased by a firm from a retailer. By the same token, exports cannot readily be purged of taxes that may have been paid on inputs. As a result, RSTs impose more intersectoral distortions than the GST imposes.

Different provinces have different sales tax systems, and this circumstance too has efficiency implications. RST rates differ across most of the provinces, and in Alberta there is no sales tax at all. Thus consumers have an incentive to shop across provincial borders in order to avoid taxation. In New Brunswick, Nova Scotia, and Newfoundland, however, the provinces' RSTs have been replaced by the harmonized sales tax (HST), which is effectively the GST with a higher rate in order to generate revenues for the provinces as well as the federal government.

## Specific Excise Taxes

The specific excise taxes that both the federal government and the provinces levy on tobacco, alcohol, gasoline, and some other products obviously discriminate against the use of these products. Some observers justify this discrimination on the ground that use of the taxed products requires the public sector to undertake expenditures for matters such as police protection, health services, and roads that it could otherwise avoid. In addition, the argument continues, use of the taxed products may give rise to adverse externalities; that is, it may impose costs on society that are not reflected in the price system. For this reason, excises on tobacco and alcohol have come to be called "sin taxes."

The trouble with this argument is that it is difficult for policy makers to identify the level of taxation appropriate for the purpose of covering the costs imposed on society by the use of the taxed products. Recent work by Raynauld and Vidal indicates that the tax rates imposed on cigarettes may be far in excess of what is required to cover the social cost of smoking.[29] Raynauld and Vidal estimate that the cost imposed by smokers on society in 1986 was $670 million. This figure includes both the additional health care costs

---

[29] See André Raynauld and Jean-Pierre Vidal, "Smokers' Burden on Society: Myth and Reality in Canada" (September 1992), 18 *Canadian Public Policy* 300-17.

and the accidental-fire costs attributable to smoking (but not the non-pecuniary costs imposed on friends and relatives). In the same year, however, the saving in health and residential care costs attributable to premature death from smoking amounted to $460 million. Thus the net social cost of smoking was $210 million. Meanwhile, society collected $3.2 billion in taxes on tobacco and realized $1.4 billion in savings in pension plan payments, for a total of $4.6 billion—over 20 times the costs! If the primary function of taxes on tobacco is to require smokers to reimburse society for the social costs of smoking, these results suggest that the taxes are far too high.

Perhaps a more important reason why products such as alcohol, tobacco, and gasoline are singled out for discriminatory tax treatment is the fact that demand for these products is relatively inelastic; consequently, they are good revenue raisers. Of course, demand for basic food is also relatively inelastic. Perhaps the difference is that food is seen as a necessity with beneficial effects, whereas tobacco, alcohol, and gasoline products are seen as being both less necessary and less meritorious. We shall discuss both sales taxes and excise taxes in more detail in chapter 5.

## Property Taxes

Municipal governments rely heavily on property taxes levied on the value of residential, commercial, and industrial properties within their jurisdictions (although in some provinces property taxes are administered provincially). The taxation of real property values can have two distorting effects. First, to the extent that property is in elastic supply, the property tax will discourage its accumulation. This consideration may be relevant in the case of buildings and physical capital, especially in the longer run, but is less likely to be so in the case of land. Of course, the quality of a given amount of land can be enhanced by clearing, drainage, improved accessibility, and so on. So one can view land too as being in variable supply.

Second, if property tax rates vary across jurisdictions, there will be an incentive to relocate from high-tax to low-tax jurisdictions. This incentive may lead to relocations of businesses not only from one jurisdiction to another within a province or from one province to another, but even from one country to another. Of course, if higher property tax rates simply reflect better local services, the incentive to relocate will be considerably lessened. We shall discuss property taxes in chapter 7.

## Transfer Payments

The federal government and the provinces make a variety of transfer payments. Federal transfers include employment insurance benefits, payments to the elderly, and refundable tax credits to low-income persons and to families. Social assistance accounts for most transfers at the provincial level. Since transfer payments are contingent on the circumstances and behaviour of recipients, they may influence recipients' labour-supply decisions, the amount of their savings, or both. To the extent that transfers provide a substitute source of income, they will reduce the incentive to work. This is especially true if the transfer received is reduced by a substantial proportion of the income earned through work, as is often the case. Particular transfer schemes can influence labour supply in a number of ways. They can affect the choice between part-time and full-time work, the labour force participation rate, job search behaviour, retirement, and hours of work. Finally, by providing a substitute source of income for retirement, or in the event of unexpected expenditure requirements or income loss (owing to ill health or layoff, for example), they reduce the need for individuals to provide for such eventualities through saving.

In practice, almost any tax or transfer system will create distortions. In principle, one could have a distortion-free tax system by taxing only items that are in fixed supply. Thus a poll tax (or head tax) is distortion-free, since it is imposed uniformly on a per-person basis and cannot be avoided (except perhaps by emigration). Similarly, taxes levied on commodities or factors for which the elasticities of demand or supply are very low do not greatly affect resource allocation or impose much distortion (for example, tobacco or alcohol taxes and land taxes). Taxes of this kind, however, though used, are not relied upon as major sources of revenue. Moreover, although they are non-distorting or efficient, they are typically regarded as being vertically inequitable, since they are not based on any index of equity such as income. They do not improve the distribution of income and may even substantially worsen it. Specific excise taxes are typically regressive not only because they are levied on goods for which demand is inelastic but also because low-income persons spend a larger portion of their incomes on these goods than do high-income persons. Inevitably, in designing a tax system, one is left with a conflict between the claims of equity and the claims of efficiency. Some balance must be reached, and reaching it is a matter for non-economic judgment.

## Economic Growth

Another criterion that one may use in judging a tax is its influence on the growth rate of the economy, including the growth rate of sectors of the economy that society may value even if they are not profitable, such as high-technology sectors. Economic growth is fostered by the accumulation of factors of production, especially capital, and by technical progress or productivity growth. Capital accumulation (investment) is particularly important, both because it provides the plant and equipment that is used to employ workers and because it can itself be a source of technical progress. New investment embodies the latest in technology and so allows new technologies to be introduced into the economy. New investment may also enhance the skills of workers in ways that spread to other sectors of the economy. Of course, investment in information, technology, and research and development (R & D) directly enhances productivity. *Endogenous growth theory* emphasizes the tenet that markets themselves may not provide the correct incentives for investment, especially investment in knowledge-related assets.[30] The argument is that part of the returns to the investment accrue to participants in the economy other than the firm undertaking the investment. If investors do not appropriate the full rewards of their investment, they tend to do too little of it. By this reckoning, anything that enhances investment is beneficial.

One of the principal ways in which the tax system influences growth is by affecting the accumulation of capital. Capital accumulation results from investment, and the quantity of investment is determined by the workings of the capital market. Taxation that either reduces the demand for investment or reduces the supply of savings (domestic and foreign) used to finance the investment will reduce the amount of investment undertaken by the private sector and thereby slow down economic growth.

The personal income tax applies to most forms of capital income (interest, dividends, and capital gains) to some extent. The forms of investment that the tax tends to favour, such as owner-occupied housing, are largely outside the sectors of the economy that are most conducive to technological innovation. Since capital income is the return to saving, taxing capital income tends to discourage saving and thus may retard growth. We say "may" because in an open economy any reduction in domestic saving as a source of financing may simply be made up by foreign saving, and investment may be unaffected.[31] If the taxation of capital income retards saving and growth, and if equity implies the inclusion of all forms of capital income in the tax base, then a conflict arises between the claims of equity and the claims of growth. One can avoid the disincentive to save only by exempting capital income from the tax base or, equivalently, by exempting savings and taxing consumption, an approach we shall discuss below.

Another possible disincentive to save arises from the system of public pensions, which, in Canada, includes the Canada and Quebec pension plans and old age security. A large part of personal saving is saving for retirement; public pensions, by reducing the need for personal retirement income, may reduce the desire to accumulate savings in private pensions. In that case, if public pensions are not funded and their funds not invested, as private pension funds are, investment and economic growth may decline. Again, however, in an open economy a reduction in domestic savings may not lead to a reduction in investment if foreign financing is available for profitable projects.

---

[30] Important early contributions to endogenous growth theory are Paul M. Romer, "Increasing Returns and Long-Run Growth" (October 1986), 94 *Journal of Political Economy* 1002-37; and Robert E. Lucas Jr., "On the Mechanics of Economic Development" (January 1988), 22 *Journal of Monetary Economics* 3-42. For a recent survey of the literature, see Philippe Aghion and Peter Howitt, *Endogenous Growth Theory* (Cambridge, Mass.: MIT Press, 1998).

[31] For a detailed discussion of this point, see Robin W. Boadway, Neil Bruce, and Jack M. Mintz, *Taxes on Capital Income in Canada: Analysis and Policy*, Canadian Tax Paper no. 80 (Toronto: Canadian Tax Foundation, 1987).

On the demand side of the capital market, taxation can reduce the incentive for firms, domestic and foreign, to undertake capital investment. For example, by reducing the marginal rate of return to corporations from investing, the corporate income tax reduces corporate investment. The personal income tax has the same effect on investment by unincorporated businesses. As we mentioned earlier, however, whether or not business income taxes do reduce the marginal rate of return to capital depends on the nature and generosity of the deductions they allow for capital costs and on any other incentives they may provide, such as investment tax credits. We shall consider the effect of business taxation on investment in detail in chapter 4.

The tax system also affects economic growth through its treatment of investment in risky projects. Although risky projects have a higher variability of return than safe projects, they also have higher expected rates of return. The tax system can influence the incentive for both households and firms to undertake risks by its treatment of the returns from risky ventures. The most important consideration here is whether the system treats losses symmetrically with gains; that is, whether it allows a full loss offset or its equivalent. One type of risky activity that merits special consideration is expenditure on research and development. R & D is important for economic growth because it is a source of technological change. The tax system affects the incentive to undertake R & D through its treatment of R & D expenditures and subsidies for R & D expenditures. We shall discuss this matter further in chapter 4.

Finally, the tax system can influence growth by influencing the quality of the labour force. It can do this by either encouraging or discouraging investment by individuals in the acquisition of skills and knowledge—that is, human capital. The return from investment in human capital is typically a higher wage rate, which is subject to personal income tax. If the costs of acquiring these skills (for example, educational expenses) are not fully deductible, there will be a disincentive to acquire them. Of course, many skills are acquired through the heavily subsidized public education system, so the individual does not bear the full cost of their acquisition. Skills may also be acquired through on-the-job training and other employer-provided opportunities. Since employers can typically deduct the full costs of employee training, the tax system may be said to encourage activities of this kind.

## Administration Costs

The final criterion for a good tax is administrative simplicity. One must not lose sight of the fact that there are significant costs associated with administering taxes, both collection costs accruing to the government and compliance costs imposed on taxpayers. The more complicated is the tax, the more costly it will be to administer. For example, the more tax-paying units there are, the greater will be the costs of administration. The GST, under which most producers are taxpayers, is more costly to administer than a single-stage sales tax such as the RST, under which only retailers are taxpayers. Moreover, much of the additional cost is borne by the taxpayers themselves. Taxes or transfers that can take advantage of the administrative machinery of an existing tax are cheaper to administer than those that cannot. Thus administrative economies are achieved by having Revenue Canada administer refundable tax credits and payments to the elderly. Similarly, arrangements under which a single agency collects taxes for more than one government save both collection costs and compliance costs; examples in Canada are the tax collection agreements for income taxes, the HST, and the arrangement whereby Quebec collects both its own sales tax and the GST. What is perhaps most important, the effectiveness of enforcement can vary from tax to tax. Simpler, more transparent taxes are generally more difficult to evade than more complicated ones. Simpler taxes also provide fewer incentives to avoid taxes and therefore less incentive for taxpayers to incur socially wasteful tax-planning costs.

Any broad reform of the tax system would have to address three important sources of administrative difficulty. One is inflation. As a rule, a part of capital income is in effect compensation for inflation-induced decline in the real value of the asset, rather than a true return to the asset. Therefore a tax whose base includes capital income should index its base for inflation. Unfortunately, indexing capital income is administratively very costly indeed, much more so than simply indexing the rate structure and the size of exemptions. In other words, tax bases that include capital income, such as the personal and corporate income taxes, ideally include complex indexation components, whereas tax systems that exclude capital income, such as those based on consumption or labour income, do not require indexation. We shall return to this issue in the next section.

An ideal income tax system—that is, one with a comprehensive base— would encounter the administrative problem of accounting for some items on an imputed basis. It would be desirable to include in the income tax base accrued capital gains and imputed rents on owner-occupied housing, and to permit the costing of inventories at their replacement values and the deduction of true replacement depreciation costs of capital. The difficulty in each case is that the item to be included or deducted is not directly observable on the basis of market values. One administratively simple way to avoid some problems of this kind would be to adopt a system based on cash flows rather than conventional accrued measures of income. We shall discuss this solution in the context of the corporate income tax in chapter 4 and in the context of personal taxation later in this chapter.

Finally, administrative obstacles also arise when non-uniform tax rates are applied to different sources of income, or when some sources are treated preferentially. For example, capital gains are generally taxed at reduced rates. This gives taxpayers an incentive to devote resources to taking as much of their income as possible in the preferentially treated form in order to reduce tax liabilities. The existence of incentives of this kind has led many observers to propose a broadening of tax bases. Most proposals for flat rate taxation, which we shall discuss below, are motivated in part by this consideration.

These are the main criteria by which we shall judge the various taxes and transfers when we discuss them individually in the following chapters. In most cases, we shall be able to suggest only in a qualitative sense the extent to which each tax satisfies or violates these criteria. Ultimately, in order to assess a tax or the tax system as a whole, one must make some judgment about the relative claims of the various criteria. It is necessary to decide, for example, how much economic efficiency one is prepared to forgo in order to increase the vertical equity of the tax-transfer system. The ideal proportions will always be a matter of some dispute.

## Taxation According to the Benefit Principle

In our discussion of the principles of taxation, we ignored the use to which tax revenues are put. Like the tax system, the provision of goods and services by the public sector raises issues related to efficiency, equity, economic growth, and administrative simplicity. It is not surprising, given these parallel concerns, that the pattern of government expenditures might, for a number of reasons, affect the evaluation of taxes. The first reason is that public goods and services themselves have redistributive effects; that is, they affect the well-being of different households differently. Indeed, it might be argued that at least as much redistribution takes place through the expenditure side of the budget as through the tax side.[32] Clearly, tax policy should take into account the benefits that households obtain from public goods and services in determining the well-being of different sorts of households. Moreover, some expenditure instruments are substitutes for taxes as means of achieving redistributive goals. For example, governments may have a choice between delivering cash transfers through the tax system—for example, by means of refundable tax credits—and making either cash or in-kind transfers on the expenditure side of the budget. For the purposes of equity, therefore, one cannot avoid considering the tax system and expenditure policies in tandem. But relating taxes and expenditures might be justified on efficiency grounds as well. In particular, if taxes imposed on households are directly related to the benefits they obtain, one might argue that the taxes enhance efficiency. Basing taxes on benefits, which is referred to as the *benefit principle* of taxation, stands in contrast with basing taxes more broadly on equity considerations, which is referred to as the *ability-to-pay principle*.

The notion that benefit taxation enhances efficiency is based on the analogy with private markets. Prices established in competitive markets automatically reflect the marginal valuation that households place on the products being transacted: households are free to purchase as much of a given product as they want, and they will presumably continue to purchase it until the marginal benefit of the last increment purchased just equals the

---

[32] For evidence supporting this view, see G.C. Ruggeri, D. Van Wart, and R. Howard, *The Government as Robin Hood: Exploring the Myth* (Kingston, Ont.: Queen's University, School of Policy Studies, 1996).

marginal cost to them, which is the price. It is a widely accepted economic principle that a competitive market system will yield an efficient allocation of resources in the private sector,[33] and it is natural enough to imagine applying this principle to the public sector as well.

The problem is that the analogy does not always apply. For one thing, the quantities of many of the goods and services provided by the public sector are fixed for the households in the economy; households simply cannot buy as much or as little as they please, as they can in the private sector. Public goods such as defence services, environmental expenditures, the administration of justice, and so on must be taken as given. This being the case, benefit pricing cannot serve as a market-rationing device for these goods in the way that prices in the private sector do. Moreover, there is no way of knowing how much benefit individual households obtain from public goods of this kind. Since households do not purchase the public goods, the price mechanism cannot reveal how much they value them, as it does in the case of private goods. Thus, for some types of public expenditure at least, the benefit principle cannot be implemented.

Some types of public services, however, are similar to private products in the sense that their use might vary across households. Examples of these services include health care, social services, garbage collection, transportation, and education. In theory, one might consider applying pricing principles to these public services and thereby achieve the efficiency advantages of benefit taxation. The extent to which services of this kind should be priced is a major policy issue, and one that goes beyond tax policy considerations. A frequent argument against pricing is that some of these major public services serve redistributive objectives. They may be explicitly redistributional, as social services are; they may provide social insurance, as the health care schemes do; or they may be important for fostering equality of opportunity, as education is. The important point for our purposes here is that the decision whether to price services of this kind, and if so to what extent, does not detract from the broader objectives of the tax system. Even if selected public services did obtain some financing from user prices, there would still be a broader need for raising revenues for public services that cannot be priced, and there would still be purely redistributive goals to be achieved through the tax-transfer system.

There is, however, one dimension to benefit pricing that is important to a federation such as Canada. It can be argued that the use of benefit taxation by subnational levels of government in a federation will enhance both equity and efficiency.[34] The argument is that in a federation in which households

---

[33] For a technical discussion of this see Boadway and Wildasin, supra footnote 9, at chapter 2.

[34] For a summary of the issues involved, see Albert Breton, "Designing More Competitive and Efficient Governments," in *Defining the Role of Government: Economic Perspectives on*
(The footnote is continued on the next page.)

and firms are free to locate in whatever jurisdiction they choose the use of benefit taxation by lower-level jurisdictions will prevent households or firms from choosing one location over another purely on the basis of the net benefits that they can obtain from the public sector rather than on the basis of their productivity or preferences. It is also suggested that matching benefits to taxes increases the visibility and transparency of government operations and thus makes them more cost-effective and more responsive to local needs and desires. Finally, it is argued that competition among governments, given the mobility of households, will actually increase efficiency and enable lower-level jurisdictions to match taxes to benefits.[35] According to this view, the redistributive functions of government should be reserved for the federal government, though it might act in concert with the provinces. We shall return to the implications of federalism for tax policy in chapter 9.

## The Choice of a Personal Tax Base

Most tax revenues come from broadly based taxes, direct and indirect. In this section, we shall consider what the most appropriate broad base would be. We shall do this in the context of the personal income tax, since this tax is the largest revenue raiser for most governments. It is also the tax that is most suited to fulfilling the equity, or redistributive, role of taxation. However, many of the arguments that we shall advance here would also apply to the choice of a tax base for, say, sales taxes. In principle, sales taxes and personal taxes can be designed to have the same base. In practice, they do not have the same base, a circumstance that implies some measure of inconsistency in tax policy.

A great deal of literature has been devoted to the question of the ideal base for a personal tax in terms of the criteria for tax design outlined in the previous section. Indeed, this question was the primary concern of the Carter commission, which came out four-square in favour of using a comprehensive notion of income as the tax base. More recently, there has been a resurgence of policy interest in alternatives to income as a personal tax base. A decade after the Carter report, both the Meade committee in the United Kingdom and the US Treasury's Blueprints for Basic Tax Reform made the case for using consumption or expenditures as the personal tax base. The Economic Council of Canada echoed this proposal in its study of the Canadian tax system, which built on a suggestion by the Macdonald commission in its wide-ranging study of the Canadian economy.[36]

---

[34] Continued ...

the State, Government and Competitiveness Project Research Series (Kingston, Ont.: Queen's University, School of Policy Studies, 1994), 55-98.

[35] This view is referred to as the "Tiebout model" after the famous article by Charles M. Tiebout, "A Pure Theory of Local Expenditures" (October 1956), 64 Journal of Political Economy 416-24.

[36] United States, Department of the Treasury, Blueprints for Basic Tax Reform (Washington, DC: US Government Printing Office, 1977); Institute for Fiscal Studies, The Structure and

(The footnote is continued on the next page.)

The purpose of this section will be to survey the economic arguments for and against the three main candidates for personal tax bases—comprehensive income, consumption, and wealth. The issue is of particular relevance to Canada, since as we shall see in chapter 3 the Canadian personal income tax, like those of virtually all other countries in the Organisation for Economic Co-operation and Development (OECD), is actually a compromise between income taxation and consumption, or expenditure, taxation. This is so because the tax contains several provisions that effectively exempt part of capital income from the tax base—for example, capital income accumulated in tax-sheltered retirement savings schemes (registered retirement savings plans or RRSPs and registered pension plans or RPPs) and the imputed rent on owner-occupied housing. We shall begin by reviewing the broadest form of tax base, comprehensive income.

## The Haig-Simons-Carter Comprehensive Income Base

One approach to choosing a personal tax base is to select one that can be used to achieve the societal goals of horizontal and vertical equity. This criterion suggests a tax base that reflects how well off a person is. One widely accepted notion of a taxpayer's well-being is his ability to pay taxes, and one possibly suitable measure of his ability to pay is his comprehensive income. The concept of comprehensive income was originally formulated by Haig and elaborated by Simons, two US economists, and was subscribed to in Canada by the Carter commission.[37] It attempts to capture in one single sum a monetary measure of a consumer's economic well-being over some period. The formal definition of comprehensive income for a given year is as follows:

> Comprehensive income is the sum of current consumption plus net additions to wealth from all sources.

This definition requires that accrued income from all sources be included in the tax base, since that income can be used for either consumption or the accumulation of wealth (saving). Transfers of wealth received, including inheritances and gifts, should also be treated as income for tax purposes, since they too can be either consumed or added to wealth. Furthermore, all income, whether consumed or added to wealth, should be treated in the same way regardless of its source (that is, labour, land, or capital). The Carter commission summarized this view in the phrase "a buck is a buck." In

---

[36] Continued ...

*Reform of Direct Taxation: Report of a Committee Chaired by Professor J.E. Meade* (London: Allen and Unwin, 1978); Canada, Royal Commission on the Economic Union and Development Prospects for Canada (the Macdonald commission), *Report*, vol. 3 (Ottawa: Supply and Services, 1985); and Economic Council of Canada, *Road Map for Tax Reform: The Taxation of Savings and Investment* (Ottawa: Supply and Services, 1987).

[37] Robert M. Haig, ed., *The Federal Income Tax* (New York: Columbia University Press, 1921); Henry C. Simons, *Personal Income Taxation* (Chicago: University of Chicago Press, 1938). See also Joseph A. Pechman, ed., *Comprehensive Income Taxation* (Washington, DC: Brookings Institution, 1977).

practice, then, the comprehensive tax base should include wages and salaries, income from self-employment, rents, dividends, interest, accrued capital gains, gifts, inheritances, and transfer payments. There is no need to account expressly for the running down of wealth for the purposes of consumption, since the running down of wealth subtracts from the base an amount equal to the amount that the additional consumption adds to the base. In short, the two amounts offset one another.

Implementation of the comprehensive measure of income as a tax base involves a number of conceptual difficulties, and some implications for efficiency and growth as well. We shall deal with these matters under several headings.

## Equality of Treatment of All Sources of Income

Should all sources of income be treated equally? In the comprehensive income base, labour income is treated identically with income from the ownership of assets. Two individuals who have the same aggregate income but who are distinguished by the fact that one received it all as wages and the other received it all as rent are considered to have the same income for tax purposes. One could argue that since a person must give up leisure to earn labour income but not to earn rental income these two taxpayers should not be regarded as equals. This example reflects the problem of defining horizontal equity when some source of imputed income, in this case leisure income, is not included in the tax base. Because of the difficulty of measuring leisure income, no satisfactory method exists for its inclusion, but the problem is more general than that. Other forms of imputed income also yield consumption benefits that are difficult to include in the base and therefore make any practical income measure incomplete.

## Gifts and Inheritances

It seems clear that gifts and inheritances should be included in the income of those who receive them: like any other form of income, they can be used to finance consumption. What about the donors? Should they be allowed to deduct the bequests and gifts they give? The question depends on whether the act of giving gifts should be regarded simply as a reduction in wealth or whether it should also be treated as an act of consumption voluntarily undertaken (since the donor presumably gets some personal satisfaction from giving). Tax systems typically do not allow those who give bequests and gifts to deduct them from taxable income (unless they give them to charitable organizations, in which case the rationale is different). These donations are therefore implicitly treated as acts of consumption. It is probably also possible to argue against allowing a deduction on the ground of administrative simplicity. Nevertheless, if gifts and inheritances are included in the income of the recipients but not deducted from the income of the donors, they are in a sense subject to multiple taxation—a given inheritance is taxed when it is received and again when it is passed on to someone else.

The problem of how to treat gifts and inheritances also arises under a consumption tax base. It does so because the source of the problem is uncertainty about the meaning of "consumption" in the context of the giving of gifts or bequests. As we shall see, many of the other issues raised in this section also apply to both the consumption base and the comprehensive income base.

## Capital Gains

Capital gains ought to be included in the base as they accrue, since they represent additions to net worth that can be used to finance consumption. It is much simpler, however, to tax capital gains when they are realized by the sale of the asset concerned than it is to tax them as they accrue. To tax gains on accrual would require imputing changes in value to a taxpayer's assets when no actual transaction has taken place. Except in the case of assets with market prices, such as stocks, this procedure would be very costly to administer. Furthermore, taxing capital gains on accrual might cause liquidity problems for taxpayers, who would be faced with paying capital gains taxes on gains that have not been realized. In general, therefore, taxing capital gains on realization is the only practical alternative.

The problem with taxing capital gains only on realization is that it gives taxpayers an incentive to postpone the realization of gains in order to defer the payment of taxes. This incentive impedes the efficiency of capital markets and affords the owner of the asset what amounts to an interest-free loan on the tax owing. At the same time, there is a benefit to allowing taxpayers to choose the timing of realization. The accrual of capital gains may not be even from year to year. The taxpayer, by choosing an appropriate realization schedule, can even out the capital gains for tax purposes and avoid the inequities that arise under a progressive tax system when a taxpayer's income fluctuates from year to year. In other words, taxpayers with capital assets can engage in *self-averaging* of their income tax. Of course, because this opportunity is not afforded to other forms of fluctuating income, its availability in this case exacerbates horizontal inequity.

Another problem with taxing capital gains arises in times of inflation. As we have noted before and shall discuss in more detail below, capital gains that merely reflect changes in the general price level do not add to real purchasing power and therefore they ought not to be taxed. This is one reason why tax systems frequently give preferential treatment to capital gains (in Canada, only three-quarters of capital gains are taxed). Other reasons for preferential treatment of capital gains may include the fact that they are in part a return for the opportunity cost of risk taking, rather than a net gain to the earner. Preferential treatment of capital gains is also a crude device for taking into account the fact that capital gains on equity shares reflect a return generated by retained corporate income that has already been taxed at the corporate level. We shall discuss the so-called double taxation of corporate and personal income and its elimination by integration in chapter 4.

## Fluctuating Incomes

As we noted earlier, a progressive tax system that uses current income as the tax base treats persons with incomes that fluctuate from year to year unfavourably relative to those whose incomes are steady. Suppose that two persons have exactly the same total income over a period of three years. One person's income is the same in each year, whereas the other's income varies widely from year to year. Suppose further that marginal tax rates increase, as they do under the Canadian system, when one moves from one tax bracket to a higher one. Finally, suppose that the person with the steady income stays in the same bracket in each of the three years, whereas the person with a fluctuating income rises out of that bracket into a higher one in one of the three years. Over the three-year period this person will pay more tax than the other; yet the two persons are on average equally well off.

In short, the tax system does not satisfy the requirements of horizontal equity in this context. One remedy is to adopt the concept of "permanent income" in defining the tax base. A taxpayer's permanent income reflects the amount of consumption that he can sustain over a long period of time without running down his wealth. (Persons with fluctuating incomes should be able to even out their consumption streams by using capital markets to borrow and lend.) From an administrative point of view, however, it is very difficult to define the tax base as permanent income rather than current income. A simpler solution to the problem of fluctuating income is to adopt a system of averaging taxable incomes over a period of years. We shall discuss methods of averaging in chapter 3.

A particularly important cause of income fluctuation is retirement. The Canadian tax system allows a form of lifetime averaging through the RRSP and RPP schemes, under which savings for retirement are deductible for tax purposes and taxed when they are received in retirement. The RRSP/RPP system is more than a simple averaging mechanism, however. It also in effect allows the interest income from retirement savings to go untaxed: the capital income that accumulates on the funds in these plans is not subject to tax until it is withdrawn. As we shall see below, this arrangement amounts to taxing individuals on a consumption basis rather than an income basis. We shall examine the use of consumption as a tax base below.

## Deductions on Equity Grounds

Persons in different personal circumstances may get different amounts of satisfaction from a given amount of comprehensive income. The principle of horizontal equity suggests that an income tax system should recognize this possibility, and in practice most tax systems attempt to account for differences in circumstances through the use of deductions from income. Thus the Canadian system allows deductions for medical expenses, physical or mental handicaps, and old age. It also allows deductions for child care expenses and deductions for some of the costs of earning income, including educational costs and business expenses. We shall discuss in detail the types of deductions that the Canadian system allows against wage and salary incomes in chapter 3; deductions against business income will be discussed in chapter 4.

An issue that arises in connection with the correction of income for individual circumstances is whether to use deductions or credits for this purpose. Deductions adjust the income base before the rate structure is applied. Credits, on the other hand, are in effect part of the rate structure: they affect the tax liability of a person with a given taxable income. The value to a taxpayer of a deduction of, say, $1,000 depends upon the tax bracket the taxpayer is in: a higher-income taxpayer saves more in taxes from the deduction than does a low-income taxpayer (for a person in a 40 percent tax bracket, the saving in taxes is 0.4($1,000) = $400; for a person in a 20 percent tax bracket, the saving is only $200). A credit, on the other hand, is worth the same amount to all taxpayers. It is tempting, therefore, to argue that credits are fairer than deductions. This argument, however, overlooks the purpose of deductions. If the income tax base does not reflect a person's true ability to pay, it is not an appropriate basis for the tax. A deduction corrects the tax base so that it properly reflects ability to pay; a credit does not. We shall take up this issue again in chapter 3.

## The Tax-Paying Unit

An important issue in designing a tax system is the choice of the tax-paying unit: to whose income should the tax be applied? As we shall discuss in chapter 3, the Canadian income tax system treats the individual as the tax-paying unit. Several observers (including the Carter commission) have suggested that the family is a more appropriate unit—or, if it is not, then the tax structure should at least take family circumstances into consideration. The main argument for this view is that an individual's well-being is indicated not only by his own income but also, in part at least, by the income of other members of the family to which he belongs. Family income is usually shared among the members of the family and is used in part for expenditures on goods the members consume jointly (such as housing, furniture, and automobiles). Moreover, the day-to-day chores of maintaining a household (referred to as *household production*) provide benefits that the members of the household share. The combined benefits of the joint consumption of consumer goods and the shared use of the output of household production are sometimes referred to as "the economies of living together."

The Carter commission argued that in order to be equitable the tax treatment of single individuals and families should accord with the following principles. Two persons who earn a given amount of income should pay less total tax if they live singly than if they live as a family. Furthermore, the tax paid by the two if they live together should be independent of the proportion of income earned by each of the two (or more). Finally, an individual who earns a given income should pay more tax than a family of two or more members who earn the same income. To achieve these ends, the Carter commission proposed that the family should be adopted as a tax-paying unit, with a separate rate schedule for individuals. This recommendation, however, met with considerable controversy and general disfavour. The critics pointed out, among other things, the difficulty of defining the family unit, the problem of dealing with the dissolution of family units, and the possibility of changing (or hiding) one's living arrangements in order to avoid high marginal tax rates. More fundamental or philosophical issues were raised as well, such as whether one ought to be defined according to one's membership in a family or as an individual in one's own right.

In any case, and for whatever reason, the Canadian tax system continues to treat the individual as the tax-paying unit. There are, however, a number of elements in the income tax that recognize some of the economic consequences of living in a family, including the additional costs of supporting a family and the economies of living together. Thus there are credits for a non-working spouse and disabled dependants. There are refundable tax credits that differentiate between families and individuals. Child care expenses and educational expenses for dependent children are tax-deductible within limits. One can contribute savings for retirement to one's spouse's account. And there are provisions for spousal transfers of certain tax credits or deductions. We shall take up these topics in more detail in chapter 3.

An alternative approach to the tax treatment of families, one that is used in the United States, Germany, and France, is to allow *income splitting*. This practice involves summing the incomes of all eligible family members and dividing it equally among them. Households in the United States and Germany can split incomes between husband and wife. France permits income splitting among all family members. The effect is to reduce the income tax on married couples whose members have different incomes. The justification for this practice is similar to the justification advanced in the Carter report for using the family as the tax-paying unit—namely, that most economic decisions are made by the family as a unit. The two approaches differ significantly, however, in their treatment of family income for tax purposes: the Carter report recommended summing the incomes of the family members and applying the tax schedule to this total, whereas under income splitting total income is divided among the eligible family members and each member is taxed separately.

## Integration of the Personal Tax with the Corporate Tax

The existence within the same tax system of a personal income tax and a corporate income tax implies that some capital income might effectively be taxed twice. (Indeed, the property tax can be a third source of taxation of capital income.) For example, income subject to the corporate tax becomes dividends and capital gains for shareholders, which, under a comprehensive income tax, is taxed again to the personal level.

One way to undo this double taxation of capital income in the hands of domestic taxpayers is to integrate the personal and corporate tax systems.[38] Integration refers to mechanisms that allow individuals at least partial credit under the personal income tax for taxes deemed to have been paid on their behalf at the corporate level. There are several ways of either partially or fully integrating the personal and corporate tax systems. The present Canadian system of dividend tax credits represents one approach. We shall discuss this and other methods of integration in chapter 4.

## Administrative Difficulties

The ideal comprehensive income tax base is the sum of consumption and additions to net worth. In order to measure comprehensive income exactly, several administrative difficulties must be overcome. Three of the most important are the requirement to measure additions to wealth as they accrue, the need to account for inflation, and the need to measure types of consumption or asset incomes that take an imputed form. Some additions to wealth, such as capital gains, accrue continually without necessarily being reflected in an observable market transaction. In principle, capital gains ought to be included in taxable income as they accrue. But because they are difficult to measure on this basis, they are usually included only when they are realized, which can be long after they begin to accrue. This arrangement introduces an element of inequity into the tax system.

In periods of inflation, moreover, part of the change in asset values reflects changes in the price level rather than a change in the real purchasing power of the asset. Capital income generated on the asset will partially offset the decline in the real value of the asset and therefore should not be included in the tax base. Purging the tax base of purely inflationary changes in wealth requires a system of indexing that can be costly to administer. We shall discuss the problem of inflation in more detail below.

Finally, consumption or returns to assets may take forms that are difficult to measure. Under the present tax system, a person who owns housing but rents it out will be taxed on the rent obtained (and will incur rental costs on the housing), whereas a person who owns the housing he occupies obtains no rental income (and incurs no rental costs). Horizontal equity requires that the imputed rent that accrues to owner-occupiers be included in the tax base, but imputed rent is difficult to measure. Problems also arise in obtaining true measures of the capital income earned from personal businesses and the imputed capital income obtained from human capital investment. In each case, the difficulty lies in measuring the costs of the capital used to produce the income, especially the depreciation costs. One advantage of using

---

[38] The desirability of undoing the double taxation depends on one's view of the role of the corporate tax. See chapter 4.

consumption rather than income as a tax base is that administrative difficulties of this kind are avoided. We turn to this subject now.

## Consumption or Expenditure as a Tax Base

Although comprehensive income is widely accepted as an equitable measure of the ability to pay taxes and is the concept that underlies the income tax systems in Canada and most other countries, there has been a continuing policy interest among economists in the use of aggregate consumption as a tax base. Indeed, as we shall see in chapter 3, there are several provisions in the current income tax system that actually make the tax base a mixture of comprehensive income and personal consumption.

Several arguments have been advanced for preferring consumption to income as a personal tax base. One is that consumption is a better indicator of a taxpayer's well-being than income is, since it is consumption, not income, that ultimately yields satisfaction. As Kaldor put it in his classic study,[39] taxpayers should be taxed according to what they take out of the "social pot" (consumption) rather than what they put into it (income). Note that this equity argument for consumption taxation does not extend to the issue of vertical equity. Whether the *base* for personal taxation is income or consumption, one can achieve any desired degree of progressivity through the choice of a rate structure to apply to that base. The point is an important one, since it is often argued, misleadingly, that because the consumption tax base excludes capital income, which tends to be more important for high-income earners than for low-income earners, a consumption tax would be less fair than an income tax.

Another argument is that a tax on income discourages saving by taxing its return (interest, dividends, capital gains), whereas a tax on consumption does not. To put the matter in another way, by taxing the return to saving an income tax taxes future consumption at a rate higher than the rate at which it taxes present consumption (the interest rate is simply the market price of future consumption). Whether the removal of the distortion of saving would improve the overall efficiency of the tax system is unclear, since it is only one of many distortions. For example, both income taxation and consumption taxation favour leisure over work effort. Economic theory holds that in an economy in which more than one distortion exists the removal of one of the distortions does not guarantee that efficiency will improve. Indeed, if one distortion partially offsets the effects of another, elimination of the first distortion might reduce efficiency. Thus the fact that an income tax both discourages labour supply (or encourages leisure) and discourages saving for future consumption may actually make it more efficient than a consumption tax, which discourages labour supply alone. If future consumption and leisure tend to be complementary, imposing a tax on future consumption amounts to an indirect way of taxing leisure. Consequently, it may be efficient to tax

---

[39] Nicholas Kaldor, *An Expenditure Tax* (London: Allen & Unwin, 1955).

capital income, since to do so is equivalent to taxing future consumption. This argument implies only that capital income should bear some tax, not that it should bear tax at the same rate as labour income. It is highly debatable whether the personal income tax system should, as it currently does, tax capital income and labour income at the same rate.

A third argument for a consumption tax, and in some respects the most compelling, is that it is easier on the whole to administer an ideal consumption tax than it is to administer an ideal comprehensive income tax. Indeed, as we have already implied, an ideal comprehensive income tax is virtually impossible to implement because of the difficulty of measuring various sorts of asset incomes accurately, especially on a real accrued basis. As we shall see, these problems are largely avoided by personal consumption taxation, since its base effectively excludes capital income. How it does this will become more apparent when we outline the basic structure of the consumption tax.

In principle, the base for a consumption tax should be simply the taxpayer's flow of consumption services over the tax year; it is this flow that yields satisfaction for the consumer. It would be difficult, of course, to measure consumption directly, since this would require taxpayers to keep track of all of their expenditures over the tax year. In principle, it would be possible to measure the flow of consumption services indirectly, but even that would be difficult. Fortunately, there are two other bases that are equivalent to consumption services in present value terms and are much easier to administer— consumption expenditures on a cash-flow basis and non-capital income. We shall discuss each of these three alternatives in turn.

## The Consumption-Services Base

The annual flow of consumption services includes both the consumption of non-durable goods and services and the consumption of current services obtained from consumer durables (housing, automobiles, and so forth). One approach to measuring a taxpayer's consumption indirectly is to measure it as the difference between income and savings. If all consumption were consumption of non-durable products, there would be no distinction between consumption services and actual expenditures on consumer goods. Income less savings would be an accurate base for a consumption tax. Note that under this approach it is necessary to treat negative and positive savings symmetrically. It is necessary, that is, to add dissaving, or borrowing, to income in order to arrive at consumption.

The administrative advantages of consumption taxation over income taxation are readily apparent. They are twofold. First, the appropriate measure of income in calculating consumption is income on a cash-flow or realization basis rather than on an accrual basis. In particular, capital income that has accrued as, say, capital gains but is not realized need not be included in the base, since by definition accrued income that is not realized is not consumed, but saved. In other words, consumption expenditures are themselves the difference between realized income and realized current savings.[40] Accounting for income and savings on a realization basis avoids the difficulty of including capital gains on an accrued basis, as an ideal comprehensive income tax would have to do.

The second administrative advantage of consumption taxation is that there is no need, as there is under income taxation, to index the base for inflation (we shall discuss the general problem of indexing for inflation later in this chapter). Once again, the tax base is actual current consumption expenditures measured as the difference between current realized income and savings. The problem of indexation of the base simply does not arise (the rate structure, however, must be indexed, to prevent bracket creep). The absence of a need to index the base for inflation will become more evident when we discuss the last of the three alternative consumption bases.

In addition to providing these advantages, the use of consumption services as a tax base also poses certain problems. For one thing, the time profile of the tax base differs from that of the income tax. A typical individual consumes more than he earns early in life, is a net saver during his middle years, and spends at least some of his savings once he has retired. A consumption tax imposes larger tax liabilities during the earlier years when the typical individual is already in debt. Paying the tax would involve either cutting back on consumption expenditures or going further into debt. The latter alternative, although perhaps the more desirable of the two, may not be feasible given the market imperfections that may exist in the personal loans market. The income tax avoids this liquidity problem.

However, the main difficulty with using consumption services as a tax base, one that in fact precludes their use, is the difficulty of measuring the flow of services from consumer durables. Again, the consumption-services tax base should be realized income less the net accumulation of both financial and real wealth (including consumer durables) plus the current services of consumer durables (the imputed rent on housing, for example). This formula provides a measure of consumption that includes both expenditures on non-durables and the consumption services of durables in the tax year. Since the services of durables are difficult to measure, this tax base is not feasible. Fortunately, one can achieve the same effect by treating durable purchases in a slightly different manner.

## The Expenditure Base

The expenditure base avoids the need to include the services of consumer durables explicitly in the tax base by including expenditures on all consumer goods, durable or not, on a cash-flow basis. Thus the expenditure base

---

[40] Note that all three of the bases that we consider in this section should include in realized income any bequests or gifts received. Whether or not the giving of gifts and bequests should be treated as a running down of financial wealth and subtracted from the tax base depends on whether or not one views the bequest or gift giving as an act of "consumption" by the donor. As we mentioned earlier, this problem also arises with the income tax.

and the consumption-services base differ in their treatment of consumer durables: the flow of services occurs over the useful life of a durable consumption good, but the expenditures are incurred when the durable is acquired. In the case of non-durables, one can think of expenditures and services as being basically equivalent over the tax year.

Like the measurement of consumption, the measurement of expenditures must be approached indirectly. One can calculate annual expenditures on consumer goods indirectly as the difference between nominal realized income and net purchases of financial and real non-consumer assets. The expenditure tax base differs from the consumption-services tax base only in its treatment of consumer durables. In principle, consumer durables are deducted from the consumption-services base and their future consumption services are included in it. Thus purchases of housing are deducted and the imputed rent on owner-occupied housing is included. This base's operation is basically analogous to the current tax treatment of RRSPs and RPPs, which allows taxpayers to deduct savings for retirement in financial assets but includes the proceeds of the funds in the tax base when they are taken out for consumption. If there were no limitations on the use of RRSPs and RPPs, the tax system would be equivalent to a consumption-services tax system. Under the expenditure tax base, neither thing is done. Since the value of consumer durables purchased should equal the present value of future consumer services, the expenditure base is equivalent to the consumption-services base in present-value terms.

A numerical example will illustrate this point. Suppose that the interest rate is 10 percent. Consider an automobile that yields annual flows of consumer services of $10,000, $7,700, $3,630, and $2,662 over the four years of its useful life. The present value of this stream of services is $10,000 + $7,700/1.1 + $3,630/1.21 + $2,662/1.331 = $22,000. The price of an automobile is $22,000, assuming competitive markets. An expenditure base would include the full purchase price of the automobile in the year of purchase, $22,000. The consumption-services base, in principle, would allow a deduction for the purchase price but include the annual flows of service benefits as they accrued each year. As the example shows, the present value of these flows would simply be the initial purchase price. Again, however, since consumer services are very difficult to measure, a consumption-services base would not be feasible.

The expenditure base retains the advantages of the consumption-services base in that it requires no indexation and measures income only on a realization basis and not on an accruals basis. However, since consumer durables must be purchased before they can be consumed, expenditure tax liabilities would be more uneven over time than would consumption tax liabilities; they would also fall more heavily on taxpayers early in their lives. Quite apart from the liquidity problems that an expenditure tax would present to taxpayers in their early years, the requirement for some averaging provisions is evident. It is this unevenness in the time profile of the expenditure tax that leads us to consider the final alternative.

## The Capital-Income-Exempt Base

A third tax base that is equivalent in present-value terms to consumption is an income base that exempts capital income. Unlike an expenditure tax base, this base does not allow a deduction for capital asset accumulation; however, the capital income on the assets is not taxable. Since the value of an asset equals the present value of its future returns plus repayment, this base has the same present value as the expenditure and consumption bases. Consider, for example, the purchase of an asset that costs $10,000, yields 10 percent interest for each of two years, and then is repaid. Under an expenditure tax system, the taxpayer deducts $10,000 from taxable income initially, then includes in taxable income $1,000 in the first year and $11,000 (interest plus principal) in the second year. The present value of this stream is just zero ($-\$10,000 + \$1,000/1.1 + \$11,000/1.21$). Under a capital-income-exempt tax base, there is neither a deduction at the beginning nor any inclusion of interest and principal later on. Thus the present value in this case is also zero. Both systems effectively shelter savings from taxation. The only difference is in the time streams of the two tax bases. Under an expenditure tax, the tax base is reduced in years of saving and increased later in years of dissaving. Under the capital-income-exempt option, the tax base is larger in earlier years and smaller in later years. For this reason, the treatment of savings under the latter base is often referred to as the *tax-prepaid* approach: savings are made out of after-tax income.

The capital-income-exempt, or tax-prepaid, system possesses the same advantages as the other approaches to consumption taxation. There is, again, no need to index capital income; in this case, capital income is not taxable. As well, income need not be measured as it accrues, but only as it is realized. In addition, however, an income tax base that exempts capital income avoids the liquidity problems of both the expenditure and consumption bases. Tax liabilities tend to be more closely timed to when the consumer is best able to finance them; that is, in periods of higher income.

## A Combined System of Consumption Taxation

The expenditure tax approach and the tax-prepaid approach treat the accumulation of assets in different ways. Although the two approaches are equivalent in present-value terms, there are some differences between them that would justify having elements of each in the same tax system. First, some assets would be easier to administer on an expenditure basis than on a tax-prepaid basis, and for others the reverse would be true. Consumer durables, obviously, would be easier to treat on a tax-prepaid basis, since it would avoid the need to measure the imputed income that they generate. In fact, it would be easier to treat any asset whose return takes an imputed form on a tax-prepaid basis—life insurance assets are an example. On the other hand, investment in human capital and in unincorporated businesses would be easier to deal with on an expenditure (cash-flow) basis. Much of the cost of human capital investments has the form of forgone earnings; given an expenditure approach, it would be very difficult *not* to exempt this cost. It would be difficult to treat an unincorporated business on a tax-prepaid basis, since to do so would involve deducting the capital income from the base, and it would be virtually impossible to distinguish the capital income from the owner's labour income. Second, for assets that are treated on an expenditure basis, records must be kept so that when the asset is run down its proceeds become taxable; that is, these assets have to be *registered*.[41] In the case of some assets, such as liquid assets, this requirement would pose an administrative inconvenience. Providing the option to treat these assets on a tax-prepaid basis would avoid the inconvenience. Finally, given the differences between the time streams of tax liabilities under the two approaches, incorporating both of them in a single tax system would allow the stream of tax liabilities to be evened out. In fact, if taxpayers were permitted to treat some assets as pre-paid and some as registered, they could engage in self-averaging and smooth out their tax liabilities or relieve their liquidity problems as they saw fit. Because of these considerations, all proposals for personal consumption taxation advocate a mixed system that combines the tax-prepaid approach with the expenditure tax approach.

The upshot of this discussion is that a consumption tax base or its equivalent is not only feasible but also possesses certain highly desirable structural features that would make it easier to administer than a comprehensive income tax. Nonetheless, one should not overestimate the economic differences between a consumption tax and an income tax. Over a taxpayer's lifetime, there is typically little difference between cumulative income and cumulative expenditures. The two would be identical if the tax system included net inheritances and gifts in taxable income but did not treat them as consumption, by their donors. If there were a reasonable system of averaging to eliminate the differences in tax treatment that arise from the different time profiles of the income and consumption bases, the main difference between the two bases would be that a consumption base avoids the distortion of savings that occurs under an income tax. If avoiding this distortion is deemed to be an efficient thing to do, given all of the other distortions that taxes impose, then one might unambiguously favour a consumption tax over an income tax. There may, of course, be reasons for specifically wanting to encourage savings, such as to increase the rate of economic growth. The presence of this motive would support the argument for consumption taxation.

## Wealth as a Tax Base

Wealth has a natural appeal as a measure of the economic status of an individual, since it can be either put to use as a source of income or run down as consumption. For several reasons, however, it has never been regarded as a practical base for the major personal tax. The most important reason is that

---

[41] The US Treasury's *Blueprints for Basic Tax Reform*, supra footnote 36, referred to assets of this kind as "designated assets."

many forms of wealth have no readily available market value, so that arbitrary and costly assessments would have to be made each time the tax was paid. A particularly difficult case is that of the value of human wealth, or the economic value of an individual's abilities. Except in rare cases (for example, professional athletes), there is no market in human wealth. Compliance would also be difficult to enforce in the case of items such as liquid assets and personal possessions. For this reason, the only tax typically imposed on wealth is the property tax levied on real property, which we shall discuss in chapter 7. In any case, a tax on wealth would ultimately be almost equivalent to a tax on income, since the market value of wealth is generally taken to be the present value of the stream of income that the wealth generates. Little would be gained by taxing wealth rather than income.[42]

## Inflation and Indexation

The persistence of inflation over the 1970s and 1980s brought to the forefront the need for appropriate indexation of the tax system. The requirement for indexation applies mainly to income taxes, both personal and corporate. It is useful to consider three main structural problems that inflation causes for the tax system, all of which we have alluded to earlier in this chapter. The first is that part of the capital income that a taxpayer receives in inflationary periods does not reflect a genuine increase in purchasing power or comprehensive income. Instead, it represents compensation for the fact that the real value of the taxpayer's assets has been eroded by inflation. Second, since the income tax base is defined in nominal terms, a taxpayer's taxable income will rise from year to year purely on account of inflation. If the rate structure is progressive, the taxpayer may be pushed into a higher tax bracket and end up paying higher real taxes solely because of inflation. This phenomenon is referred to as *bracket creep*. The final problem concerns the treatment of capital costs in the calculation of taxable business income under both the personal and corporate tax structures. Since the deduction for the depreciation of an asset (the so-called *capital cost allowance*) is a proportion of the original purchase price of the asset, inflation will reduce the real value of the deduction. Thus the deduction will not reflect the real depreciation incurred in using the asset. Similarly, since inventory usage is written off at an earlier purchase price (as required under first-in, first-out accounting practice), the writeoff will not reflect the real cost of using up inventories. At the same time, since businesses can write off the nominal interest costs on debt as a capital expense, inflation makes it possible for them to write off more than the real cost of debt finance. Let us consider the implications of these problems in more detail.

---

[42] A complete discussion of the case for and against wealth taxes in Canada may be found in Jack M. Mintz and James E. Pesando, eds., "The Role of Wealth Taxes in Canada" (September 1991), 17 *Canadian Public Policy* (entire issue).

# Illusory Capital Income

As we mentioned above, a taxpayer's comprehensive income is defined as the sum of current consumption plus net additions to wealth. To put the matter differently, it is the amount of consumption that the household can potentially undertake in a given period and still have its wealth intact at the end of the period. The nominal income of the household typically consists of labour income (wages, salaries, commissions, income from self-employment, and so forth) and capital income of various sorts, including interest, rents, dividends, and capital gains. In periods of inflation, all nominal labour income can be thought of as a component of comprehensive income but all nominal capital income cannot. Part of the latter simply offsets a loss in the real value of the asset that is yielding the capital income, given that the value of the asset is fixed in nominal terms. Indeed, if the inflation were expected to occur, the nominal rate of return on an asset would rise by enough to offset the inflation-induced erosion of the real value of the asset. By our definition of comprehensive income, this inflationary component of capital income cannot be part of income, since it merely compensates the taxpayer for the fall in his wealth.

An example may clarify this account. Consider a taxpayer who purchases a $10,000 bond that bears a simple rate of interest of 5 percent in the absence of inflation and that is not amortized. At the end of one year, interest of $500 accrues and the principal of the bond remains at $10,000. If, instead, debtors and creditors alike expect an inflation rate of 5 percent, both sides will willingly accept a 10 percent interest rate on the bond. In this case, the interest payment at the end of the year is $1,000, of which $500 compensates for the fall in the real value of the principal over the period (5 percent of $10,000) and $500 represents real interest. The individual's comprehensive income in this case is $500: if the individual consumes $500 of his nominal capital income and saves the rest, the real value of his wealth is unchanged. Another useful way to calculate real interest income is to subtract from the taxpayer's nominal interest income ($1,000) the fall in the real value of principal (0.05 × $10,000).

Alternatively, the asset that yields capital income may itself be indexed to the price level. Consider again the $10,000 bond. The rate of interest on the bond does not rise with inflation, but the real value of the principal is adjusted for inflation so that it stays intact. If the interest rate and the inflation rate are both 5 percent, the creditor will receive $500 in interest at the end of one year, and the value of the principal will have increased by 5 percent of $10,000 to $10,500. This result is equivalent to the result in the first example, since the creditor in that example could invest his $500 inflation premium at the going interest rate and thus raise the nominal value of his principal to $10,500 as well. In both cases, the comprehensive income is just the real interest received.

With these points in mind, we can now discuss how the income tax system ought to account for the "illusory" capital income that arises from inflation.

Non-capital income poses no problem, since it is not earned by holding physical assets whose value will change with inflation. Capital income arises, generally speaking, from three sources—debt, equity, and real property. If debt is unindexed, the taxpayer ought to be allowed to deduct from nominal interest income the inflation-induced fall in the value of the principal, calculated as the inflation rate times the principal. In the case of indexed debt, only the interest component need be included in income. The nominal capital gain that arises from the indexation of the principal should not be part of taxable income. The same rules should apply to debtors who are able to treat interest payments as expenses of earning income. Only the real value of the interest expenses should be deductible.

In the case of equity capital, the capital income takes the form of dividends and capital gains on the value of the shares held. One might argue that shares are like indexed assets—that rises in share values reflect inflation and dividends reflect a real rate of return. It is not necessarily that simple, however: inflation might be reflected in both higher nominal dividend payments, and nominal capital gains on the asset. More generally, the inflation will be reflected in either the capital gain in the value of the equity shares, the dividend, or some combination of the two. A comprehensive income tax system would account for this inflation by reducing nominal taxable income on equity (the sum of dividends and capital gains) by the inflationary gain (the inflation rate times the initial share value). Matters get slightly complicated under a system that is not comprehensive—for example, one that does not fully tax capital gains on accrual. If the system taxes capital income only in part, then it should exempt the inflationary component of capital income only in part as well. Obviously, the proper indexation of equity income for inflation is administratively complex.

The final type of capital income is rental income from real property. In this case, comprehensive income would include both the rental income itself plus any accrued capital gain on the real property. The appropriate indexation of the tax base, again assuming that all nominal components of capital income were fully taxable, would be to allow as a deduction the fall in the real value of the property owing to inflation.

To summarize, an income tax system should purge nominal capital income that is included in the tax base of any illusory income—that is, any income that reflects a fall in the real value of wealth. If the system fully taxes all capital income on a comprehensive basis, it can eliminate illusory income by allowing a deduction equal to the inflation rate times the nominal value of assets in each period. If the system does not tax all capital income, it should allow the inflation deduction only against the components of taxable income that are actually taxable. On the other hand, if capital income is exempt from taxation, as it effectively is under a personal consumption tax system, no indexation of the base is necessary. As we have mentioned, the absence of any need for indexation is one of the administrative advantages of a consumption tax. Under the existing tax system, no indexation is necessary for sheltered forms of capital income such as income from RRSPs and RPPs.

# Bracket Creep

Increases in nominal incomes because of inflation can cause taxpayers to move into higher tax brackets; it can also cause taxpayers who were not in a tax-paying position before the inflation to become taxable. Tax liabilities, therefore, can rise as a percentage of income simply because of inflation. Since we presumably do not want inflation alone to increase the real tax payments of taxpayers, this outcome is an undesirable one.

Bracket creep can affect both households and firms, incorporated or unincorporated, regardless of the form their income may take. It is a problem for both income tax and personal consumption tax systems. The way to deal with it is to index all exemptions, deductions, credits, and tax-bracket limits at the rate of inflation but otherwise to leave the rate structure unchanged. Presumably, one should also index any transfer payments received, including refundable tax credits.

# Deductions for Capital Expenses

Just as a tax system should account for the impact of inflation on asset values if it includes capital income in its base, so it should account for the effects of inflation on assets that are used in the course of earning business income. In arriving at taxable income, businesses ought to be allowed to deduct the true imputed costs of earning the income. Inflation poses no problem in the case of current costs; in the case of capital costs, however, two problems arise. The first has to do with the calculation of the costs of using up physical capital. If a firm uses depreciable capital to produce income, it should be able to deduct the actual amount of depreciation of the capital over the tax period. Tax systems usually account for capital depreciation by allowing a depreciation deduction—a so-called capital cost allowance—that represents a given proportion of the undepreciated value of the capital stock. In principle, this amount should represent the loss in value of the capital stock over the period—that is, the amount that the firm would have to spend to replace the depreciated capital. If there is inflation, however, and if the capital cost allowance is based on the original purchase cost of the asset, the deduction will be less than the sum of money required to replace the depreciated capital. Thus depreciation should be based on the replacement cost of the capital rather than the original cost. The same principle applies to other sorts of capital. For example, the cost of using up inventories should be the inventories' replacement cost rather than their original purchase cost.

The other problem that arises with inflation concerns the deduction for the costs of financing the holding of assets. The problem is basically the reverse of the problem of the illusory capital income generated by inflation. Just as the tax base should include only real capital income, so businesses should be allowed to deduct only the real costs of finance. To allow businesses to deduct nominal interest, for example, would be equivalent to allowing them to deduct not only real interest but also a proportion of their real principal. The inflationary component of interest payments actually represents an implicit repayment of part of the principal of the debt used to finance capital expenditures.

The administrative complexities involved in indexing business income for inflation can be rather significant. We shall discuss them in detail in chapter 4. There we shall also consider an alternative tax base for business income—the so-called cash-flow tax base, which in present-value terms is equivalent to a tax on the true economic income (or rent) generated by the firm but which overcomes many of the administrative and measurement problems of using income as a tax base, including the need to index capital costs.

## The Rate Structure and Flat Rate Tax Proposals

As we mentioned earlier, the degree of progressivity of the tax system reflects a judgment about the tradeoff between vertical equity and the disincentive effects of progressive taxation. The past several years have seen a series of proposals for broadening the base and making the rate structure both lower and less progressive. The most extreme proposals of this kind call for the replacement of the existing base and rate structures with a "flat rate" income tax.[43] Two primary considerations have led the proponents of flat rate taxation to advance it as an alternative to the present income tax system.

The first consideration is the complexity of the existing tax system. The proponents of a flat rate tax argue that the existing tax system includes too many deductions, exemptions, and other types of preferential treatment (so-called tax expenditures)—more than are called for on standard horizontal equity grounds. In addition to detracting from the equity of the tax system, the presence of these different ways of treating different sources of taxable income considerably increases the administrative and compliance costs of the tax system. Taxpayers are induced to devote resources, including the services of lawyers and accountants, to the goal of obtaining as much of their income as possible in sheltered forms. Most proposals for flat rate taxation involve a considerable broadening of the base. At the limit, they would allow only basic personal exemptions and exemptions for dependants. Quite apart from its equity and administrative advantages, a broadening of the base would permit a general lowering of tax rates.

---

[43] For a summary of flat rate tax proposals in Canada, see Michael A. Walker, *On Flat-Rate Tax Proposals* (Vancouver: Fraser Institute, 1983). For an explicit proposal, see Dennis Mills, *The Single Tax* (Toronto: Hemlock Press, 1990). A discussion of the issues may be found there and in Joseph J. Minarik, "A Flat Rate Income Tax for Canada?" in *Report of Proceedings of the Thirty-Fourth Tax Conference*, 1982 Conference Report (Toronto: Canadian Tax Foundation, 1983), 37-52. The seminal proposal for a flat tax came from Robert E. Hall and Alvin Rabushka, *The Flat Tax*, 2d ed. (Stanford, Calif.: Hoover Institution Press, 1995). It included not only a move to a flat tax but also a change from income to consumption as the base—that is, base narrowing rather than base broadening. For an analysis, see Joel Slemrod and Jon Bakija, *Taxing Ourselves: A Citizen's Guide to the Great Debate Over Tax Reform* (Cambridge, Mass.: MIT Press, 1996).

Of course, a broader base might also have some disadvantages. Many of the deductions that are currently in the tax system may be there for particular reasons of horizontal equity: to reflect the cost of earning income, or the extraordinary expenditures involved in raising a child. One would have to weigh the gains in simplicity that eliminating them would bring against the loss in horizontal equity. On the other hand, some of the deductions and credits currently in effect do actually make the tax system less equitable, including the credits for charitable donations and political contributions, the deductions for medical and dental expenses, educational deductions, and—depending on where one stands on the income-versus-consumption-base debate—perhaps the deductions for RRSP and RPP contributions as well.

The second consideration behind the flat rate proposals is the level of marginal tax rates under the current rate structure. Most proposals call for a single marginal tax rate and a given level of exemptions. Economists have referred to this scheme as a *linear progressive income tax*, since it has a fixed marginal tax rate but increasing average tax rates.[44] The marginal tax rate necessary to raise a given amount of revenue and the progressivity of the tax both increase with the level of exemptions. Flat rate tax proposals generally propose marginal tax rates in the neighbourhood of 20 to 25 percent.

Thus a flat rate tax system would differ significantly from the present system in terms of breadth of base, rate of progressivity, and marginal tax rates. However, it is the lowering of the marginal tax rate on taxable income for most taxpayers that is really the sine qua non of flat rate tax proposals. The use of a single marginal rate would have obvious administrative advantages, and the proponents of flat rate taxation argue that a lowering of marginal tax rates would have substantial and positive incentive effects: it would encourage taxpayers to work more, save more, invest more, and take more risks; moreover, it would reduce the incentive that now exists to under-report taxable income. Against these incentive effects must be set the fact that a flat rate tax would probably make the tax system less progressive. Estimates for both Canada and the United States suggest that this would be the case.[45]

How one should regard the arguments for replacing the existing rate structure with a flat rate tax depends on two sorts of judgments. One is an empirical judgment: How strong, in fact, are the incentive effects of taxation?

---

[44] The average tax rate is the ratio of taxes paid to taxable income. The marginal tax rate is the additional tax paid on an incremental dollar of income received. A linear progressive tax system can be expressed by the equation $T = t\,(Y - E)$, where $T$ is total taxes, $t$ is the marginal tax rate, $Y$ is income, and $E$ is an exemption level. Both $E$ and $t$ are the same for all individuals. The average tax rate is $T/Y$. The equation shows that even though the marginal tax rate is constant, the average tax rate rises with income.

[45] See Walker, supra footnote 43; Joel Slemrod and Shlomo Yitzhaki, "On Choosing a Flat-Rate Income Tax System" (March 1983), 36 *National Tax Journal* 31-44; and Roger S. Smith, "Base Broadening and Rate Changes: A Look at the Canadian Federal Income Tax" (1984), vol. 32, no. 2 *Canadian Tax Journal* 277-93.

Unfortunately, we have no good empirical evidence about these so-called supply-side effects. The other is the value judgment to which we have already referred: What is the appropriate tradeoff between equity and efficiency? Individuals can rationally disagree about how progressive the tax system should be.

## Tax Expenditures

The tax system is a complicated thing. This is inevitable, given the large variety of economic transactions that take place in the economy. Any broad tax base will include many of these transactions. Equally important, some transactions will be excluded. They may be excluded because they are deemed not to be suitable objects of taxation, or because policy makers, for policy reasons, have explicitly chosen to treat them favourably. It may also be administratively difficult to include some items that in principle one would like to include. These considerations make the job of legislators difficult. Tax policy must ultimately be enshrined in legislation, and legislators must therefore be informed enough to make judgments about what tax measures should be put into law.

The concept of a *tax expenditure* has been devised as a way of informing legislators, government officials, and the public about the quantitative effects of the various forms of preferential treatment found in the tax system. The term "tax expenditure" refers to the fact that tax preferences, like direct expenditures, achieve policy objectives at a cost to the treasury. Unlike direct expenditures, however, they are not subject to formal scrutiny by legislators. Direct expenditures are routinely debated as part of the annual budget placed before Parliament. Tax expenditures are not subject to the same accountability, even though some of them accomplish similar objectives. For example, an investment tax credit for research and development may accomplish much the same objective as a direct government grant, but the latter appears on the expenditure side of the government budget and the former appears as a reduction in revenue. The cost of providing the investment tax credit is a tax expenditure.

In order to make tax expenditures more transparent and accountable to Parliament, the Department of Finance routinely calculates them in detail and publishes the results. These calculations, however, refer only to federal taxes and only to the personal income tax, the corporate income tax, and the GST. Thus they give only a partial view of tax expenditures in the tax system as a whole. Below, we shall review the tax expenditures reported by the Department of Finance in 1997. First, however, it is necessary to consider how the department defines tax expenditures under each of the three main federal taxes.

Tax expenditures represent tax revenues forgone as a result of preferential tax treatment. In order to estimate tax expenditures, one must have a *benchmark tax system* in mind; that is, a tax system in which tax expenditures would be zero. Choosing a benchmark tax system requires judgments about what should or should not be a normal part of the tax system. The Department of Finance has chosen a benchmark system with a very broad base, so that it can denominate as tax expenditures as wide an assortment of tax elements as possible. The argument is that those who would choose a more restrictive benchmark system can choose to ignore the additional tax expenditures that this breadth brings about. To give a simple example, the only non-refundable tax credits that the benchmark income tax system provides are those that do not differentiate among taxpayers. Thus the personal tax credit that all taxpayers receive is part of the benchmark tax system, whereas the disability credit appears as a tax expenditure. Those who prefer to regard the disability tax credit as being part of the benchmark system can ignore the tax expenditure that results from it. Even for them, however, the tax expenditure calculated might be informative, since it indicates the cost of the preferential treatment of the disabled that the tax system provides. The Department of Finance's benchmark tax systems are rather complex, but the principles behind the benchmark system for each tax type are as follows.

## The Benchmark Personal Income Tax System

The benchmark personal income tax system includes all elements of income measured on a nominal basis, including wages and salaries, income from unincorporated businesses, and all forms of capital income. Elements that are intended to account for inflation, such as the preferential treatment of capital gains, are tax expenditures. Some elements of the personal tax system that are intended to avoid double taxation in the overall tax system, such as the dividend tax credit, are part of the benchmark and so are not tax expenditures. The existing rate structure, including surtaxes and tax brackets, is part of the benchmark. The basic personal credit is part of the benchmark rate structure, since it applies to all taxpayers, but, as we have mentioned, all selective tax credits are tax expenditures. The tax unit is the individual, so elements of the tax that relate to families and dependants are tax expenditures. The tax year is the calendar year, and any tax deferrals are treated as tax expenditures on a net basis. Thus in the case of RRSPs and RPPs current-year tax expenditures equal the current deductions for contributions to the plan less the current tax liabilities on funds taken out of the plans.

## The Benchmark Corporate Income Tax System

The benchmark corporate tax base includes all revenues less deductions normally given (such as those for depreciation and interest). The rate is taken to be the basic federal corporate tax rate, including surtaxes. The special rates afforded to small businesses and manufacturing and processing are tax expenditures. The tax unit is the single corporate entity, so any tax preferences that apply within corporate groups or to individual establishments within a corporation are tax expenditures. Like the benchmark personal tax, the benchmark corporate tax includes income on a nominal basis, so preferential treatment of capital gains is a tax expenditure. The non-taxation of intercorporate dividends, however, is regarded as a special measure to avoid double taxation and so is part of the benchmark. The tax-paying period is the fiscal year. Any measures that allow corporations to defer taxes, such as accelerated depreciation, are treated as tax expenditures, again on a net basis.

## The Benchmark Goods and Services Tax System

The benchmark GST base is simply defined as all final consumption expenditures in Canada at the general GST rate of 7 percent. Deviations from this include products that bear no GST, such as food, prescription drugs, and medical devices; products that are exempt from tax at the final stage (but bear some tax at earlier stages), such as residential rents, medical and dental services, municipal transit, and legal aid; and tax rebates available to municipalities, universities, schools, and hospitals (the so-called MUSH sector). In addition, the GST credit available to low-income families through the income tax system is a tax expenditure (rather than part of the benchmark rate structure).

On the basis of this benchmark system, the Department of Finance calculates detailed tax expenditures for each type of tax. Tables 2.2, 2.3, and 2.4 report the more substantial tax expenditures for each of the three tax types. The tables include both estimates for 1994 and projections for 1998. As table 2.2 shows, the most significant tax expenditures under the personal income tax are the child tax benefit, net RRSP and RPP contributions, the spousal credit, the non-taxation of employer-paid health and dental benefits, and the age credit. Table 2.3 shows that the most important tax expenditures under the corporate income tax are the low tax rates for small business and manufacturing and processing activities, the tax credit for scientific research and experimental development (SR & ED), the partial exclusion for capital gains received by corporations, the exemption of some interest payments from the non-resident withholding tax (available for residents of tax treaty countries), and the so-called resource allowance. The last item, however, is intended to compensate for the non-deductibility of provincial royalties and mining taxes and on balance it virtually does so. Table 2.4 shows that the main tax expenditures under the GST are the GST credit, the zero-rating of food, the tax exemption of residential rents, and the tax rebates for municipalities and housing. We shall be in a better position to evaluate the case for and against these various tax expenditures after we have reviewed the major types of taxes, which is the task we turn to next.

The next five chapters will consider individually the main taxes used by Canadian governments, federal, provincial, and local. We shall try in each chapter to accomplish three basic objectives. The first is to describe the existing provisions of each tax in enough detail to make it possible to judge their principal effects. Our second objective is to present the economic effects of each tax in a way that is accessible to readers who do not have a detailed knowledge of the methods and techniques of modern economic analysis. This task will sometimes be difficult, since the economics literature whose essence we shall attempt to distil is often highly technical. Nonetheless, we feel that

**Table 2.2   Personal Income Tax Expenditures over $250 Million, 1994 and 1998 (Projected)**

| | 1994 | 1998 |
|---|---|---|
| | *$ millions* | |
| Tuition fee credit | 185 | 255 |
| Education and tuition fee credits transferred | 205 | 300 |
| Spousal credit | 1,190 | 1,225 |
| Equivalent-to-spouse credit | 470 | 470 |
| Child tax benefit | 5,240 | 5,650 |
| $500,000 lifetime capital gains exemption for farm property | 470 | 305 |
| $100,000 lifetime capital gains exemption | 8,815 | |
| Partial inclusion of capital gains | 385 | 445 |
| Deduction of limited partnership losses | 295 | 245 |
| Non-taxation of employer-paid health benefits | 1,270 | 1,500 |
| Disability credit | 275 | 275 |
| Medical expense credit | 260 | 355 |
| Non-taxation of GIS and spouse's allowance | 260 | 280 |
| Non-taxation of social assistance benefits | 705 | 620 |
| Non-taxation of workers' compensation benefits | 585 | 610 |
| Treatment of alimony and maintenance payments | 260 | 255 |
| Age credit | 1,290 | 1,350 |
| Pension income credit | 325 | 365 |
| Registered retirement savings plans | | |
|     Deduction for contributions | 4,785 | 7,195 |
|     Non-taxation of investment income | 3,565 | 5,825 |
|     Taxation of withdrawals | −1,620 | −2,300 |
| Registered pension plans | | |
|     Deduction for contributions | 4,890 | 6,170 |
|     Non-taxation of investment income | 9,540 | 12,250 |
|     Taxation of withdrawals | −4,010 | −6,310 |
| $500,000 lifetime capital gains exemption for small businesses | 1,725 | 685 |
| Non-taxation of capital gains on principal residences | | |
|     Partial inclusion rate | 1,795 | 1,010 |
|     Full inclusion rate | 2,390 | 1,350 |
| Charitable donations credit | 900 | 1,250 |

Source: Canada, *Tax Expenditures 1997* (Ottawa: Department of Finance, 1997).

informed debate on the important issues of taxes and transfers requires that these arguments be understood as fully as possible by all participants in the debate, whether they be economists, lawyers, accountants, or members of any other profession. Our third objective in each chapter is to indicate ways in which—in our opinion or in the opinion of others—the structure of the tax under discussion conflicts with the economic objectives of society. It goes without saying that not all readers will agree with our judgment in these matters.

Finally, no examination of the tax system in Canada would be complete without some consideration of the complementary system of transfer payments to individuals. An additional chapter, therefore, will pursue the same objectives in the context of a discussion of the transfer payments made by the three levels of government.

**Table 2.3   Corporate Income Tax Expenditures over $250 Million,
1994 and 1998 (Projected)**

|  | 1994 | 1998 |
|---|---|---|
|  | *$ millions* | |
| Low tax rate for small businesses | 2,390 | 2,770 |
| Low tax rate for manufacturing and processing | 1,080 | 1,650 |
| SR & ED investment tax credit | 835 | 1,015 |
| Atlantic investment tax credit | 100 | 250 |
| ITCs claimed in current year but earned in prior years | 220 | 285 |
| Partial inclusion of capital gains | 540 | 635 |
| Royalties and mining taxes | | |
|    Non-deductibility of Crown royalties and mining taxes | −440 | −495 |
|    Resource allowance | 510 | 575 |
| Exemptions from non-resident withholding tax | | |
|    Interest on deposits | 400 | 430 |
|    Interest on long-term corporate debt | 515 | 555 |

Source: Same as table 2.2.

**Table 2.4   GST Tax Expenditures over $250 Million,
1994 and 1998 (Projected)**

|  | 1994 | 1998 |
|---|---|---|
|  | *$ millions* | |
| Zero-rated goods and services | | |
|    Basic groceries | 2,595 | 2,960 |
|    Prescription drugs | 275 | 315 |
| Tax-exempt goods and services | | |
|    Long-term residential rent | 1,450 | 1,670 |
|    Health care services | 340 | 455 |
|    Education services (tuition) | 340 | 410 |
| Tax rebates | | |
|    Rebates for municipalities | 530 | 565 |
|    Rebates for hospitals | 275 | 270 |
|    Rebates for schools | 290 | 300 |
|    Housing rebate | 520 | 565 |
| Tax credits | | |
|    GST credit | 2,785 | 2,950 |

Source: Same as table 2.2.

# 3

# The Personal Income Tax

## Introduction

Personal income taxes were introduced in Great Britain in the 19th century and in the United States in 1913. In Canada, the federal personal income tax was initially imposed in 1917 as a temporary measure to help finance the cost of World War I. Because the tax was relatively easy to collect and encountered only limited criticism, however, it was retained after the war. The personal income tax is now used by all of the provincial and territorial governments as well as by the federal government. In fact, this tax yields more revenue than any other tax or non-tax revenue source in Canada (see chapter 1). The personal income tax is generally regarded as the most equitable of all taxes. If carefully structured and adequately administered, it is an important tool of economic policy in any highly developed industrial society.

## The Structure of the Federal Income Tax

The personal income tax is imposed under the provisions of the Income Tax Act. It regards the individual rather than the family as the tax-paying unit. Table 3.1 summarizes the steps that an individual follows in calculating his personal income tax liability.[1] Box A lists the sources of income that the individual must report for income tax purposes. Box B lists the deductions from total income that he may claim in calculating net income. Box C lists the deductions from net income that produce taxable income. Box D lists the marginal federal tax rates that apply to taxable income for the purpose of calculating federal tax liability before non-refundable tax credits are deducted. Box E describes the non-refundable tax credits that the taxpayer may claim in calculating federal tax liability. Box F shows how the net federal tax is calculated. Briefly, the calculation involves the subtraction of all non-refundable federal tax credits (from box E) from the federal tax calculated in box D.

## Income

Three concepts of income appear in sequence on a taxpayer's federal tax return—total income, net income, and taxable income. *Total income* includes all forms of income that an individual is required to report for tax purposes

---

[1] This discussion highlights the economic effects of taxing personal income. It does not cover the legal and accounting implications of personal income taxation. For details on the latter, refer to accounting or legal texts on taxation.

### Table 3.1   Determination of Federal Personal Income Tax
### Liability

| |
|---|
| Box A: *Total income* consists of the following:<br>employment income, old age security pension, Canada or Quebec pension benefits, other pension and superannuation income, employment insurance benefits, taxable amount of dividends, investment and annuity income, net rental income, taxable capital gains, registered retirement savings plan (RRSP) income, self-employment income, and other income. |
| Box B: *Net income* is obtained by subtracting the following *deductions* from total income (box A):<br>registered pension plan contributions, registered retirement savings plan contributions, Saskatchewan pension plan contributions, annual union and professional dues, child care expenses, attendant care expenses, business investment losses, moving expenses, support payments, carrying charges and interest payments, exploration and development expenses, other employment expenses, and other deductions. |
| Box C: *Taxable income* is obtained by subtracting the following *deductions* from net income (box B):<br>employee home relocation loan deductions, stock option and shares deductions, limited partnership losses of other years, non-capital losses of other years, net capital losses of other years, capital gains deduction, northern residents' deductions, and additional deductions. |
| Box D: *Federal tax calculation before the deduction of non-refundable tax credits*:<br>Federal tax rates are applied to taxable income (box C) to calculate federal tax liability before deduction of non-refundable tax credits. Federal marginal tax rates are<br>• 17% of all taxable income of $29,590 or less,<br>• 26% of all taxable income between $29,591 and $59,180, and<br>• 29% of all taxable income over $59,181. |
| Box E: *Non-refundable tax credits*:<br>Two types of non-refundable tax credits are deducted from the tax calculated in box D in arriving at federal tax payable before surtaxes. Credits of the first type are deducted to determine basic federal tax, which is used as the base for calculating provincial income taxes payable. These credits include the basic personal amount, the age amount, the spousal or equivalent-to-spouse amount, the amount for infirm dependants age 18 or older, Canada or Quebec pension plan contributions, employment insurance premiums, pension income deduction to a maximum of $1,000, disability amount to a maximum of $4,233, tuition and education, interspousal transfers, medical expenses exceeding specified amounts, charitable donations, and the dividend tax credit. The second group of non-refundable tax credits have no impact on provincial tax liability but are deducted in calculating federal tax liability. These include federal political contributions, the investment tax credit, the labour-sponsored funds tax credit, and the foreign tax credit. |
| Box F: *Federal tax payable* is obtained by subtracting the non-refundable tax credits (box E) from the federal tax liability calculated in box D and adding the federal surtax. The federal surtax is 5% of all federal taxes in excess of $12,500. |

Sources: Revenue Canada, *1997 General Income Tax Guide* (Ottawa: Revenue Canada, 1997) and *1997 General Income Tax Forms* (Ottawa: Revenue Canada, 1997).

(box A of table 3.1). Legislation in 1971 and 1987 narrowed the gap between the economic definition of comprehensive income[2] and the definition of total income for tax purposes, but a number of important differences remain. First, total income does not include all money income. The most notable exclusion is 25 percent of realized capital gains. Other exclusions are income from savings through private pensions, registered retirement savings plans, and life insurance; some fringe benefits received by employees from employers (for example, contributions to pension plans); gifts and inheritances; $500 of scholarship income; lottery winnings; the goods and services tax credit; federal child tax benefits; provincial child tax credits or benefits; allowances for newborn children received from the Régie des rentes du Québec and Quebec family allowances, compensation received from a province or territory by victims of criminal acts or motor vehicle accidents; and allowances and disability pensions or dependants' pensions paid for war service. In addition, there are three types of tax-exempt income—workers' compensation benefits, social assistance payments, and net federal allowances (guaranteed income and spousal allowances).[3] Second, the emphasis that the definition of total income places on money income means that it excludes most types of non-monetary income, such as unrealized capital gains; the value of home-produced goods consumed by the producer; the value of housewives' services; income in kind; and the net imputed income arising from the ownership of durable goods, such as the net rental value of owner-occupied homes.

*Net income* is the figure obtained by subtracting a number of personal deductions from total income (box B). These deductions fall into three broad categories—deductions for pension contributions subject to ceilings based on income, deductions for expenses of earning employment income, and a variety of other deductions.[4] *Taxable income*, which is the base on which federal income tax liability is calculated, is obtained by subtracting a number of additional deductions (box C) from net income.[5]

Both income from unincorporated businesses and income from wages and salaries are subject to personal income taxation, but the determination of net income for tax purposes is not identical in the two cases. For one thing, unincorporated businesses, like incorporated businesses, can deduct from

---

[2] Richard Goode, "The Economic Definition of Income," in Joseph A. Pechman, ed., *Comprehensive Income Taxation* (Washington, DC: Brookings Institution, 1977), 1-36.

[3] These items are referred to as tax-exempt income because although they must be reported as income on the federal income-tax form (lines 144, 145, and 146) many recipients may deduct them in full (line 250).

[4] For more detail, see Revenue Canada, *1997 General Income Tax Guide* (Ottawa: Revenue Canada, 1997) (form 5006-G).

[5] Ibid.

income all of the costs of earning income, whereas individuals whose income derives from employment can deduct relatively few of these costs.[6]

Both residents of Canada and non-residents who earn income in Canada are taxed, but there is an important distinction between them. Non-residents pay Canadian income tax solely on their Canadian income, whereas residents of Canada must pay Canadian taxes on their world income. To avoid double taxation of the same income, however, residents are allowed credits against Canadian income taxes for all income taxes paid to foreign countries.

Although the current income tax base in Canada is not comprehensive, the gap between total income before allowable deductions and total personal income has closed over the past 40 years. In 1955, as table 3.2 shows, total income for tax purposes was more than $14 billion or slightly more than 66 percent of personal income. In 1980, however, total income exceeded 80 percent of total personal income. By 1995, total income for tax purposes had grown to $530 billion and was slightly less than 80 percent of personal income. Some of the discrepancy between personal income and total income for tax purposes is attributable to the exclusion from total income of imputed income and some forms of money income.[7] In addition, an indeterminate but no doubt considerable amount of income received by taxpayers is either not reported or underreported in taxable income. Some of this underreporting is not in violation of the Income Tax Act, however, since individuals without taxable income are not required to file tax returns.

Table 3.3 records taxable income as a percentage of both total personal income and total income for tax purposes for selected years from 1955 to 1995. The table clearly illustrates the impact of the 1987 tax reform, which, beginning in 1988, converted all exemptions and a number of deductions[8] into tax credits. In other words, moneys that had previously been deducted from taxable income were now taxed, and a variety of tax credits were applied against the resulting tax liability. Since the credits were, for most taxpayers, less generous than the exemptions and deductions had been, the result of the change was a marked increase in tax revenue.

## Deductions

Deductions are expenses or allowances that are subtracted from total income for tax purposes in order to arrive at taxable income. Most of the current

---

[6] Farmers and fishers are allowed to calculate their taxable income according to slightly different guidelines. See Revenue Canada, *Farming Income Tax Guide* (Ottawa: Revenue Canada, annual) (form T4003) and *Fishing Income Tax Guide* (Ottawa: Revenue Canada, annual) (form T4004).

[7] The growth of the hidden or underground economy is not an explanatory factor because its size is excluded from both measures of income.

[8] For a discussion of exemptions and deductions before the 1987 tax reform, see Robin W. Boadway and Harry M. Kitchen, *Canadian Tax Policy*, 2d ed., Canadian Tax Paper no. 76 (Toronto: Canadian Tax Foundation, 1984), chapter 2.

**Table 3.2  Comparison of Personal Income and Total Income for
Tax Purposes for Selected Years from 1955 to 1995**

|  | Personal income, $ million[a] | Total income assessed, $ million[b] | Total income for tax purposes as a percentage of personal income |
|---|---|---|---|
| 1955 ... | 21,438 | 14,199 | 66.2 |
| 1960 ... | 29,883 | 20,484 | 68.5 |
| 1965 ... | 42,118 | 30,049 | 71.3 |
| 1970 ... | 68,222 | 50,825 | 74.5 |
| 1975 ... | 138,578 | 110,353 | 79.6 |
| 1980 ... | 248,890 | 200,551 | 80.6 |
| 1983 ... | 343,052 | 265,241 | 77.3 |
| 1986 ... | 427,262 | 327,712 | 76.7 |
| 1989 ... | 550,180 | 431,845 | 78.5 |
| 1992 ... | 621,776 | 490,508 | 78.9 |
| 1995 ... | 666,542 | 530,085 | 79.5 |

[a] From Canada, Department of Finance, *Economic Reference Tables 1996* (Ottawa: the department, 1996), reference table 13. [b] From Revenue Canada, *Tax Statistics on Individuals* (Ottawa: Revenue Canada, annual).

**Table 3.3  Taxable Income as a Percentage of Personal Income and
Total Income for Tax Purposes for Selected Years from
1955 to 1995**

|  | Taxable income, $ million[a] | Taxable income as a percentage of personal income[b] | Taxable income as a percentage of total income for tax purposes[c] |
|---|---|---|---|
| 1955 ...... | 6,105 | 28.5 | 43.0 |
| 1960 ...... | 9,727 | 32.6 | 47.5 |
| 1965 ...... | 16,484 | 39.1 | 54.9 |
| 1970 ...... | 33,621 | 49.3 | 66.2 |
| 1975 ...... | 68,520 | 49.4 | 62.1 |
| 1980 ...... | 126,840 | 51.0 | 63.2 |
| 1983 ...... | 162,809 | 47.5 | 61.4 |
| 1986 ...... | 201,788 | 47.2 | 61.6 |
| 1987 ...... | 219,700 | 47.6 | 62.2 |
| 1988 ...... | 360,872 | 71.3 | 91.7 |
| 1989 ...... | 395,300 | 71.8 | 91.5 |
| 1992 ...... | 432,155 | 69.5 | 88.1 |
| 1995 ...... | 463,570 | 69.5 | 87.5 |

[a] From Revenue Canada, *Tax Statistics on Individuals* (Ottawa: Revenue Canada, annual). [b] Calculated from data in Canada, Department of Finance, *Economic Reference Tables 1996* (Ottawa: the department 1996), reference table 13, and taxable income. [c] Calculated from data in Revenue Canada, supra footnote a; Department of Finance, supra footnote b; and taxable income.

allowable deductions, listed in boxes B and C of table 3.1, may be categorized as deductions for pension contributions, deductions for the costs of earning income, and a variety of deductions intended to address specific circumstances or activities.

Between 1955 and 1987, as table 3.4 shows, total deductions grew from $6.5 billion to $118.3 billion, or from $1,315 to $6,632 per taxable return. Over the same period, total deductions fell from 51.5 to 34.8 percent of total

## Table 3.4 Deductions and Non-Refundable Tax Credits
### for Selected Years from 1955 to 1995

|  | Deductions | | | Non-refundable tax credits | | |
|---|---|---|---|---|---|---|
|  | $ million | As a percentage of total income | Per taxable return | $ million | As a percentage of basic federal tax | Per taxable return |
| 1955 ... | 6,477 | 51.5 | 1,315 | | | |
| 1960 ... | 8,851 | 47.6 | 1,513 | | | |
| 1965 ... | 11,865 | 41.9 | 1,656 | | | |
| 1970 ... | 15,675 | 31.8 | 1,707 | | | |
| 1975 ... | 34,352 | 33.8 | 2,862 | | | |
| 1980 ... | 62,917 | 33.6 | 4,261 | | | |
| 1983 ... | 83,143 | 34.0 | 5,433 | | | |
| 1986 ... | 112,383 | 35.7 | 6,795 | | | |
| 1987 ... | 118,337 | 34.8 | 6,632 | | | |
| 1988 ... | 31,297 | 8.4 | 1,780 | 18,398 | 39.3 | 1,047 |
| 1989 ... | 34,786 | 8.5 | 1,918 | 19,385 | 36.4 | 1,069 |
| 1992 ... | 42,005 | 9.3 | 2,161 | 21,926 | 38.6 | 1,128 |
| 1995 ... | 47,039 | 9.8 | 2,293 | 21,271 | 33.8 | 1,037 |

Source: Calculated from data in Revenue Canada, *Tax Statistics on Individuals* (Ottawa: Revenue Canada, annual).

income. Again, the figures for 1988 and subsequent years reflect the impact of the replacement of exemptions and some deductions by non-refundable tax credits. In 1988, total deductions dropped to $31.3 billion, or $1,780 per taxable return or 8.4 percent of total income. The introduction of non-refundable tax credits in that year allowed individuals to deduct $18.4 billion from their income tax payable (column 5). The increase in deductions between 1988 and 1995 was largely attributable to growth in contributions to registered retirement savings plans. Over the same period, non-refundable tax credits grew in absolute terms but declined as a percentage of basic federal tax.

Table 3.5 shows the distribution of total deductions by income group. In 1995, for example, the lowest quintile (20 percent) of taxpayers claimed 6.8 percent of all deductions, whereas the highest quintile claimed 48.4 percent. The pattern is similar for each of the individual deductions except those in the category "additional deductions," which includes the deductions for "tax exempt" income—income that derives from programs designed to assist low-income earners and that is included as income in one section of the income tax form and deducted in another section.

### The Rationale for Deductions

Although the justification for permitting a given type of personal deduction is not always clear, the deductions that the system presently allows seem to have three main purposes: to encourage savings for retirement (deductions for registered retirement savings plan and registered pension plan contributions); to remove from income expenses incurred in earning income (deductions for union and professional dues, child care expenses, and employment expenses); and to encourage investment (deductions for investment

**Table 3.5  Percentage of Deductions Claimed by Income Quintile, 1995**

| Income quintile | Registered pension plan contributions | Registered retirement savings plan contributions | Union and professional dues | Child care expenses | Carrying charges/ interest expense | Other employment expenses[a] | Other deductions[b] | Capital gains deduction | Additional deductions[c] | Total deductions |
|---|---|---|---|---|---|---|---|---|---|---|
| First ......... | 0.3 | 0.7 | 1.4 | 3.7 | 2.0 | 0.8 | 3.5 | 0.3 | 17.8 | 6.8 |
| Second ....... | 0.6 | 2.2 | 2.5 | 8.0 | 2.3 | 1.9 | 4.1 | 0.2 | 36.6 | 13.9 |
| Third ........ | 4.2 | 8.5 | 8.8 | 23.3 | 5.8 | 8.6 | 10.4 | 1.0 | 23.8 | 13.4 |
| Fourth ....... | 25.1 | 22.2 | 29.1 | 36.5 | 12.1 | 19.8 | 20.3 | 2.8 | 9.7 | 17.4 |
| Fifth ......... | 69.9 | 66.4 | 58.2 | 28.5 | 77.8 | 68.9 | 61.6 | 95.7 | 12.0 | 48.4 |
| Total ......... | 100.0 | 100.0 | 100.0 | 100.0 | 100.0 | 100.0 | 100.0 | 100.0 | 100.0 | 100.0 |

[a] Includes travel expenses, cost of an office and wages to an assistant, expenses paid to earn commission income, cost of meals up to 50%, lodging while employed away from home, power-saw expenses, motor vehicle costs, cost of supplies, and expenses paid to earn income from artistic activities. [b] Includes legal and accounting fees, capital cost allowances for Canadian motion picture films and videotapes, repayments of income amount, depletion allowances, Saskatchewan provincial plan contributions, moving expenses, cleric's residence, family maintenance and child support deduction, Canadian exploration and development expenses, attendant care expense, and allowable business investment loss. [c] Includes the vow of perpetual poverty deduction, 50% benefits from United States social security income, other years' restricted farm losses, income exempt under a tax treaty, tax-exempt income (workers' compensation payments, social assistance payments and net federal supplements), and some additional miscellaneous deductions.

Source: Calculated from data in table 2 in Revenue Canada, *Tax Statistics on Individuals: 1995 Tax Year* (Ottawa: Revenue Canada, 1997).

losses and for interest expenses and carrying costs on funds borrowed for investment purposes).

## Pension and Retirement Income Deductions

Registered pension plans (RPPs) and registered retirement savings plans (RRSPs) have similar features and are designed to meet both social and economic objectives. The main social goal is to provide an adequate level of income for people upon retirement (and also to reduce government expenditure for this purpose). In addition, the RRSP scheme allows individuals to average their incomes over their lifetimes. The economic objective is to encourage savings, and thus to increase the supply of funds available for investment. In terms of tax design, the tax treatment of RRSP and RPP contributions and the capital income earned thereon is equivalent to defining part of the personal tax base as expenditure rather than income. As we mentioned in chapter 2, one way in which to design an expenditure tax is to exempt from the tax base all asset accumulation. In effect, RRSPs and RPPs exempt from the tax base funds that are used to accumulate certain forms of assets (assets for retirement purposes). Thus they have the effect of making the personal tax to some extent an expenditure tax. Removal of all ceilings on contributions to retirement savings plans would lead to an even closer approximation of an expenditure tax base.

Individuals may deduct from total income RRSP contributions of up to 18 percent of their earned income in the preceding year,[9] to a maximum of $13,500 per year, unless they are accruing benefits in an RPP or a registered deferred profit-sharing plan (DPSP). This maximum limit will apply until 2002, and indexing of the limit to account for inflation is scheduled to begin in 2004. For members of RPPs and DPSPs, allowable RRSP contributions are reduced by a pension adjustment (PA). The PA is the value of employee pension benefits that accrued to the tax filer during the previous year. In the case of money purchase plans, the PA equals employee contributions plus employer contributions. In the case of benefit-defined plans, it is determined by the "nine-times" formula; that is, each percentage point of income accrued for future pension benefits is treated as being equivalent to an RRSP contribution of 9 percent of income. In addition to these normal contributions, a number of special rollovers are permitted to RRSPs from RPPs and DPSPs. Furthermore, an individual may roll retiring allowances (up to specific limits) into an RRSP without incurring tax. An individual may carry unused RRSP contribution room forward indefinitely. As well, a married individual may contribute either to his own plan or to one in the name of the spouse, but only up to the limit for the contributing individual.

Table 3.6 shows the distribution of pension deductions across income groups. Note that in every income group the percentage of tax filers contributing to

---

[9] Earned income differs from taxable income. For a discussion of the difference, see Revenue Canada, *RRSPs and Other Registered Plans for Retirement Guide* (Ottawa: Revenue Canada, annual) (form T4040).

**Table 3.6  Distribution of Pension Deductions, 1995**

| Income group, $ | Registered retirement savings plans | | | Registered pension plans | | |
|---|---|---|---|---|---|---|
| | Percentage of all returns claiming deduction | Average claim, $ | Deductions as a percentage of total income | Percentage of all returns claiming deduction | Average claim, $ | Deductions as a percentage of total income |
| Loss-10,000 ....... | 3.4 | 1,169 | 0.9 | 1.4 | 311 | 0.1 |
| 10,001-20,000 ..... | 13.8 | 1,724 | 1.7 | 5.2 | 487 | 0.2 |
| 20,001-30,000 ..... | 32.9 | 2,254 | 3.0 | 20.3 | 959 | 0.8 |
| 30,001-40,000 ..... | 47.7 | 2,906 | 4.0 | 36.5 | 1,530 | 1.6 |
| 40,001-50,000 ..... | 57.5 | 3,630 | 4.7 | 44.8 | 2,100 | 2.1 |
| 50,001-60,000 ..... | 64.2 | 4,292 | 5.1 | 48.8 | 2,751 | 2.5 |
| 60,001-70,000 ..... | 69.4 | 5,174 | 5.6 | 49.4 | 3,354 | 2.6 |
| 70,001-80,000 ..... | 73.7 | 6,539 | 6.5 | 43.3 | 3,497 | 2.0 |
| 80,001-90,000 ..... | 76.1 | 7,943 | 7.1 | 38.5 | 3,620 | 1.6 |
| 90,001-100,000 .... | 77.3 | 9,061 | 7.4 | 33.5 | 3,800 | 1.3 |
| 100,001-150,000 ... | 77.6 | 11,149 | 7.3 | 25.5 | 4,092 | 0.9 |
| 150,001-250,000 ... | 76.8 | 13,274 | 5.4 | 17.0 | 4,596 | 0.4 |
| 250,001 + ......... | 74.6 | 15,165 | 2.2 | 8.1 | 4,779 | 0.1 |
| Average .......... | 27.9 | 3,695 | 4.0 | 17.8 | 1,897 | 1.3 |

Source: Same as table 3.5.

RRSPs is higher than the percentage contributing to RPPs. In addition, the percentage of taxpayers who contribute to RRSPs is highest at the upper end of the income scale, whereas the highest percentage of contributors to RPPs occurs in the $40,000 to $80,000 range. For both deductions, the average claim per return increases as income increases. The value of the average RPP claim, however, is less than that of the average RRSP claim, a result that is not surprising in view of the higher limits and more voluntary nature of the RRSP program (participation in an RPP is frequently a condition of employment). As a percentage of total income, RPP deductions are highest in the middle of the income range and RRSP deductions are highest toward the upper end of the range but decline sharply over the last two income groups.

## Deductions for Expenses of Earning Income from Employment

In theory, the most justifiable deductions are those allowed for the cost of earning income. Two types of allowable expenses must be distinguished here. The first are the allowable expenses of earning business or financial income. The personal tax system treats these expenses in exactly the same manner as the expenses of earning corporate income, which will be discussed fully in chapter 4. These expenses are allowed only to the extent that they reflect actual costs of earning taxable income. For example, interest costs are deductible only to the extent that they are incurred as a cost of earning taxable income. They are not deductible if they refer to loans acquired in order to purchase housing or other durables or purchase tax-sheltered financial assets (such as RRSPs and registered education savings plans—RESPs). The second type of allowable expenses are those associated with employment income as distinct from business or corporate income. These expenses include union and professional dues, child care expenses, and other employment expenses, such as the costs of travel, tools, and supplies.[10]

Union and professional dues are essential costs of earning income, and the tax system has justifiably allowed their deduction for some time. More recently, the system has permitted a deduction for child care expenses for children under 16 or children who have a mental or physical infirmity. A taxpayer may claim these expenses only if they are incurred in order to enable the taxpayer or his spouse to earn income from employment or self-employment; to enroll in an educational program at a secondary school, college, university, or other designated educational institution for at least 10 hours per week for at least three consecutive weeks; to take an occupational training course for which the taxpayer or his spouse receives a training allowance; or to conduct research or similar work for which the taxpayer or his spouse receives a grant. In 1998, Revenue Canada raised the maximum deductible child care expense to $7,000 for each eligible child who is under 7 years of age or who has a physical or mental impairment. For each eligible child over 7 but under 17 or who has a lesser physical or mental infirmity, the maximum was increased to $4,000. The deduction must be claimed by the spouse with the lower income.

Since its inception, the deduction for child care expenses has been plagued with problems and inconsistencies. Difficulties have arisen in separating personal child care expenditures from those necessary to earning an income. Parents who take care of their own children while earning an income are not allowed a deduction, whereas working parents who hire someone to look after their children are. In addition, it is debatable whether there should be a limit per child. Ordinary business expenses are not generally limited to a maximum amount, and one may question the appropriateness of upper limits in this instance. Perhaps the limit was imposed in order to avoid the tax loss that might result from large deductions by high-income earners who have less need of this subsidy than do lower-income taxpayers yet are likely to incur more child care expenses.

The category "other employment expenses" covers a broad range of items. They include travel expenses, the cost of relocation for work purposes, the cost of an office, wages paid to an assistant, expenses paid to earn commission income, the cost of meals up to 50 percent, lodging expenses while employed away from home, power-saw expenses, motor vehicle costs, cost of supplies, and expenses paid in order to earn income from artistic activities.

Table 3.7 shows the distributional pattern of the expense deductions in 1995. The percentage of taxpayers who claimed union and professional dues was much higher than the percentage who claimed child care expenses or other employment expenses. The average claim for other employment expenses, however, was higher than the average claim for professional and union

---

[10] For a list of other employment-expense deductions, see the table 3.5, footnote a.

**Table 3.7  Distribution of Deductions for Expenses Incurred in Earning Income from Employment, 1995**

| Income group, $ | Union and professional dues | | | Child care expenses | | | Other employment expenses | | |
|---|---|---|---|---|---|---|---|---|---|
| | Percentage of all returns claiming deduction | Average claim, $ | Deductions as a percentage of total income | Percentage of all returns claiming deduction | Average claim, $ | Deductions as a percentage of total income | Percentage of all returns claiming deduction | Average claim, $ | Deductions as a percentage of total income |
| Loss-10,000 | 6.5 | 113 | 0.2 | 1.5 | 1,372 | 0.4 | 0.3 | 1,358 | 0.1 |
| 10,001-20,000 | 12.5 | 182 | 0.2 | 3.7 | 2,057 | 0.5 | 1.1 | 2,093 | 0.2 |
| 20,001-30,000 | 27.8 | 305 | 0.3 | 6.7 | 2,620 | 0.7 | 2.6 | 2,480 | 0.3 |
| 30,001-40,000 | 41.4 | 432 | 0.5 | 6.3 | 3,010 | 0.6 | 4.2 | 2,967 | 0.4 |
| 40,001-50,000 | 50.6 | 548 | 0.6 | 5.1 | 3,505 | 0.4 | 5.3 | 3,439 | 0.4 |
| 50,001-60,000 | 54.7 | 629 | 0.6 | 3.9 | 3,517 | 0.3 | 6.4 | 3,799 | 0.4 |
| 60,001-70,000 | 51.8 | 688 | 0.6 | 3.4 | 3,821 | 0.2 | 7.6 | 4,210 | 0.5 |
| 70,001-80,000 | 43.5 | 665 | 0.4 | 3.1 | 4,027 | 0.2 | 9.6 | 5,135 | 0.7 |
| 80,001-90,000 | 37.1 | 648 | 0.3 | 2.8 | 4,245 | 0.1 | 10.9 | 6,668 | 0.9 |
| 90,001-100,000 | 31.0 | 647 | 0.2 | 2.2 | 4,570 | 0.1 | 10.6 | 7,223 | 0.8 |
| 100,001-150,000 | 23.7 | 757 | 0.2 | 2.4 | 4,185 | 0.1 | 10.4 | 9,627 | 0.8 |
| 150,001-250,000 | 14.9 | 732 | 0.1 | 1.9 | 4,724 | 0.0 | 9.9 | 15,038 | 0.8 |
| 250,001 + | 10.2 | 790 | 0.0 | 1.2 | 4,978 | 0.0 | 8.3 | 20,671 | 0.3 |
| Average | 23.6 | 420 | 0.4 | 4.0 | 2,635 | 0.4 | 2.6 | 3,854 | 0.4 |

Source: Same as table 3.5.

### Table 3.8 Distribution of Deductions for Cost of Earning Investment Income, 1995

| Income group, $ | Carrying charges and interest expenses | | | Capital gains deduction | | |
|---|---|---|---|---|---|---|
| | Percentage of all returns claiming deduction | Average claim, $ | Deductions as a percentage of assessed income | Percentage of all returns claiming deduction | Average claim, $ | Deductions as a percentage of assessed income |
| Loss-10,000 ....... | 2.8 | 415 | 0.3 | 1.0 | 4,281 | 0.0 |
| 10,001-20,000 ..... | 9.4 | 248 | 0.2 | 1.2 | 1,999 | 0.0 |
| 20,001-30,000 ..... | 17.5 | 308 | 0.2 | 1.3 | 5,995 | 0.1 |
| 30,001-40,000 ..... | 23.2 | 375 | 0.3 | 1.3 | 8,365 | 0.1 |
| 40,001-50,000 ..... | 28.9 | 467 | 0.3 | 1.4 | 13,309 | 0.1 |
| 50,001-60,000 ..... | 34.0 | 587 | 0.4 | 1.6 | 16,607 | 0.2 |
| 60,001-70,000 ..... | 40.3 | 804 | 0.5 | 1.7 | 23,972 | 0.2 |
| 70,001-80,000 ..... | 45.8 | 1,019 | 0.6 | 1.0 | 25,118 | 0.3 |
| 80,001-90,000 ..... | 49.3 | 1,317 | 0.8 | 1.3 | 34,646 | 0.5 |
| 90,001-100,000 .... | 52.7 | 1,652 | 0.9 | 1.9 | 44,634 | 0.9 |
| 100,001-150,000 ... | 56.0 | 2,592 | 1.2 | 4.0 | 66,569 | 2.2 |
| 150,001-250,000 ... | 61.9 | 5,064 | 1.7 | 7.9 | 117,692 | 5.0 |
| 250,001 + ......... | 69.2 | 17,300 | 2.3 | 13.4 | 229,158 | 5.9 |
| Average .......... | 15.8 | 782 | 0.5 | 0.3 | 46,980 | 0.6 |

Source: Same as table 3.5.

dues or for child care expenses. Altogether, deductions for expenses incurred in earning income amount to approximately 1 percent of total income.

In evaluating employment expenses, it is often difficult to separate personal expenditures from the true costs of earning an income. Has a given individual changed his residence in order to be closer to his place of employment, or was his motive simply a personal desire to live in another home? Are the child care expenses incurred in a given instance of a consumptive nature or necessary costs of earning income? The government recognizes the difficulties raised by deductions of this kind but nevertheless allows them.

### Deductions for Expenses of Earning Investment Income

In general, taxpayers can deduct carrying charges and interest expenses that they incur in borrowing money in order to earn investment income. They cannot, however, deduct service charges or interest on loans that they have invested in RRSPs, RPPs, or RESPs. It is possible to deduct up to $500,000 in capital gains realized on the disposition of agricultural property and $500,000 in capital gains realized on the disposition of qualifying small business corporation shares. Cumulative net investment losses, however, may reduce the net taxable capital gains otherwise eligible for the capital gains deduction.

Table 3.8 shows the distribution of these deductions across income groups. Not surprisingly, the percentage of returns that claim these deductions increases as income rises. The average size of the claim increases with income as well, and so does the percentage of income that the deductions represent.

The rationale for allowing these deductions is similar to the rationale for allowing deductions for the costs of earning business income. Specifically, if expenses associated with earning labour income from self-employment are deductible, then the costs of earning investment income should also be deductible.

## "Other Deductions"

This category covers a range of deductions that are rationalized by an intention either to aid taxpayers in specific circumstances or to promote specific activities. It includes capital cost allowances for Canadian motion picture films and videotapes; depletion allowances; and deductions for Saskatchewan provincial pension plan contributions, moving expenses, partial expenses of clerical residences, family maintenance and child support payments, Canadian exploration and development expenses, attendant care expenses, allowable business investment losses, and legal and accounting fees.

## Federal Tax

An individual's federal income tax liability, before deductions for non-refundable tax credits, is calculated by applying the federal marginal tax rates to taxable income. The federal tax rates are graduated by a bracket system. The income scale is divided into three tax brackets,[11] and marginal tax rates (the rate of tax on the last dollar of taxable income) are applied to the taxable income in each bracket.[12] For 1998, the federal tax rate was 17 percent on the first $29,590 of taxable income, 26 percent on taxable income between $29,591 and $59,180, and 29 percent on all taxable income in excess of $59,180.[13] Non-refundable tax credits are then subtracted from the tax calculated according to the rate schedule.

The tax brackets and a few non-refundable tax credits (specifically, credits for the basic amount, married or equivalent amount, infirm dependants over 17 years of age, individuals over age 64, and the disabled) are indexed annually by an amount that is equivalent to any increase in the consumer price index in excess of 3 percent. Annual inflation has not exceeded 3 percent, however, since 1992. Consequently, the value of the tax brackets and the dollar value of the tax credits have not changed since then.

---

[11] There were 18 tax brackets before 1972, 13 in 1972, and 10 in 1981; there have been 3 since 1987.

[12] For a historical discussion of post-war marginal and average tax rates, see Roger S. Smith, "The Personal Income Tax: Average and Marginal Tax Rates in the Post-War Period" (1995), vol. 43, no. 5 *Canadian Tax Journal* 1055-76.

[13] The effective marginal tax rates for individuals differ from those reported in this paragraph for the following reasons. The 1999 federal budget increased the basic allowance and eliminated the 3 percent surtax for all taxpayers. As well, marginal tax rates are affected by the goods and services tax credit, CPP/QPP contributions, and employment insurance contributions.

Federal personal income tax liability may include a surtax. The surtax rate of 5 percent applies to the basic federal tax in excess of $12,500. Because the surtax is calculated after the basic federal tax, it does not affect provincial personal income tax liability.

## Non-Refundable Tax Credits

Non-refundable tax credits reduce personal income tax liability. If the total value of these credits exceeds the amount of tax payable, however, the taxpayer does not get a refund for the difference. Refundable tax credits, which we shall discuss briefly below, do refund this difference to the taxpayer.

Taxpayers have access to two types of non-refundable tax credits in calculating federal tax payable. The first type consists of credits that are deducted from taxes payable in calculating basic federal tax (the base for determining provincial income tax liability). Three different tax-credit rates apply to the credits in this group. The most widely used rate, 17 percent (equal to the lowest marginal tax rate), applies to credits for the basic personal amount, the age amount, the spousal or equivalent-to-spouse amount, the amount for infirm dependants age 18 or older, Canada or Quebec pension plan (CPP/QPP) contributions, employment insurance premiums, the pension income amount (to a maximum of $1,000), the disability amount up to a maximum of $4,233), tuition and education expenses, the interest portion of student loan repayments, interspousal transfers, and medical expenses in excess of specified amounts. For charitable donations, the tax-credit rate rises from 17 percent for the first $200 of donations to registered charities to 29 percent (equal to the highest federal marginal tax rate) for all donations in excess of $200. Finally, the dividend tax credit is equal to 13.33 percent of the grossed-up amount of all dividends received.

The use of non-refundable tax credits is a relatively recent phenomenon in Canada. Apart from the dividend tax credit, the current credits were all introduced in 1988. Between 1988 and 1995, their value for taxable returns grew from $18.4 billion to $21.3 billion. Over the same period, however, their value as a proportion of basic federal tax payable fell from 39.3 to 33.8 percent (see table 3.4).

Table 3.9 illustrates the distribution of these non-refundable tax credits (apart from the dividend tax credit, since the base for its calculation differs from the base for the others) by income group in 1995. A comparison of this table with table 3.5 shows that these tax credits, taken as a group, were much more evenly distributed across income groups than deductions were. This observation does not apply, however, to all of the individual credits. Thus the credit for charitable donations largely benefited higher-income taxpayers, as did, to a lesser extent, the credits for CPP/QPP and unemployment (now known as employment) insurance contributions. The age tax credit deliberately favoured lower-income taxpayers (it diminishes in value as income increases). The remaining credits were more evenly distributed across all income quintiles.

**Table 3.9 Percentage of Tax Credits Claimed by Income Quintile, 1995**

| Income quintile | Basic personal amount | Age amount | Spousal or equivalent-to-spouse amount | CPP/QPP contributions | Unemployment insurance[a] contributions | Pension income amount | Disability amount | Tuition fees and education amount | Inter-spousal transfers | Medical expenses | Charitable donations | Total credits |
|---|---|---|---|---|---|---|---|---|---|---|---|---|
| First ....... | 19.8 | 10.2 | 9.8 | 1.6 | 2.3 | 2.6 | 11.9 | 18.7 | 5.8 | 3.2 | 0.6 | 16.0 |
| Second ... | 20.0 | 37.7 | 16.1 | 4.4 | 4.7 | 12.9 | 22.1 | 19.8 | 20.8 | 15.2 | 3.9 | 18.8 |
| Third ...... | 20.0 | 34.4 | 23.2 | 14.6 | 14.0 | 33.6 | 29.5 | 17.5 | 36.9 | 30.6 | 12.9 | 20.8 |
| Fourth ...... | 20.1 | 15.9 | 23.3 | 33.7 | 31.6 | 29.6 | 21.1 | 15.8 | 23.7 | 25.7 | 21.4 | 21.3 |
| Fifth ....... | 20.1 | 1.7 | 27.6 | 45.7 | 47.4 | 21.3 | 15.4 | 28.2 | 12.7 | 25.2 | 61.3 | 23.1 |
| Total ....... | 100.0 | 100.0 | 100.0 | 100.0 | 100.0 | 100.0 | 100.0 | 100.0 | 100.0 | 100.0 | 100.0 | 100.0 |

[a] Now known as employment insurance.

Source: Same as table 3.5.

The second group of non-refundable tax credits have no impact on provincial tax liability but are deducted in calculating federal tax liability. The credits in this group are the federal political contributions tax credit, the investment tax credit, the labour-sponsored funds tax credit, and the credit for foreign tax paid.

Taxpayers whose non-refundable credits exceed their tax liabilities may transfer to a spouse any part of the following amounts that they do not need in order to reduce their federal income tax to zero: the age amount, the pension amount, the disability amount, and the tuition and education amounts (to a maximum of $5,000). A student may also transfer excess tuition and education amounts to a parent or grandparent or to a parent or grandparent of his spouse.

## The Rationale for Non-Refundable Tax Credits

Regardless of the original rationale behind each of the non-refundable tax credits, there appear to be a number of arguments for them: first, to protect low-income individuals who have little or no tax-paying capacity (the credits for the basic amount, the age amount, and the spousal or equivalent-to-spouse amount); second, to relieve hardships if a number of non-discretionary or involuntary expenses are not deductible (the credits for medical expenses and for the disability amount); third, to allow for contributions to public social insurance programs designed to protect individuals in specific circumstances (the credit for CPP/QPP contributions); fourth, to encourage voluntary support of certain socially desirable activities (the credit for charitable donations); fifth, to deduct the expense associated with earning future income (the credits for tuition fees and education amounts); sixth, to preserve the spending power of pension income received by the elderly or the retired (the credit for the first $1,000 of pension income); seventh, to encourage investment (the investment tax credit and the credit for labour-sponsored funds); eighth, to avoid double taxation (the foreign tax credit). The following discussion will consider the various non-refundable tax credits in terms of this classification.

## Tax Credits Applicable to the Calculation of Basic Federal Tax

These non-refundable tax credits are deducted from taxes payable on taxable income in order to arrive at "basic federal tax." Basic federal tax is used in determining provincial income tax liability in all provinces except Quebec, which administers its own personal income tax system.

### Protection of Low-Income Individuals

There are three tax credits that may be said to provide income-tax relief to low-income earners. Every taxpayer is eligible for the credit for the so-called basic personal amount of $7,131 (1999 value).[14] A taxpayer may also claim a credit for a dependent spouse—a credit whose value diminishes as the spouse's income increases. Taxpayers who are at least 65 years old may claim a further amount; again, the value of the claim declines as income rises.

Table 3.10 shows the distribution of these three tax credits by income group in 1995. Not surprisingly, 100 percent of taxpayers claimed the basic amount. The tax credit for each taxpayer, regardless of level of income, equalled $1,098 (17 percent of the basic amount in 1995 of $6,456). The tax savings realized from the use of this credit were proportionately higher for low-income taxpayers than they were for high-income taxpayers. Only a small proportion of taxpayers claimed the age amount. Since this amount is designed to fall with income, both its value and the percentage savings in taxes declined as income increased.

Except in the lowest income group, the percentage of taxpayers who claimed a spousal or equivalent-to-spouse tax credit was relatively constant at about 20 percent. Although the value of this credit was similar across income groups it generated proportionately greater savings in taxes for low-income taxpayers than for high-income taxpayers.

A major justification for the tax credit for the basic personal amount is to protect those who have no tax-paying capacity. This rationale for the credit is debatable on at least two grounds. First if the intention is to protect some minimum standard of living, then the basic amount falls short of its goal: it bears little relation to any minimum standard determined on the basis of widely accepted criteria. Second, if the purpose of the basic amount is to protect a minimum standard of living for low-income individuals, then why is it also available to middle- and high-income individuals? Perhaps the personal tax credit, like the age and spousal tax credits, should decline in value as income increases.

## Medical Expenses and Disability

The income tax credits for medical expenses and the disability amount are designed to mitigate expenses that are unusually high, represent some degree of hardship, and do not as a rule contribute to consumption enjoyment. A taxpayer is entitled to a tax credit for either the amount by which medical expenses exceed $1,614 or the amount by which medical expenses exceed 3 percent of net income, whichever is less. This credit is applicable to expenses incurred by the taxpayer, his spouse, and his dependants.

A taxpayer may claim a disability tax credit of 17 percent on an amount of up to $4,233 if he is subject to prolonged suffering from severe mental or physical impairment. Like the credit for medical expenses, this tax credit may be claimed for a dependant.

---

[14] In this chapter tax credits, unless otherwise stated, equal 17 percent of the amounts reported or claimed.

**Table 3.10 Distribution of Tax Credits Intended To Protect Low-Income Individuals, 1995**

| Income group, $ | Basic amount | | | Age amount | | | Spousal or equivalent-to-spouse amount | | |
|---|---|---|---|---|---|---|---|---|---|
| | Percentage of all returns claiming tax credit | Average tax credit, $ | Percentage of tax saved through use of tax credit | Percentage of all returns claiming tax credit | Average tax credit, $ | Percentage of tax saved through use of tax credit | Percentage of all returns claiming tax credit | Average tax credit, $ | Percentage of tax saved through use of tax credit |
| Loss-10,000 . . . . . . . . . . | 100.0 | 1,098 | 96.8 | 0.1 | 590 | 54.9 | 7.5 | 739 | 60.4 |
| 10,001-20,000 . . . . . . . . | 100.0 | 1,098 | 62.9 | 0.3 | 592 | 22.2 | 16.0 | 767 | 15.9 |
| 20,001-30,000 . . . . . . . . | 100.0 | 1,098 | 33.2 | 0.2 | 578 | 4.4 | 17.6 | 732 | 5.5 |
| 30,001-40,000 . . . . . . . . | 100.0 | 1,098 | 22.0 | 0.1 | 395 | 1.1 | 17.8 | 745 | 3.3 |
| 40,001-50,000 . . . . . . . . | 100.0 | 1,098 | 15.5 | 0.1 | 151 | 0.2 | 19.3 | 757 | 2.4 |
| 50,001-60,000 . . . . . . . . | 100.0 | 1,098 | 11.9 | 0.0 | 134 | 0.0 | 20.7 | 759 | 1.9 |
| 60,001-70,000 . . . . . . . . | 100.0 | 1,098 | 9.7 | 0.0 | 233 | 0.0 | 22.4 | 770 | 1.7 |
| 70,001-80,000 . . . . . . . . | 100.0 | 1,098 | 8.1 | 0.0 | 225 | 0.0 | 22.3 | 799 | 1.4 |
| 80,001-90,000 . . . . . . . . | 100.0 | 1,098 | 7.0 | 0.0 | 417 | 0.0 | 22.9 | 769 | 1.2 |
| 90,001-100,000 . . . . . . . | 100.0 | 1,098 | 6.1 | 0.0 | 339 | 0.0 | 22.7 | 766 | 1.0 |
| 100,001-150,000 . . . . . . | 100.0 | 1,098 | 4.7 | 0.0 | 264 | 0.0 | 20.2 | 755 | 0.7 |
| 150,001-250,000 . . . . . . | 100.0 | 1,098 | 2.8 | 0.0 | 298 | 0.0 | 19.5 | 765 | 0.4 |
| 250,001 + . . . . . . . . . . . . | 100.0 | 1,098 | 1.0 | 0.0 | 391 | 0.0 | 17.8 | 769 | 0.1 |
| Average . . . . . . . . . . . . | 100.0 | 1,098 | 26.2 | 0.1 | 550 | 2.6 | 15.0 | 753 | 3.6 |

Source: Same as table 3.5.

Table 3.11 shows that although the average tax credit for medical expenses rose with income in 1995 the tax savings from this credit fell as a percentage of tax as income increased. The percentage of taxpayers who used this credit was higher at the two ends of the income scale than it was in the middle of the scale. The percentage of taxpayers who claimed a tax credit for disability and the average tax credit claimed were both much the same across all income groups. The proportionate reduction in tax liability, however, was greatest for low-income earners.

Two reasons are usually given for allowing tax credits for medical expenses and disability. First, unavoidable large expenses may create severe hardships, especially for low-income earners. Second, it is highly unlikely that such expenses are incurred for purely consumptive purposes.

Given the latter ratonale, is it appropriate to limit claims to medical expenses in excess of a minimum threshold such as 3 percent of net income? By limiting access to the tax credit in this way, the tax authorities avoid the administrative costs of processing a large number of itemized claims; yet medical expenses do represent a drain on a taxpayer's discretionary income and should therefore be deductible from taxable income regardless of their amount. A change in the current provisions to this effect would improve the overall equity of the tax system.

## Social Insurance

Two tax credits fall under the category of credits for social insurance payments, the credit for Canada or Quebec pension plan contributions and the credit for employment insurance (previously called unemployment insurance) contributions. The Canada and Quebec pension plans were introduced in 1966. Their basic rationale is similar to the rationale that underlies the RPP and RRSP schemes, from which they differ by being more or less compulsory rather than voluntary (though participation in an RPP may be a condition of employment). The unemployment insurance (UI) program was introduced in 1941, but benefits under the program were excluded from taxable income until 1972. The rationale for including this source in taxable income is that it is appropriate to tax an individual's command over goods and services, whether this command is exercised or not.

As table 3.12 shows, the percentage of taxpayers who claimed credits for CPP/QPP and UI payments in 1995 was relatively high, a consequence of the largely compulsory nature of the two plans.[15] The value of the average tax credits for these payments was fairly low, as were the taxes saved as a result of the credits.

Although a certain amount of tax deferment may occur under both plans, it appears to be important only in the case of the CPP/QPP. Tax deferment does

---

[15] The contributory rates are described in chapter 6.

Table 3.11   Distribution of Tax Credits for Medical Expenses
and Disability Amount, 1995

| | Medical expenses | | | Disability amount | | |
|---|---|---|---|---|---|---|
| Income group, $ | Percentage of all returns claiming tax credit | Average tax credit, $ | Percentage of tax saved through use of tax credit | Percentage of all returns claiming tax credit | Average tax credit, $ | Percentage of tax saved through use of tax credit |
| Loss-10,000 ....... | 2.6 | 120 | 8.0 | 1.4 | 181 | 6.6 |
| 10,001-20,000 ..... | 10.1 | 230 | 3.5 | 3.2 | 744 | 3.5 |
| 20,001-30,000 ..... | 9.9 | 286 | 1.3 | 3.0 | 1,065 | 1.4 |
| 30,001-40,000 ..... | 6.7 | 310 | 0.5 | 2.0 | 1,267 | 0.6 |
| 40,001-50,000 ..... | 5.0 | 397 | 0.3 | 1.9 | 1,114 | 0.3 |
| 50,001-60,000 ..... | 3.6 | 470 | 0.2 | 1.5 | 1,187 | 0.2 |
| 60,001-70,000 ..... | 3.3 | 533 | 0.2 | 1.7 | 989 | 0.2 |
| 70,001-80,000 ..... | 4.1 | 637 | 0.2 | 1.6 | 1,249 | 0.2 |
| 80,001-90,000 ..... | 4.2 | 650 | 0.2 | 1.5 | 1,446 | 0.2 |
| 90,001-100,000 .... | 3.9 | 864 | 0.2 | 1.3 | 1,812 | 0.1 |
| 100,001-150,000 ... | 5.3 | 967 | 0.2 | 1.9 | 1,321 | 0.1 |
| 150,001-250,000 ... | 6.6 | 863 | 0.2 | 2.0 | 1,152 | 0.1 |
| 250,001 + ......... | 7.1 | 1,629 | 0.1 | 1.5 | 1,440 | 0.0 |
| Average .......... | 6.5 | 280 | 0.6 | 2.2 | 833 | 0.6 |

Source: Same as table 3.5.

Table 3.12   Distribution of Tax Credits for CPP/QPP and
Unemployment Insurance,[a] 1995

| | CPP/QPP | | | Unemployment insurance | | |
|---|---|---|---|---|---|---|
| Income group, $ | Percentage of all returns claiming tax credit | Average tax credit, $ | Percentage of tax saved through use of tax credit | Percentage of all returns claiming tax credit | Average tax credit, $ | Percentage of tax saved through use of tax credit |
| Loss-10,000 ....... | 27.6 | 17 | 11.4 | 37.6 | 21 | 17.9 |
| 10,001-20,000 ..... | 51.1 | 47 | 3.6 | 47.8 | 58 | 4.1 |
| 20,001-30,000 ..... | 73.8 | 92 | 3.0 | 69.3 | 108 | 3.3 |
| 30,001-40,000 ..... | 82.6 | 133 | 2.8 | 77.6 | 156 | 3.0 |
| 40,001-50,000 ..... | 87.0 | 145 | 2.1 | 82.6 | 190 | 2.6 |
| 50,001-60,000 ..... | 89.3 | 146 | 1.6 | 84.5 | 202 | 2.1 |
| 60,001-70,000 ..... | 90.5 | 147 | 1.3 | 84.3 | 205 | 1.7 |
| 70,001-80,000 ..... | 89.2 | 149 | 1.1 | 80.0 | 205 | 1.3 |
| 80,001-90,000 ..... | 87.7 | 151 | 0.9 | 76.4 | 203 | 1.1 |
| 90,001-100,000 .... | 85.8 | 155 | 0.8 | 70.9 | 202 | 0.8 |
| 100,001-150,000 ... | 83.5 | 164 | 0.6 | 59.5 | 197 | 0.5 |
| 150,001-250,000 ... | 82.7 | 179 | 0.4 | 47.0 | 190 | 0.2 |
| 250,001 + ......... | 79.2 | 171 | 0.1 | 41.0 | 191 | 0.1 |
| Average .......... | 59.2 | 95 | 1.8 | 58.3 | 114 | 2.1 |

[a] Now known as employment insurance.

Source: Same as table 3.5.

not appear to be a problem in the case of the employment insurance (EI) scheme, since there is no uniform statutory link between a person's EI contribution today and future benefits, if received. This plan is designed to protect against an economic hardship.

## Charitable Donations

Tax credits are permitted for charitable donations and gifts to the government as long as total donations do not exceed 75 percent of net income. In certain circumstances, the limit may be higher.[16] Unlike medical expenses, charitable donations are not a necessity of life and are voluntary. Any justification for allowing this claim must therefore be made in terms of the donations' social benefits.[17]

Table 3.13 shows that both the percentage of taxpayers who claim this tax credit and the estimated value of the credit are highest for the higher income groups. The percentage of taxes saved as a result of using this tax credit is less than 1 percent, for all income groups except the lowest.

If one accepts the economic principle that deductions or tax credits should be permitted only for the purpose of alleviating economic hardships or offsetting expenses incurred in earning an income, then a tax credit for charitable donations cannot be justified. Donations are of a consumptive nature and are undertaken on a purely voluntary basis. As well, they may be inefficient in a resource allocation sense, since they provide an incentive for taxpayers to contribute to certain types of organizations or activities. One might argue, therefore, that charitable deductions should be abolished, however unlikely this outcome might be. Major attacks on this position would surely come from charitable organizations, which would fear substantial losses in their revenue, and from policy makers who argue that one objective of social policy is to encourage financial contributions to "worthwhile" organizations so that governments themselves do not have to support them.

For some time, there has been an interest in the extent to which the tax system affects charitable giving. There are two ways in which taxes may play a role in this context. First, any reduction in disposable income as a result of taxes reduces most personal expenditures, including charitable donations. Under a progressive tax system, in which the effective average tax rate rises as income rises, this effect of taxes will be greatest for high-income receivers. Second, by allowing a taxpayer a tax credit of 17 percent on the first $200 of charitable giving and 29 percent on the remainder, the personal tax system reduces the price of charitable contributions relative to the prices of other goods and services. Thus, for each dollar of giving over $200, the

---

[16] For a discussion of these circumstances, see the *1997 General Income Tax Guide*, supra footnote 4, at 39-40.

[17] For a discussion of this point and a number of other effects of the tax system on charitable donations, see R.M. Bird and M.W. Bucovetsky, *Canadian Tax Reform and Private Philanthropy*, Canadian Tax Paper no. 58 (Toronto: Canadian Tax Foundation, 1976).

**Table 3.13  Distribution of Tax Credits for Charitable
Donations and Government Gifts, 1995**

| Income group, $ | Percentage of all returns claiming tax credit | Estimated average tax credit, $ | Estimated percentage of tax saved through use of tax credit |
|---|---|---|---|
| Loss-10,000 | 2.8 | 15 | 1.2 |
| 10,001-20,000 | 18.2 | 31 | 0.9 |
| 20,001-30,000 | 31.2 | 38 | 0.5 |
| 30,001-40,000 | 39.7 | 41 | 0.4 |
| 40,001-50,000 | 48.9 | 41 | 0.4 |
| 50,001-60,000 | 56.2 | 50 | 0.3 |
| 60,001-70,000 | 61.0 | 58 | 0.3 |
| 70,001-80,000 | 64.1 | 69 | 0.4 |
| 80,001-90,000 | 66.8 | 84 | 0.4 |
| 90,001-100,000 | 67.3 | 100 | 0.4 |
| 100,001-150,000 | 71.8 | 138 | 0.4 |
| 150,001-250,000 | 74.8 | 224 | 0.4 |
| 250,001 + | 75.5 | 867 | 0.6 |
| Average | 26.1 | 53 | 0.4 |

Note: Because the tax credit is 17 percent for the first $200 of donations and 29 percent for the remainder, it is not possible to calculate the average credit and percentage of tax saved from the published data. The figures here are estimates that assume a 29 percent tax credit; consequently, they slightly overstate the amounts. They do, however, reflect the distribution of credits across income groups.

Source: Same as table 3.5.

taxpayer receives a federal tax credit of 29 cents. When the provincial tax is added, the tax credit may be 50 cents or more, depending on the taxpayer's taxable income and province of residence.

## Tuition Fees and Education

A taxpayer may claim a tax credit for tuition fees (including athletic and health-service fees paid on top of post-secondary tuition) in excess of $100 for courses taken at the post-secondary level or for courses intended to develop or improve one's skills in an occupation. As well, for 1998 and beyond, a student may claim an education amount of $200 for each month or part of a month of enrolment in a qualifying educational program. If the student does not need all of his tuition and education amounts to reduce federal income tax to zero, he may either carry the unused portion forward and claim it in future years or transfer it to his spouse or a parent or grandparent, or to a parent or grandparent of his spouse, for use in the current year. If the credit is transferred to someone else, the maximum transferable credit available is $850 for both tuition and education combined. Beginning in 1999, a further tax credit is allowed for interest paid on student loans.

Because students can transfer unused tax credits for tuition fees and education amounts to other taxpayers, the percentage of returns that claim this credit is fairly uniform across all income groups (table 3.14). The average tax credit tends to be higher for those in the higher income groups,

**Table 3.14  Distribution of Tax Credits for Tuition Fees
and Education Amount, 1995**

| Income group, $ | Percentage of all returns claiming tax credit | Average tax credit, $ | Percentage of tax saved through use of tax credit |
|---|---|---|---|
| Loss-10,000 ......... | 9.2 | 291 | 42.6 |
| 10,001-20,000 ....... | 10.0 | 257 | 3.8 |
| 20,001-30,000 ....... | 10.3 | 217 | 1.0 |
| 30,001-40,000 ....... | 11.1 | 197 | 0.6 |
| 40,001-50,000 ....... | 13.4 | 220 | 0.5 |
| 50,001-60,000 ....... | 15.9 | 246 | 0.5 |
| 60,001-70,000 ....... | 16.9 | 272 | 0.4 |
| 70,001-80,000 ....... | 17.4 | 301 | 0.4 |
| 80,001-90,000 ....... | 17.0 | 318 | 0.4 |
| 90,001-100,000 ...... | 16.3 | 339 | 0.3 |
| 100,001-150,000 ..... | 15.5 | 355 | 0.2 |
| 150,001-250,000 ..... | 15.6 | 409 | 0.2 |
| 250,001 + ........... | 14.4 | 421 | 0.1 |
| Average ............ | 11.0 | 252 | 0.9 |

Source: Same as table 3.5.

whereas the proportionate reduction in taxes that results from this credit is higher for taxpayers in lower income groups.

The current treatment of tuition and education costs raises the question whether a tax credit should be permitted at all. Does a student incur these expenses in order to increase his personal consumption? Or does he incur them in order to increase his future earning power? To the extent that the expenses enhance personal consumption, they are no different from other personal consumption expenses, for which tax credits are not allowed. On the other hand, to the extent that they are an expense of earning future income, they are analogous to an outlay for tangible capital. To not allow a deduction or tax credit, then, would be to discriminate against investment in human capital.

### The Pension Income Tax Credit

A tax credit, equal to 17 percent, is permitted on the first $1,000 of pension or annuity income received annually. Table 3.15 illustrates the distribution of this tax credit across income groups. If one omits taxpayers with incomes under $10,000, the percentage of taxpayers who make this claim is roughly the same across income groups. Since the tax credit is restricted to 17 percent of $1,000, its absolute value is the same for all taxpayers. As a percentage of taxes saved, the credit is highest for low-income taxpayers.

An objective of the pension tax credit is to preserve the spending power of individuals who receive income from pension plans. Although this goal is laudable, it could also be achieved through a return to full indexation of the personal income tax structure. Full indexation was introduced in 1974 to prevent the erosion of individual income by inflation, but it was later abandoned. Annual inflation must now exceed 3 percent before indexation

### Table 3.15  Distribution of Tax Credits for Eligible Pension Income Amount, 1995

| Income group, $ | Percentage of all returns claiming tax credit | Average tax credit, $ | Percentage of tax saved through use of tax credit |
|---|---|---|---|
| Loss-10,000 ......... | 1.8 | 140 | 6.6 |
| 10,001-20,000 ....... | 14.7 | 160 | 3.5 |
| 20,001-30,000 ....... | 19.0 | 168 | 1.4 |
| 30,001-40,000 ....... | 14.9 | 168 | 0.6 |
| 40,001-50,000 ....... | 12.3 | 168 | 0.3 |
| 50,001-60,000 ....... | 10.6 | 168 | 0.2 |
| 60,001-70,000 ....... | 9.8 | 168 | 0.2 |
| 70,001-80,000 ....... | 11.5 | 168 | 0.2 |
| 80,001-90,000 ....... | 13.2 | 168 | 0.2 |
| 90,001-100,000 ...... | 14.1 | 169 | 0.1 |
| 100,001-150,000 ..... | 15.0 | 167 | 0.1 |
| 150,001-250,000 ..... | 13.7 | 167 | 0.1 |
| 250,001 + ........... | 13.3 | 165 | 0.0 |
| Average ............ | 11.4 | 164 | 0.6 |

Source: Same as table 3.5.

takes effect. Alternatively, the purchasing power of individuals would be better preserved through a system of transfer payments to the poor or, as has been suggested occasionally, the introduction of a negative income tax (see chapter 8).

Although the pension tax credit may be preferable on vertical equity grounds to the pension deduction used before 1988, it is doubtful whether this tax credit is necessary for high-income earners or whether it achieves its intended distributional consequences.

### Interspousal Tax Credits

In any year, a taxpayer may claim the unused portion of his spouse's tax credits for age, pension, disability, tuition, and education. As table 3.16 shows, roughly the same percentage of taxpayers claim this credit in every income group. However, both the absolute value of the credit and the percentage savings in taxes attributable to the credit decline as income increases.

Interspousal tax credits are justifiable on equity grounds if the family is the unit for taxing income (see chapter 2 and the discussion later in this chapter). If the individual is defined as the tax-paying unit, support for the credits on equity grounds is less defensible.

### The Dividend Tax Credit

Taxpayers may claim a dividend tax credit equal to 13.33 percent of grossed-up dividends (125 percent of actual dividends) received from taxable Canadian corporations. The purpose of this credit is to relieve some of the double taxation on shareholders of corporate source income (see chapter 4). Given that dividend income is mainly earned by higher-income individuals, it

**Table 3.16   Distribution of Interspousal Tax Credits, 1995**

| Income group, $ | Percentage of all returns claiming tax credit | Average tax credit, $ | Percentage of tax saved through use of tax credit |
|---|---|---|---|
| Loss-10,000 ......... | 1.0 | 427 | 10.2 |
| 10,001-20,000 ....... | 4.6 | 506 | 3.5 |
| 20,001-30,000 ....... | 4.4 | 502 | 1.0 |
| 30,001-40,000 ....... | 3.1 | 434 | 0.3 |
| 40,001-50,000 ....... | 2.6 | 396 | 0.2 |
| 50,001-60,000 ....... | 2.2 | 350 | 0.1 |
| 60,001-70,000 ....... | 2.2 | 354 | 0.1 |
| 70,001-80,000 ....... | 2.4 | 329 | 0.1 |
| 80,001-90,000 ....... | 2.3 | 333 | 0.1 |
| 90,001-100,000 ...... | 2.3 | 310 | 0.0 |
| 100,001-150,000 ..... | 2.6 | 298 | 0.0 |
| 150,001-250,000 ..... | 2.5 | 260 | 0.0 |
| 250,001 + .......... | 2.2 | 287 | 0.0 |
| Average ........... | 3.0 | 467 | 0.4 |

Source: Same as table 3.5.

is not surprising to note, in table 3.17, that the percentage of returns claiming this credit increases toward the upper end of the income scale. Both the value of the average tax credit and the percentage of taxes saved by income group also increase as income rises.

## Total Non-Refundable Tax Credits for Calculating Basic Federal Tax

Table 3.18 summarizes the distribution by income group in 1995 of all of the tax credits that we have discussed to this point. As the table shows, every tax return claimed at least one tax credit. The absolute value of the credits increased with income, but the percentage of taxes saved as a consequence of using credits decreased with income.

## Non-Refundable Tax Credits Not Applicable to the Calculation of Basic Federal Tax

The tax credits discussed above affect provincial taxes payable; the tax credits discussed here have no impact on provincial tax liability. They include tax credits for federal political contributions, investment tax credits, labour-sponsored funds tax credit, and the foreign tax credit.

• *The tax credit for federal political contributions.* The tax credit for contributions to federal political parties is 75 percent of the first $100 contributed, 50 percent of all contributions between $100 and $550, and 33.33 percent of all contributions over $550. Both individuals and businesses may use this credit.

• *The investment tax credit.* This credit may be used by both individuals and businesses and is applicable for the purchase of new buildings, machinery, or equipment that are used to promote economic growth and encourage

## Table 3.17  Distribution of Dividend Tax Credit, 1995

| Income group, $ | Percentage of all returns claiming tax credit | Average tax credit, $ | Percentage of tax saved through use of tax credit |
|---|---|---|---|
| Loss-10,000 ......... | 2.4 | 90 | 5.6 |
| 10,001-20,000 ....... | 4.4 | 188 | 1.3 |
| 20,001-30,000 ....... | 7.8 | 375 | 1.3 |
| 30,001-40,000 ....... | 10.1 | 473 | 1.2 |
| 40,001-50,000 ....... | 12.9 | 458 | 1.0 |
| 50,001-60,000 ....... | 16.5 | 560 | 1.1 |
| 60,001-70,000 ....... | 20.6 | 649 | 1.3 |
| 70,001-80,000 ....... | 25.5 | 843 | 1.7 |
| 80,001-90,000 ....... | 30.0 | 1,039 | 2.1 |
| 90,001-100,000 ...... | 33.3 | 1,310 | 2.5 |
| 100,001-150,000 ..... | 39.4 | 1,953 | 3.4 |
| 150,001-250,000 ..... | 46.1 | 3,186 | 3.8 |
| 250,001 + .......... | 57.3 | 11,742 | 5.6 |
| Average ........... | 8.0 | 759 | 1.9 |

Source: Same as table 3.5.

## Table 3.18  Distribution of Total Tax Credits, 1995

| Income group, $ | Percentage of all returns claiming tax credit | Average tax credit, $ | Percentage of tax saved through use of tax credit |
|---|---|---|---|
| Loss-10,000 ......... | 100.0 | 1,245 | 97.2 |
| 10,001-20,000 ....... | 100.0 | 1,599 | 71.2 |
| 20,001-30,000 ....... | 100.0 | 1,667 | 43.1 |
| 30,001-40,000 ....... | 100.0 | 1,704 | 30.5 |
| 40,001-50,000 ....... | 100.0 | 1,766 | 22.8 |
| 50,001-60,000 ....... | 100.0 | 1,838 | 18.4 |
| 60,001-70,000 ....... | 100.0 | 1,930 | 15.9 |
| 70,001-80,000 ....... | 100.0 | 2,057 | 14.2 |
| 80,001-90,000 ....... | 100.0 | 2,187 | 13.0 |
| 90,001-100,000 ...... | 100.0 | 2,344 | 12.3 |
| 100,001-150,000 ..... | 100.0 | 2,764 | 11.1 |
| 150,001-250,000 ..... | 100.0 | 3,689 | 9.0 |
| 250,001 + .......... | 100.0 | 10,637 | 8.6 |
| Average ........... | 100.0 | 1,612 | 34.4 |

Source: Same as table 3.5.

scientific research and experimental development in certain areas of Canada in qualifying activities such as farming, fishing, logging, or manufacturing. There is a series of conditions that must be adhered to in calculating this tax credit.

• *The labour-sponsored funds tax credit.* This credit is available to the first registered holders of approved shares of capital stock in a prescribed labour-sponsored venture capital corporation (LSVCC). The allowable credit cannot be more than 15 percent of the net cost of the shares (that is, the amount paid for the shares minus any government assistance other than federal or provincial tax credits on the shares) to a maximum tax credit of $750. LSVCCs are mandated to invest in small and medium-sized businesses with no more than $50 million in assets and no more than 500 employees. If the LSVCC is also registered provincially, a taxpayer may be entitled to a provincial tax credit as well.

• *The foreign tax credit.* Canadian taxpayers are required to report worldwide income in estimating their Canadian tax liability. This credit allows them to offset taxes paid on foreign income; otherwise, they would be subject to taxation on the same amount of income in both countries. The credit applies to both individual income and business income.

The investment and labour-sponsored funds tax credits are intended to provide incentives to increase investment and expand economic activity—a deliberate policy objective of the federal government and one that may have merit. The tax credit for foreign taxes paid is needed to relieve the double taxation that arises when two countries impose taxes on the same income. The tax credit for political contributions is difficult to support. It cannot be justified on the basis of promoting economic growth, reducing the cost of earning income, or contributing to broader tax or social policy objectives. It was implemented in order to support politicians and political parties, and because it is much more generous than the other tax credits it provides significant tax savings for those who use it.

## Provincial Income Tax

Under the Federal-Provincial Fiscal Arrangements and Established Programs Financing Act, 1977,[18] the federal government collects income tax revenue for the provinces as long as the provinces accept the federal tax base and rate structure. To be more specific, the provinces agree to include in income the same items as the federal government includes in its base and to accept the deductions, tax credits, and rate structure established by the federal government. Each province may specify its own income tax rate as a percentage of basic federal tax payable. In addition, the federal government will administer provincial tax credits that in its judgment do not disrupt the harmony of the personal tax system. All of the provinces except Quebec follow this procedure. Quebec levies and collects its own personal income tax revenue.[19] In 1979, the Northwest Territories and the Yukon Territory were brought into the tax collection agreements.[20]

---

[18] For a historical discussion of these arrangements and those that went before and have come after, see David B. Perry, *Financing the Canadian Federation, 1867 to 1995: Setting the Stage for Change*, Canadian Tax Paper no. 102 (Toronto, Canadian Tax Foundation, 1997).

[19] The Quebec system differs from the federal system mainly in having five tax brackets instead of three, different marginal tax rates, and different values for non-refundable tax credits. For a detailed discussion of the differences between the federal and Quebec personal income tax systems, see Karin Treff and David B. Perry, *Finances of the Nation 1997* (Toronto: Canadian Tax Foundation, 1997), 3:13-15.

[20] For more detailed information on provincial income taxes, see ibid., at chapter 3.

### Table 3.19   Provincial Personal Income Tax Rates, Applied as Percentages of Basic Federal Income Tax Payable

|                        | 1987 | 1990 | 1993 | 1995 | 1997 |
|------------------------|------|------|------|------|------|
| Newfoundland           | 60.0 | 62.0 | 69.0 | 69.0 | 69.0 |
| Prince Edward Island   | 55.0 | 57.0 | 59.5 | 59.5 | 59.5 |
| Nova Scotia            | 56.5 | 59.5 | 59.5 | 59.5 | 58.5 |
| New Brunswick          | 58.0 | 60.0 | 62.0 | 64.0 | 63.0 |
| Quebec                 | na   | na   | na   | na   | na   |
| Ontario                | 50.0 | 53.0 | 58.0 | 58.0 | 48.0 |
| Manitoba               | 54.0 | 52.0 | 52.0 | 52.0 | 52.0 |
| Saskatchewan           | 50.0 | 50.0 | 50.0 | 50.0 | 50.0 |
| Alberta                | 46.5 | 46.5 | 45.5 | 45.5 | 45.5 |
| British Columbia       | 51.5 | 51.5 | 52.5 | 52.5 | 51.0 |
| Northwest Territories  | 43.0 | 44.0 | 45.0 | 45.0 | 45.0 |
| Yukon                  | 45.0 | 45.0 | 50.0 | 50.0 | 50.0 |

na   not applicable.

Note: Provincial surtaxes (1997) as percentages of provincial tax payable—Newfoundland: 10% on provincial tax payable over $7,900; Prince Edward Island: 10% on provincial tax payable over $5,200; Nova Scotia: 10% on provincial tax payable over $10,000; New Brunswick: 8% on provincial tax payable over $13,500; Quebec: 5% on provincial tax payable between $5,000 and $10,000 and 10% on amount in excess of $10,000; Ontario: 20% on provincial tax payable between $4,555 and $6,180; Manitoba: 2% on net income over $30,000 plus a flat tax of 2% of net income; Saskatchewan: 10% on sum of basic provincial tax and flat tax less than $4,000 and 25% on sum of basic provincial tax and flat tax over $4,000 plus 2% flat tax on net income; Alberta: 8% on amount payable over $3,500 plus 0.5% of net income; British Columbia: 30% on amount between $5,300 and $8,745 and 54.5% on amount payable over $8,745; Yukon: 5.0 % on amount payable over $6,000.

Source: Karin Treff and David B. Perry, *Finances of the Nation 1997* (Toronto: Canadian Tax Foundation, 1997), chapter 3.

Table 3.19 illustrates the variation in the provincial tax rates for selected years from 1987 to 1997. In 1997, Alberta's rate was the lowest, at 45.5 percent of basic federal tax payable, and Newfoundland's rate was the highest, at 69 percent. Over the decade from 1987 to 1997, as the table shows, the provincial tax rate declined in some of the provinces and increased in others. Ontario has announced that by 1999 its tax rate will be down to 41.5 percent of basic federal tax payable.

The provinces employ various tax credits and tax deductions to promote investment that is designed to foster growth in provincial gross domestic product, to promote investment in specific investments such as labour-sponsored venture capital corporations (LSVCCs), to encourage home ownership, to encourage contributions to provincial political parties, and to remove some of the sales tax and property tax burden on low-income individuals.[21]

## Refundable Tax Credits and the Child Tax Benefit

The federal government and some of the provinces provide refundable tax credits. They differ from non-refundable tax credits in that they are payable

[21] Ibid., at chapter 3.

to individuals who may not have taxable income; again, non-refundable credits are deducted from tax liability but any excess is not refundable to the taxpayer. Since these credits are designed to deliver socially desirable programs through the tax transfer system (see chapters 8 and 9), recipients are not required to report the moneys received for tax purposes. Federal refundable tax credits include the federal sales tax credit (goods and services tax or GST) and the child tax benefit.

The federal sales tax credit (applied after calculation of the basic federal tax) provides relief from the GST for low-income families and individuals. In 1997, the credit provided $199 per adult and $105 per dependant under age 18. There is also a supplementary credit for single individuals that in 1999 is equal to 2 percent of net income in excess of $7,131 to a maximum of $105. The GST credit is reduced by 5 percent of net family income over $25,921.

In 1998, the federal child tax benefit provided a payment of $1,020 for each of the first two children, an additional $75 for each child in excess of two, and an additional $213 for each child under the age of 7 (the last amount is reduced by 25 percent of child care expenses). As well, there is a federal supplement of $605 for one child, reduced by 12.1 percent of the amount of family net income in excess of $20,921; $1,010 for two children, reduced by 20.2 percent of family net income over $20,921; and $1,010 for the first two children plus $330 for each additional child, reduced by 26.8 percent of family net income over $20,921. These federal benefits are combined with provincial and territorial programs into a single monthly payment. Payments vary across the provinces and territories, but in every instance they decline as family income rises.[22]

Some provinces too offer refundable tax credits. Sales tax credits that diminish as net family income rises exist in Quebec, Ontario, and British Columbia. Vanishing property tax credits are offered in Quebec, Ontario, and Manitoba. Other refundable provincial tax credits include one for child care expenses in Quebec, a cost-of-living tax credit in Manitoba, a family employment tax credit in Alberta, and a tax credit for dependent children in New Brunswick; all of these credits diminish as net family income increases.[23]

Refundable tax credits (which we shall discuss in more detail in chapter 9) have increased in importance over the past two decades as the federal government and the provinces have moved toward a more closely integrated tax and transfer system for delivering social programs.

## The "Alternative Minimum Tax" (AMT)

The income base, deductions, tax rates, and tax credits that we have discussed to this point ultimately generate federal and provincial income-tax liability. There is, as well, an "alternative minimum tax" (AMT) in Canada. It

---

[22] Karin Treff and David B. Perry, *Finances of the Nation 1998* (Toronto: Canadian Tax Foundation, 1998), 9:7-9.

[23] Ibid., at 3:11-17.

is calculated on a different tax base and is payable if it exceeds tax calculated in the normal manner as described above. The AMT was introduced in the early 1980s, mainly for political reasons, to ensure that higher-income individuals did not reduce their tax liability to very low levels or even zero through the use of eligible tax deductions or concessions. Very briefly, the tax base for the AMT includes RPPs, RRSPs, and DPSPs and a number of tax incentives; 100 percent, rather than 75 percent, of net capital gains; and the actual amount of taxable Canadian dividends, rather than the grossed-up amount. An exemption of $40,000 is subtracted from the AMT tax base and a tax rate of 17 percent is applied to the remainder; this calculation yields the federal minimum tax, from which is subtracted the basic minimum tax credit (the sum of personal, charitable donations, education, disability, employment insurance, and CPP non-refundable tax credits for the year—no other tax credits are deductible) and the foreign tax credit. The provincial tax is calculated as a percentage of federal tax, just as in the ordinary case. Federal and provincial surtaxes are payable in the same way as in the standard case. A taxpayer can carry forward the excess of AMT over regular tax for up to seven years to reduce regular tax as long as the regular tax exceeds the minimum tax.[24]

## Tax Revenue

Table 3.20 shows that personal income tax revenue, federal and provincial, grew between 1955 and 1995 from almost $1.3 billion to almost $111 billion. In 1955, the revenue from the tax represented 6.1 percent of personal income and 10.3 percent of total income for tax purposes; by 1995, these figures had risen, respectively, to 16.6 percent and 23.2 percent. Over the same period, the average tax per return in current dollars increased from $364 to $7,906. If one eliminates inflationary increases, by deflating by the consumer price index and using 1986 dollars, tax revenue per return grew from $1,695 to $5,922. Like the increase in relative importance of other taxes over the past few decades, the growth in personal income tax revenues reflects the increasing role of government in the provision of goods and services in Canada. Similarly, growth in the proportion of income tax revenue that goes to the provinces reflects the growing relative importance of the provinces. Their share of all personal income tax revenue grew from 2.2 percent in 1955 to 42.6 percent by 1995.

## Evaluation

Like other taxes, the personal income tax may be evaluated in terms of equity or fairness, economic efficiency, and ease of administration.[25]

---

[24] Ibid., at 3:10-11.

[25] We discussed the criteria of growth and stabilization in chapter 2 but ignored them in this chapter because they refer to macro or aggregate issues rather than individual-taxpayer issues.

**Table 3.20  Personal Income Tax Revenue for Selected Years from 1955 to 1995**

| | Federal income tax revenue, $ million | Provincial income tax revenue, $ million | Total income tax revenue, $ million | Provincial revenue as a percentage of total revenue | Total income tax revenue as a percentage of personal income | Total income tax revenue as a percentage of total income for tax purposes | Total income tax per taxable return—current dollars | Total income tax per taxable return—constant dollars |
|---|---|---|---|---|---|---|---|---|
| 1955 | 1,269 | 28 | 1,297 | 2.2 | 6.1 | 10.3 | 364 | 1,695 |
| 1960 | 1,917 | 62 | 1,979 | 3.1 | 6.6 | 10.7 | 451 | 1,902 |
| 1965 | 2,612 | 743 | 3,355 | 22.1 | 8.0 | 11.8 | 586 | 2,279 |
| 1970 | 6,302 | 2,509 | 8,811 | 28.5 | 12.9 | 17.9 | 1,153 | 3,719 |
| 1975 | 12,278 | 5,741 | 18,019 | 31.9 | 13.0 | 17.7 | 2,122 | 4,801 |
| 1980 | 19,131 | 13,009 | 32,140 | 30.5 | 12.9 | 17.2 | 3,244 | 4,828 |
| 1983 | 26,809 | 19,642 | 46,451 | 42.3 | 13.5 | 19.0 | 4,554 | 5,145 |
| 1986 | 37,503 | 24,875 | 62,378 | 39.9 | 14.6 | 19.8 | 4,975 | 4,975 |
| 1989 | 50,642 | 34,001 | 84,643 | 40.2 | 15.4 | 20.6 | 6,316 | 5,540 |
| 1992 | 59,398 | 41,524 | 101,222 | 41.3 | 16.3 | 22.4 | 7,470 | 5,831 |
| 1995 | 63,707 | 47,194 | 110,901 | 42.6 | 16.6 | 23.2 | 7,906 | 5,922 |

Sources: Data in columns 2, 3, and 4 taken from Statistics Canada, *National Income and Expenditure Accounts*, various years, catalogue no. 13-001-XPB. Columns 5 to 9 calculated from data in columns 1 to 3 and from data in Revenue Canada, *Tax Statistics on Individuals* (Ottawa: Revenue Canada, annual).

# Equity

The fairness or equity of the personal income tax is frequently judged by comparing effective tax rates—personal income taxes payable as a percentage of total income—across all taxpayers. Although the determination of equity depends ultimately on a value judgment (see chapter 2), the personal income tax is generally deemed to be horizontally equitable if taxpayers with similar taxable incomes face similar effective tax rates. Similarly, it is generally perceived to be vertically equitable if higher-income taxpayers face higher effective tax rates. Horizontal equity can be achieved under any system of credits, deductions, and tax rates as long as taxpayers who are equally well off are treated in exactly the same way. Vertical equity, on the other hand, can be achieved through a system of progressive marginal tax rates such as the one used in Canada. Deductions and tax credits also play an important role in determining the extent to which the tax system is progressive. Alternatively, progressivity can be secured through the use of a flat rate of tax with a specific level of tax-exempt income (see chapter 2).

Personal incomes before income taxation and federal transfers are less equally distributed today than they were in 1971. As a result of the tax reforms of 1972, 1981, and 1987, however, income after personal income taxes and federal transfers is more equally distributed now than it was in 1971.[26] This increase in the progressivity (or reduction in the regressivity) of the personal income tax system is a result of the substitution of tax credits for exemptions and some deductions, the broadening of the tax base, and the increase in transfer payments to individuals, including refundable GST credits and child tax benefits. Tax credits, as we noted earlier in this chapter, primarily benefit lower- and middle-income individuals; their value and allocation tend to counter the regressivity of most deductions.[27] The tax base has been broadened over the past decade by eliminating the $100,000 lifetime capital gains exemption, increasing taxation of certain employee benefits, reducing the share of employment-related expenses that are exempt from taxation, and introducing income testing for the age credit. As well, the federal government has abolished the non-refundable tax credit for dependants in order to enhance the child tax benefit for low-income families through the introduction of refundable but disappearing tax credits.[28] The introduction of the disappearing and refundable child tax benefits and GST credits has moved Canada toward a negative income tax system. Indeed, the combination of refundable tax credits targeted to low-income families and government expenditures directed to health and education have done more to equalize incomes than have progressive marginal tax rates.[29]

---

[26] See Smith, supra footnote 12.

[27] France St-Hilaire, "For Whom the Tax Breaks" (1996), vol. 2, no. 2 *Choices: Public Finance* 1-47.

[28] Ibid., at 38.

[29] See Smith, supra footnote 12, at 1076.

## Economic Effects

The personal income tax is a tax on the income generated for individuals from the use of productive factors of production; that is, it is a *general factor tax*. Its primary economic impact is on the market for these factors of production, and in particular on the willingness of households to supply them. Analysis of the economic effects of personal income taxation has concentrated on its effects on the supply of labour or work effort, on the supply of capital or savings, and on the willingness to undertake risk. In addition, the tax may provide households with an incentive to substitute untaxed activities for taxed ones. For example, households may substitute activities that yield imputed income for activities that yield monetary income (for example, household activities for market activities). This section will briefly review these potential influences of the personal income tax on individual decisions.

One theme that runs through the entire literature on the influence of the income tax is the ambiguity of the effect of the tax on the supply of various factors of production. Since the income tax taxes the reward from supplying a factor of production, it reduces the income of the individual. This is the so-called *income effect* of the tax. One might expect the individual to respond to this effect by supplying more of the factor of production in order to recover some of his previous purchasing power. On the other hand, in reducing the reward for each unit of the factor that the individual supplies, the tax reduces the marginal return or price for additional supplies of the factor and thus creates a disincentive to supply more of the factor. This effect on prices is called the *substitution effect*. The overall impact of the tax is the result of the offsetting influences of the income and substitution effects, and it is impossible to predict on theoretical grounds which effect will be stronger.

Matters are complicated by the fact that the personal income tax is progressive, so that the income and substitution effects differ from group to group. The more progressive the tax is, the stronger the adverse substitution effect will be for high-income groups relative to low-income groups, but the stronger the income effect will be as well. Different income groups will react differently, but we cannot predict on a priori grounds the direction of the overall effect; that is a matter for empirical investigation. We shall next consider each of the main ways in which the tax influences economic decisions.

### The Influence of the Personal Income Tax on Work Effort

The reward for supplying labour (or forgoing leisure) is the wage rate. The personal income tax reduces by the magnitude of the marginal tax rate both the total earnings from a given amount of labour (the income effect) and the reward for each additional hour worked (the substitution effect). Either effect can dominate; the only predictable factor is that for a given amount of tax payment (that is, holding the income effect constant), the individual will work more the lower is his marginal tax rate. The effect of the tax on work effort is especially hard to predict, since individuals cannot usually vary their work habits at will. As a rule, hours worked per day are institutionally determined. In this case, the tax can operate only in the longer run, by influencing contractually agreed-upon hours of work. The fact that, over time, hours of work have been declining and wage rates have been rising would seem to suggest that reductions in wage rates caused by taxes may actually increase work effort. This inference would not be warranted, however, since many other factors, such as technical progress and higher standards of living, have contributed to this inverse relation between hours worked and wage rates. It has been argued, too, that taxes provoke a "spite" effect that discourages work effort. In the shorter run, tax-induced changes in work patterns may occur among the self-employed or among those who work overtime, at casual jobs, or on second jobs. In addition, income taxes may affect the work patterns of secondary workers such as additional family members—a potentially important source of labour supply.

The income tax also influences the allocation of labour among various types of work. Since the tax applies to monetary income but not to imputed income, it should create an incentive to substitute the latter for the former. Thus, one would expect the tax to cause some increase in household work at the expense of market work (and hence a reduction in the labour-force participation rate of housewives) and a substitution of lower paying, more pleasant jobs for higher paying, less pleasant ones. There is, however, little evidence that the income tax influences work effort in this way. Labour-force participation rates for females have increased over the past 25 years,[30] and the proportion in lower paying, less pleasant service-sector jobs has grown relative to the proportion in higher paying, more pleasant skilled occupations.[31]

Most of the available empirical analysis of the supply of labour by persons who are able to vary their hours of work was completed in the early 1980s or before, when marginal tax rates in Canada were higher and more numerous and payroll taxes were virtually non-existent.[32] Since that time, the combination of lower marginal rates, fewer marginal tax brackets, and a more comprehensive tax base has narrowed the spread of the after-tax/transfer incomes of Canadians and thus made the influence of the personal income tax on labour supply more difficult to determine empirically. On the other hand, the emergence of payroll taxes in recent years has produced a body of literature that addresses the extent to which payroll taxes have affected labour supply. We shall discuss this literature in chapter 6.

In reality, most individuals are unlikely to make work-related decisions on the basis of their marginal tax rates alone, primarily because they are unaware of them. Work habits tend to be ingrained and are not easily changed. Indeed, as we noted earlier, many taxpayers are not in a position to

---

[30] Canada, Department of Finance, *Economic Reference Tables, August 1995* (Ottawa: the department, 1995), reference table 30.

[31] Ibid., at reference table 36.

[32] For a review of this literature, see Boadway and Kitchen, supra footnote 8, at 42-46.

alter the number of hours worked in response to tax changes, nor is it obvious that they would alter them if they could. Several additional factors undoubtedly influence work effort, of which the most important is probably the scale of the individual's fixed financial commitments (consumer debt and the like). Large commitments tend to increase the supply of labour (for example, both partners may take jobs and some individuals may work at more than one job); small commitments are likely to have the opposite effect. Finally, the enjoyment, prestige, recognition, and influence derived from working may have a greater impact on the supply of labour than personal income taxes have.

## The Influence of the Personal Income Tax on Savings

Individuals save in order to have funds for consumption use at a later date (or for bequests to their heirs). There are two economic reasons for delaying consumption. One is that the pattern of an individual's income over his lifetime does not usually coincide with his desired pattern of lifetime consumption. Over a lifetime, individuals typically earn less than they consume in early years, when they are purchasing consumer durables; earn more than they consume in the middle years, when they are paying off prior debts and saving for retirement; and earn much less than they consume in retirement. Individuals plan their consumption patterns on the basis of what they can afford to consume over their lifetimes. This is the essence of the so-called lifetime-income or permanent-income hypothesis of savings. According to this hypothesis, any permanent reduction in an individual's expected lifetime income—say, via increased income taxes—will reduce the individual's consumption over his lifetime. Thus, saving for future consumption will fall. This is the income effect of the personal income tax on savings decisions. Given that the government wants to divert a specific sum of revenue from private sector use to public sector use, this income effect is unavoidable.

The other reason for delaying consumption is the reward for delaying it—that is, the rate of return on the funds saved. This return will take the form of an interest rate in the case of debt or dividends and capital gains in the case of equity. The higher is the rate of return, the lower will be the "price" of future consumption, since each dollar of saving now will provide more future consumption. One might therefore expect an increase in the rate of interest to increase the demand for future consumption. It may also increase the number of dollars saved—but on the other hand it may not, since it now takes less savings to provide the same amount of future consumption. Thus the effect on savings of changes in the interest rate—owing, say, to the taxation of capital income—is ambiguous. This is not to say that a tax on the return to savings is not distortionary. It does distort a household's choice between present and future consumption by discouraging the latter. This distortion, however, is not exactly reflected in the observed saving behaviour of households.

As we noted in chapter 2, it is possible to design a tax system that avoids the distorting effect on savings of capital income taxation. A consumption-based tax would not distort the savings decision, since it would be equivalent to a tax that exempted capital income from its base. A tax of this kind would also have certain administrative advantages over income taxation, such as the absence of a requirement to account for income on an accrual basis and the lack of a need to index capital income. A disadvantage of a tax that exempted capital income is that its base would be smaller than that of a comprehensive income base and so its rate would have to be higher to raise the same amount of revenue. Thus it might increase the disincentive to supply labour. In addition, because a consumption tax would exclude capital income from its base, it might be viewed as being less equitable than an income tax—particularly so given that income from savings is heavily concentrated among higher-income groups.

In evaluating the impact on savings of the Canadian personal income tax, it ought to be recognized that the income tax base is not comprehensive, although it is closer to being comprehensive than it was a decade ago. In fact, the present personal income tax falls somewhere between a comprehensive income tax and an expenditure or consumption tax. This is so because the tax system effectively exempts some capital income from the tax base. Only three-quarters of capital gains (minus capital losses) are taxed. Income earned on deposits in registered education savings plans are not taxed until they are withdrawn.[33] Registered retirement savings plan contributions and registered pension plan contributions are deductible within prescribed limits. Retirement saving also obtains the benefit of the $1,000 deduction applicable to pension income. All of this is equivalent to the treatment of savings under an expenditure tax system; indeed, the tax system would be an expenditure tax if these exemptions were unlimited. On the other hand, the benefits of these exemptions are offset in part by the fact that the dividend tax credit, which is intended to be a credit for corporation taxes paid on behalf of shareholders, does not apply to dividends earned on the savings in these plans.

Another type of capital income that is exempt from taxation is the net imputed rent on owner-occupied housing (and other consumer durables as well). In 1995, the gross imputed rent on owner-occupied dwellings in Canada was estimated to be $74.4 billion.[34] If the net imputed rent equalled 10 percent of the gross, it would exceed $7 billion dollars—a major source of savings. Of course, although capital income of this kind is exempt, the interest incurred in financing the assets that yield this income is not deductible. This too is equivalent to what would occur under a consumption tax system.

---

[33] The federal government's budget of February 28, 1998 increased the eligible contributions to a RESP to $4,000 annually, with a lifetime limit of $42,000 per child. As well, the government introduced a grant equal to 20 percent of up to $2,000 in annual contributions (maximum of $400 per year) for children up to the age of 18. The individual's contribution to the RESP is not deductible, but the interest earned on the annual contributions plus the grant accumulates tax-free. It is taxable in the hands of the recipient when withdrawn.

[34] Taken from Statistics Canada, *National Economic and Financial Accounts: Quarterly Estimates, 4th Quarter, 1995*, catalogue no. 13-001 XPB, table 16.

Again, our point here is that the tax system goes part of the way toward being a consumption tax by virtue of its partial exemption of capital income. At the same time, as we discussed in chapter 2, capital income that is taxed suffers from the tax system's failure to index capital income for inflation. Since part of the income from capital is simply a premium to compensate for the fall in the real value of the asset that results from inflation, the tax system is in fact taxing part of the value of the asset itself as well as its real return. Unless rates of return rise by enough to cover both the inflation and the tax on inflationary gains, this effect will represent an additional distorting tax on savings.

Income taxation may also alter the composition of savings. For example, the preferential treatment of capital gains, the deduction of RRSP contributions, and the exclusion of interest earned on registered education contributions may encourage individuals to save in certain ways in order to minimize their tax burden. Table 3.21 shows how the composition of savings and the relative importance of overall personal savings changed between 1971 and 1995. Personal savings absorbed 6.8 percent of personal disposable income in 1971, 14.8 percent in 1984, and 8.2 percent in 1995. The greatest change in the relative importance of the various savings categories over this period occurred in the case of RRSPs. They accounted for 0.5 percent of personal disposable income in 1971 and 4.1 percent in 1995. Contributions to the CPP/QPP grew from 0.9 percent of personal income to 1.3 percent, and contributions to RPPs increased from 1.3 to 1.4 percent of personal income. Although there may not be a definitive explanation for the change in the composition of savings since the early 1970s, it appears that many individuals or families have adjusted their savings patterns to take advantage of the available tax savings. Thus contributions to the CPP/QPP, and the RRSP and RPP schemes accounted for 40 percent of all savings in 1971 but 83 percent of all savings in 1995.

## The Influence of the Personal Income Tax on Risk Taking

In addition to affecting the aggregate amount of savings of households, the income tax can influence the allocation of savings between risky and riskless investments[35] and therefore the amount of investment undertaken in risky ventures. A conventional way to characterize the risk of an asset is by the variability or spread of its possible return, usually measured by the statistical concept called the *variance*. (The variance is the sum of the squares of the deviations of each possible outcome from the expected or mean outcome, each weighted by the probability of the outcome.) When deciding upon a portfolio allocation, an individual will take account of the expected return on

---

[35] A riskless investment is one for which payment of the rate of return is certain. A risky investment is one for which payment of the rate of return is not as certain. The deviation in the rates of return on these two assets will reflect, in some sense, the difference in the probability of each investment's actually making its expected payment.

**Table 3.21  Total Personal Savings and Savings Components as
Percentages of Personal Disposable Income,
Selected Years from 1971 to 1995**

|  | 1971 | 1980 | 1984 | 1988 | 1993 | 1995 |
|---|---|---|---|---|---|---|
| Canada Pension Plan/ |  |  |  |  |  |  |
| Quebec Pension Plan . . . . . . . . . . | 0.9 | 0.9 | 0.9 | 1.0 | 1.2 | 1.3 |
| Registered retirement savings |  |  |  |  |  |  |
| plans . . . . . . . . . . . . . . . . . . . . . | 0.5 | 1.8 | 1.9 | 2.7 | 3.6 | 4.1 |
| Registered retirement plans . . . . . . | 1.3 | 1.5 | 1.4 | 1.3 | 1.4 | 1.4 |
| Registered home ownership |  |  |  |  |  |  |
| savings plans . . . . . . . . . . . . . . . | na | 0.3 | 0.2 | na | na | na |
| Other . . . . . . . . . . . . . . . . . . . . . . | 4.1 | 8.8 | 10.4 | 4.9 | 3.2 | 1.4 |
| Total . . . . . . . . . . . . . . . . . . . . . . | 6.8 | 13.3 | 14.8 | 9.9 | 9.4 | 8.2 |

na   not available.

Sources: Calculated from data in Revenue Canada, *Tax Statistics on Individuals* (Ottawa:
Revenue Canada, selected years); and Canada, Department of Finance, *Economic Reference
Tables, August 1995* (Ottawa: the department, 1995), reference table 13.

each asset and the variance of the asset. Those assets with a higher risk
(variance) will be held only if they have an expected rate of return high
enough to compensate for the risk. The expected rates of return on various
assets on the market will reflect the risk differentials among the assets. Let us
consider two assets, a risk-free one, and a risky one, with expected rates of
return of 10 percent and 15 percent respectively (in the absence of taxation).
The 5 percent differential is the risk premium on the risky asset: it is the
premium required to compensate savers for the variability of possible returns.
Investment financed by the risky asset will have higher expected profits, but
more variability, than will risk-free investment.

The taxation of capital income influences risk-taking by affecting both the
expected return on an asset and the asset's riskiness. Consider the special
case of a tax system that treats gains and losses symmetrically—that is, one
that refunds losses in the same proportion as it taxes gains. Under a system of
this kind, referred to as a tax with full loss offsets, the expected return on
assets is reduced in proportion to the tax rate, but so is the variance. It has
been demonstrated in the economics literature[36] that one cannot deduce on
theoretical grounds whether or not a tax with full loss offsets would cause
households to reallocate their portfolios in favour of less risky assets.

Income taxes do not usually treat gains and losses symmetrically. To the
extent that gains give rise to tax payments that are greater than the tax reductions saved on losses, the tax system provides a disincentive to risk taking
relative to a system that provides full loss offsets. Yet even with only partial
loss offsetting the impact of the tax on risk taking is ambiguous. There are
two ways in which a tax system may treat gains and losses asymmetrically.

---

[36] See, for example, Jan Mossin, "Taxation and Risk-Taking: An Expected Utility
Approach" (February 1968), 35 *Economica* 74-82.

First, under a system with increasing marginal tax rates, the rate at which gains are taxed may be higher than the rate at which losses reduce taxes. Second, a tax system that does not allow for full loss offsetting at the personal level will discriminate against individuals who incur losses. The problem of asymmetry in the treatment of gains and losses is particularly important for businesses and is discussed further in chapter 4.

There is no empirical evidence on the actual effect of income taxation on risk-taking in Canada. Under current tax law, however, a number of specific rules have been established to foster risk taking and hence investment. Thus only three-quarters of capital gains are included in income for tax purposes and three-quarters of capital losses may be deducted from capital gains. If the losses in a particular year exceed the gains, they may be carried forward indefinitely until all capital losses have been absorbed. Before 1972, capital gains were excluded altogether from income taxation, so one might expect risk taking and investment to have decreased since then; but given the loss-offset provisions and the fact that only three-quarters of the gain is taxed, it is uncertain whether any decrease has actually occurred. Another way in which the government shares risk with investors is by allowing them to deduct contributions to RRSPs and RPPs and taxing the income from these funds only when they are withdrawn. Finally, the tax system allows taxpayers to offset business losses against future gains or other income over an indefinite period. In any case, most of Canada's investment is undertaken by large corporations and institutions rather than by individuals; consequently, the personal income tax structure may have little impact on the actual level of risk taking and subsequent investment.

## Summary

Although it is difficult to quantify precisely the effects of most tax provisions on economic behaviour, it is clear that the provisions we have discussed may very well provide incentives or disincentives to behave in certain ways. At the same time, it must be noted that we have not discussed all of the provisions that are designed to elicit certain kinds of behaviour. All of the various individual deductions, tax credits, and exclusions contribute to the incentive effects of the personal income tax.

## Administration and Compliance

As we noted in chapter 2, administration costs depend on a number of factors, including both the complexity of the tax and the number of taxpayers involved. The personal income tax is far more complex than most of the other taxes in Canada and covers more taxpayers directly than any other tax. The tax's complexity, evident in the variety of income sources subject to tax and the range of allowable deductions and tax credits, is attributable in large part to the fact that it is expected to perform a number of tasks—to generate revenue for funding public goods and services, to redistribute income, to provide incentives for specific activities, and to promote investment and economic growth.

One estimate puts the cost of administering the combined federal/provincial personal income tax system, unemployment insurance premiums, and Canada/Quebec pension plan contributions at about 1 percent of the total revenues generated from these sources.[37] This figure is relatively low, given the complexity of the tax, and its lowness is probably attributable to the large amount of revenue generated by the tax and to the fact that the tax system is based, by and large, on self-enforcement. Taxpayers are required to report their own income, and the percentage of taxpayers who are audited is relatively small. Compliance by individuals who earn only wage and salary income is high because their opportunities for tax avoidance or evasion are minimal; audits are seldom required. The opportunities for evasion or non-compliance are greater for the self-employed and the owners of businesses, who can with relative ease slip into the hidden or underground economy. Although it is difficult to find solid evidence on the extent of non-compliance with the personal income tax system, there is recent evidence to suggest that the underground economy has grown in recent years, but less because of the personal income tax system, perhaps, than because of the Canadian governments' increased dependance on indirect taxation.[38] In general, the level of tax morality in Canada is high relative to the levels in many other countries.

## Issues

Over the past two or three decades, the personal income tax system in Canada has become more equitable and allocatively efficient. The tax base is more comprehensive than it used to be, and the after-tax distribution of tax income across all income ranges has narrowed. There remain, however, a number of issues that deserve further attention here.

## Exclusions

If an income tax base is to be truly comprehensive, it must include all forms of income regardless of source and whether realized or accrued. Any violation of this principle results in a narrower tax base and higher statutory tax rates than would otherwise be required to raise the same amount of revenue. Since the omitted items are not evenly distributed across income groups, some taxpayers gain by their omission and others lose. Although any exclusion violates this basic principle of equity, an exclusion may be justifiable if it serves important social or economic goals that cannot be served by other means. The exclusion of some forms of income may also be appropriate if the administrative and compliance costs of including them are excessive. With

---

[37] François Vaillancourt, *The Administrative and Compliance Costs of the Personal Income Tax and Payroll Tax System in Canada, 1986,* Canadian Tax Paper no. 86 (Toronto: Canadian Tax Foundation, 1989), 82-84.

[38] Roderick Hill and Muhammed Kabir, "Tax Rates, the Tax Mix, and the Growth of the Underground Economy in Canada: What Can We Infer?" (1996), vol. 44, no. 6 *Canadian Tax Journal* 1552-83.

these points in mind, we shall consider the more important "monetary income" items excluded from the Canadian income tax base in the following discussion.

## Capital Gains

Capital gains (and losses) were excluded from taxation in Canada until 1972, when the federal government adopted legislation that required taxpayers to include in their annual taxable income one-half of all realized capital gains received during a tax year. Since that time, a number of major changes have taken place in the tax treatment of capital gains, of which the most recent was the elimination in 1994 of the $100,000 lifetime capital gains exemption.[39] Currently, individuals are required to include in annual income 75 percent of their net capital gains (realized gains minus capital losses). If losses exceed gains, 75 percent of this net loss may be used to reduce taxable gains of other years. It cannot be used to reduce other sources of taxable income in the current year or other years. Net capital losses may be carried back three years and offset against taxable capital gains in those years. Alternatively, if a taxpayer has no previous capital gains against which to deduct current capital losses, these losses may be carried forward indefinitely and applied against future taxable capital gains. For securities donated to Canadian charities, the donor is taxed on 37.5 percent of the gain rather than 75 percent.

Revenue Canada defines a capital gain (loss) as a gain (loss) obtained from the sale of a capital asset that cannot be included in the tax base under any other definition of income.[40] Some gains from the sale of capital assets, however, are excluded from the base. First, a capital gain realized on the sale of a taxpayer's principal residence and up to one-half hectare of surrounding land is exempt. Second, capital gains realized on working farm land are not taxed if the farm is passed on to the owner's spouse or his children (special conditions may apply in the latter case). Third, if certain conditions are met, disposition of farm property and shares in small businesses qualify for a $500,000 lifetime exemption. Fourth, gains realized on the sale of personal-use items such as paintings, antiques, and books are taxable only to the extent that the proceeds from their sale exceed $1,000. Any asset that yields less than this sum is excluded.[41] Losses on items of this kind, however, are allowed only against gains from items of the same class. Personal-use items such as furniture and cars, which generally depreciate with use and cost over $1,000, are subject to tax on any gain, but losses are not allowed on these items. They are not allowed because the property is deemed to depreciate

---

[39] For a discussion of the $100,000 lifetime capital gains exemption, see the articles on "The Canadian Experience of the Lifetime Capital Gains Exemption" (November 1995), 21 special supplement *Canadian Public Policy* (entire issue).

[40] For a detailed discussion, see Revenue Canada, *Capital Gains Tax Guide* (Ottawa: Revenue Canada, annual) (form T4037).

[41] In other words, the adjusted cost basis (defined as the cost of acquiring the asset plus the cost of any improvement in its value) used in calculating the tax on gains realized on the sale of items of this kind cannot be less than $1,000.

CANADIAN TAX POLICY

### Table 3.22  Taxable Capital Gains by Income Group, 1995

| Income group, $ | Percentage of taxpayers who reported taxable capital gains | Average taxable gain reported, $ | Taxable capital gains as a percentage of total income for tax purposes |
| --- | --- | --- | --- |
| Loss-20,000 ........ | 2.5 | 1,125 | 0.3 |
| 20,001-40,000 ....... | 4.7 | 1,846 | 0.3 |
| 40,001-60,000 ....... | 8.2 | 2,760 | 0.5 |
| 60,001-80,000 ....... | 13.1 | 4,417 | 0.9 |
| 80,001-100,000 ...... | 19.5 | 7,624 | 1.7 |
| 100,001-150,000 ..... | 27.3 | 17,374 | 4.0 |
| 150,001-250,000 ..... | 36.9 | 39,506 | 7.8 |
| 250,001 + .......... | 50.2 | 140,724 | 13.6 |
| Average ........... | 4.9 | 7,444 | 1.4 |

Source: Calculated from data in table 9 in Revenue Canada, *Tax Statistics on Individuals: 1995 Tax Year* (Ottawa: Revenue Canada, 1997).

through personal use—the loss is defined as a personal expense. A possible advantage of excluding all assets under $1,000 is the avoidance of the administrative costs involved in processing and reviewing a large number of claims.

Table 3.22 illustrates the skewed distribution of taxable capital gains for 1995. Although slightly fewer than 5 percent of taxpayers claimed capital gains, more than 50 percent of taxpayers with incomes in excess of $250,000 claimed some capital gains and only 2.5 percent of all taxpayers with incomes of less than $20,000 claimed any. Not surprisingly, the average taxable gain increased as income increased. Finally, taxable capital gains accounted for less than 1 percent of all income for taxpayers with incomes of less than $80,000 but almost 14 percent of all income for taxpayers with incomes of more than $250,000.

The current tax treatment of capital gains raises at least two important questions. First, should capital gains be treated differently from wage and salary income? Second, does the fact that they are treated differently lead to distortions in the allocation of resources? The preferential tax treatment afforded to capital gains has been criticized on the ground that it leads to an unfair distribution of the tax burden. As long as income forms the tax base, income received from capital gains can purchase the same goods and services as income from wages and salaries; therefore, the argument runs, the two types of income should be treated similarly for tax purposes. Horizontal equity would be achieved between recipients of these two sources of income, however, only by excluding inflationary increases in capital gains from the tax base and taxing all gains on an accrual basis. The present system's failure to exclude inflationary increases from the tax base through indexation is unfair, since it means that taxpayers are taxed on gains that do not increase their real income or real purchasing power (see chapter 2). Further inequities arise from the fact that capital gains are currently taxed in Canda not as they accrue but when they are realized. One consequence of this arrangement is the possibility of bunching of income—gains that have accrued over several years may be taxed in a single year at progressive rates,[42] leading to a tax burden larger than it would be under an accrual system. In the absence of any income tax averaging scheme in Canada (see below), this inequity goes unaddressed. As well, taxation on a realization basis provides an incentive for taxpayers to hold onto their assets and thus defer taxes until the assets are sold (all gains are deemed to be realized at time of death even if they are not sold). Taxpayers who do this have an advantage over those who, for whatever reason, must sell their assets.

Although full indexation of capital gains would remove the inequity created when illusory gains (strictly attributed to price) are taxed and should be relatively easy to implement, taxation on an accrual basis may be impractical. Some assets, such as shares of private corporations, are difficult to value on an accrual basis. As well, taxation of accruals might force liquidation of assets to pay the tax.[43]

To answer the question whether the current tax treatment of capital gains leads to a misallocation of resources is essentially to determine whether it causes individuals to behave in ways that lead to lower levels of economic activity than would exist under a distortion-free tax of equal yield. A system that taxes capital gains does result in a lower net return and a smaller supply of funds for investment purposes than there would be under a system that excluded capital gains from the tax, but it is difficult to demonstrate that the current treatment of capital gains in Canada has reduced risk taking and the supply of capital sufficiently to harm the Canadian economy. To gain some insight into this, consider the impact of the $100,000 lifetime capital gains exemption that was abolished in 1994. An important policy objective of this exemption was to encourage investment in fixed and intangible assets and small business ventures by reducing the amount of capital gains subject to tax.[44] A recent study, however, suggests that the exemption did not stimulate investment by large public corporations to a significant degree.[45] This finding implies, conversely, that the removal of the exemption has not led to a significant decrease in investment.

Critics of capital gains taxation have argued that it inhibits economic growth by reducing investors' willingness to assume risk. Evidence on this point is difficult to obtain, but it is not obvious that the effect of the capital gains tax on risk taking has been adverse. The existence of full loss-offset provisions and the reduction over the past few years in the number of tax brackets and marginal tax rates have done much to maintain, if not encourage, risk

---

[42] The reduction in the number of tax brackets and marginal tax rates in the late 1980s may have reduced this effect.

[43] Jack Mintz and Stephen R. Richardson, "The Lifetime Capital Gains Exemption: An Evaluation" (November 1995), 21 special supplement *Canadian Public Policy* S1-12, at S10.

[44] Ibid., at S5.

[45] Kenneth J. McKenzie and Aileen J. Thompson, "The Impact of the Capital Gains Exemption on Capital Markets," ibid., S100-15.

taking by investors. Furthermore, another study of the effects of the $100,000 lifetime capital gains exemption suggests that it did not lead to increased risk taking as measured by the extent to which individual investors increased equity holdings and firms altered their debt/equity ratios.[46]

It has also been suggested that capital gains taxation, and specifically the taxation of gains from the sale of stocks, encourages investors to hold onto their stocks in order to avoid or postpone tax. If this effect is substantial, then it may limit the supply of funds for new ventures and thereby retard economic growth. Under Canadian law, however, the gains or losses on assets are deemed to be realized for tax purposes when the owner of the assets dies, a provision that may well reduce the "locked-in" effect. Deemed realization at death does not occur in the case of a bequest to a joint survivor (a person who owned the asset jointly with the deceased person before the latter's death), which is not subject to tax, or in the case of family farms or businesses, to which a $500,000 lifetime capital gains exemption applies. The usual rationale for the $500,000 lifetime capital gains exemption is that farmers and owners of small businesses tend to invest their savings in their farms or businesses rather than in tax-assisted registered retirement plans. How valid is this rationale? One study concludes that the exemption can in fact be viewed as a way of allowing farmers to accumulate assets for retirement on a tax-free basis.[47] The evidence is less supportive of the exemption, however, in the cse of owners of small businesses, who in general can, and do, put sufficient income into RRSPs to meet their retirement needs. A further issue, of course, is whether this special treatment should be restricted to farmers and small business owners or whether it should be extended to others who might be limited in their accumulation of wealth for retirement purposes.

Finally, the provision whereby only 37.5 percent of the gain on securities donated to charities is recorded as taxable income is an attempt to encourage contributions to the charitable sector so that it may provide necessary services for needy individuals and thus remove the necessity for government provision.

Given the difficulties of taxing capital gains on an accrual basis, the absence of a full indexation scheme, and the lack of evidence to suggest that the tax on capital gains has reduced the supply of investment funds and risk taking, the current policy of including three-quarters of capital gains income may be as close as it is possible to come to achieving horizontal equity and not signficantly distort the allocation of society's resources.

## Life Insurance

Life insurance policies may be designed in a number of ways, but all policies have one or both of the following features: protection against economic loss

---

[46] Vijay M. Jog, "The Lifetime Capital Gains Exemption: Corporate Financing, Risk Taking and Allocation Efficiency," ibid., S116-35.

[47] Vijay M. Jog and Huntley Schaller, "Retirement Income and the Lifetime Capital Gains Exemption: The Case of Qualified Farm Property and Small Business Corporation Shares," ibid., S136-58.

owing to premature death and savings in the form of reserves accumulated out of premium payments, which earn interest for the benefit of the insured. Under current Canadian tax law, the proceeds received by a beneficiary because of premature death of the insured are not included in the beneficiary's income tax base. Although this omission violates the principles of equity and neutrality, it may be unwise for other reasons to include these funds in taxable income. Essentially, the arguments for and against taxing the proceeds from insurance are as follows. On the one hand, insurance proceeds are intended to replace at least part of the income that the insured person would have received had he continued to work. Since earned income is included in the tax base, it follows that insurance proceeds too should be taxable. Averaging provisions (which do not exist currently in Canada), if properly designed, would alleviate the heavy income tax burden that a lump-sum payment generates under progressive tax rates. On the other hand, it might be unfair to tax the beneficiary at the time of death of the insured, since this is frequently a time of economic loss for the family. There may also be a social interest in encouraging individuals to look after their dependants, and the exclusion of insurance benefits will presumably act as a stimulant to that end.

If a life insurance policy is surrendered or matures before the death of the insured, he receives a portion of his original premium (the savings element) plus interest earned on these funds. The portion of the premium that is returned is not taxable, but the interest and (if applicable) dividends are subject to tax. For whole-life policies that meet specific conditions,[48] annual interest income can accumulate tax-free until the policy is redeemed. Once the policy is redeemed, however, the taxpayer must include all accumulated interest income in his tax base in the year in which it is received. In the case of term policies, annual interest and dividend income is taxed on an accrual basis.

The tax treatment of term policies accords more closely than that of whole-life policies with the requirements of horizontal equity, but it would be improved by excluding the inflationary component of interest payments from taxable income. As in the case of other forms of savings, the taxation of nominal accrued annual returns means that the recipient is taxed on inflation-induced interest income. The tax treatment of whole-life insurance policies, which excludes the interest from taxable income until it is realized, is similar to the tax deferment under the RRSP and RPP schemes and similar arguments apply.

## Other Money Income

The following items are currently excluded from income for tax purposes: gifts and inheritances,[49] $500 of scholarship income, lottery winnings, the

---

[48] Tax deferral on accrued income is available for most whole-life policies purchased for protection and paid for by premiums over 20 years or more as long as the policy provides significant amounts of insurance protection relative to the income buildup.

[49] For a discussion of wealth taxation, see chapter 9.

GST credit, federal child tax benefit payments, provincial child tax credits or benefits, allowances for newborn children received from the Régie des rentes du Québec, Quebec family allowances, compensation received from a province or territory by victims of criminal acts or motor vehicle accidents, and allowances, disability pensions, and dependants' pensions paid for war service. There has been little public discussion of the merits of excluding these items, but policy makers and others who have considered the subject may feel that the exclusion of these income sources is justified either by the hardships suffered by the recipients or by the administrative difficulties associated with capturing them in the tax base. Nevertheless, their exclusion violates the objective of achieving a horizontally equitable tax system: individuals or families who receive income of this type may pay lower taxes than others with the same amount of income from taxable sources. Since it would improve the overall distribution of the tax burden to include these forms of income in the tax base, they should be included—even if including them necessitates an increase in the absolute level of government transfers to correct for low incomes.

It might be difficult to enforce the inclusion of some of these income components, such as gambling profits and gifts. The inclusion of lottery winnings, scholarships, and bursaries, however, would be easy to administer and police. Lottery winnings are, by and large, unexpected, and given appropriate averaging provisions should logically be included in the tax base.

It is difficult on economic grounds to justify the continued exclusion of $500 of bursary and scholarship income. The exclusion violates the principle of equity and discriminates in favour of students who receive income in this form. Although there may be a social justification for favourable tax treatment of students, it would be better to limit this favourable treatment to allowing the deduction of educational costs and tuition fees. This provision applies to all students and does not, as the exclusion of some scholarship income does, give rise to the inequity that results when similar students with identical total incomes have different taxable incomes.

## Imputed Income

The income tax base is narrower than it need be not only because it excludes various forms of money income but also because it excludes certain kinds of imputed income. The most important form of imputed income is the net imputed rent on owner-occupied dwellings. Net imputed rent is defined as gross imputed rent minus the expenses of home ownership—property taxes, interest on mortgage debt, depreciation, repairs and maintenance, and casualty insurance. The omission of net imputed income from taxable income discriminates in favour of homeowners and against renters. The part of the owner's income that takes the form of imputed net rent is free of tax, whereas the renter must use taxable income to pay his full housing costs. In addition, an investor in an owner-occupied house is favoured over other investors.

This discrimination is illustrated by the following example. Three individuals earn identical incomes ($50,000) and hold equivalent amounts of wealth ($100,000) in different forms. One individual's wealth is represented by the $100,000 house in which he lives. The second individual's wealth is invested in an identical $100,000 house that he owns subject to a $50,000 mortgage. His remaining $50,000 is invested in securities. The third individual rents an identical house for $12,000 per year and invests his $100,000 in securities. The first individual's home-ownership expenses (property taxes, depreciation, repairs, and insurance) amount to $4,000, leaving him with a net imputed rent of $8,000 ($12,000 of gross rental value minus $4,000 of expenses). For the mortgage owner, home-ownership expenses total $8,000 ($4,000 for the above expenses plus $4,000 for interest payments on the mortgage), leaving him with a net rental income of $4,000. In addition to his salary, he receives $4,000 of investment income from securities with a market value of $50,000. The renter, on the other hand, receives $8,000 of investment income on securities valued at $100,000, plus his annual income of $50,000. All three individuals have identical incomes of $58,000 in the economic sense but unequal incomes for tax purposes. The renter and mortgage owner must include investment income in taxable income, while the owner and to a lesser extent the mortgage owner can exclude their imputed net income. Among owner-occupants, the exclusion favours those with higher incomes more than those with lower incomes; this is so because the value of an exclusion from taxable income varies directly with the marginal tax rate, which in turn varies directly with income. Similar arguments could be made for the inclusion of net imputed rent on all consumer durables.

|  | Owner | Mortgage owner | Renter |
|---|---|---|---|
| Annual income ............... | $ 50,000 | $ 50,000 | $ 50,000 |
| Wealth .................... | 100,000 | 100,000 | 100,000 |
| Gross rental value ............ | 12,000 | 12,000 | 12,000 |
| Home ownership expenses ....... | 4,000 | 8,000 | — |
| Net rental value ............. | 8,000 | 4,000 | — |
| Income from securities .......... | — | 4,000 | 8,000 |
| Economic income ............. | 58,000 | 58,000 | 58,000 |
| Taxable income .............. | 50,000 | 54,000 | 58,000 |

Although the exclusion of net imputed rent violates the economic principle of neutrality by discriminating in favour of home ownership, the subsidy it provides tends to be rather inefficient. It favours high-income earners over low-income earners and it does not provide the latter, who are already exempt from tax, with more disposable income. In spite of this subsidy, it is highly likely that many Canadians view home ownership as an expense rather than as an investment from which they can obtain a positive annual return. It appears that non-tax factors, such as the rise in real income that accompanies home ownership, the availability of mortgage financing, and the general satisfaction of owning a home are much more influential than tax considerations are in encouraging home ownership.[50]

---

[50] Although the proposed deduction for mortgage interest and property taxes might encourage home ownership, it would also create more distortions in the present system. The deductions would amount to claiming expenses of earning income (imputed rent) that itself was

(The footnote is continued on the next page.)

Imputed income has never been included in the tax base in Canada or the United States. It was included in England until 1963. The problems that led to its removal there were not entirely specific to England; they included the practical problems involved in administering any scheme of this kind. How, for example, does one distinguish between a repair and a permanent improvement? How does one establish gross rental value in the absence of market transactions? Because of these administrative problems and the extreme public outcry that would emerge if imputed net rent were taxed, it is almost certain that it will not be included in the tax base in Canada, at least not in the foreseeable future. Indeed, the Royal Commission on Taxation,[51] as thorough as it was in outlining a comprehensive tax base, recommended that net imputed rent on owner-occupied homes not be included in the base because its inclusion was administratively infeasible.

There are other non-cash exclusions to which imputed values could be attached. For example, goods and services that are produced and consumed by the same individual are theoretically part of income. The Canadian tax system attempts to capture at least part of the value of some goods of this kind. Thus farmers are required to include in their income an estimate of the value of all produce grown and consumed at home. This figure is almost always understated; it is unlikely, though, that the time and effort required to enforce stricter regulations would be worth the improvement in equity that might be achieved. The consumption of one's own services, such as dressmaking, gardening, painting, plumbing, and carpentry, also qualifies as a form of income; the most obvious example is that of housewives' or spouses'/partners' services. The value of the service at home is excluded from taxable income, but identical work for payment away from home is included in taxable income. Once again, practical difficulties preclude the inclusion of these items in taxable income.

Although the exclusion of certain activities from the tax base provides an incentive to undertake these activities rather than other, taxable activities, this distortion may be acceptable given the difficult, if not impossible, task of accurately evaluating the wide range of non-market activities.

## Fringe Benefits

The magnitude of the fringe benefits of employment that are excluded from the tax base is impossible to measure. Fringe benefits include many items that increase the economic power of the employee but that are directly provided or partially or fully paid for by the employer. They range from direct payments for dental and extended health care plans, employment insurance premiums, and pension plan contributions to amenities such as air

---

[50] Continued ...

not taxed. The deduction would also be inequitable, since its value would increase with income—all the more so, owing to the progressivity of the tax.

[51] Canada, *Report of the Royal Commission on Taxation* (Ottawa: Queen's Printer, 1966).

conditioning and recorded music. Other non-taxable benefits include food and lodging while the employee is at a temporary site, certain automobile use, disability-related employment benefits such as transportation to and from work, and employee benefits as part of a retirement compensation arrangement (subject to certain limits).

Ideally, all forms of compensation from employment, whether in kind or in cash, would be included in the tax base. As to the problem of proper valuation, the best approach is to record the benefit at market value. This amount may be more than the recipient would be willing to pay for the benefit if he were given the choice of purchasing it or not purchasing it, but it is not the responsibility of the tax system to accommodate this difficulty. Instead, the individual should arrange to receive full value for the benefit received, either by demanding a cash payment or by obtaining additional remuneration to compensate for the difference between the cost of the benefit and its value to the individual net of taxes.

Although valuation and general administration problems would make it difficult to include all fringe benefits in the tax base, a variety of contributions made by the employer on the employee's behalf have been brought into the employee's tax base over the past few years. They include, among other things, premiums paid for group term life insurance, the full value of subsidized board and lodging and other personal expenses provided, interest on interest-free or low-interest loans to employees, and membership dues or participation fees paid for employees in recreational and social clubs (lodges, golf courses, and convention facilities). The continued exclusion of the employer's contributions to the employment insurance plan and registered pension plans is acceptable, since they are deductible by the employee in any case.

## Tax Credits Versus Deductions

The tax reform of 1987 replaced all exemptions and some deductions with tax credits, but a number of deductions were retained (see table 3.5). Support for deductions as opposed to tax credits is strongest among higher-income taxpayers, for whom deductions generate greater tax savings than tax credits do. Table 3.23 illustrates this point with an example based on four hypothetical taxpayers in four different income brackets, each of thom receives a deduction of $10,000. It is apparent from the table that the value of the deduction in terms of tax savings is more important to high-income earners than it is to low-income earners. Replacement of a deduction with a tax credit limits the tax savings to the same dollar amount for all taxpayers. In this example, each taxpayer would receive a tax credit of $1,000—that is, a credit equal to the tax paid on the first $10,000 of taxable income.

The use of tax credits rather than deductions, it has been argued, enhances equity. This argument is based, however, on a particular norm that suggests that equity is increased when all taxpayers are granted the same absolute tax relief (in terms of taxes saved) per dependant, regardless of their level of income. In addition, the allowance of a tax credit for a given activity instead

**Table 3.23   Tax Savings from Deductions for Hypothetical Taxpayers**

| Income group, $ | Marginal tax rates, % | Total income for tax purposes | Tax payable on total income for tax purposes | Dollar value of deduction | Taxable income | Tax payable on taxable income | Tax savings from deduction |
|---|---|---|---|---|---|---|---|
| | | | | *dollars* | | | |
| 0-20,000 ....... | 10 | 20,000 | 2,000 | 10,000 | 10,000 | 1,000 | 1,000 |
| 20,001-40,000 .. | 20 | 40,000 | 6,000 | 10,000 | 30,000 | 4,000 | 2,000 |
| 40,001-60,000 .. | 30 | 60,000 | 12,000 | 10,000 | 50,000 | 9,000 | 3,000 |
| 60,001-80,000 .. | 40 | 80,000 | 20,000 | 10,000 | 70,000 | 16,000 | 4,000 |

of a deduction gives taxpayers less of an incentive to undertake that activity; thus tax credits are less distortive than deductions are. Finally, the use of tax credits instead of deductions generates more tax dollars for the government.

The choice between tax credits and deductions should depend on the policy objectives to be achieved. Credits should be used when the objective is to increase the progressivity of the tax system. Indeed, the substitution of tax credits for most deductions in Canada, over the past two decades, has narrowed the after-tax distribution of income. Additional progressivity would be achieved by replacing the non-refundable tax credits with refundable tax credits such as those that already exist for the GST and child tax benefits. Non-refundable tax credits are of no assistance to individuals without taxable income and do nothing to redistribute income. Replacing them with refundable tax credits would move the tax-transfer system closer to being a comprehensive negative income tax system. Deductions, on the other hand, should be used when the objective is to adjust or alter the tax base; for example, all expenses associated with earning income should be treated as a deduction (see the discussion of this subject in chapter 2).

## The Tax Treatment of Savings

The tax treatment of savings in Canada varies widely across the various types of savings. Contributions to RRSPs and RPPs are deducted from income for tax purposes, but a tax credit is provided for compulsory contributions to the CPP/QPP. Annual accrued interest earned on funds contributed to registered education savings plans (RESPs) and on a portion of premiums paid for some whole-life insurance policies are excluded from annual taxation. Three-quarters of all net capital gains (gains minus losses) are taxable, but farmers and small business owners are eligible for a $500,000 lifetime capital gains exemption. Tax incentives are provided for tax shelters such as flowthrough shares, film shelters, and LSVCCs—the effective tax rate in these cases may even be negative. The net imputed rent on owner-occupied housing is excluded from taxation. Dividend income from Canadian sources is taxed at a lower rate than interest income.

**Table 3.24  Representative Effective Marginal Tax Rates
by Type of Savings, Ontario, 1993**

| Savings source | Taxable income of $25,000 | Taxable income of $45,000 | Taxable income of $100,000 |
|---|---|---|---|
| | | *percent* | |
| Interest income .............. | 27.37 | 41.86 | 52.35 |
| Dividend income ............ | 7.39 | 25.50 | 35.36 |
| Capital gains | | | |
| Shares ................... | 17.32 | 27.03 | 34.31 |
| Real estate .............. | 14.21 | 22.56 | 29.03 |
| Small business and farm | | | |
| (under $500,000) ........ | 0.00 | 0.00 | 0.00 |
| Owner-occupied dwellings ..... | 0.00 | 0.00 | 0.00 |
| RRSP/RPP ................ | 0.00 | 0.00 | 0.00 |

Source: Jack M. Mintz and Thomas A. Wilson, "Private Provision of Retirement Income: Tax Policy Issues," in Keith G. Banting and Robin Boadway, eds., *Reform of Retirement Income Policy: International and Canadian Perspectives* (Kingston, Ont.: Queen's University, School of Policy Studies, 1997), 209-39, at 227, table 4.

Table 3.24 shows the effective marginal tax rates in Ontario in 1993 for the major types of savings. These rates range from zero percent for contributions to RRSPs and RPPs, owner-occupied housing, and farms and small businesses to over 50 percent for interest income in the highest taxable income bracket. In fact, interest income faces the highest effective marginal tax rate in all taxable income levels.

This differential treatment of different forms of savings, though it has been questioned on occasion, has been defended on a variety of grounds. Thus the rationale for deducting RRSP and RPP contributions is to encourage individuals to save for retirement and, hence, reduce the need for government transfers to the elderly. The main benefit of RPPs and RRSPs is the value of the tax deferred on both the principal and annual earnings. An example will illustrate this point. Assume that a taxpayer is subject to a 30 percent marginal tax rate at all times. In the absence of taxation, $1 of today's income invested at 10 percent (compounded annually) will grow to a value of $6.73 in 20 years. If the investor pays tax at the end of 20 years, he will be left with $4.71. However, if the investor is required to pay tax on the dollar before he invests it (as in the case of a non-registered plan) and on the interest earned each year as it is earned, he will receive only $2.71 after 20 years.

The tax credit for compulsory contributions to the CPP/QPP has the same rationale as the deduction for RRSPs and RPPs. The net rent on owner-occupied dwellings is excluded from taxation for a variety of reasons, not the least of which is the public outcry that would arise if the government taxed this source of income. The exclusion of interest earned on RESPs is intended to increase savings and, subsequently, investment in post-secondary education. The exclusion of one-quarter of capital gains is intended in part to increase savings and investment. The taxation of dividend income at a lower rate is intended to remove the double taxation of corporate source income. The special tax incentives offered through tax shelters are intended to increase investment in specific types of business ventures.

Given the variety of tax incentives or deductions for savings, a number of questions arise, not the least of which is whether any savings should be taxed. Consumption-tax advocates argue that taxing consumption is both more efficient and fairer than taxing income. It is more efficient because unlike income taxation it does not favour present consumption over future consumption and thereby discourage saving. It is fairer because it taxes individuals according to what they take out of the common pool rather than what they contribute. One can also achieve vertical equity under a consumption tax, by taxing consumption at progressive marginal rates.

Those who support income as the tax base argue that any annual increase in one's ability to command goods and services should be taxed. Horizontal equity is achieved when all forms of income, regardless of source, are included in the tax base, and vertical equity is achieved by setting up a progressive tax structure. Allocative efficiency, however, is better served by consumption taxation, which removes the distortions created by the income tax and specifically by the taxation of savings, which discriminates against future consumption and results in too little saving.[52]

The current pattern of savings in Canada, as shown in table 3.21, suggests that at present most savings are tax deductible (the table omits the value of owner-occupied housing). This finding supports the contention that the income tax treatment of savings has moved closer over the past few years to a consumption base. This move would be completed and the remaining distortion (the incentive for taxpayers to alter their behaviour in order to reduce their taxes) would be eliminated without substantially reducing government revenues by exempting all forms of savings from tax.

It is unlikely, however, that government officials, policy makers, or the general public would support the complete removal of all forms of savings from taxation. It would take only one news story about one taxpayer who earned $100,000 in interest income and paid no tax to terminate any movement in this direction.

Although the fact that some types of savings receive preferential tax treatment is seldom criticized, there has been some criticism of the tax system's differential treatment of CPP/QPP contributions, for which it allows tax credits, and RRSP and RPP contributions, for which it allows deductions.

The deductibility of RRSP and RPP contributions discriminates in favour of taxpayers in the higher marginal tax brackets, who are better able than lower-income taxpayers are to take advantage of retirement savings plans.

---

[52] See chapter 2 for a fuller discussion of income versus consumption as the tax base.

One proposed remedy for this discrimination is to treat RRSP and RPP contributions in the same manner as CPP/QPP contributions—that is, to allow tax credits rather than deductions for the former as well as the latter. This solution, however, would not necessarily be more equitable or allocatively efficient than the current arrangement. Inequities would arise if the tax rate at the time of contribution was lower than the rate at the time of withdrawal. Consider, for example, an individual in a 25 percent bracket who makes an RRSP contribution that will earn a return of 10 percent. This contribution generates a tax credit of 25 percent. When the funds are withdrawn, however, the individual's marginal tax rate is 45 percent. In other words, the individual receives a tax savings of 25 percent before retirement only to face a tax rate of 45 percent after retirement. This is equivalent to a wealth tax of 20 percent and is well in excess of the annual 10 percent return on the asset. If tax rates were expected to increase over time, taxpayers would have an incentive either to hold savings outside of RRSPs and RPPs or to save less.[53]

Another suggestion for altering the tax treatment of RRSPs and RPPs is to tax the income earned by RPPs and RRSPs. This solution too, however, may not improve allocative efficiency or equity, since a number of other forms of savings are either tax-free or taxed at a negative rate (see table 3.24). Other solutions call for the imposition of a penalty on early withdrawals from RRSPs or for reductions in RRSP contribution limits. Both of these proposed arrangements are inferior to the current system. A penalty for early withdrawals would reduce individuals' flexibility in using RRSPs to average their income or to finance unexpected expenditures before retirement. As well, if individuals felt that their RRSP contributions were locked in, they might be discouraged from using RRSPs as a means of saving for retirement. The government has maintained limits on RRSP contributions primarily because the existence of the limits improves vertical equity, increases government revenues, and may not reduce savings.[54] Nevertheless, this policy has its deficiencies. It discriminates against those who do not have the opportunity to use RPPs, and it reduces the individual's opportunities to average his income if he is confronted with a loss of his job or unexpected expenditures.[55]

The treatment of savings for retirement purposes has improved significantly over the past two decades, though certainly further reform is possible. Thus the Economic Council of Canada recommended some years ago that the limit on RRSP contributions be increased to 30 percent and indexed thereafter

[53] Jack M. Mintz and Thomas A. Wilson, "Private Provision of Retirement Income: Tax Policy Issues," in Keith G. Banting and Robin Boadway, eds., *Reform of Retirement Income Policy: International and Canadian Perspectives* (Kingston, Ont.: Queen's University, School of Policy Studies, 1997), 209-39, at 232.

[54] Christopher Ragan, "Progressive Income Taxes and the Substitution Effect of RRSPs" (February 1994), 27 *Canadian Journal of Economics* 43-57.

[55] For a detailed discussion of these points, see Mintz and Wilson, supra footnote 53, at 232-33.

to the average annual change in the industrial wage. The federal budget of 1996, however, indicated that the current limit of $13,500 will stay in effect until 2002 and that indexation of this limit will not take place until 2004.

In summary, although the supporters of consumption taxation argue that all forms of savings should be excluded from taxation, this is not likely to happen in Canada in the foreseeable future. Income is entrenched as the tax base, and, that being the case, preferential treatment must be provided for savings if they are to be excluded from taxation. At the moment, there appears to be considerable support for the preferential treatment of savings for retirement income, education, home ownership, and job-creating and investment activities. Criticism has emerged, however, of the use of deductions rather than tax credits for RRSP and RPP contributions. Again, although the use of tax credits for many deductions has increased the progressivity of the tax system, their use for RRSP and RPP contributions might increase allocative inefficiency and, for certain taxpayers, inequity as well. There are, however, two changes that would improve the treatment of retirement savings—an increase in the RRSP contribution limit and indexation of the limit.

## Averaging

In the absence of an averaging scheme, progressive income tax rates lead to a heavier taxation of fluctuating income than of an equal sum of income distributed evenly over a number of years. For example, a taxpayer who earned $80,000 of taxable income in 1997 and nothing in 1998, and who had non-refundable tax credits of $1,700 in each year, would have had a federal tax liability, including federal surtaxes, of $17,801.74 (at 1997 rates) in the first year and nothing in the second year, for a total of $17,801.74 over both years. If the same total taxable income had been spread evenly over two years, the taxpayer's federal taxes would have been $6,217.70 per year for a total of $12,435.40, some $5,366 less.

The lack of an averaging scheme, therefore, leads to inequities and discriminates against activities that are likely to result in fluctuating incomes. "Taxpayers usually do not and cannot arrange their business and personal affairs to conform with the calendar. Annual income fluctuations are frequently beyond the control of the taxpayer, yet he or she is taxed as if twelve months were a suitable horizon for decisionmaking."[56] Authors, artists, composers, professional athletes, and people whose extended training significantly shortens their working lives are all penalized by the single-tax-year system: they may spend several years on little or no income while writing a book, perfecting a piece of art, composing a musical score, developing an athletic skill, or training for a specialized occupation, and yet all of their income from these activities will be taxable in the year in which it is received.

---

[56] Joseph A. Pechman, *Federal Tax Policy*, 3d ed. (Washington, DC: Brookings Institution, 1977), 116.

Income-tax averaging was once permitted in Canada,[57] but the 1981 federal budget and the tax reform of 1987 explicitly removed it from the tax system. The use of RRSPs permits limited income tax averaging for individuals whose incomes fluctuate over their lifetime. In years of relatively high income, a taxpayer can reduce his taxable income by contributing to an RRSP. In years of relatively low income (owing to retirement or unemployment, for example), he may withdraw funds from his RRSP without penalty, although he must pay income taxes on the amount withdrawn. RRSPs are useful as an averaging vehicle, but because of their contributory limits they do not provide perfect averaging.

There is a strong case for the restoration of income-tax averaging, and it should apply to all taxpayers regardless of occupation or levels of income. Given the computerization of tax recording and collection, an averaging system would be fairly easy to administer and simple to understand. Indeed, it could even be based on a five-year moving average if tax authorities did not want to extend it over all tax years.

## Indexation

We discussed in chapter 2 the need to index a tax system that uses income as its base. In particular, we noted that the failure to index the personal income tax system leads to the taxation of "illusory gains" and that the existence of progressive marginal tax rates leads to "bracket creep." Fortunately, there are some provisions in the Canadian tax system that remove the tax from illusory gains. For example, the taxation of inflationary gains on capital income is partially mitigated by the fact that some capital income goes untaxed. One-quarter of net capital gains is excluded from income taxation as is the first $500,000 of capital gain on farms and small businesses. Those who are aged 65 or more can claim a tax credit for $1,000 of pension income. The imputed income from consumer durables (for example, housing) is not taxed. In addition, capital income accumulated in RRSPs and RPPs is not taxable, so indexation is not an issue in this context. Interest earned on funds deposited in RESPs or on a portion of the premiums for whole-life insurance policies is excluded from annual taxation. The nominal increase in capital income from other sources is fully taxable.

The problem of bracket creep would be eliminated by full indexation of the personal tax structure. At the moment, the annual indexing factor in Canada[58] is the amount by which the inflation rate (measured by the consumer price index) exceeds 3 percent. This factor applies, moreover, only to the three tax brackets and some of the amounts on which tax credits are based (the personal amount, the age amount, the spousal or equivalent-to-

---

[57] For a discussion of earlier income tax averaging schemes, see Boadway and Kitchen, supra footnote 8, at 111-14.

[58] Full indexation of the marginal tax brackets and exemptions was introduced in 1973, but subsequent changes have eroded it.

spouse amount, the amounts for infirm dependants age 18 or over, and the disability amount).[59] All of the deductions and some of the credits are ineligible for indexation—their values or limits are set by explicit government policy through the budgetary process. For example, the value of the $1,000 pension-income credit for the elderly has eroded over time, as have the contribution limits for RRSPs and RPPs. Extensions of these limits would increase the fairness of the tax system, and full indexation would exclude the taxation of illusory income, but either measure would lead to further revenue loss by the government. Conversely, the failure to implement full indexation has generated increases in government revenue by virtue of inflation alone, modest as the rate of inflation has been over the past few years. A recent study notes that over the past decade the value of deductions has increaed by less than 8 percent, whereas consumer prices have increased by 34 percent.[60] In the course of the decade, the federal government received about $10.4 billion more in revenue than it would have received had full indexation remained in place (the provinces benefited as well). Most of the additional revenue came from increases in income taxes as taxpayers moved into higher brackets. The federal government also saved money by paying less to lower-income Canadians in old age security payments, disability benefits, the GST credit, and the child tax benefit; the thresholds for these benefits have been frozen since 1992.

Whether one views the reinstatement of full indexation of the personal tax system as a pressing issue depends, in part, on one's attitude toward debt financing. Some might argue that the additional revenue obtained as a result of bracket creep has been a welcome source of finance for addressing the deficits of the past and for paying off some of the debt overhang. Bracket creep is not an unfair way of raising tax revenues to pay for what are after all postponed tax liabilities built up in the past. Others, however, might argue that obtaining additional tax revenues in this way has partially absolved the government from the need to reduce expenditures and to get the overall tax burden down to levels more comparable with levels in the United States.

## Progressivity

The personal income tax system is progressive when the effective rate of tax varies directly with income; that is, when the percentage of income paid in taxes increases as income rises. This result may be achieved through either the application of progressive marginal rates to the income tax base[61] or the combination of a proportional or flat rate tax and exemptions and deductions.

---

[59] The inflation rate has not exceeded 3 percent since 1992; hence, there has been no change since then in these values.

[60] Finn Poschmann, *Inflated Taxes, Deflated Paycheques* (Toronto: C.D. Howe Institute, December 1998).

[61] The three federal marginal tax rates and their corresponding tax brackets are noted in table 3.1.

Although the rationale for progressive personal income taxation is the achievement of vertical equity, there remains the thorny issue of how progressive the personal income tax system should be. Clearly, there is no scientific basis for establishing the appropriate degree of progressivity and no magic formula for the "right" rate structure. Tradeoffs play a dominant role in the setting of tax rates—the higher the tax rate is, the greater is the economic inefficiency and the lower is the level of national output.[62]

Recognizing that high marginal tax rates create harmful disincentives and reduce economic output, the federal government has reduced the number of tax brackets and narrowed the spread of marginal rates over the past 50 years (see table 3.25). It has also broadened the tax base, replaced all exemptions and some deductions with non-refundable tax credits, and introduced a refundable child tax credit and the GST credit. The combination of these changes has produced an after-tax-transfer distribution of income that is narrower now than it was 25 years ago. Of course, the question whether the current marginal tax rate structure is the correct one cannot be answered, since there is no unequivocal benchmark with which we can compare the current rate structure. A former member of the Department of Finance who made up "dozens of rate schedules for successive Ministers of Finance" may have put the matter as succinctly as possible when he stated that "[a]fter much humming and hawing and staring at the ceiling this citizen will finally put his finger on one schedule and simply say 'that one looks about right'— and that is it. It is as simple and unsophisticated as that."[63]

## The Tax-Paying Unit

The current tax system in Canada is based on the individual rather than the family as the tax-paying unit, but it includes several provisions that depart from this basis. The tax credit for a spouse, the interspousal tax credits for age, pension, disability, tuition, and education, the opportunity for an individual to contribute to a spouse's RRSP, and the fact that refundable tax credits (the GST credit and the child tax benefit) are based on a definition of net family income all suggest a partial recognition of the family as the tax-paying unit. Some provincial refundable tax credits are also based on family income.

How the tax system should treat differences in family size and circumstances is one of the more vexing questions of tax policy. It raises not only the standard equity and efficiency issues, but also social policy issues and the issue of responsibility for the well-being of family members: should this responsibility rest entirely with individuals, or should society assume some share of it? In addressing these issues, policy makers must distinguish between single-adult families and two-adult families, two-adult families with one earner and those with two earners, and families with children and

---

[62] Smith, supra footnote 12, at 1071.

[63] A. Kenneth Eaton, *Essays in Taxation*, Canadian Tax Paper no. 44 (Toronto: Canadian Tax Foundation, 1966), 27.

Table 3.25    Combined Federal and Provincial Personal Income
Marginal Tax Rates for Selected Years from 1949 to 1997

| Taxable income, $ | 1949, % | 1973, % | Taxable income, $ | 1987, % | Taxable income, $ | 1997, % |
|---|---|---|---|---|---|---|
| 1 | 15.00 | 4.58 | 1 | 9.00 | 1 | 26.35 |
| 501 | 15.00 | 5.49 | 1,321 | 24.00 | 29,591 | 40.30 |
| 1,001 | 17.00 | 24.80 | 2,640 | 25.50 | 59,181 | 44.95 |
| 2,001 | 19.00 | 26.10 | 5,280 | 27.00 | 63,438 | 46.40 |
| 3,001 | 19.00 | 27.41 | 7,919 | 28.50 | | |
| 4,001 | 22.00 | 27.41 | 10,560 | 28.50 | | |
| 5,001 | 22.00 | 30.02 | 13,198 | 30.00 | | |
| 6,001 | 26.00 | 30.02 | 15,839 | 30.00 | | |
| 7,001 | 26.00 | 32.63 | 18,477 | 34.50 | | |
| 8,001 | 30.00 | 32.63 | 21,119 | 34.50 | | |
| 9,001 | 30.00 | 35.24 | 23,756 | 37.50 | | |
| 10,001 | 35.00 | 35.24 | 26,398 | 37.50 | | |
| 11,001 | 35.00 | 38.91 | 29,038 | 37.50 | | |
| 12,001 | 40.00 | 38.91 | 31,678 | 37.50 | | |
| 14,001 | 40.00 | 43.93 | 36,953 | 45.00 | | |
| 15,001 | 45.00 | 43.93 | 39,597 | 45.00 | | |
| 24,001 | 45.00 | 48.95 | 63,347 | 51.00 | | |
| 25,001 | 50.00 | 48.95 | 65,994 | 51.00 | | |
| 39,001 | 54.00 | 56.12 | 102,950 | 51.00 | | |
| 40,001 | 59.00 | 56.12 | 105,589 | 51.00 | | |
| 60,001 | 64.00 | 61.34 | 158,384 | 51.00 | | |
| 90,001 | 69.00 | 61.34 | 237,575 | 51.08 | | |
| 125,001 | 74.00 | 61.34 | 329,965 | 51.08 | | |
| 225,001 | 79.00 | 61.34 | 593,937 | 51.00 | | |
| 400,001 | 84.00 | 61.34 | 1,055,888 | 51.00 | | |

Note: In 1949, only the federal government occupied the personal income tax field. Since 1972, provincial taxes, except in Quebec, have been levied as a percentage of the basic federal tax. The 1973 calculated rates are the federal tax rates grossed up by 30.5 percent of the basic federal tax to reflect the combined provincial and federal marginal rates. The provincial rate for 1987 is assumed to be 47 percent. The provincial rate for 1997 is assumed to be 52 percent.

Source: Karin Treff and David B. Perry, *Finances of the Nation 1997* (Toronto: Canadian Tax Foundation, 1997), 3:7, table 3.5.

families without children. Our discussion will consider four general arguments relevant to the tax treatment of families, each of which has potential implications for tax policy design. Some of these implications are conflicting, so in the end a judgment must be made about which of them are the more relevant.

## Family Income Versus Individual Income

Even if one accepts the view that taxpayers are individuals, and that an individual's tax liability depends on how well off he is, one is obliged to consider how family circumstances affect individuals' well-being. The most obvious consideration in this context is simply that the individuals in a family share a common family budget. If we assume that the family arrangement is an amicable or cooperative one,[64] this consideration suggests that family income should be pooled for tax purposes and each person taxed as if his income were his per-capita share of family income. Indeed, a recent study suggests that the adoption of income splitting in Canada would improve horizontal equity for couples relative to singles and for one-earner families relative to two-earner families.[65] As well, it would integrate tax policy and social policy—although (as noted below) economic, administrative, and social objections to taxing on the basis of the family unit would likely be significant. A system that allowed full income splitting within the family would be similar to the system in the United States.

The Canadian tax system does not permit full income splitting, but the opportunity to use tax credits for one's spouse effectively reduces tax liabilities for two-adult families if only one spouse is working. The fact that full income splitting is not permitted may well have to do with the issues discussed in the next subsection.

It should be noted that the argument for income splitting, like the arguments considered below, presumes that the tax system is progressive—that because of the combination of credits and exemptions and a graduated rate structure average tax rates rise with real income. In a purely proportional tax system, there would be no need to account for family differences on equity grounds. In the case of taxes such as the GST, family characteristics come into play only to the extent that the tax system attempts to make the tax progressive. Thus the GST credit specifically takes family size into account, as does the child tax benefit.

## Household Production

An important issue from an economic perspective is the taxation of imputed income from household production. Most persons presumably engage in household chores such as preparing meals, gardening, laundering, house maintenance, and so on. In principle, the services represented by these activities could be acquired on the market, in which case those supplying them would be subject to taxation. If all individuals devoted comparable amounts of time to household chores, no issues related to taxation would arise. However, since some persons systematically devote more time to household chores than others do, the issue of horizontal equity arises. This issue is particularly relevant in the case of two-adult families, especially if only one partner is in the work force. The stay-at-home partner, presumably,

---

[64] Not all economists view the family in these terms. Some treat the family arrangement as simply a matter of convenience that participants enter into to achieve gains from exchange. According to this view, sharing is not equal and cooperative but rather a result of bargaining in which those with more economic strength gain the most.

[65] Kenneth J. Boessenkool and James B. Davies, "Giving Mom and Dad a Break: Returning Fairness to Families in Canada's Tax and Transfer System," *Commentary* 117 (Toronto: C.D. Howe Institute, November 1998).

is engaging in significant amounts of (unpaid) household production. Horizontal equity suggests that this production should be accounted for in the income tax system. In practice, it is very difficult to measure the value of unpaid household production; even if measurement were possible, monitoring to verify it would not be easy, since there is no market transaction involved. Thus the best that can be done is to adopt somewhat ad hoc presumptive measures to account for situations in which household production is likely to be relevant.

At the level of generality, if one accepts the argument that household production should be taxed, the standard prescription is to impose a higher tax liability on single-earner two-adult families than on two-earner families with the same total income. At the same time, one might want single-earner two-adult families to pay less than half the taxes of two-earner families that earn twice as much, given that one wants the tax system to be progressive at the individual level. If taxes are levied on individuals, as they are in Canada, these objectives are partially accomplished by not allowing income splitting in single-earner families and by the use of spousal credits. Whether the amounts are precisely sufficient is, of course, a matter of judgment. Unfortunately, the elimination of the working supplement for the child tax benefit program means that those in the work force no longer receive assistance to offset their reduced time for household production.

The non-taxability of household production has similar implications for the taxation of two-adult one-earner families vis-à-vis one-adult families. For a given income, a taxpayer with a non-working spouse should pay less tax than a single taxpayer, since the couple's income must support two adults rather than one. On the other hand, if the single-earner couple's income is half the income of the single taxpayer, given the presumption of significant household production they should pay more than half as much tax as the single taxpayer. Finally, if the single-earner pair have twice the income of the single person, presumably one would want them to pay more than twice as much tax. Again, these general prescriptions are satisfied by a tax system that is progressive at the individual level but provides credits for non-working spouses.

Although the treatment of non-working spouses in the current system accords with the spirit of the arguments for income splitting and taxing household production, the issue of income splitting is still unresolved in the case of two-earner families. There seems to be no good economic reason why income splitting should not be allowed between two working spouses. There may be social reasons. Income splitting treats families as arrangements under which the members pool their incomes and draw on them mutually. It might be objected that this implicitly subordinates the independence of the two partners in a marriage.

Any attempt to design the tax system so that taxpayers with a working partner are treated differently from taxpayers with a non-working partner brings its problems. For one thing, it raises the question of the kinds of partnerships that should be treated as families for tax purposes. If an expansive definition is used, there is then the administrative issue of monitoring living arrangements to verify if a non-working partner is in the household.

## Economies of Living Together

Another argument that is potentially relevant to the tax treatment of the family is the argument that various economies arise when individuals live together: family members share consumer durables, and they can specialize in different household chores. This argument, if accepted, might suggest that two income earners should be taxed more heavily if they live together than if they live apart. The current tax system makes no effort to apply this principle, and quite apart from the fact that applying it would be difficult administratively it is not clear that living arrangements as such should be a factor in tax policy. They are entered into voluntarily and presumably reflect the tastes of the participants.

## Costs of Raising Children

An issue that is extremely difficult to resolve on economic grounds is that of the tax treatment of the costs of raising children. Given the previous argument about the sharing of family income, a household with children should pay less tax than a household with the same income but without children, simply because there are more family members. This outcome could be achieved through a basic tax credit or deduction to compensate parents for the non-discretionary costs of raising children, such as the costs of providing them with food, clothing, and shelter. Unfortunately, no such deduction or credit currently exists in Canada. This failure to provide assistance may reflect a perception that children provide some household production and jointly consume household services with other members of the family. The tax system does allow credits for medical and dental expenses and educational expenses incurred on behalf of children, but these credits are available for all persons in the family: they are not intended specifically for children.

The most important exception to the tax system's general failure to compensate for the costs of raising children is the provision of tax credits for the costs of child care where there is no stay-at-home parent. A horizontal equity justification for this credit is that child-care expenses constitute a cost of earning income. In order to enter the labour force, parents must make some arrangements for child care. Moreover, the providers of child care are themselves typically taxable, so the deduction does not entail that the provision of child care is tax-free. It has recently been advocated, especially by the Reform Party, that the tax benefits of the child care expense deduction be extended to stay-at-home parents. One argument for this change is that the tax system as it stands discriminates against families with a stay-at-home parent. This argument is readily dismissed on the ground that child care by a stay-at-home parent involves untaxed household production, which is favoured already. If stay-at-home parents are allowed a child care expense deduction, then the imputed income on which the deduction is based should be taxable in the hands of the stay-at-home parent.

A more serious and controversial argument for extending the child care expense deduction to stay-at-home parents is that parents should be rewarded for staying at home to take care of their children (presumably over and above the reward associated with the non-taxability of their household production). There are several variants of this argument, all of which stand or fall on social judgments rather than economic ones. One variant is simply that the traditional family should be supported as an important institution in society. A second is that children, especially those from disadvantaged backgrounds, have higher chances of success and impose less of a social and economic burden on society in the future if they are raised by a stay-at-home parent. A third variant is even more controversial. It is that society itself has a responsibility to ensure that all children, regardless of their means, have equal opportunities. This argument raises the fundamental question whether the ultimate responsibility for children rests with their parents or with society at large.

In summary, a major problem with the current system is that it fails to recognize the non-discretionary expenses of raising children. One way of overcoming this inequity would be to restore the universal deduction for children. Equity would be further improved without increasing anyone's tax burden if this change were accompanied by an equivalent reduction in the deduction for child care expenses.[66] Whether these non-discretionary expenditures should be treated as a deduction or as a tax credit depends on the desired policy objectives. A credit should be used if the objective is to increase progressivity, and a deduction should be used if the objective is to adjust the tax base. A second way of achieving similar results would be to universalize the child tax benefit.[67]

## Harmonization of Federal and Provincial Income Taxes

As we have seen, both the federal government and the provinces levy income taxes. If they did so completely independently, taxpayers would not only bear the burden of paying two taxes on their incomes but also have to comply with two separate tax systems and file two tax returns. Moreover, the existence of wholly separate federal and provincial income taxes could well impose distortions in the internal common market, distortions that would cause capital and businesses to be misallocated among provinces and perhaps preclude each province from undertaking those activities for which its resources are most suited. Finally, different standards of vertical equity might apply across the provinces. Provinces might well engage in beggar-thy-neighbour competition in order to attract desirable factors of production and businesses and to discourage burdensome factors of production from locating in their

---

[66] Ibid.

[67] John Richards, "Avoiding Poverty Traps," *The National Post*, March 25, 1999.

jurisdictions. For these reasons, economists have stressed the importance of harmonizing income taxes among jurisdictions in a federation.[68]

As we have seen, the income tax system is largely harmonized through the tax collection agreements (TCAs). All of the provinces except Quebec participate in these agreements, under which the federal government agrees to collect taxes for a province provided that the province abides by the federal income tax base and rate structure. Each participating province is allowed to choose a provincial tax rate to apply to basic federal taxes, so that the federal rate structure applies automatically. Taxpayers file a single return that covers both their federal and their provincial taxes, and the federal government assumes responsibility for tax collection, including auditing, enforcement, and bad debts. Moreover, the provinces are allowed more latitude than simply to set a single tax rate. The federal government is willing to administer tax credits, including refundable ones, on their behalf for a small fee, provided that the credits are judged (by the federal government) not to be costly to administer, not to discriminate against non-residents of the relevant province, and not to distort the interprovincial allocation of resources. All participating provinces make considerable use of this provision, especially to provide tax relief for low-income persons. Since these credits are applied after tax liabilities have been determined, they do not compromise the common base or rate structure. There has been some deviation from the common base, however, in provinces that have been allowed to apply flat rate taxes on personal income under the TCAs (Alberta, Manitoba, and Saskatchewan).

This system of harmonization has served the federation well for most of the post-war period. As the provinces occupy a larger and larger share of the income tax room, however, there are definite signs of strain. The demand for special tax credits has increased rapidly in recent years, and the federal government has accepted most of them, despite the fact that some of these credits compromise the common base and create incentives for business activities to choose one province over another. Moreover, the provinces themselves have expressed discontent with their relative lack of flexibility under the TCAs. They argue that because they must abide by the federal base and rate structure they have relatively little independent tax-policy initiative. They cannot, for example, implement local preferences for redistribution by choosing a province-specific rate structure or by defining the base as broadly or narrowly as they choose. Moreover, they argue, the federal government is prone to making unilateral and unannounced changes to the base or rate structure that affect provincial tax revenues in unanticipated ways. Some provinces have even contemplated leaving the TCAs in order to have more say over the income taxes they levy.

---

[68] The case for harmonizing income taxes is discussed more fully in Robin Boadway and Neil Bruce, "Pressures for the Harmonization of Income Taxation Between Canada and the United States," in John B. Shoven and John Whalley, eds., *Canada-U.S. Tax Comparisons* (Chicago: University of Chicago Press, 1992), 25-74.

Various proposals have been made to give the provinces more flexibility and tax policy independence without forsaking the administrative advantages of a common tax administration. Most of these proposals involve retaining the common tax base but allowing provinces more discretion over their rate structures. The starkest way of doing this would be to let the provinces apply rate structures of their own choosing to the common base—a shift from the present "tax-on-tax" system to a "tax-on-base" system. Indeed, the federal government has recently agreed to this approach. The provinces will be permitted either to continue with the existing personal TCAs or, beginning in 2002, to set their own rate structures and to use their own tax credits, within limits (see chapter 9). This agreement will certainly allow provinces to implement their own systems of tax progressivity, but it also creates the potential for provinces to compete with one another in the matter of rate structures, with the objective of attracting higher-income taxpayers. A less dramatic way of affording the provinces some say in their rate structures would be to retain the common rate structure but give the provinces the right to choose at least some of their own basic credits for personal or demographic purposes. Now that personal circumstances are taken into account through the use of tax credits rather than deductions, provincial preferences can be accommodated without compromising the common base. As always, there is a tradeoff, in this case between the advantages of having a harmonized income tax system (administrative simplicity, equity, and efficiency of the internal economic union) and the disadvantages of not having one (increased collection and compliance costs, and greater inefficiency and inequity induced by independent provincial tax policy choices and interprovincial tax competition). One thing is clear, however: the greater is the income tax room occupied by the provinces, the greater will be the pressures for disharmonization. This is a factor that must be taken into consideration in deciding how decentralized the federation should be, and how important the income tax should be in the federal government's tax mix.

# 4

# The Corporate Income Tax

## Introduction

The corporate income tax is currently the fourth largest source of own-source revenue for both the federal government (about 10 percent of revenue in fiscal year 1995-96) and the provinces (just over 6 percent). Personal income taxes, general sales taxes, and payroll taxes all raise more revenues at both levels of government. This was not always the case. In the early 1950s, corporate income taxes accounted for about one-quarter of total federal and provincial revenues. Their gradual decline in importance since then is accounted for in part by a decline in corporate profits as a percentage of GDP, from over 13 percent in 1950 to less than 8 percent today.[1] The decline also reflects a larger trend: governments in many countries around the world have reduced their corporate tax rates in response to growing international competitive pressures and the increasing mobility of capital and businesses.

The corporate income tax is but one of many taxes imposed on businesses in Canada. Owners of unincorporated businesses are taxed under the personal income tax, as we have seen. Some businesses are liable for annual capital taxes, federal and provincial. Resource industries face special provincial levies. As subsequent chapters will show, businesses incur payroll taxes, sales and excise taxes and, not least important, property taxes and other levies to local governments. Our emphasis in this chapter will be on the corporate income tax, but we shall also touch on business taxes that we do not cover elsewhere, particularly resource and capital taxes. Many of the same economic principles apply to these taxes as apply to the corporate tax.

We shall begin by reviewing the provisions of the existing corporate tax system. We shall then discuss the economic effects of the tax. Finally, we shall consider policy issues and options, including those proposed by the Mintz committee.

## Current Provisions

The authority for the federal corporate income tax is the Income Tax Act, the same act of Parliament as governs the personal income tax. It is not surprising, therefore, that many of the provisions that apply to business income under the personal tax also apply under the corporate tax, including the

---

[1] These figures are reported in Canada, *Report of the Technical Committee on Business Taxation* (Ottawa: Department of Finance, April 1998) (herein referred to as "the Mintz committee report," after the chair of the committee, Jack Mintz).

definition of taxable income and the menu of deductions. In fact, the two taxes differ in their treatment of business income only in the matter of rates: the income of personal (unincorporated) businesses is taxed at personal rates, whereas corporate income is taxed at corporate income tax rates. All of the provinces levy their own corporate taxes, although the federal government collects the tax for seven of them—all except Alberta, Ontario, and Quebec—under the tax collection agreements. Since the structure of provincial corporate taxes (though not the rates) corresponds closely to the federal structure, much of our discussion will centre on the latter. We shall, however, discuss the workings of the tax collection agreements.

The Income Tax Act is a "living document"—one that undergoes frequent revisions as circumstances change. Many of these revisions are technical or are minor changes designed to achieve specific policy objectives. From time to time, however, the government undertakes a major revision of the system. The post-war period has seen three important episodes of reform. The first occurred in 1972, in the wake of the famous Carter report. The 1981 budget introduced a lesser, but still significant, set of revisions. In 1987, the federal government initiated a major reform of the corporate tax, the first part of a broader reform of the Canadian income and sales tax systems. The 1987 reform, responding to the imperative of an increasingly open and competitive international environment, sought to make the corporate tax system more neutral and less intrusive. Like reforms launched by some of Canada's major competitors, such as the United States and the United Kingdom, it opened an era of broader bases and lower rates. The intention was to remove at least some of the preferential treatment that the existing system afforded to particular activities and industries. As we shall see, many instances of preferential treatment remain, and the thrust of the Mintz committee recommendations is to take the next step by removing them and further lowering the tax rates.

The federal corporate tax is imposed on the taxable income (defined below) of all corporations resident in Canada and non-resident corporations that carry on business in Canada.[2] The taxable income of resident corporations includes both income earned inside Canada and income earned outside Canada. In the case of non-resident corporations, only income earned inside Canada is taxable (including taxable capital gains on the sale of Canadian property). The tax-paying status of a business is therefore much like that of an individual under the personal income tax. Unincorporated businesses are not subject to the corporate tax; their income is taxed directly as the personal income of their owners. Unincorporated businesses include partnerships and proprietorships, professional practices, farms, and fishing operations.

---

[2] According to Canadian tax law, a corporation is considered to be resident in the country in which its central control and management are situated. Unincorporated businesses assume the residency of their owners as determined by the personal tax system (that is, the owners' place of residence on December 31 of the tax year).

Canadian owners of corporations are subject to personal taxation of the income that they obtain from corporations. This arrangement, naturally, gives rise to concerns about double taxation, which are dealt with by measures that are intended to integrate the corporate and personal taxes. We shall discuss the integration of the two taxes in detail later in the chapter.

Corporate income tax payable is calculated in much the same way as personal income tax payable. Corporations are taxed on an annual basis, but the tax year for a corporation, unlike the tax year for an individual, does not necessarily coincide with the calendar year. A corporation's tax year is the fiscal year for which the accounts of its business are usually made up. The corporation arrives at an annual figure for taxable income by deducting from total revenues earned certain costs of earning the income, exempt income, and other deductions (such as incentives for particular expenditures). It then applies the rate structure to taxable income in order to arrive at federal tax payable and provincial tax payable. The rate structure encompasses not just the relevant federal and provincial tax rates, but also various tax credits that both levels of government implement to reduce tax liabilities selectively. If a corporation operates in more than one province, then in order to determine provincial tax liabilities it is necessary to attribute to each province the portion of the corporation's taxable income that originates there. In practice, this is difficult to do precisely, so the tax authorities use an *allocation formula* to allocate the taxable income among the provinces. The proportion of taxable income that the formula allocates to a province is an average of the proportion of the firm's sales in the province and the proportion of the firm's payroll in the province.[3] A detailed description of the calculation of a corporation's tax liabilities follows.

Some provisions of the corporate tax apply in different ways to different types of corporations, so before we examine the process of calculating corporate tax liabilities in more detail it is appropriate to identify the several types of corporations that are distinguished for the purposes of the tax. A *public corporation* is a resident corporation that has the ability to raise capital in the public capital market by selling its shares. This category includes not only all corporations actually listed on prescribed stock exchanges (that is, the Calgary, Canadian, Montreal, Toronto, and Vancouver exchanges) but also unlisted corporations that satisfy a number of conditions equivalent to those satisfied by listed corporations. These conditions have to do with the number of shareholders, the dispersal of ownership, the public trading of shares, and size. Subsidiaries of public corporations are treated as public corporations for tax purposes. *Private corporations* are resident corporations that do not satisfy the conditions for being public corporations and are not controlled by a public corporation or corporations. A resident

---

[3] This allocation formula is adhered to both by the provinces that have harmonized their corporate taxes with the federal corporate tax by means of tax collection agreements and by the provinces that administer their own corporate taxes.

corporation controlled by an individual through a trust or trusts is considered private. A *Canadian corporation* is one that is incorporated in Canada or has been resident in Canada continuously since June 18, 1971. Finally, a *Canadian-controlled private corporation* (CCPC) is a private Canadian corporation that is not controlled by a non-resident person or persons or by a public corporation or corporations. Control in this context is Canadian ownership of at least 50 percent of the voting shares.

The distinction between an *active business* and a *non-active business* is also relevant. A corporation is said to be engaging in an active business if its activities require expenditures of time, labour, and attention by its employees, and if these expenditures are a significant determinant of the income earned by the corporation. A corporation that derives its income wholly or primarily from financial investments is not engaged in an active business.

## Total Revenue

The total revenue of a corporation engaged in the production of goods and services includes the accrued value of its sales during its tax-paying year. (Investment income earned by corporations, such as interest, dividends, capital gains, and royalties, may also be taxable; we shall consider the treatment of investment income below.) As we have mentioned, total revenue includes sales by resident corporations anywhere in the world and sales by non-resident corporations from business carried on in Canada. Note that total revenue from the sale of goods and services is not the same thing as total value of production. They differ from one another according to the accumulation or the using up of inventories. Deductions for the cost of holding inventories are discussed below. Note also that total revenue is not the same as cash receipts from the sale of output. Under the existing system, revenues (and costs) are accounted for on an *accrual* basis rather than a *cash-flow* basis. That is, the firm adds the revenues when it transacts the sale rather than when it receives the payment. The difference between accrued revenues and cash received is known as *accounts receivable*. This difference is a shortfall of revenues that must be financed by the firm in exactly the same manner as the outlays of the firm. Indeed, any negative cash flow incurred by the firm, such as through the purchase of capital equipment that will generate future revenues, must be financed by the firm. The tax treatment of this financing, whether it takes the form of borrowing from outsiders or using the funds of shareholders, is an important element of the tax system.

## Deductions from Taxable Income and Exempt Income

Firms are allowed to deduct certain expenses that are deemed to be costs of earning income.[4] There are two general criteria for these deductions: they

---

[4] The rules that we outline in the following discussion are also used to determine the taxable income of unincorporated businesses. The latter, however, is subject to the personal income tax rather than to the corporate income tax.

must be made for the purpose of gaining or producing income for the corporation, and they must be "reasonable in the circumstances." There are also two basic types of deductible expenses: *current expenses* and *capital expenses*. Current expenses are expenses that are incurred in order to produce current income from the property or the business of the firm; that is, the output is produced as the expenses are incurred. A capital expense is a once-and-for-all expense—one that brings into being an asset of permanent and enduring advantage. Both types of expenses are deductible on an accrual basis; that is, the firm deducts the expenses when the inputs are used to produce income rather than when they are paid for. Current expenses are fully deductible in the year in which they are incurred. Capital expenses are deducted over the useful life of the capital purchased. Any difference in timing between the purchase of an input and the payment for it is known as an *account payable*. In addition, certain other deductions are allowed for specific types of expenditures. Finally, some types of corporate income are exempt from tax and so are excluded from the base.

If the deductions in any given year exceed revenues, the firm is earning negative taxable income. This may occur because the firm is engaging in heavy capital expenditures that will generate revenues only later on, or because it is suffering a setback in its current revenues. The tax law includes provisions for the spreading of negative tax liabilities, referred to as *tax losses*, over years in which taxable income is positive. Tax losses incurred in a given year may be carried backward to reduce taxable income earned in the previous three years or forward to reduce taxable income earned in the subsequent seven years. In the former case, the firm obtains a refund of taxes previously paid; in the latter case, the firm's subsequent tax liabilities are reduced. There is no interest factor associated with either the carry backward or the carry forward. Capital losses, or losses that arise from losses in the value of financial assets when they are sold, may also be carried backward for three years but only against past capital gains, but they can be carried forward against future capital gains indefinitely. Other measures in the tax system allow for other limited forms of loss offsetting. Corporations that are engaged in a variety of business operations may use losses in some lines of business to offset gains in others, a provision that gives them an advantage over smaller, more specialized firms. Unlike the United States or the United Kingdom, however, Canada makes no provision for the transfer of losses between individual corporations with common ownership. Finally, as we shall see, some tax credits are refundable immediately even for taxpayers that are otherwise in a loss position.

The existing system, though it recognizes the existence of tax losses, does not provide *full loss offsetting*—that is, the symmetric treatment of all gains and losses under the tax. The equivalence is less than exact because the postponement of tax reductions to future years in which positive taxable income is earned involves an element of forgone interest. Under full loss offsetting, negative tax liabilities incurred in a given year would be either fully refundable or could be carried forward (indefinitely) with interest. The absence of full loss offsetting puts at a disadvantage those firms prone to make losses—those engaged in risky ventures, those engaged in a narrow line of business, and those undertaking large capital expenditures. The issue is of some importance in practice. In every year between 1965 and 1985, according to the Mintz committee report, at least 45 percent of corporations in Canada did not have positive taxable incomes. Between 1985 and 1993, accumulated tax losses rose from $68.5 billion to $115 billion. In 1994, moreover, businesses were in a position to claim only about 10 percent of the previous year's total carryforward.

## Current Expenses

All costs of a current nature are deductible in the tax year in which they accrue. Accounting for current costs is a relatively straightforward matter. Current costs generally include all expenditures made for the production of income in the same year in which they were made. The more common current expenses are wages and salaries, rents for properties used in business, raw materials and goods purchased, fuel, hire prices for capital equipment that is leased rather than purchased, accounting and legal fees on income-earning activities, vehicle expenses, insurance premiums, annual licence fees, management service fees, advertising, losses owing to fire or theft, discounts on purchases, and club entertainment fees (if used to earn income). The amounts claimed must be "reasonable." If the expenditures are for the production or acquisition of goods for inventory, they are not deductible until the goods are taken out of inventory and used to produce income. As well, most taxes paid are not deductible. Exceptions to this rule are taxes that are levied independently of the revenue or profits of the firm. For example, municipal property taxes on land and buildings are deductible if the property is used to produce income. Sales and excise taxes paid on goods purchased are also deductible; in the case of the goods and services tax (GST), the taxes are actually creditable against taxes collected on sales.

Certain employer contributions on behalf of employees are deductible as expenses. Employer contributions to registered pension plan funds are deductible in amounts up to a maximum amount per employee each year. If pension plans include life insurance benefits, the premiums paid by the employer are deductible. Canada Pension Plan contributions paid on behalf of employees are deductible. In 1997, these contributions were 2.925 percent of wages per employee for earnings between $3,500 and $35,800 (employees matched that contribution). Employment insurance contributions on behalf of employees are also deductible. In 1997, these contributions were 4.06 percent of the first $39,000 of annual earnings (employees paid 2.90 percent of the same base).

Some conceptual problems may arise, however, in distinguishing current inputs from capital inputs. For example, is the purchase of an automobile for the use of employees a current cost or a capital cost? Since the automobile is an asset, its purchase is classified as a capital cost. On the other hand, there are some expenditures that clearly lead to ongoing revenues and yet which are treated as current costs. Examples include advertising and marketing expenditures and the costs of training employees. These costs are deductible as current costs out of practical necessity. It would be difficult to treat them as capital costs and spread them over the life of their usefulness.

## Capital Cost Allowances

As we mentioned above, capital expenditures are purchases of assets, which are used to produce income in the future. One can classify assets broadly into four types: depreciable assets (for example, buildings and machinery), depletable and renewable resource properties, non-depreciable assets (for example, land), and inventories. Each type is subject to its own separate tax treatment. Generally speaking, however, the tax system allows two sorts of deductions for capital purchases: a deduction for interest costs incurred on debt issued to purchase the capital, and a deduction for the imputed cost of the loss in value of the asset through use. The using up of the capital is referred to as its depreciation, and the deduction that the tax system allows for depreciation is called a *capital cost allowance* (CCA).

A capital cost allowance is an amortization of initial outlay on depreciable capital over its useful or service life. There are three sorts of depreciation—tax, book, and economic. *Tax depreciation* is simply the amount of depreciation allowed by the capital cost allowance. *Book depreciation* is the depreciation rate that a firm's accountants use in writing down capital for accounting purposes. It is meant to correspond to the rate at which the capital is actually wearing out. Tax depreciation and book depreciation will differ if the CCA incorporates an incentive to investment—for example, if it is accelerated.[5] The acceleration of CCAs creates a distinction between taxable income and book profits and thus gives rise to the phenomenon of *deferred taxes*. Given accelerated tax depreciation, tax payments will be lower initially than they would be if book depreciation were used, but this reduction in taxes is recouped at a later date. The taxes are not forgone, but merely deferred. Finally, *economic depreciation* is the rate at which the *value* of an asset falls from one year to the next. Assets will depreciate in real value owing to wear and tear, obsolescence, increases in their own prices, and increases in the price level—that is, inflation. In periods of inflation, book depreciation, which is based on the original cost of assets, will be lower than economic depreciation, which is based on replacement cost. Economic depreciation is a concept that economists use; unfortunately, it is difficult to measure accurately, since there is typically no reliable market price for capital that

---

[5] Some corporations use a formula for calculating book depreciation that is different from the formula used for tax purposes. The tax system generally uses the declining balance method, which gives higher depreciation in earlier years of an asset's life. Some corporations use the straightline method, which gives the same amount of depreciation in each year. We shall discuss the differences between the two approaches below.

is in use. Likewise, book depreciation and tax depreciation are usually based on arbitrary measures of the useful life of different forms of capital.

Capital cost allowances are established according to a set of rates laid down in the Income Tax Act. The procedure for calculating the capital cost allowance is as follows. Normally, a firm writes off assets according to the *declining balance method*, also referred to as exponential depreciation. Firms may, however, write off some types of assets in accelerated fashion by using the *straightline method*. Under the declining balance method, one obtains the CCA for a given year by applying a set rate of depreciation to the undepreciated original cost of the asset. Consider, for example, a machine purchased for $100,000 that is assigned a depreciation rate, or CCA, of 10 percent. In the first year, the CCA is (0.1 × $100,000) or $10,000. The undepreciated balance is $100,000 − $10,000 = $90,000. This figure becomes the book value of the capital for tax purposes. In year two, depreciation is 10 percent of the undepreciated book value, or (0.1 × $90,000) = $9,000, and the undepreciated balance on the books is $90,000 − $9,000 or $81,000, and so on. Table 4.1 shows the sequence of depreciation allowances for the first six years of an asset's life under the declining balance method. The straightline method, by contrast, applies a given rate of depreciation to the original cost until the asset is fully depreciated; in other words, the writeoff is the same in each year. For example, if a straightline rate of depreciation for a $100,000 asset is 10 percent, the writeoff is $10,000 per year for 10 years. The difference between the two methods, as figure 4.1 shows, is in the time profile of depreciation.[6]

The Income Tax Act identifies 33 categories of assets. Some assets are categorized by type (for example, buildings, computer software), and some by use (for example, manufacturing and processing assets, pollution-control equipment). The declining balance method applies to almost all asset categories, at rates that range from 4 to 100 percent. A few categories are eligible for the straightline method. Each asset category is assigned to a class with a specific CCA rate. For example, machinery and equipment are assigned to class 8, which has a 20 percent depreciation rate, whereas brick, stone, and cement buildings are in class 3, which has a 5 percent depreciation rate. The assignment of assets to classes is meant to conform roughly to actual rates of depreciation, as reflected in the useful life of the asset. In computing its capital cost allowances, a firm pools all assets of a given class together. When the firm acquires additional assets of a given class, it simply increases the undepreciated balance for that class by the cost of the asset.

---

[6] The United States permits a third method of calculating depreciation, the *sum-of-years-digits* method. The proportion of the original asset value allowed as depreciation each year is the number of years of depreciation still remaining divided by the sum of years of life. For example, a 10-year asset has a sum of years of 10 + 9 + 8 + ... + 3 + 2 + 1 = 55. The depreciation allowances for successive years are 10/55, 9/55, 8/55, ... 3/55, 2/55, and 1/55.

**Table 4.1   Sequence of Depreciation Allowances for Six Years**

| Year | Undepreciated cost | Capital cost allowance |
|------|--------------------|------------------------|
| | *dollars* | |
| 1 | 100,000 | 10,000 |
| 2 | 90,000 | 9,000 |
| 3 | 81,000 | 8,100 |
| 4 | 72,900 | 7,290 |
| 5 | 65,610 | 6,561 |
| 6 | 59,049 | 5,905 |

**Figure 4.1   Annual Capital Cost Allowance Calculated by Two Methods**

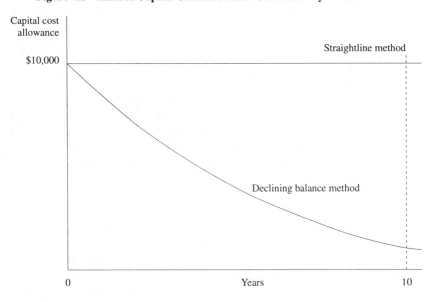

Before the tax reform of 1981, a firm was allowed to claim a full year's CCA on an asset in the tax year in which it was acquired, even if the firm had used the asset for only part of the tax year. Now, however, a firm may write off only one-half of the normal CCA in the year in which the asset is acquired. This provision applies to all asset classes.

### Specific Rules

A number of specific rules apply to the use of capital cost allowances. The most important are as follows:

• *Eligibility.* To be depreciable, an asset must be for business use only and must be used in the current year to produce income. In other words, assets that are held idle or that are used for pleasure are not depreciable. If a firm uses an asset such as a car for both business and pleasure, it may apply CCA only to a proportion of the cost of the asset equivalent to the proportion of time that the asset was used for business during the tax year.

• *Electing not to claim an allowance.* Firms are not obliged to claim any of the CCA for which they are eligible in any given year. For example, if a firm is in a tax-loss position, it may elect not to claim its full depreciation and leave the undepreciated balance for any asset class intact for use in future years.

• *Service lives.* Under the declining balance method, the undepreciated balance becomes smaller and smaller over time but never actually disappears. Once the asset goes out of use, however, the firm may write off the undepreciated balance for that asset in its entirety (provided that it is the only asset remaining in its class). This arrangement ensures that the original cost of the asset is fully written off over the useful life of the asset. If the last remaining asset in a given class is scrapped, a *terminal loss* is created, which the taxpayer may claim in its entirety.

• *Patents and licences.* Patents, franchises, concessions, timber rights, and licences granted for limited periods are income-earning assets and so may be depreciated. The base used is the cost actually incurred for the rights.

• *Ineligible purchases.* As we mentioned above, depreciation is not allowed on properties that are not used to produce income (although this status may vary from year to year). In addition, no depreciation is allowed on current expenses, inventories, land, or dining, sporting, or recreational facilities. Finally, no depreciation is allowed on oil and gas wells, bituminous sands or oil sands deposits, base or precious metal deposits, or non-bedded industrial mineral deposits. These resource deposits benefit from the special tax treatment of resources that we shall discuss later in this section.

• *Rental and leasing properties.* Taxpayers may not use CCAs on rental and leasing properties to create a loss against non-rental income, although they may use losses on rental properties to offset gains on other rental properties. This provision is intended to prevent taxpayers from using rental properties to shelter income from other sources. It does not apply to corporations whose principal business is life insurance or the leasing, renting, developing, or sale of real property.

• *Recapture of depreciation.* If an asset is disposed of and the proceeds of the disposition differ from the undepreciated balance, taxable income must be adjusted to account for the fact that the amount of depreciation given does not correspond to the actual fall in value of the asset. If the undepreciated balance exceeds the revenue from disposing of the asset, the taxpayer may claim a deduction equal to the difference, or a *terminal loss*. On the other hand, if the proceeds of the disposition exceed the undepreciated balance, the excess must be "recaptured" as taxable income. This is done by reducing the undepreciated balance of the appropriate asset class. If the balance is insufficient, the remainder is included immediately as taxable income. Consider, for example, an asset that was originally purchased for $100,000 and whose value CCAs have depreciated to $40,000. Suppose the asset is sold for $60,000. Since this amount exceeds the undepreciated balance by $20,000, the latter amount is recaptured. If there are other assets of the same depreciation class, the $20,000 is recaptured by reducing the undepreciated balance for the class by that amount. If there are no assets of the same class, the taxpayer must add $20,000 to taxable income. In this case, the depreciation is recaptured immediately.

A special case arises if the disposition of the asset yields an amount in excess of the original cost. In this case, there is not only a recapture of depreciation but also a capital gain. For example, suppose that the asset in the above example sells for $120,000. The entire $60,000 of depreciation is recaptured either against the undepreciated balance of other assets of the same class or as income. In addition, the $20,000 capital gain is subject to tax. Since three-quarters of capital gains are taxable, $15,000 is added to taxable income.

### Special Provisions

The above discussion applies to depreciation in normal cases. The federal government has from time to time introduced special treatment under the CCA provisions in order to provide incentives (or disincentives) for the purchase of assets for particular uses or by particular industries. These special provisions are normally temporary. The main current ones are as follows:

• *Research and development (R & D) investment.* The Canadian tax system, like those of most other countries, includes incentives for R & D expenditures. The argument is that these expenditures provide benefits to the economy over and above those obtained by the firms that incur the expenditures. The incentives take two forms—accelerated depreciation and investment tax credits (we shall discuss the latter below). These incentives are available for what are referred to as scientific research and experimental development (SR & ED) activities, which include basic research, applied research, and experimental development. Both capital and current expenditures on SR & ED (except for expenditures on land and buildings) may be deducted immediately, or "expensed." Any expenditures not claimed in a given year may be carried forward indefinitely. This amounts to extremely rapid accelerated depreciation.

• *Accelerated depreciation in mining.* There are several instances of rapid writeoff of capital expenditures in the mining industries. Exploration expenses incurred in Canada may be deducted immediately and carried forward indefinitely, as may preproduction development expenses. Canadian development expenses may be written off at the rate of 30 percent, and so may purchases of resource properties. Finally, expenditures on structures and equipment for new mines or major mine expansions may be written off immediately.

• *Accelerated depreciation in oil and gas.* Similar, though less generous, incentives apply to the oil and gas industry. Canadian exploration expenses may be written off immediately and carried forward indefinitely. Canadian development expenditures may be written off at 30 percent. In oil and gas, unlike mining, preproduction development expenditures are treated as development expenditures and may be written off at 30 percent. The costs of acquiring oil and gas resource properties may be written off at 10 percent. We shall consider the special tax treatment of the resource industries in more detail below.

• *Generous depreciation rates in manufacturing.* The corporate tax system has traditionally favoured manufacturing and processing industries. Until the 1987 income tax reform, firms in these industries could deduct expenditures for machinery and equipment on a straightline basis at a rate of 50 percent. The 1987 reforms eliminated this tax preference but replaced it with a fairly favourable declining balance rate of 30 percent. As we shall see below, manufacturing and processing also benefit from other forms of preferential treatment.

## Interest Deductibility

The other cost of holding capital assets is the interest incurred (or interest forgone) in financing the capital, since the funds tied up could have been used to earn interest elsewhere. In computing its taxable income, a firm may deduct interest payments made during its taxation year. Interest is deductible on money borrowed for the purpose of earning income from a business or property, including money borrowed to purchase shares. Notice that the deduction is for the full amount of nominal interest paid, even if a part of the interest is simply an inflation premium—that is, compensation for the fall in the real value of the asset owing to inflation.

The so-called *thin capitalization provisions* limit the interest deductible on debt owed to "specified" non-residents—that is, non-resident persons or corporations that own more than 25 percent of the shares of any class in the corporation. The proportion of interest paid that these non-residents may claim as a deduction is expressed by the following fraction:

[Debt held by specified non-residents − (3 × equity)]/debt held by specified non-residents

As one can see, the fraction is larger the greater is the quantity of debt held by specified non-residents relative to the value of their equity. The thin capitalization provisions provide a way, though a rather rough one, of preventing foreign corporations from avoiding Canadian corporate taxes. A foreign corporation that owns Canadian subsidiaries pays a full 38 percent tax on the return to equity, plus any surtaxes in place (see below). If it can hold its assets in the firm as debt, however, it may deduct the full interest cost of the debt and pay only the withholding tax on non-resident income of 25 percent (or less in the case of residents of tax-treaty countries). In the absence of the thin capitalization provisions, therefore, there would be an incentive to set up a corporation with limited equity capital and finance most of its investments with interest-deductible debt.

Interest payments are a rough indicator of one of the opportunity costs of purchasing capital equipment: the outlay of funds on capital assets yields a stream of returns over the life of the asset, but at the same time interest on the funds invested is forgone. The deductibility of interest on debt, however, does not necessarily capture all of the opportunity costs, in the form of forgone interest, of holding capital. The capital may have been financed not by debt, but by the issue of equity (shares) or by retained earnings, neither of which results in deductible interest costs. Dividend payments to shareholders are not deductible, although the costs incurred in issuing or selling the shares are deductible (including legal, accounting, and printing costs but not dealers' commissions). Thus the financing of capital by equity involves an opportunity cost in the form of forgone interest by the shareholders. We shall discuss the economic implications of this state of affairs later in the chapter. For now, it is enough to note that the absence of a deduction for the cost of equity financing implies that the corporate tax is a tax on the equity income generated by corporations for their shareholders.

## The Treatment of Inventories

Inventories held by a firm are a form of asset, and for tax purposes their acquisition is a capital expense. Inventories include both production inputs purchased from other firms and goods-in-process held as stocks for eventual sale. The costing of inventories for tax purposes is done on an accrual basis. This means that a firm may not deduct the cost of acquiring inventories when they are purchased; it may deduct the cost only when the inventories are taken out of storage and used. Given costing on an accruals basis, there are three sorts of costs associated with the holding and use of inventories. First, there are the costs of storing the goods. These costs are deductible when they are incurred. Second, there are the costs, in the form of interest incurred or forgone, of financing the stock of inventories. As in the case of other forms of capital, only incurred interest costs are deductible. Finally, there are the actual costs of the goods held in inventory. These costs are deducted, when the inventory is used, according to *first in, first out* (FIFO) accounting principles. That is, when an item of a given kind is taken out of inventory and used, a deduction is allowed equal to the acquisition cost of the oldest item of that kind that is held in inventory. Note that the acquisition cost can be either the cost of purchasing the good from another firm or the cost of producing it (including wages, materials, and so forth) by the firm itself.

The use of FIFO accounting for inventories implies that in times of inflation the deduction for the use of an inventory is less than the replacement value of the inventory. Given inflation, in other words, the allowable deduction will be less than the true imputed cost of using the inventory.

## Scientific Research and Experimental Development Expenditures

The corporate tax treats scientific research and development expenditures liberally. All current SR & ED expenditures, whether they are incurred in

Canada or elsewhere, may be deducted fully. Eligible expenditures include both expenditures on research undertaken by the firm itself and payments to other institutions for research undertaken on its behalf. If the expenditures are to be eligible, the research must be scientific. Other types of research including market research, product testing, and the like are not considered to be scientific research. As we mentioned above, capital SR & ED expenditures that are undertaken in Canada are also fully deductible in the year in which they are incurred. Capital expenditures undertaken in Canada in order to acquire property, other than land, that is to be used for scientific research are deductible according to the capital cost allowances established for the class into which they fall. Research expenditures are, of course, of a capital nature to the extent that they lead to the acquisition of knowledge that is useful in producing output over a number of years. Nonetheless, they are not treated as capital expenditures for tax purposes. Obviously, the allowance of an immediate deduction for expenditures of this kind provides some incentive to undertake them.

As we shall discuss later, both current and capital SR & ED expenditures are also eligible for partially refundable investment tax credits. The current credit rate is normally 20 percent, but it is enhanced to 35 percent for smaller Canadian controlled private corporations (CCPCs). The credits reduce the amount of SR & ED expenditures that the firm may deduct.

## Charities

Registered charities are exempt from income taxation and may issue receipts to taxpayers who make donations to them. As we discussed in chapter 3, the income tax system allows taxpayers to claim credits for charitable donations, within limits, against their income tax liabilities. To be registered, a charity must satisfy several criteria that have to do with the nature of activities it undertakes, the use of its income, and the expenditure of its donations. There are two types of charities, *charitable organizations* and *charitable foundations*, and slightly different rules apply to each.

Charitable organizations are organizations that devote all of their resources to charitable activities (for example, the relief of poverty, the advancement of religion or education, or activities intended to the benefit of the community as a whole). They may be corporations, trusts, or other organizations. They are allowed to undertake business activities that are related to their charitable activities.

A charitable organization may give up to 50 percent of its income (net of capital gains and losses) to other charities. The receiving charity then includes these donations in its own income. Finally, a charitable organization is obliged to spend in each tax year 80 percent of the receipted donations that it received in the preceding year. Failure to do this may result in a revocation of registration and all of the tax advantages that registration entails.

Charitable foundations are corporations or trusts that are operated solely for charitable purposes—usually, their primary activity is to make donations to other charities. The tax rules that apply to a foundation depend on whether it is a *public foundation* or a *private foundation*. A charitable foundation is public if at least 50 percent of its directors and trustees deal at arm's length, and if no more than 75 percent of its capital was obtained from one individual or group of individuals. Otherwise, it is a private foundation.

Public foundations, like charitable organizations, are allowed to carry on a related business. They may incur no debt and may not acquire control of any corporation. Unlike charitable organizations, they may disburse as much of their annual income as they wish to other charities. They are, however, subject to minimum expenditure requirements. Each year, they must expend the greater of two amounts: 80 percent of the receipted donations received in the previous tax year and 90 percent of the current year's income (net of capital gains and losses). They may generally carry forward disbursements in excess of 90 percent of income in a given year as expenditures for the following three years. In computing income, the foundation may take a reserve equal to the current year's income. The reserve must be included in the following year's income.

Private foundations may not carry on a related business, and they are subject to somewhat different disbursement requirements. The capital of a private foundation is divided into *qualified investments* (those used in the work of the foundation) and *unqualified investments* (all of the rest). In the case of qualified investments, the disbursement quota is 90 percent of the income earned by the investments in the current year. In the case of unqualified investments, the quota is the greater of 5 percent of the investments' market value (evaluated at the beginning of the tax year) and 90 percent of the income from the investments during the tax year.

### Intercorporate Dividends

Dividends received by Canadian public corporations are exempt from taxable income. The purpose of the exemption is to avoid the double taxation that would otherwise arise, since dividends are paid out of income that has already been taxed at the corporate level. Capital gains on shares held in other companies, however, are taxable, despite the fact that they too may arise from after-tax income.

Dividends received by private corporations are subject to a 33⅓ percent tax, referred to as a part IV tax because it is specified in that part of the Income Tax Act. When the corporation pays out the dividends to its shareholders, however, its corporate tax on those dividends is refunded. Part IV tax acts as a disincentive to accumulate tax-free dividends in a private corporation, such as an investment holding company, in order to defer personal tax payments. The 33⅓ percent part IV tax rate happens to be nearly equivalent to the rate at which someone in the top federal tax bracket would pay personal income tax on dividends received. Consider, for example, a person who receives a dividend of $100 from Canadian sources. This dividend is grossed-up by 25 percent to $125 and added to taxable income. For a person with a 46 percent tax rate, approximately the top personal rate in 1997, tax payable is

0.46 × \$125, or \$58. The taxpayer then claims a dividend tax credit of 0.2 × \$125, or \$25, and thus is left with a net tax payment of \$58 − \$25, or \$33.

Dividends that Canadian corporations, public or private, receive from foreign affiliates (subsidiaries) that carry on an active business in tax-treaty countries are tax-free. This is so because, presumably, foreign taxes have already been withheld against them. As we shall discuss below, no foreign tax credit is allowed for these taxes. For branch-plant operations abroad, income earned is fully taxable under the Canadian corporation income tax and credit is allowed for foreign income taxes paid. Any repatriation of earnings is simply an internal transfer of funds and has no tax implications.

## Investment Income

Apart from dividends and capital gains, the investment income of public corporations is treated as ordinary income. Dividends received by public corporations, as we mentioned above, are exempt, and like the personal tax the corporate tax requires the inclusion of only three-quarters of capital gains in income. The sale of a business is treated as a capital gain rather than as ordinary income.

In the case of private corporations, the situation is somewhat more complicated. All of their investment income, excluding dividends received from foreign affiliates and including three-quarters of capital gains, is fully taxed as non-active business income. The taxation of this income, however, is fully integrated with the taxation of shareholders' income under the personal income of shareholders—that is, full credit is given for corporate tax paid through a combination of tax refunds to the corporation and the dividend tax credit applicable to personal income. Thus investment income flows through private corporations to their shareholders without bearing any corporate tax. We shall discuss the integration of the corporate and personal taxes further below.

Financial corporations, which receive a considerable part of their income as investment income, are subject to other special provisions, which we shall discuss below as well.

## Cooperatives

Although most cooperatives are incorporated, they receive special treatment under the corporate tax. Some producers' marketing cooperatives, even if they do earn income, are non-income-earning in the eyes of the law, which deems them to be simply agents of the producers. The income earned by these cooperatives is passed on to shareholders and is treated as their income for tax purposes. Non-profit or charitable cooperatives, like other non-profit or charitable corporations, are exempt from tax.

Cooperatives whose income is taxable—so-called *patronage cooperatives*—obtain the benefit of the small business tax rate discussed later in this chapter. They can also take advantage of a tax provision that allows the deduction of dividends paid to patrons on the basis of their volume of business with the firm. In fact, all corporations are allowed to deduct patronage dividends against taxable income, but ordinary corporations are obviously not in a position to make much use of this provision.

There are limits to the amount of patronage dividends that a cooperative may deduct. If patronage dividends are not paid to non-members of the cooperative, they may be deducted only against the income earned from members. Dividends that are paid to non-members may be deducted only if they are paid at the same rate as dividends paid to members. Patronage dividends must be given prior advertisement to members and must be paid on the basis of patronage, although they may vary with the class, grade, or quality of products. They must also be paid within 12 months of the end of the relevant tax year. They do not, however, have to be paid in cash but may instead be credited as a security and used for the (tax-free) internal financing of the cooperative. Patronage dividends paid as securities are placed in a revolving fund and paid out or repurchased in the order in which they were put in. Finally, some provinces require cooperatives to set aside a percentage of their income as a reserve subject to tax.

Patronage dividends in excess of $100 paid to a Canadian resident in a single tax year are subject to a withholding tax of 25 percent. The tax is credited to the member when the patronage dividend is taxed in his hands. The withholding tax compensates for the benefit of the possible delay between the earning of income by the cooperative and its taxation in the hands of the member. Patronage dividends received on account of consumer purchases are not taxable in the hands of recipients. All others are. Patronage dividends, however, are not eligible for the dividend tax credit.

## Financial Institutions

There are many kinds of incorporated financial institutions. Their function in the economy is to act as intermediaries between savers and lenders. They accept the savings of the public in the form of deposits or premiums and use the proceeds to make loans for the purpose of earning investment income. We have already dealt with the tax treatment of private corporations that earn investment income. The tax system looks favourably upon the intermediary or flowthrough role of private corporations, and the tax treatment of their investment income—that is, non-active business income—is fully integrated with the tax treatment of their shareholders' income. There is therefore no "double taxation" of this form of business income.

Several types of financial institutions, however, are public corporations and are taxed accordingly—for example, chartered banks, trust companies, credit unions, and insurance companies. All of the rules applicable to the taxation of corporate income apply to them. They pay the full corporate tax rate on taxable income, which includes interest earned and three-quarters of capital gains but excludes intercorporate dividends. They may deduct interest paid on the deposits they hold. Individual types of financial corporations are also subject to various special tax provisions:

• *Chartered banks* may deduct from income a reserve to cover losses on loans and bad and doubtful debt up to a reasonable amount. That amount is calculated as a moving average of the bank's loan losses in the past five years. Banks need not withhold tax on interest payments to non-residents on their foreign currency deposits, or on interest payments in Canadian currency on Canadian dollar deposits paid by a branch or office outside Canada. Banks, other deposit-taking institutions, and life insurance companies must pay a special capital tax. Ordinary income tax liabilities are creditable against it, so it acts as a *minimum tax*; that is, a tax to ensure that the institution does not escape corporate taxes in any given year. All of the provinces also levy capital taxes on banks and trust and loan companies.

• *Credit unions, caisses populaires, and savings and credit unions* are subject to a lower rate of corporate tax identical to the rate applied to small businesses, which we shall discuss later in this section. They may deduct a reserve of a prescribed amount (currently 1.5 percent) based on certain assets (bonds, debentures, agreements of sale, mortgages, and debt owing). This provision serves the same purpose as the banks' deduction for bad debt. The reserve taken in one year is included in taxable income in the following year, when a new reserve is deducted. In addition, these institutions may deduct all payments that they allocate to members in proportion to their borrowing during the year. These payments are equivalent to patronage dividends, which we discussed above; they are, accordingly, not eligible for the dividend tax credit in the hands of members.

• *Insurance corporations.* Although life insurance corporations are deemed to be public corporations for tax purposes, they are subject to several special provisions. They may deduct dividends received from taxable Canadian corporations apart from dividends on term preferred shares acquired in the ordinary course of business. They may allocate capital gains to particular policy holders, who are then deemed to have realized the gain. Investment income that life insurance companies earn on behalf of their policy holders is taxed at a flat rate of 15 percent, and the mortality gains that are paid out to policy holders from reserves are tax-free. Resident life insurance companies are not taxed on business income earned outside Canada and are not allowed credits for foreign taxes paid. They may deduct a policy reserve for each class of policy holders. Insurance corporations of all types that receive all of their premiums from charitable organizations, churches, and schools are tax-exempt, as are those that receive at least one-half of their premium income from farmers and fishers.

• *Investment and mutual fund corporations.* Corporations (including mutual fund corporations) are deemed to be investment corporations if they are Canadian public corporations and meet certain conditions regarding their ownership—no shareholder may own more than 25 percent of the issued capital stock—and the source of their income—for example, 80 percent of their property must consist of financial assets, 95 percent of their income must be derived from these assets, 85 percent of their revenue must be from Canadian sources, and less than 25 percent of their income may be interest income. Investment and mutual fund corporations may distribute capital gains by means of special capital gains dividends and through redemption of their shares. Share redemptions and capital gains dividends are treated as capital transactions and are taxed as capital gains in the hands of shareholders.

## Resource Producers

Corporations involved in the production of minerals, oil, and gas are liable for corporate income tax on their taxable income at the usual rates. Their taxable income is calculated in much the same way as that of other corporations, but there are several special provisions that affect their deductions for capital costs and for other types of taxes paid; these provisions are discussed here. Resource corporations are usually also subject to additional forms of taxation at both the federal and provincial levels; we shall discuss this subject later in the chapter.

Three types of provisions under the corporate income tax allow resource companies generous writeoffs for capital costs. First, as we mentioned earlier, mining companies obtain accelerated depreciation on capital used in starting or expanding mines and for the costs of exploration and the costs of developing resource properties. Second, the corporate tax allows an additional deduction known as a *resource allowance* against resource income. Third, firms may pass exploration and development expenditures through the firm to its owners by means of a device known as a *flowthrough share*. This device enables the owners of a firm in a loss position to take immediate benefit of the writeoff, which would otherwise be carried forward by the firm. The following subsections expand on this summary.

### Exploration, Resource Development, and Acquisition Expenses

Corporations that are in the business of producing non-renewable resources are allowed to write off all exploration expenses in Canada immediately. Exploration expenses include any expense incurred in determining the existence, location, and extent of a non-renewable resource. Pre-production development expenses for new mines, but not for new oil and gas wells, are also treated as exploration expenses and may be deducted immediately. Firms may write off the development costs of Canadian mining properties and of oil and gas wells at a declining balance rate of 30 percent. They may write off the costs of acquiring Canadian mineral resource properties at a declining-balance rate of 30 percent and the costs of acquiring oil and gas leases and wells at a rate of 10 percent. The limit on these deductions in any one year is the amount of income earned before loss carryforward deductions and after the deduction of dividends received from taxable Canadian corporations. The firm may carry any unclaimed balance forward indefinitely to the income of future years. If the corporation is part of an association or syndicate, it may claim its share of the expenses of the association.

The corporate tax also allows a partial deduction for foreign exploration and development expenses. All resident corporations (whether resources are their principal business or not) can deduct exploration and development expenses incurred outside Canada to the extent of their income from foreign sources. If this income is less than 10 percent of expenses, the firm may apply the balance of the 10 percent against other income.

Since expenditures for exploration and development contribute to the earning of income in the future, it is reasonable to argue that they are in fact capital expenditures rather than current expenditures. They represent the cost of acquiring an asset—a mineral deposit, for example—that is used up over time. By this reckoning, the tax provisions for the immediate deduction of exploration expenses and the rapid writeoff of development expenses (at rates that generally bear no relation to the useful life of the asset) give the resource industries a considerable advantage relative to other industries. We shall discuss the justification for this and other advantages afforded to the resource industries later in this chapter.

## The Resource Allowance

Before 1974, resource companies were allowed to deduct provincial resource taxes and royalties from taxable income. This deduction is no longer allowed: it was argued that it encouraged provincial governments to increase their levies on resource taxes, since part of the cost of any increase would be borne by the federal government rather than the firm. Instead, corporations and individuals are allowed a so-called resource allowance—a deduction of 25 percent of their "net profits" from resource production, defined as profits calculated before the deduction of exploration and development expenditures and interest.

This change in the federal tax treatment of provincial royalties was one result of a dispute between the federal government and the provinces over the rents accruing from resources. According to the British North America Act of 1867, especially as revised by the Constitution Act of 1982, resources are under the authority of provincial governments. With the great rise in oil and gas prices in the 1970s, however, conflict arose over the treatment of resource revenues under the scheme of federal-provincial equalization, whereby the federal government transfers funds to the less well-off provinces according to the shortfall of their tax bases relative to a national standard, and over the extent of provincial rights to collect resource revenues.[7] Unlike other tax sources, oil and gas revenues had not been fully equalized, since to

---

[7] For an account of the equalization system and federal-provincial fiscal relations generally, see Robin W. Boadway and Paul A.R. Hobson, *Intergovernmental Fiscal Relations in Canada*, Canadian Tax Paper no. 96 (Toronto: Canadian Tax Foundation, 1993).

equalize them would be very costly to the federal government. Meanwhile, the federal government had claimed a share in the revenues from oil and gas, first by imposing an export tax on oil and gas to keep domestic prices down and later by levying taxes on them as part of the national energy program. The disallowance of provincial royalties as deductions further increased federal resource revenues. Finally, the federal government successfully challenged in the courts the resource tax that Saskatchewan levied on oil companies, arguing that it interfered with interprovincial trade and was a direct tax on non-residents of the province. These issues were resolved in part by the constitutional amendments of 1982, which explicitly gave the provinces the right to tax their non-renewable resources as they saw fit. The non-deductibility of provincial resource levies remains in place, however, as does the incomplete equalization of provincial oil and gas revenues. A full account of these issues would take us too far afield.

### Flowthrough Shares

Oil and gas and mining corporations may finance their exploration and development expenditures by issuing *flowthrough shares*, which are essentially instruments for allowing the owners of corporations in a loss position to obtain refundability of those losses. The mechanism is straightforward. When flowthrough shares are issued, the shareholders who purchase them are entitled to reduce their personal incomes by the tax deductions that the corporation would otherwise claim on exploration and development expenditures, which as we have seen are generous. In turn, the corporation forgoes the right to claim these expenses against its own income: the corporation is deemed to have renounced the exploration and development expenses to the new shareholders. Flowthrough share financing is open to all oil and gas corporations for any Canadian exploration and development expenses, including Canadian oil and gas property expenses, but it is primarily useful to corporations that are in a loss position (such as many junior exploration companies) and so cannot obtain refundability of their losses. In fact, flowthrough shares serve as an indirect means of introducing loss offsetting into the corporate tax system selectively for resource firms.[8]

## The Rate Structure

Once one has obtained the tax base, taxable income, by deducting all allowable expenses from the firm's revenues, one applies a corporate tax rate to this base to obtain the firm's tax liability. The corporate tax rate has varied frequently over time, and it can vary according to the circumstances of firms. To begin with, there is the general corporate tax rate applied by the federal government, which was 38 percent in 1997. For income earned in a province,

---

[8] For an analysis of the effects of flowthrough shares, see Vijay M. Jog, Gordon J. Lenjosek, and Kenneth J. McKenzie, "Flowthrough Shares: Premium-Sharing and Cost-Effectiveness" (1996), vol. 44, no. 4 *Canadian Tax Journal* 1016-51.

**Table 4.2   Federal and Provincial Corporate Income Tax Rates, 1987 and 1997**

| | 1987 | | | 1997 | | |
|---|---|---|---|---|---|---|
| | Small business | Manufac- turing and processing | General | Small business | Manufac- turing and processing | General |
| | | | *percent* | | | |
| Federal . . . . . . . . . . . . . | 15 | 30 | 36 | 12 | 21 | 28 |
| Newfoundland . . . . . . . . | 10 | 16 | 16 | 5 | 5 | 14 |
| Prince Edward Island . . . | 10 | 15 | 15 | 7.5 | 7.5 | 16 |
| Nova Scotia . . . . . . . . . . | 10 | 15 | 15 | 5 | 16 | 16 |
| New Brunswick . . . . . . . | 5 | 15 | 15 | 7 | 17 | 27 |
| Quebec . . . . . . . . . . . . . | 3.22 | 5.5 | 14 | 5.91 | 9.15 | 16.71 |
| Ontario . . . . . . . . . . . . . | 10 | 14.5 | 15.5 | 9.5 | 13.5 | 15.5 |
| Manitoba . . . . . . . . . . . | 10 | 17 | 17 | 9 | 17 | 17 |
| Saskatchewan . . . . . . . . | 10 | 17 | 17 | 8 | 17 | 17 |
| Alberta . . . . . . . . . . . . . | 5 | 8 | 14 | 6 | 14.5 | 15.5 |
| British Columbia . . . . . . | 9.51 | 15 | 15 | 9 | 16.5 | 16.5 |
| Northwest Territories . . . | 10 | 10 | 10 | 5 | 14 | 14 |
| Yukon . . . . . . . . . . . . . | 5 | 10 | 10 | 6 | 2.5 | 15 |

Source: Karin Treff and David B. Perry, *Finances of the Nation 1997* (Toronto: Canadian Tax Foundation, 1997), 4:4, 4:8, and 4:9, tables 4.2, 4.4, and 4.5.

this rate is reduced by 10 percent, leaving 28 percent. Each province applies its own rate to corporate income earned in its jurisdiction. The basic federal rate of 28 percent for income earned in the provinces is reduced to 21 percent for manufacturing and processing firms and to 12 percent for small firms. Each province too has a preferential rate for small firms, and some also have a lower rate for manufacturing and processing firms. Table 4.2 shows the federal and provincial rates in 1997.

The corporate tax rates currently in place are relatively low by post-war standards. In 1987, the general federal tax rate was 46 percent, and for a period in the 1960s it was 50 percent. The major income tax reform of 1987 broadened the base and reduced the rates in order to make the corporate tax less intrusive in business decision making and the corporate tax rate compar- able to those of our major international competitors. The Mintz committee has recommended further base broadening, so that the rate can be brought down to 33 percent, and elimination of the preferential manufacturing and processing rate.

Each of these deviations from the general federal rate requires some separate discussion.

### The Tax Abatement to Provinces

Canada is a federation in which considerable fiscal power lies with the provinces. The provinces have both significant expenditure responsibilities and independent legislative authority to raise revenues through taxation.

Unlike the subnational units in most other federations, the provinces share virtually all of the major tax bases with the federal government. The corporate income tax is one of the tax bases occupied jointly by the federal government and the provinces. Thus firms must comply with corporate taxes not only at two levels of government, but also, possibly, in more than one province at the same time.

In order to avoid the enormous compliance costs, collection costs, and inefficiencies that would arise if corporate tax systems varied significantly across jurisdictions, the provinces and the federal government have adopted measures intended to harmonize their corporate taxes. All of the provinces except Alberta, Ontario, and Quebec participate in tax collection agreements with the federal government under which the latter collects corporate taxes on behalf of the provinces and the provinces apply their own tax rates to a base set by the federal government. Even in the provinces that administer their own corporate taxes, the provincial tax agrees fairly closely with its federal counterpart; in particular, these provinces' tax bases are quite similar to the federal one. Moreover, all of the provinces abide by the same rules for allocating taxable income among jurisdictions, the so-called allocation formula. According to this formula, a corporation's income is allocated among jurisdictions, including foreign jurisdictions, according to the average of revenues received and wages and salaries paid in each jurisdiction. For taxable income allocated to a province, the provincial corporate tax rate applies; for taxable income allocated to foreign sources, the general federal rate applies. In order to facilitate this allocation, the federal government abates or reduces its general tax rate by 10 percentage points—that is, from 38 to 28 percent—in taxing income earned within a province. The provinces are then free to select their own provincial corporate tax rate. As table 4.2 shows, their rates are similar but not identical.

## The Small Business Rate

All Canadian-controlled private corporations are taxed at a preferential rate on the first $200,000 of their active business income. This so-called *small business deduction* reduces their corporate tax rate to between 20 and 24.5 percent on this income, depending on the province in which the income is earned. (Small businesses are also liable for temporary corporate surtaxes, which are discussed further below.) The small business deduction is available to all CCPCs, but it is phased out for CCPCs with capital that exceeds $10 million. The evidence suggests, however, that the bulk of the total deduction claimed is claimed by small firms. The Mintz committee calculated that 90 percent of the small business deduction went to firms whose total business income was no greater than $200,000.[9]

---

[9] Mintz committee report, supra footnote 1, at 5.9, table 5.3. During the 1970s and early 1980s, the small business deduction was subject to a cumulative limit.

The purpose of the small business deduction is to compensate small businesses for some of the disadvantages they presumably face in establishing themselves and competing with larger firms. It is argued, for example, that outside financing is more costly for small firms than for large ones. This is so in part because many small firms are relatively new firms with little credit history. Lenders will typically not have enough information about these firms to judge their prospects and will therefore extend loans to them only on terms that assume a relatively high level of risk. The problem is compounded by the fact that small businesses are more risky as a rule than larger ones. They tend to be more specialized and less able to diversify their risk internally, and they often operate in areas which are innovative but uncertain. The riskiness of small businesses puts them at a disadvantage in another respect as well: as we have noted, the tax system does not treat risky enterprises favourably, since it does not treat tax losses symmetrically with profits. Small firms also face a proportionately larger burden of business taxes that are not profit-related than larger businesses do. These taxes include property taxes, payroll taxes, and commodity taxes levied on purchases. Finally, many of the costs of complying with the tax system are much the same for all firms, regardless of size; consequently, they place a relatively heavier burden on small firms than on large ones. These costs include not only the costs of filing the various tax forms, but also the costs of preparing for the possibility of tax audits. Compliance with the GST in particular is alleged to be disproportionately costly for small businesses. The small business deduction helps to offset these disadvantages, though it is useful only if the firm is in a tax-paying position.

The small business tax rate also melds nicely with the personal tax system. As we shall see later, the combination of the small business deduction, the dividend tax credit, and the partial exemption for capital gains roughly ensures that for small businesses the corporate tax is fully integrated with the personal tax. In effect, the owners of small private corporations are ultimately taxed as if their firms were unincorporated businesses. This arrangement removes any incentive for a firm to decide to incorporate for tax reasons alone.

## The Manufacturing and Processing Tax Rate

The federal government taxes manufacturing and processing profits earned in Canada at the very favourable rate of 21 percent. (The small business rate does not distinguish manufacturing and processing from other activities.) In addition, five provinces—Newfoundland, Prince Edward Island, Quebec, Ontario, and Alberta—all offer preferential rates; the most generous rates apply in the first three of these provinces.

The preferential tax treatment of manufacturing and processing reflects a tradition in Canadian industrial policy that has been part of our history since the government of Sir John A. Macdonald used tariff protection to encourage the development of a viable manufacturing sector and thus develop the national economy. Recent years, however, have seen a shift in circumstances that has called preferential industrial policies into question. The manufacturing sector has certainly matured since the early years of the Canadian economy and it is not clear that it still needs special treatment. The advent of freer trade has afforded opportunities elsewhere in the world for Canadian manufacturing industries to establish market penetration, so it is no longer necessary to protect the domestic market. More generally, economic policy has come to recognize the importance of allowing industries to exploit their comparative advantages unfettered by tax considerations. In addition, the structure of industry is changing rapidly. Some of the most dynamic and rapidly growing industries are in the services sector. It is not at all clear that they should have to operate at a tax disadvantage relative to manufacturing and the resource industries. For all of these reasons, the issue of the tax treatment of manufacturing and processing relative to the tax treatment of other industries is on the table. The 1987 income tax reform went some way toward eliminating preferential treatment of manufacturing and processing by removing a number of the generous accelerated depreciation provisions available to them. The Mintz committee has recommended that the federal government take the next step and eliminate the manufacturing and processing tax rate. We shall return to this issue later in the chapter.

## The Corporate Surtax

From time to time, the federal and provincial governments levy temporary *surtaxes* over and above the regular tax rate. In recent years, for example, governments anxious to raise additional amounts of revenue in order to reduce budgetary deficits have resorted to surtaxes on income taxes, both corporate and personal. A surtax is a "tax on a tax": it is calculated as a percentage of the normal tax liability. In 1997, the federal corporate surtax was 4 percent of the basic federal tax rate of 28 percent, or $0.04 \times 28 = 1.12$ percentage points of corporate tax. This surtax applies equally to small businesses and to manufacturing and processing; that is, the deductions for these firms do not affect the surtax liability. With the surtax, then, the federal tax rate is 29.12 percent, the manufacturing and processing rate 22.12 percent, and the small business rate 13.12 percent.

Some provinces also levy their own surtaxes. For example, in 1997 Quebec levied a surtax of 2.8 percent of all corporate taxes payable. Ontario imposes a surtax of 4 percent on the excess over $200,000 of taxable incomes of CCPCs. This surtax effectively phases out the preferential small business tax in the case of large CCPCs.

## Investment Tax Credits

From time to time, governments use tax credits to encourage investment. Tax credits are typically calculated as a percentage of the investment and are used to reduce taxes otherwise payable. Some tax credits are refundable; others may be carried forward if the firm cannot use them in a given year. Before the income tax reform of 1987, the corporate tax system allowed a general investment tax credit of 7 percent on all investments in Canada; much higher rates applied to investments in high-unemployment regions such as Atlantic Canada and the Gaspé region of Quebec. The reform eliminated the general investment tax credit, but the credit for Atlantic Canada and the Gaspé region remained; it is referred to as the Atlantic Canada investment tax credit (AITC).

The tax credit rate under the AITC is 10 percent of qualifying investments, which include buildings, machinery, and equipment used in farming, fishing, logging, mining, oil and gas, or manufacturing and processing. The AITC reduces tax liabilities, but it also reduces the base for capital cost allowances for the investments concerned. Critics (such as the Mintz committee) argue that the increase in investment achieved by the AITC is not sufficient to justify the high revenue cost of the program. They also point out that the AITC's base is relatively narrow, and that it excludes the important growing areas of services and high-tech computer-oriented industries. The Mintz committee recommended the abolition of the AITC and the introduction of more direct incentive measures in its place.

The only other sizable investment tax credit offered by the federal government is one for research and development. We have already shown that SR & ED spending benefits from liberal capital cost allowances. All SR & ED spending, capital and current, is eligible for a general tax credit of 20 percent; for small CCPCs, the figure is 35 percent. The credit reduces current taxes, but it also reduces the deduction that can be claimed for SR & ED in the following year. The standard carryback periods of 3 years and carryforward of 10 years apply, but some refundability is allowed as well. Up to 40 percent of the SR & ED tax credit is refundable for large corporations and unincorporated businesses, while the credit is fully refundable for small CCPCs. All of the provinces allow immediate writeoffs of SR & ED expenditures, and several offer SR & ED tax credits as well, with rates that range from 10 to 15 percent. All in all, the Canadian tax regime for R & D is the most generous among OECD countries.

Some provinces offer other sorts of investment tax credits as well. Manitoba, Saskatchewan, and Prince Edward Island provide general non-refundable investment tax credits. Quebec offers investment tax credits for worker training and investments in small businesses. Ontario, too, has an investment tax credit for training, and also a capital tax credit for banks that invest in small businesses.

## The Foreign Tax Credit

Corporations resident in Canada that earn income from branch plant operations outside Canada may be subject to corporate income tax in the country in which the income is earned. This income is also taxable in Canada. In order to avoid double taxation, the Income Tax Act allows firms a tax credit against Canadian corporate taxes for foreign business income taxes paid to other national governments or their political subdivisions (for example, states of the United States). Firms may carry these credits forward for up to five years.

The situation is somewhat different in the case of income earned from foreign subsidiaries of Canadian firms that operate in tax treaty countries. In this case, the income accruing to the Canadian firm takes the form of repatriated dividends. Since these dividends enter Canada tax-free, no foreign tax credit is allowed for foreign taxes paid on the income that generated the dividends. This treatment of dividends from subsidiaries differs from their treatment in the United States. There, dividends received from subsidiaries are taxable and a tax credit is given for foreign taxes deemed to have been paid on their account. If tax rates abroad are lower than US tax rates, this provision will give firms an incentive to postpone taxes by retaining earnings in the subsidiary rather than repatriating them. No such incentive exists in the Canadian system.

## Other Tax Credits

The federal government and the provinces also offer a variety of less important tax credits. They include federal tax credits for charitable donations, federal and provincial tax credits for gifts to Canada and the provinces, and, less justifiably, perhaps, federal and provincial tax credits for political contributions. The federal government offers a tax credit for provincial logging taxes paid, as do British Columbia and Quebec. Alberta offers a royalty tax credit on oil royalties paid in the province, as well as deductibility of royalties from taxable income. British Columbia and Saskatchewan offer a tax credit for the amount of provincial tax that arises from the federal disallowance of resource royalties as an expense. Finally, British Columbia, Nova Scotia, Quebec, Ontario, Manitoba, Saskatchewan, and the federal government all offer tax credits for film production.

## Capital Taxes

Both the federal government and the provinces levy capital taxes, that is, annual taxes based on some measure of the value of capital in the firm. Although these taxes are not corporate taxes as such, they act as supplements to the corporate tax and are interwoven with it to some extent. Federal and provincial capital taxes differ somewhat, so we shall describe each in turn.

The federal government levies two capital taxes. One is a general capital tax that applies to the value of a corporation's capital in excess of $10 million. The value of capital for this purpose includes both shareholders' equity and debt; an investment allowance ensures that capital is not counted in more than one corporation. The rate of tax is 0.225 percent of capital, but the corporate surtax may be credited against the capital tax. The crediting is applicable to the three preceding and seven succeeding years if it is not exhausted in the current year. This arrangement implies that the capital tax serves in part as a *minimum corporate tax*—in other words, as a tax that ensures that corporations pay some tax whether they are profitable or not, but that is offset to the extent that the corporate tax is being paid. It is, of course, a minimum tax only for large corporations; smaller firms are relieved of what is otherwise a tax that is insensitive to a firm's profits.

The second form of federal capital tax is applicable only to financial institutions. It is applied at a rate of 1 percent to capital between $200 million and $300 million and at a rate of 1.25 percent of capital in excess of $300 million. "Capital" for this purpose as well includes shareholders' equity and debt, but it excludes deposits. This capital tax, too, acts as a minimum tax, since corporate tax liabilities can be offset against the tax. Temporary surtaxes have been levied on the capital tax of financial institutions from time to time.

The provinces levy an array of capital taxes. All of the provinces except Newfoundland, Prince Edward Island, and Alberta levy general capital taxes; the rates vary from 0.19 percent in Nova Scotia to 0.64 percent in Quebec. In addition, all of the provinces levy capital taxes on financial institutions—generally at rates of about 3 percent, a figure that is substantially higher than the federal rate. Provincial corporate taxes are not creditable against provincial capital taxes, so the latter do not act as minimum corporate taxes in the way that the federal capital taxes do. On the other hand, unlike federal capital taxes, provincial capital taxes are deductible against federal and provincial corporate taxable income. It has been argued, indeed, that this is one reason why their rates are relatively high. Accepting this argument, the Mintz committee recommended that the deductibility of provincial capital taxes be eliminated. It also recommended that federal and provincial capital taxes be harmonized, in much the same way as corporate taxes are now harmonized, in order to achieve more uniformity of capital tax bases and reduce collection and compliance costs.

## The Withholding Tax

Payments by a resident corporation to non-resident shareholders or creditors are subject to a withholding tax. The general withholding tax rate is 25 percent, but lower rates apply to payments to residents of countries with which Canada has a bilateral tax treaty—countries that include Canada's major trading partners. The treaty rates vary with the type of payment. Recent treaty negotiations have settled on 5 percent for dividends, 10 percent for interest, and no withholding for certain types of royalties. In the past, typical rates were 15 percent for dividends and interest and 10 percent for royalties. Interest paid by a Canadian resident corporation to a non-resident at arms' length is exempt from the withholding tax, a provision that facilitates access by Canadian corporations to world capital markets.

## An Overview of Differential Tax Treatment

The corporate tax system is fairly complicated. It is not surprising, therefore, that it applies unevenly across the economy. The corporate tax burden can

**Table 4.3  Average Effective Federal Corporate Tax Rates
by Industry and Size of Firm, 1993 and 1994**

| Industries | Overall | Large corporations | Small corporations |
|---|---|---|---|
| | | *percent* | |
| Agriculture, forestry, and fishing . . . . . . . . | 8 | 12 | 7 |
| Mining . . . . . . . . . . . . . . . . . . . . . . . . . . . . | 6 | 6 | na |
| Oil and gas . . . . . . . . . . . . . . . . . . . . . . . . | 16 | 16 | na |
| Manufacturing . . . . . . . . . . . . . . . . . . . . . . | 16 | 17 | 13 |
| Construction . . . . . . . . . . . . . . . . . . . . . . . . | 14 | 20 | 12 |
| Transportation and storage . . . . . . . . . . . . . | 14 | 15 | 10 |
| Communications . . . . . . . . . . . . . . . . . . . . . | 17 | 17 | na |
| Public utilities . . . . . . . . . . . . . . . . . . . . . . | 26 | 26 | na |
| Wholesale trade . . . . . . . . . . . . . . . . . . . . . | 20 | 24 | 14 |
| Retail trade . . . . . . . . . . . . . . . . . . . . . . . . | 16 | 20 | 14 |
| Deposit-taking institutions . . . . . . . . . . . . . | 26 | 26 | na |
| Other finance . . . . . . . . . . . . . . . . . . . . . . . | 15 | 14 | 19 |
| Other services . . . . . . . . . . . . . . . . . . . . . . | 16 | 21 | 14 |
| All industries . . . . . . . . . . . . . . . . . . . . . . | 16 | 14 | 14 |

na  not applicable.

Note: Tax rates include federal income and capital taxes. Average tax rates are presented as ratios of financial accounting income of profitable companies.

Source: Canada, *Report of the Technical Committee on Business Taxation* (Ottawa: Department of Finance, April 1998), table 4.1.

vary across industries, across provinces, between public corporations and private corporations, between Canadian firms and foreign firms, and across types of activities. We shall later discuss some of the implications of differences in the tax treatment of different corporations. Our task here is to convey some idea of the broad magnitude of the various tax concessions, preferential rates, and the like.

Table 4.3 shows the average effective federal corporate tax rates paid by the various industries in the Canadian economy in 1993 and 1994. These rates were calculated by simply dividing federal corporate and capital taxes by the book profits of profitable corporations, averaged over the two years. The table shows how the average tax burden varies across industries. Rates are relatively low in the resource and manufacturing sectors and relatively high in the tertiary and financial sectors. These differences reflect several different features of the tax system and some features of the industries themselves as well. The generous capital cost allowances and writeoffs for resources obviously reduce the effective tax rates for the resource and manufacturing industries, and manufacturing benefits further from the preferential statutory rate for that sector. The small business deduction is more important to agriculture, forestry and fishing, construction, and retail trade than to other sectors. Other influences are less apparent. The deductibility of interest payments favours firms that rely on debt financing over those that rely on equity. Firms that invest in machinery and equipment receive more generous writeoffs than firms that invest in inventories or buildings. Presumably the extent to which these advantages apply varies systematically from industry to industry, but this variation is not apparent from the aggregate data in table 4.3.

The table is insufficient in other respects as well. It includes only federal taxes; presumably provincial taxes would magnify the differences. It includes only profitable companies—a consideration that is likely to be more important in relation to some industries than others. Finally, it takes no account of the fact that a portion of corporate tax liabilities is recouped through tax provisions at the personal level, such as the dividend tax credit and the preferential treatment of capital gains, that are intended specifically to integrate the personal and corporate taxes. In spite of these shortcomings, however, the data in table 4.3 make it clear that the corporate tax system is far from even-handed in its treatment of various sectors.

## Relief from Double Taxation: Integration with the Personal Income Tax

One of the most controversial consequences of the corporate tax is the alleged double taxation of shareholders to whom after-tax corporate income ultimately accrues. The equity income of a corporation is taxed first by the corporate income tax and again, when dividends are distributed or capital gains are realized, by the personal income tax. To the extent that the corporate tax has not been shifted to purchasers of the corporation's output through higher prices or to suppliers of inputs through lower prices, the shareholder's return on capital is indeed taxed twice. The last section of this chapter will discuss the inequities that are said to arise from the double taxation of corporate income and some proposed remedies. This section will outline the present extent of relief from double taxation.

In discussing this problem, it is useful to distinguish between the treatment of corporations that earn active business income and those that earn non-active (financial) income. We shall consider the former first. As we mentioned above, all equity income of public corporations, except dividends received and capital gains, is fully taxed at a combined federal and provincial rate of slightly over 40 percent. Dividends received are tax-free (to avoid "triple" taxation, since they have already been taxed as the distributing corporation's income), and only three-quarters of capital gains are taxed. Two provisions of the personal income tax provide partial relief from double taxation to taxpayers who receive income from Canadian corporations: the dividend tax credit and the taxation of only three-quarters of capital gains.

The dividend tax credit rate has varied over the years, in parallel with changes in the corporate tax rate itself. Currently, the dividend tax credit rate is 25 percent of dividends received, which compensates shareholders for 20 percentage points of corporate tax. An example will clarify this point. Consider a taxpayer who receives a dividend of $100 from Canadian sources. The dividend tax credit system uses a *gross-up and credit* procedure. The dividend is first grossed-up by 25 percent to yield $125 of notional gross dividends. The grossed-up dividends are added to the taxpayer's taxable income. After the taxpayer has calculated his taxes owing, he subtracts from them a credit equal to $25, the amount by which the dividends have been grossed-up. This tax credit is equivalent to the tax that the dividend-paying corporation would have paid had it faced a tax rate of 20 percent; that is, if the corporation had earned pre-tax income of $125 and paid corporate tax at a rate of 20 percent, it would have been able to pay a dividend of $100. Thus a dividend tax credit of 25 percent calculated according to the gross-up and credit method fully integrates the dividends if the latter have been paid out by a firm whose tax rate is 20 percent. This rate is roughly equal to the tax rate for CCPCs that can claim the small business deduction.

For large corporations, the 25 percent dividend tax credit "underintegrates" the corporate and personal taxes, at least if the corporation is in a tax-paying position. Suppose, for example, that a large corporation pays a tax rate of 40 percent. In this case, a dividend of $100 requires before-tax corporate income of $167, of which $67 (= 0.4 × $167) is paid as corporate tax. Since the taxpayer receives only a dividend tax credit of $25, less than half the tax paid is reimbursed.[10] To achieve full integration in this case, the dividend tax credit rate would have to be 67 percent. That is, the dividends would have to be grossed-up by $67, an amount equivalent to the amount of corporate taxes that have been paid. Of course, if the corporation is not in a tax-paying position, the dividend tax credit "overintegrates." That is, it gives shareholders a credit for dividends paid on income from which no corporate tax has been withheld. "Overintegration" may also occur if a corporation's deductions from its taxable income reduce its tax liabilities significantly.

Full and exact integration of dividend income is not feasible, since it would require varying the dividend tax credit rate to match the tax rate for each corporation that paid dividends. Even so, the advantages of integration would not extend to all shareholders. Low-income taxpayers who are in a non-tax-paying position but who receive dividends—for example, pensioners who rely on capital income—cannot use the dividend tax credit. Neither can shareholders who receive dividends on tax-exempt assets such as pension fund holdings. The credit is not refundable, and it cannot be carried forward.

---

[10] In fact, the tax credit on $25 on dividends is not exactly $25, owing to the fact that the credit is calculated sequentially for the federal and provincial governments. The actual method of calculating the dividend tax credit is as follows. Dividends are grossed-up by 25 percent as mentioned. Federal taxes are then calculated, and a tax credit of 13⅓ percent of the grossed-up dividend is given against federal taxes. Provincial taxes are then calculated as a percentage of federal taxes, thus compounding the tax credit. For example, the Ontario statutory tax rate in 1997 was 48 percent of federal taxes. Thus the dividend tax credit was 13⅓% + (0.48 × 13⅓%) = 19.73% of grossed-up dividends, or $24.66. This is roughly equivalent to a system that gives a tax credit equal to the amount of grossing up of dividends. The amount of difference varies from province to province. Our discussion here and in later sections will ignore this complication and simply assume that the tax credit given is the same as the amount that is added to dividends when they are grossed up.

On the other hand, if shareholders are able to shift the incidence of the corporate tax to other factors of production or consumers, there is no need to reimburse them through the dividend tax credit. It has been argued that in a world with open capital markets, this shifting does indeed normally take place.[11] We shall return to the arguments for and against integration later in this chapter.

Shareholders may also obtain income from corporate ownership in the form of capital gains. Although there is no "capital gains tax credit," the partial exemption of capital gains under the personal tax serves as a partial method of integration. Consider again our example of a receipt of $100 in shareholder income, this time in the form of capital gains. Only three-quarters of the $100 is taxable, so $75 is added to the shareholder's tax base. If the shareholder is in the 50 percent tax bracket, his tax liability on the capital gains is $37.50 and his after-tax income is $62.50. This result is equivalent to his having received $125 before tax and having paid the full 50 percent tax on this amount. In the case of this taxpayer, in other words, it is equivalent to full integration of capital gains income from a corporation that faces a tax rate of 20 percent, since a corporation in this position would need $125 of before-tax income to pay out a dividend of $100. If the $125 had been paid directly to the shareholder, the latter would have incurred the tax liability of $62.50. Thus full integration occurs only if two conditions are met: the taxpayer must be in the 50 percent tax bracket and must receive the capital gain from a corporation that is subject to a 20 percent corporate tax rate. For lower-income taxpayers, the partial exemption of capital gains offers less compensation. Indeed, all of the problems associated with the integration of dividend income arise in this context as well.

This discussion has ignored an important feature of the tax treatment of capital gains—the fact that they are not taxed until realization. Shareholders of corporations can defer paying personal taxes on equity income by retaining their funds within the corporation and not realizing any capital gains. Consequently, if the personal tax rate exceeds the corporate tax rate, as it is likely to in the case of small businesses, it may pay entrepreneurs to incorporate. Incorporation allows them to shelter capital income that would have been subject to immediate personal taxation had the firm remained unincorporated.

In order not to discourage individuals from receiving investment income through private corporations (or public corporations controlled by one individual or related group of individuals), the tax laws have essentially provided for the full integration of all investment income of these corporations. At the same time, certain provisions exist that prevent individuals from using the private corporation as a tax-deferring device. As we mentioned earlier, private corporations must pay a 33⅓ percent tax on dividends received on portfolio investments (the so-called part IV tax). When the

---

[11] See, for example, Robin Boadway and Neil Bruce, "Problems with Integrating Corporate and Personal Income Taxes in an Open Economy" (1992), 48 *Journal of Public Economics* 39-61.

dividends are paid out, the tax is effectively returned to the firm in the form of a tax credit of $1 for every $4 of dividends paid out.

To summarize this discussion, double taxation arises only in the case of the income of public corporations that are subject to the full corporate tax rate and in the case of the active business income of private corporations that are not eligible for the small business tax rate. Indeed, in many cases the provisions intended to prevent double taxation result in undertaxation, especially if the corporation is able to shift the corporate tax to consumers. In some cases, however, the corporate tax may result in significant overtaxation, such as when shareholders are tax-exempt or in a non-tax-paying position. We shall return to this subject later in this chapter.

## Corporate Tax Collection Agreements (TCAs)

Businesses in Canada may operate under several tax jurisdictions at the same time. In order to avoid administrative complexity, double taxation, and wasteful tax competition, it is important that the business taxes imposed by different jurisdictions share some basic features. In the case of the corporate tax, this result has been achieved through a combination of historical evolution and the formal harmonization arrangements referred to as the tax collection agreements. Since World War II, the system of corporate taxes has gradually evolved from one in which the federal government had sole authority to one in which the provinces have gradually come to occupy a substantial share of the corporate tax room while continuing to accept federal administration and federally defined harmonization of the tax.

The TCAs for the corporate tax formalize the system of harmonization for the seven participating provinces (all of the provinces except Alberta, Ontario, and Quebec). Their mechanics are remarkably simple. The participating provinces agree to allow the federal government to administer their provincial taxes. The federal government collects taxes on behalf of the provinces and assumes responsibility for compliance through its auditing activities. Thus a business that operates in an agreeing province files only one tax return. The provinces, for their part, must accept the federal tax base. They may, however, choose their own tax rates, and, if they wish, their own small business and manufacturing and processing deductions as well. The provincial tax rate applies directly to the federal tax base (under the TCAs for the personal income tax, the provincial tax rates apply to the federal taxes payable). The federal government will also administer—for a fee—tax credits legislated by the provinces, provided that in its judgment the tax credits are relatively simple to administer, do not distort interprovincial trade, and do not discriminate against out-of-province firms.

An important part of the corporate tax harmonization arrangements is the allocation formula, which determines the share of corporate income to be attributed to each jurisdiction in the case of a corporation that operates in more than one province or abroad. As we noted earlier, the formula is a simple one: the share of a corporation's taxable income that is allocated to a given province is the average of the shares of its payroll and its revenues at point of sale that are attributable to its permanent establishments in the province. (Special rules apply to transportation and to the finance and insurance industries.)

The provinces that participate in TCAs benefit from having the federal government administer their taxes and yet retain the right to set the provincial tax rate. The disadvantage is that provinces are not free to choose their own tax bases. The base is set unilaterally by the federal government, usually as part of the federal budget process and within its tradition of budget secrecy. As well, the participating provinces must rely on the federal tax authorities to perform audits and some provinces have argued that these authorities may be more diligent when there are federal revenues at stake rather than provincial ones. For these reasons, Alberta, Ontario, and Quebec have opted to administer their own corporate tax systems (Quebec alone administers its own personal income tax as well). Nonetheless, their tax bases do not vary significantly from the federal base, and to avoid double taxation they abide by the same allocation formula as well. No doubt the similarity between the federal system and the systems even in the non-participating provinces is a consequence of the fact that the corporate tax system as a whole has evolved from a system that the federal government designed in the first instance, when it was sole occupant of the corporate tax field.

## Other Federal and Provincial Taxes on Resources

In addition to applying provincial and federal corporate taxes and municipal property taxes (see chapter 7) to natural resources and resource properties, the federal government and the provinces levy a variety taxes that apply specifically to natural resources. The purpose of these taxes is simply to obtain a share of the rents that accrue to resources. In the case of the federal government, resource taxes apply mainly in the territories and to offshore exploitation of resources, both areas of federal jurisdiction. The provinces have the right to raise revenues from resources located within their own boundaries. We shall concentrate here on the three main sources of resource revenues—oil and gas production, mining, and forestry. Other sources are water power, hunting, fishing, and trapping. Resource-revenue regimes tend to vary significantly across both jurisdictions and resource type. Nor is there any analogue of the TCAs for resources. Our discussion will be fairly cursory.

### Oil and Gas

The common form of levy applied to oil and gas is the *royalty*, which can be viewed as a charge for extracting oil or gas from the ground. Royalties, unlike income taxes, are typically levied on the volume or value of oil and gas extracted.

The federal government levies a royalty of a variable rate on oil and gas production within its jurisdiction—except in the case of oil and gas production off the shores of Newfoundland and Nova Scotia, which has been turned over to those provinces under the Atlantic accords. The rate rises from 1 percent of revenues to 5 percent over the first six years of production or until the initial investment has been recovered, whichever comes sooner. After that, the rate is 5 percent of revenues or 30 percent of net cash flow, whichever is greater.

Practice among the provinces varies considerably. In Alberta and Saskatchewan, the royalty rate depends on whether the oil and gas is old or new; in the case of oil, it also depends on whether the oil is heavy or non-heavy and on whether it comes from enhanced recovery, oil sands, or conventional wells. Finally, the royalty rate increases with production level and price. In British Columbia as well, oil royalty rates depend on whether the oil is old or new and rise with production levels. Natural gas royalty rates vary with the type of well and the selling price but not with the volume of production. These are the main oil and gas producing provinces at present, but Newfoundland and Nova Scotia will become significant producers as their offshore deposits are exploited.

## Mining

The federal government also uses a royalty regime to obtain revenues from mining production from federal lands in the territories. The royalty is based on the value of production above a minimum, and the rate rises with the value of production (from 3 to 12 percent). There is a three-year royalty holiday for new mines.

All mineral-producing provinces also levy taxes of one form or another on mining. Most commonly, the tax is levied on profits or income from mining operations, but there are also taxes on acreage, assessed value, land rentals, royalties, and licences. Manitoba and Saskatchewan also tax processing profits. The taxes may be applied either at a fixed rate or at a rate that increases with the income from the resource. A brief description of the provincial mining regimes follows:

• *British Columbia*: In the case of coal, the higher of 17.5 percent of net income and 7.5 percent of revenues. In the case of most other minerals, the higher of 13 percent of net income and 2 percent of revenues.

• *Alberta*: A royalty of 10 percent on the value of placer minerals extracted. A graduated royalty on metallic minerals of 1 percent of revenues until costs are recovered and then the higher of 1 percent of revenues and 12 percent of net revenues. Charges for leases and permits.

• *Saskatchewan*: A flat rate of 12.5 percent on the profits from mining and processing. Royalties on the value of production of uranium, potash, coal, and several other minerals.

• *Manitoba*: A flat rate of 20 percent on the profits from mining and processing. Exploration permits and development leases.

• *Ontario*: A tax of 20 percent on profits in excess of $500,000. An acreage tax of $4 per hectare on mining lands.

• *Quebec*: A flat rate of 18 percent on profits from mining operations with an annual credit of $90,000. Licences for prospecting, exploration, leasing, and renting mineral lands.

• *New Brunswick*: A tax of 2 percent on net revenues starting in the third year of operation. A tax of 16 percent on net profits over $100,000, with a deduction of 25 percent of research expenditures. Fees for prospecting, claims, and leases.

• *Nova Scotia*: No metallic mineral mines. A tax of 33⅓ percent on income from gypsum over $5,000 and royalties on other minerals. Licences for exploration and development.

• *Newfoundland*: A flat rate of 15 percent on net income less royalty and rental payments. A tax of 20 percent on revenue from leases to third parties. A charge for mineral holdings of $12.50 per hectare. Fees for Crown land applications and leases.

### Forestry

All of the provinces charge for the use of timber rights on Crown lands and levy ground rents as well. The rates vary widely among provinces. Quebec and British Columbia also tax profits from logging, both at a rate of 10 percent. Quebec exempts the first $10,000 of profits, British Columbia the first $25,000. Both provinces, however, provide special credits against federal and provincial corporate income taxes that ensure that the logging tax imposes no additional tax burden. Most provinces also levy a *stumpage fee*, which is based on the quantity of timber cut from Crown lands. Finally, several provinces use licences to control the exploitation of forests.

## The Economic Effects of Corporate Taxation

The corporate income tax is basically a tax on the net income accruing to equity capital in the corporate sector of the economy. Since the same capital income is taxed in the hands of its owners under the personal income tax, the income from holding equity in corporations appears to be subject to double taxation. As we have shown, the double taxation is mitigated by the integration provisions of the corporate and personal taxes. These provisions integrate fully corporate incomes that qualify for the small business deduction; dividends paid out of corporate income that has borne a higher rate is less than fully integrated. To the extent that double taxation remains, the corporate tax might be expected to have an adverse effect on the incomes of capital owners and to influence their decisions to accumulate and hold capital for particular uses. Both the effect of the corporate tax on the division of national income between capital owners and others—that is, its incidence—and the effect of the tax on the accumulation of capital and its allocation to various uses—that is, its efficiency effects—have been the subject of considerable analysis and investigation in the economics literature. We shall discuss each of these matters in turn. Our discussion will refer mainly to the part of the tax that is not undone by integration.

# The Incidence of the Corporate Tax

The legal incidence of the corporate tax is roughly on the return to equity capital (net of deductions for capital costs) in the corporate sector of the economy—that is, on the income earned by shareholders from the ownership of shares in corporations. This does not imply that shareholders bear the ultimate burden or incidence of corporate taxation in the sense that their incomes would be greater by the full amount of the tax if the tax were absent. The corporate tax will not fall entirely on shareholders if the gross (or taxable) income of corporations is higher in the presence of the tax than it would have been in its absence. As we discussed in chapter 2, the tax may be shifted if gross income rises to cover part or all of the tax levied. Since gross income is the difference between total revenue and allowable costs, any shifting of the tax must take the form of either increased total revenue or reduced costs. An increase in total revenue would be accomplished by shifting the burden of the tax to consumers in the form of higher prices, so-called *forward shifting*. Alternatively, *backward shifting* of the tax occurs if the tax induces a reduction in the prices for other factors of production, such as labour. There have been many approaches to studying the incidence of taxes. We outline them here, beginning with statistical studies.

## Econometric Esimates of Corporate Tax Incidence

Early analysis of the shifting of the corporate tax concentrated on the observed relationship between profits or rates of return and corporate tax rates over time. In a celebrated study, Krzyzaniak and Musgrave[12] tested statistically the relationship between corporate tax rates on the one hand (the independent or exogenous variable) and the rate of return to capital on the other (the dependent or endogenous variable). They concluded that the US corporate tax was fully shifted in the form of higher before-tax profits. Whether the shifting was forward or backward could not be determined. Subsequent work has disputed this finding of 100 percent shifting, mainly on statistical grounds. The strongest argument against these results, put forward by Cragg, Harberger, and Mieszkowski,[13] is that the observed close relationship between the rate of return on capital and the corporate tax rate is a misleading indicator of the extent to which corporate tax changes themselves account for the observed changes in rates of return. They suggest that other exogenous changes occurring in the economy caused the rate of return to change, and that these changes were correlated with the tax changes. Because

---

[12] Marian Krzyzaniak and Richard A. Musgrave, *The Shifting of the Corporation Income Tax: An Empirical Study of Its Short-Run Effect upon the Rate of Return* (Baltimore: Johns Hopkins Press, 1963).

[13] John G. Cragg, Arnold C. Harberger, and Peter Mieszkowski, "Empirical Evidence on the Incidence of the Corporation Income Tax" (December 1967), 75 *Journal of Political Economy* 811-21. See also M. Krzyzaniak and R.A. Musyrave, "Corporation Tax Shifting: A Response" (July-August 1970), 78 *Journal of Political Economy* 768-73, and John G. Cragg, Arnold C. Harberger, and Peter Mieszkowski, "Corporation Tax Shifting: Rejoinder" (July-August 1970), 78 *Journal of Political Economy* 774-77.

these variables were not included in the regression equation, their effect on the rate of return was picked up by the tax variable. When Cragg, Harberger, and Mieszkowski add as explanatory variables the employment rate and a dummy variable for the mobilization and war years, the effect of the corporate tax shrinks considerably; indeed, it becomes statistically insignificant. Several studies of this sort have been done for the United States and other countries, but no consensus has emerged on the actual extent of tax shifting. Various studies have obtained results that range anywhere from no shifting to full shifting of the corporate tax.[14]

A similar methodology was applied to Canada by Spencer,[15] who used data for the periods 1935 to 1939 and 1948 to 1964 in testing the influence of corporate tax rates on the rate of return to the Canadian manufacturing sector. He postulated that the gross rate of return to capital—that is, gross profits divided by the capital stock—depended on the rate of corporate tax and a number of other variables, including the change in consumption divided by gross national product (GNP), the inventory-to-shipment ratio, government revenue divided by GNP, exports divided by GNP, and the ratio of actual output to potential output. A statistical regression of the relationship between the gross rate of return and these variables yielded the result that the tax was approximately fully shifted. That is, any increase (or decrease) in corporate taxes appeared to be fully recaptured in higher (or lower) profits before tax.[16]

Subsequently, Dusansky and Tanner[17] performed a rather more sophisticated analysis of tax shifting in Canadian manufacturing industries over the same periods. They argued that Spencer's independent variables were not exogenous; rather they were determined within the economic system along with the rate of return to capital. By treating these variables as if they were exogenous, therefore, Spencer's analysis had produced biased and inconsistent results. Dusansky and Tanner dealt with this problem by treating the rate-of-return relationship as one of many in the system and using the statistical technique of two-stage least squares to estimate it. In addition, they used a set of variables somewhat different from the set that Spencer had used.

---

[14] For a complete survey of the empirical studies, see Balbir S. Sahni and T. Mathew, *The Shifting and Incidence of the Corporation Income Tax* (Rotterdam: Rotterdam University Press, 1976).

[15] Byron G. Spencer, "The Shifting of the Corporation Income Tax in Canada" (February 1969), 2 *Canadian Journal of Economics* 21-34.

[16] More accurately, the hypothesis of full shifting of the tax in the short run could not be rejected. Note that the inclusion of the ratio of actual to potential output as an explanatory variable meets the objections raised by Cragg, Harberger, and Mieszkowski, supra footnote 13. In any case, Spencer found this variable not to be correlated with the tax rate. His study was subsequently criticized on statistical grounds by Lévesque, who nonetheless obtained virtually the same results. See Robert Lévesque, "L'incidence de l'impôt sur le revenu des sociétés canadiennes: commentaire" (February 1970), 3 *Canadian Journal of Economics* 158-63 and the "Reply" by Spencer, ibid., at 164-67.

[17] Richard Dusansky and J. Ernest Tanner, "The Shifting of the Profits Tax in Canadian Manufacturing, 1935-65" (February 1974), 7 *Canadian Journal of Economics* 112-21.

They assumed that the rate of return to capital depended on the tax rate, the inventory-to-sales ratio, the cost of materials, wage costs, annual changes in output per man, the labour-capital ratio, and the ratio of actual GNP to potential GNP. Each of these variables depended in turn on another set of exogenous variables.[18] From the statistical evidence, Dusansky and Tanner concluded that the corporate tax was approximately 75 percent shifted.

In an earlier study, Lévesque[19] had attempted to determine whether tax shifting depended on the structure of the industry. He used cross-section data for 31 industries during the period 1948-1952 in analyzing the relationship between changes in profit rates following tax changes and industry concentration ratios (defined as the percentage of employees accounted for by the leading three firms in the industry in 1948). The argument was that the more concentrated an industry is the greater is its ability to shift taxes forward to consumers. Although Lévesque did find a relationship between concentration and shifting that was similar in magnitude to the relationship found by Dusansky and Tanner, the attempt to explain profit rates was not successful overall. It is not clear, therefore, how much faith to put in Lévesque's results.

## Open-Economy Considerations

The problems that vex attempts to isolate the effects of corporate taxation on gross income from time series data are not the only factors that cast doubt on the reliability of the Canadian statistical studies. Another factor is the studies' failure to address the implications for the incidence of the corporate tax of the relative "openness" of the Canadian economy. "Openness" can refer to either the capital market or the market for products.[20] Since capital can flow into and out of the Canadian economy relatively freely, capital would not be invested here if it did not obtain a rate of return that was comparable, after the application of the corporate tax, to the rate of return available elsewhere. In other words, the after-tax return to capital in Canada is more or less fixed; it can respond to only a limited extent to circumstances in Canada, including the existence of the corporate tax. The precise extent to which Canadian capital markets face fixed rates of return is not clear. There is some evidence that Canadian rates of return do respond somewhat to purely Canadian influences, such as the availability of Canadian finance, especially

---

[18] The exogenous variables included annual advertising expenditures, the short-term interest rate, government expenditures, exports, imports, and statutory tax rates.

[19] R.J. Lévesque, *The Shifting of the Corporate Income Tax in the Short Run*, Studies of the Royal Commission on Taxation no. 18 (Ottawa: Queen's Printer, 1967).

[20] "Openness" can also refer to international movements of labour, but owing to constraints on immigration labour is much less mobile than other capital goods. Even so, the advent of free trade in North America has enhanced the ability of highly skilled labour to move across borders. International mobility of labour imposes constraints on the extent to which such labour can be forced to bear taxes. This circumstance, however, has implications for the ability of governments to impose progressive taxes rather than for the incidence of the corporate tax.

in the case of small firms.[21] Nonetheless, it seems clear that Canadian rates of return are heavily influenced by the rates available abroad, and to the extent that this is the case the corporate tax must be shifted away from capital and onto prices or wages. Note that this does not rule out there being a rate of return on capital in Canada different from rates in other countries (owing to country-specific risk factors, exchange rate uncertainty, inflation, and so forth). It simply suggests that the size of the difference will not be determined by the supply of Canadian funds.

The incidence of the corporate tax also depends on the extent of the openness of markets for products. To the extent that Canadian corporations sell their output on world markets at fixed prices, the tax cannot not be shifted forward onto prices. If both export and import prices are fixed and the net return to capital is fixed, the corporate tax must either be shifted backward onto labour and other factors that are not mobile internationally or force capital to move out of industries that produce traded commodities and into industries that produce non-traded commodities, where it can be shifted onto prices. However, in order to assess the impact of the corporate tax on rates of return in Canada, we would have to know a great deal more than we do now about how the return to corporate capital is tied to world financial markets, and about the ability of Canadian firms to influence the prices of products they sell.

The implications for tax policy of open capital markets in Canada are potentially profound. If capital markets are open, then taxes levied on firms, such as the corporate tax, will cause the before-tax rate of return on investment to rise. This result will distort investment decisions and thereby cause investment to fall. At the same time, personal taxes levied on capital income will cause the after-tax rate of return on savings to fall and hence discourage saving. Given open capital markets, then, a system of integration that works through the personal tax system, such as the dividend tax credit system in Canada, will achieve the reverse of its intended result: instead of undoing the corporate tax, with its distorting effect on investment, it will undo the personal tax on dividends. This result will, to be sure, prevent the distortion of saving decisions, but only at the price of contradicting what one presumes to be the intent of the personal income tax system. We shall return to these issues in the last section of this chapter.

## General Equilibrium Incidence Analysis

Another strand of the tax-incidence literature has concentrated on the effects of the corporate tax on resource allocation among industries. We discussed this type of analysis, known as *general equilibrium analysis of tax incidence*, in chapter 2, but it will do to recapitulate the main points of that discussion

---

[21] See the summary in Kenneth J. McKenzie and Aileen J. Thompson, *The Economic Effects of Dividend Taxation*, Working Paper 96-7 (Ottawa: Department of Finance, Technical Committee on Business Taxation, 1996).

here.[22] A tax imposed on corporate income initially reduces the rate of return on capital employed in the corporate sector of the economy. If capital markets are operating competitively, capital will move out of the corporate sector and into the unincorporated sector. Because of the assumed property of diminishing marginal returns to capital, the return to capital will initially fall in the unincorporated sector and rise in the corporate sector. The reallocation of capital will continue until the economy reaches a new equilibrium in which the after-tax returns to capital in the corporate and unincorporated sectors are identical. In this way, the burden of the tax will be shifted in part to capital owners in the unincorporated sector. This result implies that the corporate tax does not discriminate against owners of corporations in favour of owners of unincorporated business. The workings of the capital market spread any part of the tax that falls upon capital across all capital owners.

Again, part of the tax may also be shifted backward to labour or forward to consumers. When capital reallocates from the corporate to the unincorporated sector, labour requirements will decline in the corporate sector and increase in the unincorporated sector. If the unincorporated sector uses more capital relative to labour than the corporate sector does, then the corporate sector will release more labour than the unincorporated sector can absorb at the going wage rate. Consequently, the wage rate will decline. Conversely, if the corporate sector is relatively capital intensive, the reallocation of labour and capital will cause the wage rate to rise. In this case, capital could bear more than 100 percent of the tax.

Another way in which the tax can be shifted to labour is through its effect on the aggregate amount of capital available. So far we have considered the effect of a reallocation of a given amount of capital among industries and have assumed that the aggregate amount of capital available would not be influenced by the tax. In fact, if the corporate tax tends to reduce the rate of return to capital, the rate of capital accumulation through investment will decline. If less capital is available per unit of labour, the wage rate will fall and the return to capital will rise. In this way, part of the burden of the tax will be shifted to labour over time. Given this effect, some authors have argued, a revenue-neutral increase in the corporate tax rate and a reduction in the personal tax rate might actually make labour worse off and capital owners better off in the long run.[23]

---

[22] Arnold C. Harberger pioneered this type of analysis. See his seminal study, "The Incidence of the Corporation Income Tax" (June 1962), 70 *Journal of Political Economy* 215-40. For useful surveys of the Harberger model, see George F. Break, "The Incidence and Economic Effects of Taxation," in Alan S. Blinder, Robert M. Solow, George F. Break, Peter O. Steiner, and Dick Netzer, *The Economics of Public Finance* (Washington, DC: Brookings Institution, 1974), 119-237; and Peter Mieszkowski, "Tax Incidence Theory: The Effects of Taxes on the Distribution of Income" (December 1969), 7 *Journal of Economic Literature* 1103-24.

[23] See, for example, Martin Feldstein, "Incidence of a Capital Income Tax in a Growing Economy with Variable Savings Rates" (October 1974), 41 *Review of Economic Studies* 505-

(The footnote is continued on the next page.)

So far we have outlined the incidence of the corporate tax on the "source" side; that is, its effect on the returns to factors of production—labour and capital. In addition, the taxation of capital in the corporate sector may affect the "use" side of individual budgets. To be specific, if the tax causes the price of goods produced by the corporate sector to rise relative to those produced elsewhere, then persons who devote relatively large proportions of their incomes to purchasing goods produced in the corporate sector will bear a relatively larger share of the tax.

The overall incidence of the corporate tax will be the sum of the tax's incidence on the source side of individual budgets and its incidence on the use side. The exact sharing of the burden will depend on the ease with which capital may be substituted for labour in both the corporate sector and the unincorporated sector,[24] on the relative capital intensities of the two sectors, and on the elasticities of consumer demand for the output of the two sectors. Harberger concluded that in the US economy as a whole capital bears almost the entire burden of the corporate tax; more recent work by Shoven and Whalley supports this conclusion.[25] Boadway and Treddenick, who used a general equilibrium model that incorporated 56 industries and inputs for capital, labour, and materials, found that in Canada too capital owners bear virtually all of the burden of the corporate tax;[26] Lee had similar results.[27] This conclusion directly contradicts the results of the time series studies cited above, by Krzyzaniak and Musgrave and by Spencer. Of course, the two types of studies are very different from one another. For example, the general equilibrium tax incidence analyses are completely static, since they take no account of the effect of the corporate tax on the aggregate amount of capital available, whereas the time series studies are at least implicitly dynamic, since they use actual data over a period of time. It cannot be said, however, that the results of one type of study are more compelling than the results of the other type. Taken together, they leave the question of the incidence of the corporate tax very much up in the air.

---

[23] Continued ...

13; Ronald E. Grieson, "The Incidence of Profits Taxes in a Neo-Classical Growth Model" (February 1975), 4 *Journal of Public Economics* 75-85; and Robin Boadway, "Long-Run Tax Incidence: A Comparative Dynamic Approach" (July 1979), 46 *Review of Economic Studies* 505-11.

[24] The more substitutable capital is for labour, the less will be the required change in relative factor returns required to absorb the factors released from the corporate sector in different proportions from those used in the unincorporated sector.

[25] John S. Shoven and John Whalley, "A General Equilibrium Calculation of the Effects of Differential Taxation of Income from Capital in the U.S." (November 1972), 1 *Journal of Public Economics* 281-321.

[26] Robin Boadway and John Treddenick, "A General Equilibrium Computation of the Effects of the Canadian Tariff Structure" (August 1978), 11 *Canadian Journal of Economics* 424-46.

[27] J.T. Marshall Lee, "The Effects of Taxes on Resource Allocation and Distribution of Income in Canada: A General Equilibrium Analysis" (PhD thesis, Queen's University, 1983).

## Impact Incidence Studies

One other procedure has been adopted as a means of estimating corporate tax incidence. It is to assume some pattern of shifting and deduce from this pattern how the incidence of the tax is allotted among income groups, given the existing distribution of capital (and labour) among income groups. This procedure typically estimates the incidence of each of the taxes taken together, the corporate tax being only one of them. As we noted in chapter 2, there have been several incidence studies of this sort, of which the most recent is one by Vermaeten et al.[28] On the basis of certain incidence assumptions, they calculate the proportion of "broad income" paid as taxes for each decile of income, where broad income includes market income (adjusted for inflation), various types of non-market income, and government transfers. In the case of the corporate income tax, their "standard" incidence assumption is that the tax is borne by owners of corporate capital. They also calculate a regressive case in which half of the corporate income tax is shifted to consumers. The half that is shifted is distributed among the various income groups according to the proportion of each group's income that is spent on consumer goods produced by the corporate sector. The half that is not shifted is distributed among the income groups according to the proportion of each group's income that derives from dividend payments.

In the standard model, the incidence of the corporate income tax attributions is close to zero for the first six income deciles, rises slightly over the next three, and then rises dramatically in the highest decile. The progressivity of the tax decreased gradually decade by decade between the 1950s and the 1980s. Under the regressive assumption, in which half of the tax burden is shifted to consumers, the tax is regressive in the lower income ranges and slightly progressive in the higher ranges. This outcome is explained by the fact that lower-income persons spend more in proportion to their income than higher-income income persons do. The half of the burden that is not shifted falls on shareholders' income: as a percentage of total income, corporate-source income is higher for high-income groups and low-income groups (into which many retired persons fall) than it is for middle-income groups.

The main problem with studies of this kind is that they simply assume a pattern of shifting instead of estimating it. As Whalley has shown, and as we discussed in chapter 2, one can obtain vastly differing incidence results by varying the shifting assumptions.[29] In addition, these studies ignore any repercussions the tax may have on the production side of the economy—that is, its incidence on the source side. They also ignore the general equilibrium

---

[28] Arndt Vermaeten, W. Irwin Gillespie, and Frank Vermaeten, "Who Paid the Taxes in Canada, 1951-1988?" (September 1995), 21 *Canadian Public Policy* 317-43.

[29] John Whalley, "Regression or Progression: The Taxing Question of Tax Incidence" (November 1984), 17 *Canadian Journal of Economics* 654-82.

effects of tax changes and simply assume fixed pre-tax incomes.[30] Finally, the shifting assumptions themselves often imply that markets are not effective at allocating resources. For example, the assumption that part of the corporate tax is partly shifted and part is borne by corporate owners (but not by owners of unincorporated businesses) implies that the rate of return on corporate and unincorporated capital can differ. As we argued above, if the corporate tax is borne by capital owners, the operations of capital markets should ensure that it is borne by capital owners in both sectors.

## The Effect of the Corporate Tax on Resource Allocation

The corporate tax can distort the allocation of resources in the economy to the extent that it affects the marginal returns from different activities differently. For example, as we have noted, it can affect the level of investment in the corporate sector and hence distort the allocation of capital between the corporate sector and the unincorporated sector. Since the tax does not treat all corporations identically, it can also distort the allocation of capital among industries within the corporate sector and among firms of different sizes. Finally, it can distort households' decisions to save and to take risks. We shall discuss all of these potential distortions in this section, but first it is worth considering the more fundamental question of the impact of the tax on marginal, as opposed to average, returns to capital: it is the tax's influence on marginal returns that makes it distorting.

A corporate tax will fall on one or more of three bases, depending on its structure. First, the tax may be a tax on the *economic profits* or *rents* generated by the firm. Second, it may be a tax on the return to capital in the corporate sector. Third, it may be a tax on risk taking and entrepreneurship. The economic profit of a firm is the difference between its total accrued revenue and its total imputed costs. The latter include all current costs (for example, labour and materials) and all imputed costs associated with the use of capital, such as true replacement depreciation, the replacement value of inventories used, the reduction in value of depletable assets through use, and the full imputed costs of financing all asset holdings (interest on debt and required rate of return on equity), including any risk premiums. Economic profit, in short, is any earnings over and above the earnings that are required to compensate the firm for the inputs used. These additional earnings can arise from a variety of sources, including monopoly or oligopoly power, special advantages of the firm (such as location), and the ownership of natural resources. If a corporate tax base is to reflect economic profits exactly, the tax must allow firms to deduct from total earnings the true opportunity costs of all resources used in the production process. If the tax base does reflect economic profits exactly, the corporate tax will be non-distorting or *neutral*. It will not impinge upon the return required to compensate

---

[30] For a comparison between the impact incidence and general equilibrium approaches, see Lee, supra footnote 27.

the firm for its use of resources and so will not induce the firm to employ fewer resources. Furthermore, investments that are just marginal will bear no tax, since they earn no economic profit. Only inframarginal investments will yield taxable income. In terms of neutrality, then, a corporate tax whose base was economic profits would be a perfect tax. The extent to which a tax deviates from neutrality is conventionally measured by the marginal effective tax rate, a concept that we discuss below.

The actual tax system is almost certainly not neutral in its treatment of economic profits, mainly since actual deductions for capital costs almost certainly do not reflect true imputed capital costs. The capital cost allowances for physical capital do not reflect true depreciation rates. It is likely that the percentage rates used in calculating CCAs exceed the rates at which the capital is actually used up, especially in the case of firms that obtain accelerated depreciation.[31] During periods of inflation on the other hand, CCAs do not reflect the replacement costs of depreciating capital, since they are based on the asset's original cost. Writeoffs for capital costs are especially rapid in the case of depletable assets—that is, non-renewable natural resources.

The present corporate tax system also falls short of neutrality in its treatment of the costs of financing capital. Only the interest on assets that are financed by debt is deductible, not the "forgone" interest on assets that are financed by equity. Since the imputed costs of capital are not fully deductible from the tax base, the tax must fall to some extent on the return to capital in the corporate sector. To this extent at least, the tax is distorting and will induce the allocative effects outlined below. During periods of inflation, however, the tax's failure to allow a deduction for imputed interest will be offset in part by the fact that the tax system allows the deduction of nominal interest rather than real interest. Since part of nominal interest payments reflect a compensation to creditors for the fall in the real value of the principal owing to inflation, the ability to write off the inflationary portion of interest payments is equivalent to being able to write off part of the repayment of the principal in real terms.

Finally, part of a corporation's profits might represent a return to certain "imputed" factors of production, of which the most important are risk and entrepreneurship. To the extent that the returns to a corporation are risky, the owners of the corporation must bear a cost of risk taking, for which they are compensated in the form of higher returns. If these returns are taxed entirely as income—that is, if no deduction is allowed for the opportunity costs of taking a risk—the tax will discriminate against risk taking. In fact, the corporate tax does implicitly attempt to account for risk through the system of loss offsetting. Unless loss offsetting is perfect, however, so that losses are treated symmetrically with gains, the disincentive to risk taking will remain (we shall discuss this point further below). Similar reasoning applies to any

---

[31] This point is discussed in some detail in the Mintz committee report.

other imputed cost that is not deductible from the tax base, such as entre-preneurship. The tax will discourage its use in the corporate sector.

These considerations indicate that the corporate tax does have some impact on marginal rates of return and therefore does distort resource allocation. Of course, all of the above effects are mitigated to the extent that the corporate tax is integrated with the personal tax—indeed, if the corporate tax were perfectly integrated, it would be completely undone and would have no effect at all. We have already mentioned the fact that perfect integration would be difficult to achieve in an open economy, and we shall return to the question of integration in the next section. The remainder of this section considers the various ways in which the corporate income tax may distort decision making and resource allocation in the economy as a whole, assum-ing that it is at least in part a tax on the marginal return to capital, especially equity capital, in the corporate sector.

## The Corporate Sector Versus the Unincorporated Sector

The corporate tax is imposed only on incorporated firms. The income of unincorporated firms is taxed only as personal income in the hands of the owners of the firms. Corporate source capital income is taxed at both the cor-porate level and the personal level, except to the extent that it is integrated. The effect of this discriminatory treatment is to cause some resources to be employed in the unincorporated sector rather than in the corporate sector. As we discussed earlier, capital will be reallocated to the unincorporated sector until its net return is equalized everywhere. The reallocation of capital to the unincorporated sector will attract other factors, such as labour, with the result that the entire unincorporated sector (mainly service industries and portions of agriculture and fishing) will grow at the expense of the corporate sector. Harberger's seminal study estimated that in the absence of the US corporate tax there would have been between 20 and 40 percent more capital in the corporate sector in the United States and correspondingly less capital in the unincorporated sector.[32] This estimate, however, is no more than sugges-tive, since it is based upon a priori guesses about the degree of sub-stitutability of labour for capital in production, and about the elasticities of consumer demand for corporate and non-corporate output.

The implication of this tax-induced reallocation of factors from the corporate to the unincorporated sector is that the economy is not using its resources in the most efficient possible way. Since capital owners will reallocate capital until the after-tax return is identical everywhere, the before-tax return will be greater in the corporate sector, owing to the corporate tax, than it is elsewhere. From a social point of view, consequently, too little

---

[32] Arnold C. Harberger, "Efficiency Effects of Taxes on Income from Capital," in Marian Krzyzaniak, ed., *Effects of Corporation Income Tax* (Detroit: Wayne State University Press, 1966), 107-17.

capital is being used in the corporate sector and too much in the unincorpo-rated sector. The fact that the before-tax return is larger in the corporate sector means that national output would be increased if capital were reallocated from the unincorporated to the corporate sector. The loss to society from this misallocation of capital is known as the *welfare cost* of corporate taxation. Harberger estimated that the welfare cost of the US corporate tax was equivalent to between 2.5 and 7 percent of corporate tax revenues (or from 0.1 to 0.6 percent of GNP).[33]

The decision to incorporate may itself be influenced by the structure of the corporate tax. In the absence of taxes, firms incorporate because of the advantages of incorporation—limited liability of the shareholders for the debt of the firm and access to equity markets for financing. These advantages are presumably of special importance to large firms, and it is not likely that the existence of the corporate tax has much influence on their decisions about incorporation. In the case of small firms, however, there are several ways in which the corporate tax might influence the decision to incorporate. For example, to the extent that the corporate tax is not integrated with the personal tax, the double taxation of capital income will impose a tax cost on incorporation. In Canada, this consideration is not likely to be an important one, since in the case of small corporations, as we have seen, there is close to full integration of the two taxes. Indeed, if anything, the corporate tax may provide a mild incentive for small firms to incorporate: income that is retained and reinvested in the corporation escapes current personal taxation, unlike the income of unincorporated business.

## The Differential Treatment of Industries Within the Corporate Sector

As we discussed in the first section of this chapter, the corporate tax treats different industries differently. Some industries pay lower tax rates than others pay; some are allowed more generous deductions than others are allowed. In some cases, the preference for certain industries is explicit. Manufacturing and processing industries face advantageous tax rates. Re-source industries benefit from the rapid writeoffs for exploration and development expenditures. In other cases, general rules work to the advan-tage of particular industries. Canadian-controlled private corporations face relatively low tax rates. CCAs for machinery and equipment are more liberal than CCAs for, say, buildings. Investments financed by debt are favoured over those financed by equity. R & D expenditures obtain both rapid writeoffs and tax credits. Cooperatives may deduct consumer patronage dividends that are not taxable in the hands of recipients. All of these measures provide

---

[33] For a comprehensive survey of welfare cost distortions estimated in the literature, see John B. Shoven and John Whalley, "Applied General-Equilibrium Models of Taxation and International Trade: An Introduction and Survey" (September 1984), 22 *Journal of Economic Literature* 1007-51.

incentives for capital and other productive inputs to locate in some industries or firms rather than others until all after-tax returns are equalized. From a social efficiency point of view, the differential tax treatment of industries under the corporate tax implies that there will be too little activity in highly taxed industries relative to other industries.

It is not immediately apparent how different industries fare under the existing corporate tax system, and there is relatively little evidence of the effect of corporate taxation on the allocation of resources among industries in Canada. In a model that uses a general equilibrium methodology that is basically the same as the one pioneered by Harberger, Boadway and Treddenick have computed the effect on resource allocation in Canada of the distortions induced by the corporate tax.[34] They find, surprisingly, that the corporate tax structure discriminates against most mining industries, all processing industries, and most manufacturing industries (especially alcohol, machinery, motor vehicles, chemicals, and miscellaneous manufacturing). The tax favours most service industries and agriculture—presumably because they are in large part unincorporated. Unfortunately, these results are speculative. They derive from a static model of the economy with given stocks of capital. The analysis includes no statistical estimation and ignores dynamic considerations. Furthermore, the study calculates effective corporate tax rates rather crudely as average effective corporate tax rates by simply taking the ratio of total corporate taxes paid to total capital income in each industry. The study assumes that depreciation is the same in all industries, and because of limitations of the data corporations and unincorporated businesses are lumped together. Recent work on marginal effective tax rates, reported below, indicates that average tax rates can be very different from effective marginal tax rates, which are the proper measure of the distorting effect of the corporate tax.

## Interprovincial Distortions

Provincial corporate income tax rates vary somewhat from province to province, and this variation will distort the allocation of resources among provinces. The extent of this distortion is extremely difficult to assess, but there are reasons to suppose that it is not very great. For one thing, the difference between the highest provincial rate and the lowest is only 6 percentage points; for another, the provinces with higher tax rates may provide correspondingly higher levels of public services to corporations.

Perhaps more important is the fact that different provinces have different mixes of corporations. The same factors that give rise to interindustry distortions will distort the interprovincial allocation of capital. If it is true, as the Mintz committee says, that resource and manufacturing industries are treated favourably relative to services and tertiary industries, this circumstance will

---

[34] Boadway and Treddenick, supra footnote 26.

undoubtedly affect some provinces more than others. For example, the three westernmost provinces rely heavily on resources, and Ontario and Quebec rely heavily on manufacturing.

One other potential source of interprovincial resource misallocation is the wide variation in the treatment of resource industries across provinces. As we noted above, some provinces levy taxes on resource profits, whereas others levy ad valorem or per-unit royalties on production. In addition, some provinces' rates are graduated, others are not, and the average rates vary considerably from province to province. These differences in treatment are likely to influence the distribution of investment in resource industries across the various provinces. Unfortunately, no empirical analyses are available to indicate the magnitude of the distortion involved.

## The Effect of the Corporate Tax on the Financial Structure of Corporations

So far we have concentrated on the way in which the corporate tax influences the allocation of aggregate resources among uses. The remainder of the section considers how the tax affects the incentive for individual firms to undertake productive activities.

The first step in any productive undertaking is the financial decision. In financing their capital expenditures, firms use a variety of financial instruments, all of which can be classified as either debt or equity. The choice of a financial structure depends on a variety of factors, including the relative costs of debt and equity finance to the firm, as determined by financial markets; the availability of internal financing to the firm, as determined by its cash flow; and the tax treatment of the costs associated with each of these methods of financing.

The corporate tax influences the financial structure and the cost of finance of the firm mainly because it favours the use of debt over equity finance. The costs of debt finance—that is, interest—are deductible from taxable income, but the costs of equity finance are not. Thus firms have an incentive to substitute debt finance for equity finance. Of course, there is a limit to the extent to which they can do this. As a firm's contractually fixed interest obligations increase relative to equity, the firm's riskiness to shareholders and creditors increases as well. The relative variability of the residual return to shareholders rises, and so does the probability of bankruptcy. As a result, the rate of return required to compensate equity holders may rise and the interest rate demanded by lenders to the firm will rise. It will become more and more costly for the firm to substitute debt for equity despite the tax advantages of doing so. Eventually, the rise in the cost of finance will overcome the tax advantage of increasing the debt-equity ratio. The firm will end up with more debt than it would have incurred in the absence of the tax, but it will not rely entirely on debt finance. Overall, however, the interest deductibility provision will result in more bankruptcy than is desirable from a social point of view.

Because the tax system allows firms to deduct nominal interest on debt rather than real interest, debt finance can be even more attractive during inflationary periods. The fact that nominal interest includes an inflationary component designed to compensate creditors for the fall in the real value of their assets means that during inflation firms can actually deduct part of their principal from taxable income.

Personal taxes too can affect the cost of finance and the choice between debt and equity. The personal tax system treats the income from debt (interest) differently from the income from equity (dividends and capital gains). In general, because of the dividend tax credit and the preferential treatment of capital gains, interest is taxed more heavily at the personal level than is equity income. Thus the personal tax tends to offset the advantage to debt finance conferred by the corporate tax. The personal tax is also likely to affect a firm's choice of a method of equity finance. On the one hand, if equity finance is obtained from new equity issues rather than retained earnings, existing shareholders may receive additional dividends. On the other hand, earnings that are retained rather than paid out as dividends yield capital gains to existing shareholders. Since capital gains tend to be taxed less heavily at the personal level than dividends, shareholders will prefer as a rule to obtain equity finance from retained earnings rather than new share issues. In general, indeed, the tax system discourages the paying-out of dividends. This is sometimes referred to as the *trapped equity effect* of the tax system.

Besides providing an incentive for firms to use retained earnings rather than new equity finance, the tax advantage for retained earnings favours firms that have internal sources of finance over those that do not. Thus, the tax system favours mature firms over small, immature ones. Moreover, by providing an incentive to keep funds within a corporation rather than pay them out as dividends, the system provides an incentive for takeovers—firms with excess funds may use them to take over firms with a shortage of funds and thereby keep the funds in the corporation.

The impact of the personal tax on the cost of finance is tempered considerably by the openness of Canada to world capital markets. The returns that Canadian residents receive on their savings must conform to the rates set on international capital markets; otherwise the funds would move elsewhere to obtain the going return. Consequently, it has been argued, the costs of finance that Canadian firms must pay before the application of personal tax are likely to be more or less fixed, especially for larger firms. According to this view, which is a fairly compelling one, the imposition of Canadian personal taxes will merely reduce the after-tax return to Canadian savers rather than increase the cost of finance to firms. Only taxes levied on the firm will affect the latter. Just how open Canadian capital markets are is an important but unanswered empirical question. One might expect the returns for widely traded debt and equity instruments to conform closely to the returns on international markets. In the case of private corporations, this outcome is less certain. In their case, personal taxes may have a significant impact on the cost of finance.

## The Effect of the Corporate Tax on Investment

One of the most important effects of the corporate tax is its effect on the investment decision of the firm and thus collectively on aggregate investment. The decision to invest depends ultimately on the rate of return that a firm can obtain on additional, or "marginal," units of investment. To the extent that the corporate tax affects this marginal rate of return, it will also affect the amount of investment that firms wish to undertake—and in fact it is likely that the tax does influence the rate of return on marginal investments. This is so because the gross returns to the investment (revenues net of current costs) are taxable but the true costs of using the capital are not deductible. For example, the costs of equity finance are not deductible, nor are the true replacement costs of inventory usage, and capital cost allowances may not reflect true economic depreciation.

The analysis of the effects of corporate taxation on investment has been the subject of a large body of empirical literature, especially with application to the United States. The seminal work was carried out by Jorgenson and his associates, who developed the so-called *neoclassical theory of investment* upon which much of the theoretical and empirical literature has been based.[35] According to this theory, firms will wish to accumulate capital until the additional revenue generated by the last increment of investment (the "marginal revenue product") over a given period just equals the full economic cost of holding the capital for the same period. The latter is referred to as the *user cost of capital* and includes the cost of financing the marginal investment (after tax), the true economic depreciation arising from obsolescence, wear and tear, and capital gains; and the tax saving arising from tax writeoffs for capital costs during the period. A corporate tax system affects the decision in two ways. First, it reduces the marginal revenues to the firm from investment by taxing them. Second, it reduces the user cost of capital, or the marginal cost of holding the capital, by allowing tax savings through the mechanism of deductions for capital costs, in particular deductions for interest and depreciation. It has been established in the economics literature that if the present value of the writeoffs for capital, including any investment tax credits, just equals the initial purchase price, the tax will not affect the profitability of the marginal investment and so will not affect the incentive to invest.[36] The tax is said in this case to be neutral: it will reduce the marginal revenues and the marginal costs of holding capital by the same

---

[35] Dale W. Jorgenson, "Capital Theory and Investment Behavior" (May 1963), 53 *The American Economic Review* 247-59; Robert E. Hall and Dale W. Jorgenson, "Tax Policy and Investment Behavior" (June 1967), 57 *The American Economic Review* 391-414; and Dale W. Jorgenson, "Econometric Studies of Investment Behavior: A Survey" (December 1971), 9 *Journal of Economic Literature* 1111-47. For a critical survey of the neoclassical approach, see Robert S. Chirinko, "Will the Neoclassical Theory of Investment Please Rise? The General Structure of Investment Models and Their Implications for Tax Policy," in Jack M. Mintz and Douglas D. Purvis, eds., *The Impact of Taxation on Business Activity* (Kingston, Ont.: Queen's University, John Deutsch Institute for the Study of Economic Policy, 1987), 109-67.

[36] This is demonstrated in Robin W. Boadway, "Corporate Taxation and Investment: A Synthesis of the Neo-Classical Model" (May 1980), 13 *Canadian Journal of Economics* 250-67.

proportion. If the value of writeoffs is lower, investment will be discouraged, and vice versa. We shall present some evidence below of the direction and magnitude of the distortion imposed by the corporate tax on marginal investments of various sorts.

Tax changes influence the incentive to invest through their effect on the user cost of capital relative to revenues. Any measure that increases the relative user cost of capital will discourage investment, and any measure that makes it cheaper to hold capital will encourage investment. Such measures include changes in capital cost allowances, the introduction of various investment incentives, and changes in the tax rate itself. Any acceleration of the capital cost allowance for a particular type of capital increases the present value of these deductions and so reduces the present value of future tax payments. In other words, because tax payments are postponed, the present value of an investment plan is increased. An investment tax credit offsets corporate tax liabilities by a given percentage of the investment. It may or may not affect the subsequent stream of capital cost allowances. Investment tax credits in Canada typically reduce the base for future depreciation writeoffs by the amount of the credit; they thereby reduce, but do not eliminate, the incentive effect of the credit.

Accelerated depreciation and investment tax credits have slightly different incentive effects. Although both increase the present value of tax deductions, the accelerated depreciation scheme is of more value for long-lived investments and the investment tax credit is of more value for short-lived investments. On the one hand, an investment tax credit equal to a given percentage of investment may be claimed every time an investment is undertaken. In the case of investments with a short life, therefore, it may be claimed frequently. On the other hand, accelerated depreciation schemes allow firms with long-lived investments to claim deductions earlier in the life of the asset. This consideration will be of greater value to the firm in present value terms the longer-lived the asset is and hence the further into the future normal deductions may be spread.

Most empirical work in this area is based on investment demand equations derived from the neoclassical theory of investment and follows the methodology of Jorgenson.[37] In its simplest version, this methodology assumes that the decision to invest depends on changes in output (the so-called *accelerator effect*) and on the user cost of holding capital, which we discussed above. To be more precise, observed investment is assumed to have been determined by the past and present values of these variables, values that reflect both lags in decision making and installation and expectations about future output and prices.

The results derived from analyses of this kind are mixed. In studies of the US corporate tax in the 1960s, Jorgenson and his associates found that over

---

[37] Jorgenson, "Capital Theory and Investment Behavior," supra footnote 35.

40 percent of the increase in net investment in manufacturing equipment in 1963 could be attributed to a 7 percent investment tax credit introduced in 1962. Similarly, the adoption of accelerated depreciation methods in 1954 and of a reduction in service lives in 1962 had led to a significant increase in aggregate investment. A tax rate reduction in 1964, however, had had no positive effect on investment. A subsequent study by Bischoff agreed that the investment tax credit had provided substantial stimulation to investment but argued that the accelerated depreciation had produced hardly any effect.[38] A great many studies—too many to describe here—have been undertaken in the United States, not all of which have yielded the same results.[39]

In 1976, Gaudet, May, and McFetridge used the basic Jorgenson approach to study the effect on investment of the Canadian corporate tax.[40] They estimated the statistical dependence of the capital stock in manufacturing on current and past values of both manufacturing output and the user cost of capital. As we have mentioned, the dependence of the capital stock on changes in tax parameters such as tax incentives for investment will be reflected in the effect of the tax changes on the user cost of capital. Gaudet, May, and McFetridge found that the user cost was a significant determinant of the capital stock, although the lag associated with its operation was somewhat longer than the lag associated with output-induced changes in capital accumulation. They concluded that the Canadian government could influence, with a lag, the decision of firms to invest in capital by changing the corporate tax rate or providing tax incentives. Their study performed no simulations to establish the likely magnitude of these effects.

Two subsequent studies in the 1970s—one by McFetridge and May and the other by Harman and Johnson—confirmed these results.[41] The former study estimated a statistical relationship between capital demanded and several variables, including the relative costs of labour and capital services, the level of output, and lagged values of capital demanded. McFetridge and May then used the estimated relationship to simulate the impact of various tax incentive and disincentive measures that had been undertaken since 1950 to influence investment in machinery and equipment in Canadian manufacturing industries. Their results confirmed that investment is sensitive to tax changes, but with a lag. For example, an increase of 15 percent in the base for

---

[38] Charles W. Bischoff, "The Effect of Alternative Lag Distributions," in Gary Fromm, ed., *Tax Incentives and Capital Spending* (Washington, DC: Brookings Institution, 1971), 61-125.

[39] See the survey in Chirinko, supra footnote 35.

[40] G.O. Gaudet, J.D. May, and D.G. McFetridge, "Optimal Capital Accumulation: The Neo-Classical Framework in a Canadian Context" (August 1976), 58 *Review of Economics and Statistics* 269-73.

[41] D.G. McFetridge and J.D. May, "The Effects of Capital Cost Allowance Measures on Capital Accumulation in the Canadian Manufacturing Sector" (July 1976), 4 *Public Finance Quarterly* 307-22; and F.J. Harman and J.A Johnson, "An Examination of Government Tax Incentives for Business Investment in Canada" (1978), vol. 26, no. 6 *Canadian Tax Journal* 691-704.

capital cost allowances in December 1970 caused net investment to increase by about 9 percent in 1972 and 4 percent in 1973. An accelerated depreciation provision introduced in May 1972 caused net investment to rise by 3.55 percent in 1973, 6.42 percent in 1974, and 7.15 percent in 1975. Typically, a tax incentive has its initial impact one year after it is introduced and its modal impact in the third year. McFetridge and May concluded that because of the lags involved investment incentives were not a suitable instrument for short-term stabilization. Yet one should not, perhaps, draw too strong a policy conclusion from their results, since they are based on annual rather than, say, quarterly data. Moreover, there is still some debate in the literature about the reliability of the basic Jorgenson approach to estimating investment expenditures.

Harman and Johnson obtained results similar to those of McFetridge and May for the magnitude and the timing of the impact of investment incentives. They also found that the tax revenue lost owing to the measures was of the same order of magnitude as the amount of investment induced. Thus the 1972 accelerated depreciation and tax reduction induced an estimated increase in investment of $313.3 million and an estimated loss in tax revenues of $568.2 million—results that cast doubt on the efficacy of these tax incentives.

## The Effect of the Corporate Tax on Aggregate Savings

A large proportion of capital income is saved, both by shareholders and, in the form of retained earnings, by the corporation itself. Since the corporate tax is a direct tax on the capital income from which the savings are generated, one might suppose it to have a greater adverse impact on savings than other taxes have. There is, however, little empirical evidence to support this supposition and some reasons to be cautious about it. One cannot infer from the fact that a large part of corporate income is saved that taxes on corporate income are paid largely at the expense of savings. For one thing, the corporate tax may be shifted from capital income to consumers and to other factors of production, in which case after-tax income will be the same as it would be in the absence of the tax. This consideration is especially relevant in Canada, whose capital markets are relatively open to international capital flows. As we argued earlier, if an economy is small and open and capital flows freely across its borders, the after-tax rates of return that corporations must pay to their shareholders and creditors are predetermined by international markets and are not affected by the corporate tax. In this extreme case, the tax is completely shifted elsewhere and rates of return to savers are unaffected.

Even if the tax is not completely shifted and does reduce corporate income, its implications for savings may not be as drastic as one might think. Although corporate retained earnings are completely saved, they are saved on behalf of shareholders. If shareholders recognize that corporations are doing less saving on their behalf, they may react by consuming less and saving more of their other income. In this case, shareholders are said to "see through the corporate veil." Empirical evidence for the United States and the United Kingdom tends to support the view that shareholders' personal savings are influenced to a considerable extent by corporate retained earnings. For example, Poterba found that an incremented increase in corporate savings in the United States is accompanied by a reduction of personal savings of between 50 and 75 percent.[42] Much more evidence is required, however, before one can say with any confidence how the corporate tax affects savings.

## The Effect of the Corporate Tax on Risk Taking

As we mentioned earlier, since part of corporate taxable income may reflect a return required to compensate shareholders for the bearing of risk—that is, a cost of risk bearing that is a legitimate cost of earning income—the corporate tax may be thought of as being in part a tax on risk borne by the shareholders. At the same time, the loss-offset provisions in the corporate tax are quite liberal. Consequently, although the tax may reduce the gains from risky ventures, it may also reduce the losses. In effect, the government shares in the risk of the enterprise. If loss offsetting were perfect—that is, if the tax system credited losses immediately—one could view the corporate tax as being simply a means by which the government becomes a silent partner in the corporation, sharing with it all gains and losses symmetrically.

Given these considerations, it is difficult to say what effect the tax has on corporations' willingness to assume risk. From the point of view of a corporation, the tax reduces the possible variability of returns (both up and down) and increases, to a corresponding degree, the variability of government tax revenues. At the same time, the tax will reduce the average or mean expected return. Consequently, the tax may very well induce the decision makers of the corporation to assume more risk—that is, seek higher and more variable returns than they would seek in the tax's absence. Given the liberality of the offset provisions, there is no a priori basis for the popular notion that the tax must reduce risk taking by corporations.[43] Evidence of the effect of taxation on risk taking is virtually non-existent, but it would be incorrect to presume that the corporate tax generally discourages risk taking.

There are, however, some specific circumstances in which the tax system may put firms that are engaged in risky enterprises at a disadvantage. Small,

---

[42] See J.M. Poterba, "Tax Policy and Corporate Saving" (December 1987), *Brookings Papers on Economic Activity* 455-503. For earlier results, see Martin S. Feldstein, "Tax Incentives, Corporate Saving, and Capital Accumulation in the United States" (April 1973), 2 *Journal of Public Economics* 159-71; and Martin Feldstein and George Fane, "Taxes, Corporate Dividend Policy and Personal Savings: The British Postwar Experience" (November 1973), 55 *Review of Economics and Statistics* 399-411.

[43] This is a well-known result in the public finance literature and originated with Evsey D. Domar and Richard A. Musgrave, "Proportional Income Taxation and Risk Taking" (May 1944), 58 *Quarterly Journal of Economics* 388-422. See the earlier discussion of the subject in the context of the personal tax in chapter 2. An extension of the analysis to the corporate tax appears in Jack M. Mintz, "Some Additional Results on Investment, Risk Taking, and Full Loss Offset Corporate Taxation with Interest Deductibility" (November 1981), 96 *Quarterly Journal of Economics* 631-42.

growing firms are frequently subject to more risk than larger firms are. They are often in risky lines of business, and they have less opportunity than larger firms do to diversify across other products. The loss-offset provisions, though liberal, may be insufficient to offset the riskiness that these firms face. If they go bankrupt, they lose the advantage of the loss-carryforward provisions. Even if they do not go bankrupt, they may not be able to offset their losses for a long time. This disadvantage compounds the disadvantage relative to larger, more stable firms that small firms already have in obtaining financing. The issue is one of some importance, since small, risky firms may be responsible for a disproportionately large share of innovation and job creation. It is unfortunate and costly to society, therefore, if the tax system puts them at a disadvantage.

The loss-offset provisions also fail to compensate firms sufficiently for what is called *capital risk*.[44] The term refers to the risk that firms face because of fluctuations in the price of their capital goods. Capital cost allowances are based on the original purchase price of capital goods. If the price of capital goods increases, CCAs will not cover the cost of replacing them. (Of course, if prices fall, CCAs will more than cover replacement costs.) The tax system fails to capture this source of uncertainty; that is, government does not share capital risk in the way that it shares *output risk*, or risk that arises from a change in the value of sales by the firm.

## Corporate Taxation and Inflation

The corporate tax is not indexed for inflation, and the question arises whether the existence of inflation exacerbates the distortion that the corporate tax imposes on investment. At issue is the impact of inflation on the value of the writeoffs permitted to the firm and hence on the tax base. In theory, the impact of inflation on the incentive to invest is ambiguous. On the one hand, capital cost allowances are based on the historic cost rather than the replacement cost of investments and inventories are deductible according to FIFO accounting principles rather than at replacement cost. Consequently, the real value of these deductions falls with inflation, causing real tax payments to rise. On the other hand, firms are allowed to deduct nominal rather than real interest payments. As we mentioned earlier, the inflationary component of the interest rate reflects an inflation-induced fall in the real value of the principal. Thus the corporate tax provisions implicitly allow firms to write off part of the principal of their debt in addition to real interest. An indexed system would allow depreciation at replacement cost and the deductibility of real financial costs.

Whether inflation increases or reduces the corporate tax distortion depends on the relative magnitudes of the disadvantages of historic capital

---

[44] The notion of capital risk was first analyzed by Jeremy I. Bulow and Lawrence H. Summers, "The Taxation of Risky Assets" (February 1984), 92 *Journal of Political Economy* 20-39.

cost accounting and the advantages of nominal interest deductibility. This is an empirical question that can only be resolved by investigating the actual experience of firms. Some light can be shed on it by the calculation of marginal effective tax rates, a technique that has become a staple of tax policy analysis in Canada and one that provided the basis for many of the recommendations of the Mintz committee. We conclude this section by summarizing some work that has been done in this area.

## Measuring the Effective Tax Rate in Canada

We have mentioned that the corporate tax affects the investment decision of firms by changing the rate of return that they can obtain on marginal investments. A marginal investment is one that generates revenues just sufficient to cover the full costs, including the imputed cost of any shareholders' funds used to finance it. If marginal investments bear tax, there will be a disincentive to invest: the only projects that will be profitable are those that cover not only the costs of investing but also the tax liabilities they create. An investment that is marginal under the tax will have a higher rate of return than one that would be marginal in the absence of the tax. (Inframarginal investments that have a higher rate of return will also bear a tax liability.) Although it is conventional to expect the tax to impinge upon the marginal investment and to impose a disincentive on the investment decision of the firm, in principle the corporate tax could instead be subsidizing marginal investments. It all depends on the generosity of writeoffs for capital costs and the magnitude of tax credits. If the present value of the future writeoffs arising from one unit of investment (including capital cost allowances, interest deductions, and the benefit of any investment tax credit) exceeds the initial cost of the investment, the tax will actually subsidize investment at the margin.

One must be careful to distinguish between the impact of the tax on marginal rates of return and its impact on inframarginal rates of return. In the context of the incentive to invest, it is the rate of return at the margin that is important. It is possible for the tax to subsidize investment at the margin and yet yield positive tax revenues from inframarginal investments. Moreover, the incentive effect can vary significantly by type of investment and sector.

A body of empirical work in Canada and elsewhere has attempted to identify the direction and measure the magnitude and direction of the distortion imposed by taxes on the rate of return to marginal investments. This distortion, the so-called *marginal effective tax rate* (METR),[45] is measured as the

---

[45] The Canadian work began with Robin Boadway, Neil Bruce, and Jack Mintz, "Taxation, Inflation and the Effective Marginal Tax Rate on Capital in Canada" (February 1984), 17 *Canadian Journal of Economics* 62-79. For an international perspective, see Mervyn A. King et al., *The Taxation of Income from Capital: A Comparative Study* (Chicago: University of Chicago Press, 1983). A survey of the literature may be found in Robin W. Boadway, "The Theory and Measurement of Effective Tax Rates," in *The Impact of Taxation on Business Activity*, supra footnote 35, 60-98.

difference between the gross (before-tax) rate of return on investment and the net (after-tax) rate of return received by savers. Both the corporate tax and the personal tax will influence the size of the distortion. In measuring the gross rate of return, it is assumed (following the neoclassical theory of investment) that firms will invest until the rate of return just equals the user cost of capital net of depreciation. In other words, the latter is used as a proxy for the gross rate of return. The net return is the return obtained by the debt and equity holders of the firm.[46] The METR is usually expressed as a proportion of the gross rate of return. It thus measures the share of the return on the marginal investment that accrues as taxes to the government; the remainder represents the return to private investors.

The original work of Boadway, Bruce, and Mintz measured this distortion for various types of capital (machinery, buildings, inventories, and land) on the basis of aggregate annual data for the years 1963 to 1978. They then broke the METR down into the portion attributable to corporate taxation and the portion attributable to personal taxation. This decomposition is especially relevant in the context of an open economy, in which the corporate tax mainly affects the investment decision and the personal tax affects savings. Their results indicated that the corporate tax structure imposed its largest distortion on inventories, but that otherwise the METR was significantly lower than statutory tax rates were. (An investment tax credit in place during the study period substantially reduced the METR.) The personal tax was somewhat more distorting than the corporate tax, except in the case of savings, such as savings for retirement, that were sheltered from personal taxes. The advent in the 1970s of high rates of inflation did not appear to affect the magnitude of the METR except in the case of inventories. It is important to emphasize that these results were obtained from highly aggregated data. Nevertheless, they do reinforce the theoretical result that neither the corporate tax nor the tax's failure to account for inflation necessarily discriminates against investment. Again, the tax's effect on investment depends on the generosity of its system of writeoffs for capital costs.

---

[46] The formal derivation of the METR is rather technical. In brief, its components are as follows for the case of depreciable capital. The before-tax user cost of capital is given by $(r + d)(1 - z)/(1 - u)$, where $r$ is the cost of finance to the firm, $u$ is the corporate tax rate, $d$ is the economic depreciation rate, and $z$ is the present value of future capital cost allowance deductions on a dollar's worth of capital. The firm will invest until the before-tax marginal revenue from the last unit of investment just equals this user cost. The rate of return on the marginal investment, then, is this marginal revenue less the depreciation rate, or $R = (r + d)(1 - z)/(1 - u) - d$. This result is referred to as the before-tax marginal rate of return on investment. The after-personal-tax rate of return on savings is given by $S = \beta i(1 - t) + (1 - \beta)\rho$, where $t$ is the personal tax rate on interest income, $\beta$ is the proportion of investment financed by debt, $i$ is the interest rate on debt, and $\rho$ is the after-tax rate of return on equity to the shareholders, taking account of dividend and capital gains taxation. The METR is then defined as $(R - S)/R$: the share of the rate of return on the marginal investment accruing to the tax authorities. Measurement of the METR requires estimating the parameters that constitute $R$ and $S$ for various types of investments.

Tax policy proposals have come to be heavily influenced by METR calculations. The corporate income tax reform of 1987 was accompanied by METR calculations on a sector-by-sector basis; they indicated the need for reforms designed to make the corporate tax system more neutral. Subsequently, the Mintz committee used detailed METR calculations to substantiate its argument for the need to eliminate some of the remaining tax provisions that favour some industries relative to others. Table 4.4 shows a selection of the METRs computed for the Mintz committee for different types of capital, different industries, and different sizes of firm. These data indicate a number of instances of differential tax treatment across industries, where the taxes include federal and provincial corporate and capital taxes and also provincial sales taxes on capital goods. The METRs are all substantially below the statutory rates, reflecting the fact that deductions for capital costs reduce the tax burden on marginal investments. Not surprisingly, the METRs for small businesses are lower than those for large ones—a consequence of the small business tax deduction. For large firms, inventories tend to have the highest METRs; they are followed by land and structures. Inventories apparently suffer from the use for tax purposes of FIFO tax-accounting methods, whereas machinery obtains favourable capital cost allowances. The METRs for research and development are negative, an outcome that reflects both the high initial writeoffs for R & D and the SR & ED tax credit. The METR for exploration and development, though positive, is very low, again because of rapid writeoffs. The METRs in the resource industries and in manufacturing are relatively low, and the METRs in construction and the service industries are relatively high.

These METRs indicate the size of the distortion that taxes on business income impose on marginal investments and therefore the magnitude of the disincentive to invest. The Mintz committee also considered the burden of all taxes that are imposed on business inputs. Table 4.5 shows for various industries the percentage of capital costs that consist of taxes on capital and the percentage of labour costs that consist of taxes on labour. Taxes on capital again include federal and provincial corporate and capital taxes and, as well, provincial sales taxes on business inputs. Taxes on labour include federal and provincial payroll taxes paid by employers, net of any benefits of earmarked programs. The table indicates that the share of costs taken as taxes is much larger in the case of capital costs than it is in the case of labour costs. It also confirms the finding that capital taxes favour small firms and firms in the resource and manufacturing sectors. The differential effects of taxes on labour are much less pronounced.

## Structural Problems of the Corporate Income Tax

This section will consider a variety of proposals for reforming the corporate income tax. Few taxes have received more attention from policy advisers and academic economists alike. The decades since the renowned Carter report of 1966 have seen a number of important studies of the corporate tax and

**Table 4.4   Marginal Effective Tax Rates by Industry, Size of Firm, and Capital Type, 1997**

| | Large business | Small business |
|---|---|---|
| | *percent* | |
| Industries | | |
| Agriculture, fishing, and trapping .......... | na | 7.9 |
| Forestry ............................. | 28.8 | 12.6 |
| Mining ............................. | 8.7 | na |
| Oil and gas ......................... | 5.5 | na |
| Manufacturing ....................... | 17.9 | 7.6 |
| Construction ........................ | 37.0 | 17.5 |
| Transportation ...................... | 27.9 | 15.7 |
| Communications ..................... | 23.9 | 20.2 |
| Public utilities ...................... | 30.3 | 14.7 |
| Wholesale trade ..................... | 32.1 | 15.5 |
| Retail trade ......................... | 33.8 | 16.4 |
| Other services ...................... | 27.6 | 10.1 |
| Assets | | |
| Structures .......................... | 24.2 | 8.3 |
| Machinery ........................... | 19.6 | 17.9 |
| Land ............................... | 25.3 | 9.2 |
| Inventory .......................... | 37.6 | 16.5 |
| Exploration and development ............. | 0.2 | na |
| Research and development ............... | −28.0 | −39.8 |

na   not applicable.

Source: Canada, *Report of the Technical Committee on Business Taxation* (Ottawa: Department of Finance, April 1998), table 3.1.

**Table 4.5   Effective Tax Rates on Input Costs, 1997**

| | Large business | | | Small business | | |
|---|---|---|---|---|---|---|
| Industries (non-financial) | Capital costs | Labour costs | Total | Capital costs | Labour costs | Total |
| | *percent* | | | | | |
| Agriculture, fishing, and trapping .... | na | na | na | 8.9 | −5.4 | 1.6 |
| Forestry ...................... | 45.4 | −5.2 | 0.9 | 14.5 | −5.4 | −2.9 |
| Mining ....................... | 13.3 | 2.7 | 5.7 | na | na | na |
| Oil and gas ................... | 8.0 | 1.4 | 4.5 | na | na | na |
| Manufacturing ................. | 27.0 | 3.2 | 8.8 | 9.8 | 3.0 | 4.6 |
| Construction .................. | 59.9 | −0.6 | 5.5 | 21.5 | −0.9 | 1.7 |
| Transportation ................ | 39.5 | 3.2 | 8.3 | 19.0 | 2.9 | 5.3 |
| Communications ............... | 35.2 | 4.4 | 15.4 | 27.3 | 4.0 | 10.8 |
| Public utilities ................ | 44.4 | 4.5 | 26.9 | 17.4 | 4.2 | 12.0 |
| Wholesale trade ............... | 51.7 | 3.6 | 10.4 | 19.4 | 3.3 | 5.7 |
| Retail trade ................... | 53.0 | 3.0 | 7.5 | 20.3 | 2.6 | 4.3 |
| Other services ................. | 39.5 | 2.7 | 9.7 | 12.2 | 2.3 | 4.3 |
| All non-financial firms ............ | 33.3 | 2.8 | 9.4 | 14.6 | 2.4 | 5.1 |

na   not applicable.

Source: Canada, *Report of the Technical Committee on Business Taxation* (Ottawa: Department of Finance, April 1998), table 3.2.

proposals for its reform. Two influential studies in the 1970s were the Meade report in the United Kingdom and the US Treasury's *Blueprints for Basic Tax Reform*,[47] which, in part, inspired proposals for capital tax reform by the now-defunct Economic Council of Canada.[48] In addition, the academic economics journals have published a variety of analytical papers about the economic effects of corporate taxation and their implications for reform.[49] Several countries have attempted major legislative reforms of their corporate tax systems. In Canada, reforms in 1981 and 1987 have preceded the current challenge, represented by the Mintz committee proposals, to undertake further reforms suitable to the realities of rapidly changing times.

Two important points emerge from the literature and the reform experience of the past 30 years. The first is that the economist's view of the corporate tax has evolved considerably since the time of the Carter report. The second is that the current views of academic economists appear to be at variance with the views of many other tax experts, including those in government. At any rate, the reforms that governments have proposed and undertaken have diverged substantially from the concerns that have dominated the academic literature. Until recently, one might argue, the views of policy specialists dominated the reform agenda, but with the advent of a new international economy characterized by open capital markets the views of academic economists have gained more prominence. It is possible to view the Mintz committee report as an attempt to fuse academic views of corporate tax policy with the realities and complexities of the real world.

To set the stage, it is useful to begin this section with a broad overview of the rationale for the corporate tax and the implications of this rationale for the structure of the ideal tax. This discussion will suggest many ways in which the tax might be reformed; it will also provide a framework within which one can assess the existing system and recent and proposed reforms. We shall then turn to some of the more specific shortcomings of the corporate tax referred to in the literature, concentrating especially on the ways in which the system affords preferential treatment to some activities or institutions relative to others.

---

[47] Institute for Fiscal Studies, *The Structure and Reform of Direct Taxation: Report of a Committee Chaired by Professor J.E. Meade* (London: Allen & Unwin, 1978); and United States, Department of the Treasury, *Blueprints for Basic Tax Reform* (Washington, DC: Government Printing Office, 1977).

[48] Economic Council of Canada, *Road Map for Tax Reform: The Taxation of Savings and Investment* (Ottawa: Supply and Services, 1987).

[49] For a summary of the academic literature, see A.B. Atkinson and J.E. Stiglitz, *Lectures on Public Economics* (London: McGraw-Hill, 1980); *The Impact of Taxation on Business Activity*, supra footnote 35; and Robin W. Boadway, Neil Bruce, and Jack M. Mintz, *Taxes on Capital Income in Canada: Analysis and Policy*, Canadian Tax Paper no. 80 (Toronto: Canadian Tax Foundation, 1987).

## The Rationale for the Corporate Income Tax

The corporate tax falls on capital income that is typically taxed again when the income is passed on to households in the form of dividends and capital gains. A natural question to ask is, Why tax corporate income at all? Why not rely solely on the personal income tax? There are two fundamental rationales for the taxation of income at the level of the corporation (apart from its being a useful source of tax revenues). The first is that it may be desirable to tax some forms of capital income *at source* if these forms of income would otherwise escape full taxation by the personal income tax. Thus a corporate tax may be useful for its *withholding function*. The Carter report stressed this function and in fact judged it to be the only real function of the corporate tax. The second rationale for a corporate tax, and the one stressed in the economics literature, is that a tax on corporate income can be an ideal tax on efficiency grounds, since if it is properly designed it will strike only the rents or pure economic profits of corporations and impose no distortions on the economy. Thus a corporate tax might also function as a *pure profits tax*.

Obviously, an ideal corporate tax would function as both a withholding tax and a tax on pure profits. The difficulty is that the ideal structure for one purpose differs from the ideal structure for the other purpose. The existing system reflects this dilemma. Some provisions appear to have been designed with withholding in mind and others with taxing profits in mind, but the system fails to reconcile the two functions and performs neither of them as effectively as it might. Part of our purpose here is to suggest how a corporate tax might be structured with both functions in mind.

### The Withholding Function

The withholding function arises from the recognition that corporations are ultimately owned by individuals, and that any tax imposed is ultimately borne by individual taxpayers. If it were possible to tax all capital income fully and immediately under the personal income tax, there would be no need to use the corporate tax as a withholding device. Two types of capital income escape full or immediate taxation at the personal level, capital gains income and income that accrues to non-residents. Firms invariably retain some of their income and reinvest it, instead of paying it out as dividends. The retained income increases the value of real capital in the firm and gives rise to capital gains on the shares held. If capital gains were taxed as they accrued, the benefits obtained by shareholders would be taxed immediately. Taxation on accrual is not feasible, however, so capital gains are instead taxed on realization. Thus shareholders can effectively postpone payment of the tax by not realizing the capital gain arising from the retained earnings. A withholding tax on retained earnings at the corporate level would prevent this result. In this case, of course, since the tax would be intended only to withhold tax revenues in advance and not to function as an additional tax, some credit for taxes paid would have to be given at the personal level—that is, the corporate tax would have to be integrated with the personal income tax.

The Canadian personal tax system does not tax non-resident households on capital income they earn in Canada. Consequently, a case can be made for withholding against this income at source. The ideal withholding tax for this purpose would be one that applied only to corporate source income accruing to foreigners. In practice, since it is not possible to distinguish at source the corporate income that will accrue to foreigners, withholding must apply to all capital income, including that accruing to domestic residents. The tax withheld from domestic residents must then be credited to them by a system of integration of personal and corporate taxes. Notice that the withholding of capital income for the purpose of withholding against non-residents includes withholding against retained earnings. In other words, it accomplishes both of the functions of withholding.

If one were designing a corporate tax solely with the withholding function in mind, the design of the tax would be as follows. Suppose that it is desirable to withhold against all forms of capital income accruing to foreigners. Again, this means that the withholding tax will have to apply to all forms of capital income at source. The income of the firm that eventually ends up as capital income for households is simply the "value added" of the firm less wage payments—that is,

net capital income = revenues − current costs − true depreciation at replacement cost − inventory usage at replacement cost.

This would be the proper tax base for a corporate tax designed to withhold against all capital income.

Since some of the income generated by the corporation might appear as dividends, interest, or capital gains in the hands of residents, it would be necessary to integrate the personal tax with the corporate tax to prevent the double taxation of the same income. The simplest way to achieve integration would be via a system of gross-ups and credits similar to the existing dividend tax credit system but applicable to all forms of capital income at the personal level. The rate of gross-up would be $1/(1 - u)$, where $u$ is the corporate tax rate, and the value of the tax credit should be $u$ times the grossed-up dividend. This type of integration would completely nullify the effects of the corporate tax as far as domestic residents are concerned. The tax would ultimately be payable only by non-residents. In the process, the taxation of all corporate income at source would effectively withhold tax on capital gains as they accrued via retained earnings and thus achieve the other goal of withholding as well.

The present system deviates from this ideal withholding tax in several ways. First, it does not withhold against all capital income. In particular, since interest is deductible, taxes are not withheld against interest at the corporate level. Domestic asset holders are liable to taxation on interest payments at the personal level, but foreigners are subject only to withholding taxes, whose rates are lower than personal tax rates. Thus the treatment of interest is more favourable than the treatment of dividends and capital gains.

Second, the withholding that is done is done imperfectly. The tax system does not allow true depreciation at replacement cost or inventory usage at replacement cost as an ideal withholding tax would. Finally, the present scheme of integration is far from perfect. Since interest is not withheld against, it is proper that no gross-up and credit apply to it. A full gross-up and credit system should apply, however, to all equity income withheld against that is eventually realized by residents. No such system applies at present to capital gains income, which is not explicitly integrated at all,[50] or to dividends and capital gains obtained by non-taxed institutions or individuals, such as pension funds or registered retirement savings plans (RRSPs). The portion of capital income that is integrated is not fully integrated, since the dividend tax credit system grosses up dividends at a rate less than the full corporate tax rate paid on them. Moreover, personal tax applies the same dividend tax credit rate to all dividends, regardless of the rates of tax that the corporations paying the dividend have paid. The existing system, in short, is far from being an ideal withholding tax. We shall return to the question of integration later in this section.

There is another, more fundamental consideration. In an economy that is heavily exposed to international capital markets, it is not clear that corporate taxes withheld at source can fulfil a withholding function. Take the extreme case in which Canadian rates of return on asset holdings must conform with those determined on international capital markets. In this case, no tax imposed on a corporation can affect the after-tax return that must be paid to the firm's creditors, whether they are shareholders or lenders. The corporate tax merely increases the pre-tax rate of return that investments must earn and thereby reduces the incentive to invest. The tax itself will be shifted from capital owners to non-capital factors of production, especially labour, and the income of these factors will be reduced accordingly. By this reckoning, withholding serves little purpose. Integration of corporate tax payments through the personal tax simply compounds the problem. Measures such as the dividend tax credit cannot undo any personal tax that has been applied on savings at the personal level without also undoing the corporate tax. One is left with a corporate tax that discourages investment and a dividend tax credit that undoes the personal tax on savings—effects precisely the opposite of those intended. Thus, to the extent that Canadian rates of return are determined on international capital markets, the corporate tax cannot fulfil a withholding role and integration is counterproductive!

There is one objection to this argument against the withholding role of the corporate tax, and it is an objection that has been historically powerful. If

---

[50] One could argue, as the Mintz committee has done, that the exemption of one-quarter of capital gains from the income tax serves as a form of partial integration. This exemption, however, applies to all capital gains from all sources, domestic or foreign, corporate or non-corporate. Moreover, the Department of Finance treats the partial capital gains exemption, but not the dividend tax credit, as a tax expenditure, which indicates that the Department of Finance does not view the exemption as an integration device.

foreign governments provide a tax credit against corporate taxes paid by their resident firms abroad, then the corporate tax serves as a method of simply transferring tax revenues from foreign treasuries to the Canadian treasury. As long as Canadian corporate tax rates do not exceed the rates of foreign tax-crediting regimes, they will be offset by a tax credit, and thus the tax withheld becomes a "free" source of tax revenue for the Canadian treasury. On the other hand, although the United States offers tax credits to US corporations that operate in Canada, not all countries observe the same policy. Any attempt to impose a corporate tax on foreign corporations whose countries do not offer credits will result in the tax's being shifted back to Canadians and in a reduction in investment. In any case, the foreign tax credit is offered only when the firm repatriates dividends. This being the case, the tax offsetting will be deferred, and the Canadian tax will not be fully offset by the foreign tax credit. Thus even this argument for withholding has its limitations. One is left with fundamental doubts about the main rationale for corporate taxes.

## The Pure Profits Tax Function

The other function of the corporate tax is the one stressed in the economics literature.[51] Economists have long recognized that if the corporate tax base were properly defined, the corporate tax would be an ideal, non-distorting tax. The ideal design requires that the corporate tax base be equivalent to pure economic profits.

In principle, it is easy to state how this should be achieved. Pure profits are the difference between the accrued revenues of a firm and the full imputed costs of producing those revenues. The revenue side of the equation should include all sales as they accrue rather than as they are realized (as is the case under the existing system). The cost side is somewhat more complex. It should include the true imputed or opportunity costs of all resources used in producing output—that is, the costs of using any input that could otherwise have been used elsewhere in the economy. In the case of current inputs, these costs include the costs on an accrual basis of labour, materials, business services, and so forth, as in the existing system. In the case of capital inputs, whose use stretches over several tax periods, an imputation of the cost of using the input should be made in each period. In the case of depreciable capital, the imputed cost should be the true rate of depreciation at replacement cost (that is, the loss in value owing to obsolescence and wear and tear evaluated at replacement cost) plus the cost of financing the asset in real terms (that is, the real interest cost in the case of debt financing and the real rate of return required on equity in the case of equity financing) less any real capital gains from holding the asset. In the case of non-depreciable

---

[51] This function is summarized in more detail in Boadway, Bruce, and Mintz, supra footnote 49. See also Robin W. Boadway, Neil Bruce, and Jack M. Mintz, "The Rationale for and the Design of the Corporation Income Tax" (1984), vol. 86, no. 2 *The Scandinavian Journal of Economics* 286-99.

capital (for example, land), only the real costs of financing less real capital gains should be deductible. In the case of inventories, both the replacement costs on items taken out of inventory and the real cost of financing the holding of inventories should be deductible. Renewable resources are similar to inventories and should be treated analogously. Finally, in the case of depletable assets, the deduction should be the real cost of financing the asset plus the accrued fall in the value of the asset as the asset is depleted.

Since this tax base would not include any item that represented a payment for an input used in the production process, a tax on this base would be a tax on pure profits or rent. The tax base would reflect profits arising out of the monopoly power or the special advantages of a firm, such as location, and it would reflect all pure rents on natural resources, including rents from land. Firms that earned no economic profits would pay no tax, and the tax would not affect the production decisions of firms that did earn economic profits. Marginal investments would bear no tax: the METR would be zero. Only inframarginal profits would be subject to tax.

Unfortunately, this "ideal" tax has a major shortcoming. Some of the items of imputed cost are not readily observable, since they do not correspond to market transactions. This consideration makes a tax of this kind difficult, if not impossible, to administer. The unobservable items include the true depreciation rate on depreciable capital; the real cost of finance, especially equity finance; capital gains on depreciable capital held; replacement values of inventory used; and the loss in value of depletable assets through use. There is, however, a tax base that is equivalent to the pure economic profits of a firm in present-value terms but much easier to administer. The tax base is the cash flow of the firm, and a tax levied on this base is referred to as a *cash-flow tax*. The cash flow of a firm that earns business income is the difference between the actual revenues it receives on a cash-flow basis and its capital and current expenditures, also on a cash-flow basis. It can be shown that such a tax base has the same present value as a tax base defined to be pure profits. Thus, a tax levied on this base would be non-distorting.[52]

A cash-flow tax is much easier to administer than a pure profits tax because only realized flows enter its base, and they are easy to observe. Capital costs are expensed as investment occurs. There is no need to impute interest or depreciation during the life of the capital. Furthermore, there is no need under a cash-flow system to correct for inflation. Cash-flow taxation does, however, have one disadvantage, at least in the view of the tax authorities. Tax writeoffs occur much earlier under cash-flow taxation than they do under the present system, so tax payments are postponed. Indeed, when a firm is undertaking investment, its taxable cash-flow may well be negative. The postponement of tax liabilities should not really be a problem, however,

---

[52] For an extension of this analysis to firms earning financial income, see Robin W. Boadway, Neil Bruce, and Jack M. Mintz, "On the Neutrality of Flow-of-Funds Corporate Taxation" (February 1983), 50 *Economica* 49-61.

since the present value of tax receipts under a cash-flow tax is the same as it is under imputed-profits taxation. The greater likelihood of negative tax liabilities, however, emphasizes the need under any corporate tax for full loss offsetting provisions. Otherwise, the tax will not be efficient. Nor is it difficult to combine cash-flow taxation with the principle of full loss offsetting. One can simply apply the principle of cash-flow taxation whenever cash flows are positive but allow firms to carry forward all cash-flow tax losses with full (nominal) interest payments. This solution overcomes many of the disadvantages of cash-flow taxation that the tax authorities identify, such as the need for refundability of negative tax liabilities, while retaining a simple and efficient source of revenues.[53]

Unlike corporate tax collections under a withholding tax, collections under a pure profits tax need not be integrated with the personal tax system. Indeed, crediting shareholders for corporate taxes paid would effectively undo the purpose of the tax, which is to give the government a share of the pure profits of the economy. Nor could one design a personal tax that taxed pure profits alone, since pure profits can only be discerned at source. At the personal level, capital income that arises from pure profits cannot be distinguished from other capital income.

The present system goes some distance toward being a tax on pure profits. It taxes revenues on accrual and attempts to allow capital deductions on an accrual basis. Some capital items are written off on a cash-flow basis, including the acquisition costs of depletable assets (for example, exploration and development expenditures), scientific research and development expenditures, advertising expenditures, investments in human capital, and the acquisition of intangibles, all of which are expenditures that lead to the accumulation of assets with future income-earning potential. However, the present tax also differs in several significant ways from a tax on pure profits. It allows firms to deduct only interest costs, not the costs of equity finance. It provides depreciation allowances that permit firms to write off capital before its service life is exhausted. It is not indexed, so firms can deduct nominal interest rather than real interest. It provides for depreciation at historic cost rather than replacement cost, and for the writing off of inventories at first in, first out values.

## Summary

Once again, it is unfortunate that the ideal structure for a corporate tax designed to perform a withholding function differs from the ideal structure for a corporate tax designed to tax pure profits. The most important differences are the following:

---

[53] This modified system of cash-flow taxation is presented in detail in Robin Boadway and Neil Bruce, "A General Proposition on the Design of a Neutral Business Tax" (July 1984), 24 *Journal of Public Economics* 231-39. They indicate that any time path of tax revenues can be allowed, as long as all postponed untaxed cash flows are carried forward with interest.

• The ideal tax base for withholding would allow no deductions for the costs of finance (unless it were desired for political reasons not to withhold against interest, in which case interest could be deductible). The ideal base for pure profits taxation would allow full deduction of all financial costs.

• Corporate taxes collected from domestic residents for withholding purposes should be credited under the personal tax system. Corporate taxes collected as pure profits should not be integrated in this manner.

• More generally, to the extent that rates of return on capital are determined on international capital markets, the case for the corporate tax as a withholding device is suspect but its role as a tax on pure profits remains.

• A tax on pure profits can be levied on a cash-flow basis, or on a cash-flow basis combined with loss carryforwards with interest. A withholding tax cannot.

These differences do not mean that it is impossible to design a corporate tax capable of accomplishing both ends. With some care, it can be done. Once appropriate rates for withholding and for pure profits taxation are determined, the combination of the two tax systems into one structure can be accomplished by an appropriate aggregation of the two bases and rates.[54] Alternatively, it may be more appropriate to view the corporate tax as basically a withholding tax and apply a pure profits taxation scheme to industries in which there are thought to be considerable rents (for example, resource industries). This is essentially what the provinces do in having provincial resource taxes alongside their corporate taxes. What is probably most important is simply that policy makers, in assessing corporate tax reforms, be aware that the tax has these two possible roles.

The present tax is neither a passive withholding tax nor a non-distorting pure profits tax. It is probably better characterized as being partially a withholding tax and partially a tax on the equity capital income of corporations. Because it taxes equity capital at source and also because its provisions differ over sectors and activities, it probably distorts the allocation of resources in the economy. These characteristics of the tax suggest, in fact, that it has functions quite apart from its withholding function or any function as a tax on pure profits. For example, it is possible to view corporate taxes as compensation for the many services corporations obtain from the public sector, such as education of its workers, public sector infrastructure, and the protection of property rights. The Mintz committee has recognized this function as a valid rationale for the tax. It would be difficult, however, to design satisfactory tax policy on the basis of this rationale. For one thing, it is virtually impossible to identify the benefits that accrue to corporations (or to any other entities, for that matter) from public goods and services. For another, the principle of benefit taxation conflicts with the broader equity

---

[54] For a detailed discussion of how this may be done, see Boadway, Bruce, and Mintz, "The Rationale for and the Design of the Corporation Income Tax," supra footnote 51.

objectives of taxation that we discussed in chapter 2. Finally, imposing taxes on corporations is no guarantee that corporations will pay those taxes. In an open economy, as we have seen, it is likely that the bulk of corporate taxes are shifted elsewhere.

Another supplementary role for the corporate tax is as an instrument for industrial policy—that is, for encouraging certain industries at the expense of others. Economists have traditionally eschewed industrial policies, largely because they question whether governments can identify which industries will be "winners" in the future and which will be "losers." They suggest that the allocation of resources should be determined by markets rather than by governments. They do, however, recognize that tax incentives may be appropriate for activities that provide extra-market, or external, benefits to the economy at large. For example, firms may develop new knowledge, produce new products, or train new managers—activities whose benefits are dissipated in part to other firms. The Canadian tax system provides incentives for investment in some activities that generate external benefits. However, the system has traditionally also been used for broader industrial policy objectives, such as the encouragement of particular industries and the encouragement of investment in depressed regions. The Mintz committee took the view that the tax system should not be used for these purposes. It argued that if the government wished to provide incentives it should provide them by more direct means, such as grants (presumably despite the administrative costs and discretionary decision making that direct support requires). For the time being, in any case, distortions that arise from policy interventions are a fact of the tax system. The following subsections discuss some of these distorting effects in more detail.

## Corporations Versus Unincorporated Businesses

The above discussion suggested that the corporate tax is to some extent a tax on the return to equity capital in the corporate sector rather than either a withholding tax or a tax on the economic profits of the firm (or a combination of the two things). To the extent that this is the case, the tax distorts the allocation of capital between taxed firms and untaxed firms. Since the corporate tax rate is quite high, this distortion may be quite large. Moreover, if the existence of the corporate tax amounts to a bias in favour of unincorporated firms, the provisions of the tax favour small, Canadian-controlled corporations over large public corporations. Here we shall deal with the general issue of how large corporations are treated relative to other businesses; in the next subsection, we shall look specifically at the preferential treatment of small corporations.

Owners of corporations are taxed at the corporate level and then taxed again at the personal level, when corporation income is transformed into personal income as dividends or capital gains. Owners of unincorporated businesses are taxed only at the personal level. Thus the corporate tax provides a strong incentive to allocate capital to the unincorporated sector. If capital is mobile among industries, it will tend to be allocated so that the gross-of-tax return in the corporate sector is sufficiently greater than the gross return in the unincorporated sector to cover the additional tax liability. Since the return to capital tends to decline as the amount of capital employed increases, the corporate tax will cause relatively too little capital to accumulate in the corporate sector and too much in the unincorporated sector.

There are, however, several considerations that tend to mitigate the severity of this distortion. First, the decision to incorporate lies with the firm itself. If the advantages of incorporating (for example, limited liability and access to capital markets) outweigh the disadvantages of paying the tax, the firm will incorporate. Second, partnerships, even if they are incorporated, may elect to be treated as partnerships for tax purposes. Third, Canadian-controlled private corporations enjoy the benefits of the small business tax rate and the generous integration provisions outlined earlier in this chapter. The magnitude of the distortion is mitigated, therefore, to the extent that private corporations are in closer competition with unincorporated businesses than are public corporations. Finally, public corporations themselves obtain the benefit of generous writeoff provisions and at least partial integration. Thus, as we noted earlier, the marginal effective tax rate that a public corporation faces may be much lower than the statutory rate; for some industries, indeed, it may be negative.

The main disadvantage of treating corporations differently from other firms for tax purposes is the resultant misallocation of capital among sectors—that is, the inefficiency induced by the corporate tax. One might also be concerned about the fairness or equity implications of the tax. It is important to note, however, that even though the statutory rate of tax is different for corporations than it is for unincorporated businesses this circumstance does not imply discrimination against owners of corporations in terms of horizontal equity. The operation of capital markets tends to make the net-of-tax return to capital the same everywhere, with the result that the burden of the corporate tax is spread to all owners of capital alike and not merely to those in the corporate sector. Thus the tax may be more reasonably viewed as one that discriminates against all capital income and in favour of labour income (although in an open economy such as Canada, as we have shown, the tax is likely to be shifted to labour). Whether this method of taxing income is equitable or inequitable depends upon whether one regards the ability to pay taxes out of capital income as being greater or less great than the ability to pay taxes out of labour income. Some have argued that on the ground of horizontal equity one ought to favour labour income over capital income, since the earning of labour income involves a loss of leisure and the earning of capital income does not. The earning of capital income does, however, involve a cost to owners of capital. It involves the postponement of consumption in order to save for the future and, as well, the incurring of various degrees of risk.

Despite the inefficiency of the capital allocation to which it gives rise, the corporate tax continues to be levied in Canada and elsewhere for several reasons. First, it is a still a lucrative relatively easily administered source of tax revenue. Its elimination would require governments to raise tax revenue elsewhere, perhaps at a greater cost. Its extension to unincorporated business in order to eliminate the discriminatory treatment of corporations would involve an immense increase in administrative costs. In addition, small businesses could presumably avoid the tax with relative ease: their owners would merely have to take their profits in the form of higher salaries for themselves as managers.

Second, to the extent that the tax falls on the pure profits of firms, it is an ideal tax from an efficiency point of view. If all of the costs of operating (including imputed costs such as risk taking) were deductible, the tax would fall only on pure profits and would be non-distorting.

Third, a substantial proportion of the capital in Canada is foreign-owned. Most foreign investment in Canada comes from countries whose governments collect corporate income tax on the foreign operations of their domestic firms and give a tax credit for corporate income taxes paid abroad. The elimination of the Canadian corporate tax would simply extinguish the tax credit, and foreign-owned firms would become liable only for foreign taxes. This outcome would be equivalent to a transfer of tax revenues from the Canadian government to foreign governments. (Where the Canadian tax rate had exceeded the foreign tax rate, part of the gain from the elimination of the Canadian tax might accrue to the firm itself.) In other words, the corporation tax acts as a withholding tax against the income earned by foreigners through corporations operating in Canada.

Finally, to the extent that the ultimate incidence of the corporate tax is on capital owners, the tax may be thought of as a fair one in terms of vertical equity. If one of the aims of the tax system is to redistribute incomes from higher to lower income groups, the corporate tax may provide some rough assistance to this end, given that the proportion of ownership of capital rises as income rises. Of course, it is far from being an ideal tool for redistributing income.

Could the corporate tax achieve all these useful ends without distorting the allocation of capital? As we mentioned earlier, neither an ideal withholding tax nor an ideal tax on pure profits would distort investment decisions. An ideal withholding tax would be perfectly integrated with the personal income of resident owners and would generate from the income of corporations only the net revenues attributable to non-resident owners. The present system, however, is less than fully integrated. If the federal government wished as well to share in the rents generated in the corporate sector, it could do it with relative ease by imposing a separate cash-flow tax on sectors where pure rents might be present. One obvious candidate for this treatment is the resource sector, which is already subject to various taxes over and above the corporate income tax. (As we shall discuss below, none of these taxes succeed in collecting rents in a non-distorting manner.) With a little ingenuity, the government could even devise a corporate tax that achieved simultaneously the goals of withholding, integration, and pure profits taxation.

Under any form of the tax, however, the role for withholding might be a very limited one indeed, given that rates of return in Canada are largely determined abroad and corporate taxes are as a result likely to be shifted largely to labour and other factors.

## The Treatment of Small Businesses

Small business corporations have long enjoyed preferential treatment under the corporate tax. Before 1972, *all* corporations were entitled to pay a reduced tax rate on an initial amount of annual taxable income. For example, in 1971, the tax rate of 21 percent was applicable to the first $35,000 of profits of all corporations. There were some problems with this provision. For one, it gave corporations an incentive to split into as many tax-paying entities as possible in order to take advantage of the small business tax rate as often as possible. This loophole was gradually closed, and now only one deduction is allowed for affiliated firms. A more important problem, however, was the fact that the equivalent of the present small business deduction was available to all corporations, large or small, public or private, foreign or domestic. Since the special rate was intended as an incentive to encourage the growth of small businesses, it was inefficient to give it to all firms. Large corporations did not need it, and it artificially supported and perhaps perpetuated small, stagnant firms.

The Carter report had recommended abolishing the small business rate entirely as part of its overall recommendation for fully integrating the corporate and personal taxes. The federal government's measured response to the Carter report, the *White Paper on Taxation*, retreated significantly from the full-integration proposal. The white paper did, however, recommend the retention of full integration in the case of small businesses—or, more accurately, closely held corporations. Closely held corporations would be taxed at full rates, the gross-of-tax income would be allocated to shareholders for inclusion in their personal tax bases, and full credit would be given to individuals for corporate tax paid on their share of profits. Capital gains, however, would be fully taxed.

Despite the provision for full integration, some critics argued the proposals would affect small businesses adversely. Under the existing system, small business income that was taxed at the lower rate could be retained in the corporation and reinvested. No personal tax would be levied until it was taken out as dividends. Accordingly, a low-tax source of funds was available for investment in the growth of these businesses. Under the white paper proposals, a higher tax rate would apply and corporate income would be immediately integrated with personal income. There would be no postponement of the tax. The fact that capital gains would be fully taxed offered further discouragement. In fact, the preferential treatment of small businesses would be practically eliminated.

After considerable debate, the tax reforms actually implemented retained the principle of preferential treatment. The new law limited the special tax rate—now the small business tax rate—to private Canadian corporations (CCPCs). Public corporations, because they had full access to capital markets, were deemed not to require the lower rate. The omission of foreign corporations was justified on the ground that any tax cut to them would benefit mainly the governments of other countries, especially the United States. As well, it was considered to be in the social interest to encourage Canadian enterprises. A new provision placed a limit on the amount of total profit for which a firm could claim the lower tax rate over time. This provision prevented a prolonged dependence of less efficient small businesses on special treatment under the tax laws. The upper limit was abandoned in 1984, and today all CCPCs are eligible for the small business tax rate indefinitely.

As we noted earlier, several arguments have been advanced for the special treatment of small businesses. It is alleged that because of capital market imperfections small businesses are less able to generate outside funding than large ones are and must rely more heavily on internally generated funds. The costs of financing may well be higher for small firms, since the transaction costs per dollar of loan may be higher for smaller loans. Small firms also have limited access to equity markets. They may have no credit record, or they may be involved in new enterprises that potential creditors find hard to evaluate. Along similar lines, it is argued that small businesses encounter certain setup (or "infant industry") costs, such as the cost of acquiring the experience they need in order to compete with established firms. This argument provides some justification for placing a limit on the total income eligible for taxation at the lower rate, since presumably the requirement to acquire experience is temporary. Finally, it is often argued that small businesses contribute to the stability of society and therefore ought to be supported.

Many of these arguments are, of course, very difficult to substantiate, but probably the most substantial problems facing growing firms are cash-flow problems. Their smallness and immaturity may indeed make it relatively difficult for them to obtain external financing. The reduced tax rate for small businesses, however, does very little to get more cash into the hands of small firms. The tax system does not allow large tax writeoffs in early years of high investment (except in the form of investment tax credits or accelerated depreciation, which are typically available to large and small firms alike), but even if it did the writeoffs would not help small firms' cash flows much. The tax advantage of early writeoffs is less under a low tax rate than it is under a higher rate. Moreover, the existing loss-offset provisions do not allow cash credits for firms in negative taxable income positions. In short, small firms would have better cash flows if they faced higher rates of tax but could obtain accelerated writeoffs for capital costs and cash refunds of losses through effective loss offsetting. Immediate refundability of tax losses, in fact, would be the single reform that would best address the financing problems of small firms. It would also reduce the income tax system's present bias against risky investments by small firms, which are typically unable to self-insure by diversifying internally.

An alternative strategy for assisting small businesses through the tax system would be to make more use of the principle of flowing through certain tax preferences owing to a corporation to its shareholders. Currently, oil and gas and mining firms may issue flowthrough shares in order to finance exploration and development expenditures. The tax deduction for these expenditures can be "flowed through" to the purchasers of the shares, for use at the personal tax level when the firm is in a loss position and so cannot take immediate advantage of the deduction under the corporate tax. It might be possible to apply this principle to the end of relieving the financing problems of small businesses.[55]

As a means of helping small businesses to thrive, then, the small business deduction has its limitations. It does, however, allow small businesses to be treated on a par with unincorporated businesses, given the existing dividend tax credit. In other words, the present system does provide more or less full integration for small firms and thereby eliminates the incentive to firms to remain unincorporated for purely tax reasons.

## Deductions for Capital Costs

The corporate tax system allows deductions for depreciation (capital cost allowances) and interest costs, and from time to time it also allows special deductions or tax credits as investment incentives. If the system allowed deductions for all economic costs, including imputed costs, the tax would fall on pure profits or rents alone and would not distort the allocation of resources. To put the matter in another way, if the system allowed the deduction of true economic depreciation and the imputed costs of risk and entrepreneurship, the corporate tax would be a tax on equity income properly defined. Since the equity income of all firms would be treated comparably, the distortions across industries and assets that the present tax imposes would disappear.

Since, however, no market prices exist for imputed costs (for example, the costs of risk bearing and entrepreneurship), it is administratively difficult to impute them as costs to be deducted from corporate income. Suppose, for example, that lenders require, say, a 15 percent interest rate to induce them to lend money to a risky business if they can get 10 percent on less risky assets (for example, government bonds). The additional 5 percent is the opportunity cost of taking the risk and is termed the *risk premium*. In principle, the risk premium ought to be allowed as a capital cost incurred by the equity owners of the firm. Because it is difficult to measure the risk premium, however, it is not allowed as a capital cost for tax purposes (unless it is included in interest

---

[55] An alternative to the lower tax rate would be to permit businesses to borrow against their tax liabilities by paying their taxes in interest-bearing notes. See G. David Quirin and Kerr Gibson, *Investment for Growth—Where Are Incentives Needed?* (Montreal: Canadian Economic Policy Committee, 1971).

actually paid). It appears that there is no practical way to prevent the tax from introducing a distortion against factors of production, such as risk, whose return takes the form of imputed income.

Similar problems arise in the case of deductions for capital costs. Consider an outlay of $100,000 to purchase a machine. After one year's use, owing to wear and tear and obsolescence, the machine will probably be worth less than $100,000 (ignoring inflation). This reduction in the value of a capital good, or its depreciation, constitutes, with the cost of financing, the cost involved in using that capital asset. However, since the actual expenditure on a capital asset is incurred in the initial year of its acquisition, whereas the services obtained from the asset are typically stretched over several years, there is no cash payment that corresponds to the value of the capital services used up in a given year. If there were a second-hand or rental market for every type of capital asset, it would be possible, though certainly difficult, to determine the annual value of capital services with reasonable accuracy. Annual rental cost, for example, would cover approximately the loss in market value plus the imputed interest each year. Some capital assets are, in fact, leased or rented, and their rental expenses are deductible as current costs to the user firm and treated as income to the leasing firm. As a rule, however, the current market values of capital assets are not determinable, so the tax authorities rely instead on a schedule of depreciation rates or capital cost allowances for various types of assets based on estimates of asset lives. There is no way of knowing how closely the CCA for a particular type of asset approximates its true rate of depreciation. The Mintz committee argued that capital cost allowances often overstate the true depreciation rate. These rates have been in place for some time, and owing to the rapidity of technological innovation the service lives of assets are generally shorter now than they were in the past.

The depreciation rate allowed for a particular asset will influence the desire of firms to invest in that asset. The depreciation claimed by a firm represents income on which no tax is paid. The more rapidly a firm is allowed to depreciate the cost of an asset, the earlier will the tax reduction accrue, and thus the greater will be the present value of the tax savings from depreciation. In other words, tax reductions yield a benefit in the form of interest earned or interest not forgone, and the earlier the reductions accrue the greater the benefit will be. Therefore, any measure that tends to speed up the tax savings attributable to depreciation reduces the cost of investing in the asset and so encourages investment.

This is the rationale for accelerated depreciation schemes that the tax authorities have made available from time to time. Before the 1987 income tax reform, accelerated depreciation was available to investment in machinery and equipment by manufacturing and processing firms. Firms could write off investments, under the straightline method, at 50 percent per year. By reducing the depreciation period to two years, the scheme permitted firms to postpone some of their taxes owing to subsequent years. This arrangement was equivalent to granting the firm an interest-free loan equal to the amount of the postponed tax payment for the duration of the postponement.

Although an accelerated depreciation scheme such as the one previously in existence for manufacturing and processing provides an incentive for all firms to invest more, it provides relatively more incentive for investment in long-lived assets. This is so because the present value of the tax postponement that accrues to a given dollar of outlay on capital equipment will be greater the longer the life of an asset is. The simple example in table 4.6 will illustrate this point. Consider two investments of $100,000, one in an asset that lasts three years and the other in an asset that lasts five years. Assume a corporate tax rate of 50 percent, an interest rate of 5 percent, and, for simplicity's sake, straightline depreciation. A firm would ordinarily claim depreciation of $33,333 per year for the three-year asset and $20,000 per year for the five-year asset. Suppose, however, that the tax authorities have implemented a two-year accelerated depreciation scheme, so that the writeoffs for both assets are, instead, $50,000 per year for two years. In the case of the three-year asset, the firm writes off an additional $16,667 in each of the first two years. Since the tax rate is 50 percent, tax savings of $8,333 occur in each of the two years; that is, the firm pays $8,333 less in tax than it would have paid under the ordinary depreciation schedule. In the third year, however, when the depreciation is exhausted, the firm faces an additional tax liability of $16,667. In the case of the five-year asset, the firm writes off an additional $30,000 in each of the first two years, and receives a tax saving of $15,000 per year. In the last three years, taxes are $10,000 per year higher than they would be under ordinary depreciation. Computation of the present value of all the tax changes for each asset, given an interest rate of 5 percent, shows that the present value of the tax savings under the accelerated depreciation scheme is $1,150 in the case of the three-year asset and $4,220 in the case of the five-year asset.[56]

In contrast to accelerated depreciation, investment tax credit schemes favour short-lived assets over long-lived assets. An investment credit permits firms to write off a proportion of the initial outlay immediately as an expense. Some countries allow the credit in addition to the normal depreciation provisions; in Canada, the base for depreciation may be reduced by the investment tax credit. The qualitative effects are the same in either case, so for simplicity we assume that full depreciation is also allowed. In this case, an investment tax credit of 10 percent allows a firm that undertakes $100,000 of new investment an immediate tax reduction of $10,000. Since the value of

---

[56] On the other hand, if the firm continually replaces depreciating capital in order to keep the amount of capital it holds intact, it is possible to design accelerated depreciation schemes that will increase the rate of return from investing in assets of all durabilities in the same proportion. This possibility is discussed in David F. Bradford, "Tax Neutrality and the Investment Tax Credit," in Henry J. Aaron and Michael J. Boskins, eds., *The Economics of Taxation* (Washington, DC: Brookings Institution, 1980), 281-98, and Arnold C. Harberger, "Tax Neutrality in Investment Incentives," ibid., 299-313.

**Table 4.6  Comparison of Accelerated Depreciation Schemes
for Assets with Different Service Lives**

|  | Regular depreciation | Accelerated depreciation | Difference in tax |
|---|---|---|---|
|  |  | *dollars* |  |
| Three-year asset |  |  |  |
| Year 1 ............ | 33,333 | 50,000 | −8,333 |
| Year 2 ............ | 33,333 | 50,000 | −8,333 |
| Year 3 ............ | 33,333 |  | 16,667 |
|  | Present value of tax difference = −1,150 | | |
|  |  |  |  |
| Five-year asset |  |  |  |
| Year 1 ............ | 20,000 | 50,000 | −15,000 |
| Year 2 ............ | 20,000 | 50,000 | −15,000 |
| Year 3 ............ | 20,000 |  | 10,000 |
| Year 4 ............ | 20,000 |  | 10,000 |
| Year 5 ............ | 20,000 |  | 10,000 |
|  | Present value of tax difference = −4,220 | | |

an investment tax credit depends on the initial outlay and not on the length of life of the asset, this method of encouraging investment does not lead to larger tax savings if the investment is in long-lived assets rather than short-lived assets. Indeed, investment tax credit schemes favour investment in short-lived assets, since the firm can claim the credit every time an asset is replaced.

## Indexation of the Corporate Tax Base

A further problem arises in accounting for capital costs in periods of inflation. As we discussed in chapter 2, an inflation-proof corporate income tax would have to index capital cost allowances, inventory costs, and financial costs. We shall consider each of these elements in turn.

In principle, the capital cost allowance should reflect the reduction in value of a depreciable asset through use over the year. Or, equivalently, it should reflect the amount of replacement expenditure that would have to be undertaken in a year to maintain the value of the depreciable asset. Depreciation for tax purposes is based on original or historic cost—that is, on the cost of the asset when it was originally purchased. In periods of inflation, historic cost will be less than replacement cost and depreciation based on historic cost will not be sufficient to replace worn-out assets at the now-higher prices.

For example, consider an asset costing $1 million purchased in year zero and depreciated by the straightline method at 20 percent. Suppose the inflation rate is 10 percent. After one year of use, $200,000 may be claimed as depreciation. Because of the 10 percent inflation, however, the cost of the asset if purchased one year later would be $1.1 million (assuming its price rose at the same rate as average prices in the economy). Thus the replacement expenditure required to maintain the value of a one-year asset would be 0.2 ×

$1.1 million = $220,000, which exceeds the tax depreciation allowed. Basing depreciation on replacement values would overcome this problem.

A similar problem arises with inventory costing. Under the present system, items used out of inventory are costed on a first in, first out basis. In periods of inflation, the FIFO accounting cost of inventories used will be less than the replacement cost, so the writeoff allowed for the use of inventory will be less than the amount required to replenish the stock of inventory. A system of costing inventory use at replacement cost would avoid this difficulty.

In the case of interest costs (or any financial costs), inflation has the opposite impact. Firms are allowed to deduct the full nominal interest payments on debt. Since part of the nominal interest payment reflects compensation for a loss in real value of principal, the firm is in fact being allowed to write off part of its principal against taxable income. A fully indexed tax system would allow firms to deduct only the real cost of finance in calculating taxable income, and only real interest receipts would be taxable at both the corporate and personal levels.

As we suggested earlier, however, there is a simpler method of dealing with the problem of accounting for capital costs during periods of inflation, one that obviates the need to estimate true replacement depreciation, the replacement cost of inventory, and real financial costs. This method is simply to permit firms to expense capital costs immediately. The present value of the immediate writeoff of capital expenditures with no interest deductibility is exactly the same as the present value of true replacement depreciation and full real interest deductibility (based on both debt financing and equity financing). The two schemes would also yield the same present value of tax revenues to the government, though the time pattern would be different in each case. Tax payments under a scheme of immediate writeoff would be lower in earlier years and higher in later years than tax payments under an indexation scheme; in earlier years, they might even be negative. It is not surprising that economists have long advocated immediate writeoff as an efficient way of expensing capital assets. One disadvantage of it is that fast-growing firms could defer the tax for as long as investment was equal to income. In addition, a scheme of full loss offsetting would be mandatory if immediate writeoffs were to be effective.

An example will illustrate the equivalence of the two schemes in present value terms. Consider an asset worth $1 million that depreciates by a constant amount over five years. Assume an interest rate of 10 percent and a tax rate of 50 percent. Table 4.7 shows the time stream of writeoffs for depreciation and interest (assuming full interest deductibility on the value of the capital) and the tax savings per year over the five-year life of the asset. The present value of the depreciation and interest deductions over the five-year life of the asset is $1 million. This figure, of course, is just the original cost of the asset: immediate expensing of the $1 million cost will give the same present value of writeoffs for capital. Similarly, the present value of the tax savings from the writeoffs is $0.5 million, which is the same as the tax savings

**Table 4.7  The Equivalence Between True Depreciation Combined
with Full Interest Deductibility and Immediate Expensing
of Investment**

| Year | Depreciation deduction (20 percent of $1 million per year) | Interest deduction (10 percent of undepreciated capital) | Tax saving (20 percent of interest and depreciation deductions) |
|---|---|---|---|
| | | *dollars* | |
| 1 ............. | 200,000 | 100,000 | 150,000 |
| 2 ............. | 200,000 | 80,000 | 140,000 |
| 3 ............. | 200,000 | 60,000 | 130,000 |
| 4 ............. | 200,000 | 40,000 | 120,000 |
| 5 ............. | 200,000 | 20,000 | 110,000 |

Present value of depreciation and interest deductions =
  $300{,}000/1.1 + 280{,}000/(1.1)^2 + 260{,}000/(1.1)^3 + 240{,}000/(1.1)^4 + 220{,}000/(1.1)^5 =$
  $1,000,000.
Present value of depreciation and interest deductions =
  $150{,}000/1.1 + 140{,}000/(1.1)^2 = 130{,}000/(1.1)^3 = 120{,}000/(1.1)^4 = 110{,}000/(1.1)^5 =$
  $500,000.

from the immediate writeoff of $1 million. The only difference is that with immediate writeoff the tax savings all occur in the initial year, whereas under the true depreciation and interest-deduction scheme the tax savings occur throughout the life of the asset. Thus, the time streams of tax revenues to the government will differ, but the two streams will have the same present values.

Suppose, now, an inflation rate of 10 percent. Indexation of the tax system requires that depreciation deductions be at replacement value and that real interest be deducted on the replacement value of the undepreciated capital stock. In the example, the inflation causes depreciation deductions to rise by 10 percent per year. Interest deductions are obtained by applying the real interest rate, 10 percent, to the replacement value of the undepreciated capital stock. The latter is obtained by revaluing the undepreciated capital stock upward by the 10 percent inflation rate each year. The stream of depreciation and interest deductions is then discounted by the nominal interest rate, which in the example is 21 percent (10 percent plus 10 percent plus 0.1 times 10 percent). As the reader can verify, the present value of depreciation and interest deductions thus calculated would be $1,000,000.

## Preferential Treatment of Resource Industries

The non-renewable resource industries (mining and oil and gas) have long enjoyed special treatment under the corporate tax. They currently enjoy a number of tax advantages that reduce the effective corporate tax rate on equity capital in these industries below rates on equity in other industries (indeed, the rate can easily be negative). One advantage is the ability to write off expenditures on exploration and development immediately, even though they may be thought of as expenses incurred in the acquisition of an asset—a mine or a well—that will yield services over a period of years. The advantage to the firm of the allowance of immediate expensing rather than ordinary depreciation is that it postpones tax payments and thus reduces their present value. Moreover, by taking advantage of flowthrough share financing, which is available to the resource sector alone, resource firms can obtain the benefits of immediate writeoffs for exploration and development expenses even if they are in a loss position. Flowthrough share financing, as we have seen, allows a firm to pass its exploration and development expenses on to its shareholders, who can use them as personal tax deductions. Resource industries also enjoy the advantage of rapid writeoff of the costs of acquiring resource properties, though again, they are essentially capital costs of acquiring assets that can have a fairly long life. Note that these rapid write-offs do not reduce the interest deductions that a resource firm can claim on the basis of its debt financing. Yet it is a principle of tax accounting that if immediate expensing of capital costs is allowed there is no need to give interest deductions as well. Finally, resource firms also obtain the resource allowance, although this allowance is in lieu of deductibility of provincial royalties and mining taxes.[57]

The case for these generous deductions must rest on a more general case for affording preferential tax treatment to the resource industries. We shall consider here some of the arguments that have been advanced for preferential treatment in this case.

## Risk

It is often argued that corporate taxation discriminates against resource industries, since a relatively large part of the profit in those industries represents a payment for the cost of risk taking. Mining and petroleum ventures are said to incur a high degree of risk, owing to uncertainties about the sizes of deposits and about the prices of resources on world markets. Although it is doubtlessly true that resource ventures are risky, it is also true that mechanisms are available whose use may reduce the risk to shareholders considerably. For one, firms may engage in *risk pooling*; that is, they may engage simultaneously in several lines of risky activity, which may be less risky as a group than any of them is individually. The aggregate risk associated with a group of risky outcomes will be less than the sum of the risks of the outcomes taken individually provided that the probabilities of the outcomes of the various ventures are not correlated with one another.

For many firms, the opportunities for risk pooling by diversifying their business activities may be quite limited. Diversification by firms, however, is not the only way of reducing the risk associated with resource ventures.

---

[57] Resource firms were previously also allowed a deduction referred to as a depletion allowance, which reflected the running down of their resource properties. This allowance, however, amounted to a double deduction on assets that already had been written off, so it was repealed with the 1987 income tax reform.

Shareholders themselves may reduce risk by diversifying their ownership of assets purchased on stock markets. Since stock markets are relatively well-organized and competitive, there is no apparent reason why risks may not be reduced in this way. These considerations weaken the case for special treatment of resource industries on the ground of risk, even if it is true that resource ventures are more risky than other ventures. In fact, since risk is hard to measure, there is no way of knowing whether or not the costs of risk taking are greater in the resource industries than they are elsewhere. Given this uncertainty, the question whether resource industries merit special treatment on the ground of risk cannot be answered one way or the other.

## Financial Capital Requirements

The exploration and development activities of the resource industries require large amounts of financial capital, especially since the less expensive deposits have already been discovered and developed. Much of this capital comes from the internal funds of the companies themselves, and many of the companies are international. It is argued, therefore, that the tax laws should not prevent resource firms from having sufficient funds from current operations to finance their necessary and growing expenditures. A related argument is that if Canadian tax treatment of resource industries is harsher than the tax treatment of these industries in other countries funds will be diverted elsewhere; for example, since the United States has a system of depletion allowances and preferential treatment of resource industries, it is argued that Canada, too, should have such a system.

These arguments are very difficult to assess. A case cannot be made on economic grounds for favouring an industry simply because other nations do. It is a precept of international trade theory that introducing a domestic distortion makes a country worse off regardless of the external circumstances facing it: industries should develop according to their comparative advantage as determined by markets rather than as a result of government intervention. As to the capital-requirements argument, it must rely on the possibility that capital market imperfections of some sort prevent those markets from generating external financing sufficient to meet the resource industries' large demand for funds. It would be difficult to substantiate this possibility empirically.

## Informational Externalities

Another argument is that the exploration activities of one firm benefit other firms as well insofar as the information obtained by one firm is of use to the other firms. These benefits are known as "informational externalities." In deciding on the level of exploration, an individual firm will weigh the expected benefits to itself against the expected costs and will ignore benefits that may accrue to others (for which it will not be compensated). Therefore, firms will engage in less than the socially desirable amount of exploration. To the extent that this is true, it would justify favouring the activities that contribute to the externality. One could justify the fast writeoff of exploration expenses on this ground, but it would be difficult to base a case on it for rapid writeoff of development expenses or of the costs of acquiring resource properties allowances.

## Social Overhead Capital

Resource industries often provide a great deal of social overhead capital (towns, houses, roads, and so forth) to employees in order to attract them to the industry. It is not clear, however, that this fact justifies special treatment of the resource sector. Since the provision of social overhead is necessary to attract the labour force from other industries, it may simply represent a legitimate expense of doing business, analogous to a wage cost. If so, firms should be able to deduct its cost as an expense of doing business. At the same time, the resource industry benefits from the infrastructure provided by government, such as transportation facilities. In terms of benefits from social capital, the resource industry may be receiving a net advantage.

## Tariff and Freight Structures

Finally, it is argued that the existing tariff and freight structures heavily favour manufacturing industries and that resource industries ought to be duly compensated. The establishment of preferential tariff and freight structures for manufacturing was undertaken for the express purpose of fostering manufacturing activity at the expense of other sectors, including resource industries. Consequently, any preferential treatment of the resource industries to offset the effects of these policies would frustrate their intended aim. On the other hand, if it were decided that the protection afforded to manufacturing by the tariff and freight structures was unjustified, the appropriate policy would be to dismantle those structures. And in fact, the transportation sector has been gradually deregulated in recent years.

In summary, then, it would seem that the case for preferential treatment of resource industries on economic grounds is not a strong one.

## The Taxing of Resource Rents

An important source of structural problems associated with the taxation of the resource industries is the provincial taxation of these industries. As we have seen, the provinces levy a wide variety of taxes on resource industries, including profit taxes at various rates on minerals, royalties on minerals and natural gas, and fees for the use of Crown lands for exploration, production, and timber. The constitution assigns resources to the independent control of the individual provinces, so uniformity of structures or rates across provinces is not a likely prospect. Nonetheless, there are some important economic considerations that the design of resource taxation should take into account.

The purpose of resource taxation is to capture at least part of the rent or economic value of resources on provincial lands. The rent from extracting a resource is the difference between the total revenue generated from its sale and the total costs incurred in extracting it. A tax system that imposes a tax on rent thus defined will succeed in capturing part of the rent. Provincial resource taxes that tax profits are appropriate, therefore, for taxing the rents from the resources.

As we have seen, it is relatively easy to construct a profit tax base that accounts for the true opportunity costs of extracting the resource. The simplest way to do this is to define the tax base as the cash flow of the resource-producing corporation. The tax base would be all revenues realized from the sale of output (including resource properties) less the sum of current costs, fixed capital costs, exploration and development costs, and acquisition costs, all on a cash-flow basis. A tax of this kind could exist side-by-side with a corporate income tax designed as a withholding tax. The cash flow tax might be levied solely at the provincial level. As we have mentioned, it would be necessary to complement the cash-flow tax with a system of complete loss offsetting to retain the efficiency of the tax, given the fact that cash-flow taxation tends to push tax revenues into the future. Complete loss offsetting would be accomplished by applying an interest rate to loss carryforwards.

If cash-flow taxation were judged to be undesirable—say, from a government revenue point of view—it would still be possible to design a profits tax that approximated a tax on the flow of rents. A profits tax, of course, would be more difficult to design and administer. It would be necessary to include all revenues, and to deduct current costs, on an accrual basis. Inventory use would be deducted at replacement cost, and depreciable capital would be allowed a capital cost allowance based on replacement cost. Resource properties themselves would be deductible as they were depleted on a replacement cost basis, and no deductions would be allowed on expenditures undertaken to obtain the resources; this exclusion would extend to exploration and development expenditures, which would be viewed as capital expenditures. All financial costs (including the costs of both debt and equity) would be deductible on a real basis. This scheme is similar to what resource economists call *rate-of-return taxation*.[58]

As our discussion of resource taxation has shown, none of the current resource taxes that are designed to capture rents even approach this ideal. The federal and provincial corporate income taxes are inadequate as rent-capturing devices because the exemptions they provide for capital and resource costs are generally much higher than the true imputed costs. Provincial resource taxes are often not really income taxes at all but rather royalties based upon total value of production (ad valorem royalties) or on total quantity produced (per-unit royalties). This approach is not appropriate for the taxation of resource rents, since there is no necessary relationship between total revenues or total output and profits. Indeed, since royalties do

---

[58] For a discussion of the concept of rate-of-return taxation, see Nancy Olewiler, *Rate-of-Return Taxation of Minerals*, Discussion Paper no. 317 (Kingston, Ont.: Queen's University, Institute for Economic Research, 1978).

not take costs into account, it is entirely possible for a royalty scheme to tax profits at a rate of more than 100 percent. Thus a royalty is a distortionary tax and will discourage the production of the resource, whereas a tax on rents, if levied correctly, is a neutral tax.[59]

An alternative way of capturing resource rents is through the sale of leases to exploit the resources on Crown lands. If the leases are sold competitively, the revenues generated will be the expected resource rents less any discount for the risk involved in not being certain of the value of the resources on the property leased. There will be no need to levy taxes to capture the rents on the resources once they are extracted. If taxes do exist, they will be capitalized into the price that firms are willing to pay for the leases and lease revenues will fall accordingly. The main difference between the marketing of property rights (ex ante) and the taxing of resource profits (ex post) is that in the former case the private operator bears all of the risk associated with the extraction of the resource and in the latter case the government bears part of the risk. If the government is more efficient at pooling risk than private operators are, then the ex post method will be preferable to the ex ante method. No convincing evidence is available that helps us to discern which method of bearing the risk is preferable.

A method of taxing resource rents that is equivalent to obtaining revenue through the sale of leases is in situ taxation. This is taxation levied on the value of a resource deposit in the ground—that is, before it has been exploited. The market value of the deposit should reflect the expected future stream of rent adjusted for risk. Taxing a portion of that value is equivalent to taxing part of the rent ex ante. An in situ tax that is levied periodically (for example, annually) rather than once and for all will be distorting, since it will create an incentive to extract all of the resource as quickly as possible. Alternatively, if a firm is not intent on exploiting all discoveries in a short time, the tax may discourage exploration.

## Some Other Structural Problems

The corporation income tax is a complex entity that could easily be the basis for an entire book on its own. We have discussed the major structural problems of the tax at some length; here we will briefly consider possible solutions to some of the less important structural problems, most of which we have mentioned earlier in this chapter.

---

[59] For an analysis of the METR in the resource industries, see Robin Boadway and Ken McKenzie, "The Treatment of Resource Industries in the 1987 Federal Tax Reform," in Jack Mintz and John Whalley, eds. *The Economic Impacts of Tax Reform*, Canadian Tax Paper no. 84 (Toronto: Canadian Tax Foundation, 1989), 286-325; and Robin W. Boadway, Kenneth J. McKenzie, and Jack M. Mintz, *Federal and Provincial Taxation of the Canadian Mining Industry: Impact and Implications for Reform* (Kingston, Ont.: Queen's University, Centre for Resource Studies, 1989).

## Loss Offsetting

The system of loss offsetting, though improved in recent years, is still less than perfect. Firms in a non-tax-paying position with tax credits owing cannot obtain a tax credit in years in which their tax payable is negative (unless their past incomes allow them to use the carryback provision). This restriction is particularly unfortunate for rapidly growing firms that are undertaking large volumes of new investment and for small firms, which because of capital market imperfections may face cash flow restrictions. The ideal system would be one in which firms receive negative tax payments when their tax payable is negative. Refundability of negative tax liabilities would make cash available to firms precisely when they most need it. An alternative approach would be to allow firms to carry losses forward with interest; this approach would be equivalent in present value terms to refundability of losses, though it would not help the cash-flow position of firms that were undertaking large investments.

If refundability of losses were implemented, it would have to be with the vigilance of the tax collection authorities. As with refundable credits, it would be important to ensure that the expenditures leading to the losses or credits were actually undertaken. Problems can arise if refundability is allowed on the basis of expected losses or expenditures. The scientific research tax credit enacted in the early 1980s led to excessive claims for credits to undertake expenditures that never came to pass.

## Differential Provincial Corporate Income Taxes

One of the dangers at present is that the tax system will become more fragmented by additional provinces' setting up their own corporate tax systems with different bases and different rates. Resource taxes already vary markedly from province to province, as do some of the credits that the federal government administers for the provinces under the tax collection agreements, such as R & D and film production tax credits. A multiplication of provincial corporate tax regimes would induce tax competition, which impedes the efficient allocation of capital within the national economy. Indeed, the provinces might use their corporate tax systems to engage in self-defeating "beggar-thy-neighbour" policies in an effort to attract capital from each other. The emergence of independent systems would also increase compliance and collection costs. It is difficult, however, to see how this outcome might be prevented, given the extent to which fiscal responsibility has been decentralized to the provinces in recent years. The present system of tax collection agreements, which ensures a common tax base and not-too-different tax rates, is a good one, but its maintenance will require a great deal of cooperation among governments, something that is becoming increasingly difficult to achieve in an increasingly decentralized federation.

## Intercorporate Flowthrough of Capital Income

To avoid double taxation, the corporate tax system allows the deduction of intercorporate dividends on receipt and of interest on payment. Capital gains, however, the other form that capital income can take, are not protected by any flowthrough provisions. The income that generates capital gains (for example, retained earnings and windfall profits) is taxed at source. Then, when a shareholding corporation realizes this income as capital gains, it is taxed again, albeit at three-quarters of the usual rate. To be perfectly consistent, the system should allow deductibility of intercorporate capital gains as well as of intercorporate dividends. Since capital gains are not deductible, the cost of equity income is higher than it would otherwise be. It is not obvious why this anomaly in the corporate tax system exists.

## The Financial Structure of Corporations

The tax system offers several inducements that may affect the choice of a source of corporate financing. Thus the deductibility of interest encourages firms to favour debt over equity as a source of financing. Within the category of equity finance, the difference at the personal level between the tax treatment of dividends and the tax treatment of capital gains implies that retained earnings and new equity issues are not treated uniformly. Because the capital gains exemption is somewhat more generous than the dividend tax credit, it is generally argued that the tax system favours retained earnings over new equity issues. Since dividends are only taxed on realization and their realization can be deferred without limit, the effective tax rate on dividends may in fact be much lower than the effective tax rate on capital gains. To avoid these distorting influences on the financial structure of corporations, the corporate tax system would have to treat debt and equity on a par (as would be the case under either an ideal withholding system or a pure profits tax). In addition, the personal tax would have to treat capital gains, dividends, and interest uniformly, which might be difficult.

## Integration Procedures

The personal tax provisions for avoiding double taxation suffer from shortcomings similar to those of the comparable corporate tax provisions. Like income earned by corporations, interest received by individuals is taxable at the personal level, a provision that reflects the fact that no tax is withheld on interest income at the corporate level. Dividends paid to individual shareholders are taxable, but some credit is given for taxes paid at the corporate level by means of the dividend tax credit. There are four problems with this approach. First, like corporations, resident individuals receive no explicit credit for corporate taxes withheld on capital gains. One might argue that the three-quarters taxation of capital gains is equivalent to a credit, but this provision is not limited to capital gains obtained from Canadian corporations. In principle, if one believes in integration as a policy objective—and we have shown that there is some question about the validity of integration in an open economy—capital gains should be treated on par with dividends and be afforded a tax credit. Second, the dividend tax credit is not available on certain sheltered forms of income such as pension funds and RRSPs. Yet if these funds are invested in corporations, tax on the income they earn is withheld at source. Thus the tax system favours interest income over equity income on funds invested in these sheltered forms. If the sheltering of these forms of retirement income was done with the full intention of letting them accrue capital income tax-free, the lack of integration provisions partially undoes this intention. Third, the dividend tax credit is not refundable and cannot be carried forward or backward; consequently, it is ineffective for taxpayers in a non-tax-paying position—that is, low-income taxpayers. There is no apparent justification for this state of affairs. Fourth, the dividend tax credit does not provide complete integration—a point we shall investigate more completely in the final section of the chapter.

## The Integration of the Corporate and Personal Income Taxes

One of the major issues considered by the Carter commission in its study of the taxation of income in Canada was the so-called double taxation of income that is alleged to exist as a result of the corporate income tax. Once again, the essence of the problem is that income of corporations is taxed twice—once by the corporate tax and again, when dividends are received and capital gains on shares of Canadian corporations are realized, by the personal income tax. There is some relief from double taxation in the form of the dividend tax credit and the fact that capital gains are partially exempt from taxation. As we shall show, these measures do not exactly offset the corporate tax payable, and the question naturally arises whether there are alternative, more appropriate ways to integrate the two taxes and thus eliminate the double-taxation problem.

There are, however, two issues that ought to be settled first, and they are whether double taxation of the owners of corporations is actually occurring and whether, even if it is, integration really is desirable. From a purely accounting or legal point of view, there is no doubt that both the corporate income tax and the personal income tax apply to the resident shareholders of public corporations and some private corporations. It may appear, therefore, that corporate source income is treated unfairly and that it should not be taxed at all at the personal level—that is, that corporate and personal taxation should be fully integrated. This point of view is, however, a naïve one, for three reasons. First, since capital markets in Canada are reasonably competitive and efficient, they ensure that the net-of-tax return to capital is the same in all uses, corporate or otherwise. If it were not, it would be in time, since investment would eventually change the allocation of capital over firms until net rates of return were the same everywhere. This fact implies, as we noted earlier, that the incidence of the corporate tax is spread over all capital owners and does not fall just on those in the corporate sector. There is no justification, then, for treating owners of corporate income differently from other owners of income. For that matter, the incidence of the corporate tax may well be shifted largely or entirely to labour, in which case there is no double-taxation problem.

Second, proposals to integrate the corporate tax and the personal tax fully are ultimately equivalent to proposals to do without the tax revenue generated by the corporate tax. It is not clear that one would want to do away with the corporate tax as a revenue-raising device. It may be a much more efficient way of raising revenues than the available alternatives would be. At least part of the corporate tax falls on the pure profits of corporations. If all of the costs of using capital and other factors of production were deductible, it would be a perfectly efficient tax from an economic point of view. Obviously, not all of these costs are deductible, but enough are to ensure that the tax can be fairly efficient or non-distorting. If one aim of the corporate tax system is to tax pure profits or rents, then the part of the corporate tax that falls on rents should not be integrated. One argument against this role for the corporate tax is that it is horizontally inequitable, since the corporate tax then falls more heavily on persons who obtain part of their capital income as the rents of corporations than it falls on others. For the purposes of this section, however, it is useful to view the corporate tax not as a pure profits tax but rather as a tax on all capital income that has the unfortunate side effect of causing capital to be reallocated to the non-corporate sector. There may be equity reasons for taxing capital income relatively more heavily than labour income. The corporate tax is one way of doing this, although it could probably be done more efficiently through the personal income tax system.

Third, and perhaps most important, as we have repeatedly stressed, the case for integration—and, more generally, for the corporate tax as a withholding device—loses much of its force in an open economy setting. If capital markets in Canada are highly open to the rest of the world, rates of return in Canada, suitably adjusted for risk, will have to conform with those elsewhere. Otherwise, both domestic and foreign investors will simply take their funds elsewhere. This being the case, taxes imposed on a corporation will have to be absorbed entirely by someone other than the corporation's shareholders; most likely they will be largely shifted to labour. The result will be a state of affairs in which the presence of the corporate tax reduces investment and capital owners effectively do not bear any corporate tax. If, on top of this, domestic shareholders receive the benefits of integration through the personal tax system, the effect will be simply to undo partially whatever taxes have been levied on equity income at the personal level. The corporate tax will not be undone. Thus, integration becomes essentially pointless in terms of its alleged purpose.

The upshot of this discussion is that the case for integrating the personal and corporate taxes is not as strong as the simple arguments for integration would imply. It certainly cannot be based upon the notion that owners of public corporations are treated unfairly relative to other capital owners. All capital owners effectively bear the same burden under the corporate tax. The corporate tax is essentially a tax on capital income that yields a substantial amount of revenue and that discriminates against capital accumulation in the corporate sector. Integration of the tax system, to the extent that it is not vitiated by open-economy considerations, tends to offset those effects, and full integration is equivalent to eliminating the corporate tax altogether. In an open economy, integration becomes essentially pointless. Nonetheless, it is worth considering the merits of various forms of integration, since they are very much part of the ongoing policy discussion.

With those provisos in mind, let us consider the alternative methods proposed in the literature for integrating the corporate and personal income taxes, beginning with the most complete method—the partnership approach.

## The Partnership Approach

This approach attempts to fully integrate the corporate and personal income taxes. There are two variants of it. The first is simply to abolish the corporate income tax, prorate the income of the corporation to its owners, and require the owners to pay individual income tax on their share of corporate income in the year in which it accrues. All corporate income is thus treated as personal income. The disadvantage of this method is that it might cause liquidity problems, since it implies that individuals would have to pay tax on income they had not yet received (the income retained by the corporation). Individuals might be forced to liquidate shares or the corporation might reduce its retained earnings, so corporate savings would be discouraged.

The alternative approach, which avoids these difficulties, is the one recommended by the Carter commission. The corporation would pay the corporate tax, then allocate both its distributed income and its retained income on paper among its shareholders. The shareholders would then add to their taxable income their allocated shares of the corporate income before tax and treat the tax paid by the corporation as having been paid on their behalf (that is, they would credit it against personal tax payable). The corporation would, in effect, act as a withholding agent of the owner. Some administrative problems would arise when shares changed hands more than once during the year, but the corporate and personal taxes would be fully integrated and the effects of the corporate tax would be completely offset.

In judging the merits of tax proposals, it is convenient to consider their relative treatment of persons in different groups or tax brackets. Table 4.8 illustrates the partnership approach to integration on this basis.[60] The example assumes for simplicity that all corporate income is distributed to shareholders and that the corporate tax rate is 50 percent; the reader can easily amend the example to allow for lower tax rates. The table examines the relative treatment of shareholders in six income tax brackets ranging from 0 to 50 percent who receive $1,000 of corporate source income. Column 6 shows the tax that would be paid on the $1,000 in the absence of the corporate tax, or, equivalently, under the partnership approach. This is simply the tax that results from applying the personal tax rate to the capital income

---

[60] This approach is similar to the one discussed in Joseph A. Pechman, *Federal Tax Policy*, rev. ed. (Washington, DC: Brookings Institution, 1971), 105-48.

Table 4.8  Comparison of Partnership Approach with No-Integration Case

| Marginal tax rate (percent) | Pre-tax corporate income (1) | Corporate tax (50% tax rate) (2) | Dividend received (3) | Shareholder individual income tax (4) | Total tax burden (5) | Tax paid under partnership approach (6) | Additional tax burden (7) |
|---|---|---|---|---|---|---|---|
| | | | | *dollars* | | | |
| 0 | 1,000 | 500 | 500 | 0 | 500 | 0 | 500 |
| 10 | 1,000 | 500 | 500 | 50 | 550 | 100 | 450 |
| 20 | 1,000 | 500 | 500 | 100 | 600 | 200 | 400 |
| 30 | 1,000 | 500 | 500 | 150 | 650 | 300 | 350 |
| 40 | 1,000 | 500 | 500 | 200 | 700 | 400 | 300 |
| 50 | 1,000 | 500 | 500 | 250 | 750 | 500 | 250 |

Note: It is assumed that there are no retained earnings.

generated. Column 5 shows the amount that would be paid under a corporate tax with no integration.[61] The difference between columns 5 and 6 is column 7, the additional tax burden borne by each income group that is attributable to the corporate tax. As the table shows, an absence of integration is very regressive, since the additional tax burden that it imposes, as a proportion of capital income earned, falls as the marginal rate rises.

One can judge the equity of the tax integration system by the way in which the burden is reduced for various income groups. There is a strong case for the partnership approach on the ground of equity, since in removing all of the tax burden shown in column 7 it removes a greater amount from the lower-income groups than from the higher-income groups.

## The Dividend Exclusion Method

This method of integration, like all of the methods that follow, provides only partial integration. The shareholder is allowed to deduct part or all of the dividends received from taxable income. One can deduce the effect on different income groups of complete deductibility of dividends relative to the effect of a fully integrated system from table 4.8. Since dividends are not taxable, column 4 becomes all zeros and total tax payable becomes $500 by each income group. The additional tax burden attributable to this partially integrated corporate tax is reduced by the elements of the original column 4. The amounts in column 7 become $500, $400, $300, $200, $100, and $0. These amounts represent the additional burden imposed by a dividend exclusion tax scheme relative to a fully integrated scheme. Note that the amount by which partial integration reduces the additional tax burden increases with income. The additional tax burden for persons above the 50 percent tax bracket would actually be negative, since they would be getting back more in personal taxes than would be paid in corporate taxes on their behalf. Clearly, this is a very inequitable way of providing partial integration. This is true, in fact, of all schemes that use deductions, since the value of deductions rises with the marginal tax rate. The partial exemption of capital gains raises the same problem.

## The Dividend-Received Tax Credit Method

The obvious alternative to dividend exclusion is a tax credit given on the basis of dividends received. Before the tax reform of 1972, this was the method used in Canada. Individuals could deduct from tax payable 20 percent of dividends received from Canadian corporations.

Under the 20 percent dividend tax credit system, the numbers in column 4 of table 4.8 are all reduced by (0.2 × $500) or $100. Since persons in the zero

---

[61] This table and those that follow ignore the shifting of the tax that takes place. Nonetheless, it is useful for illustrating the relative burdens placed upon various income groups under various systems.

tax bracket do not pay tax, they get no benefit. Those in the 10 percent bracket obtain a credit of only $50. All of the others' additional burdens are reduced by $100, so column 7 becomes $500, $400, $300, $250, $200, and $150. This is a more equitable remedy than the dividend deduction, since it benefits all groups by the same amount, but the additional burden that this partly integrated tax imposes relative to a fully integrated one is still highly regressive.

## The Dividend-Paid Deduction Method

This method, used in the 1930s in the United States, allows corporations to deduct all or part of their dividends from taxable corporate income. It has the obvious effect of discouraging corporations from retaining earnings.

Suppose that corporations are allowed to deduct 50 percent of dividends from taxable income. In table 4.8, then, the corporate taxable income on $1,000 of fully distributed profits becomes $500, so tax payable—column 2—becomes $250. The shareholder receives a dividend of $750—column 3— and pays tax accordingly. After working through the columns, one arrives at the following figures for column 7: $250, $225, $200, $175, $150, and $125. That is, the partial integration reduces the additional burden imposed by an unintegrated system by one-half. This method is more equitable than the previous methods of partial integration, since it reduces the burden for low-income groups by greater amounts than they do.

## The Withholding Method

Withholding is the method of integration currently used in Canada. Part of the corporate tax paid on dividends is withheld as a tax in respect of the shareholders, who receive a credit for the amount that has been withheld. This method is effectively the same as the dividend-paid deduction method, though some authors have suggested that it avoids the disincentive for corporations to retain earnings that the latter method creates.[62] It may be true that a corporation has no the direct disincentive to retain earnings if corporate tax payments are reduced at the personal tax level rather than at the corporate tax level, but if the corporation is acting in the interest of its shareholders, it will respond to either method of integration in much the same way.

An example will illustrate the withholding method as it is currently used in Canada. Table 4.9 shows the effect of the existing 25 percent dividend tax credit under the assumption that all corporate profits are paid out as dividends.[63] Again, the pre-tax corporate income is $1,000 and the corporate tax rate is 50 percent. The dividend received of $500 is grossed up by the tax

---

[62] See, for example, Pechman, supra footnote 60.

[63] As we noted earlier, the tax credit given is not exactly 25 percent of dividends received, owing to the fact that the tax credit is divided between the federal and provincial levels of government and varies with provincial tax rates. We ignore this complication here.

**Table 4.9  Withholding Method—25 Percent Rate with All Profits Distributed**

| Marginal tax rate (percent) | Dividend received (1) | Grossed-up dividend added to personal income (2) | Personal income tax before credit (3) | Personal income tax payable after credit of $250 (4) | Total tax burden (5) | Additional tax burden (6) | Percentage of additional tax burden removed (7) |
|---|---|---|---|---|---|---|---|
| | | | | *dollars* | | | |
| 0 ................ | 500 | 625 | 0 | −125 | 375 | 375 | 25 |
| 10 ............... | 500 | 625 | 62.5 | −62.5 | 437.5 | 337.5 | 25 |
| 20 ............... | 500 | 625 | 125 | 0 | 500 | 300 | 25 |
| 30 ............... | 500 | 625 | 187.5 | 62.5 | 562.5 | 262.5 | 25 |
| 40 ............... | 500 | 625 | 250 | 125 | 625 | 225 | 25 |
| 50 ............... | 500 | 625 | 312.5 | 312.5 | 687.5 | 187.5 | 25 |

credit rate of 25 percent to give ($500 × 1.25) = $625. This amount is added to taxable income, tax payable is calculated (column 3), and a credit is given of (0.25 × $500) = $125 (column 4). The table assumes that even people in the low tax brackets receive the full credit, which is not the case in practice if they do not have sufficient other income. The total tax burden (column 5) is then $500 plus personal tax, assuming a 50 percent corporate tax rate. The additional tax burden is column 5 less the amount that would have been paid in the absence of the corporate tax—that is, under full integration. Finally, column 7 compares column 6 with column 7 of table 4.8 to calculate the proportion of the additional tax burden created by the corporate tax that the dividend tax credit removes. The reduction is proportionately the same for all income groups, just as it is with the dividend-paid deduction. If the dividend tax credit were 100 percent, all of the additional burden would be removed.

This illustration ignores the fact that corporate profits are partially retained and partially distributed. To see what this means, assume that one-half of profits after tax are distributed and one-half are retained. Furthermore, assume that the half that are retained show up as capital gains to the shareholder and are realized. Table 4.10 indicates the effect of the tax system on individuals of various tax brackets in these circumstances. Once again, we assume corporate profits before tax of $1,000 and a corporate tax rate of 50 percent. The combined system of a 25 percent dividend tax credit and the inclusion of three-quarters of capital gains as taxable income yields a tax burden, given by column 8, over and above the personal tax burden that would arise in the absence of the corporate tax (or under a fully integrated system). Column 9 shows the percentage by which this additional tax burden is less than the burden imposed by a wholly unintegrated system. Owing to the inclusion of taxable capital gains, the amount of tax removed in this case is less than the amount removed in the case in which all profits are distributed (table 4.9). From the shareholder's point of view, therefore, distribution of profits is preferable to retention of profits. Moreover, the pattern of reduction of the tax burden is much more regressive in this case than it is under most other methods of integration. The percentage of additional income removed is higher for the higher income groups. On equity grounds, therefore, the current system of integration in Canada is worse than are most of the alternatives that we have considered here.

Finally, recall that under the current Canadian tax system the 25 percent dividend tax credit is given on all dividends received from Canadian corporations regardless of the amount of tax that has been paid on the corporate income. If the corporation has paid relatively little tax (for example, because of the depletion allowance or accelerated depreciation) shareholders might be "overcompensated" for corporate taxes paid. By amending table 4.9, one can calculate the effect of allowing the full dividend tax credit on income that has been taxed at only 10 percent, for whatever reason. In this case, the corporate tax paid on dividends of $500 is $55.56, rather than $500. The total tax burden figures in column 5 are therefore $444.44 lower than they were in the original calculation, and the additional tax burden is $444.44 less. The

**Table 4.10  Withholding Method—25 Percent Rate with One-Half of Profits Distributed**

| Marginal tax rate (percent) | Dividend received (1) | Grossed-up dividend (1.25 × $500) (2) | Taxable capital gains (0.75 × $250) (3) | Income for tax purposes (col. 2 + col. 3) (4) | Income tax before credit (5) | Tax payable after credit of $62.50 (6) | Total tax burden (col. 6 + $500) (7) | Additional tax burden (8) | Percentage of tax burden removed (9) |
|---|---|---|---|---|---|---|---|---|---|
| | | | | | *dollars* | | | | |
| 0 . . . . . . . . . . . . . | 250 | 312.5 | 187.5 | 500 | 0 | -125 | 375 | 375 | 25 |
| 10 . . . . . . . . . . . . . | 250 | 312.5 | 187.5 | 500 | 50 | -75 | 425 | 325 | 27.8 |
| 20 . . . . . . . . . . . . . | 250 | 312.5 | 187.5 | 500 | 100 | -25 | 475 | 275 | 31.3 |
| 30 . . . . . . . . . . . . . | 250 | 312.5 | 187.5 | 500 | 150 | 25 | 525 | 225 | 35.7 |
| 40 . . . . . . . . . . . . . | 250 | 312.5 | 187.5 | 500 | 200 | 75 | 575 | 175 | 41.7 |
| 50 . . . . . . . . . . . . . | 250 | 312.5 | 187.5 | 500 | 250 | 125 | 625 | 125 | 50.0 |

percentage of the additional tax burden that is removed in this case is 136 percent—that is, more than full credit is given for the corporate tax paid. This result, though inequitable, may not be undesirable, since presumably the tax incentives were put in place in order to encourage the corporation's activity. To offset the benefits partially by not allowing the full dividend tax credit would be to detract from the usefulness of the original incentive.

## Tax Reform: Recommendations of the Mintz Committee

The Mintz committee was appointed in 1996 with a mandate to assess the business tax system and recommend ways in which to make it more conducive to economic growth and job creation, to simplify its structure (and thereby reduce the costs of collection and compliance), and to enhance its fairness. The business tax system was taken to include all taxes levied on businesses, including federal and provincial corporate and capital taxes, payroll taxes levied on employers, property taxes, and sales taxes on business inputs. Relying heavily on the detailed calculation of METRs, the committee argued that the main deficiencies of the existing system are as follows:

• Statutory corporate tax rates on non-manufacturing businesses are higher in Canada than they are in the countries that are our main competitors, with the exception of the continental European countries. In Canada, the average statutory rate is 43 percent; in the United States it is 39 percent and in the United Kingdom 32 percent. Canada's higher rate discourages non-manufacturing companies from locating here and encourages multinational corporations to shift profits out of Canada by borrowing in Canada in order to increase their interest deductions and hence reduce their tax bases.

• METRs vary across industries in Canada, a circumstance that distorts the allocation of resources, increases the costs of collection and compliance, reduces fairness, and requires tax rates for non-preferred businesses to be high. In particular, the service industries, which are the source of much employment growth, are at a tax disadvantage relative to the manufacturing and resource industries.

• The present system exhibits an unhealthy reliance on taxes that are insensitive to profits, and that therefore cause economic inefficiency, are unfair, and impede the growth of small firms and those whose profits are temporarily low.

The committee concluded that it could best address these problems and fulfil its mandate by proposing reforms aimed at one overriding objective: the creation of a more neutral tax system with internationally competitive rates. Greater neutrality could be achieved by reducing the differences among the METRs faced by different businesses, and this would require scourging the business tax system of provisions that favour some activities over others. This objective is very much in line with the principles behind the 1987 income tax reforms (and with reforms in other countries as well)—to broaden the base and reduce the rates. This outcome would in itself simplify the system and reduce collection and compliance costs, but, there are other measures that could also be taken to make the administration of the business tax system smoother. They include enhancing the harmonization of federal and provincial taxes. The following discussion reviews the main recommendations of the Mintz committee. Note that many of the recommendations that accept elements of the status quo are as important as those that reject it.

## A Reduction in Corporate Tax Rates

In order to make the Canadian statutory tax rate comparable to statutory rates in the United States and the United Kingdom, the committee proposed a reduction in the general rate from the current 38 percent to 33 percent. Of this, 20 percent would be the federal general rate and 13 percent would be the abatement available on corporate income earned in the provinces. Corporate income surtaxes would be eliminated. The provincial abatement of 13 percentage points implies that the provinces would reduce their rates by an average of 1 percentage point. In this context, as in others, the committee appealed to the provinces to adopt measures that would complement those of the federal government. Of the various goals set by the committee, however, the provincial rate reduction is likely to be one of the most difficult to achieve, given that each province has independent decision-making authority over corporate tax rates.

In opting for lower corporate tax rates, the committee accepted the view that rates in Canada should conform with those set abroad. Since personal marginal tax rates are considerably higher than the proposed 33 percent corporate tax rate, the reformed corporate tax would not be able to withhold fully against the income of domestic shareholders. In recommending the rate reduction, therefore, the Mintz committee departed significantly from the Carter report's emphasis on the corporate tax's role as a withholding tax. The committee's view is consistent with the notion that in an open economy the case for withholding on behalf of domestic shareholders loses much of its appeal.

## The Elimination of Some Corporate Tax Preferences

A reduction in the corporate tax rate would in itself reduce the revenues obtained from the tax. The committee's whole package of proposed reforms, however, is designed to be revenue neutral. The rate reduction would be "financed" by the removal of a number of tax preferences. Under the Mintz committee proposals, therefore, the preferential tax rate for manufacturing and processing, currently 31 percent, would be eliminated. The general federal small business rate would increase slightly, from 12 percent (13.12 percent with the surtax in effect) to 14 percent; the provincial abatement of 10 percent on top of that would remain. On the other hand, in order to reward small businesses according to the employment they provide, 20 percent of the employer's share of employment insurance contributions could be credited against the corporate income tax. This change would effectively bring the rate down to as little as 11 percent for some firms. Thus the existing tax preference for small businesses, at least in the case of those that create and maintain jobs, would be considerably enhanced.

Capital cost allowance rates that are too generous relative to economic depreciation would be reduced. This change would especially affect items such as manufacturing and processing assets, heavy moving equipment, and vessels. More generally, the committee called for a review of the existing capital cost allowance rates in order to ensure that they match economic depreciation rates. Along the same lines, it recommended that the rapid writeoff of development costs in mining and oil and gas be reduced from 30 percent to 25 percent, that the immediate writeoff of capital costs for new mines be replaced by the standard 25 percent rate, and that the cost of acquiring new mining properties be reduced to 10 percent to make it comparable with the treatment of oil and gas properties. The resource allowance, which is a deduction in lieu of the deductibility of provincial royalties and taxes, would be retained, but the base to which the allowance applies would be narrowed by extending it to include the deduction of all exploration, development, and interest costs. Finally, the writeoffs for research and development, which are among the most generous in the world, would be reduced. Immediate deductibility of SR & ED assets would be eliminated. The committee's presumption was that this array of measures would substantially reduce the wide variation in METRs across activities and industries. In particular, it would eliminate the preferential METRs for manufacturing and processing and the resource industries.

The committee would also reduce the generosity of some tax credits. In particular, it would eliminate the Atlantic investment tax credit and reduce the SR & ED tax credit for large corporations from 20 percent to 15 percent. At the same time, to recognize the important role played in R & D by small businesses, and their difficulties in attracting financing, the committee proposed that they be able to obtain a full refund of the SR & ED tax credit offered to them, which would be 27 percent instead of the current 35 percent. In general, these proposals, though relatively minor, are consistent with the argument made throughout the committee's report that the tax system should not be used to deliver special preferences to particular industries. Tax preferences delivered through the tax system tend to be costly (since they are available to all, whether they are needed or not), and they introduce complexity into the tax system. There is also an underlying presumption in the report that governments should eschew the use of tax preferences because it should be left to the market to determine the allocation of resources. In cases where clear arguments for assistance can be made, the committee suggested that direct grants be used instead of tax preferences. This would represent a major departure from past practice. The Canadian business tax system has traditionally been a vehicle for the delivery of industrial policies, and investment tax credits have been prominent among the instruments used for this purpose. Detractors will argue that the delivery of assistance through direct grants would introduce a need for administrative discretion and, with it, the possibility of political interference.

## Enhancement of the Integration of Personal and Corporate Taxes

Despite the fact that the Mintz committee argued for a reduction in corporate tax rates to match rates in competing jurisdictions, it explicitly accepted the traditional withholding rationale for the corporate tax—its use as a device for precluding shareholders from deferring personal income taxes by retaining and reinvesting income in the corporation. Having accepted the tax's withholding role, the committee naturally wished to maintain and even enhance the provisions for integration of the corporate income tax with the personal income tax.

The committee identified the main devices for integrating the corporate and personal taxes as being the dividend tax credit, the partial exemption of capital gains, the tax-free flow of intercorporate dividends, and the special provisions related to the investment income of CCPCs. The committee argued that this system has a number of satisfactory features. In particular, the dividend tax credit roughly fully integrates income that has been subject to the small business tax rate, though it undercompensates for income that has been subject to the full corporate tax rate. Similarly, the taxation of three-quarters of capital gains roughly integrates for high-income taxpayers corporate source income that has been subject to the small business tax rate. The investment income of CCPCs is also more or less fully integrated.

The main deviations from perfect integration seem to be the following. First, integration is available on corporate source income at the same dividend tax credit rate regardless of the tax that has been paid at the corporate level. For example, if dividends are paid by tax-loss firms, which is certainly conceivable, a dividend tax credit is available. Second, some recipients of dividends do not receive the dividend tax credit, either because they are tax-exempt (for example, pension funds) or because they are in a non-tax-paying position. Moreover, dividends received by low-income households that are not in a tax-paying position are effectively not credited, since the credit is non-refundable. The treatment of capital gains too leads to inequities and inefficiencies. Unlike dividends, capital gains are integrated—to the extent that they are integrated at all—by an exemption rather than by a credit, an arrangement that favours higher-income taxpayers. In addition, the one-quarter exemption does not apply to interfirm capital gains. Finally, one could argue that the one-quarter exemption does not, in fact, serve as an integration device: government tax-expenditure calculations do not treat it as one. It applies to all capital gains received, and not just those from Canadian corporations.

The Mintz committee's recommendations address only one of these deficiencies—the receipt of the dividend tax credit in excess of corporate taxes that have been levied. The main proposal for improving integration is to institute a joint federal-provincial corporate distribution tax (CDT). This would be a tax of 25 percent levied on all corporate dividend payments. Ordinary federal and provincial corporate taxes would be fully creditable against the CDT, with a 3-year carrybackward and 10-year carryforward provision. Special provisions would ensure that the CDT did not impede the tax-free flow of intercorporate dividends, or the full integration of investment income of CCPCs. The CDT would function as a withholding device to ensure that the dividend tax credit was available only on taxes that had been previously paid. In achieving that objective, however, it would also effectively undo any reduced tax rates that corporations might face for any reason—it would undo the reduced rates, that is, whether they were attributable to tax preferences or to the firm's being in a tax-loss position because of growth or bad luck. The main issue to be addressed in assessing the CDT proposal is whether reduced tax rates, which may be in place for good policy reasons, should be effectively undone by a device of this kind. The committee's view is that tax preferences should not be used, period. Therefore, anything that defangs them should be implemented. Not all observers will agree with that assessment.

In dealing with overintegration, the Mintz committee chose not to deal with its opposite, underintegration. It proposed no relief for dividends (or capital gains) received by tax-exempt institutions, or for dividends received by taxpayers in a non-tax-paying position. The logic of integration would suggest that the benefit of integration should be extended to both categories of recipients. The committee also failed to address the anomalous treatment of capital gains relative to dividends. It explicitly favoured retaining the existing treatment of capital gains (though it did propose phasing out the $500,000 lifetime capital gains exemption for farm property and CCPCs).

A more general matter at issue is the relevance of withholding, and indeed the relevance of integration measures of any kind, in an open economy. In a fully open economy, as we argued earlier, withholding against domestic shareholders serves no purpose. The after-tax rate of return to shareholders must conform with the rate of return on international markets; consequently, taxes levied on corporate equity income will be shifted to immobile factors, such as labour. Nor does withholding, or integration generally, undo the distortion of economic decisions imposed by the corporate tax. Since integration operates through the personal tax system rather than the corporate tax system, it serves only to reduce taxes payable on equity income at the personal level and leaves the distortion associated with the corporate tax in effect. The only valid role for withholding in an open economy is withholding against the income of foreign corporations that can avail themselves of tax credits in their home countries. Although capital markets in Canada may not be fully open, they are nonetheless "quite" open. This being the case, a major rethinking of the role of the corporate tax may be in order.

### Changes in the Taxation of International Capital Income

The Mintz committee expressed some concern about leakages from the Canadian tax revenue base through international transactions, and proposed a number of measures designed to deal with the problem. Full consideration of these proposals would take us too far afield, so we shall simply summarize them here. The aim of the main proposals is to reduce taxpayers' ability to claim interest deductibility in Canada for investments undertaken abroad.

Under the proposed measures, therefore, Canadian taxpayers would no longer be able to claim interest deductibility on interest in investments in foreign affiliates. In addition, non-Canadian firms' ability to shift interest expenses to related Canadian businesses would be restricted by a tightening up of the thin capitalization provisions, which, as we discussed earlier, restrict the amount of shifted interest that may be deducted. Finally, the proposed provisions would limit the definition of foreign affiliates to affiliates in which Canadian corporations have significant equity interest. The right to repatriate income from transactions with foreign affiliates without tax would be limited to affiliates that enjoy tax-treaty status.

## Improvements in Federal-Provincial Tax Harmonization

The Mintz committee recognized that in a federation in which the provinces and the federal government both occupy a mobile and complicated tax base such as corporate income it is highly desirable to harmonize the taxes of the two levels of government as closely as possible. Harmonization reduces compliance and collection costs, prevents self-defeating and distortionary tax competition among provinces, and discourages unproductive private sector tax planning. To improve harmonization, the committee proposed that all 10 provinces join the tax collection agreement system for the corporate tax. This proposal, obviously, requires the 3 non-complying provinces—Alberta, Ontario, and Quebec—to join, something that only they can decide. The committee also recommended that provincial and federal capital taxes be harmonized, if possible through a system of tax collection agreements. At the least, the committee argued, the two levels of government should adopt a common base for each of the two taxes, and a common method for allocating them to each jurisdiction. Given common tax bases, any tax incentives or requirements for additional revenue should be achieved through tax rates or credits, not through changes in the bases.

## Adoption of the User-Pay Principle

Finally, the Mintz committee addressed the concerns about profit-insensitive taxes by proposing the use of benefit taxation to help alleviate the problem. The committee singled out two particular taxes for possible application of the "user-pay principle"—employment insurance (EI) premiums and the federal excise tax on motive fuels.

The committee noted that there is no relation between the EI contribution rate and the amount of a firm's claims, either past or expected, on EI benefits. Thus firms are not penalized for excessive layoffs. Since they are not, they have an incentive to use layoffs rather than, say, reduced hours of work or accumulation of inventories in the face of a temporary downturn in demand. To counter this subsidy to layoffs, the committee proposed that the federal government move in the direction of *experience rating* EI contributions. Under an experience-rated EI system, a firm's payroll tax rate would be related to its past layoff experience. Economists have frequently recommended experience rating EI premiums, and the EI legislation permits it. Nevertheless, experience rating has not been used. The committee did not recommend the imposition of full experience rating, but only that the federal government discourage overuse of the EI system by giving some weight to firms' past layoff experience in setting employer premiums. Nor did it recommend that individual payroll tax rates be subject to experience rating, though from an economics point of view there is really no distinction between employer and employee contributions. Full experience rating would imply that there is no "insurance" component to EI, since each firm would contribute enough to cover its own employees' use of benefits. Exactly how much experience rating is ideal is a difficult issue and one that the committee did not address.

In discussing the federal excise tax on motive fuels, the committee emphasized the strategy of taxing different fuels differently as a means of internalizing the externalities that arise from air pollution. It has been argued that the fuel excise tax may be thought of as a user price for the benefits that vehicle users obtain from the road system. As a benefit tax, however, the excise tax is rather indirect; in any case it is not obvious why benefit taxation should apply to roads and not to other public goods and services, such as higher education, public telecommunications, and so on. The committee argued that, as a tax on pollution, the federal excise tax is not particularly efficient. It focuses on one type of pollutant, motive fuels, to the exclusion of others, such as coal. The committee proposed that the federal fuel excise tax be replaced with a more broadly based environmental tax that would be related more directly to the emission of pollutants and to the damage that pollutants do to the environment. This change would significantly rationalize the excise tax on fuels without necessarily affecting the amount of revenues that it generates. Like many of the committee's other proposals, this proposal would ideally involve the cooperation of the federal government and the provinces, since they have a joint interest in the objectives of environmental taxation and in the resources that would ultimately be taxed. The committee did not discuss the rationalization of the other main excise taxes, the "sin" taxes on alcohol and tobacco products, though presumably these too might be candidates for reform.

# 5

# Commodity Taxes

## Introduction

Commodity taxes in Canada are frequently criticized as being regressive and less than uniform in their application to the vast array of goods and services on which they are imposed. Nevertheless, they are important sources of revenue for both the federal government and the provinces.[1] Federal commodity taxes consist of the goods and services tax, a number of specific excise taxes, excise duties, and customs duties. The most significant commodity taxes at the provincial level are general sales taxes, fuel taxes, and alcoholic beverages and tobacco taxes.

Table 5.1 shows that since the early 1970s federal commodity taxes have accounted for between one-fifth and one-quarter of the federal government's own-source revenue. The much-discussed goods and services tax (GST), and its predecessor before 1991, the federal manufacturers' sales tax (MST), have been the most important sources of federal commodity-based revenue over the past few decades. By fiscal year 1995-96, the GST accounted for more than 66 percent of federal budgetary revenues from commodity taxation. Fuel taxes, alcoholic beverage and tobacco taxes, and customs duties (tariffs), by comparison, each accounted for between 9 and 13 percent of commodity-based revenues. The "other" category in table 5.1 includes the air transportation tax and a variety of miscellaneous charges; it accounted for the remaining 2 to 3 percent of federal commodity-based taxes and charges.

The most important commodity tax at the provincial level is the sales tax. Although it is non-existent in Alberta and the Northwest Territories and its rate varies from province to province (see table 5.2), it is by far the most important source of commodity-tax revenue in all of the provinces that use it. In 1996-97, as table 5.3 shows, the sales tax accounted for between 64 and 78 percent of all commodity-based revenues in each of the provinces except Alberta. In the provinces with sales taxes, fuel taxes accounted for a further 15 to 27 percent of the total, and alcoholic beverage and tobacco taxes for between 4 and 13 percent.

---

[1] Satya Poddar and Morley English, "Fifty Years of Canadian Commodity Taxation: Key Events and Lessons for the Future" (1995), vol. 43, no. 5 *Canadian Tax Journal* 1096-1119.

**Table 5.1  Federal Government Revenue from Commodity Taxes for Selected Fiscal Years**

| Tax source | 1970-71 | | 1980-81 | | 1990-91 | | 1995-96 | |
|---|---|---|---|---|---|---|---|---|
| | Millions of dollars | Percentage of total | Millions of dollars | Percentage of total | Millions of dollars | Percentage of total | Millions of dollars | Percentage of total |
| General sales tax[a] | 2,281 | 56.2 | 5,429 | 50.0 | 16,700 | 59.7 | 22,130 | 66.5 |
| Motive fuel tax | — | — | 454 | 4.2 | 2,975 | 10.6 | 4,180 | 12.6 |
| Alcoholic beverages and tobacco tax | 887 | 21.9 | 1,510 | 13.9 | 3,305 | 11.8 | 2,896 | 8.7 |
| Customs duties | 815 | 20.1 | 3,188 | 29.4 | 4,150 | 14.8 | 3,270 | 9.8 |
| Other | 73 | 1.8 | 270 | 2.5 | 856 | 3.1 | 794 | 2.4 |
| Total | 4,056 | 100.0 | 10,851 | 100.0 | 27,986 | 100.0 | 33,270 | 100.0 |
| Commodity taxes as a percentage of own-source revenue | 26.2 | | 20.2 | | 21.7 | | 23.4 | |

— not applicable.

[a] The manufacturers' sales tax was replaced by the federal goods and services tax on January 1, 1991.

Sources: Statistics Canada, *Public Finance Historical Data, 1965/66-1991/92*, catalogue no. 68-512; and Statistics Canada, *Public Sector Finance*, catalogue no. 68-212 XPB.

**Table 5.2   Provincial Sales Tax Rates for Selected Years**

|                         | 1967 | 1983 | 1998 |
|-------------------------|:----:|:----:|:----:|
|                         |      | *percent* |   |
| Newfoundland .......................... | 6 | 12 | 8 |
| Prince Edward Island .................... | 5 | 10 | 10 |
| Nova Scotia .......................... | 5 | 10 | 8 |
| New Brunswick ........................ | 6 | 10 | 8 |
| Quebec .............................. | 8 | 9 | 7.5 |
| Ontario .............................. | 5 | 6 | 7 |
| Manitoba ............................ | 5[a] | 7 | 7 |
| Saskatchewan ......................... | 4 | 5 | 7 |
| Alberta .............................. | — | — | — |
| British Columbia ...................... | 5 | 7 | 7 |

— not applicable.

[a] Introduced on June 1, 1967.

Sources: Robin W. Boadway and Harry M. Kitchen, *Canadian Tax Policy*, 2d ed., Canadian Tax Paper no. 76 (Toronto: Canadian Tax Foundation, 1984), 258; and Karin Treff and David B. Perry, *Finances of the Nation 1998* (Toronto: Canadian Tax Foundation, 1998), 5:4.

# The Structure of Federal Commodity Taxes[2]

## The Goods and Services Tax (GST)

The federal goods and services tax[3] (GST) replaced the manufacturers' sales tax[4] (MST) on January 1, 1991. As we noted in chapter 1, the GST is a form of value-added tax (VAT) and is similar to the VATs used in most other industrialized countries, though it is more comprehensive than most other VATs. The GST is a destination-based tax: imports are fully included and exports are exempt. It is based on a broad range of consumer goods and services, but not on investment expenditures or government expenditures. The current rate of tax is 7 percent.

The GST applies to goods and services at every stage of production and distribution. Businesses are allowed tax credits for all GST paid on goods and services, including investment goods, that they purchase in the course of their operations. The final consumer, however, cannot claim tax credits. In general, the tax is equivalent to a uniform tax on final consumption—it is calculated by multiplying the final selling price of a taxable good or service

---

[2] For a historical discussion of federal consumption taxes, see J. Harvey Perry, *Taxation in Canada*, 5th ed., Canadian Tax Paper no. 89 (Toronto: Canadian Tax Foundation, 1990), chapters 9 to 11.

[3] Karin Treff and David B. Perry, *Finances of the Nation 1998* (Toronto: Canadian Tax Foundation, 1998), 5:1-3.

[4] For a description of the MST and the inequities and distortions that it created, see John Whalley and Deborah Fretz, *The Economics of the Goods and Services Tax*, Canadian Tax Paper no. 88 (Toronto: Canadian Tax Foundation, 1990), chapters 3 to 5; and Robin W. Boadway and Harry M. Kitchen, *Canadian Tax Policy*, 2d ed., Canadian Tax Paper no. 76 (Toronto: Canadian Tax Foundation, 1984), 260-61 and 279.

Table 5.3   **Provincial Revenue from Major Commodity Taxes, 1996-97[a]**

| | General sales tax | | Gasoline and motive fuel taxes | | Alcoholic beverages and tobacco taxes | | Total,[b] millions of dollars |
|---|---|---|---|---|---|---|---|
| | Millions of dollars | Percentage of provincial consumption tax revenue | Millions of dollars | Percentage of provincial consumption tax revenue | Millions of dollars | Percentage of provincial consumption tax revenue | |
| Newfoundland | 556.4 | 71.7 | 118.0 | 15.2 | 102.0 | 13.1 | 776.4 |
| Prince Edward Island | 129.3 | 71.9 | 27.2 | 15.1 | 22.5 | 12.5 | 179.9 |
| Nova Scotia | 747.0 | 71.7 | 203.4 | 19.5 | 86.0 | 8.3 | 1,042.0 |
| New Brunswick | 734.0 | 78.4 | 161.8 | 17.3 | 38.0 | 4.1 | 936.2 |
| Quebec | 5,299.9 | 73.2 | 1,487.8 | 20.5 | 428.2 | 5.9 | 7,241.9 |
| Ontario | 9,766.9 | 73.1 | 2,476.9 | 18.5 | 817.0 | 6.1 | 13,368.3 |
| Manitoba | 820.0 | 71.2 | 218.6 | 19.0 | 109.7 | 9.5 | 1,151.0 |
| Saskatchewan | 847.4 | 63.6 | 365.5 | 27.4 | 117.3 | 8.8 | 1,331.8 |
| Alberta | — | | 545.0 | 60.3 | 317.0 | 35.1 | 904.1 |
| British Columbia | 3,059.0 | 69.1 | 805.0 | 18.2 | 475.0 | 10.7 | 4,429.1 |
| All provinces | 21,959.9 | 70.0 | 6,409.2 | 20.4 | 2,512.7 | 8.0 | 31,360.7 |

—   not applicable.
[a] Estimates. [b] As well as the three major taxes listed here, this total includes a few miscellaneous commodity taxes.

Source: Karin Treff and David B. Perry, *Finances of the Nation 1998* (Toronto: Canadian Tax Foundation, 1998), 5:5, table 5.2.

by 7 percent. The tax does not, however, apply to all goods and services in the same way. Some goods are zero-rated, some are exempt, and some are eligible for rebates.

In the case of *zero-rated* goods and services, no tax applies to the final selling price but sellers can claim tax credits for all tax paid on purchases at intermediate stages of production and distribution. Effectively, the full value of the good or service escapes tax. Goods that fall into this category include basic groceries (but not snack foods, non-fruit beverages, prepared foods, or restaurant meals), prescription drugs, medical devices, and exports. Products that are normally purchased only by farmers, such as seeds and fertilizers, are zero-rated, and so are most sales by farmers. Provincial and territorial governments are zero-rated because the constitution prevents the federal government from taxing provincial governments. Purchases by treaty Indians on reserves are zero-rated, as are purchases by organizations and individuals with diplomatic immunity.

In the case of *exempt* goods and services, no tax is imposed on the final selling price and sellers cannot claim tax credits for purchases of inputs. In this case, the tax component in the final selling price is less than it would be if the good were taxable (since the value added at the exempt stage escapes tax), but greater than it would be if the good were zero-rated. Sales made by small businesses or traders (defined as those with gross annual sales revenue under $30,000) and infrequent sales by private individuals (sale of a used car, for example) are exempt. Some specific goods and services are exempt as well; they include most health and dental services, rented residential accommodation (but not temporary accommodation), financial services, day care services, local public transit, and most educational services. New homes are fully or partially taxable,[5] but resold homes are exempt.

*GST rebates* exist for specific sectors or services. A partial rebate of GST is granted to municipalities, universities and colleges, schools, and hospitals—the MUSH sector. The following table shows both the rebate rates and the effective tax rate for the components of this sector:

|  | Rebate rate | Effective tax rate |
|---|---|---|
|  | percent | |
| Municipalities ................ | 57.14 | 3.0 |
| Universities and colleges ......... | 67 | 2.31 |
| Schools ..................... | 68 | 2.24 |
| Hospitals ................... | 83 | 1.19 |

As well, all of the GST on books purchased by schools, universities, libraries, and charities is rebated. Government-funded registered charities and non-profit organizations receive a 50 percent rebate on all taxable purchases.

---

[5] New homes that cost more than $450,000 are taxed at 7 percent. Those that cost less than $350,000 qualify for a rebate of 2.5 percentage points. The rebate is phased out between $350,000 and $450,000.

Tourists may apply for a full rebate of the GST they pay on accommodation and on most consumer goods that they take out of the country.

Finally, low-income individuals and families are eligible for relief from the GST in the form of a refundable sales tax credit applied against income. In 1997, the credit provided a maximum of $199 per adult and $105 per dependant under 18, and there was a supplementary credit for single adults that was phased in at a rate of 2 percent of net income in excess of $6,456 to a maximum of $105. The total credit was reduced by 5 percent of net family income over $25,921, and it disappeared once an individual's income exceeded $30,000 and family income exceeded $35,000. Beginning in 1999, however, the income thresholds were increased to correspond with the increase in the basic personal amount, from $6,456 to $7,131, and hence in the tax credit for that amount.

## Excise Taxes and Duties

Excise taxes were initially introduced as taxes on luxury items. Over time, however, their scope and breadth of coverage has expanded, and as table 5.4 shows they now apply to a fairly large number of items.[6] When the GST was introduced in 1991, excise tax coverage diminished somewhat—some items that had been subject to excise taxes were now included in the GST base instead. Excise taxes are imposed as fixed amounts per unit or as ad valorem (percentage) taxes based on the manufacturer's selling price. These taxes are in addition to the GST.

Unlike excise taxes, which are levied on both domestic and imported goods, excise duties[7] are applied only to domestic alcohol and tobacco products (see table 5.4). The imposition of these duties on domestic goods alone does not, however, provide an advantage for foreign-produced items imported into Canada, since customs duties (tariffs) are imposed on these imported products at a rate that more than compensates for their exclusion from excise duties. In certain cases, both excise taxes and excise duties apply to the same product; tobacco and cigars are two products that bear both charges.

## Customs Duties (Tariffs)

Customs duties are imposed on a wide range of products imported into Canada. Their basic purpose is to protect Canadian-produced goods from cheaper foreign products, but as table 5.1 shows they also generate a significant sum of revenue for the federal government.

In Canada, customs duties consist of both specific and ad valorem rates that vary with respect to the product and the country from which the good is

---

[6] For a list and more detailed description of federal excise taxes and duties, see supra footnote 3, at 5:9-14.

[7] Excise duties are applied to the manufacture and distribution of certain products over which the federal government exercises some control through licensing requirements.

## Table 5.4 Federal Excise Tax Rates and Excise Duties, 1998

| Excise tax rates | | Excise duties | |
|---|---|---|---|
| Gasoline (motor and aviation)[a] | $0.085 per litre | Distilled spirits | $11.066 per litre of alcohol |
| Diesel and aviation fuel | $0.04 per litre | Mixed beverages up to 7% alcohol | $0.2459 per litre |
| Cigarettes[b] | $0.13388 per 5 cigarettes | Beer | |
| Manufactured tobacco[b] | $10.648 per kilogram | Up to 1.2% alcohol | $2.591 per hectolitre |
| Cigars[b] | 50% | 1.2% to 2.5% alcohol | $13.9909 per hectolitre |
| Tobacco sticks[b] | $0.01465 per stick | Over 2.5% alcohol | $27.985 per hectolitre |
| Wines | | Cigarettes | |
| Alcohol, 1.2% or less | $0.0205 per litre | Up to 1,361 grams per 1,000 | $27.475 per 1,000 |
| Alcohol, 1.2% to 7% | $0.2459 per litre | Over 1,361 grams per 1,000 | $29.374 per 1,000 |
| Alcohol, over 7% | $0.5122 per litre | Cigars | $14.786 per 1,000 |
| Automobile air conditioners | $100 per unit | Manufactured tobacco | $18.333 per kilogram |
| Jewellery | 10% | Raw leaf tobacco | $1.572 per kilogram |
| Watches, clocks | 10% | Tobacco sticks | $18.333 per 1,000 |

[a] Effective 1989, leaded gasoline is taxed at a rate that is 1 cent per litre higher than the rate shown for unleaded gasoline. Since 1985, gasoline used for commercial purposes has qualified for a rebate of 1.5 cents per litre. [b] Rates on tobacco products apply to all provinces and territories except Prince Edward Island, Nova Scotia, New Brunswick, Quebec, and Ontario—see table 5.6 in *Finances of the Nation 1997* for a list of federal and provincial cigarette taxes.

Source: Karin Treff and David B. Perry, *Finances of the Nation 1998* (Toronto: Canadian Tax Foundation, 1998), 5:10, tables 5.4 and 5.5.

imported. For instance, under the North American free trade agreement (NAFTA) introduced on January 1, 1994, tariff barriers between Canada, the United States, and Mexico were eliminated according to an agreed-upon schedule. As well, the Uruguay round of the general agreement on tariffs and trade (GATT), completed in December 1993, reduced tariffs on a number of Canadian exports and reduced the protection from imports for goods such as eggs, poultry, and dairy products. The recent formation of the World Trade Organization (WTO) to replace the general agreement on tariffs and trade (GATT) should lead to more multilateral trade agreements and even less reliance on tariffs.

## The Structure of Provincial Commodity Taxes

Provincial governments levy a number of commodity-based taxes,[8] of which only the most significant are discussed here.[9] This discussion, it must be emphasized, does not concentrate on details; rather, it highlights the similarities and differences among the provinces in their taxation of retail sales and excise taxes, with an emphasis in the latter case on the excise taxes that apply to tobacco products and fuel. The other provincial commodity-based taxes generate relatively small, although not unimportant, sums of money; they include land transfer taxes (a tax on the transfer of property used in New Brunswick, Ontario, Manitoba, and British Columbia), land speculation taxes (Quebec), amusement taxes (based on the price of admission and used in Prince Edward Island, Nova Scotia, New Brunswick, and Ontario) and taxes on pari-mutuel betting in every province, although off-track betting is subject to tax only in Nova Scotia, Saskatchewan, and British Columbia. None of these minor taxes, however, are discussed in this book.

## General Sales Taxes

All of the provinces and territories except Alberta and the Northwest Territories levy taxes on retail sales of consumer goods or consumer goods and services. British Columbia, Saskatchewan, Manitoba, and Ontario administer their sales taxes themselves and determine their own rates and bases. Unlike the GST base, these bases generally exclude services. The sales tax in Prince Edward Island is applied at a rate established by the province but on the same tax base as is used for the GST. In Newfoundland, New Brunswick, and Nova Scotia, the federal government administers a harmonized federal-provincial sales tax (HST) that applies at a uniform rate to the GST base. Finally, Quebec has a sales tax (QST) that covers a range of goods and services similar to the GST base. In addition to administering its own sales tax, Quebec administers

---

[8] See Perry, supra footnote 2, at chapter 15, for a historical discussion.

[9] Other activities that generate revenue for provincial governments but that are not discussed here include licence fees for motor vehicle operation, registration fees for vehicles, commercial licences, fines for motor vehicle infractions, revenue from liquor control boards, and amusement taxes.

the GST in Quebec on behalf of the federal government.[10] We shall first discuss the provincial sales taxes that are not harmonized with the GST. It is useful to think of these taxes as a single tax—the retail sales tax (RST)—with bases and rates that vary somewhat from province to province.

## Retail Sales Tax (RST)[11]

Retail sales tax is levied on the consumer but collected by the vendor, who remits it to the province. RST applies to the selling price of all goods sold for final use or consumption except those specifically exempted by law. For a few classes of goods, including food, prescription drugs, medical appliances, most books, and children's clothing, exemption is the rule in àll of the provinces. Considerable variation exists in the treatment of other consumer goods. Most provinces exempt certain thermal insulation materials and energy conservation devices. Adult clothing and footwear receive limited exemptions in a few provinces, and several provinces exempt yard goods and clothing patterns. All of the provinces except Ontario exempt magazines and periodicals and some classroom and students' supplies.

Exemptions for production goods also vary across the provinces. All of the provinces exempt farm machinery and equipment; farm products, seeds, and crops; farm livestock and feed; and fertilizers and the like. Exemptions for production machinery, production consumables, and processing materials are becoming the norm, but differences do exist across the provinces. Saskatchewan is the only province that does not tax prepared meals (subject to a minimum price).

Although there is considerable interprovincial variation in the use of exemptions, and hence interprovincial variation in the retail sales tax base,[12] the rationale for most of these exemptions is fairly straightforward. Taxation of some items (food and prescription drugs) would place a heavy burden on low-income groups. Other exemptions are provided in order to encourage the consumption of specific items (insulation materials for example), and still others are provided in order to eliminate multiple taxation and its associated problems (such as the exemption of production machinery).

In addition to the general retail sales tax rate, many provinces apply separate tax rates on specific goods and services, including alcoholic beverages, restaurant meals, and telephone services.[13] The following provinces apply special sales taxes on alcoholic beverages:

---

[10] Richard M. Bird and Pierre-Pascal Gendron, "Dual VATs and Cross-Border Trade: Two Problems, One Solution?" (July 1998), 5 *International Tax and Public Finance* 429-42.

[11] For more detail on this subject, see supra footnote 3, at 5:3-8.

[12] James M. Dean, "A Note on Interprovincial Variations in the Base for the Retail Sales Tax" (1989), vol. 37, no. 4 *Canadian Tax Journal* 1017-19.

[13] For more details, see supra footnote 3, at 5:7.

• Prince Edward Island applies its retail sales tax plus a 25 percent tax on all retail purchases.

• Quebec levies an 8 percent tax on alcoholic beverages sold in licensed establishments. The regular sales tax rate applies to other alcoholic beverages. Beer and weak cider served in taverns are exempt from the retail sales tax.

• Ontario imposes a sales tax of 12 percent on purchases from liquor stores and 10 percent on purchases in licensed establishments.

• Manitoba levies a 12 percent tax on liquor but none on beer.

• British Columbia's tax on liquor is 10 percent.

Similar interprovincial variation occurs in the tax treatment of telephone and telecommunication services, prepackaged computer software, advertising, insurance premiums, laundry and drycleaning services, and utility services, including petroleum fuels and electricity. There are other, less important variations as well.[14]

## The Harmonized Federal-Provincial Sales Tax (HST)

The HST effectively replaces the GST and the RST with a single multistaged sales tax whose base mirrors the GST. Goods and services sold in the three participating provinces, including those imported from outside the three provinces, are liable for a tax of 15 percent, of which 7 percent is for the normal GST and 8 percent accrues to the provinces. Products sold by firms in these provinces to firms in other provinces ("exports") pay the tax required in the latter. Input tax credits are then given according to the actual tax paid on input purchases—those made in HST provinces obtain full credit for the HST paid, whereas any that have been made in other provinces receive only the GST credit. The HST is administered centrally by Revenue Canada on behalf of the participating provinces. The revenue obtained by the 8 percent provincial levy is allocated among the three provinces according to estimates of provincial aggregate consumption provided by Statistics Canada. The system is essentially a revenue-sharing system in which the provinces obtain a fixed share of revenues generated by the HST. They have no independent discretion in the choice of the provincial tax rate or the base, although the federal government consults with them about both matters.

## The Quebec Harmonized Sales Tax (QST)

The Quebec harmonized sales tax (QST) differs significantly from the HST. In this system, Quebec retains its own sales tax, so it can choose its own base and rate structure. But there is a single tax-collecting authority, in this case the Quebec Revenue department. Like the HST, the QST is a destination-based sales tax, but the procedure for implementing it is slightly different. All sales in Quebec to Quebec residents are subject to both the GST and the

---

[14] Ibid., at 5:8, for more detail.

QST, whose rate is 7.5 percent. Non-residents pay only the GST. On purchases from outside the province, firms pay only GST but households are supposed to pay both GST and QST. QST is collected on imported purchases by firms when the purchases are used as inputs and then taxed on resale. Input tax credits are available for all GST and QST paid on inputs purchased in Quebec. Since inputs purchased elsewhere have not paid the QST, they receive no credit. This arrangement, referred to as the *deferred payment system*, was adopted in order to economize on administrative costs. An arrangement of this kind is possible only in a multistage tax system.

## Excise Taxes

By far the most important provincial excise taxes are those that apply to tobacco and gasoline. These taxes are in addition to the special sales taxes that the provinces levy on these goods under their sales tax systems.

### Tobacco

Every province levies a special tax, on either a per unit or ad valorem basis, on cigarettes, cigars, and tobacco. This tax is over and above the federal excise taxes and duties on tobacco products. Most provinces also subject tobacco products to the provincial sales tax. As table 5.5 shows, the special rates (over and above provincial and federal sales taxes) vary considerably from province to province. It should be noted that in 1994 both the provincial rates and the federal rates were reduced in five provinces (Prince Edward Island, Nova Scotia, New Brunswick, Quebec, and Ontario). This was done to counter a boom in cigarette smuggling and the ensuing loss of tax revenue in these provinces.

### Gasoline

In addition to the federal excise tax of 8.5 cents per litre[15] (see table 5.4), motor fuel is taxed at the point of sale by every province and territory. Prince Edward Island, Nova Scotia, British Columbia, and the Northwest Territories use ad valorem rates, and the remaining provinces and the Yukon use fixed rates.

As in the case of other provincial consumption taxes, fuel tax rates, allowable exemptions, refunds, and rate reductions for specific uses vary from province to province. Table 5.6 shows the interprovincial variation in provincial fuel tax rates in 1998. Note that provincial fuel taxes per litre of unleaded gasoline ranged from 9 cents in Alberta to 16.5 cents in Newfoundland. In the case of aviation fuel, provincial fuel taxes ranged from 0.7 cents per litre in Newfoundland and Prince Edward Island to 3.5 cents in Saskatchewan. Some provinces also tax some or all of the following fuels: motive fuel; diesel (fuel oil); propane and butane; and marine, diesel, and locomotive fuel.

---

[15] A rebate system provides partial relief for certain users such as the handicapped.

## Table 5.5  Federal and Provincial Cigarette Taxes, 1998[a]

| | Federal | | Provincial tobacco tax | Total |
|---|---|---|---|---|
| | Excise tax | Excise duty[b] | | |
| | *dollars per carton of 200 cigarettes* | | | |
| Newfoundland .......... | 5.35 | 5.50 | 22.00 | 32.85 |
| Prince Edward Island[c] ..... | 4.65 | 5.50 | 12.64 | 22.79 |
| Nova Scotia[c] ............ | 4.65 | 5.50 | 9.04 | 19.19 |
| New Brunswick[c] ......... | 4.45 | 5.50 | 7.68 | 17.63 |
| Quebec[c] ............... | 2.25 | 5.50 | 5.94 | 13.69 |
| Ontario[c] ............... | 2.65 | 5.50 | 4.70 | 12.85 |
| Manitoba .............. | 5.35 | 5.50 | 16.00 | 26.85 |
| Saskatchewan ........... | 5.35 | 5.50 | 16.80 | 27.65 |
| Alberta ................ | 5.35 | 5.50 | 14.00 | 24.85 |
| British Columbia ........ | 5.35 | 5.50 | 22.00 | 32.85 |
| Northwest Territories ...... | 5.35 | 5.50 | 25.20 | 36.05 |
| Yukon ................ | 5.35 | 5.50 | 16.40 | 27.25 |

[a] Does not include federal GST and provincial sales taxes, where applicable. [b] On cigarettes up to 1,361 grams per 1,000. [c] Federal and provincial taxes on cigarettes were reduced in 1994.

Source: Karin Treff and David B. Perry, *Finances of the Nation 1998* (Toronto: Canadian Tax Foundation, 1998), 5:11, table 5.6.

## Table 5.6  Provincial Fuel Taxes, 1997

| | Unleaded gasoline | Motive fuel | Diesel (fuel oil) | Propane and butane | Aviation fuel | Marine, diesel, and locomotive fuel |
|---|---|---|---|---|---|---|
| | *cents per litre* | | | | | |
| Newfoundland ........ | 16.5 | — | 16.5 | 7.0 | 0.7 | 3.5 |
| Prince Edward Island ... | 13.0 | — | 13.5 | — | 0.7 | — |
| Nova Scotia .......... | 13.5 | — | 15.4 | 7.0 | 0.9 | 1.1 |
| New Brunswick ....... | 10.7 | 13.7 | — | 6.7 | 2.5 | 4.3 |
| Quebec ............. | 15.2 | — | 15.2 | — | 3.0 | 3.0 |
| Ontario ............. | 14.7 | — | 14.3 | 4.3 | 2.7 | 4.5 |
| Manitoba ........... | 11.5 | 10.9 | — | 5.7 | 3.2 | 7.45 |
| Saskatchewan ........ | 15.0 | — | 15.0 | 9.0 | 3.5 | 15.0 |
| Alberta ............. | 9.0 | 6.5 | 9.0 | 6.5 | 1.5 | 6.0 |
| British Columbia ...... | 11.0 | 11.5 | — | — | 3.0[a] | 3.0 |

— not applicable.

[a] Decreased to 2 cents per litre on April 1, 1999.

Source: Karin Treff and David B. Perry, *Finances of the Nation 1998* (Toronto: Canadian Tax Foundation, 1998), 5:13, table 5.8.

## Lotteries

In the 25 years since lotteries were legalized in Canada, they have grown into a multibillion dollar industry. The federal government had access to lotteries throughout the 1970s, but in 1985 the provinces received exclusive control over lotteries, slot machines, and video devices. In return for having vacated this revenue field, the federal government receives annual payments from the provinces. Many provinces also permit gambling activities for charitable or religious purposes.[16] Many hospitals run lotteries to finance the acquisition of specialized equipment. Municipalities in some provinces (Ontario, in particular) are involved in charity casinos—a means of raising revenues locally for charitable causes.

Lotteries are legal monopolies that are price-setters. They benefit from legislation that prohibits any form of privately operated lottery. Approximately 50 percent of gross lottery sales goes to the prize pool, a further 13 to 22 percent covers costs, and between 30 and 35 percent remains as economic profit for the use of provincial governments, hospitals, or charities.[17]

Consumers' appetite for lottery products is seemingly unending, and revenues are constantly increasing. Governments have been quick to seize onto this apparently painless way of producing revenue, which is especially attractive in a time when other forms of "visible" taxation are politically difficult. Total sales in the Canadian lottery market, which amounted to $51 million in 1971, had by 1986 grown to $2.6 billion.[18] In 1996, the Ontario Lottery Corporation alone had sales of more than $2.1 billion and made $665 million available to the Ontario government.[19] According to one estimate, approximately 68 percent of all Canadian households purchased one or more lottery products in 1992.[20]

Lotteries have been with us for the better part of three decades, large-scale casino developments are a relatively new phenomenon. In a climate in which governments are scrambling to meet their financial obligations and there is considerable resistance to tax increases, many governments and citizens see casinos as an attractive way of raising new revenues and creating jobs. For instance, the Casino de Montréal generated $36 million in profits in the first three months of operation, and the temporary casino in Windsor generated over $73 million in provincial taxes between May 1994 and January 1995.[21]

---

[16] Vancouver Board of Trade, *Report by the Gaming Task Force* (Vancouver: Vancouver Board of Trade, 1994).

[17] John R. Livernois, "The Taxing Game of Lotteries in Canada" (December 1986), 12 *Canadian Public Policy* 622-27, at 622.

[18] Ibid.

[19] Ontario Lottery Corporation, *Annual Report, 1996* (Sault Ste. Marie, Ont.: Ontario Lottery Corporation, 1996), 20.

[20] Estimated from the 1992 Statistics Canada, *Survey of Family Expenditures* (Ottawa: Statistics Canada, 1994).

[21] Lennart E. Hendriksson, "Hardly a Quick Fix: Casino Gambling in Canada" (June 1996), 22 *Canadian Public Policy* 116-28, at 117.

# Evaluation

## Criteria

Any evaluation of a specific consumption tax[22] will use several criteria, of which the most important, perhaps, is economic efficiency: the tax should not distort patterns of production or consumption and thereby lead to a misallocation of resources. A second criterion is equity: the tax should also be analyzed in terms of its distributional impact on individuals in different income groups. Finally, the tax should be easy to administer.

Although all three of these criteria are important, it is virtually impossible to satisfy all of them simultaneously. The adoption of one tax instead of another may lead to a more equitable distribution of the tax burden but create more serious distortions in the allocation of resources. Or a tax designed to improve economic efficiency may generate excessive administrative costs. It is up to policy makers, therefore, to decide which criterion is to be given priority.

### Economic Efficiency

If one assumes that in the absence of taxes the allocation of society's resources is perfect, and if the imposition of a specific consumption-based tax leads to a form of consumption or production behaviour different from the behaviour that would exist in the absence of taxes, then the tax is said to be economically inefficient or non-neutral, with the effect that it will generate a misallocation of society's resources. On the other hand, if distortions exist in the absence of the tax, then the imposition of the tax may actually improve the overall allocation of society's resources.

In order to be completely neutral, a given tax must affect all forms of economic behaviour in exactly the same way. If consumption taxes are applied uniformly to all purchases of goods and services, they will not distort the pattern of consumption, but they may distort the overall ratio between consumption and leisure: since the tax makes goods and services more expensive, it gives consumers an incentive to substitute leisure for consumption.

Consumption taxes in Canada are not, in fact, imposed at uniform rates on all goods and services. Some services are not included in the tax base, certain categories of goods are exempt, and goods are not all taxed at the same rate. Thus consumers have an incentive to adjust their purchases by substituting untaxed goods and services for taxed goods and services. The distribution between consumers and producers of the resultant burden of the tax will depend on the extent to which the quantity demanded and supplied of taxed items is sensitive to price changes. If demand for the taxed items is highly

---

[22] This evaluation deals with the specific consumption taxes and duties outlined in this chapter. It does not deal with, for example, the question of the relative advantages of general consumption taxes and income taxes. For this discussion, see chapter 2.

insensitive or supply highly sensitive to price changes, most of the burden will be borne by consumers. If the opposite conditions prevail, most of the burden will fall on producers. If the tax does not alter consumption and production patterns, there will be no shifting of factors of production away from the taxed sector and therefore no change in the allocation of resources. If, instead, the tax leads to a decrease in demand for the taxed items, there will be a reduction in the factors of production employed in the taxed industry and hence a change in the allocation of resources. In the absence of other taxes, the new allocation of resources will be less efficient than the old one. As we noted in chapter 2, economists refer to a tax-induced loss in economic efficiency as the excess burden of the tax (deadweight loss), since consumers or producers, or both, are not as well off as they would have been had the same amount of revenue been raised by a tax that did not alter patterns of consumption and production.

Much of the preceding paragraph assumes that in the absence of consumption taxation the allocation of resources would be optimal. Reality is quite different. Given the presence of other taxes, for example, the introduction or extension of a consumption tax may actually improve economic efficiency by correcting distortions that existed previously. On balance, it may be difficult to determine whether a specific consumption-based tax, as one component of an overall tax system, is good or bad on efficiency grounds. The analysis in this chapter of specific taxes or duties will attempt nonetheless to assess some of the more important economic effects of the current consumption tax structure in Canada.

## Equity

There are two criteria that can be used to evaluate the fairness or equity of consumption taxes. One is benefits received. According to this criterion, fairness is achieved when every person who receives similar benefits pays similar taxes. This is the principle that is generally used in evaluating the fairness of user fees.[23] In the case of consumption taxes, this principle is applicable only to some specific excise taxes; for most consumption taxes, there is no obvious link between taxes paid and benefits received.

The second criterion, and the one employed in this chapter, is ability to pay. Under this criterion, horizontal equity is achieved when people with similar incomes pay similar taxes. Vertical equity is achieved when high-income earners pay appropriately higher taxes than do low-income earners— although the definition of "appropriately" in this context is a subject of considerable controversy among the tax-paying public. Since specific consumption taxes or duties are imposed as an absolute amount or a fixed percentage of the selling price of specific items, many observers argue that

---

[23] See chapter 7 for a discussion of this point.

these taxes are not progressive in their impact on taxpayers. In other words, because the percentage of income that a consumption tax absorbs is larger for a poor taxpayer than it is for a wealthy taxpayer, the tax violates the principle of vertical equity. Moreover, since people with identical incomes may differ in the extent to which they prefer taxed items to untaxed items, consumption taxes also fail to achieve horizontal equity: they discriminate against consumers who, for one reason or another, spend a larger percentage of their income on taxable items than other consumers do.

Some observers have argued that because discussions of vertical equity generally measure tax liability as a percentage of annual income rather than permanent or lifetime income they overstate the regressivity of consumption taxes. The difficulty is that it is probably not possible, given the data currently available, to develop reliable measures of lifetime income.

## Ease of Administration

A tax should not be costly to collect, it should be clearly understood by the taxpayer, and it should be easy to administer. Consumption taxes tend to meet these criteria better than most other taxes, mainly because the number of people who collect and report the tax is relatively small, the accounting systems are generally well developed, and the tax base and rate structure is usually relatively simple and easy to understand.

## The Goods and Services Tax (GST)

Few critics of the GST (and its provincial counterparts, the HST and the QST) object to the tax in principle. What the critics do object to is the current structure of the tax, which, they argue, falls well short of realizing any of the three criteria discussed above: in its present form, the GST is neither equitable, economically efficient, nor administratively simple. For the most part, as this section will show, the tax's shortcomings are attributable to its failure to treat all goods and services in the same manner.

To begin with, the GST violates both horizontal and vertical equity. The exclusion of some goods and services from the tax base and the preferential treatment of others violate the principle of horizontal equity: since taxpayers with similar incomes have different degrees of preference for taxed, untaxed, or preferentially taxed activities, they pay different amounts of tax. The GST violates the principle of vertical equity because it is levied at a fixed rate, with the result that lower-income individuals pay proportionately more in taxes than do high-income earners. To offset some of this vertical inequity, the GST exempts a small range of goods and services and imposes lower effective rates on selected sectors (that is, the MUSH sectors). There is also a refundable tax credit that is intended to remove some of the tax's regressivity. This credit, however, is based on income rather than on the amount of GST paid and may go to people who purchase relatively few taxable products and services.

Empirical evidence on the distributional impact of the GST is scarce. A number of studies of value-added taxes (VATs) in European countries have attempted to measure the extent to which the use of exemptions or lower rates for "necessities" (such as basic groceries or prescription drugs) reduces the taxes' regressivity.[24] The results indicate that the application of differential rates has little effect on the distribution of the burden of the tax. The distribution is much the same whether necessities are zero-rated (as in the United Kingdom), taxed at a lower rate (as in the Netherlands), or taxed at the standard rate (as in Denmark and Norway). In all cases, the burden appears to be broadly proportional in relation to consumption and somewhat regressive in relation to annual income; the reason for this result is that the consumption patterns of the various income groups tend to converge.[25] Since exemptions and preferential rates seem to do little to correct the regressivity of general consumption taxes, one may well wonder about the wisdom of complicating the GST with differential rates and seriously ask whether it might not be better to provide assistance for the poor through income transfers elsewhere in the fiscal system.

A Canadian study completed before the substitution of the GST for the manufacturers' sales tax (MST) estimated both the impact of this substitution on economic growth and its distributional impact across income groups.[26] The study concluded that the GST would be fairly progressive in its impact on family incomes of up to $35,000 and roughly proportional in its impact on incomes above $40,000.[27] A second study concluded that taxpayers with incomes of less than $30,000 would be relatively worse off under the GST than they were under the MST and that all other taxpayers would be slightly better off.[28] A third study concluded that the refundable tax credit for low-income earners makes the GST proportional across a wide range of consumption.[29]

The use of differential rates also leads to a misallocation of resources. Differences in effective tax rates lead to differences in relative prices, and these differences, in turn, lead to more purchases of the exempt goods and fewer purchases of the taxed goods than there would be if all goods faced the same rate. Thus the distortion of relative prices leads to a movement of factors of production from more highly taxed activities to less highly taxed activities and hence results in changes in factor prices. Resources move from their

---

[24] Sijbren Cnossen, "What Rate Structure for a Goods and Services Tax? The European Experience" (1989), vol. 37, no. 5 *Canadian Tax Journal* 1167-81.

[25] Ibid., at 1172-73.

[26] Patrick Grady, "An Analysis of the Distributional Impact of the Goods and Services Tax" (1990), vol. 38, no. 3 *Canadian Tax Journal* 632-43.

[27] Ibid., at 637-43.

[28] G.C. Ruggeri and K. Bluck, "On the Incidence of the Manufacturers' Sales Tax and the Goods and Services Tax" (December 1990), 16 *Canadian Public Policy* 359-73.

[29] Jack M. Mintz and Thomas A. Wilson, "Options for the Goods and Services Tax" (Fall 1994), 3 *Canadian Business Economics* 27-36, at 27.

most profitable use to less profitable uses, and total output ends up being lower than it would be under a uniform tax rate.[30] The economic loss is aggravated by the practice of making up the revenue losses that result from setting low or zero rates on some goods and services and by setting higher rates on other goods and services. In fact, it has been estimated that the severity of tax distortions increases as the square of the tax rate that causes them.[31] In other words, the higher is the standard tax rate required to maintain revenue, the more serious are the distortions and the greater the loss of potential output.

Finally, the exemption of some goods and the use of lower effective tax rates for purchases made by municipalities, universities, schools, and hospitals has significantly increased the complexity of the tax.[32] As well, the choice of a low threshold, $30,000, for exempting small businesses has increased both the administrative costs borne by governments and the compliance costs borne by the private sector. In fact, it has been estimated that the compliance costs are 16 percent of sales for businesses with revenues of less than $100,000 and 3 percent of sales for businesses with revenues of more than $1 million.[33]

## The Retail Sales Tax (RST)

Most observers agree that retail sales taxes are regressive, in spite of the exemption from the RST base in most jurisdictions of essential items such as prescription drugs, shelter, food, and children's clothing. The extent of the regressivity, however, is uncertain. As in the case of the GST, any estimate of the regressivity of the RST depends on the concept of income that the analysis uses as the basis for measuring effective tax rates across income groups and on the shifting assumptions that it uses in allocating the tax burden among these groups.[34] The extent to which the results accord with reality, then, depend on the extent to which the assumptions reflect reality. Studies that assume that sales taxes are shifted forward to consumers have found the RST to be regressive. Studies that assume that the tax falls on recipients of

---

[30] See Cnossen, supra footnote 24, at 1175-76.

[31] For a discussion of these effects of differential rates, see John Kay and Michael Keen, "Alcohol and Tobacco Taxes: Criteria for Harmonisation," in Sijbren Cnossen, ed., *Tax Coordination in the European Community* (Deventer, The Netherlands: Kluwer, 1987), 85-111.

[32] For a detailed discussion of the complexity of the GST, see Richard M. Bird, "Cost and Complexity of Canada's VAT: The GST in International Perspective" (January 3, 1994), 8 *Tax Notes International* 37-47.

[33] Canada, House of Commons, Standing Committee on Finance, *Replacing the GST: Options for Canada* (Ottawa: Queen's Printer, June 1994).

[34] John Whalley, "Regression or Progression: The Taxing Question of Incidence Analysis" (November 1984), 17 *Canadian Journal of Economics* 654-82; and Nadarajah and Wernerheim, infra footnote 39.

factor income have found it to be progressive.[35] Two fairly recent simulation studies[36] based on micro data reached different conclusions about the incidence of sales taxation in Canada as a whole. One study found sales and excise taxes to be regressive across the entire income distribution.[37] The other found that low- and high-income taxpayers faced below-average effective tax rates, whereas middle income taxpayers faced above-average tax rates. The latter results suggest that these taxes are progressive over the low income range, proportional over the middle income range, and regressive over the high income range.[38] The two studies had different results because they used different measures of income and different assumptions about government transfers to individuals. A more recent simulation study of the incidence of Newfoundland's consumption taxes over the period 1984 to 1992 concluded that they were largely and increasingly regressive.[39]

In addition to its incidence effects, the current structure of retail sales may produce a number of allocative distortions. First, the failure to include all goods and services in the tax base is distortive in that it encourages individuals to purchase untaxed items in preference to taxed items. The differential treatment of goods and services is justified only if it serves to control or internalize externalities or improve the after-tax distribution of income.

Second, the differences in the base and rate structure from one province to the next might provide an incentive for consumers to purchase items where they are not taxed or are taxed at a lower rate. An empirical study of the impact of RST rate differences on transborder sales in Canada considered the adjacent cities of Ottawa and Hull. The study used data for 1971, when the RST rate in Ontario was 5 percent and the rate in Quebec was 8 percent. The results suggested that this 3-percentage-point difference was not large enough to make it worthwhile for Hull residents to shop in Ottawa.[40]

To the extent that industrial machinery or production equipment is subject to provincial sales taxes in some provinces and not in others, industries are encouraged to alter their production or distribution methods or to move to

---

[35] For a summary of pre-1980 Canadian studies, see Jean-Marie Dufour and François Vaillancourt, "Provincial and Federal Sales Taxes: Evidence of Their Effect and Prospect for Change," in Wayne R. Thirsk and John Whalley, eds., *Tax Policy Options in the 1980s*, Canadian Tax Paper no. 66 (Toronto: Canadian Tax Foundation, 1982), 408-36.

[36] Frank Vermaeten, W. Irwin Gillespie, and Arndt Vermaeten, "Tax Incidence in Canada" (1994), vol. 42, no. 2 *Canadian Tax Journal* 348-416; and G.C. Ruggeri, D. Van Wart, and R. Howard, "The Redistributional Impact of Taxation in Canada" (1994), vol. 42, no. 2 *Canadian Tax Journal* 417-51. For a summary of pre-1980 studies, see Boadway and Kitchen, supra footnote 4, at 267-69.

[37] Vermaeten et al., supra footnote 36, at 375.

[38] Ruggeri et al., supra footnote 36, at 444.

[39] K.S. Nadarajah and C. Michael Wernerheim, "Incidence and Distribution: Newfoundland's Consumption Tax Revisited" (1995), vol. 43, no. 6 *Canadian Tax Journal* 2035-57.

[40] Dufour and Vaillancourt, supra footnote 35, at 423-25.

lower-tax areas. Taxation of business inputs may lead to a misallocation of resources if effective tax rates exceed the marginal cost of public services consumed. As well, taxation of business inputs may produce a cascading effect, in which the tax on the input is passed through to a final selling price that is higher than it would be under an equal-yield sales tax imposed on the final selling price.

Further problems may arise if consumers can purchase items out-of-province and pay tax on them at a rate lower than the rate in the province where they live. Legally, a consumer is required to pay the sales tax at the prevailing rate in his or her home province, but in spite of attempts to police interprovincial and international purchases there is doubtless some evasion. It is not likely, however, that the loss of revenue or economic efficiency on this account is very large. Large distributors and mail-order houses generally collect sales tax revenue for the appropriate government from the purchaser. Automobiles or trucks must be registered in the home province and are taxed at the time of registration. In any case, the sheer distance for most people from one taxing jurisdiction to the next and the general inconvenience of organizing out-of-province purchasing activities make serious problems in this area unlikely. It is not likely, moreover, that many industries choose a given location simply in order to escape retail sales taxes on industrial machinery, since this cost would amount to a very small percentage of total production costs. Other factors, including proximity to markets, raw materials, and labour markets, are undoubtedly more important determinants of industrial location.

## Excise Taxes and Duties

The federal government and all of the provinces have long levied excise taxes on alcohol, tobacco, and gasoline. Otherwise, the list of products to which specific excise taxes and duties apply has changed substantially over the past few decades. Revenue generation has always been an important motive for the imposition of excise taxes, particularly in the case of excise taxes on alcohol, tobacco, and gasoline (because of the relatively inelastic demand for those goods over a wide range of tax rates), but specific taxes and charges have been introduced for other reasons as well, such as to limit the consumption of specific goods, to control externalities, or to tax those who benefit from a specific service.

We shall discuss these rationales below. First, however, it is appropriate to consider the equity effects of excise taxation.

If one uses ability to pay as a basis for determining the fairness of a consumption tax, then a given tax is unfair to the extent that individuals with similar incomes spend different proportions of their incomes on taxable items. If, instead, the basis for determining fairness is benefits received, then a given consumption tax is unfair to the extent that differences in taxes paid are not reflected in differences in benefits received. With the possible exception of the federal air transport tax, which may be defensible on the basis of the benefits-received criterion, the existing specific excise taxes are difficult to defend under either fairness criterion.

The unfairness of excise taxes might be defensible if the taxes can be justified on other grounds. Thus one rationale for some excise taxes is that they discourage the consumption of items whose use is socially or economically harmful. For example, the excise taxes on tobacco and alcohol have been defended on the ground that the use of these goods generates costs that society as a whole must bear: alcohol consumption leads to automobile accidents and hence higher insurance rates; both alcohol and tobacco are responsible for illnesses that increase health and medical costs. If these taxes did in fact limit the consumption of the taxed items, then they could lead to an improvement in the distribution of the overall tax burden. In reality, however, few observers believe that the current rate structure of alcohol and tobacco taxation significantly discourages consumption of these products. Demand for alcohol and tobacco tends to be inelastic, and increases in alcohol and tobacco taxes generate increased revenues. Moreover, the availability of lower-priced alternatives to the taxed goods, such as smuggled cigarettes[41] and "brew-your-own" wine and beer (to which the alcohol-specific excise taxes do not apply) limits the extent to which governments can increase these taxes.

Some excise taxes are specifically intended to discourage the consumption of selected items. For example, the purpose of the $100 federal tax on air conditioners in automobiles is to control the purchase of non-essential items that use scarce resources—oil and gas.

The rationale for excise taxes imposed in lieu of charges for government services, such as motor fuel taxes and related motor vehicle licence fees, is similar to the rationale for user charges—the taxes on vehicles and fuel are essentially charges for the use of roads. Although not all of the benefits from highways and roads accrue directly to their users, it is felt that enough direct benefits arise to justify specific taxes. These taxes may produce a better allocation of resources between alternative transportation systems than would exist in their absence. For example, if railroads were forced to finance all costs from their own revenue and roads were largely subsidized by general tax levies, then road users would be favourably treated relative to railroad users. Thus there is a case for a specific tax on all individuals who benefit from this particular public good.

---

[41] In 1994, the federal government and five provincial governments (see table 5.5) lowered their tax rates on cigarettes in an effort to stop cigarette smuggling and the ensuing loss in tax revenues.

Finally, a number of excise taxes and duties have been imposed rather haphazardly in terms of both the items taxed and the rates applied. The only rationale for their imposition, if it can be called a rationale, is that they provide revenue without generating any serious public criticism. The excise tax that the federal government imposes on watches, clocks, and jewellery (at a 10 percent rate) falls into this category; though it was originally imposed as a luxury tax—that is, as a tax on goods not essential to a basic standard of living—it does not in fact improve the overall allocation of society's resources. It is useful only as an uncontentious revenue source.

The imposition of selective excise taxes or duties may distort an individual's consumption pattern, but this result is not necessarily undesirable on efficiency grounds. Some distortions may even be beneficial. If the imposition improves the overall allocation of society's resources, it should be encouraged. If it reduces the consumption of an item whose use generates harmful effects that are ultimately borne by members of society who may never have directly consumed this good, then it should be lauded. If it encourages consumers to purchase items that consume less of society's scarce resources, it should be supported. This discussion supposes, however, that it is possible to establish rates that accurately reflect the costs of consuming particular goods and control that consumption. In fact, most excise taxes have no function apart from their revenue-generating capacity.

The existence of a wide array of excise taxes and rates is a symptom of the fiscal fragmentation that has resulted from the federal and provincial governments' attempts to intervene in the economy through the tax system. The overall structure of the excise tax system is difficult to fathom, and the haphazard and inconsistent nature of the system leads one to the conclusion that there is no sound economic or political rationale for much of it. The system is unnecessarily complex and inefficient: it applies per-unit levies to some goods and ad valorem levies to others; to some goods, such as cigarettes and fuel, both the federal government and the provinces apply both excise taxes and duties. Application of a single tax rate to all goods of similar character would improve the overall efficiency of the system and reduce enforcement and compliance costs. Further improvement might result from giving the responsibility for these taxes to just one level of government, and indeed a strong argument might be made in favour of giving most, if not all, excise taxes and duties (excluding customs duties) to the provincial governments. This transfer would eliminate administrative duplication and provide the provinces with more independent revenue. It would, however, require much more cooperation between the federal government and the provinces than they are usually able to achieve.

## Lotteries

A major criticism of government-run lotteries is that the implicit taxation associated with them is fundamentally regressive in ability-to-pay terms. Some observers doubt whether the monopoly profits derived from lottery sales ought to be regarded as a form of implicit taxation, since they come from voluntary expenditures.[42] Yet lottery profits are generated by state-owned enterprises and are no different from the revenues that arise from the consumption of alcohol, tobacco, or any other taxed product. Indeed, the implicit lottery tax[43] is exactly analogous to an excise tax at a very high rate.[44] This high tax rate may be partial justification for the non-taxation of lottery winnings under the income tax.

Studies of the regressivity of implicit lottery taxes in Canada have used two measures to determine regressivity. One measure is income elasticity. If this elasticity is less than one, the tax is deemed to be regressive in its impact on consumers. If it is greater than one, the tax is deemed to be progressive. The second measure is the Suits index.[45] The value for this index can range from −1 to +1; the former number indicates extreme regressivity and the latter extreme progressivity. A value of zero indicates a proportional tax. Table 5.7 shows the income elasticity coefficients and the Suits index values derived in four studies conducted between 1987 and 1998. All four studies concluded that the implicit lottery tax is regressive, and the changes calculated by the Suits index values from study to study suggest that the regressivity is increasing.

The study results indicate that lottery expenditures are more regressive than the existing taxes on alcohol and less regressive than those on tobacco. The implicit lottery tax is more regressive than either the personal income tax or retail sales tax.[46] It is worth noting, however, that excise taxes are almost always more popular (or less unpopular) than the more general taxes, in spite of their greater regressivity. Finally, it has been observed that higher-income individuals tend to favour lotteries whose profits are spent on specific projects (hospital equipment, for instance) over other lotteries.[47]

## The Reform of Commodity Taxation

The existence of the inequities and inefficiencies outlined above has generated some discussion about further major reforms of consumption taxes. In

---

[42] C.T. Clotfelter and P.J. Cook, *Selling Hope: State Lotteries in America* (Cambridge, Mass.: National Bureau of Economic Research, Harvard University Press, 1989), chapter 11.

[43] We are unaware of any studies of the incidence of casino spending, including slot machines and video display devices.

[44] Livernois, supra footnote 17; and Clotfelter and Cook, supra footnote 42.

[45] Calculation of this index is identical to calculation of the Gini coefficient. It is defined as $S = 1 - (L/K)$, where $L$ is the area under a Lorenz type curve and $K$ is the area under the diagonal. To calculate the area under the Lorenz type curve, the accumulated percentage of taxes paid is plotted against the percentage of after-tax income ranked in ascending order. See Daniel B. Suits, "Gambling Taxes: Regressivity and Revenue Potential" (March 1977), 30 *National Tax Journal* 19-35.

[46] François Vaillancourt and Julie Grignon, "Canadian Lotteries as Taxes: Revenues and Incidence" (1988), vol. 36, no. 2 *Canadian Tax Journal* 369-88.

[47] Livernois, supra footnote 17.

**Table 5.7   Regressivity of the Implicit Tax on Lottery
Expenditures—Income Elasticities
and the Suits Index**

| Study | Province(s)/city | Year | Income elasticity | Suits index |
|---|---|---|---|---|
| Livernois (1987)[a] | Edmonton, Alberta ....... | 1983 | 0.72 | −0.10 |
| Vaillancourt and Grignon (1988)[a] | Atlantic Canada ......... | 1982 | 0.54 | −0.13 |
| | Quebec ............... | 1982 | 0.48 | −0.14 |
| | Ontario ............... | 1982 | 0.36 | −0.18 |
| | Western Canada ......... | 1982 | 0.41 | −0.17 |
| | Canada ............... | 1982 | — | −0.18 |
| Kitchen and Powells (1991)[b] | Atlantic Canada ......... | 1986 | 0.80 | −0.21 |
| | Quebec ............... | 1986 | 0.70 | −0.13 |
| | Ontario ............... | 1986 | 0.78 | −0.19 |
| | Manitoba/Saskatchewan .. | 1986 | 0.73 | −0.19 |
| | Alberta ............... | 1986 | 0.92 | −0.16 |
| | British Columbia ........ | 1986 | 0.71 | −0.18 |
| | Canada ............... | 1986 | — | −0.18 |
| Edwards (1998)[b] | Atlantic Canada ......... | 1992 | 0.82 | −0.11 |
| | Quebec ............... | 1992 | 0.68 | −0.21 |
| | Ontario ............... | 1992 | 0.71 | −0.23 |
| | Man./Sask./Alberta ...... | 1992 | 0.73 | −0.19 |
| | British Columbia ........ | 1992 | 0.73 | −0.17 |
| | Canada ............... | 1992 | 0.79 | −0.22 |

—   not applicable.

[a] Uses before-tax income. [b] Uses after-tax income.

Sources: John R. Livernois, "The Taxing Game of Lotteries in Canada" (December 1986), 12 *Canadian Public Policy* 622-27; François Vaillancourt and Julie Grignon, "Canadian Lotteries as Taxes: Revenues and Incidence" (1988), vol. 36, no. 2 *Canadian Tax Journal* 369-88; Harry Kitchen and Scott Powells, "Lottery Expernditures in Canada: A Regional Analysis of Determinants and Incidence" (1991), vol. 23, no. 12 *Applied Economics* 1845-52; and Greg Edwards, "Lottery Expenditures in Canada: Who Buys Lottery Tickets?" (honours essay, Trent University, Department of Economics, Peterborough, Ontario, 1998).

particular, discussion has centred on the merits of replacing the GST with one or more alternatives.[48] More recently, harmonization of the GST and the provincial retail sales taxes has surfaced as an issue. Other important issues are the appropriateness of refundable credits as a means of removing some of the sales tax burden on low-income individuals, the impact of consumption taxes on cross-border shopping and smuggling, and the extent to which consumption-based taxes have contributed to the underground economy. Finally, arguments have surfaced in support of replacing the current excise

[48] See, for example, Mintz and Wilson, supra footnote 29, at 31-34; Poddar and English, supra footnote 1, at 1113-15; Richard Bird, *Where Do We Go From Here: Alternatives to the GST* (Toronto: KPMG Centre for Government, 1994); and Peter Dungan, Jack M. Mintz, and Thomas A. Wilson, "Alternatives to the Goods and Services Tax" (1990), vol. 38, no. 3 *Canadian Tax Journal* 644-65.

tax on gasoline with a more rational environmental tax based on pollution damage. Although there may be additional topics, this list covers the more salient issues, which provide the matter for the remainder of this chapter.

## Replacing the GST[49]

Before the federal election in 1993, the Liberal party committed itself to replacing the GST with an equal-revenue alternative, and it appears that this promise prompted many citizens to vote for the Liberals at election time. Although promising to scrap the GST proved to be politically popular, the Liberals have never followed through on the promise, for, as they discovered, the real trick is to come up with an equal-yield alternative that is politically, economically, and fiscally sound. Two alternatives that have been suggested are greater use of personal income taxes and greater use of payroll taxes. Neither of these possibilities, however, is likely to be realized. Any attempt to make greater use of income taxes, which are already high in relation to income taxes in the United States, our major trading partner, would provoke serious political opposition. Payroll taxes are lower in Canada than they are in the United States; nevertheless, fear of becoming less competitive internationally would lead the business community to oppose increases in this area as well. Furthermore, to increase dependence on income or payroll taxes while reducing dependance on the existing commodity-tax base would be to move away from a system that includes a broad mix of taxes and in which commodity-based taxes play an important role. Quite apart from political opposition to greater dependence on either income taxes or payroll taxes, there are some economic arguments against these alternatives to the GST.

### Increased Income Taxes

It has been suggested, on occasion, that the federal government eliminate the GST and make up the lost revenue by increasing personal income taxes. This could be done either by increasing income tax rates (possibly by imposing an income surtax on high-income earners)[50] or by broadening the income tax base (by taxing all of the imputed income from owner-occupied housing, 100 percent of capital gains, lottery winnings, and fellowship or scholarship income or, alternatively, by reducing tax expenditures).[51] The proponents of this change argue that it would simplify the tax system by eliminating one tax source, eliminate the difficulties associated with harmonizing federal and provincial sales taxes (see the discussion in the next section), make the tax system more progressive, bring commodity tax rates in Canada more closely

---

[49] This discussion concentrates on non-consumption-based alternatives.

[50] Neil Brooks, *Searching for an Alternative to the GST*, Discussion Paper no. 90.C.1 (Ottawa: Institute for Research on Public Policy, February 1990).

[51] Neil Brooks, "An Alternative to the GST," paper prepared for the meetings of the Canadian Economics Association and Canadian Association of Business Economists (mimeograph, Calgary, June 1994).

in line with those in the United States, and, possibly, lead to a reduction in consumer prices.

The opponents of this position, however, argue that an increase in income taxes would discourage saving and investment,[52] with the result that the elderly would become more dependent on government support and the Canadian economy more dependent on foreign borrowing. It would also lead to more emigration of skilled labour and to increased tax evasion. These considerations should not be treated lightly; indeed, they outweigh the advantages of placing greater dependence on income taxes.[53]

## Increased Payroll Taxes

Proponents of higher payroll taxes as a replacement for the GST commonly argue that the tax base is similar for both taxes. Under the GST, a firm remits taxes on the basis of the difference between its taxable sales and its taxable benefits. This difference, it is argued, is essentially the value added as measured by the firm's total payroll including employee benefits, or the same tax base as is taxed under a payroll tax. Further, a comparison of tax rates in Canada and the United States shows that consumption taxes are higher in Canada and payroll taxes are lower; hence, a move to higher payroll taxes and lower consumption taxes would bring the Canadian system closer to the US system.[54]

Those who oppose the substitution of increased payroll taxes for the GST make the following arguments.[55] First, the GST and payroll tax bases are not identical. The payroll tax base is narrower than the GST base, since unlike the latter it excludes consumption derived from economic rents (returns in excess of the opportunity cost of inputs). Second, since payroll taxes do not apply to returns to capital, it would be necessary to introduce a "cash-flow" tax[56] in order to prevent firms from paying their employees, and the self-employed from paying themselves, in the form of dividends and other kinds of capital income. Third, since the GST is a destination-based tax that applies to domestic consumption only (exports are exempt), regardless of where earnings and economic rents are incurred, and the payroll tax is an origin-based tax on the earnings of labour sourced in Canada, the payroll tax provides an

---

[52] See chapter 2 for a fuller discussion of this point.

[53] Dungan, Mintz, and Wilson, supra footnote 48, at 652-55; Mintz and Wilson, supra footnote 29, at 29-30; and Whalley and Fretz, supra footnote 4, at 126.

[54] Jonathan R. Kesselman, "Assessing a Direct Consumption Tax To Replace the GST" (1994), vol. 42, no. 3 *Canadian Tax Journal* 709-803, at 789-80.

[55] For a summary of these arguments, see Mintz and Wilson, supra footnote 29, at 30-31.

[56] Kesselman, supra footnote 54, at 720-21. Briefly, the cash-flow method allows full deduction of the cost of all capital acquired in the period but no deduction for interest expenses. It does, of course, allow the deduction of the cost of intermediate inputs and labour inputs. For the self-employed and for shareholders in closely held corporations, the cash flow without a deduction for proprietor's salary is the most appropriate way to measure the individual's total return. This calculation prevents tax avoidance through the payments of dividends or other means. See the discussion in chapter 4 for more detail.

incentive for firms to avoid tax by shifting production to other countries and importing their products into Canada. Fourth, payroll taxes have already increased significantly in recent years (although they have fallen within the last two years), and there is evidence to suggest that this increase has contributed to the rise in structural unemployment.[57] Further increases would almost certainly generate a huge outcry from the business community, which maintains that any increases in payroll taxes would drive up production costs and make their products less competitive in international markets.

## Harmonization of the GST and the RST[58]

With the introduction of the GST in 1991, retailers and consumers were faced with two overlapping consumption-tax regimes, one federal and one provincial. Moreover, the two regimes' bases and rate structures differed significantly. The GST taxed most goods and services at a uniform rate, whereas the provincial RSTs applied mainly to goods, with exemptions that varied across provinces. This double system was recognized as being both inefficient and unnecessarily costly to administer. The inefficiencies arose largely at the provincial level. The narrow bases of the RSTs discriminated in favour of services and against goods. Also, the fact that the RSTs were single-stage retail taxes led to the inadvertent inclusion in their bases of business inputs, a result that distorted relative producer prices within a province and increased costs for products exported from the province. It was therefore a stated objective of the federal government to induce the provinces to harmonize their RSTs with the federal GST.

This objective has been met only in part. Three provinces (New Brunswick, Newfoundland, and Nova Scotia) have adopted a fully harmonized sales tax (HST) system; and Quebec has harmonized the GST with its own separate multistage tax (the QST).[59]

As an approach to harmonization, the QST has a major advantage relative to the HST system—the province retains the ability to set its own rate structure and base. Of course, it does this at a cost, namely the increased collection and compliance costs associated with operating two value-added tax systems side-by-side. The problem of imposing a VAT in a setting in which there are no border controls to ensure that imports are fully taxed and exports appropriately exempted has long been a major stumbling block—especially in the European Union, whose members continue to maintain their own independent VAT systems even as border controls are being dismantled. Some observers have recommended the Quebec system as a model for a VAT

---

[57] Stephen S. Poloz, *The Causes of Unemployment in Canada: A Review of the Evidence*, PEAP Policy Study 94-5 (Toronto: University of Toronto, Institute for Policy Analysis, 1994). Also, see the discussion in chapter 6.

[58] This issue is discussed in more detail in chapter 9.

[59] Both of these taxes were described earlier in this chapter.

in a federation where border controls do not exist.[60] The system for handling cross-border transactions operates on a self-assessment basis: firms are required to declare their sales to non-resident purchasers who are not liable for the tax. The fact that the GST is collected with the QST is said to provide a check to ensure the honest reporting of firms. On the other hand, the fact that the tax is collected provincially rather than federally presumably introduces its own costs. Some taxpayers will have to deal with two separate tax administrations. And it might be argued that provincial tax auditors will be more vigilant in monitoring measures that effect their own province's tax revenues than in monitoring those that affect tax revenues in other provinces.

The QST is relatively young, and experience will show how costly it is in administrative terms as a system of harmonization, especially if other provinces decide to adopt similar systems. Nonetheless, the QST shows that harmonization of a VAT system in a federation without internal border controls is feasible.[61]

## Refundable Sales Tax Credits

The federal government offers a refundable sales tax credit that declines in value as taxable income increases. This tax credit does not directly offset federal income tax liability; it is instead paid out in quarterly instalments during the following fiscal year. As well, three provinces provide refundable sales tax credits directly against provincial income tax liability in order to remove some of the alleged sales tax burden on lower-income individuals. In Quebec, the tax credit is $104 per adult and $31 per dependent child, and these amounts are reduced by 3 percent of family income. The maximum value of the credit in Ontario is $100 per adult and $50 for each dependent child, and the value of the allowable credit diminishes as family income increases. Seniors receive a separate refundable tax credit for sales and property taxes. In British Columbia, the refundable sales tax credit is $50 per person, subject to a phase-out rate of 2 percent of net income over a threshold that varies with family size.[62]

It is somewhat misleading to refer to these arrangements as sales tax credits, since their value bears no obvious relation to the value of sales taxes paid by the individual. Instead, the credit varies with the income of the taxpayer and number of his dependants and diminishes as income increases. The motive behind refundable sales tax credits—to provide tax relief for low-income individuals and families—may be laudable, but their use involves serious costs in terms of economic inefficiency and administrative complexity. Quite apart from this consideration, as we noted earlier, refundable sales tax credits are not a very effective means to their intended end. Concerns about income distribution would be better addressed through the income transfer

---

[60] Bird and Gendron, supra footnote 10.

[61] Sales tax harmonization is discussed further in chapter 9.

[62] Supra footnote 3, at chapter 3.

system, which could more accurately identify needy recipients and provide policy makers with a clearer indication of the true cost of income-redistribution programs. But whether or not sales tax credits should be used, they are used; if we take their use as a given, what can be done to improve them?

The continuing concern of most policy makers and much of the general public that sales taxes are highly regressive has led to a number of suggestions for replacing the present system of sales tax credits with arrangements that might be more effective in reducing the tax burden on low-income earners. One suggestion involves the application of a tax credit against the income tax liability of a tax filer. Under this scheme, a sales tax would be imposed on all purchases; at the end of the year, the taxpayer could claim a credit against his or her income tax for the sales tax paid on a prescribed set of items, including food, shelter, prescription drugs, and clothing. If the scheme required taxpayers to supply receipts for all purchases, it would be administratively complex; however, the use of high-speed computers might make it feasible. Another approach would be to use estimates of consumption expenditures according to family size, age of dependants, and other factors.[63] Alternatively, a tax credit that was not directly associated with the amount of consumption expenditures but that had a fixed absolute value for all taxpayers or that decreased in absolute value as income increased would provide relatively more relief for low-income taxpayers than for high-income taxpayers and would be fairly easy to integrate with the present income tax system. Although this credit would not be a specific sales tax credit, it would introduce more progressivity into the overall tax system. This credit system is currently used for the GST rebate and some provincial tax credits.

The current sales tax regime's use of exemptions leads to inequities among members of the same income group: because some items are taxed and some are not, taxpayers whose total incomes are identical and who spend identical amounts on consumption may pay different amounts of tax. The current system also is inequitable among different income groups, since an exemption is worth more to higher-income taxpayers than it is to lower-income taxpayers. Two tax credit schemes offer plausible alternatives to the use of exemptions. The first, an itemized tax credit plan, would allow taxpayers to deduct credits for certain allowable purchases from income taxes payable. This arrangement would eliminate some of the existing disincentives against buying taxable items. Under the second scheme, taxpayers would receive a credit whose value depended on income. Taxpayers with identical incomes would receive the same absolute relief regardless of their expenditure patterns. In this case, the relative prices of taxed and untaxed items would not be altered and so the relief would not create an incentive to purchase untaxed items rather than taxed items.

---

[63] The use of average data to calculate tax relief is unlikely to generate a horizontally equitable tax system, yet it may be necessary if one is to avoid a number of potentially expensive administrative problems.

The implementation of an itemized tax credit plan would provide the same absolute relief for individuals who had different incomes but whose consumption expenditures were the same and would thus yield relatively more relief for low-income taxpayers than for high-income taxpayers. A tax credit of a fixed amount or one that decreased as income increased would have the same effect. Finally, it should be noted that the present system's use of both exemptions and tax credits makes little economic sense, since it is likely in some cases to provide more relief than is necessary.

## Cross-Border Shopping and Smuggling

If neighbouring jurisdictions have different sales tax rates and exemptions, and if these differences result in different selling prices for similar goods, an incentive exists for consumers either to purchase products from the jurisdiction with the lowest rates or to engage in smuggling and avoid the tax altogether. To what extent do consumption-tax rates differ from province to province and, what is more important, between Canada and the United States? Does the existence of these differences in fact encourage either cross-border shopping or smuggling?

Table 5.8 shows the sales tax rates in the Canadian provinces and the bordering US states. The Canadian rates combine the GST and provincial tax rates; there is no federal sales tax in the United States, so the US rates are the state sales tax rates only.[64] Excise taxes and duties as well tend to be higher in Canada than in the United States. Regardless of the province, however, when the excise and sales tax differentials are combined, Canadian consumption-tax rates exceed those in the United States, frequently by a considerable amount.

The question whether consumption-tax differentials encourage cross-border shopping and smuggling has been the subject of discussion for some time, but especially since the introduction of the GST. Substitution of the GST for the manufacturers' sales tax increased the effective tax rates on many services and non-durable goods and lowered the rates on many capital goods not imported by consumers and on consumer durables, such as automobiles, furniture, and appliances—goods that are, in any case, difficult to smuggle. This concern about the impact of the GST on cross-border shopping and smuggling centres on goods and services that Canadians consume in the United States (such as tourist services) and non-durables (such as clothing, cigarettes, and liquor).[65]

One of the first studies to address the impact of the GST on cross-border shopping estimated that the tax would increase relative prices, on average, by 3.8 percent; this was on top of an estimated 16 percent price advantage that already existed in favour of US products. In addition, the study estimated that

---

[64] There are some city sales taxes in the United States, especially in the larger metropolitan areas. They are not reported in table 5.8.

[65] Mintz and Wilson, supra footnote 29, at 28.

**Table 5.8  Sales Tax Rates in the Canadian Provinces and
the Neighbouring US States, 1997**

| Canada | | United States | |
|---|---|---|---|
| Province | Total sales tax rate (%)[a] | Neighbouring state(s) | Total sales tax rate (%)[b] |
| Newfoundland .......... | 15.0 | Maine ................. | 6.0 |
| Prince Edward Island ..... | 17.0 | | |
| Nova Scotia ........... | 15.0 | | |
| New Brunswick ......... | 15.0 | | |
| Quebec .............. | 13.5 | Maine ................. | 6.0 |
| | | New York[c] .............. | 4.0 |
| | | New Hampshire .......... | 0.0 |
| | | Vermont .............. | 5.0 |
| Ontario .............. | 15.0 | Michigan ............... | 6.0 |
| | | Minnesota[c] ............. | 6.5 |
| | | New York[c] .............. | 4.0 |
| | | Wisconsin[c] ............. | 5.0 |
| Manitoba ............. | 14.0 | Minnesota[c] ............. | 6.5 |
| | | North Dakota ............ | 5.0 |
| Saskatchewan ........... | 14.0 | Montana ............... | 0.0 |
| | | North Dakota ............ | 5.0 |
| Alberta .............. | 7.0 | Montana ............... | 0.0 |
| British Columbia ........ | 14.0 | Idaho .................. | 5.0 |
| | | Montana ............... | 0.0 |
| | | Washington[c] ............ | 6.5 |

[a] GST of 7 percent plus provincial retail sales tax rate. [b] State sales tax only—there is no federal sales tax. [c] Local tax rates are additional.

Sources: Karin Treff and David B. Perry, *Finances of the Nation 1997* (Toronto: Canadian Tax Foundation, 1997), 5:4 for Canadian provincial sales tax rates; and CCH, *State Tax Guide* (Chicago: CCH) (looseleaf), table of rates, 60-100.

the GST-induced price increase would expand cross-border traffic by 2 million shoppers annually and reduce domestic demand in 1991 by about $1 billion, or 0.15 percent of gross domestic product (GDP).[66] A later study indicated that cross-border shopping had been increasing before the implementation of either the free trade agreement (1988) or the GST (1991). Appreciation of the Canadian dollar and a rise in per capita income during the late 1980s had done more to stimulate cross-border shopping than had the

[66] Reported in G.C. Ruggeri and D. Van Wart, "Overoptimism and the GST: A Critical Comment on the Hamilton and Kuo General Equilibrium Analysis" (1992), vol. 40, no. 1 *Canadian Tax Journal* 148-61, at 159-60. The estimated effect of the GST on cross-border shopping was obtained from Revenue Canada, Customs and Excise, *Relative Prices and Same Day Travellers* (Ottawa: Revenue Canada, 1990).

GST, though the latter had given it an additional boost.[67] A third study estimated the impact of the GST on both border and non-border communities. It concluded that in border communities as much as 60 percent of the GST burden was shifted backward into lower payments for factor suppliers, whereas in non-border communities, the GST was shifted forward into higher consumer prices. The degree of backward shifting depended on international consumer mobility.[68] All of these studies, however, referred to the late 1980s and the early 1990s; since then, the incentives for cross-border shopping other than the existence of the GST have diminished. For example, the Canadian dollar has depreciated considerably over the past decade (from about 88 cents US to about 68 or 69 cents US), and the federal government now collects provincial retail sales taxes at international border points.

## The Underground Economy

There is general agreement that the underground economy has grown over the past three or four decades,[69] but little agreement about the extent to which it has grown or about how the responsibility for this growth should be allocated between direct taxes (personal income and payroll taxes) and indirect taxes (provincial sales taxes and the GST). One study estimates that the underground economy grew between 1964 and 1995 by between 3 and 11 percent of GDP. The study does not determine whether changes in direct taxes had more or less to do with this growth than changes in indirect taxes. It does conclude, however, that improvements in tax compliance are not likely to be achieved by shifts toward indirect taxes and away from direct taxes.[70] A second study finds that the underground economy did not exceed 4.5 percent of GDP in 1993.[71] A third offers an estimate of 8 to 11 percent of GDP in the same year.[72] The latter study also argues that since 1991 the largest single factor in the growth of the underground economy has been the GST.[73] There have been other factors as well, however, including under-reporting of personal incomes and hence underpayment of personal income

---

[67] Livio Di Matteo, "Determinants of Cross-Border Trips and Spending by Canadians in the United States: 1979-1991" (Spring 1993), 1 *Canadian Business Economics* 51-61.

[68] Michelle Boisvert and Wayne Thirsk, "Border Taxes, Cross-Border Shopping, and the Differential Incidence of the GST" (1994), vol. 42, no. 5 *Canadian Tax Journal* 1276-93.

[69] Rolf Mirus, Roger S. Smith, and Vladimir Karoleff, "Canada's Underground Economy Revisited: Update and Critique" (September 1994), 20 *Canadian Public Policy* 235-52; and Roderick Hill and Muhammed Kabir, "Tax Rates, the Tax Mix, and the Growth of the Underground Economy in Canada: What Can We Infer?" (1996), vol. 44, no. 6 *Canadian Tax Journal* 1552-83.

[70] Hill and Kabir, ibid., at 1577-78.

[71] Don Drummond, Mireille Éthier, Maxime Fougère, Brian Girard, and Jeremy Rudin, "The Underground Economy: Moving the Myth Closer to Reality" (Summer 1994), 2 *Canadian Business Economics* 3-17, at 6.

[72] Peter S. Spiro, "Estimating the Underground Economy: A Critical Evaluation of the Monetary Approach" (1994), vol. 42, no. 4 *Canadian Tax Journal* 1059-81.

[73] Ibid.

taxes, a growing tolerance (by the tax-paying public) for tax evasion, and an increasing tendency to avoid specific excise taxes (those on tobacco, alcohol, and jewellery, in particular).[74]

Estimates of the size and the growth of the underground economy and the contribution of different taxes to it are, in fact, only estimates. What is less doubtful, however, is that the federal government was overly optimistic when it suggested that the GST would actually reduce tax evasion. This does not mean that the GST is an inherently bad tax. In any highly industrialized economy, there is considerable merit in a tax system that includes a broad mix of taxes, and the GST is an important component in the tax mix in Canada. What appears to be necessary to reduce tax evasion in Canada is an improved administrative effort—that is, more auditing and other measures to increase compliance.[75]

## Replacing Current Fuel Taxes with an Environmental Tax

Although the current federal and provincial excise taxes on motive fuels—gasoline, diesel, and jet fuel—can be viewed as taxes on emissions, they were not designed with environmental objectives in mind and therefore are not allocatively efficient. Instead, they were introduced to raise revenue and encourage national self-sufficiency in petroleum production. A recent study recommends that fuel excise taxes vary with the amounts of emissions that the various fuels produce or with the amounts of environmental damage that they cause.[76] The existing fuel tax structure creates incentives to use untaxed or undertaxed sources of emissions and thus leads to a misallocation of society's resources.[77]

---

[74] Drummond et al., supra footnote 71.

[75] Peter S. Spiro, "Evidence of a Post-GST Increase in the Underground Economy" (1993), vol. 41, no. 2 *Canadian Tax Journal* 247-58.

[76] Canada, *Report of the Technical Committee on Business Taxation* (Ottawa: Department of Finance, April 1998), chapter 9.

[77] See chapter 9 for a fuller discussion of environmental taxation in a broader context.

# 6

# Payroll Taxation

## Introduction

Canada has one of the most diverse payroll tax systems in the world. The ten provinces, the two territories (soon to be three), and the federal government all employ payroll taxes in one form or another. Payroll taxes are imposed on labour earnings only—all other forms of income, including returns to capital, business, and financial investments, are excluded. Labour earnings include wages and salaries and, sometimes, fringe benefits. Some payroll taxes are imposed on earnings from self-employment and others are not. Payroll taxes may be levied on the employer, the employee, or both. Payroll taxes may use exemptions, floors, and ceilings. The tax base may be either an individual's labour earnings or the firm's total payroll, and the rate applied to the base is typically a flat rate. Payroll taxes are relatively simple in design and operation.[1]

Federal payroll taxes consist of premiums for employment insurance (formerly called unemployment insurance) and Canada/Quebec pension plan contributions. Provincial payroll taxes include workers' compensation premiums, which are collected in every province, and taxes on payrolls to help finance either health care or post-secondary education or both; Quebec, Manitoba, Ontario, Newfoundland, and the Northwest Territories all levy taxes of this kind. Alberta and British Columbia, by contrast, partially fund hospital and medical care through premiums levied on participants. The remaining provinces and the Yukon fund their health care programs through general revenues.

Although payroll taxes, as we noted in chapter 1, are relatively less important in Canada than they are in many other industrialized countries, they have been the fastest growing source of tax revenue in Canada over the past three decades. In 1961, as table 6.1 shows, payroll taxes in Canada were equivalent to 1 percent of gross domestic product (GDP); by 1993, the figure had grown to 5.8 percent. Payroll taxes grew faster in Quebec over this period than in any other province, rising from 1.1 percent of gross domestic provincial product (GDPP) to 6.9 percent. Ontario was close behind: the increase there was from 1 percent of GDPP to 6.1 percent. By contrast,

---

[1] For a detailed description and analysis of payroll taxes in a number of countries, including Canada and its provinces, see Jonathan R. Kesselman, *General Payroll Taxes: Economics, Politics, and Design*, Canadian Tax Paper no. 101 (Toronto: Canadian Tax Foundation, 1997); and Jonathan R. Kesselman, "Payroll Taxes Around the World: Concepts and Practice" (1996), vol. 44, no. 1 *Canadian Tax Journal* 59-84.

payroll taxes amounted to 4.1 of GDPP in Saskatchewan and 4.2 percent of GDPP in Alberta in 1993.

Table 6.1 also illustrates the growth of payroll taxes as a percentage of federal and provincial government revenues. For Canada as a whole, the percentage of government revenues generated from payroll taxes on employers and employees rose from 4.1 percent in 1961 to 14.4 percent in 1993. There is considerable interprovincial variation, however, in the importance of payroll taxes. Their importance is greatest in Ontario and Quebec, where they accounted for, respectively, 16.9 and 15.9 percent of government revenues in 1993. Even in the provinces where they are least important, Saskatchewan, Prince Edward Island, and New Brunswick, they accounted for, respectively, 9.2, 9.4, and 9.6 percent of government revenues in 1993.

The relative importance of payroll taxes has increased over the past three decades because of the introduction of the Canada and Quebec pension plans in 1966 and provincial payroll taxes for health, post-secondary education, or both in Quebec in 1970, Manitoba in 1982, Ontario in 1990, Newfoundland in 1990, and the Northwest Territories in 1993.[2] Workers' compensation premiums were introduced in 1910, and unemployment insurance was introduced in 1940. Of interest here is the increase in effective tax rates that has accompanied this increase in payroll taxation. Since the tax bases and coverage of provincial payroll taxes vary widely from province to province, an interprovincial and intertemporal comparison of legislated tax rates would be meaningless. Instead, table 6.2 for selected years from 1961 to 1993 provides estimates by province of *effective* payroll tax rates—that is, the total payroll tax revenues raised in each province expressed as a percentage of total wages and salaries. For Canada in its entirety, the effective payroll tax rate rose from 2.11 percent in 1961 to 6.48 percent in 1981 and 11.6 percent in 1993. Quebec's payroll tax rate, at 14 percent in 1993, was the highest, and Alberta's, at 9.42 percent, was the lowest.

Unemployment insurance (UI), now employment insurance (EI), and Canada Pension Plan and Quebec Pension Plan (CPP/QPP) contributions accounted for the bulk of payroll taxes in 1993. The effective tax rate for UI contributions was 5.15 percent, and the rate for CPP/QPP contributions was 3.25 percent (table 6.3). Recent proposals to increase employment insurance and CPP/QPP contributions will, if adopted, increase effective payroll tax rates. There is plenty of opportunity, moreover, for further effective rate increases, since some provinces have not yet entered the payroll tax field and the others are more likely to raise than lower the rates for the payroll taxes they already levy.[3]

---

[2] Note that the data in tables 6.1 and 6.2 exclude the Northwest Territories.

[3] Livio Di Matteo and Michael Shannon, "Payroll Taxation in Canada: An Overview" (Summer 1995), 3 *Canadian Business Economics* 5-22.

**Table 6.1  Payroll Taxes[a] in Canada and the Provinces, 1966 and 1993**

| | 1961 | | 1971 | | 1981 | | 1993 | |
|---|---|---|---|---|---|---|---|---|
| | As a % of GDPP[b] | As a % of government revenue[c] | As a % of GDPP | As a % of government revenue | As a % of GDPP | As a % of government revenue | As a % of GDPP | As a % of government revenue |
| Newfoundland | 1.3 | 4.6 | 2.2 | 5.1 | 3.2 | 6.9 | 6.0 | 10.9 |
| Prince Edward Island | 1.0 | 3.3 | 2.1 | 4.5 | 3.1 | 6.3 | 5.1 | 9.4 |
| Nova Scotia | 1.2 | 4.6 | 2.3 | 5.8 | 3.6 | 7.5 | 5.0 | 10.8 |
| New Brunswick | 1.2 | 4.5 | 2.4 | 5.6 | 3.5 | 6.8 | 5.0 | 9.6 |
| Quebec | 1.1 | 4.1 | 2.3 | 6.6 | 4.7 | 11.8 | 6.9 | 15.9 |
| Ontario | 1.0 | 4.0 | 1.8 | 5.4 | 2.9 | 8.7 | 6.1 | 16.9 |
| Manitoba | 0.9 | 3.8 | 2.0 | 5.9 | 2.7 | 7.9 | 5.6 | 12.9 |
| Saskatchewan | 0.8 | 3.3 | 1.3 | 4.5 | 2.1 | 5.7 | 4.1 | 9.2 |
| Alberta | 0.8 | 4.0 | 1.7 | 5.6 | 2.2 | 5.7 | 4.2 | 11.2 |
| British Columbia | 1.1 | 4.6 | 2.1 | 6.7 | 3.1 | 9.8 | 4.7 | 11.5 |
| Canada | 1.0 | 4.1 | 2.0 | 5.9 | 3.3 | 8.9 | 5.8 | 14.4 |

[a] Provincial payroll taxes (workers' compensation premiums in every province plus payroll taxes for health and/or post-secondary education in Quebec, Manitoba, Ontario, and Newfoundland) and federal payroll taxes (employment insurance—formerly unemployment insurance premiums—and Canada and Quebec pension plan contributions) by province.  [b] Gross domestic provincial product.  [c] Provincial and federal government revenue combined.

Source: Zhengxi Lin, Garnett Picot, and Charles Beach, "What Has Happened to Payroll Taxes in Canada over the Last Three Decades?" (1996), vol. 44, no. 4 *Canadian Tax Journal* 1052-77.

**Table 6.2  Effective Tax Rates by Province and for Canada
for Selected Years from 1961 to 1993**

|  | 1961 | 1971 | 1981 | 1993 |
|---|---|---|---|---|
| Newfoundland | 2.35 | 4.12 | 6.12 | 12.14 |
| Prince Edward Island | 2.11 | 4.39 | 6.56 | 9.99 |
| Nova Scotia | 2.41 | 4.48 | 6.62 | 10.39 |
| New Brunswick | 2.40 | 4.37 | 6.39 | 10.16 |
| Quebec | 2.15 | 4.43 | 8.76 | 14.00 |
| Ontario | 2.07 | 3.42 | 5.45 | 11.70 |
| Manitoba | 1.74 | 3.87 | 5.44 | 11.90 |
| Saskatchewan | 1.92 | 3.70 | 5.96 | 9.74 |
| Alberta | 2.03 | 3.75 | 5.88 | 9.42 |
| British Columbia | 2.33 | 4.11 | 6.22 | 9.46 |
| Canada | 2.11 | 3.86 | 6.48 | 11.60 |

Note: Effective tax rates equal total payroll tax revenues in each province as a percentage of total wages and salaries.

Source: Same as table 6.1.

**Table 6.3  Effective Payroll Tax Rates for Canada
for Selected Years from 1961 to 1993**

| Component | 1961 | 1971 | 1981 | 1993 |
|---|---|---|---|---|
| Unemployment insurance | 1.41 | 0.91 | 2.58 | 5.15 |
| Canada and Quebec pension plans | — | 2.15 | 2.22 | 3.25 |
| Workers' compensation | 0.70 | 0.59 | 1.04 | 1.54 |
| Health and/or post-secondary education taxes | — | 0.21 | 0.63 | 1.66 |
| Total | 2.11 | 3.86 | 6.48 | 11.60 |

Note: Effective tax rates equal total payroll tax revenues in each province as a percentage of total wages and salaries.

Source: Same as table 6.1.

# The Structure of Federal Payroll Taxes

The federal government levies two payroll taxes—employment insurance, known until recently as unemployment insurance, and Canada/Quebec pension plan contributions.

## Employment Insurance

The unemployment insurance program has been reformed and amended many times since its inception in 1941.[4] Originally, the federal government met all administrative expenses and augmented the unemployment insurance account with a grant equal to one-fifth of combined employer and employee contributions. Since 1990, however, the system has been funded entirely by employer and employee contributions. The federal government may authorize repayable

---

[4] For a historical discussion, see Zhengxi Lin, "Employment Insurance in Canada: Recent Trends and Policy Changes" (1998), vol. 46, no. 1 *Canadian Tax Journal* 58-76.

advances to the account when it is in a deficit position. In 1997, the program was renamed the employment insurance (EI) program.

In setting the tax rate to be applied to employers and employees, the federal government uses as a benchmark a statutory rate that is based on a three-year average of the program's costs. When the program is projected to run a cumulative deficit, the actual rate will be higher than the statutory rate. When the program is projected to run a surplus, as is currently the case, the actual rate will be lower than the statutory rate.

Before 1998, contributions were based on weekly earnings up to a given limit ($845 per week in 1996 and 1997). In 1998, the basis for the program became annual earnings rather than weekly earnings. The employee's contribution rate is now (1999) 2.55 percent, and the employer's rate is 3.57 percent (1.4 times the employee's rate). Thus of insurable earnings to a maximum of $39,000 annually, the maximum contributions are $994.50 for an employee and $1,392.30 for an employer. Contribution rates and maximum amounts have fallen over the past few years,[5] primarily because the benefits under the program have been reduced and the program has become less expensive to operate.[6] A special two-year program was introduced for 1997 and 1998 to provide relief to all firms with employer premiums of less than $60,000 in 1996. In 1997, eligible firms paid virtually no employer premiums for new employees, and in 1998 the premiums paid by eligible firms were reduced by 25 percent.

## Canada Pension Plan and Quebec Pension Plan Contributions

The Canada Pension Plan (CPP) came into effect on January 1, 1966, and pension payments began in January 1967. The plan operates in all parts of Canada except Quebec, which has its own pension plan. The provisions of the Quebec Pension Plan (QPP), however, are very similar to those of the federal plan. CPP benefits supplement rather than replace private retirement pension plans.[7] Coverage is compulsory for most employees and self-employed persons. Contributions are not required from persons under the age of 18 or over 69, pensioners, armed forces personnel, certain provincial government employees, casual or migratory workers, and certain other employees.[8]

---

[5] In 1994, the contribution rates were 3.07 percent for employees and 4.298 percent for employers; these rates were applied to insurable earnings to a maximum of $780 per week; the 1996 rates were 2.95 percent (employees) and 4.13 percent (employers) of insurable earnings to a maximum of $845 per week; the 1997 rates were 2.9 and 4.06 percent of insurable earnings to a maximum of $845 per week.

[6] EI benefits are discussed in chapter 8. It should be noted here, however, that there is only a weak connection between a worker's contributions and expected benefits.

[7] CPP/QPP benefits are discussed in chapter 8. CPP/QPP benefits are more closely related to contributions than are EI benefits, since each individual has his own CPP/QPP account.

[8] Karin Treff and David B. Perry, *Finances of the Nation 1997* (Toronto: Canadian Tax Foundation, 1997), 9:15.

In 1997, the employee and employer each contributed 2.925 percent of pensionable earnings to the plan and self-employed persons contributed 5.85 percent of pensionable earnings. Pensionable earnings were defined as earnings between $3,500 and $35,800 per year or a maximum of $32,300. The upper income limit increases each year in line with the increase in the average industrial wage. The maximum employee and employer contribution for 1997 was $944.78 ($1,889.55 for the self-employed). Like the upper income limit, contributory rates have increased from year to year.[9]

In December 1997, concern about the CPP's inability to generate sufficient revenues to fund future pension benefits led the government to legislate higher contributory rates. The legislation stipulates the rates for each year up to 2007. Initially, these rates will generate a surplus, and it is anticipated that as a result of investing this surplus and using the returns, contributory rates will be lower in the long run than they would otherwise be.

## The Structure of Provincial Payroll Taxes

Provincial payroll taxes consist of workers' compensation premiums, which are paid in every province and the two territories, and general payroll taxes in Newfoundland, Quebec, Ontario, Manitoba, and the Northwest Territories.

### Workers' Compensation Premiums

Employers pay provincial payroll taxes in the form of workers' compensation premiums in order to fund provincially administered workers' compensation boards. In all jurisdictions but three (Prince Edward Island, Nova Scotia, and the Northwest Territories), the tax rates vary by industry and occupation and may be experience-rated at the firm level. Across Canada, there is considerable variation in the industrial classification system and application of the tax. Thus the number of separate assessment rates varies from only 5 in the Yukon to 357 in Quebec. The use of experience-rating means that different employers in the same industry may pay different rates. As well, some business operations may be classified into two or more industry groups with different assessment rates.[10]

Although the rates may vary across industries and occupations within industries, they are generally set at levels sufficient to cover the projected costs of accidents incurred by the rate group in each year. Additional surcharges may be added to cover costs of past unfunded accidents. As table 6.4 shows, average assessment rates rose in every province between 1966 and 1994.

---

[9] In 1994, for example, the combined rate was 5.2 percent and the maximum amount of income subject to the CPP was $31,000; in 1996, the figures were 5.6 percent and $31,900.

[10] For a more detailed discussion, see François Vaillancourt, *The Financing of Workers' Compensation Boards in Canada, 1960-1990*, Canadian Tax Paper no. 98 (Toronto: Canadian Tax Foundation, 1994).

**Table 6.4  Workers' Compensation Average Assessment Rates, 1966-1994**

|  | 1966 | 1976 | 1986 | 1991 | 1994 |
|---|---|---|---|---|---|
| Newfoundland | 1.62 | 1.42 | 1.79 | 2.92 | 3.18 |
| Prince Edward Island | na | na | 1.32 | 1.95 | 2.07 |
| Nova Scotia | 1.16 | 1.18 | 1.19 | 1.66 | 2.54 |
| New Brunswick | 1.97 | 1.48 | 1.77 | 2.04 | 2.15 |
| Quebec | 1.39 | 1.86 | 2.04 | 2.32 | 2.75 |
| Ontario | 1.23 | 1.75 | 2.59 | 3.20 | 3.01 |
| Manitoba | 0.67 | 1.10 | 1.67 | 2.25 | 2.12 |
| Saskatchewan | 1.53 | 2.21 | 1.37 | 1.63 | 1.67 |
| Alberta | 1.44 | 1.47 | 1.59 | 1.85 | 2.13 |
| British Columbia | 1.30 | 1.83 | 2.19 | 1.82 | 2.42 |

na  not available.

Source: Livio Di Matteo and Michael Shannon, "Payroll Taxation in Canada: An Overview" (Summer 1995), 3 *Canadian Business Economics* 7.

## Provincial Health and Post-Secondary Education Taxes

Newfoundland, Quebec, Ontario, and Manitoba levy payroll taxes that are ostensibly used to help finance health care and post-secondary education. Except in Quebec, however, the revenues generated by these taxes go into general funds and can be used for any purpose. The Northwest Territories' payroll tax is much the same but no claim is made for it as a tax designed to raise revenue for a specific purpose. Unlike the federal payroll taxes, none of the provincial or territorial taxes set limits on the wages or salaries subject to taxation.

Where payroll taxes are used, they have become large revenue generators. In 1996, they produced almost $3.8 billion in provincial revenues in Quebec and $2.7 billion in Ontario. Payroll taxes were the third largest revenue source in Quebec, the fourth largest in Ontario, Newfoundland, and Manitoba, and the fifth largest in the Northwest Territories.

Table 6.5 summarizes the provincial payroll taxes. Quebec, the first of the provinces or territories to levy payroll taxes, introduced its tax in 1970. The Northwest Territories, which brought in its tax in 1993, is the most recent entrant. In 1996, the legislated basic tax rate ranged from 4.26 percent in Quebec to 1.95 percent in Ontario to 1 percent in the Northwest Territories. Ontario, Manitoba, and Newfoundland provide relief for small business in the form of lower effective tax rates. Quebec and Ontario tax net incomes from self-employment, but Ontario is scheduled to eliminate this tax in 1999. Although the provincial payroll taxes apply to all employers, including non-profit and quasi-public organizations and all levels of government, some distinctions are made. Newfoundland, for example, taxes employers in the renewable resource sector at the reduced rate of 1 percent. Commercial truckers based in Manitoba that provide services to out-of-province employers are taxed at a reduced rate, as are Quebec businesses in the international financial services sector.[11]

---

[11] See Kesselman, *General Payroll Taxes*, supra footnote 1, at chapter 5 for a detailed and excellent discussion of provincial payroll taxes.

**Table 6.5  Summary of Features of Provincial Payroll Taxes, 1996**

|  | Quebec | Manitoba | Ontario | Newfoundland | Northwest Territories |
|---|---|---|---|---|---|
| Name of tax . . . . . . . . | Health services fund (HSF) contributions | Health and post-secondary education tax levy | Employer health tax (EHT) | Health and post-secondary education tax | Payroll tax |
| Date initiated . . . . . . . | November 1970 | July 1982 | January 1990 | August 1990 | July 1993 |
| Projected revenues for 1996-97 ($ millions) . . . . . . . . | 3,762 | 206.5 | 2,665 | 71.6 | 12.1 |
| Rank of payroll tax in province's taxes[a] . . . . . . . . . . . | Third, after PIT and RST | Fourth, after PIT, RST, and GFT | Fourth, after PIT, RST, and CIT | Fourth, after RST, PIT, and GFT | Fifth, after PIT, CIT, TT, and GFT |
| Tax rate for 1996 (%) . . . . . . . . . . . | 4.26[b] | 2.25 | 1.95 | 2 | 1[c] |
| Tax relief for small business . . . . . . . . . . | None | $750,000 exemption; rate of 4.5% on payroll from $750,000 to $1,500,000 | In 1998, the first $300,000 was exempt; in 1999, the first $400,000. | $100,000 exemption | None |
| Self-employed coverage . . . . . . . . . | Yes, above $5,000 (includes other non-employment income); 1% rate with ceiling. | No | In 1998, the amount of total self-employment income above $40,000 was taxed at graduated rates. This provision is to be eliminated in 1999.[d] | No | No |

(The table is concluded on the next page.)

**Table 6.5  Concluded**

| | Quebec | Manitoba | Ontario | Newfoundland | Northwest Territories |
|---|---|---|---|---|---|
| Exempt or tax-preferred sectors ... | International financial services | Commercial truckers get tax reduction for out-of-province employment. | None | Renewable resource sectors (fishing, forestry, and farming) are taxed at rate of 1%. | None |

[a] PIT = personal income tax; CIT = corporate income tax; RST = retail sales tax; GFT = gasoline and fuel tax; TT = tobacco tax. [b] Employers are required to spend the equivalent of 1 percent of their payroll on worker training or pay the difference in tax. [c] This tax rate is applied to employers rather than employees. [d] Graduated rate structure of 0.98% below $200,000 to 1.95% at $400,000 to be retained for public sector employees.

Source: Jonathan R. Kesselman, *General Payroll Taxes: Economics, Politics, and Design*, Canadian Tax Paper no. 101 (Toronto: Canadian Tax Foundation, 1997), 122-23.

## Incidence and Employment Effects

Increasing reliance on payroll taxes has not emerged without its critics. In particular, politicians and businessmen alike have criticized payroll taxes on the ground that they are "job killers."[12] This and other criticisms generate a number of questions: Who bears the burden of a payroll tax? What are the employment effects of payroll taxes? Should they be earmarked for specific government expenditure programs such as social security? Do they have an impact on our international competitiveness? Are they difficult to administer? These questions are the basis for the remainder of this chapter.

### Incidence, or Who Bears the Tax?

A commonly accepted view among taxpayers is that payroll taxes imposed on employers are borne by employers and those imposed on employees are borne by employees. This view, of course, ignores the possibility or the extent to which the employer or employee is able to shift the tax onto someone else. The tax could be shifted in one or more of the following ways. It could be passed on to labour in the form of lower takehome wages (that is, wages lower than they would be in the absence of the tax) or it could be passed on to consumers in the form of higher product prices; or it could be shifted to owners of capital (including land) in the form of lower rates of return. The following discussion separates its consideration of these possibilities into a theoretical analysis and empirical results.

### Theoretical Analysis

Our attempt to determine who pays the tax begins with the partial equilibrium model depicted in figure 6.1.[13] $D$ and $S$ represent the aggregate demand and supply curves for labour for a specific industry or sector. In the absence of a payroll tax, $W_0$ represents the equilibrium wage and $N_0$ represents the equilibrium level of employment (the intersection of the $D$ and $S$ curves is noted by $E_0$). Assume that a general payroll tax, $t$, is imposed on the employer. The result is that the demand curve decreases to $D^1$ and the level of employment to $N_1$ (equilibrium moves to $E_1$). The before-tax wage rate rises from to $W_0$ to $W_r$, and the after-tax wage rate falls from $W_0$ to $W_n$. The tax burden is borne by both the employer, who pays more ($W_r - W_0$), and the employee, who receives less ($W_0 - W_n$). Alternatively, assume that a payroll tax of the same rate, $t$, is imposed on the employee. In this case, the labour-supply curve shifts upward to $S^1$ and the result is a new before-tax wage of $W_r$ and an after-tax wage of $W_n$ (equilibrium is at $E_2$). Thus the incidence of a tax imposed on the employee is identical to the incidence of a tax at the same

---

[12] For a discussion of this view, see Di Matteo and Shannon, supra footnote 3; and Jonathan R. Kesselman, "Payroll Taxes in the Finance of Social Security" (June 1996), 22 *Canadian Public Policy* 162-79, at 162-63.

[13] For a more thorough theoretical discussion, see Kesselman, *General Payroll Taxes*, supra footnote 1, at 55-70.

**Figure 6.1   The Impact of a General Payroll Tax on the Wage Rate and Employment**

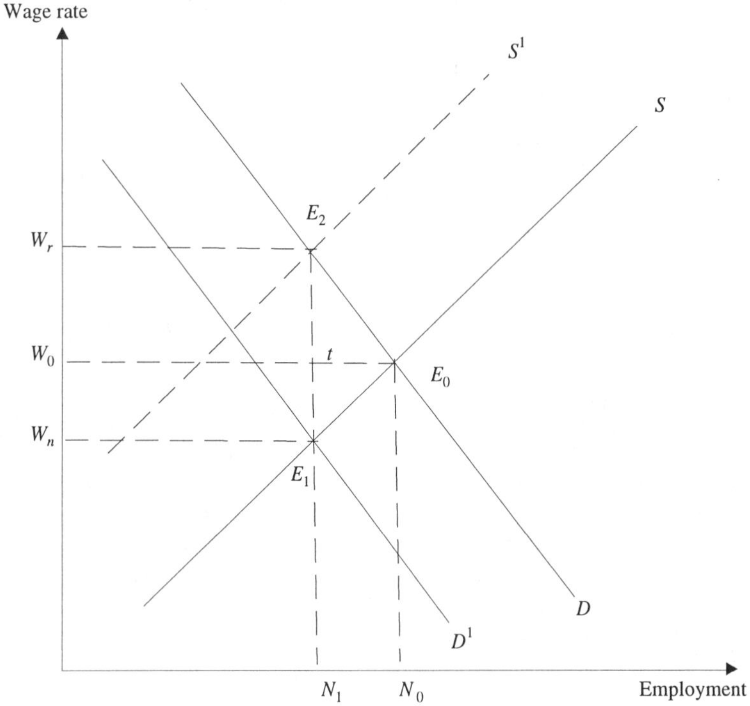

Wage rate

Note: $t$ = tax rate = $E_2E_1$ = $W_rW_n$.

rate imposed on the employer ($W_r - W_0$ on the employer and $W_0 - W_n$ on the employee). Regardless of the legal incidence of the tax (that is, whether it is imposed on employers or employees), its economic incidence (final resting place) is the same. The effect on employment is also the same ($N_0$ to $N_1$).

The distribution of the burden between employers and employees depends on the elasticities of demand and supply for labour. Thus the more inelastic the supply of labour is relative to the demand curve, the larger is the employees' share of the total tax burden. The employees' share also increases with the elasticity of the demand for labour relative to the supply curve. Conversely, the share borne by employers increases with the elasticity of supply and with the inelasticity of demand.

The short-run incidence of general payroll taxes[14] will differ from their long-run incidence. In the short run, since labour demand and supply are

---

[14] With a general payroll tax, there is no direct link between the tax paid and the benefits received from the revenues collected. A general payroll tax is also not experience-rated—as are, for example, workers' compensation premiums.

slow to adjust, wages will be fairly inflexible; consequently, the tax will likely be borne primarily by the employer if it is imposed on the employer and by the employee if it is imposed on the employee. In the long run, as labour demand and supply change, the incidence of the tax is likely to shift. It is the long-run incidence that is of particular relevance for government policy decisions, and it is the long-run incidence that is discussed here.

The partial equilibrium analysis in figure 6.1 ignores the impact of payroll taxes on other labour markets or on product prices or returns to capital. It is useful primarily because it illustrates the circumstances in which payroll taxes will fall mainly on employees or mainly on employers and because it suggests that the long-run incidence of the tax will be the same whether it is imposed on employees or on employers.

If we extend the partial equilibrium analysis of figure 6.1 to include other labour markets, the long-run incidence of payroll taxes may depend on the extent to which labour is mobile and different employers face different effective payroll tax rates. If labour is mobile, workers who incur the largest net wage decrease because of the tax will, in the long run, transfer to employers from which they can secure a higher net wage—that is, exempt employers or those that face lower effective tax rates. This shift will reduce labour supply in the sectors where the net impact on wages is greatest and increase it in exempt sectors or in sectors where the decrease in the net wage is less severe. Under this scenario, labour adjustment continues until the net wage for comparable jobs is the same everywhere. In other words, labour in every sector bears part of the tax, in the sense that wages everywhere are lower than they would be in the absence of the tax.

To the extent that employers cannot pass the payroll tax on to employees, they will pass it on either to consumers, in the form of higher product prices, or to investors, in the form of lower rates of return to capital. The extent to which employers can pass along payroll taxes in the form of higher product prices depends on market conditions. If product prices are determined in world markets (through international competition), then employers in a single jurisdiction (a province, for example) that has increased payroll taxes may not, for fear of losing business, shift the increase forward onto prices. If, however, employers in this jurisdiction have some control over product prices, they may shift some of the tax onto prices. Similarly, within any jurisdiction, employers who have control over prices (that is, employers who are not subject to interprovincial or international competition) may be able to shift some of the tax increase onto consumers, whereas employers without control will not be able to recover the tax increase by increasing their selling prices. For example, it may be easier for service sector industries (consulting, legal, accounting, and the like) to recover payroll tax increases through higher fees than it is for manufacturers to recover them through higher prices, since service fees tend to be determined locally but many product prices are subject to national or international constraints.

An employer may also pass part or all of a payroll tax increase on to capital owners, in the form of lower rates of return. This will happen if product prices are determined in international markets and the employer initially absorbs the payroll tax increase as an increase in production costs. In order to retain the previous profit margin without passing the tax on to employees, the employer would have to pass the tax back to capital owners in the form of lower rates of return. Given international or interprovincial mobility of capital, differential decreases in rates of return will be reflected in capital shifts, and this shifting will continue until the net rates of return in comparable sectors are the same. In effect, all capital owners bear the tax.

The above analysis ignores the use that is made of the tax revenue. If the revenue is used to reduce other taxes or government deficits, or for increased government spending, it may alter the demand for or the supply of labour and thus affect the incidence of the tax. For example, if the payroll tax replaces a tax borne entirely by employees, its imposition will lead to an increase in workers' disposable income and a subsequent reduction in their labour supply. In figure 6.1, this change implies a leftward shift in the labour supply curve and thus less of a reduction in the net wage received by employees and a smaller share for employees—and a larger share for employers—of the burden of the payroll tax.

Which of these scenarios for the incidence of general payroll taxes best describes the situation in Canada? By and large, Canada operates in the global economy, so capital in Canada is highly mobile and product prices generally are influenced, if not determined, by interprovincial and international market conditions. Thus it is unlikely that a general payroll tax increase in one province or in the country as a whole would be shifted forward in the form of higher product prices or lower rates of return. Labour, then, is left as the most likely recipient of the tax increase.[15] Payroll tax increases will be reflected in wages and salaries that are lower than they would be in the absence of the tax.

Instead of a general payroll tax, let us consider the incidence of a benefits-linked tax imposed on the employer.[16] If there is a very tight tax-benefit linkage, and if employees recognize the value of the benefits and subtract them fully from their expected gross wage, then the employees will bear the entire burden of the tax.

In this case, however, no distortions will arise—the tax will have no effect on wage rates and employment. This outcome is illustrated by figure 6.2. $D$ and $S$ represent the original aggregate demand for and supply of labour, and the initial equilibrium wage is $W_0$ and employment is $N_0$. Imposition of a benefit-linked payroll tax on the employer at the rate of $t$ reduces the demand to $D^1$; this reduction by itself reduces employment to $N_1$, and the tax will be shared between the employer and the employee according to the relative elasticities of labour demand and supply. Given a benefit-linked tax and

---

[15] Frank Vermaeten, W. Irwin Gillespie, and Arndt Vermaeten, "Tax Incidence in Canada" (1994), vol. 42, no. 2 *Canadian Tax Journal* 348-416, at 366.

[16] See Kesselman, *General Payroll Taxes*, supra footnote 1, at 67-68.

Figure 6.2    The Impact of a Benefit-Linked Payroll Tax on the
              Wage Rate and Employment

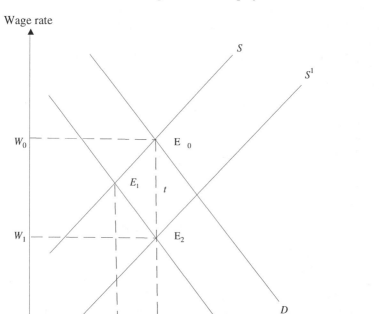

Note: $t$ = tax rate = $E_0E_2$ = $W_0W_1$.

workers who value these benefits fully, the workers will lower their supply
curve to reflect the value of the benefits. The labour supply, in this instance,
will shift rightward to $S^1$, equilibrium will shift to $E_2$, and employment will
return to its original level of $N_0$. The gross wage will return to $W_0$, but the net
wage will be $W_1$. Thus the tax has no impact on employment or the before-tax
wage rate. The employee bears the full burden of the tax.

Under different circumstances, however, employees may not bear the full
burden of a benefit-linked tax. If workers do not fully value all benefits (with
the result that supply lies between $S$ and $S^1$) and employers pay the full cost
(as reflected in $D^1$), the equilibrium level of employment will be less than $N_0$
and the payroll tax will be shared between the employer and the employees
according to the relative elasticities of the demand and supply for labour. A
similar result will arise if the employer does not pay the full costs of the
benefit-linked payroll tax.

The conclusion that labour bears almost all of the payroll tax burden may
not apply if the payroll tax on the employer is experience-rated and the tax

revenue is used to fund a specific liability, such as workers' compensation.[17] Employers' inability in this case to shift increases in tax rates onto workers arises from the fact that employees may incur higher risks of injury in working for high-risk employers. In this case, in contrast to the case of benefit-linked payroll taxes, it is a disbenefit for employees to work for employers with higher tax rates. In figure 6.2, this situation would be depicted as a shift in the supply curve to the left of $S$, which would imply a reduction in the firm's ability to shift the tax onto employees.

Since the elasticities of labour demand and labour supply are important in determining who bears the final burden of payroll taxes, the next section reviews the literature on these elasticities.

## Elasticity Estimates

A study of aggregate demand and supply elasticities in labour markets in Ontario estimated that 90 percent of the burden of the provincial payroll tax is borne by labour.[18] A more recent study estimated that a 1 percent rise in the average payroll tax in Canada would raise real wage costs to employers by 0.56 percent and lower the net wage received by employees by 0.44 percent.[19] Other studies have produced other results, and no estimates have emerged that are widely regarded as being correct.[20] Indeed, it has been argued that, for several reasons, any estimates of labour elasticities based on the conventional model must be treated with caution.[21]

To begin with, the model assumes that all labour markets are competitive. For the approximately 35 percent of the Canadian workforce that is covered by collective agreements, however, it is collective bargaining, not competition, that determines wages.[22] Much of the theoretical literature on union behaviour suggests that labour may not bear a general payroll tax even when the supply of labour is highly inelastic; instead, increased payroll taxes lead to higher wage demands.[23] When union behaviour is analyzed, however, this result is not always observed. It has been suggested, in fact, that collective bargaining may produce the same result as that in figure 6.1. It works in this way: employers attempt to share the cost of an employer payroll tax with their unionized workers by extracting agreement from the unions to accept

---

[17] Ibid., at 80-81.

[18] Bev Dahlby, "Payroll Taxes," in Allan M. Maslove, ed., *Business Taxation in Ontario* (Toronto: University of Toronto Press in cooperation with the Ontario Fair Tax Commission, 1993), 80-170, at 108.

[19] Di Matteo and Shannon, supra footnote 3, at 19.

[20] Ibid., at 20.

[21] For a detailed discussion of these reasons, see Dahlby, supra footnote 18, at 108-13.

[22] Di Matteo and Shannon, supra footnote 3, at 15.

[23] A.J. Oswald, "The Economic Theory of Trade Unions: An Introductory Survey" (1985), vol. 87, no. 2 *The Scandinavian Journal of Economics* 160-93; and John Creedy and Ian M. McDonald, "Models of Trade Union Behaviour: A Synthesis" (December 1991), 67 *The Economic Record* 346-59.

smaller wage increases, whereas unions try to shift the employee portion of the payroll tax onto employers through higher wages.[24]

Second, the demand and supply model assumes that real wages are flexible and adjust in response to changing payroll taxes. In reality, however, nominal wages are fixed in the short run because of minimum-wage laws and union contracts. Consequently, an unanticipated increase in payroll taxes may lead to reductions in employment greater than those that the competitive model would predict, and the incidence of the increase would differ accordingly. As for the long run, one study concludes that it may take several years for the impact of an increase to be felt. Specifically, it notes that even if the supply of labour is perfectly inelastic some of the short-run burden will fall on capital, and that this result will persist for years.[25]

Third, the conventional model assumes that all employers are taxed at the same rate. As we have shown earlier in this chapter, this is clearly not the case—effective tax rates differ for various structural reasons.

Fourth, the conventional model described above suggests that real wages will adjust to eliminate all unemployment. Efficiency wage models have challenged this assumption. To put the matter briefly, these models argue that firms may increase productivity or reduce costs by paying higher wages in order to reduce labour turnover, increase employee morale, and reduce shirking by employees. If an employer's response to a payroll tax increase is to pay higher wages to cover these additional costs, the employer will bear proportionately more of the tax than the conventional model predicts.

Given the shortcomings of the conventional demand and supply model for estimating elasticities, it may be that the burden of payroll taxes on labour is smaller than the results obtained by studies that use this model suggest. In fact, estimates based on this method of determining the incidence of payroll taxes are inferior to estimates that have emerged from the econometric literature, whose results are summarized in the next section.

## Econometric Evidence

In 1993, Bev Dahlby completed an extensive and critical Canadian review of the econometric literature on payroll taxation.[26] Dahlby began by reviewing a number of studies that estimated the impact of payroll taxes on wages and employment (owing to a dearth of Canadian studies at that time, almost all of the studies dealt with other countries). He then combined the results of these

---

[24] David Wilton and David Prescott, *The Effects of Tax Increases on Wage and Labour Costs*, Discussion Paper 93-29 (Kingston, Ont.: Queen's University, School of Policy Studies, 1993).

[25] Daniel S. Hamermesh, "Factor Market Dynamics and the Incidence of Taxes and Subsidies" (December 1980), 95 *Quarterly Journal of Economics* 751-64, at 761.

[26] Dahlby, supra footnote 18, at 113-33. Kesselman, *General Payroll Taxes*, supra footnote 1, at 71-81, also provides an excellent summary of the literature.

studies with predictions that he obtained from the competitive labour market model on the basis of reasonable estimates for the demand and supply elasticities of labour. He concluded "that labour bears over 80 percent of the employer payroll tax burden in the long run."[27]

Two other reviews have reached similar conclusions. Hamermesh concludes that "the lack of convincing direct estimates of payroll tax shifting and the well-established values of the labour supply and demand elasticities suggest that there is only small scope *in the long run* for a payroll subsidy to increase employment, or for a payroll tax to reduce it. Barring substantial improvement in empirical studies of tax incidence, we must tentatively infer that most of the burden of payroll taxes is on wages."[28] Marchildon, Sargent, and Ruggeri find that "in the short run, ... employers will bear from 50 to as much as 100 percent of the tax" and "in the long run these effects diminish as the tax burden is shifted onto employees. In the long run employees bear almost the full burden of payroll taxes."[29]

Besides these general reviews, there are four empirical studies that have used Canadian data to estimate the incidence of payroll taxes. The results of these studies, like the results of incidence studies for other taxes, differ for a variety of reasons, including differences in the period covered, the nature of the data used, the type of payroll tax considered, and the choice of methodology. A study by Prescott and Wilton based on union contracts signed between 1979 and 1992 finds that employee payroll tax increases did not lead to higher wage rates but that higher employer payroll taxes were associated with higher wage settlements.[30] On the other hand, a more recent study by Beach, Lin, and Picot, who use employer payroll tax data in examining the variation in effective payroll tax rates across provinces and over time, concludes that "the employer payroll tax is associated with a highly significant downward shift in the labour demand curve that is more consistent with full shifting of the tax back onto labour than with no or only partial shifting."[31] The difference between the results of the two studies is, however, more apparent than real, since it arises from differences between the payroll taxes considered in the studies and the tax bases on which they were imposed. Indeed, similar variations in the incidence of payroll taxes have been found in other countries and are supported by economic theory. For

---

[27] Dahlby, supra footnote 18, at 133.

[28] Daniel Hamermesh, *Labour Demand* (Princeton, NJ: Princeton University Press, 1993), 172-73.

[29] Lori Marchildon, Timothy C. Sargent, and Joe Ruggeri, "The Economic Effects of Payroll Taxes: Theory and Empirical Evidence" (mimeograph, Department of Finance, Economic Studies and Policy Analysis Division, Ottawa, February 1966), 16.

[30] David Prescott and David Wilton, "The Effects of Tax Increases on Negotiated Wage Increases in the Canadian Private Sector" (December 1996), 28 *Applied Economics* 1495-1503.

[31] Charles Beach, Zhengxi Lin, and Garnett Picot, "The Employer Payroll Tax in Canada and Its Effects on the Demand for Labour" (mimeograph, Queen's University, Department of Economics, Kingston, Ont., May 1995), 38.

instance, a firm that faces competitive labour and product markets cannot shift a tax rate that is higher than the rate for other firms in the same market. A tax rate that is similar for every firm, however, can be shifted partially or fully onto labour.[32] A study by Vaillancourt and Marceau supports this point: they conclude that uniform payroll taxes are borne partially or fully by labour in the form of lower wages, whereas firm-level variations in tax rates (under experience-rated programs such as workers' compensation) are likely to be borne by employers.[33]

Finally, a study by Abbott and Beach, which uses provincial data to estimate both employment and wage effects of changes in employer payroll tax rates, concludes that an increase in the employer's tax rate of 1 percentage point would lead to an annual reduction in an employee's wage of 1.7 to 3.5 percent.[34] The authors express caution about this result, however, since data on earnings and effective payroll taxes are not easily estimated. Although this result differs from the results in the empirical literature on labour supply, which uses an inelastic supply curve, it may be consistent with an efficiency model, in which labour is supplied along a more elastic no-shirking condition curve. Alternatively, the difference may be attributed to the calculation of the effective tax rates in the presence of ceilings, or to the endogenous nature of the tax variable, which overstates the effect on wages and employment.[35]

In summary, then, although the evidence is not entirely uniform or conclusive,[36] it suggests that general payroll taxes tend to be passed on to employees and that firm- or sector-specific payroll taxes are more likely to be borne by employers.

## Employment Effects

Employers and some politicians frequently criticize payroll taxes on the ground that they lead to higher involuntary unemployment. In fact, however, the empirical research suggests that in general this is not the case, at least in the long run. Where the evidence suggests that the payroll tax is borne almost entirely by employees, it follows that there is very little long-run impact on

---

[32] Kesselman, *General Payroll Taxes*, supra footnote 1, at 76 and 80-81.

[33] François Vaillancourt and Nicolas Marceau, "Do General and Firm-Specific Employer Payroll Taxes Have the Same Incidence?" (October 1990), 34 *Economic Letters* 175-81.

[34] Michael Abbott and Charles Beach, "The Impact of Employer Payroll Taxes on Employment and Wages: Evidence for Canada, 1970-93," in Michael Abbott, Charles Beach, and Richard Chaykowsi, eds., *Transition and Structural Change in the North American Labour Market* (Kingston, Ont.: Queen's University, IRC Press, 1997), 154-234.

[35] Kesselman, *General Payroll Taxes*, supra footnote 1, at 76-77.

[36] For a discussion of the caveats surrounding the shifting of employer payroll taxes, see Canada, *Report of the Technical Committee on Business Taxation* (Ottawa: Department of Finance, April 1998), 3.15.

employment.[37] In figure 6.1, this state of affairs would imply a highly inelastic labour supply curve and a highly elastic demand curve. An increase in the payroll tax would lead to a marginal increase in the gross wage rate and a much larger reduction in the net wage rate. Employment would fall very little. Where the employer bears some or all of the payroll tax, as in the case of experience-rated payroll taxes, the employment effect will be more noticeable. In fact, one estimate suggests that a 1 percentage point increase in the average payroll tax rate in Canada in 1994 would have produced a loss of 40,600 jobs in the long run.[38] An earlier study also concluded that employer payroll taxes in Canada create unemployment.[39] Specifically, this study stated that between 1971 and 1988 the natural rate of unemployment grew by 1.5 percentage points as a result of increases in payroll taxes. This increase in the unemployment rate exceeded the increase attributed to unionization or to increases in the unemployment insurance rate. Further, this study suggests that personal income taxes and direct taxes do not have a significant impact on unemployment and that a revenue-neutral shift from payroll taxes to other taxes would lead to a reduction in the natural rate of unemployment.[40]

Employment results may be different, however, for payroll taxes that are closely linked to benefits. One Canadian study[41] estimates the effects on employment of four payroll taxes—employment insurance, CPP/QPP, workers' compensation, and provincial general payroll taxes. Each of these taxes has a different tax-benefit linkage. The results suggest that the CPP/QPP has a positive employment effect, but that increases in any of the other three taxes have negative employment effects. The study concludes that the difference arises because the tax-benefit linkage is stronger in the case of the CPP/QPP than it is in the cases of the other taxes.

Payroll taxes also affect employment by setting ceilings above which earnings are not taxed (employment insurance, the CPP/QPP, and workers' compensation all have ceilings of this kind). The ceilings generate differences in marginal tax rates; for example, the marginal employer tax rate on an extra hour worked by a worker with earnings above the ceiling is zero, whereas the marginal tax rate is positive if earnings are below the ceiling. Thus employers have an incentive to employ highly paid workers and have current workers work more hours rather than hire additional workers—in other words, to favour full-time employment over part-time employment.

---

[37] Beach, Lin, and Picot, supra footnote 31; and Jonathan Gruber, "The Incidence of Payroll Taxation: Evidence from Chile" (1997), vol. 15, no. 3 (special supplement, part 2) *Journal of Labor Economics* S72-S101.

[38] Di Matteo and Shannon, supra footnote 3, at 19.

[39] David Coe, "Structural Determinants of the Natural Rate of Unemployment in Canada" (March 1990), 37 *International Monetary Fund Staff Papers* 94-115.

[40] Ibid., at 108-13.

[41] Richard Archambault and Douglas Hostland, *Payroll Taxes and Employment in Canada: Some Evidence from Provincial Data*, Working Paper no. W96-7E (Ottawa: Human Resources Development Canada, Applied Research Branch, 1996).

One Canadian study, however, finds that payroll taxes play a relatively minor role in determining overtime work hours; in fact, they explain only one-sixth of the total change in hours worked.[42]

## Evaluation of Payroll Taxes

This section addresses the distributional (equity) impact of payroll taxes, their impact on the allocation of resources (efficiency), their administration and compliance costs, and a few other relevant topics.

## Equity

The distributional impact of a tax is a consequence of its incidence. The determination of the incidence of a tax is the determination of who, in the last analysis, pays the tax. The distributional impact of a tax depends upon whether the tax is progressive, proportional, or regressive in its impact on those who ultimately pay it. Two Canadian studies have found that payroll taxes are slightly progressive for lower-income families, more or less proportional for middle-income families, and slightly regressive for higher-income families.[43] These results are not surprising, given the structure of most payroll taxes. For lower-income families, the tax-free range for CPP/QPP contributions results in increasing effective rates as income rises to the maximum contribution level. Effective tax rates decline, however, once income passes the maximum contribution levels for CPP/QPP and employment insurance, and so these taxes are regressive over the higher income range. The regressivity is exacerbated by the fact that wages and salaries tend to decline as a percentage of income as income rises.

## Economic Efficiency

Payroll taxes that are not clearly linked to benefits may be allocatively inefficient if they exclude certain sectors or activities or if they apply at different rates to different sectors or activities. This inefficiency may be justified, however, if practical or administrative problems (such as low compliance) impede the administration and collection of the tax or if the differential treatment is designed to accommodate specific policy objectives or offset other distortions. Before we consider some potential distortions created by the existing system of payroll taxes and changes that could improve their allocative efficiency, it should be noted that payroll taxes may be the most efficient and distortion-free taxes in Canada. Nevertheless, they have some shortcomings in efficiency terms that should be discussed.

---

[42] Bob Billings, "What's Behind the Rise in Overtime?" (mimeograph, Department of Finance, Economic Analysis and Forecasting Division, Ottawa, October 1995).

[43] Vermaeten, Gillespie, and Vermaeten, supra footnote 15; and G.C. Ruggeri, D. Van Wart, and R. Howard, "The Redistributional Impact of Taxation in Canada" (1994), vol. 42, no. 2 *Canadian Tax Journal* 417-51.

## Incomplete Coverage or Differentials in Effective Tax Rates

Provincial payroll taxes in Canada cover a broad range of industry sectors and types of employment. The few exceptions to this coverage include tax relief for small business in Newfoundland, Ontario, and Manitoba, tax relief for the self-employed in Quebec and Ontario (until 1999), and exempt or tax-preferred sectors in Quebec, Manitoba, and Newfoundland. Otherwise, the provincial payroll taxes cover full-time and part-time workers in the private, public, quasi-public, and non-profit sectors alike. They do not differentiate between the commercial and industrial sectors, or between corporate and unincorporated businesses, or between the different levels of the public sector.[44] In general, no other major tax administered by either the provinces or the federal government is so uniform in its coverage.

Limited as they are, the exceptions to uniform coverage do change the effective rate of payroll taxation across a wide range of sectors and activities. Consider the following examples of distortions that can arise. If small businesses or the self-employed receive preferential treatment, incentives exist for firms to operate as a series of smaller businesses or to purchase inputs from independent contractors in order to minimize the tax. Uneven effective tax rates, as we noted earlier, lead to shifts in labour from more heavily taxed areas to those areas that are less heavily taxed, an outcome that produces a deadweight loss or excess burden for society.[45] Similar distortions arise if payroll taxes are imposed only on wages and not on full-compensation packages (wages plus fringe benefits, including pension contributions and the like) and only up to a ceiling.

Small business is one sector that some provinces have singled out for special relief (see table 6.5). Payroll taxes for small businesses, it has been argued, should be lower than payroll taxes for large businesses for the following reasons. First, small firms tend to be more labour-intensive than large firms. Second, payroll costs as a percentage of overall costs tend to be higher for small firms than for large ones. Third, payroll taxes as a percentage of total taxes are higher for small firms. Finally, the small business sector has been responsible for most of the job growth in Canada over the past two decades.[46]

None of the arguments in favour of special treatment of the small business sector or any other sector or activity justify the creation of differential effective payroll tax rates. Differential rates create distortions and lead to efficiency losses that could be avoided if general payroll taxes were imposed

---

[44] For more detail on this see Jonathan R. Kesselman, "Canadian Provincial Payroll Taxation: A Structural and Policy Analysis" (1994), vol. 42, no. 1 *Canadian Tax Journal* 150-200.

[45] Dahlby, supra footnote 18, at 140; and Kesselman, *General Payroll Taxes,* supra footnote 1, at 88-92.

[46] Dahlby, supra footnote 18, at 146-52.

on all labour earnings (full compensation) at a uniform rate.[47] Where special assistance is justified, it should be provided in the form of cash grants that do not alter relative prices or create incentives in favour of certain sectors or activities. The cost of assistance would then be apparent, and taxpayers and decision makers could decide whether the tax cost of the special treatment were merited. If special treatment is provided through the tax system, no one really knows its true cost.

## Experience Rating

Workers' compensation premiums are experience-rated; that is, the higher is the potential liability of a work-related injury, the greater is the effective tax rate. Similarly, CPP/QPP benefits are directly related to the premiums paid. Programs of this kind link taxes and benefits more directly than do general payroll taxes and therefore represent a better allocation of society's resources, since those who are most likely to receive the benefits are those who will pay higher taxes for their availability. Although it may not be possible to experience-rate all payroll taxes, it would clearly make sound economic sense to extend experience rating to the employment insurance program—as has been done in the United Kingdom and the United States, among other places.

The EI system currently treats all industries the same, regardless of their patterns of employment. This means that it favours industries with unstable employment patterns, since these industries' contributions fall short of their benefits. Industries with stable employment are effectively subsidizing those with unstable employment, including both seasonal industries, whose pattern of employment is predictable, and risky industries with randomly fluctuating demand for output. The result is a distortion in the allocation of resources in favour of unstable industries.[48] Although there may be some risk-smoothing function that justifies this state of affairs in the case of risky industries, no such argument can be made for seasonal industries. The latter do not involve any risk, since their patterns of output over the year are predictable. In addition, the costless availability of EI benefits induces firms, with the implicit acquiescence of workers, to increase temporary layoffs and to substitute layoffs for reductions in hours worked or even wage reductions.[49] The existence of EI benefits that are unrelated to contributions also increases the likelihood that firms will hire secondary workers on a temporary basis during peak output periods, in the knowledge that these workers may be eligible for EI benefits when the period is over.

---

[47] This was a recommendation in Ontario, *Fair Taxation in a Changing World: Report of the Ontario Fair Tax Commission* (Toronto: University of Toronto Press in cooperation with the Ontario Fair Tax Commission, 1993), 478.

[48] Miles Corak and Wendy Pyper, *Workers, Firms and Unemployment Insurance*, Statistics Canada catalogue no. 73-505E.

[49] Oliver Franke and Derek Hermanutz, "Employment Insurance: Returning to Insurance Principles" (Summer 1997), 5 *Canadian Business Economics* 61-72, at 69.

Experience rating of EI premiums would have some important beneficial effects from an efficiency point of view.[50] First, it would relate contributions more closely to the level of stability of employment in an industry and thus reduce the system's tendency to favour industries with unstable output patterns. In other words, it would move the system closer to being a true insurance system. Second, because experience rating would make it costly for firms to lay workers off, it would reduce their incentive to use temporary layoffs instead of reductions in hours of work in periods of low demand. Full experience rating would eliminate the incentive altogether, but even partial rating would reduce it somewhat. Finally, experience rating would make it more difficult for individuals to obtain work for the purpose of building up EI benefits, since employers would have a reduced incentive to hire temporary workers. Given this reduced incentive, it would be in an employer's interest to identify, and not hire, those who were likely to quit after a short spell of employment. Of course, if firms could not accurately identify these persons, experience rating would create a disincentive to hire persons who might be suspected of wanting only temporary work, such as married women and students, but who were in fact seeking long-term employment. Quite apart from this consideration, the fact that experience rating would discourage firms from hiring people who specifically require temporary work is a reason to limit the range of its application.

It is possible to estimate the impact on employment and output of these effects. A recent Canadian simulation study based on 95 industrial sectors estimates that the adoption of an experience-rated EI scheme similar to the one used in the United States would reduce aggregate unemployment by 2.2 percentage points and increase GDP by 2.2 percent. Unemployment would decline in 72 of the 95 sectors.[51]

Since it is the firm that makes the decisions about layoffs, the premiums under an experience-rated EI scheme should apply to employers only.[52] Thus an experience-rated EI program would be very similar to workers' compensation, under which the employer pays fully experience-rated premiums. The base for experience rating under an employment insurance scheme is usually either the firms' rate of layoffs or the benefits claimed by employees who have been either laid off or fired without good cause.

A recent Department of Finance report proposes a scheme of partial experience rating of employer contributions to the EI program that would

---

[50] Thomas J. Courchene, *Social Canada in the Millennium: Reform Imperatives and Restructuring Principles* (Toronto: C.D. Howe Institute, 1994); Franke and Hermanutz, supra footnote 49; and Alice Nakamura, John Cragg, and Kathleen Sayers, "The Case for Disentangling the Insurance and Income Assistance Roles of Unemployment Insurance" (Fall 1994), 3 *Canadian Business Economics* 46-53.

[51] Louis Beausejour, Munir A. Sheikh, and Baxter Williams, "Experience Rating Employment Insurance Contributions" (1998), vol. 24, no. 3 *Canadian Public Policy* 388-93.

[52] Franke and Hermanutz, supra footnote 49, at 69.

give weight to the employer layoff experience on an employer-by-employer basis.[53] Under this proposal, in addition to the specific rates for individual employers, a single contribution rate would continue to apply to all employers, but it would be reduced over time. Total employer contribution rates would not exceed the maximum rate applicable in 1998. Employers with superior layoff experience relative to a reference level would see their contribution rates drop, subject to a floor. The federal government has considered the use of experience-rated contributions for employers in the past but rejected the idea because of protests from certain sectors of the economy. The current proposal's cap on contribution rates may make it more salable to those sectors.

## Labour-Intensive Sectors

A criticism frequently made against payroll taxes is that they discriminate against labour-intensive sectors or industries and favour capital-intensive activities. If payroll taxes are borne by employees, as the evidence presented earlier suggests, there will be no incentive in favour of capital-intensive sectors, since the tax is simply reflected in lower take-home wages for employees and not in higher wages paid by employers. Further, even if part of the tax is borne by employers, in the long run this portion will be reflected in higher costs of producing capital goods and non-capital goods alike. No difference will arise between the relative costs of producing capital and non-capital goods, and hence there will be no distortion between labour-intensive and capital-intensive activities.

## Visibility and Accountability

Payroll taxes on employers are much less visible than payroll taxes on employees and therefore more acceptable politically, even though the empirical evidence suggests that employees ultimately bear most of the tax burden (in the case of general payroll taxes) regardless of who pays the tax initially. A problem with invisible taxes is that they tend to be less accountable and hence less efficient than visible taxes. Accountability is best secured when those who pay taxes are able to link their marginal tax liability with the value of marginal benefits received from government expenditures financed by these taxes. Application of the tax to employers creates the possibility of less accountability and hence more taxation and more extensive spending on programs than would exist if all payroll taxes were deducted directly from employees' wages. Direct deduction from employees would provide the basis for a closer link between taxes paid and program benefits and thus potentially lead to a better allocation of resources. On the other hand, it may be that the low visibility of provincial payroll taxes on employers is precisely the reason why they are popular as a means of financing social security programs, in spite of the lack of benefit linkages.[54]

---

[53] Supra footnote 36.

[54] Kesselman, supra footnote 12.

## Administration and Compliance

There are two related issues here: the ease and the cost of administering the tax, and the ease and the cost of complying with the tax. In Canada, the administration of payroll taxes is simpler than the administration of virtually every other major tax. The tax bases for the CPP/QPP and EI are broad and are clearly defined, and the rates on taxable earnings are uniform. The administration of these programs is further simplified by the fact that under both of them the employer remits both the employer's contribution and the employees' contributions, and by the fact that they are both linked with the administration of the income tax. Workers' compensation premiums may be the most complicated of the payroll taxes, because of the variation in assessment rates, but the program has been in existence long enough to make its administration fairly straightforward. Because payroll taxes create little in the way of administrative problems, they are relatively cheap to collect. Thus the estimated cost of administering Ontario's general payroll tax in 1992-93 was 0.38 percent of the revenue generated by the tax.[55] For Newfoundland's general payroll tax, the estimated cost in 1993 was 0.5 percent of the revenue collected. These costs are considerably lower than are the costs of administering other taxes.

The ease of administering payroll taxes may be attributed, in part at least, to the willingness of taxpayers to comply with them. Payroll taxes compare well with other major taxes in this respect. As Jonathan R. Kesselman has noted, "the incentives for employers to comply with a payroll tax are similar to those for withholding income tax from employees; only when the gross payments to workers are reported will they be tax-deductible as business expenses."[56] Employer payroll tax is a tax-deductible item. There is also some evidence that compliance is greater the closer is the relation between income taxes and payroll taxes—improving compliance with one improves compliance with the other.[57] According to one estimate, the compliance costs associated with the Canadian payroll tax system amounted in 1986 to 3.5 percent of the federal and provincial taxes remitted.[58] A more narrowly focused study reports that the compliance costs for small businesses are 3 percent of the federal and provincial taxes remitted.[59] Finally, it has been estimated that the costs of complying with provincial taxes amount to between 0.7 and 1.4 percent of the tax revenues.[60]

---

[55] Kesselman, supra footnote 44, at 182.

[56] Kesselman, *General Payroll Taxes*, supra footnote 1, at 54.

[57] James Alm, "Noncompliance and Payroll Taxation in Jamaica" (July 1988), 22 *The Journal of Developing Areas* 477-95, at 493.

[58] François Vaillancourt, *The Administrative and Compliance Costs of the Personal Income Tax and Payroll Tax System in Canada, 1986*, Canadian Tax Paper no. 86 (Toronto: Canadian Tax Foundation, 1989), 82-84.

[59] Plamondon and Associates Inc., *Business Compliance Costs for Federal and Provincial Payroll Taxes* (Ottawa: Revenue Canada, 1997), 8.

[60] Robert E. Plamondon and David Zussman, "The Compliance Costs of Canada's Major Tax Systems and the Impact of Single Administration" (1998), vol. 46, no. 4 *Canadian Tax Journal* 761-85, at 769.

The possibility of non-compliance (evasion) is greatest in the case of business proprietors and the self-employed, because of the relative ease with which they may enter the underground or hidden economy. This is a problem whose complete eradication is unlikely; the real issue is whether an alternative to the payroll tax, such as an indirect tax, would generate less underground activity. Recent evidence suggests, however, that the underground economy has grown since Canadian governments have become relatively more dependent on indirect taxes.[61] If this is true, the suggestion that some alternative indirect tax should replace the payroll tax loses considerable credence. It may be argued that more, not less, weight should be placed on payroll taxes in order to minimize overall tax evasion and increase tax compliance.

## Other Issues

### Earmarking

For the purposes of this discussion, an earmarked tax is one whose revenues are allocated to a specific program and fund the entire cost of this program.[62] In Canada, workers' compensation premiums are earmarked, since they are allocated to a fund for workers who are injured or disabled at work and the fund is intended to finance the full costs of the program. Since 1990, the EI system has been funded entirely by employer and employee contributions, but although these contributions go into a separate account, that account falls within the general consolidated revenues of the federal government and amounts in excess of the requirements of the EI system may be used for other purposes. Thus EI premiums are earmarked only in part. CPP/QPP contributions, on the other hand, are fully earmarked, since they are assigned to a specific fund and all contributions, and the return on these contributions, are intended to fund pension payments for current and future beneficiaries. Provincial payroll taxes, while labelled as taxes for health, post-secondary education, or both, are contributions to general funds and bear no direct relationship to provincial expenditures on either health or post-secondary education. Thus they are not earmarked.

Those who support earmarking do so because it creates a link between the cost of a program and the tax rate necessary to fund it. This link means that a taxpayer can more clearly relate the benefits from a program to the costs of providing the program and decide for himself whether the program is worth the cost. Whenever a link is forged between marginal costs and marginal benefits, the allocation of resources will be more efficient than it is under

---

[61] Roderick Hill and Muhammed Kabir, "Tax Rates, the Tax Mix, and the Growth of the Underground Economy in Canada: What Can We Infer?" (1996), vol. 44, no. 6 *Canadian Tax Journal* 1552-83.

[62] For an extensive discussion of the different definitions and implications of earmarking, see Wayne R. Thirsk and Richard M. Bird, "Earmarked Taxes in Ontario: Solution or Problem?" in Allan M. Maslove, ed., *Taxing and Spending: Issues of Process* (Toronto: University of Toronto Press in cooperation with the Ontario Fair Tax Commission, 1994), 129-84.

general revenue funding. The opponents of earmarking, on the other hand, argue that it can lead to rigidity in budgetary decisions and overspending because of an unwillingness to review periodically the relative benefits of alternative uses of public funds.[63]

Given the arguments for and against earmarking, the workers' compensation and employment insurance programs appear to be the strongest candidates for this treatment, especially if they are combined with experience rating. The case for earmarking pension plan contributions is less strong. The arguments for earmarking general payroll taxes are almost non-existent.

## Tax Deductibility

The federal budget of 1991 introduced a proposal, not yet enacted, to curtail the deductibility of provincial payroll and capital taxes in calculating federal corporate income tax liability. This proposal, reiterated in a 1998 Department of Finance report,[64] is a response to the fact that the proliferation of provincial payroll taxes in recent years has reduced federal corporate tax revenues, since employers are entitled to deduct payroll taxes as a business expense.

The proposal to eliminate the deductibility of payroll taxes deserves comment. First, property and sales taxes are allowed as deductible business expenses—why not allow a deduction for payroll taxes? Second, the federal government's budgetary proposal assumes that payroll taxes are borne by employers. If a general payroll tax is in fact borne by labour, full deductibility will not reduce federal corporate tax revenues, since employers will face the same wage costs after the tax (the after-tax wage received by employees plus the payroll tax) as before the tax (the wage received by employees before the tax was shifted onto them). Third, if payroll taxes do result in higher employment costs for businesses, making them non-deductible may lead to job losses, especially for low-income workers. It might be added that this is a big issue for the provinces. Certainly, the availability of the deduction is alleged to have been influential in inducing provinces to use payroll taxes for funding provincial health programs.

## International Competitiveness

The business community and some politicians frequently argue that payroll taxes imposed on employers inhibit the ability of Canadian business to compete in international markets.[65] Employer payroll taxes, according to their critics, are a business expense that increase the cost of goods sold in international markets. The issue of tax competition is, however, extremely complex. It has less to do with the impact of any single tax than with the

---

[63] Kesselman, *General Payroll Taxes*, supra footnote 1, at 93-94; and Dahlby, supra footnote 18, at 153-54.

[64] Supra footnote 36, at 11.14.

[65] Tax competition, as it apples to the overall tax system, is discussed in chapter 9.

impact of all taxes. It depends, moreover, on the availability of the public services (human and physical infrastructure, for example) funded by these taxes. Firms in jurisdictions where high taxes coincide with high levels of public services can be just as competitive as firms in low-tax jurisdictions with low levels of public services.

Tax competition is discussed in more detail in chapter 9; our interest here is in the impact of payroll taxes on competitiveness. At the moment, there is really no solid evidence to support allegations that payroll taxes in Canada inhibit competition. Canadian payroll taxes tend to bear lower effective rates than similar taxes in most countries with which Canadian businesses compete.[66] Furthermore, if payroll taxes are borne by labour, as the evidence tends to suggest they are, they will not, in the long run, be reflected in higher product prices and Canadian business competitiveness will not be inhibited. If, however, employers bear the tax in the short run or if they bear some of the long-run tax burden, as in the case of firm-specific payroll taxes, the tax may be reflected not in higher prices internationally, but rather in exchange-rate adjustments arising from a lower value for the Canadian dollar.

## Summary

Although provincial general payroll taxation in Canada is relatively new, provincial payroll taxes for workers' compensation, employment insurance, and Canada and Quebec pension plan contributions have been around for some time. For a variety of reasons, payroll taxes have much to contribute. They are simple in conception and application, involve low compliance costs for business and low administrative costs for government, and are not vulnerable to much abuse. The payroll tax is a good candidate for a tax to decentralize to the provinces, given that labour is relatively immobile and the tax need not be harmonized (see chapter 9). Further, the available evidence suggests that general payroll taxes are borne mainly by labour, although firm-specific payroll taxes are likely to be borne, partially at least, by employers. Finally, payroll taxes as they are currently applied in Canada create fewer distortions and tend to be more efficient than any other tax in the Canadian tax system.

---

[66] Kesselman, *General Payroll Taxes*, supra footnote 1, at 12-19.

# 7

# Property and Local Taxation

## Introduction

Property taxation, in one form or another, is the oldest system of taxation in existence. In Canada, it was initially a tax on selected types of property, but by the early 1900s it had evolved into a comprehensive tax on real and personal property and income.[1] During the first few decades of this century, rapid urbanization and the consequent need for more local government services led to even greater use by municipalities of real property taxes, taxes on personal property, poll taxes, and income taxes. Some municipalities attempted to increase their revenues by introducing a business tax—that is, an additional tax on the real property base for commercial and industrial properties.

Matters are rather different now. Municipalities no longer have access to the income tax base. In almost every province, personal property taxes have been abandoned either through the elimination of personal property from the property tax base or through the inclusion of personal property in the real property tax base. Poll taxes have disappeared as a source of local government revenue. The business tax has been replaced in most provinces by higher property tax rates on commercial and industrial properties. Despite the differences between property taxation as it was when it was introduced and as it is today, there are also many similarities: exemptions existed then and still do, taxpayers could appeal their assessments then and can appeal them now, and the problem of standardizing property assessment is as intractable now as it was in the beginning.

Today, property taxes, which include taxes on real property, special assessments, business taxes, and local improvement levies, are the exclusive domain of provincial governments and local authorities (that is, municipal governments and school boards) and constitute the third largest source of tax revenue for Canadian governments (after personal income taxes and general sales taxes). Between 1971 and 1996, as table 7.1 shows, property taxes in Canada increased from almost $3.5 billion to more than $33.4 billion. Over the same period, property taxes grew from 3.6 percent of gross domestic provincial product (GDPP) to 5.4 percent.

---

[1] For a more detailed discussion, see J. Harvey Perry, *Taxation in Canada*, 5th ed., Canadian Tax Paper no. 89 (Toronto: Canadian Tax Foundation, 1990), 211.

341

**Table 7.1   Property Tax Revenues[a] as a Percentage of Gross Domestic Provincial Product for Selected Years from 1971 to 1996**

| | 1971 | | 1981 | | 1991 | | 1996 | |
|---|---|---|---|---|---|---|---|---|
| | $ millions | % of GDPP | $ millions | % of GDPP | $ millions | % of GDPP | $ millions | % of GDPP |
| Newfoundland . . . . . . . . . . | 10 | 0.8 | 59 | 1.2 | 146 | 1.6 | 183 | 1.8 |
| Prince Edward Island . . . . . . | 7 | 2.7 | 19 | 1.9 | 52 | 2.5 | 105 | 4.3 |
| Nova Scotia . . . . . . . . . . | 89 | 3.7 | 210 | 2.7 | 437 | 2.5 | 600 | 3.2 |
| New Brunswick . . . . . . . . . | 40 | 2.2 | 137 | 2.2 | 362 | 2.7 | 516 | 3.6 |
| Quebec . . . . . . . . . . . . | 838 | 3.5 | 2,193 | 2.7 | 4,884 | 3.1 | 7,050 | 5.0 |
| Ontario . . . . . . . . . . . . | 1,484 | 3.7 | 4,137 | 3.2 | 11,493 | 4.1 | 16,318 | 6.9 |
| Manitoba . . . . . . . . . . . | 152 | 3.9 | 548 | 4.2 | 1,009 | 4.4 | 1,130 | 5.1 |
| Saskatchewan . . . . . . . . . | 159 | 4.6 | 437 | 3.0 | 832 | 4.0 | 935 | 4.5 |
| Alberta . . . . . . . . . . . | 273 | 3.5 | 1,114 | 2.1 | 2,236 | 3.1 | 2,953 | 4.5 |
| British Columbia . . . . . . . | 422 | 4.1 | 1,677 | 3.7 | 2,536 | 3.1 | 3,802 | 4.7 |
| Total / average[b] . . . . . . . | 3,477 | 3.6 | 10,548 | 3.0 | 24,026 | 3.6 | 33,416 | 5.4 |

[a] Provincial, school board, and local property taxes. [b] Includes Yukon Territory and Northwest Territories.

Sources: Calculated from Statistics Canada, *Provincial Economic Accounts, Annual Estimates, 1961 to 1995*, catalogue no. 13-213D and data from Statistics Canada, Financial Management Systems (FMS), mimeograph, 1998.

The relative importance of property taxes varies from province to province. In Newfoundland, property taxation accounted for 1.8 percent of GDPP in 1996. In Ontario, Manitoba, and Quebec, it accounted, respectively, for 6.9, 5.1, and 5.0 percent of GDPP. The relative importance of property taxes in a given province depends on a variety of factors, including the range of services funded by property taxes (education and social services in some provinces and not in others), the availability of refundable personal income tax credits (used in some provinces but not in others), and the division of expenditure responsibilities between municipal and provincial governments (provinces in which municipalities have more expenditure responsibilities vis-à-vis the province generally rely more heavily on property taxes). Table 7.2 notes the relative importance of property taxes for provincial, municipal, and school board purposes in 1996. By 1996, several provinces had moved into the property tax field and further moves have occurred since then. At present, Prince Edward Island imposes a uniform property tax on all property owners, New Brunswick levies a property tax on non-residential (commercial or industrial) property, Manitoba levies a property tax on residential and non-residential property (the latter bears a higher rate), Alberta levies a tax on non-residential property, British Columbia levies a property tax on both residential and non-residential property, and since 1998 Ontario has levied a provincial property tax on residential property. In general, provincial involvement in property taxation varies directly with the extent of the province's involvement in funding primary and secondary schooling.[2] Provincial involvement also occurs where provincial governments have assumed responsibility for levying property taxes in unorganized areas, most notably British Columbia.

Even where there is some provincial involvement in the property tax field, the property tax is the only tax of any substantive revenue importance that is available to municipalities. Municipalities obtain the bulk of their revenue from property taxes, user fees (sales of goods and services), and grants; additional revenue comes from fines, penalties, fees, permits, and investment income. As table 7.3 shows, the relative importance of each of the three main revenue sources changed substantially between 1971 and 1996. Municipal property taxes rose in relative importance in all provinces except Ontario. (changes since 1996 have led to increased dependence on property taxes in this province as well). Grants became relatively less important in all provinces and user fees became more important. This is a trend that is likely to continue across the country.

Growing taxpayer resistance to property tax increases and reductions in provincial grants have compelled municipalities to exploit alternative

---

[2] Harry M. Kitchen, *Property Taxation in Canada*, Canadian Tax Paper no. 92 (Toronto: Canadian Tax Foundation, 1992), chapter 1; and Harry Kitchen and Douglas Auld, *Financing Education and Training in Canada*, Canadian Tax Paper no. 99 (Toronto: Canadian Tax Foundation, 1995), chapter 2. Ontario has recently implemented a property tax for funding education.

### Table 7.2  Relative Importance of Provincial, School Board, and Municipal Property Taxes, 1996

|                          | Local | Provincial | School boards | Total |
|--------------------------|-------|------------|---------------|-------|
|                          |       | *percent*  |               |       |
| Newfoundland ............ | 98.3  | 1.7        | 0.0           | 100.0 |
| Prince Edward Island ...... | 44.4  | 55.6       | 0.0           | 100.0 |
| Nova Scotia .............. | 100.0 | 0.0        | 0.0           | 100.0 |
| New Brunswick ........... | 54.8  | 45.2       | 0.0           | 100.0 |
| Quebec .................. | 89.4  | 0.0        | 10.6          | 100.0 |
| Ontario ................. | 45.8  | 0.0        | 54.2          | 100.0 |
| Manitoba ................ | 50.1  | 19.2       | 30.7          | 100.0 |
| Saskatchewan ............ | 49.7  | 0.1        | 50.2          | 100.0 |
| Alberta ................. | 53.9  | 40.0       | 6.1           | 100.0 |
| British Columbia ......... | 62.0  | 38.0       | 0.0           | 100.0 |
| Yukon Territory .......... | 89.0  | 11.0       | 0.0           | 100.0 |
| Northwest Territories ...... | 64.6  | 17.2       | 18.2          | 100.0 |
| Total average ............ | 59.1  | 9.2        | 31.7          | 100.0 |

Note: Property taxes include real propety taxes, development charges, lot levies, special assessments, business taxes, land transfer taxes, and grants in lieu of taxes.

Source: Calculated from data provided by Statistics Canada, Financial Management Systems (FMS), mimeograph, 1998.

### Table 7.3  Relative Importance of Municipal Government Property Taxes, User Fees, and Grants,[a] 1971 and 1996

|                          | 1971 | | | 1996 | | |
|--------------------------|----------------|--------------|--------|----------------|--------------|--------|
|                          | Property taxes | User fees    | Grants | Property taxes | User fees    | Grants |
|                          | *Percentage of total municipal government revenue* | | | | | |
| Newfoundland .......... | 36.1           | 6.1          | 50.9   | 50.6           | 15.6         | 30.1   |
| Prince Edward Island ...... | 34.5        | 4.6          | 59.1   | 63.8           | 21.9         | 9.2    |
| Nova Scotia ............ | 36.4           | 4.7          | 53.7   | 55.6           | 11.5         | 29.0   |
| New Brunswick ......... | 33.8           | 15.2         | 45.2   | 51.7           | 21.1         | 25.0   |
| Quebec ................ | 38.9           | 7.8          | 48.2   | 68.3           | 15.1         | 12.0   |
| Ontario ................ | 44.1           | 4.2          | 47.6   | 41.7           | 20.3         | 32.4   |
| Manitoba .............. | 39.0           | 8.2          | 44.4   | 43.1           | 19.4         | 27.9   |
| Saskatchewan ........... | 42.5           | 7.2          | 43.7   | 52.6           | 22.1         | 12.2   |
| Alberta ................ | 35.2           | 7.0          | 49.4   | 42.2           | 30.0         | 12.9   |
| British Columbia ......... | 48.0         | 6.7          | 40.9   | 50.1           | 25.0         | 13.2   |
| Total/average[b] .......... | 41.7        | 6.0          | 47.1   | 49.6           | 20.3         | 22.9   |

[a] Excludes other sources of revenue, such as permits, fines, penalties, licences, investment income, and so forth. [b] Includes Yukon Territory and Northwest Territories.

Sources: Calculated from data in Statistics Canada, *Public Finance Historical Data 1965/66-1991/92*, catalogue no. 68-512, occasional; and from data provided by Statistics Canada, Financial Management Systems (FMS), mimeograph, 1998.

revenue sources. Many municipalities have introduced more innovative property-based charges, such as development charges, special assessments and area rates, increased licence and permit fees, and an expanded range of user fees. In addition, many municipal politicians and administrators, and some policy analysts have argued that municipalities should have direct access to provincial revenue sources, especially income and sales tax revenues. This chapter will focus its discussion on issues associated with property taxation, alternative sources, and, since they are an implicit local tax, user fees.[3]

Before we proceed with this discussion, however, it is worth noting that municipal governments in some provinces have access to a few additional local tax sources, including land transfer taxes (tax applied as a specific percentage of the value of property transferred) in Nova Scotia, Quebec, and Manitoba and amusement taxes (based on admission prices) in Quebec, Manitoba, and Saskatchewan. As well, most municipalities in all provinces draw some revenue from amusements such as circuses, juke boxes, and bowling alleys through special licences or permits. Since the revenues yielded by these taxes are relatively small (although not unimportant), their application is straightforward, and they are not used in every province, they are excluded from further discussion in this book.

## Property Taxes

Since the property tax is primarily a local government tax, one's view of this tax may depend on one's view of the appropriate role of local government. If property taxes were designed as a collection of user fees,[4] local governments would assume a role very different from the one that they currently fulfil. In essence, they would become service agencies; that is, enterprises responsible only for delivering services to specific and identifiable properties. They would no longer be responsible for funding services to persons, such as schools and welfare programs, or services that provide common benefits, such as streets, street lighting, and police protection. Although the employment of user fees as the basis for financing all local government services would generate efficiency gains,[5] it is a serious question whether local governments conducted on this basis would continue to be governments at all. After all, government should by definition have some responsibility for

---

[3] Grants are not discussed in this book. For a discussion of grants, see Richard Bird and Enid Slack, *Urban Public Finance in Canada*, 2d ed. (Toronto: Wiley, 1993), chapter 8; and Robin W. Boadway and Paul A.R. Hobson, *Intergovernmental Fiscal Relations in Canada*, Canadian Tax Paper no. 96 (Toronto: Canadian Tax Foundation, 1993), chapter 3.

[4] For an excellent discussion of the implications of user charges in financing local government services, see Richard M. Bird, *Charging for Public Services: A New Look at an Old Idea*, Canadian Tax Paper no. 59 (Toronto: Canadian Tax Foundation, 1976); and Richard M. Bird and Thomas Tsiopoulos, "User Charges for Public Services: Potentials and Problems" (1997), vol. 45, no. 1 *Canadian Tax Journal* 25-86.

[5] Ibid.

redistributional activities. It is as reasonable for the citizens of Montreal, or Toronto, or Vancouver, or Halifax, or wherever, to be concerned about the distributional impact of their local government's activities as it is for them to be concerned about the distributional impact of federal and provincial taxes and expenditures.

If one discards the view that local government should be strictly a service agency and agrees that it should provide local public services whose benefits the residents within its jurisdiction enjoy in common, one comes up with a different role for local taxation. In this case, an appropriate tax is one that is based on local residents (or exported only to the extent that services are) and supplemented by grants to account for externalities (that is, benefits from local services that spill over into neighbouring communities).[6] Although there is no clear basis for determining the appropriate local tax base for funding local services that provide collective benefits, it is possible to mount arguments in defence of property taxes for this purpose—arguments unrelated to the provision of benefits to specific properties.[7]

To begin with, income and consumption taxes are currently in the domain of the provinces and the federal government. Although they may be used as a supplement to property taxes, using them to completely replace property taxes would place additional pressure on their bases.[8] Furthermore, to the extent that income and consumption taxes generate inequities and inefficiencies, using them to replace property taxes would exacerbate these distortions.

Second, given that no single tax is entirely fair and distortion free, there is considerable merit in a provincial or national tax system that employs a mix of taxes. The use of property taxes is one way to achieve this mix. Finally a property tax may have merits in its own right; that is, it may achieve important social and economic policy objectives that other taxes cannot achieve.[9]

---

[6] Under this approach, user fees or charges would be retained for funding services whose costs and benefits can be assigned to specific properties or individuals (water and sewers, and a portion of transit and recreation, for example). For an excellent discussion of the benefit model of local finance, see Richard M. Bird, "Threading the Fiscal Labyrinth: Some Issues in Fiscal Decentralization" (June 1993), 46 *National Tax Journal* 207-27.

[7] For a discussion in support of property tax funding for local public services that provide collective benefits to the local community, see John Bossons, Harry Kitchen, and Enid Slack, "Local Government Finance: Principles and Issues," an unpublished paper for the Ontario Fair Tax Commission, Toronto, 1993; Almos Tassonyi, "The Benefits Rationale and the Services Provided by Local Governments," an unpublished paper for the Ontario Fair Tax Commission, Toronto, 1993; and Paul A.R. Hobson, "Efficiency, Equity and Accountability Issues in Local Taxation," in Paul A.R. Hobson and France St-Hilaire, eds., *Urban Governance and Finance: A Question of Who Does What* (Montreal: Institute for Research on Public Policy, 1997), 113-31, at 117-18.

[8] In Manitoba, for example, municipalities receive a share of provincial personal and corporate income taxes.

[9] See Neil Brooks's commentary on the Ontario Fair Tax Commission's report in Ontario, *Fair Taxation in a Changing World: Report of the Ontario Fair Tax Commission* (Toronto:
(The footnote is continued on the next page.)

For example, in a country without a wealth tax as such, the residential property tax may be perceived as a proxy for a wealth tax. In fact, it has been suggested that property taxes are "the major representative of wealth taxation in Canada."[10]

## Tax Base and Rate Structure

The property tax system has two critical components—the tax base and the tax rate. The tax base is the assessed value of land and buildings. In some provinces, "assessed value" is preceded by an adjective such as "actual," "fair" or "real." Whatever the choice of adjective, the courts have ruled that "assessed value" refers to market value.

Although the precise components of the assessment base vary across provinces and territories, every jurisdiction treats real property—land and buildings—as the principle component of the base. Most jurisdictions also include other broadly defined property characteristics in the tax base. For example, machinery and equipment affixed to property are included in the assessment base in Newfoundland, Nova Scotia, Quebec, Ontario, Manitoba, Northwest Territories, and the Yukon. In Prince Edward Island, New Brunswick, and Saskatchewan, machinery, equipment and other fixtures are liable to property taxation only if they provide services to the buildings. In 1987, British Columbia removed all machinery and equipment from the property tax base.[11]

In every province and territory, land is taxed at its full assessed value. This is also largely true of buildings, machinery, and equipment. Municipalities in Alberta and the Yukon, however, use the replacement cost of buildings as the tax base, and municipalities in Manitoba, Saskatchewan, and the Northwest Territories tax only a percentage of the assessed value of buildings.

Machinery and equipment are exempt from property taxation in British Columbia and in municipalities in Alberta that levy a business tax. In the Yukon, they are taxed on the basis of new replacement cost. Elsewhere, machinery and equipment are generally assessed at full market value.

Quebec's definition of taxable property is broader than the other provinces' definitions are. In addition to the above-mentioned components, it includes other immovable items such as wharves, machinery foundations, handling systems, refinery and other chimneys, and anti-pollution equipment. Nova Scotia also has a relatively broad base: it includes land, buildings, and structures; trees, bushes, and shrubs; mines, excavations, and underground

---

[9] Continued ...
University of Toronto Press in cooperation with the Ontario Fair Tax Commission, 1993), 1019-38, at 1019-23.

[10] Richard Musgrave, Peggy Musgrave, and Richard Bird, *Public Finance in Theory and Practice* (Toronto: McGraw-Hill, 1987), 434.

[11] For more detail on these characteristics, see Kitchen, supra footnote 2, at chapter 2.

improvements and quarries; minerals, gas, oil, gems, salt, and gypsum; machinery and equipment; and rafts, floats, and houseboats used for residential or commercial purposes.[12]

The property tax base also varies across municipalities. Thus municipalities may vary in their tax treatment of mobile homes; in the special statutory assessment rules they apply to farmlands and/or buildings, forest lands, mines and mineral resources, public utilities, and railway tracks; and in the exemptions—total or partial, mandatory or discretionary—that they grant to various entities including various industries, schools, churches, Crown lands, public properties, homes for the aged, charitable organizations, and cemeteries.[13] This variation in special concessions produces substantial variation in the tax base across municipalities.[14] Moreover, the tax base in a specific community may change continually as "land is placed into use or changes use through development and building, or as values attached to existing assessment are revised."[15]

Once a municipality determines the amount of tax dollars that it will need from the general property tax, it derives the tax rate by dividing the required tax revenue by the taxable assessment base and expressing the result as either a mill rate or a percentage.[16] Municipalities generally have different tax (mill) rates for different categories of property (industrial, commercial, and residential) and sometimes for groups within these categories. As well, property tax rates for municipal purposes generally differ from property tax rates for school purposes.[17] Finally, as we shall discuss below, municipalities may for various reasons impose special charges or additional taxes on certain properties.

## Evaluation

In spite of increasing criticism, the (real) property tax is upheld by the fact that it has been for many years the major source of tax revenue for local governments. There have been numerous attempts in recent years to reform

---

[12] Canadian Property Tax Association, *Tax Practices Across Canada Manual*, rev. ed. (Toronto: Canadian Property Tax Association, January 1989).

[13] For a more detailed discussion, see Kitchen, supra footnote 2, at chapter 2.

[14] This is not to imply that variation is not intended. Differentials are often established deliberately through the full or partial exemption of property from the assessment base or through the use of split or variable tax (mill) rates.

[15] Ontario, *Report of the Commission on the Reform of Property Taxation in Ontario* (Toronto: Government Printer, 1977), 1.

[16] Except in some municipalities in Atlantic Canada, where the rate is expressed as a percentage, real property taxes are generally levied at rates expressed in mills per dollar of the assessed value of property. The mill rate is derived by dividing tax revenue required by total taxable assessment and multiplying this coefficient by 1,000.

[17] Kitchen and Auld, supra footnote 2, at chapter 4.

the tax[18] and eliminate its shortcomings. The latter include the variation across provinces and municipalities in assessment procedures and tax rates, the tax's less-than-comprehensive tax base, its differential treatment of different properties, the less-than-uniform application of the tax, and the traditionally assumed regressivity of the residential property tax. Some suggestions for improvement have been implemented; others have not. In any case, these problems have been the focus of most of the recent work on property taxation and deserve detailed discussion.

## Variation in Assessment Practices

Inaccuracy in determining assessment values may create unsanctioned unfairness. Since it is seldom possible to maintain assessment at full market value (owing to information delays, work pressures, and the timing of reassessment cycles), uniformity is the most important principle of assessment. In any year, this principle requires the assessment of all properties at the same fraction of market value. If the general level of assessment for a specific class of property (single residential, for example) is 80 percent of the market value and one property is assessed at 95 percent, it may be claimed that this latter property is paying more than its fair share of taxes, given identical tax rates for all properties.

Inaccurate assessment is probably the most widely publicized and the most serious administrative fault of the real property tax. Ratios of assessed value to market value vary widely both within and among municipalities and both within and among property classifications. These variations may be either non-legislated (unintentional) or legislated (intentional). Non-legislated or unintentional variations arise because it is difficult to establish market values for properties that sell infrequently and because assessors often evaluate similar properties at different rates. Legislated variations in property assessment arise because provinces wish to impose lower taxes on certain types of property.

### Non-Legislated Variation

Uneven assessment practices generate three kinds of inequities: inequities within each class of property, inequities across classes of property, and inequities across municipalities within a province.

Inequities within property classes arise when properties within a class are not assessed at the same ratio of market value. For example, suppose there are two similar homes each with a market value of $400,000. One is assessed at $30,000 (or 7.5 percent of its market value) and the other at $20,000 (or 5 percent of market value). This difference may arise from any one of several

---

[18] See, for example, *Fair Taxation in a Changing World*, supra footnote 9, at chapters 27-33; and *Report of the Commission on the Reform of Property Taxation in Ontario*, supra footnote 15.

factors. For example, homes located in the downtown area of cities tend to be underassessed relative to homes located in the suburbs. Older homes tend to be underassessed relative to newer homes. Residential dwellings of one and two units are almost always underassessed relative to multiresidential dwellings.

Inequities across property classes arise when properties in different classes are not assessed at the same ratio of market value. Thus commercial properties tend to be overassessed relative to all residential properties except multiunit dwellings but underassessed relative to industrial and manufacturing properties.[19]

Uniform assessment is critical to the functioning of any local government system that uses the assessment base to apportion the costs of delivering uniform local government services to the residents of more than one municipality.[20] If properties of equal value are assessed at different percentages of market value across a region or county, the application of a constant region- or county-wide mill (tax) rate will violate uniformity in the treatment of properties. As a result, the apportionment of costs across municipalities will fall disproportionately on the municipalities in which property taxes are a higher percentage of market value. Studies have shown that the introduction of market-value assessment on a uniform base across large geographical areas improves the funding by property taxes of regional or municipal services.[21] There is another consideration here: if one of the roles of provincial grants to municipalities is to redistribute income, then assessed property value within the municipality is likely to be the major, if not the sole, component of the grant base. To the extent that assessment practices are not uniform, these grants will not work as intended.[22]

## Legislated Variation

All of the provinces have legislation that affords special treatment to specific categories of property for assessment purposes. For example, farmland and forest lands invariably receive favourable treatment; mines and mineral resources are generally, but not always, exempt from local property taxes; pub-

---

[19] R.M. Bird and N.E. Slack, *Residential Property Tax Relief in Ontario*, Ontario Economic Research Council Studies (Toronto: University of Toronto Press, 1978), 78; and Ontario Committee on Taxation, *Report* (Toronto: Queen's Printer, 1967) (3 volumes).

[20] Niagara Region Review Commission, *Report and Recommendations* (Toronto: Ontario Ministry of Municipal Affairs, October 1989), 113.

[21] Lewis Soroka and Carey Spiece, "Market Value Assessment in Niagara: The Regional Dimension" (1995), vol. 43, no. 2 *Canadian Tax Journal* 401-14; and James M. Dean, Derek P.J. Hum, and Harvey Stevens, "Reform Revisited: The 1990 Winnipeg Reassessment" (1991), vol. 39, no. 5 *Canadian Tax Journal* 1305-12.

[22] For a thorough discussion of the problems associated with an assessment system that is not uniform in Ontario, see Enid Slack, *An Analysis of Expenditures and Revenues in the Regional Municipality of Niagara* (Niagara Falls, Ont.: Niagara Region Review Commission, 1988), 40-51.

lic utilities generally pay a tax based on gross receipts rather than on assessed property values; and railway tracks are assessed under special rules.[23]

## Variation in Effective Property Tax Rates

As we have seen, the effective property tax rate (the ratio of the property tax liability to the market value of the property) often varies across types of residential property within a community.[24] This happens whenever a property tax (mill) rate applies to residential property categories that are assessed at different percentages of market value. Effective property tax rates tend to be higher on multiunit residential dwellings than on single-unit dwellings because the former tend to be assessed at a higher percentage of market value. Effective property tax rates on older dwellings are generally lower than those on newer dwellings for the same reason. Differential treatment of this kind is a result of assessment practices rather than a deliberate policy objective of any provincial or local government. Certainly, these differences in effective tax rates have never been defended on the ground that they reflect differences in the costs or benefits of servicing different property types within the same municipality or neighbourhood. Rather, they reflect the fact that governments can more easily impose relatively high effective tax rates on some categories of property than on others. For example, owner-occupiers of single detached houses are more likely to protest against property taxation than are renters, who are often unaware of the property tax liability on their rented quarters, or commercial/industrial property owners, who may feel that they can pass the tax on to consumers of their products or employees of their firms.

Differences in effective property tax rates (tax price) may be justified if they reflect differences in the cost (production, environmental, and social) of delivering services to the various properties. In other words, if some properties or property types are more expensive to service than others are, a case can be made for differences in property tax rates. Unfortunately, current differences in effective property tax rates have arisen from differences in assessment practices and not explicitly from variations in the tax (mill) rate. Failure to correlate benefits from local government services with the extra cost (or approximation of it) of service delivery leads to a redistribution of income that is not neutral. Where taxes exceed the extra cost of delivering the service, incentives exist for people or businesses to relocate to lower-taxed areas, since the alternative is to accept lower property values. To avoid difficulties of this sort and to set the base for an efficient and fair property tax system, one should assess all properties within a municipality and a city-region at a uniform percentage of market value. One could then design

---

[23] For more detail, see Kitchen, *supra* footnote 2, at chapter 2.

[24] It must be emphasized that this comment refers to properties within a municipality. Comparisons of effective tax rates across municipalities must be treated with considerable caution, since differences will arise when some municipalities fund selected services from user fees and others fund the same services from property taxes. Where this exists, differences in effective tax rates will and should be noted.

variable mill rates to capture cost differences across properties, property types, and municipalities (or neighbourhoods within municipalities, for that matter) within the city-region.[25] Alternatively, one could capture these differences through the use of special assessment or benefiting-area charges on properties that receive more costly municipal services—a point we shall discuss below.

## Taxation of Residential Versus Non-Residential Properties

In every province, a deliberate effort (supported in many cases by provincial statutes) has been made, either through assessment differentials or differential tax rates, to impose higher taxes on non-residential properties than on residential properties. This practice creates efficiency[26] and equity concerns. For example, a study of property taxation in Ontario has suggested that the residential sector receives proportionately more benefits from local government services than the non-residential sector receives.[27] Since the non-residential sector also faces higher effective property tax rates, the study concludes that the non-residential sector in Ontario is overtaxed and the residential sector is undertaxed. More specifically, the study notes that if non-residential properties funded only the portion of local services that benefited these properties, property taxes might fall as much as 50 percent. Furthermore, if all education funding were removed from property taxes in the Ontario cities examined in the study, the property tax for the remaining services would approximate, in a crude fashion at least, a benefits-based local tax.

These findings suggest that the residential sector pays a tax price that is lower than the cost of the services that it consumes. The result is an inefficient level of output—specifically an oversupply. If local government were to make allocative efficiency a primary objective, they would eliminate the current discriminatory taxation of non-residential property. This step would also make the tax more fair, since the sector that benefited from the services would be the sector that paid for them.

## Incidence of the Property Tax

Probably the strongest and most long-standing criticism of the real property tax is that it is regressive. It has traditionally been assumed, in other words,

---

[25] This has been done in British Columbia for some time, and the practice was introduced in Ontario in 1998. Variable mill rates can help a municipality to achieve a specific land-use pattern; for example, the application of higher tax rates to suburban properties may result, at the margin, in a higher concentration of activity in the downtown core. For an evaluation of the implications of variable mill rates, see Enid Slack, "Variable Mill Rates" (mimeograph, Municipal Finance Branch, Ministry of Municipal Affairs, Toronto, January 1991).

[26] Douglas A.L. Auld, Paul Hobson, and Harry Kitchen, "Utilization of the Property Tax: An Economic Analysis," a report prepared for the Ontario Ministry of Municipal Affairs (mimeograph, Toronto, 1990).

[27] Harry M. Kitchen and Enid Slack, *Business Property Taxation*, Government and Competitiveness Project Discussion Paper no. 93-24 (Kingston, Ont.: Queen's University, School of Policy Studies, 1993).

that the tax absorbs a greater percentage of the income of low-income earners than of high-income earners. Indeed, this is the perception of most local municipal officials, taxpayers, and some analysts, even though many of the analytical studies and data do not unequivocally support this perception. In order to shed some light on the issue of property tax regressivity, the following discussion will consider on both theoretical and empirical grounds the question who pays the property tax.

Although the legal incidence of the property tax is on the owners of real property, our emphasis in this chapter, as elsewhere, is on economic incidence. With any tax, there is an incentive to avoid tax liability either by attempting to shift the tax burden to another economic agent or by shifting resources into other activities. In the case of the property tax, the owner of a rental property might attempt to shift the tax to his tenants, or the owner of a commercial or industrial property might attempt to shift the tax to consumers or to his employees. Of particular interest is the case in which property tax liability differs across jurisdictions. In this instance, other things being equal, there is an incentive to relocate to jurisdictions where the liability is less.

## In Theory

Changes in the residential property tax on owner-occupied housing will, in the short run, be borne by the owner. In the long run, however, if the tax causes the imputed net return to home ownership to fall relative to the return to other assets, homeowners will have an incentive to reduce investment in housing (for example, by reducing the level of maintenance) in favour of investment in other assets. The result will be a reduction in the net return on those other assets. Hence, some portion of the burden of the tax will be borne by all asset owners in the economy.

In the case of rental properties, landlords have an incentive to pass on changes in the residential property tax to tenants. The extent to which they are able to do this will depend on market forces (demand and supply) in the rental property market. Given a model in which the supply of capital to the housing sector is perfectly mobile and the supply of capital to land is fixed, it is generally accepted that the burden on landlords will be approximated by the amount of tax attributable to the land component in housing and that the burden on tenants will be approximated by the amount of tax attributable to the capital component in housing. Indeed, this is the essence of what has come to be known as the "traditional" view of the incidence of the property tax.[28] In the past, when capital's share in housing was thought to be

---

[28] For a more detailed discussion of both the "traditional" and "new" views of property tax incidence, see Richard M. Bird, "The Incidence of the Property Tax: Old Wine in New Bottles?" (1976), supplement *Canadian Public Policy* 323-34; Bird and Slack, supra footnote 19, at chapters 4 and 5; Henry J. Aaron, *Who Pays the Property Tax: A New View*, Studies of Government Finance (Washington, DC: Brookings Institution, 1975); Peter Mieszkowski and

(The footnote is continued on the next page.)

relatively large, this view led to the conclusion that the residential property tax was borne largely by tenants. Rapid inflation in land values in the middle and late 1980s is thought to have increased the share of the property tax burden borne by landlords. We shall demonstrate this point more fully below.

There is also an incentive to shift the burden of the non-residential property tax. Although the tax is imposed on the owners of property (in the case of the general property tax) and on tenants (in the case of the business occupancy tax, where it exists), its economic incidence may fall on one or more of the following: consumers, landowners, capital owners, and labour. The extent to which the tax is borne by each of these groups depends either on market conditions or on the mobility of land, labour, and capital. Thus the amount by which the non-residential property tax is shifted forward to consumers depends on market conditions. If commodity prices are set in world markets, it is unlikely that the tax can be shifted forward into higher commodity prices. If firms in a particular jurisdiction have some control over commodity prices, some of the tax may be shifted to consumers. Indeed, if the product or service that is being produced is exported outside the jurisdiction, consumers in other jurisdictions may also bear part of the tax. This is the problem of tax exporting, which we shall discuss below.

Let us assume for the moment that the tax is not shifted forward to the price of goods or services but that it is instead shifted back to the factors of production. The extent to which these factors bear the tax depends on their mobility—that is, their ability to avoid the tax by moving from one taxing jurisdiction to another. Thus, the degree to which the non-residential property tax is borne by capital depends on capital mobility. The mobility of capital is different, however, for different uses of non-residential property. Where there are *agglomeration economies*, or economies that result from locating near to similar activities (as there might be in the case of a trendy shopping area or the financial district of a major city), capital is relatively immobile and the tax is borne, at least to some extent, by capital owners.

The ability of businesses to shift the non-residential property tax onto labour depends on the structure of labour markets and the mobility of workers into and out of the market. It is generally believed that labour is less mobile[29] than capital, since workers who change jobs often change their

---

[28] Continued ...

George R. Zodrow, "Taxation and the Tiebout Model: The Differential Effects of Head Taxes, Taxes on Land Rents, and Property Taxes" (September 1989), 27 *Journal of Economic Literature* 1098-1146; and Kitchen, supra footnote 2, at chapter 3.

[29] A review of labour supply elasticities by Bev Dahlby, "Payroll Taxes," in Allan M. Maslove, ed., *Business Taxation in Ontario* (Toronto: University of Toronto Press in cooperation with the Ontario Fair Tax Commission, 1993), 80-170, concluded that the supply of labour is fairly inelastic. In other words, individuals' response to a change in the net wage rate is very low. Further, workers are probably more mobile within jurisdictions (for example, within a metropolitan area) than between jurisdictions, since the costs of moving within a jurisdiction are lower.

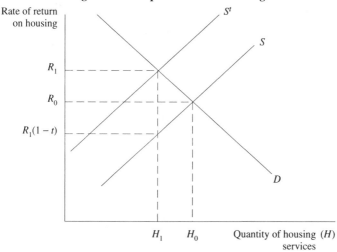

**Figure 7.1    Impact of Tax on Housing**

places of residence as well. The costs of moving (both financial and psychological) are not a factor for investors in capital.

The degree to which landowners bear the non-residential property tax depends on the supply elasticity of land. Although the supply of land in total is fixed, the supply of land in urban use or land available for specific uses may not be fixed. Further, if the property tax is borne by landowners, it is capitalized into lower property values.

The point thus far is that one can expect property taxes to affect both commodity prices (housing rentals and the prices of goods and services where real property services are an input in production) and factor returns. The "traditional" view of the property tax emphasizes the commodity price effect, whereas the "new" view of the property tax emphasizes the factor returns effect.

These general arguments may be understood in the context of simple supply-demand analysis. In figure 7.1, curve $D$ represents the demand for housing services and curve $S$ represents the supply of housing services. The vertical axis measures the annual rate of return on housing services, $R$, and the horizontal axis measures the quantity of housing services, $H$. In the absence of taxes, the equilibrium quantity and equilibrium rent are given, respectively, by $H_0$ and $R_0$. The imposition of a tax at rate $t$ increases the cost of supplying housing services by the amount of tax and therefore shifts the supply curve up to $S^t$. Equilibrium is re-established at gross rent $R_1$ and quantity $H_1$. The corresponding net rent (rent net of property taxes accruing to the landlord) is $R_1(1 - t)$. The amount of tax per unit at quantity $H_1$ is given by the difference between gross and net rents; since the gross rent paid by tenants has risen (but by less than the amount of tax liability) and the net rent received by landlords has fallen (but also by less than the amount of tax liability), the burden is said to be split between tenants and landlords.

Now, to the extent that the value of housing services supplied is derived from the services of capital and land embodied in housing, the amount of the burden of property taxation that is borne by landlords must ultimately rest on land or capital. Since housing capital is relatively mobile in the long run, this burden will tend to rest on land.

Thus the "traditional" view of property tax incidence. The logic of the "new" view[30] is easily demonstrated. A tax on land and structures will be fully borne by owners of the taxed factors if these factors have no alternative use. In that case, the tax will have no effect on commodity prices. Alternatively, in an economy that consists of a large number of independent taxing jurisdictions and in which capital is mobile between jurisdictions, capital does have an alternative use if the tax change occurs in a single jurisdiction. If, however, all jurisdictions simultaneously increase property taxes by the same proportion, the tax increase (as it relates to structures) cannot be escaped simply by relocating.

Consider a situation in which property taxes are levied in each of three independent tax jurisdictions of the same size. A condition of equilibrium is that the net return to capital will be equalized across jurisdictions as a consequence of capital mobility. Suppose that initially the net return to capital is 10 percent. Now suppose that jurisdictions $A$, $B$, and $C$ levy property taxes at 2, 3, and 4 percent respectively, so that the average rate of tax across jurisdictions is 3 percent. As a result, capital moves from jurisdictions $C$ and $B$ to the low-tax jurisdiction, $A$. Because the return to capital tends to diminish as the supply increases, this movement drives down the return to capital in the receiving jurisdiction and drives it up in the jurisdictions from which the capital has flowed. The flow of capital ceases when the net return is again equal across jurisdictions. In the new equilibrium, the gross returns are 9, 10, and 11 percent in $A$, $B$, and $C$ respectively, and the common net return to capital is 7 percent, that is, the net return has fallen by the average rate of tax across jurisdictions. To the extent that the gross return to capital has fallen in $A$, output prices fall in $A$. To the extent that the gross return to capital has risen in $C$, output prices rise in $C$. These "excise" effects on prices, however, cancel across jurisdictions, leaving just the "factor return" effect. Thus differential rates of property tax across jurisdictions can give rise to excise-type effects, but when the economy-wide effects of the tax are taken into account just the effect on factor returns remains.

The fundamental contribution of the "new" view, then, is the recognition that property tax changes, even in just one jurisdiction, will have an impact

---

[30] The proponents of the "new" view have borrowed a model of corporate tax incidence and applied it to the analysis of property taxes. For a discussion of this model and its assumptions, see chapter 4.

throughout the economy. Because differences in property taxes across jurisdictions cause interjurisdictional flows of mobile capital, changes in the tax will affect both prices and the return to capital, but the excise-type price effects will cancel across jurisdictions and only the capital-tax effect will remain.[31] This fundamental shift in the view of the property tax as another form of capital tax rather than as an excise tax has caused a reassessment of the perceived regressivity and efficiency effects of the property tax.

No matter what the effect of property taxation on the return to capital, there remains its effect on the return to immobile land. To repeat a point made earlier: the return to land will fall by the amount of the increase in tax liability. Since in recent years the share of land in housing may have increased relative to the share of capital, it is all the more important not to ignore the portion of tax that is attributable to land.

The "traditional" view, again, maintains that the burden of changes in property taxes will be borne by consumers of the services of property. This shifting assumption, combined with the fact that the share of income spent on housing varies inversely with income, has led to the conclusion that the property tax is a regressive tax—and that violates the principle of vertical equity in terms of ability to pay. The property tax is also seen as being particularly burdensome for elderly homeowners, whose current income may be insufficient to meet property tax payments. It has been shown, however, that even if the underlying shifting assumption is correct existing property tax credits, grants, and exemptions (which we shall discuss below) have done much to reduce the regressivity associated with this tax.[32]

Under the "new" view of the property tax as another form of capital tax (a tax borne by the owners of capital in the economy as a whole and by landowners), the incidence conclusion is reversed. Since capital (and land) ownership is more heavily concentrated among high-income groups than among low-income groups, the property tax may be less regressive than it is generally thought to be.

It is apparent from the foregoing discussion that the theoretical literature on the incidence of the property tax is based on a number of critical assumptions. The question is whether the assumptions accord with reality. For example, it may be incorrect to assume that capital is perfectly mobile. Ballentine and Thirsk suggested that the existence of international tax treaties makes capital less mobile internationally than the literature on property tax supposes it to be.[33] They concluded, accordingly, that a countrywide increase in Canadian property taxes would probably be borne by property owners in

---

[31] The gross return to capital is the annual rental income obtainable on a unit of capital. Correspondingly, the net return is the return net of tax liability.

[32] Peter Chinloy, "Effective Property Taxes and Tax Capitalization" (November 1978), 11 *The Canadian Journal of Economics* 740-50.

[33] J. Gregory Ballentine and Wayne R. Thirsk, *The Fiscal Incidence of Some Experiments in Fiscal Federalism: Technical Report* (Ottawa: Supply and Services, 1979).

Canada. More recent evidence, however, suggests that capital is in fact highly mobile across national borders, from which it follows that a country-wide increase in property taxes might be borne by capital owners beyond Canadian borders.

The assumption that the supply of land is fixed is also not entirely accurate, since landfill operations have proved that there is some elasticity here. Finally, the assumption that product and factor markets are perfectly competitive, so that factors of production receive payments equal to the value of their marginal product, is unlikely to accord with reality.

## In Practice

Evidence on property tax incidence falls into two categories: evidence based on aggregate data and evidence based on household data.

Studies that rely on aggregate data must make a number of assumptions about the allocation of the property tax among taxpayers across income groups. For example, if one accepts the "traditional" view of tax incidence, one assumes that the portion of the tax that falls on land is borne by landowners and that the portion of the tax that falls on improvements is borne by those who occupy the buildings. Given these assumptions, one estimates what portion of total tax revenue from non-farm residential property is generated from owner-occupied buildings and what portion is generated from rented structures (generally, a 67-33 percent split is assumed), and also what portion is a tax on land and what portion is a tax on improvements (generally, a 25-75 percent split is assumed).[34] One uses this information to generate, various series with a view to distributing types and amounts of income, and also rent payments, rental income, and the value of owner-occupied dwellings, across income classes. One then allocates the total tax payment by means of some proxy measure. In the case of homeowners, for example, the payment is determined on the basis of the home's market value. Finally, one calculates property tax as a percentage of income. The numerous assumptions, approximations, and generalizations implicit in this process should be apparent.

An examination of the results of a variety of models that use aggregate data generates the following observations.[35] All the studies suggest that the property tax is regressive at the lower level of the income scale. Under the strictest traditional assumptions, the tax is regressive for all income classes. If some of these assumptions are modified, the incidence pattern that becomes roughly proportional or slightly progressive as income increases. Models that use the "new" view and the general equilibrium models suggest that the property tax is more progressive at the upper end of the income scale. Because individuals in the higher- and lower-income groups receive proportionately more of their income in the form of capital income than do indi-

---

[34] Bird and Slack, supra footnote 19, at 62.

[35] Ibid.; and Ballentine and Thirsk, supra footnote 33, at 203.

viduals in the middle-income groups, the latter models generate a U-shaped incidence profile. The different studies ascribe different depths to the trough of the U-shaped incidence profile, but they all agree about the shape of the profile itself.[36]

What conclusions can one draw from the evidence cited? Unfortunately, none that are very useful. Whalley, in testing the robustness of these study results, found that he was able to make the property tax either more or less regressive simply by changing the shifting assumptions.[37] In fact, the most noticeable shortcoming of the incidence studies based on aggregate data is that they really do nothing to prove the validity of their assumptions. They merely illustrate what the distribution of the tax burden would be if the assumptions were true.[38]

Nor is this the only deficiency of these incidence studies. Aggregate data can yield only aggregate results: its use conceals any variation in incidence across individuals or areas. These studies also ignore important differences in tax administration and expenditure responsibilities among and within provinces. Finally, and not least, all of these studies use data that refers to a year some distance in the past.

Studies based on individual or family household data have also produced conflicting results. The earliest study, by Meng and Gillespie, used individual household data for 1978.[39] It employed five different shifting models in order to examine the distributional implications of property taxation in each of five regions[40] and in Canada as a whole. The shifting assumptions employed in these models were similar to those employed in the models cited above. For each model, the authors calculated average effective property tax rates for income deciles. They then compared these tax rates across annual income groups in order to determine the incidence pattern. Under the shifting assumptions corresponding to the "traditional" view, they found a property

---

[36] For further elaboration on this material, see Wayne R. Thirsk, "Political Sensitivity Versus Economic Sensibility: A Tale of Two Property Taxes," in Wayne R. Thirsk and John Whalley, eds., *Tax Policy Options in the 1980s*, Canadian Tax Paper no. 66 (Toronto: Canadian Tax Foundation, 1982), 384-401.

[37] John Whalley, "Regression or Progression: The Taxing Question of Incidence Analysis" (November 1984), 17 *Canadian Journal of Economics* 654-82.

[38] For an excellent summary of the assumptions used in the tax-incidence literature and how they affect the conclusions derived, see B.G. Dahlby, "The Incidence of Government Expenditures and Taxes in Canada: A Survey," in François Vaillancourt, research coordinator, *Income Distribution and Economic Security in Canada*, Collected Research Studies of the Royal Commission on Economic Union and Development Prospects for Canada, vol. 1 (Toronto: University of Toronto Press, 1985), 111-51.

[39] Ronald Meng and W. Irwin Gillespie, "The Regressivity of Property Taxes in Canada: Another Look" (1986), vol. 34, no. 6 *Canadian Tax Journal* 1417-30. The data were taken from Statistics Canada, *Family Expenditures in Canada*, vol. 3, *All Canada: Urban and Rural, 1978*, catalogue no. 62-551.

[40] Atlantic Canada, Quebec, Ontario, the Prairies, and British Columbia constitute the regions studied.

tax incidence pattern for Canada and its regions that was regressive over the lowest income deciles but more or less proportional over the middle and higher income deciles. Under the shifting assumptions associated with the "new" view, however, they found the incidence of property taxes to be mildly progressive over the lowest income deciles, more or less proportional over the middle income deciles, and progressive over the highest income deciles. In addition, this study is the only published Canadian study that has measured the variation in effective property tax rates within each income decile. This variation is one measure of the horizontal equity of the tax. In general, the results indicate that the variance in average property tax rates decreases as income increases.

Another study matched Ontario Ministry of Revenue data for household property tax liability with household income data obtained from a telephone survey of residents of the City of Toronto. This study analyzed the impact of a property tax change by income class and found the change to be progressive on average.[41]

A third study, completed by the Fair Tax Commission in Ontario, concluded that when property taxes are taken as a percentage of household income, their incidence pattern is regressive.[42] The study obtained its results by dividing household property tax liability by household income for one specific year in two municipalities (Pickering and Etobicoke). The results are similar to those of other studies that use the same methodology.

More recently, two simulation studies that used similar methodologies but individual family data for two different years (1986 and 1988) arrived at different conclusions about the incidence of the property tax. The 1986 study concluded that property taxes were regressive over the income scale,[43] whereas the 1988 study noted that property taxes were roughly proportional over the same income scale.[44] The two studies arrived at different conclusions for two reasons: first, they used different measures of family income; second, they used different assumptions in estimating the amount of tax shifted to consumption because of the indexing of government transfers.

Finally, we have conducted our own analysis of property tax incidence. Specifically we have used data from Statistic Canada's 1992 "Survey of Family Expenditure"[45] to evaluate the incidence of property taxes on the

---

[41] The study was completed by Environics Inc. for the City of Toronto in 1988.

[42] *Fair Taxation in a Changing World*, supra footnote 9, at 642-54.

[43] G.C. Ruggeri, D. Van Wart, and R. Howard, "The Redistributional Impact of Taxatoin in Canada" (1994), vol. 42, no. 2 *Canadian Tax Journal* 417-51.

[44] Frank Vermaeten, W. Irwin Gillespie, and Arndt Vermaeten, "Tax Incidence in Canada" (1994), vol. 42, no. 2 *Canadian Tax Journal* 348-416.

[45] Information drawn from the data tape includes annual family income (that is, all wages, rents, interest, dividends, profits from unincorporated business, pension income, government transfers, and other miscellaneous money receipts such as lotteries, bequests, lump-sum settlements,

(The footnote is continued on the next page.)

owners of owner-occupied dwellings.[46] Our analysis excludes renters, since property tax information is not available for this group. In fact, separating the tax on homeowners from the tax on renters has the advantage of clearly distinguishing the burden on owner-occupiers from the burden on renters. This distinction, although it has not been made in previous studies, is an important one, since the two burdens are likely to generate different affects.[47] We also omit farm properties, since the assessment-to-sales ratios used in assessing these properties are significantly different from those used in assessing residential non-farm properties.[48] Data limitations also prevent any analysis on the commercial and industrial sector.

If one measures annual property taxes[49] as a percentage of annual family income,[50] one obtains a comprehensive rather than a marginal view of incidence. This approach, in other words, considers the incidence of the existing tax burden, rather than the effect on incidence of a change in the tax.[51] Table 7.4 reports our results for all of Canada and for each province for 1992.[52] The table records the property tax as a percentage of gross annual family income, on average, for all owner-occupied dwellings within each income decile and each province. The figures suggest that if one uses annual family income as the index of equality the property tax is definitely

---

[45] Continued ...

and so forth received by all family members), the market value of owner-occupied property, homeowner's equity, and other socioeconomic and demographic characteristics as required.

[46] This includes homeowners who reported paying property tax for the entire year on the same principle residence.

[47] See D.A.L. Auld and Frank C. Miller, *Principles of Public Finance: A Canadian Text*, 2d ed. (Toronto: Methuen, 1982), 218; and Bird and Slack, supra footnote 19, at 58.

[48] See Kitchen, supra footnote 2, at chapter 2.

[49] "Property taxes" include taxes on special assessments. They exclude property tax relief schemes such as tax credits applied against income tax liability (as in Ontario, for example) or cash grants offered independently of the property tax bill (homeowner's grants, for example), since that information is not available in the data.

[50] Since expenditures on housing are a joint decision of both spouses, annual family income is the income concept employed. A potential weakness, however, of using one year's money income is that it may not generate the best measure of the real impact of the tax. It has been suggested that one can obtain a better indication of relative tax burdens by calculating the tax as a percentage of permanent income. Unfortunately, a reliable measure of permanent income cannot be obtained from the available data (one-year, cross-sectional information). A further problem—one more serious than most proponents of the "permanent income" concept recognize—is that property taxes, like most other annual expenditure obligations, must be paid annually. Thus the use of money income may not be inferior to the use of permanent income in this case.

[51] For a defence of the usefulness of viewing the incidence question in this manner, see W. Irwin Gillespie, "Taxes, Expenditures and the Redistribution of Income in Canada, 1951-1977," in *Reflections on Canadian Incomes*, selected papers presented at the Conference on Canadian Incomes, sponsored by the Economic Council of Canada, Winnipeg, May 10-12, 1979 (Ottawa: Supply and Services, 1980), 27-50.

[52] See Harry M. Kitchen, "Property Taxation as a Tax on Wealth: Some New Evidence" (1987), vol. 35, no. 4 *Canadian Tax Journal* 953-63 for 1982 results; and Kitchen, supra footnote 2, at 60-61 for 1986 results.

**Table 7.4 Property Tax as a Percentage of Gross Family Income by Income Decile and Province, 1992**

| Gross family income (deciles) | New-found-land | Prince Edward Island | Nova Scotia | New Brunswick | Quebec | Ontario | Manitoba | Sas-katch-ewan | Alberta | British Columbia | Canada |
|---|---|---|---|---|---|---|---|---|---|---|---|
| | | | | | | *percent* | | | | | |
| First | 2.26 | 10.16 | 5.69 | 3.95 | 9.08 | 12.34 | 7.62 | 8.62 | 8.45 | 12.55 | 8.66 |
| Second | 2.17 | 3.84 | 3.36 | 3.19 | 6.03 | 6.04 | 5.82 | 5.18 | 3.60 | 4.60 | 4.79 |
| Third | 1.67 | 3.22 | 3.16 | 2.43 | 4.69 | 5.17 | 4.14 | 4.47 | 3.79 | 4.66 | 4.01 |
| Fourth | 1.33 | 2.27 | 2.14 | 1.66 | 3.75 | 4.00 | 3.28 | 3.35 | 3.31 | 3.91 | 3.36 |
| Fifth | 1.08 | 1.89 | 2.05 | 1.55 | 3.47 | 3.54 | 3.38 | 3.19 | 2.75 | 2.81 | 2.92 |
| Sixth | 1.10 | 2.22 | 1.71 | 1.84 | 3.47 | 3.19 | 3.29 | 3.44 | 2.25 | 2.86 | 2.80 |
| Seventh | 1.12 | 2.01 | 1.97 | 1.46 | 2.82 | 2.94 | 2.94 | 2.59 | 2.31 | 2.25 | 2.43 |
| Eighth | 1.23 | 2.45 | 1.71 | 1.34 | 2.70 | 2.83 | 3.18 | 2.80 | 2.59 | 2.23 | 2.41 |
| Ninth | 1.27 | 1.60 | 1.71 | 1.21 | 2.32 | 2.32 | 2.44 | 2.37 | 1.98 | 2.16 | 2.26 |
| Tenth | 0.79 | 2.10 | 1.64 | 1.12 | 2.20 | 2.25 | 1.86 | 2.24 | 1.71 | 1.58 | 1.92 |

Sources: Calculated from data in Statistics Canada, "1992 Survey of Family Expenditure" (microdata set, Ottawa, 1995) and reported in Chris Cairns, "Who Pays the Residential Property Tax?" (honours essay, Trent University, Economics Department, Peterborough, Ont. 1998).

regressive especially in Ontario and British Columbia. Furthermore, the regressivity tends to be greatest over the lower income deciles.

Since most previous studies used more than one income concept in testing for regressivity, we also calculated property taxes as a percentage of a broad income base,[53] defined as family income plus imputed rent calculated as 8 percent of homeowner's equity[54] plus the value of gifts received and the value of home grown-food and fuel. We do not report the results here, since they are essentially the same as those in table 7.4.[55] The tax burden is somewhat smaller for all income deciles if one uses the broad income measure rather than gross family income, but the difference is not statistically significant (using a difference of means test) for any income decile.

Like the studies that use aggregate data, studies that use household data must be treated with caution. The difficulty in this case is that most of the studies do not take into consideration the age, wealth, or other important characteristics of households. For example, evidence on income distribution from Statistics Canada suggests that lower-income households tend to be dominated by young adults and the elderly. Young adults who are in the early stages of their income-earning careers, but who have expectations for higher incomes in the future, are likely to be housed in accommodation that reflects their expected income rather than their current income. If one were to estimate their property taxes as a proportion of future expected income, or on the basis of some measure of permanent or lifetime income, the incidence pattern would almost certainly be very different from the pattern that emerges from the usual simplified analysis. In the case of the elderly, the other group that dominates the low-income sector, the calculation of property taxes as a percentage of market value may not be a true reflection of ability to pay, since many elderly people are asset-rich but income-poor. The difficulty, of course, is that wealth held in the form of property cannot readily be used to pay property taxes. Fortunately, as we shall discuss below, there are a variety of municipal and provincial programs available for alleviating the property tax burden on low-income households.

The existing studies—both those that use aggregate data and those that use household data—may also have a more serious and fundamental shortcoming. All of these studies determine the pattern of incidence by measuring property taxes as a percentage of some definition of income (annual money income, income adjusted to reflect government expenditure and taxation policies, and so forth). As M. Mason Gaffney has observed, however, to use income as the index of equality implies that one is judging the "property tax

---

[53] This is an attempt to approximate more closely the income concept used in aggregate data studies and hence to see how the results here compare with those in other studies.

[54] This percentage was suggested by Michael C. Wolfson, "Wealth and Distribution of Income in Canada, 1969-1970" (June 1979), 25 *The Review of Income and Wealth* 129-40.

[55] See Chris Cairns, "Who Pays the Residential Property Tax?" (honours essay, Trent University, Economics Department, Peterborough, Ontario, 1998).

on the basis of how closely it resembles the income tax, in every detail. Since nothing resembles the income tax so much as the income tax, the property tax looks inferior."[56]

Given the doubtful rationale for using income as the base for measuring regressivity, it is more fruitful to discuss the incidence of the property tax as a percentage of either the owner's equity in the property (market value minus outstanding debt) or the property's market value. Thus one might argue that if the property tax is not intended to be a set of user charges it ought to be designed as a tax on wealth, one that uses the owner's equity as a proxy for wealth. Alternatively, one might argue that the appropriate measure of the incidence of the property tax would be property taxes as a percentage of market value, since in practice property taxes are based on assessed values, which are in turn related to market values. Consequently, variation in property taxes as a percentage of market value across or within jurisdictions will reflect variation in the effective tax rate.

Table 7.5 shows property tax as a percentage of homeowner's equity (market value minus outstanding mortgage) across income deciles in each province. Roughly speaking, the pattern of incidence in this table is an inversion of the U-shaped pattern in table 7.4: in Canada as a whole, property taxes as a percentage of owner's equity tend to be lower for low- and high-income families than for middle-income families.

If one calculates property taxes as a percentage of market value, it is possible to observe the extent to which effective tax rates on owner-occupied homes vary within and across provinces. If this variation is caused by differences in the level of government services provided, then communities that provide relatively few services ought to face relatively low effective tax rates. Comparisons of effective tax rates across provinces, however, must be treated cautiously since different provinces use property taxes to fund different services; thus Ontario, for example, makes more use of property taxes than the other provinces do to fund elementary and secondary education. A comparison of effective tax rates across all municipalities within a province may have more legitimacy, since municipalities within a province, by and large, use property taxes to fund similar services.

Table 7.6 shows property taxes as percentages of market value by province and income decile. What is important here is the extent to which the percentages vary or do not vary across income groups within each province. Where the percentages across all income groups within a province are constant, one can assume that assessment practices are uniform; that is, all owner-occupied residences are taxed at the same percentage of market value. The data indicate a high degree of uniformity across income deciles within each province.

---

[56] M. Mason Gaffney, "The Property Tax Is a Progressive Tax," in *Proceedings of the Sixty-Fourth Annual Conference on Taxation*, National Tax Association, 1971 (Columbus, Ohio: NTA, 1972), 408-31, at 423.

**Table 7.5 Property Tax as a Percentage of Homeowner's Equity by Income Decile and Province, 1992**

| Gross family income (deciles) | Newfoundland | Prince Edward Island | Nova Scotia | New Brunswick | Quebec | Ontario | Manitoba | Saskatchewan | Alberta | British Columbia | Canada |
|---|---|---|---|---|---|---|---|---|---|---|---|
| | | | | | | *percent* | | | | | |
| First . . . . . . . . . | 0.79 | 1.77 | 1.75 | 1.15 | 1.93 | 1.44 | 1.51 | 2.20 | 1.26 | 0.99 | 1.47 |
| Second . . . . . . . | 0.85 | 1.50 | 1.23 | 1.30 | 2.16 | 2.19 | 2.32 | 2.96 | 1.59 | 0.90 | 3.21 |
| Third . . . . . . . . | 0.25 | 1.49 | 1.54 | 2.71 | 2.76 | 2.40 | 2.08 | 3.31 | 4.66 | 1.05 | 2.42 |
| Fourth . . . . . . . | 0.94 | 1.46 | 1.70 | 1.71 | 7.28 | 2.31 | 4.14 | 6.42 | 1.99 | 1.30 | 3.21 |
| Fifth . . . . . . . . | 1.44 | 1.85 | 2.17 | 1.96 | 2.66 | 2.67 | 2.14 | 2.74 | 2.05 | 1.30 | 4.85 |
| Sixth . . . . . . . . | 0.77 | 3.43 | 2.57 | 1.97 | 3.44 | 2.59 | 4.71 | 4.66 | 2.17 | 1.36 | 2.37 |
| Seventh . . . . . . | 0.69 | 2.02 | 2.41 | 1.65 | 3.26 | 6.92 | 3.18 | 2.57 | 2.25 | 1.69 | 3.70 |
| Eighth . . . . . . . | 0.14 | 2.38 | 2.35 | 1.51 | 3.20 | 1.80 | 4.78 | 6.50 | 2.99 | 1.37 | 3.58 |
| Ninth . . . . . . . . | 1.24 | 1.86 | 2.10 | 1.64 | 3.68 | 2.82 | 4.13 | 3.67 | 1.86 | 1.47 | 2.12 |
| Tenth . . . . . . . . | 1.24 | 1.61 | 2.04 | 1.72 | 2.29 | 2.03 | 3.01 | 3.69 | 1.74 | 1.06 | 2.08 |

Sources: Same as table 7.4.

Table 7.6  Property Tax as a Percentage of Market Value of the Home by Income Decile and Province, 1992

| Gross family income (deciles) | New-found-land | Prince Edward Island | Nova Scotia | New Brunswick | Quebec | Ontario | Manitoba | Sas-katch-ewan | Alberta | British Columbia | Canada |
|---|---|---|---|---|---|---|---|---|---|---|---|
| | | | | | | *percent* | | | | | |
| First . . . . . . . . . . | 0.79 | 1.20 | 1.16 | 0.83 | 1.79 | 1.33 | 1.42 | 1.95 | 1.06 | 0.96 | 1.30 |
| Second . . . . . . . . . | 0.70 | 1.05 | 1.05 | 1.03 | 1.59 | 1.24 | 1.70 | 2.01 | 1.06 | 0.78 | 1.29 |
| Third . . . . . . . . . | 0.70 | 1.06 | 1.22 | 0.93 | 1.59 | 1.30 | 1.64 | 1.91 | 1.65 | 0.90 | 1.30 |
| Fourth . . . . . . . . | 0.65 | 1.08 | 1.06 | 0.97 | 1.78 | 1.64 | 1.64 | 2.03 | 1.19 | 1.02 | 1.36 |
| Fifth . . . . . . . . | 0.70 | 1.01 | 1.20 | 0.85 | 1.71 | 1.28 | 1.91 | 2.02 | 1.22 | 0.94 | 1.34 |
| Sixth . . . . . . . | 0.63 | 1.28 | 1.13 | 0.99 | 1.86 | 1.27 | 1.88 | 2.02 | 1.20 | 0.91 | 1.38 |
| Seventh . . . . . . | 0.75 | 1.19 | 1.29 | 0.96 | 1.83 | 1.26 | 2.00 | 1.97 | 1.19 | 0.79 | 1.40 |
| Eighth . . . . . . | 1.00 | 1.27 | 1.14 | 1.01 | 1.74 | 1.31 | 2.21 | 2.22 | 1.48 | 0.78 | 1.35 |
| Ninth . . . . . . . | 0.77 | 1.03 | 1.40 | 0.97 | 1.78 | 1.22 | 1.90 | 1.85 | 1.21 | 0.84 | 1.36 |
| Tenth . . . . . . . | 0.68 | 1.18 | 1.17 | 1.03 | 1.72 | 1.18 | 1.76 | 2.23 | 1.10 | 0.69 | 1.26 |

Sources: Same as table 7.4.

## Property Tax Relief

There are really two kinds of property tax relief—indirect and direct. Municipalities in many provinces grant indirect relief to residential properties by using split or differential mill (tax) rates to assign rates to residential properties that are lower than those on non-residential properties. In other instances, municipalities or provinces exempt specific types of property from assessment of taxation, or assess them at less than normal rates, or tax them at statutory rates of assessment that may not generate a level of revenue comparable to the level generated by other assessments. As well, the federal government and provincial governments and Crown agencies pay grants in lieu of taxes[57] on Crown properties that may be less than full or partial property taxes. The situation varies greatly among the provinces.

Every province also provides some direct property tax relief programs for individual taxpayers, and it is these relief payments that we shall consider here. Individual tax relief schemes vary considerably across Canada.[58] Provincial programs range from grants to exemptions to tax credits to deferrals. In addition, the municipalities in most provinces have jurisdictional power to enact relief schemes for poverty-stricken taxpayers. These schemes include reductions, cancellations, and refunds of property taxes. One must be cautious, however, in comparing the use of these programs across provinces. The extent of property tax relief depends largely on the extent of municipal government responsibility for expenditure and the extent to which local government services, including education, are funded by property taxes. The more important property taxes are as a revenue generator, the more extensively tax relief schemes are likely to be used.

Although the primary objective of property tax relief is to reduce the burden of property taxes on residential taxpayers in specific circumstances, it must be asked whether there is any basis for granting tax relief solely in order to offset property taxes. To be specific, if the residential property tax is not regressive, there is no reason to provide relief in order to reduce its regressivity. Furthermore, if the property tax is considered to be a tax on a component of wealth (namely, property values), there is little justification for granting relief from the tax on the basis of the taxpayer's income. Under these circumstances, arguments in favour of property tax relief are of no more relevance than arguments in favour of relief for any other tax. A single tax-relief scheme based on ability to pay and implemented by the province or the federal government might achieve greater overall equity in the tax system than any number of separate federal, provincial, and local government schemes.

---

[57] For a detailed discussion of grants in lieu of property taxes, see Kitchen, supra footnote 2, at chapter 7.

[58] For a fuller explanation of property tax relief schemes in each province, see Karin Treff and David B. Perry, *Finances of the Nation 1997* (Toronto: Canadian Tax Foundation, 1997), 6:13-15; and Kitchen, supra footnote 2, at chapter 6.

Here, however, we shall ignore the question whether property tax relief ought to be provided in the first instance and concentrate on specific property tax relief schemes, actual and proposed.

## Property Tax Credits

Five provinces, Quebec, Ontario, Manitoba, Alberta, and British Columbia, provide a property tax credit as a means of alleviating the alleged regressivity of the property tax. The value of the credit—which the federal government administers for the provinces, except Quebec—varies inversely with personal income tax liability; that is, as income tax liability increases, the value of the credit, which is subtracted from personal income taxes payable, declines.

One comprehensive analysis of the Ontario refundable property tax credit program suggests that the property tax credit is progressive in its impact on taxpayers; that is, it provides relatively greater benefits to low-income households than to high-income households.[59] A study completed for the Fair Tax Commission in Ontario reached a similar conclusion.[60] Although property tax credits are likely to be progressive, especially if they are refundable,[61] the existing credit schemes are not without shortcomings. For one thing, residents pay their property taxes during the year, yet they do not receive the tax credit until after they have filed their income tax returns on or before April 30 of the following year. The relatively long wait between payment of property taxes and receipt of the tax credit can create liquidity problems for income-poor taxpayers.

Another problem is that the definition of income used to determine eligibility for the credit may not accurately measure ability to pay. At the moment, income (as defined by the federal government) excludes some deductions such as contributions to registered retirement savings plans (RRSPs) that arguably should be included in any measure of ability to pay that is used to determine eligibility.[62]

Given the prevailing uncertainty about the regressivity of the property tax, it would be more appropriate to analyze the property tax credit as part of the general income-transfer program in the province then as a credit specifically designed to offset property tax liability. Indeed, it is unlikely that many taxpayers see any link between property taxes paid and the ensuing tax credit. After all, the credit for property taxes paid in one year is not available until the income tax return is filed in the following year. Furthermore, except in

---

[59] Bird and Slack, supra footnote 19.

[60] *Fair Taxation in a Changing World*, supra footnote 9, at 644.

[61] If a tax credit exceeds tax liability and the government reimburses the taxpayer for the difference, the tax credit is refundable. If the government does not refund the difference, the credit is non-refundable.

[62] For an extensive and thorough discussion of this point, see Bird and Slack, supra footnote 19, at chapter 7.

Quebec, the credit is administered by the federal government rather than the provinces. On the other hand, if one regards the property tax credit as a component of the provincial income-transfer system, the question arises whether the credit generates the desired redistribution of income, since it is designed to provide more relief to those with more wealth (higher property values).

In summary, uncertainty over the degree of regressivity of the property tax and the tendency of the property tax credit to provide relief that varies directly with property values argues strongly in favour of eliminating the credit[63] and using other components of the provincial government's income-transfer system to improve the overall distribution of income. Indeed, the analysis of Ontario's property tax credit program referred to above concluded that it is "difficult to argue convincingly that the property tax credit system . . . has been either terribly successful or terribly needed."[64]

## Tax Deferrals

Although property-tax-deferral programs are not widely used, local governments in some provinces have the power to implement them for specific taxpayers. Some municipalities in Prince Edward Island, Nova Scotia, and Ontario have deferral programs, and a province-wide program for senior citizens and handicapped individuals operates in British Columbia.

Under a tax-deferral program, the owner of the property is permitted to defer some or all of his property taxes on an annual basis. Depending on the program, the lost revenue will be made up from provincial payments to the municipality or from general revenues of the municipality itself. The amount of the tax deferred becomes a lien against the property and is payable to the province or the municipality when the property is transferred. As well, an interest charge usually, but not always, applies to the taxes deferred.

A number of implications arise from the use of tax deferral schemes. First, if one's ability to pay taxes is measured by a combination of income and wealth, where the property tax is viewed as a proxy for a tax on wealth, then a taxpayer who is asset-rich but income-poor could use this scheme to reduce his tax burden. In fact, tax-deferral schemes can be especially useful in alleviating cash-flow problems for income-deficient taxpayers.

Second, most tax-deferral programs are available to senior citizens only. Although one may be critical of age-dependent eligibility requirements for any income-transfer scheme, it may be administratively practical to impose restrictions of this sort. Expansion of tax-deferral programs to include the non-elderly might lead to a significant increase in the number of applicants, with the result that loans (tax deferrals plus interest charges on them) would

---

[63] Some observers recommend tax credits that are inversely related to ability to pay as a means of redistributing income.

[64] Bird and Slack, supra footnote 19, at 120.

be outstanding for a much longer period of time. According to some municipal officials, expansion might be administratively complicated and costly.[65]

Although there are some solid economic arguments in favour of tax-deferral programs, relatively few taxpayers use them. In British Columbia, for example, the number of applicants, though it is increasing, has been small. Property-tax-deferral programs tend not to be popular with taxpayers because of the strong emotional attachment that the elderly have to their homes and their desire to leave them unencumbered to their heirs.[66]

### Grants

Provincial or municipal grants designed to remove some of the burden of property taxes are available to eligible homeowners or renters in some provinces. The value of the grant may vary inversely with income, and some jurisdictions restrict eligibility to the elderly or to welfare recipients. In New Brunswick, grants are the only property tax credit scheme; in Alberta and Manitoba, grants are used in conjunction with tax credits. In British Columbia and Ontario, tax credits, deferrals, and grants are all used for various purposes.

As a mechanism for transferring income, grants should be evaluated in the same way as any other component of the overall provincial income-transfer scheme. Grants have the advantage over the current property tax credit schemes of being more directly linked with the payment of, or reduction in, property tax liability. It is also easier as a rule to direct grants specifically to individuals in need, especially in smaller communities where it is relatively easy to identify hardship cases. A grant program, however, may be more difficult to administer than a tax-credit program.

### Exemptions

In Newfoundland and Nova Scotia, it is possible in certain circumstances for taxpayers to be exempted from property taxes. Exemption effectively removes the burden of funding local services from these taxpayers and shifts it to other taxpayers. In this respect, exemptions are similar to grants, reductions, cancellations, or refunds that completely offset property tax payments.

If the exemption is available only to senior citizens, it may be deficient as a tax-relief measure since it fails to consider the recipient's ability to pay taxes. Similar deficiencies may exist if the exemption is based strictly on the taxpayer's income and ignores property values.

---

[65] Enid Slack, "An Analysis of Property Tax Relief Measures and Phase-in Mechanisms," a report prepared for the Task Force on Reassessment in Metropolitan Toronto (mimeograph, Toronto, August 1989).

[66] Bird and Slack, supra footnote 19, at 98.

## Reductions, Cancellations, and Refunds

In some provinces, the municipal act allows municipalities to refund, cancel, or reduce property taxes in special cases, generally cases of poverty or illness. These programs usually apply for one year, and taxpayers are required to apply for them annually. The lost revenues are absorbed out of general municipal revenues. Little use is made of these programs. They would appear to be most appropriate for use in smaller municipalities, where it is relatively easy to identify worthy recipients.

Although tax relief for people who are deemed to have insufficient ability to pay is an important policy objective of governments, it is not clear that local-government programs of this kind are appropriate instruments for the purposes of income redistribution. Taxpayers who are not required to pay for the consumption of local services, have every incentive to demand larger quantities of these services than is allocatively efficient. Moreover, some of the beneficiaries of these programs may be asset-rich and income-poor, and it is a question whether people with significant assets should get relief from property tax payments under any circumstances.

Provincial and federal income-transfer schemes are more appropriate than are municipal programs of this kind as means of redistributing income. Tax-deferral schemes offer a better solution to the liquidity problem for asset-wealthy homeowners.

## Assessment Credits

At present, municipalities in Canada do not use assessment credits, but they have been suggested as a possible mechanism for relieving the property tax burden on residential properties.[67] An assessment credit scheme involves the removal of a fixed amount (determined by the local council) from the market-value assessment for each property.[68] Since the amount of the credit would be the same for all properties, the scheme would in effect convert the property tax into a progressive tax. Although this scheme may appear to have some merit, it would be a suspect device unless all of the properties owned by a particular individual were aggregated. The use of assessment credits would also result in a reduced assessment base overall. It would be necessary, therefore, to impose higher tax rates in order to raise an amount of property tax dollars equal to the amount that the system raised before the assessment credit was introduced. In the case of properties with relatively low assessed values, the value of the assessment exemption would offset the higher tax rates, and the owners of those properties would be better off

---

[67] For a discussion of this topic, see Metropolitan Toronto Advisory Task Force on Assessment Reform, *Report of the Sub-Committee on Implementation Mechanisms* (Toronto: the task force, October 1987).

[68] This is similar to allowing personal income tax exemptions in a personal income tax system.

financially. In the case of properties with relatively high assessed values, the higher tax rates would more than offset the value of the assessment credit, and these taxpayers would be worse off financially.

As a relief mechanism, the assessment credit, which has the same dollar value for all residential property owners, is deficient because it is based on the assessed value of property and not on the property owner's total ability to pay.[69]

## Exemptions

One problem with the real property tax is that allowable exemptions[70] have reduced the tax base. The organizations that own exempt properties sometimes make payments in lieu of property taxes, but it is frequently suggested that the payments are less than the property taxes would be if they were allowed.[71]

The exemption of certain properties from property taxation and provisions for payments in lieu of taxes that are less than the property taxes would be discriminate in favour of the organizations that own these properties. The result is a mix of land use that may be different from the mix that would exist under equal treatment of all properties. The policy of granting tax-exempt status is difficult to support. If a sound case can be made for preferential treatment of certain organizations, then these organizations should be rewarded directly by means of grants rather than on the basis of their property holdings. Subsidization should be open and should be subject to review and amendment by elected representatives according to their interpretation of the public interest.

In spite of frequent calls for the elimination of tax exemptions, public pressure and the prospect of losing a number of municipal services supplied by the tax-exempt organizations have generally resulted in recommendations for including only some of the value of the exempt properties in the tax base.[72] Virtually all suggestions for reform, however, have recommended that all exempt property be subject to assessment and that grants in lieu of taxes, if they are to continue, be equivalent to the taxes that could be collected under a uniform and equitable property tax system. Unfortunately, these recommendations have seldom been accepted.

---

[69] Slack, supra footnote 65, at 16-17.

[70] For a listing and description of exempt properties in Canada, see Kitchen, supra footnote 2, at chapter 2.

[71] For a discussion of payments in lieu of property taxes, see Kitchen, ibid., at chapter 7. For more detail on the federal grants-in-lieu program, see Harry Kitchen and François Vaillancourt, "The Impact of the Fiscal Immunity of the Federal Crown and Its Agents: The Case of Real Property Taxes," a paper prepared for the Law Reform Commission of Canada (mimeograph, Ottawa, June 1988).

[72] For a further discussion of exempt properties, see *Report of the Commission on the Reform of Property Taxation in Ontario*, supra footnote 15, at 80-83.

## Local Property Tax Exportation

The commercial/industrial sector's ability to export the burden of its property tax to residents of other municipalities is another source of misallocation of resources.[73] Tax exportation occurs when some portion of the burden of a tax is borne by non-residents, owing to changes in either relative commodity prices or the net return to foreign-owned factors of production (inputs in the production process). For example, if higher effective tax rates on non-residential (commercial and industrial) properties lead to relatively higher prices on that community's exports to other communities, the taxing jurisdiction will have effectively shifted part of its tax burden onto residents of other communities. If the non-residential tax in every jurisdiction is exported to some extent, jurisdictions that export relatively more of the tax will be better off than jurisdictions that export relatively less of it. In particular, if the burden of the tax is shifted from residents of high-income jurisdictions to residents of low-income jurisdictions, the distribution of income among jurisdictions will become less equitable. This outcome, undesirable in itself, also runs counter to provincial equalization schemes that attempt to redistribute resources (income) from relatively high-income jurisdictions to relatively low-income jurisdictions.

The limited evidence on tax exportation in Canada refers to a sample of relatively large municipalities in Ontario.[74] This evidence suggests that in 1971 the degree of exportation ranged from a low of 16 percent of the non-residential tax burden in Ottawa to highs of 106 percent for Hamilton and 104 percent for Sault Ste. Marie. What is more important, relatively rich municipalities such as Sarnia and Brampton had relatively high exportation rates (70 and 92 percent respectively), whereas relatively poor municipalities such as Cornwall and Belleville had relatively low exportation rates (35 and 31 percent respectively). Thus in Ontario at least, the exportation of the burden of the non-residential property tax does result in an implicit transfer from relatively low-income municipalities to relatively high-income municipalities.

## The Property Business Tax

Municipalities in every province maintain either a separate municipal business tax or non-residential property taxes that are levied at a higher rate than residential taxes and thus include what would otherwise be a municipal business tax. There appears to be no sound economic rationale for the general imposition of this tax. Those who favour it argue that businesses create additional demands for local services such as police, roads, fire protection, and so forth, but it has been suggested that in reality this additional tax revenue is used to finance services whose benefits accrue primarily to the residential

---

[73] Of course, a firm's ability to export will depend on the elasticity of demand for the exported product.

[74] Thirsk, supra footnote 36.

sector. Cross-subsidization of this kind can lead to an oversupply of residential services. A more allocatively efficient but politically less acceptable alternative would be to impose higher tax rates on the residential sector, if it is indeed this sector that is collectively benefiting most from these services.[75]

Since businesses can deduct all of the expenses they incur in earning income, including business taxes, and since owner-occupiers of residential dwellings are not allowed similar deductions, it has been suggested that an extra tax on business is legitimate as a means of reducing disparities in taxes between these two categories of taxable property. It is true that owner-occupiers are not able to deduct property taxes, but it is also true that owner-occupiers are not required to include imputed income from their owner-occupied dwellings (see chapter 3) or capital gains earned on the disposal of their principal residences in their taxable income.[76] These exclusions are similar to deductions from income for tax purposes (as in the case of the business tax), since they reduce the taxable economic income of the taxpaying unit. On this basis, it is difficult to make a case for a general business tax on commercial and industrial properties.

## The Property Tax as a Capital Tax

If one ignores the public services funded by property taxes and assumes that property taxes cannot be passed along to customers in the form of higher prices for goods and services produced by the non-residential sector, then one can treat the property tax as another form of tax on business income or capital. Furthermore, if there are sectors of the economy in which the property tax is more significant than other forms of capital tax, the property tax may tend to even out the overall treatment of income from capital throughout the economy and thus reduce the distortionary effects of inter-sectoral differences in the rates of other capital taxes. There is, in fact, some evidence that the property tax does perform this important role.[77]

As we noted in chapter 4, a study by the Economic Council of Canada has estimated marginal effective rates of capital taxation for Canada in 1985.[78] Marginal effective tax rates (METRs) measure the tax payable[79] as a percentage of the pretax rate of return on a prospective marginal investment project over its lifetime. Thus they provide a measure of the disincentive imposed by

---

[75] Harry M. Kitchen, *The Role for Local Government in Economic Development* (Toronto: Ontario Economic Council, 1985).

[76] For a discussion of capital gains and imputed rent on owner-occupied dwellings, see chapter 3 in this book.

[77] See Sylvester Damus, Paul Hobson, and Wayne Thirsk, *The Welfare Effects of the Property Tax in an Open Economy*, Discussion Paper no. 320 (Ottawa: Economic Council of Canada, 1987).

[78] Economic Council of Canada, *The Taxation of Savings and Investment: A Research Report Prepared for the Economic Council of Canada* (Ottawa: Economic Council of Canada, 1987), 103 and 146.

[79] Property taxes include business taxes where they exist.

the tax system to undertake particular potential investment projects. The Economic Council's estimates indicated that municipal property taxes on the non-residential sector increased the METR on buildings relative to the METR on machinery and inventories. The industries most affected by the property tax were commercial services and construction. The property tax on businesses substantially reduced significant variations in METRs across industries attributable to the corporate income tax.[80] On the other hand, inclusion of the non-residential property tax with personal, corporate, and sales taxes as another form of capital taxation slightly increased the variation in effective tax rates across industries and assets. This result suggested that the burden of the non-residential property tax in 1985 should have been smaller than it was. Finally, the Economic Council's estimates suggested that the non-residential property tax contributed more to the overall capital tax rate on the non-financial corporate sector than did either the capital tax component of sales taxation or the corporate income tax.

The Economic Council's study also examined the effects of capital taxation on the allocation of capital between the industrial sector and residential housing: the study distinguished between owner-occupied housing and rental housing, which are treated differently from one another under Canadian income tax law. The council's calculations suggested that the overall marginal effective capital tax rate on investment in owner-occupied housing in 1985 was slightly more than 21 percent. This figure was lower than the rate calculated for investment in machinery in the corporate sector (26.4 percent) and substantially lower than rates calculated for investment in buildings and inventories (49.6 percent and 43.1 percent, respectively). The marginal effective rate for rental properties was 44.7 percent.

If these results reflect reality, then the tax system provides a stronger incentive to invest in owner-occupied housing[81] than in other assets.[82] Indeed, it has been suggested that under certain conditions society would be better off if non-residential property taxes were reduced and residential property taxes were increased.[83] This result would follow from two effects. First, a reduction in property tax rates on business would reduce the amount of property tax burden exported to non-residents. Second, since capital

---

[80] For a discussion of distortions created by the corporate tax in Canada, see chapter 4 of this book.

[81] Much of the incentive exists because of the non-taxation of imputed net rental income on owner-occupied housing.

[82] There is a need to update the Economic Council's calculations in the face of income tax reform and the replacement of the federal manufacturers' sales tax with a broadly based goods and services tax that includes expenditure on new housing. The role of the property tax in this new system is far from clear, but to the extent that tax reform has reduced the variation in effective corporate tax rates it may have significantly increased the overall distortionary impact of the property tax.

[83] Damus, Hobson, and Thirsk, supra footnote 77; and Shantayanan Devarajan, Don Fullerton, and Richard A. Musgrave, "Estimating the Distribution of Tax Burdens: A Comparison of Different Approaches" (April 1980), 13 *Journal of Public Economics* 155-82.

invested in real property is, on average, taxed at higher rates than capital invested in other factors of production, reducing business property tax rates would reduce the variation in capital tax rates. On balance, the reduction in tax exportation and the decrease in the variance in tax rates would improve the allocation of resources across the Canadian economy and thus produce overall efficiency gains.[84]

## Property Tax Capitalization

Property tax capitalization refers to the effect of local government taxes and expenditures on real estate values. Consider the case of two cities that are identical in every respect (structure, demography, and provision of local public services) except one: property taxes are higher in one city than they are in the other. If citizens are aware of this property tax differential, it will be capitalized into property values; that is, property values will be lower in the city with higher taxes. As long as property tax differentials are capitalized into property values, the tax will provide no incentive to live in one community rather than another.

If the property tax were a true benefits tax designed to fund local government services, the tax price would equal the marginal benefit from the service received and there would be no incentive to move from one community to another in order to minimize the net (expenditures minus taxes) tax burden. Indeed, under this scenario, individuals who desired more public services might move to communities with higher property taxes. Since the property tax is not a true benefit tax, however, distortions may exist and citizens may choose to relocate in order to improve their net gain. Under the current system of differential assessment practices, distortions arise if the differential in property taxes for funding similar services is not capitalized into property values. Although the jury is still out on the question of the extent to which capitalization arises[85] under assessment differentials of the type that exist in Canada a study[86] based on evidence for London, Ontario found no evidence of capitalization of property tax differentials into property values. If the differentials are not capitalized, then some properties are overtaxed and some similar properties are undertaxed.

## Local Services Funded from Local Property Taxes

The property tax should be evaluated not only in terms of the distortions that it creates in its current or potential application, but also in terms of its appropriateness as a means of funding local services. For example, it has been argued on several grounds that the property tax should be used only to fund services that primarily benefit property, and that the funding of matters

---

[84] Economic Council of Canada, supra footnote 78, at 103 and 146.

[85] For a summary of the theoretical and empirical literature on capitalization of property taxes, see Mieszkowski and Zodrow, supra footnote 28.

[86] Chinloy, supra footnote 32, at 740.

such as education and social services should not be based on local taxation. First, it is argued, these services are not services to property and hence should not be funded from taxes based on property values. Second, these services are primarily redistributive and generate benefits for society as a whole. The responsibility for broad social policy properly rests with the higher levels of government; consequently, education and social services should be funded entirely by the federal government or the provinces. Third, education and social service expenditures are growing more rapidly than most other local-government expenditures. Many municipal officials argue that the local property tax base does not have the capacity to absorb the rapidly increasing costs of these services, and that their funding should be taken over by the provincial governments, which have access to more elastic revenue sources, such as income taxes and sales taxes.

These arguments have not been unpersuasive: some provincial governments have removed funding for schools or social services from the property tax base and assumed responsibility for funding these services themselves. Yet is also possible to argue the other side of the question. For one thing, it is not easy to distinguish between people-related and property-related services.[87] Are services that deal with protection, general government, roads, or the environment related to people or to property? Even if a clear sorting out of local services into these two categories were possible, all services that accrue to property—water provision, sewage disposal, roads—are ultimately for the benefit of people. After all, a service that did not benefit local residents would not get the political support necessary for its provision.[88]

For another thing, the argument that education and social services are primarily distributive and generate benefits for all of society ignores the benefits that these services convey specifically to the residents of the local community. It is common knowledge, for example, that there are both bad schools and good schools in large metropolitan areas in Canada, and properties near good schools are valued more highly by the market. Similar comments could be made about the relation between the level of social services and property values across municipalities. Since the quantity and quality of these services affect property values, it follows that a case may be made for funding them, at least in part, from local property taxes.[89]

In addition, one might argue that local governments should be able, if they wish, to maintain education and social services at levels above those mandated by the province. For some municipalities, these services are as impor-

---

[87] For an interesting discussion of these issues, see John Graham, "The Place of the Property Tax in the Fiscal System," in Lorraine Eden, ed., *Retrospectives on Public Finance* (Durham, NC: Duke University Press, 1991), 149-67.

[88] Ontario, *Report of the Royal Commission on Metropolitan Toronto*, vol. 2 (Toronto: Ontario Government Bookstore, 1977), 186.

[89] For a more detailed defence of this position, see Kitchen and Auld, supra footnote 2, at chapter 4.

tant in their effect on the quality of life of local residents as other local government services. To shift all responsibility for education and social services to the provincial government is to remove from local governments any opportunity to make decisions about them.

Finally, in spite of the perception to the contrary held by many citizens and local government officials, there is no inherent reason why the property tax should have less revenue-generating capacity than provincial taxes have. Table 7.7 indicates that property taxes increased less as a percentage of gross domestic provincial product between 1971 and 1994 than did either provincial personal income taxes or provincial retail sales taxes. This circumstance does not by itself support a case for higher property taxes, but it does suggest that the tax base could in fact sustain higher property tax rates. No doubt the high visibility of the property tax, the common perception that it is highly regressive, and concern over a possible taxpayers' revolt have discouraged local governments from using it more extensively.

## Special Charges

This section discusses three special charges that are frequently imposed on properties to pay for local infrastructure (for specific capital projects).[90] These changes are special assessments, which can be characterized as property-related specific-benefit levies; municipal bonusing, which can be characterized as a prepayment for special privileges that benefit specific properties; and development charges or lot levies, which are prepayments for benefits that accrue to specific areas within a municipality.[91]

### Special Assessments

A special assessment is a specific charge or levy added to the existing property tax on residential or commercial/industrial properties to pay for additional or improved capital facilities that border on those properties. Examples of capital projects financed in this way are the construction or reconstruction of sidewalks, the initial paving or repaving of streets, and the instalment or replacement of water mains, sanitary sewers, or storm sewers. In each instance, the abutting property is presumed to benefit from the local improvement and is expected therefore to bear a portion or all of the capital costs.

Special assessments do not as a rule contribute significant sums of revenue to local budgets, but they are nevertheless an important means of financing local improvement projects. It is usually possible to allocate the costs of these projects according to some measure of benefits received. Thus

---

[90] For a more detailed discussion of the alternatives, see Almos Tassonyi, "Financing Infrastructure in Canada's City-Regions," in *Urban Governance and Finance*, supra footnote 7, 171-200, at 185-93.

[91] Although municipal bonusing and development charges are municipal levies imposed on new development and are often unrelated to property values, we include them here because they do constitute a tax on property.

**Table 7.7  Property Tax Revenue, Provincial Personal Income Tax Revenue, and Retail Sales Tax Revenue as Percentages of GDPP, 1971 and 1994**

| | 1971 | | | 1994 | | |
|---|---|---|---|---|---|---|
| | Property tax | Personal income tax | Retail sales tax | Property tax | Personal income tax | Retail sales tax |
| Newfoundland ........ | 0.8 | 2.0 | 3.3 | 1.5 | 5.2 | 5.4 |
| Prince Edward Island ... | 2.7 | 1.4 | 3.0 | 2.7 | 4.9 | 4.3 |
| Nova Scotia .......... | 3.7 | 2.0 | 2.8 | 2.7 | 5.0 | 3.8 |
| New Brunswick ....... | 2.2 | 2.4 | 3.0 | 2.8 | 4.7 | 4.2 |
| Quebec ............. | 3.5 | 4.3 | 2.4 | 3.4 | 7.7 | 3.3 |
| Ontario ............. | 3.7 | 2.4 | 1.7 | 4.5 | 5.1 | 2.7 |
| Manitoba ........... | 3.9 | 3.0 | 1.7 | 4.6 | 5.0 | 2.6 |
| Saskatchewan ........ | 4.6 | 1.8 | 1.8 | 4.0 | 4.6 | 2.8 |
| Alberta ............. | 3.5 | 2.3 | 0.0 | 3.4 | 3.5 | 0.0 |
| British Columbia ...... | 4.1 | 2.4 | 2.1 | 3.2 | 4.6 | 2.7 |
| Average[a] ........... | 3.6 | 2.9 | 1.9 | 3.8 | 5.4 | 2.6 |

[a] Includes the Yukon Territory and Northwest Territories.

Sources: The calculations in this table exclude all federal income and sales tax revenues. The property tax percentages are from table 7.1. Personal income and retail sales tax percentages are calculated from data in Statistics Canada, *Public Finance Historical Data 1965/66-1991/92*, catalogue no. 68-512, occasional; and Statistics Canada, *Public Sector Finance, 1995-96*, catalogue no. 68-212-XPB.

municipalities may apportion the local charges among benefiting properties on the basis of each property's frontage, its area, or its assessed value; or it may levy a uniform charge on all properties within the benefiting area. Another alternative is to base the charge directly on the benefits of the project as measured by the increase in property values that it creates.[92]

In principle, user-fee pricing of local improvements whose benefits can be assigned to specific properties is an ideal policy. In practice, however, the accurate apportionment of costs among the relevant properties may be somewhat difficult to achieve. In the case of projects whose benefits are more widespread or cannot be assigned to specific properties, funding from general revenue sources is more appropriate.

## Municipal Bonusing

Under a municipal bonusing scheme, a municipality grants a developer an increased height or density allocation if the developer agrees to some explicit condition, such as to provide subsidized housing or preserve historic buildings. Municipal experience with bonusing schemes dates back to the late 1800s, but numerous complaints about inequities and abuses led to the

[92] Bird, supra footnote 4, at 107-9; and Kitchen, supra footnote 2, at 76-77.

removal of legislated bonusing schemes in every province by the mid-1900s.[93] Municipalities continue to use bonusing schemes from time to time on their own initiative.

The difficulty is that in the absence of provincial legislation to control the use of bonusing schemes municipalities are likely to make decisions about their use on an ad hoc basis; the result will be different decisions at different times and for different people. Height or density bonuses may create inequities and inefficiencies. Planning principles that were used in establishing zoning legislation to restrict height and density were presumably designed to control urban development, servicing, and transportation. If these height and density restrictions are exchanged for "facilities, services, or matters," one may very well ask why zoning legislation was enacted in the first instance. If a municipal position on maximum densities is defensible on planning grounds, why should the need for a local day care centre, additional subsidized housing, or restoration of historic facades alter that rationale? Tradeoffs of this sort may throw all future planning principles into question and lead to further abuses.[94]

## Development Charges

Development charges are a relatively new feature of municipal finance in Canada.[95] Municipalities in Ontario have used them for the past 30 years and municipalities in British Columbia for the past 20; their use in other provinces is even more recent.

A development charge is imposed on developers, at a specific dollar amount per lot (or per hectare or acre), to finance the off-site capital costs of development.[96] The charge is usually applied to the capital costs of facilities necessitated by new development, but under certain circumstances it is applied to additional capital costs required to service redevelopment. Historically, development charges have been levied to finance "hard" services such as water supply systems, sewage treatment plants, trunk mains, and roads. In some jurisdictions, however, they have recently been expanded to finance the growth-related costs of a number of "soft" services, including education, libraries, general government, parks, recreation facilities, and schools.[97]

---

[93] For a brief history of housing schemes, see Kitchen, supra footnote 75, at chapter 3.

[94] Bird and Slack, supra footnote 3, at 111.

[95] These charges are known as development charges in Ontario, as development cost charges in British Columbia, and as lot levies, exactions, and impact fees in other jurisdictions.

[96] On-site services such as local roads, sidewalks, street lighting, sewers, and water are the responsibility of the developer. In Ontario, these services tend to be included in subdivision approval plans.

[97] The province of Ontario granted royal assent for the Development Charges Act, 1989, SO 1989, c. 58, on November 23, 1989. In essence, municipalities are permitted to impose development charges for a vast range of growth-related capital expenditures made necessary by the existence of new properties. It must be emphasized that only growth-related capital expenditures qualify for inclusion in the development charge.

In the face of increasing demands for local services, growing provincial restrictions and regulations, declining provincial grants, and downloading of provincial programs, many municipalities have seized upon development charges as a way to solve their capital budgeting problems. In their zeal to expand their use of development charges, however, municipalities have frequently not paused to consider either the appropriateness of this financing scheme or its economic impact. Any evaluation of development charges should take specific account of their incidence, equity, efficiency, and administrative effects.[98]

## Incidence

Since the development charge is imposed on new dwellings only, its final incidence will depend on the demand and supply for dwellings in the local market.[99] If the demand for housing is fairly insensitive to price increases, the developer will be able to pass the charge on, fully and immediately, to buyers of new homes. Demand is likely to be insensitive when the housing market is buoyant, as it was, for example, in the middle and late 1980s. When the housing market is not buoyant, developers tend to postpone development until it regains its buoyancy. If the price of new homes increases because of a development charge, market conditions will drive up the price of existing homes as well.

## Equity

Under the benefits-received principle, development charges will be fairest when the beneficiaries of services from publicly provided facilities are easy to identify—that is, when the cost of capital facilities that service specific properties can be determined for each property and when all benefits from the service are confined to that property. Capital expenditures on water, sewers, and local streets are examples of expenditures whose beneficiaries are easy to identify.

By the same reckoning, capital expenditures whose benefits accrue to future residents of the local community but cannot be directly associated with specific properties, should be financed from general property tax revenues. Capital expenditures that fall in this category include fire and police protection, general government, primary and secondary education, and neighbourhood parks and recreational facilities. The argument is that capital expenditures of this kind should be financed from borrowing, whose repayment

---

[98] For a more detailed evaluation of development charges, see Harry Kitchen, "Municipal Bond Financing: Issues and Alternatives" (mimeograph, Ontario Home Builders' Association, Toronto, June 27, 1990); Enid Slack, *An Economic Analysis of Development Charges in British Columbia and Ontario* (Vancouver: Laurier Institute, March 1990); Enid Slack and Richard Bird, "Financing Urban Growth Through Development Charges" (1991), vol. 39, no. 5 *Canadian Tax Journal* 1288-1304; and Bird and Slack, supra footnote 3, at 105-10.

[99] Slack, supra footnote 98, at 37-41.

would come from future property tax revenues from future beneficiaries. These revenues should be collected from the entire community unless it can be determined that the services benefit only the residents of a specific area, in which case a special area rate could be imposed.

Even if development charges adhere to the benefits-received principle, however, inequities will arise in the allocation of costs of services between current and future taxpayers.[100] The use of property taxes or user fees on new properties to finance the repayment of capital expenditures for existing properties or to finance future capital expenditures (through annual capital levies added to the general property tax), creates a serious inequity: new property owners must pay for both their own capital expenditures through development charges and the replacement of capital facilities for existing residents through annual property tax payments. To remove this inequity, municipalities should reduce their development charges by the present value of (1) all future property tax payments used for retiring the debt on similar capital projects and (2) the capital levy component of property taxes used for financing similar capital expenditures in the future.

In addition, to the extent that existing properties benefit from facilities financed by previous property owners (through moneys collected from property taxes and deposited in reserves or from annual operating revenues), a move from property taxation to development charges on new properties implies that existing property owners will receive a windfall gain: property values increase, but there is no proportionate increase in property taxes to fund local services. On the other hand, if existing property owners are obliged to pay property taxes for services to new development, there may be a legitimate concern that they are being taxed in order to provide a level of service for new properties that is higher than the level of service they receive for their own properties. Clearly, the crucial issue for public policy purposes is to determine who should bear which costs. Costs that are truly growth-related and that clearly benefit new properties only should be paid for by these properties. Furthermore, it is essential that the charge be appropriate; otherwise some property owners will receive windfall gains and others will be charged more than is fair.

Finally, if new properties fund their infrastructure on the basis of benefits received (development charges) and existing properties fund theirs on the basis of ability to pay (property tax revenues), the result is variable treatment within the municipality of properties that may be similar. Differentiation should occur on the basis of services provided rather than on the basis of whether a property is new or old.

---

[100] Ibid., at 41-42; Slack and Bird, supra footnote 98; and Bird and Slack, supra footnote 3, at 105-10.

## Efficiency

An efficient development charge must cover the full cost of delivering the service. Charges for municipal capital expenditures should consist of a capacity component, to cover the capital cost of constructing the facility, and a location or distance/density charge, to cover the capital cost of extending the service to particular properties or neighbourhoods.[101] Ideally, a charge on an individual property or on a neighbourhood will capture the extra cost of the capital facility associated with that property or neighbourhood. If the extra cost of providing services to different properties varies with the location or type of property or the nature of the capital facility provided, then for the sake of allocative efficiency the charge or levy on each property or neighbourhood should vary as well. In municipalities with a development charge, however, the usual practice is to impose an identical charge on all properties of a particular type (single residential, for example),[102] regardless of the location of the property within the community or the neighbourhood. This practice, which has been adopted for the sake of administrative simplicity, creates problems on efficiency grounds. For example, residential dwellings in low-density neighbourhoods are often subject to the same charge as residential dwellings in high-density neighbourhoods, yet it is apparent that the marginal cost per property of a given infrastructure project will be higher in a low-density area than it is in a high-density area (it will require more pipe, more asphalt, more cement, and so on, to service a property in a low-density neighbourhood).

Similarly, it may be more expensive to provide certain services to some parts of a city than it is to provide them to other parts. Thus it may be more expensive to provide a given facility in a hilly area than in a flat area or in one type of soil than in another. The application of the same charge to all properties in a given category, regardless of their location, is allocatively inefficient: some properties will be overcharged and others will be undercharged. A more efficient pricing policy, one that secures correct prices for the provision of capital facilities, would allocate the costs of infrastructure, via the development charge, to new properties that actually benefit from the infrastructure. Although it may be impractical to expect municipal officials to calculate the infrastructure cost for each new property site, there is no reason why these costs should not be calculated for each new development area (or neighbourhood, or ward). If this were done, then development charges in each area would more closely approximate the true costs of providing infrastructure for that area. Under the current practice, which applies one charge

---

[101] Paul P. Downing and Thomas S. McCaleb, "The Economics of Development Exactions," in James E. Frank and Robert M. Rhodes, eds., *Development Exactions* (Washington, DC: Planners Press, American Planning Association, 1987), 42-58, at 51-52.

[102] Different rates are imposed on different property types; for example, the rate for single residential properties is different from the rate for multiunit residential properties; commercial and industrial rates differ from one another and from residential rates as well.

across the entire community, development charges in the less expensive service areas subsidize properties in the more expensive service areas.

## Administration

In most municipalities that have enacted development charges, determination of the actual development charge has been controversial and hotly debated. Questions have arisen about what capital facilities should be included in the charge and what portion of those capital costs should be allocated to new properties.[103] Although legislation in Ontario specifically states that the capital facilities funded from development charges must be solely and strictly growth-related,[104] the general practice has been for municipalities to include as many facilities as possible and to calculate the charge, at least in part, according to what the market will bear. Indeed, in prosperous times and buoyant housing markets, municipalities may be able to set fairly sizable development charges without encountering serious protest. When times are less prosperous, however, and housing market activity is slow, the market is less willing to tolerate higher development charges, especially when they do not appear to be directly related to the cost of services received by new property owners.

## Alternatives to Market-Value Assessment

Our evaluation of property taxes has assumed that market value assessment is the tax base. Not everyone agrees that this is the most appropriate tax base, however. We shall consider two alternatives to market-value assessment: site-value assessment and unit assessment.[105]

### Site-Value Assessment

Some critics of market-value assessment advocate a move to site-value assessment (SVA) as a feasible substitute. Site-value assessment is based on a site's capacity to serve rather than on its current use. Capacity to serve is independent of what the owner does with the property.

In its purest form, SVA refers to the assessment of land only. All capital improvements (buildings, for example) are excluded from the assessment base. Under a graded SVA system, capital improvements are included in the base but are taxed at graduated rates that are lower (sometimes significantly lower) than is the rate for land; the levels of gradation will vary according to the taxing jurisdiction's policies and practices.

---

[103] For a critical examination of these concerns, see Harry Kitchen, "Development Charges: Background, Issues and an Evaluation of the City of Peterborough's Development Charges Study" (mimeograph, Peterborough Home Builders' Association, Peterborough, Ontario, August 15, 1990).

[104] See Ontario, Ministry of Municipal Affairs, *A Guide to the Development Charges Act, 1989* (Toronto: Ministry of Municipal Affairs, Municipal Finance Branch, March 1990).

[105] For a more detailed discussion, see Kitchen, supra footnote, 2, at chapter 9.

Since SVA involves property assessment practices, assessors are familiar with its operation. It entails the use of the same assessment machinery, personnel, and collection practices as current property assessment and would not create the administrative problems that would arise from the implementation of an entirely new and unfamiliar tax (for example, a poll tax). Site-value assessment differs from market-value assessment principally in requiring assessors to estimate the value of land separately from the value of buildings. In some jurisdictions, separating the assessment of land from the assessment of buildings is a practice with which assessors are already familiar. In these jurisdictions, buildings tend to be taxed at varying percentages of their assessed value, whereas land is taxed at 100 percent.

Site-value assessment is not new to Canada. It was widely used in Western Canada between 1903 and 1913. Three major reasons can be cited for its implementation then. First, it was hoped that it would lead to the breakup of large tracts of unimproved land held by absentee owners. Second, it was hoped that it would prevent land speculation. Third, it was felt that it would encourage capital improvements—that is, the construction of buildings.

Ontario experimented with site-value assessment in the early 1920s, but the system was not deemed to provide the expected benefits and was quickly abandoned. Since then, various forms of site-value assessment have been considered as alternatives to market-value assessment but have always been rejected.[106]

Under SVA, the value attached to a piece of land for tax purposes is what the land would be worth if it were employed in its best possible use in terms of economic return (an application of the opportunity-cost principle). This does not mean the best possible use in the future. It means the best possible use today.

Advocates of graded SVA argue that their system, which taxes land more heavily than buildings, has significant advantages over the current practice of taxing land and buildings at the same rate. The current system, it is alleged, discourages property improvements, since they lead to higher assessed values. Graded assessment reduces this disincentive. Indeed, it has been demonstrated that under certain circumstances greater reliance on land taxation may hasten economic development to the point where it is excessive on efficiency grounds.[107]

---

[106] For example, the Ontario Committee on Taxation, *Report*, supra footnote 19, vol. 2, recommendations 11:8-15, at 81-119; and *Report of the Commission on the Reform of Property Taxation in Ontario*, supra footnote 15, judged SVA to be inadequate and impractical. It was also rejected in "Taxing Matters: An Assessment of the Practice of Property Taxation in Ontario" (mimeograph, Toronto, 1985) and not considered by the Ontario Fair Tax Commission, supra footnote 9.

[107] Brian L. Bentick, "The Impact of Taxation and Valuation Practices on the Timing and Efficiency of Land Use" (August 1979), 87 *Journal of Political Economy* 859-68; and David E.

(The footnote is continued on the next page.)

To be more specific, graded assessment implies an emphasis on growth that may not be socially desirable, especially if preservation of heritage buildings, neighbourhood parks, or low-density development is to be encouraged. Furthermore, any incentive to speed up development may lead to problems such as downtown congestion, especially if development proceeds before other municipal objectives and goals have been carefully planned and coordinated.[108] Although it might be possible to accommodate these concerns through municipal zoning legislation, graded assessment would create considerable pressure for land conversion, and therefore for changes in zoning, because of the increased benefits (to the owner) that would arise from more intensively developed land.

Evidence on the effect of converting to a system that taxes land more intensively than buildings is scarce. A recent study evaluated the impact on local economic development in Pittsburgh, of the city government's decision in 1979-80 to restructure its property tax so that the rate on land was more than five times the rate on structures.[109] The study found that after this change Pittsburgh experienced a dramatic increase in building activity, one far in excess of any increases in other cities in the region. It stopped short, however, of concluding that the change in tax policy was responsible for the boom. Instead, it suggested that a shortage of commercial space was the primary basis for the expansion, but that the increase in land taxation had played an important supporting role by enabling the city to avoid increases in other taxes that might have impeded development. An earlier study had concluded that Pittsburgh's modified form of site-value tax did not constitute a sufficient penalty to encourage owners of underdeveloped or undeveloped property to develop. It had found, not surprisingly, that development in Pittsburgh responded to market conditions (demand for office space or buildings for corporate headquarters) and government incentives, including tax abatements and federal income tax credits. Property taxes were not an important factor in decisions.[110]

In cities that have proclaimed the success of their graded assessment schemes, much of the development that has followed the introduction of graded assessment has occurred at the expense of neighbouring municipalities that have not adopted a similar scheme. In any case, the claims of success

---

[107] Continued ...

Mills, "The Non-Neutrality of Land Value Taxation" (March 1981), 34 *National Tax Journal* 125-29.

[108] For an expression of concern over the way in which hasty, unplanned, and uncoordinated development can severely limit a municipality's policy options, see Toronto, *Final Report of the Joint Committee on Property Tax Reform* (Toronto: the committee, 1982).

[109] Wallace E. Oates and Robert M. Schwab, "The Impact of Urban Land Taxation: The Pittsburgh Experience" (March 1997), 50 *The National Tax Journal* 1-21.

[110] This study involved an analysis of real estate and assessment data in Pittsburgh from 1975 to 1985. See Michael Weir and Lillian E. Peters, "Development, Equity and the Graded Tax in the City of Pittsburgh" (June 1986), 5 *Property Tax Journal* 71-84.

must be treated with caution. The assumption behind these claims is that all new development derives from the graded tax system; virtually no account is taken of the possibility that some of the expansion may have resulted from changing market conditions, changes in the local labour market, or the receipt of state or federal grants—all of the factors that were indicated as being largely responsible for development in Pittsburgh's case.

Replacement of the current property tax system with either a graded system or one that taxed land alone would generate windfall gains[111] and losses in the short run as tax bills rose for some properties and fell for others. A recent analysis suggested that the reduction in taxes on buildings that accompanies a shift to a graded system is capitalized into higher property values and that the offsetting increased tax on land is capitalized into lower values.[112]

## Unit Assessment

Support for unit assessment—assessment based on the size of land and buildings—has emerged in response to three perceived shortcomings of market-value assessment. First, the subjective elements of market-value assessment are said to cause it to make it an inferior base for the taxation of property. Determining the market value of properties that have not been sold involves an assessor's judgment of market value—a judgment, it is alleged, that is often incorrect, especially given that assessors (and the officials who hear appeals of assessments) vary in competence and experience. Administrative inequities of this kind create a property tax system that seems arbitrary and unfair to many taxpayers. Unit assessment, it is claimed, is more objective than market-value assessment.

Second, assessment on the basis of market value penalizes homeowners who improve their property, since improvement leads to higher property taxes. Assessment on the basis of unit value does not generate penalties of this kind.

Third, market-value assessment often leads to large and rapid shifts in property values. Oscillating market values and the corresponding swings in property taxes may not reflect the ability of taxpayers to meet their property tax commitments. Unit assessment, its proponents argue, removes the cyclical swings in taxes and creates more certainty for taxpayers.

Under unit assessment, the tax base would be a combination of building area and lot area. The assessed value of a property would be its lot area times an assessment rate per square metre of lot area plus its building area times an

---

[111] Bird and Slack, supra footnote 3, at 82-83.

[112] Jan K. Brueckner, "A Modern Analysis of the Effects of Site Value Taxation" (March 1986), 39 *National Tax Journal* 49-58.

assessment rate per square metre of building area.[113] The assessment base, therefore, would take no account of variables such as location, market conditions, and quality of structures. These variables, or any others that were deemed appropriate, would instead be accommodated through the use of variable tax rates.

Unit assessment is open to criticism on several grounds. First, the argument that unit assessment would be more objective than market-value assessment is not compelling. Unit assessment would require elements of judgment or subjectivity in establishing the value assigned to land and the value assigned to buildings, and in determining the differential between these two components. In general, it is difficult to imagine that administrative problems would be any less severe under unit assessment than they are under market-value assessment. If evaluation is a problem under the existing system, then surely the solution is to improve the assessment process rather than to change it dramatically.

Second, the argument that market-value assessment is inferior to unit assessment because it deters owners from property improvements raises an empirical question that cannot be easily answered. What is likely, though, is that property improvements increase property (market) values, and owner's equity, far in excess of the annual increase in property taxes. In other words, the increase in property tax that results from property improvements under market-value assessment is unlikely to be large enough to deter property owners from attempting to increase their wealth (through higher house prices and increased owner's equity).

Third, promotion of unit assessment on the ground that market-value assessment does not fairly measure ability to pay in oscillating property markets is also less than compelling. Clearly, when properties are sold in rising property markets, capital gains (which are sometimes substantial) ensue and ability to pay increases. In the case of properties that increase in value but are not sold, the taxpayer's capacity to consume, and hence his ability to pay, likewise increases. If increases in value create financial hardships for the taxpayer, tax-relief schemes are available that may alleviate them.

Fourth, a major shortcoming of unit value is that it requires the initial determination of a value per square foot, and as circumstances change over time, subsequent changes in this value. How is the initial value to be determined and how will changes be made? Are the necessary determinations to be made by some bureaucrat or are they to be left to the market? If a bureaucrat is to make them, they are likely to be arbitrary and unfair. If the market is to make them, why not use the market value of the property (as in market-value assessment) as the base?

---

[113] Harry Kitchen, "Alternative Methods of Taxation and Assessment," a report prepared for the Task Force on Reassessment in Metropolitan Toronto (mimeograph, Toronto, August 1989), part VII.

Fifth, the general uncertainty and the high transition and dislocation costs that a switch to unit assessment would argue against its introduction. The transaction and transition costs would, in all likelihood, be substantial both for those responsible for administering the system and for those on whom the tax is imposed. The introduction of a new base would cause shifts in the tax burden and produce a new series of winners and losers; the result would be a set of distortions not previously experienced.

Finally, a number of provincial and local government commissions, committees, and reports have endorsed market value as the most desirable base for property taxation.[114] One exception was the Ontario Fair Tax Commission,[115] which recommended unit assessment in spite of a thoughtful and carefully articulated argument by one of its commissioners in favour of market-value assessment.[116]

## Alternatives to Property Taxation

Recent increases in property taxes have led to suggestions that one or more alternative taxes be considered for implementation by local governments.[117] In the case of residential properties, suggestions for taxes to supplement or replace property taxes include poll taxes, municipal income taxes, municipal sales taxes, and a municipal fuel tax.[118]

## Poll Taxes

A poll tax, sometimes called a head tax, is a tax of a specific dollar value that applies to every individual. It bears no direct relationship to property values, nor is it based on any concept of the taxpayer's ability to pay (whether wealth-based, consumption-based, or income-based). The local tax base for each municipality is directly dependent on the number of residents (adult residents if the tax only applies to adult residents).

Although poll taxes are not currently used in Canada, their use was at one time available to municipalities in every province in Canada. The poll tax's revenue yield, in total, was never large, but for the relatively few municipalities, most of them in Atlantic Canada, that employed it, it was an important revenue source. The only country that has used a local poll tax of any

---

[114] For a list, see Harry M. Kitchen, *Local Government Finance in Canada*, Financing Canadian Federation no. 5 (Toronto: Canadian Tax Foundation, 1984), chapters 8 and 9; and Kitchen, supra footnote 2, at chapter 3.

[115] *Fair Taxation in a Changing World*, supra footnote 9, at chapter 29.

[116] See ibid., at 1019-23, for a critical commentary by Neil Brooks (a commissioner).

[117] Since municipalities are creatures of the province, provincial legislation would be required to allow municipalities access to alternative tax sources.

[118] See Kitchen, supra footnote 2, at chapter 10.

significance in the recent past is the United Kingdom.[119] Problems with its administration and taxpayers' criticism, however, led to its termination.

Because property is both highly visible and highly immobile, an updated register of taxable property (land and buildings) is relatively easy to maintain and monitor for the purposes of establishing taxable value. Maintaining a register of taxable occupants, however, as the administration of a poll tax requires, is potentially more difficult, since households would develop ingenious schemes for escaping full reporting of total taxable occupants. In fact, it has been suggested that the administration costs of operating a poll tax system would significantly exceed the costs of administering and operating a property tax system.[120]

If one considers the poll tax in isolation from all other taxes, it is possible to argue that it is the most efficient tax that governments (local or otherwise) could adopt. It is a fixed charge on all eligible taxpayers; that is, taxpayers cannot legally avoid it. Since it does not change the relative price of undertaking various consumption or other types of activities, it does not provide an incentive for individuals to behave in specific ways; hence, it is economically efficient.[121]

The matter appears in a somewhat different light, however, if one evaluates local taxes as part of the system as a whole. Local taxes that are inefficient (that is, that create distortions) may correct for the inefficiencies of taxes imposed by other levels of government. For example, the federal government and the provinces tax certain types of consumption activity through their various sales and excise taxes. Since those taxes exclude the annual consumption of housing services, one might argue that they create a distortion (one type of consumption activity is favoured over other types). The property tax on residential properties may partially, if not completely, correct this distortion or inefficiency. A local tax that was perfectly neutral, such as a poll tax, would not have this corrective effect. Thus, the case for poll taxation on the ground of economic efficiency is not as strong as many of its proponents have suggested.

Finally, a poll tax would be less equitable than the current property tax. Since the amount of poll tax would be unrelated to property values, the tax

---

[119] For a detailed description of the reform package, see United Kingdom, Secretary of State for the Environment, Secretary of State for Scotland, and Secretary of State for Wales, *Paying for Local Government*, Cmnd. 9714 (London: Her Majesty's Stationery Office, January 1986); D.H. King, *Accountability and Equity in British Local Finance: The Poll Tax*, Discussion Paper no. 145 (Stirling, Scot.: University of Stirling, 1988); and Stephen Smith and Duncan Squire, *Local Taxes and Local Government* (London: Institute for Fiscal Studies, 1987).

[120] Smith and Squire, supra footnote 119, at 35.

[121] For arguments in support of a local poll tax for Canada, see Paul A.R. Hobson, "Local Government in Canada: Creature, Chameleon, Consort," in Melville McMillan, ed., *Provincial Public Finances*, vol. 2, *Plaudits, Problems, and Prospects*, Canadian Tax Paper no. 91 (Toronto: Canadian Tax Foundation, 1991), 215-39.

would fall more heavily on lower-income households than on higher-income households.[122]

## Local Income Taxation

Canadian municipalities are not without experience in gaining access to income tax revenue. Some provincial and municipal governments had been levying taxes on income for 80 years or more when the federal income tax came into existence in 1917.[123] In fact, income taxation was so important at the local level that municipal income tax revenues exceeded provincial income tax revenues in every year through 1930.[124] By the end of the 1930s, every province had adopted some form of municipal income tax. In 1941, however, the provinces entered into the wartime tax rental agreements with the federal government, under which they temporarily surrendered their and their municipalities' right to levy income taxes. Since 1941, no municipality in Canada has levied a municipal income tax. At this point, any effort by municipal governments to regain access to the income tax field would depend on the willingness of the federal government and the provinces to accede to such requests.

Some form of local income tax exists in about half of the industrialized countries that are members of the Organisation for Economic Co-operation and Economic Development (OECD).[125] In some of these countries, the central government administers and collects the tax and refunds it to the municipalities. In others, local governments have some degree of independent control over the amount of revenue generated by income taxation—some have control over the rates but not the base, others have control over both the rates and the base.[126]

There are basically two feasible approaches to the administration of a local income tax. First, municipalities might "piggyback" their income taxes onto the existing provincial income tax system by adding additional percentage points to the provincial income tax base. This alternative would oblige municipalities to accept the definition of taxable income and allowable credits used in the federal and provincial systems. Second, a local

---

[122] For an illustration of the distributional impact and support for this statement, see Kitchen, supra footnote 2, at 132-34.

[123] Sheldon Silver, "The Feasibility of a Municipal Income Tax in Canada" (1968), vol. 16, no. 5 *Canadian Tax Journal* 398-406, at 398-99.

[124] Calculated from data in Canada, *Report of the Royal Commission on Dominion-Provincial Relations*, book III (Ottawa: King's Printer, 1940), sections 1 and 3; and F.H. Leacy, ed., *Historical Statistics of Canada*, 2d ed. (Ottawa: Statistics Canada, 1983).

[125] For more detail, see John Kay and Stephen Smith, *Local Income Tax: Options for the Introduction of a Local Income Tax in the United Kingdom*, Report Series no. 31 (London: Institute for Fiscal Studies, 1988), chapter 3.

[126] For a brief discussion of alternative approaches to local income taxation, see Harry M. Kitchen, "Municipal Income Taxation—A Revenue Alternative?" Fiscal Figures feature (1982), vol. 30, no. 5 *Canadian Tax Journal* 781-86, at 783-84.

government might administer its own income tax system. Although this alternative would permit more local autonomy and flexibility than the first, it would also be more expensive to administer. Many municipalities in the United States, however, have willingly incurred these administrative costs in order to control their own tax bases.[127] Under a separate municipal income tax system, local authorities would decide what is to be taxed. For example, if only earned income were to be taxed, deduction could be at source and the tax would be similar to a payroll tax. If the base were to include unearned income as well (interest, dividends, rent, and so forth), then a more sophisticated administrative machinery would be required.

Local authorities would also have to decide whether to tax commuters and, if they did tax them, whether to treat them differently from residents.[128] Some local government services that benefit local residents collectively benefit residents of other jurisdictions as well, particularly persons who commute to work from outside the municipality. To the extent that local government services are funded from property taxes, commuters do not contribute directly to the costs of these services. Their contribution is no different from that of all other residents of the province who pay provincial taxes and thus contribute to the funding for provincial grants to municipalities. A major rationale for a local income tax deducted at source, then, is that it allows the municipality to tax commuters for some of the collective benefits they receive from the providing municipality.

If a municipal income tax were levied everywhere, the general efficiency implications of the tax would be identical to those of the existing federal and provincial personal income taxes. If, however, an income tax were imposed as a supplement to existing taxes in one municipality and not in surrounding areas, the tax might create an incentive for people to migrate to lower-tax communities.

The replacement of all or part of residential property tax revenues with personal income tax revenues would produce winners and losers. If the change were revenue-neutral, property taxes would fall and income taxes would rise. The final impact on each taxpayer (individual or unincorporated business) would depend on the extent to which higher income taxes offset lower property taxes. In reality, however, it is not certain that a change of this sort would be revenue-neutral. Municipalities might view the extra tax room in the property tax base as an opportunity to raise property taxes.

Finally, since the property tax tends to be less progressive than the income tax,[129] the introduction of a local income tax as a substitute for increased

---

[127] For a discussion, see Robert L. Bland, *A Revenue Guide for Local Government* (Washington, DC: International City Management Association, 1989), chapter 6.

[128] Most US cities in which local income taxes supplement local property taxes tax commuters and residents at the same rate.

[129] Whalley, supra footnote 37.

reliance on the property tax would almost certainly produce a more progressive distribution of the tax burden for funding local services.[130]

## Municipal Retail Sales Tax

Quebec is the only Canadian province in which municipalities have levied a retail sales tax. In fact, the retail sales tax was introduced in Canada, on May 1, 1935, by the City of Montreal. The revenues from the tax were primarily designed to meet heavy relief payments that threatened the city's ability to balance its budget. The rate was 2 percent, and it applied to all retail sales of tangible personal property except food and certain retail goods bought by manufacturers. In 1940, the province entered the retail sales tax field and, like Montreal, adopted a rate of 2 percent. The Montreal sales tax continued but was administered by the province. Several other Quebec municipalities introduced sales taxes of their own, also at the rate of 2 percent. In 1964, however, the province took over the entire sales tax field and established a uniform province-wide tax rate. Today, the retail sales tax is strictly a provincial tax in all provinces—except Alberta, where it does not exist.

A municipality that wished to levy a retail sales tax would have the same choices as one that wished to levy an income tax. That is, it might piggyback onto the existing provincial sales tax system or it might operate its own sales tax system independently of the province. In this case as well, the administrative costs of a piggyback scheme would be much less than those of an independent system. On the other hand, the savings in administrative costs would come at a price: the municipality would have less flexibility and autonomy than it would obtain from a locally designed and administered tax.

One of the primary rationales for a municipal retail sales tax as a complement to the local property tax is the same as one of the primary rationales for the income tax as a complement to the local property tax. To the extent that local government services are funded from property taxes imposed on local residents, non-residents who benefit from these services avoid direct tax contributions to their funding. The imposition of a retail sales tax would allow the local jurisdiction to use the tax system directly to recover some of the costs of providing local services (roads, streets, public transit, police protection, and so on) whose benefits go in part to non-residents.

If a municipal sales tax at the same rate and on the same base were levied in every municipality, the overall efficiency implications of the tax would be identical to those of the existing provincial retail sales tax structure. If a municipal sales tax were levied in some municipalities and not in others, so that tax rates were different across municipalities, some distortions would arise. For example, individuals would have an incentive to purchase goods and services in municipalities with lower tax rates. The existence of this

---

[130] Douglas Auld, "Alternative Methods of Funding for Education," a report prepared for the Task Force on Reassessment in Metropolitan Toronto (mimeograph, Toronto, August 1989).

incentive might have unfortunate long-run consequences for retail establishments in the higher-tax communities.

One study of the incidence of retail sales taxes in Canada concluded that the taxes were regressive even if all exempt purchases were included in the estimations.[131] It is likely that the federal goods and service tax has a similar distributional pattern.

A local retail sales tax would tend to be more regressive than a local income tax, and it would be far less successful in taxing commuters. As a means of taxing visitors, however, in order to recover some of the costs of local government services used by those individuals, a retail sales tax would be superior to an income tax (administratively, it would be impossible to impose a local income tax on visitors). Alternatively, the municipality could tax visitors for the cost of services consumed through a hotel and motel occupancy tax.

## Hotel and Motel Occupany Costs

The revenue yield from a hotel and motel occupancy tax at the local level would be unlikely to approach the yields generated by either an income or retail sales tax. Nevertheless, interest in occupancy taxes exists. Over the past two decades, in fact, many local governments in the United States have adopted them.

An occupancy or room tax would take the form of an additional levy imposed on the provincial retail sales tax rate. The tax is defended on the ground that it compensates local governments for the expanded services that they provide for tourists or visitors (for example, additional police and fire protection and extra highway and public transit capacity needed to meet weekend or peak convention and tourist demands).

Whereas local income and retail sales taxes would fall on both residents and non-residents, a hotel and motel occupancy tax would fall on visitors alone. Again, local governments might either simply piggyback a few extra percentage points onto the existing retail sales tax rate for hotel and motel rooms or set up their own administrative structures to administer and collect the tax. And again, a piggyback scheme would be administratively less expensive than an independent scheme but also less flexible.

The levying of a hotel and motel room occupancy tax in some municipalities and not others provides an incentive for individuals to stay in hotels and motels in the municipalities without the tax. If the demand for hotel and motel rooms is sensitive to price, then noticeable losses may occur. Convention arrangements, for example, are often highly cost-sensitive; consequently, a municipality that levied a motel and hotel tax might lose business to potential convention centres without a tax.

---

[131] François Vaillancourt and Marie-France Poulaert, "The Incidence of Provincial Sales Taxes in Canada, 1978 and 1982" (1985), vol. 33, no. 3 *Canadian Tax Journal* 490-510.

## Municipal Fuel Taxes

Although a number of US cities levy municipal gas taxes, the Greater Vancouver Regional District (GVRD) is the only municipality in Canada that levies a local fuel tax. Municipalities that do levy fuel taxes almost always earmark the revenues for local roads and local public transit.

A local fuel tax, like a local income tax or sales tax, could be either levied directly by the municipality or piggybacked onto the existing provincial fuel tax. The first alternative would give the municipality more autonomy than the second but would be more costly to administer. Piggybacking, under which the province would collect the tax and remit the revenues to each municipality on the basis of amounts collected in that municipality, is the more reasonable alternative.

Although a tax on fuel would affect both residents and visitors, it is more likely to be viewed as a tax on residents. Regardless of its incidence, a tax on motor fuel may be viewed as a benefits-based tax and has considerable merit, especially if the revenues are earmarked for funding local roads and public transit.

## User Fees

The benefits-based model for financing municipal services[132] assigns an important role to user fees. In particular, the model calls for their employment to finance all or a portion of the cost of services whose specific beneficiaries can be identified, provided that it is possible to allocate the services to those who are willing to pay and to exclude non-users and provided that it is possible to estimate the per-unit costs of service provision. In the case of services that provide collective benefits and cannot be allocated to specific individuals or properties, local property taxation[133]—supplemented, perhaps, by an additional tax or taxes—is a more appropriate funding tool.

User fees currently fund some or all of the costs of a range of municipal services in Canada, including water, sewers, solid waste collection and disposal, recreation, public transit and parking.[134] User fees range from fixed charges that are unrelated to consumption to charges that vary directly with quantity consumed to mixes of fixed and variable charges. In addition, the pricing structure may cover either all or only a portion of real production and delivery costs. Decisions about pricing structures and the proportion of costs to recover from user fees depend on a variety of considerations. Local tradition,

---

[132] For a defence of this model as a basis for funding municipal services, see Bird and Slack, supra footnote 3, at 66-67; and Bossons, Kitchen, and Slack, supra footnote 7.

[133] The earlier evaluation of property taxes was completed in the context of the benefits model.

[134] Tassonyi, supra footnote 7; and Mark Sproule-Jones and John White, "The Scope and Application of User Charges in Municipal Governments" (1989), vol. 37, no. 6 *Canadian Tax Journal* 1476-85 for a list of user fees and their relative importance in funding municipal services in Ontario.

the type of service, the tastes or preferences of residents, and the willingness (or lack of willingness) of local politicians and administrators to substitute prices for local taxes are all factors that may affect the choice of policies.[135]

## General Evaluation

User fees, if they are set correctly, have all the efficiency advantages of private sector prices. They serve to ration output to those who are willing to pay for the good or service, and they act as a signal to suppliers (local governments or their delivery agents)—a signal that indicates the quantity and quality of output desired. In practice, however, prices or user fees are generally not set correctly: their purpose is to raise revenue rather than to serve as a rationing and demand-signalling device. The failure to price properly has created a good deal of unplanned and implicit redistribution, much of which would be unacceptable, in all likelihood, if it were made explicit. Indeed, as Richard M. Bird has noted, "the repeated attempt to redistribute everything through inadequate and inefficient pricing may well have resulted in less overall redistribution than might otherwise have been attained."[136]

Allocative efficiency, fairness, and accountability in the provision of a specific service is achieved if the fee (price or charge) per unit equals the extra cost of the last unit of output consumed. This is the well-known principle of marginal-cost pricing.[137] In practice, however, it may be difficult to apply this pricing principle. One source of difficulty is the problem of estimating marginal cost. The determination of user fees (prices) may also be problematical in the presence of economies of scale, capacity constraints, fluctuations in demand, second-best considerations, or externalities.[138]

The task of determining marginal costs for some services may be complicated by the difficulty of identifying and quantifying the services' true economic costs.[139] Recent advancements in analytical techniques, however, should allow municipalities to overcome many of these difficulties. Even if precise cost information about a given service is difficult to attain or apportion, reliance on second-best information in setting user fees might lead to greater efficiency, fairness, and accountability in local service provision than is possible with alternatives such as local taxes, licences, permits, and so on.

---

[135] Mark Sproule-Jones, "User Fees," in Allan M. Maslove, ed., *Taxes as Instruments of Public Policy* (Toronto: University of Toronto Press in cooperation with the Ontario Fair Tax Commission, 1994), 3-38; and Kitchen, supra footnote 75, at 33-34.

[136] Bird, supra footnote 4, at 104.

[137] For detailed discussions of this pricing principle and the issues surrounding it, see Harry Kitchen, "Pricing of Local Government Services," in *Urban Governance and Finance*, supra footnote 7, 135-68; Bird, supra footnote 4; Bird and Tsiopoulos, supra footnote 4; and Sproule-Jones, supra footnote 135.

[138] Bird and Tsiopoulos, supra footnote 4, discuss this in more detail, at 52-64.

[139] See Bird and Tsiopoulos, ibid., at 52-58, for an elaboration on these problems and for an evaluation of alternative cost bases used in setting user fees.

In the case of services that display characteristics of publicly provided private goods, marginal-cost pricing will recover the full cost if the services can be provided at a constant average cost. Difficulties arise, however, in the case of services that benefit from economies of scale (per-unit costs decline as output rises): the marginal cost will be lower than the average cost, and revenues will be insufficient to recover the full costs of production. For many public utilities, for instance, significant fixed production costs result in a declining average cost. In cases of this kind, marginal-cost pricing will recover only operating costs. The recovery of fixed costs will require either a subsidy equal to this amount or the adoption of a two-part (or multipart) pricing policy. Use of a government subsidy is likely to be both politically unpopular and economically inefficient—raising the revenues to fund the subsidy is almost certain to create inefficiencies or distortions elsewhere. Adoption of a two-part pricing policy is generally the preferable alternative. Ideally, one part of the price would be a fixed charge for the privilege of using or gaining access to the facility and the other part would be a variable charge equal to the marginal cost of the last unit consumed.

Capacity constraints occur when a given infrastructure provides a limited level of service. In the context of marginal-cost pricing, problems arise if capacity is uneven and can be expanded only in discrete amounts. In these cases, services will typically be either under- or overprovided relative to the efficient level.[140] If the service is underprovided, its marginal benefit will exceed its marginal cost, hence the price will exceed marginal cost and total revenues will exceed total costs. If the service is overprovided, its marginal benefit will be less than its marginal cost; hence the price will be less than the marginal cost and total revenues will be less than total costs. The "size-of-facility" decision, therefore, is one that requires benefit-cost analysis. If the facility is too small, an efficient pricing policy will result in revenues that exceed costs—the project is self-financing. If the facility is too large, revenues from sales will not be sufficient to finance provision of the service.

A further issue in user-fee pricing is the pricing of services in peak and off-peak periods of demand. Efficient pricing may call for higher fees in peak periods and lower fees in off-peak periods. This is so because peak demand strains capacity and only lasts for a portion of the demand cycle. The marginal benefit to peak users occurs only over that portion of the demand cycle, whereas the marginal cost of capacity expansion is incurred over the entire demand cycle. The result is that the marginal benefit to peak users exceeds their marginal costs. In addition, since off-peak users gain no additional benefit from capacity expansion, the additional capacity costs should be shouldered entirely by peak users. In other words, the off-peak price should be set equal to marginal operating costs, whereas the peak price should be set equal to the sum of marginal capacity costs and operating costs.

---

[140] Tassonyi, supra footnote 90.

Second-best considerations arise in the presence of inefficient pricing policies (prices set at levels other than marginal cost) elsewhere in the system. They arise, for instance, when a municipality implements a user fee for a particular service but other services that are considered substitutes are not subject to a specific charge. Thus, road and expressway users pay nothing per trip (other than vehicle operating costs), whereas users of public transit are charged for each trip. In this instance, it might be possible to achieve efficiency gains by setting the price for public transit, the controllable sector, below the marginal cost, thereby creating an incentive for increased use of transit services and decreased use of roads and expressways, the uncontrollable sector. Pricing solutions of this kind are known as "second-best" solutions.[141]

Finally, subsidization may also be warranted if the provision of a given service generates externalities or spillover benefits that accrue to non-residents. Much of the capital and social infrastructure in a municipality benefits residents and non-residents alike, and charges (taxes) collected from local citizens may be less than the full marginal social cost. Although it is possible to impose user charges on non-residents as well, the charges may not capture capacity costs appropriately. In these circumstances, it may be preferable to provide a subsidy rather than to shift the associated costs to local residents. The standard recommendation here is that the costs be subsidized at a rate equal to the share of the benefits that accrues to non-residents.

## Specific Services[142]

Reliance on user fees is increasing in most municipalities and is likely to expand even further as a result of provincial downloading and a general reluctance to increase local property taxes. Consequently, we shall devote the remainder of our discussion of user fees to an analysis of municipal services that already depend to some extent on user fees or that have been discussed as possible candidates for user-fee financing in the future.

### Water

Water provision in Canada uses five basic rate structures: a flat rate charge, a charge based on property assessment, and three types of volume-based charges. In the case of residential properties, flat rate charges are used more widely than any of the alternatives. Some municipalities also use them for commercial properties. Flat rate charges are unrelated to water consumption. The rate structure is typically very simple, although some flat rate systems have become fairly complex. The rate often varies by type of customer; for example, the residential rate may be different from the commercial/industrial rate. The rate may also depend on characteristics of a customer's property—

---

[141] Robin Boadway, "The Role of Second Best Theory in Public Economics," in B. Curtis Eaton and Richard G. Harris, eds., *Trade, Technology and Economics: Essays in Honour of Richard G. Lipsey* (Brookfield, VT: Edward Elgar, 1997), 3-25.

[142] This section draws heavily from Kitchen, supra footnote 137, at 147-63.

number and type of rooms, number of water-using fixtures, number of residents, size of lot, presence of a swimming pool, size of service connection, and so on. Because flat rate charges are unrelated to consumption, they do not require the use of meters.

A very few municipalities use various indirect methods of charging for water that are equivalent to a flat rate charge. The charges are based on property assessment and take the form of an addition to the property tax bill, frontage charges, or special assessments.[143]

Volume-based charges require the use of meters and use one of three rate structures—constant-unit rate, declining block rate, or increasing block rate. A constant-unit rate is an equal charge per unit of consumption (cubic metre, for example) and seldom differentiates among customer classes. It is the type of volumetric charge most commonly used in Canada. A declining block rate structure generally consists of a basic or fixed service charge per period and a volumetric charge that decreases in discrete steps or blocks as the volume consumed increases. Typically, one or two initial blocks cover residential and light commercial water use, and additional blocks apply to heavy commercial and industrial uses. The fixed component of the charge often varies with the size of the service connection. Minimum charges that correspond to a minimum amount of water consumption in each billing period are common under these systems.

Under an increasing block rate structure, which a very few municipalities use, the volumetric charge increases by steps as consumption increases. Systems that use this structure do not usually include minimum billings.

## Evaluation

Since efficiency is achieved when the price is set to cover the marginal cost, the first step in water pricing is to ensure that municipalities are metered. Currently, approximately 40 percent of all municipalities use meters for residential consumers and approximately 60 percent use meters for commercial and industrial customers.[144] It is relatively easy to derive efficient prices for water: individuals can be excluded from consuming the service, reasonably precise measurements of output and cost can be obtained, and collection and administrative costs are low.[145] Currently, however, because prices are based on average costs, allocative efficiency is seldom achieved.

---

[143] D.M. Tate and D.M. Lacelle, *Municipal Water Rates in Canada—Current Practice and Prices, 1991* (Ottawa: Environment Canada, Inland Waters Directorate, 1995).

[144] Ibid.

[145] For an application of marginal-cost pricing schemes, see Michael Fortin, "The Economics of Water Conservation," in *Towards User Pay for Municipal Water and Wastewater Resources* (Washington, DC: Rawson Academy of Aquatic Science, 1990); and Roger McNeill and Donald Tate, *Guidelines for Municipal Water Pricing* (Ottawa: Environment Canada, Inland Waters Directorate, Water Planning and Management Branch, June 1990), chapters 3, 4, and 5.

As well, few municipalities include all relevant operating costs in water rates. For example, most municipalities exclude depreciation costs, although a few that do not currently include them are developing an interest in their future inclusion. Failure to incorporate depreciation means that the annual cost of capital (water plant and system) used up in the provision of water is not captured in the price. This is an increasingly significant deficiency, given that many municipalities face rising costs for infrastructure rehabilitation.[146]

As long as some operating costs are ignored and real marginal costs not measured, it may be folly to comment on the efficiency of existing volumetric pricing structures (the inefficiency of fixed charges unrelated to consumption goes without saying). Whether prices should rise with consumption, decline with consumption, or remain at a fixed rate per unit consumed is an empirical question, one that depends on the marginal cost of production and delivery.[147] If water conservation is considered to be important, however, then an increasing block rate structure would be efficient and appropriate.

The marginal cost of water supply, like the marginal costs of a number of other services, increases with distance from the source of supply. Municipalities do not, however, vary the unit price of water to reflect this circumstance. The result is that users with lower marginal costs subsidize users with higher marginal costs. If this subsidy is capitalized into land values, properties further from the source will be priced higher than they would be in its absence.[148] Finally, the failure to use peak-load prices for late afternoon and evening consumption and seasonal prices during the summer generates excessive demand at these times.

Although a few municipalities have moved toward marginal-cost pricing or expressed an interest in it, most pricing structures for residential and commercial/industrial properties deviate substantially from it. The result is both an inefficient allocation of resources, and an unfair allocation of costs. Customers whose price exceeds the marginal cost subsidize those whose price is below the marginal cost. For example, failure to differentiate between peak periods and off-peak periods means that heavy users of water at certain times of the day or year are subsidized by users whose demand for water during these times is less heavy. Failure to differentiate by distance means that users who are closer to the source subsidize users who are further from the source.

A recent study based on 77 water utilities in Ontario concluded that the marginal cost of water supply exceeded the price for water in every munici-

---

[146] For a discussion of this point, see Fortin, supra footnote 145.

[147] For a discussion of the implications of the different rate structures, see Kitchen, supra footnote 114, at 269-73.

[148] Paul B. Downing, "User Charges and the Development of Urban Land" (December 1973), 26 *National Tax Journal* 631-37, at 632.

pality studied.[149] On average, the price to residential customers was $0.32 per cubic metre and the estimated marginal cost was $0.87 per cubic metre. In the non-residential sector, the average price was $0.734 per cubic metre and the estimated average marginal cost was $1.492 per cubic metre. The result of these large discrepancies between marginal cost and price is a substantial deadweight loss per unit of output. The underpricing of water has generated a higher level of consumption than is allocatively efficient and led to a level of investment in water facilities that is higher than it would be if a more efficient pricing policy were employed.[150]

## Sewage Collection and Treatment

Sewage collection and treatment expenses are almost always recovered through surcharges on water bills. Most municipalities, including some with metered water rates, impose a flat rate charge rather than one based on sewage flow. Other municipalities set the sewer charge as a percentage of the water bill.

### Evaluation

Unless sewage charges are related to the volume of sewage discharged and treated, they are almost certain to be inefficient. The design of an optimal pricing scheme for sewage requires detailed knowledge of the incremental cost of collecting and treating it. As Bird observes, a multipart pricing structure probably best approximates the efficient pricing principle, "with, for example, a connection fee to cover per unit average costs for transmission and treatment capacity, a front footage charge to cover collection costs, and a monthly fee, preferably related to water usage, to cover out-of-pocket operating charges."[151] For that matter, the connection fees could vary with the distance of serviced areas from the sewage treatment plant.

The pricing schemes currently in use are far from optimal. There is seldom any attempt to separate the costs associated with treatment, collection, and transmission of sewage. A few municipalities, particularly the larger ones, impose a surcharge on industrial users on the assumption that industrial waste is more dense and more damaging and hence more expensive to treat than is residential sewage. Flat rate charges are inefficient because they do not reflect the marginal cost of the service provided, and the same thing may be said of charges prorated on the basis of the water bill. The assumption that water use is directly and positively correlated with sewage generation is a doubtful one; for example, one can attribute a large component of water consumption to the watering of lawns, the washing of cars, the filling of swimming pools, and many other household uses that do not generate sewage.

---

[149] Steven Renzetti, "Municipal Water Supply and Sewage Treatment: Costs, Prices and Distortions" (mimeograph, Brock University, St. Catharines, Ont., 1997).

[150] Ibid., at 19.

[151] Bird, supra footnote 4, at 125.

The study of 77 water utilities in Ontario that we cited above concluded that the average marginal cost of sewage treatment was $0.521 per cubic metre, whereas the average price was $0.128 per cubic metre.[152] As in the case of water, the discrepancy between price and marginal cost is responsible for deadweight losses and an overexpansion in sewage treatment facilities. Perhaps of greatest concern, however, is the suggestion that the underpricing of sewage treatment has discouraged the development of alternative sewage treatment technologies.[153]

## Public Transit

Municipal transit systems everywhere are financed largely by a combination of fare-box revenues, provincial grants (these are disappearing in Ontario), and local revenues (raised from property tax revenues, primarily). Some systems generate additional funds from charter/rental services, advertising, and other sources.

Concern about the size of the provincial and municipal subsidies required to cover transit systems' operating deficits has generated considerable discussion about what share of operating costs ought to be charged to transit users. Needless to say, local officials consider a number of social, economic, and political factors in setting fares. These factors include the availability of other forms of transportation, local residents' ability to pay for transit services, and local politicians' notions of acceptable levels of fares.[154] Most communities set different fares for adults, children, students, and seniors and offer discounts for monthly passes.

### Evaluation

To advocate that public-transit users pay a price equal to the full marginal cost of the service they consume would be allocatively efficient and fair only if private-transit (automobile) users were levied a charge that reflected the full marginal social cost of the facilities they use. A second-best argument applies here: since the tax, price, or fee paid by each automobile user for each trip taken is less than the marginal cost, marginal-cost pricing for public transit is not efficient. Efficiency, in this case, must be achieved by subsidizing local public transit, and the question then becomes that of establishing the correct subsidy.[155]

[152] Renzetti, supra footnote 149.

[153] G. Gardner, *Recycling Organic Waste*, Worldwatch Paper 135 (Washington, DC: Worldwatch Institute, 1997); and Sandra Postel, "Facing Water Scarcity," in Lester Brown, project director, *The State of the World 1993: A Worldwatch Institute Report on Progress Toward a Sustainable Society* (New York: Norton, 1993), 22-41.

[154] Harry Kitchen, "Urban Transportation Policy," in Richard A. Loreto and Trevor Price, eds., *Urban Policy Issues: Canadian Perspectives* (Toronto: McClelland and Stewart, 1990), 107-23.

[155] Bird, supra footnote 4, at 64-68.

The current fare structure creates economic problems both because of what it does and because of what it fails to do. Almost all municipalities fail to charge higher prices in peak hours and thus reduce the demand at these times and encourage use during off-peak hours. The result is overinvestment and greater capacity than can be justified on efficiency grounds. On the other hand, higher peak-load fares might lead to an allocatively inefficient use of private autos. More direct policies to prevent excessive auto use—such as higher charges for automobile licences, higher municipal parking fees, or effective regulations restricting use—might be more effective.

The problems generated by the absence of peak-load charges are complicated by the presence of quantity discounts. Rush-hour travellers are the primary users of these discounts, which lower their per-trip charge precisely when higher fares make more economic sense. Reduced fares for senior citizens, children, and students are also difficult to justify, especially at peak hours. Indeed, any subsidies that are supplied on the basis of age or status and are completely unrelated to income are difficult to support on efficiency and fairness grounds.

Finally, since the marginal cost of carrying a rider varies with the distance travelled, the failure of most large municipalities to use zone charges may create efficiency and fairness problems. Fixed fares imply that short-distance travellers are overpaying and long-distance travellers are underpaying; a less-than-efficient level of service is the result. They also imply that short-distance travellers are subsidizing long-distance travellers— a policy that is subject to the same criticism as the policy of providing reduced fares for seniors, children, and students.

## Public Recreation

The programs provided by municipal parks and recreational facilities that are most likely to involve user fees include skating (admissions, hourly ice rentals, and instruction), swimming (admissions, memberships, and instruction), tennis (court fees, membership, and instruction), camping (campground fees and day-camp charges), golf (greens fees, membership, and instruction), and so on. Although the relative importance of user fees in funding these services has increased in recent years, one survey of 19 municipalities in southern Ontario noted that in most instances the user fees do not take capital costs into account and, for that matter, cover only a fraction of operating costs.[156]

### Evaluation

Given the availability of private facilities and programs that may serve as substitutes for public facilities and programs, one may question whether there is any role for municipal involvement in recreational activities. The general response is that local governments provide these services for people who

---

[156] Sproule-Jones and White, supra footnote 134, at 1483.

cannot afford to pay for private services and in order to accommodate the positive externalities that recreational activities generate. To secure these objectives, the charge per activity or event is generally below operating costs. This subsidization, however, may be neither efficient nor fair. First, it can be and has been argued that local governments should not concern themselves with the issue of income distribution. Second, even if one grants that local governments should have some responsibility for income distribution, they should provide it through relief based on income or some other measure of ability to pay and not through reduced prices for everyone regardless of ability to pay. Probably the soundest basis for subsidization occurs where public recreation activities yield significant positive externalities. These externalities may take the form of a more physically fit and healthier society and hence lower medical costs for everyone. In reality, however, the externalities are unlikely to be significant. Indeed, they would probably be greater under an alternative and equally subsidized scheme of improved health and educational programs.

Since the largest portion of the benefits from recreational services accrue directly to users, these services should be priced so that they extract sufficient revenues to cover a comparable portion of the costs. Unfortunately, the public sector has not adopted many aspects of private sector pricing for similar services. Private suppliers, faced with the prospect of recovering all costs through their pricing structures, have recognized the advantages of an annual fixed levy plus an admission charge for each use of the facility. Municipalities virtually never follow this approach and therefore neither cover costs nor use their scarce resources efficiently.

Except in a few cases, such as arena rentals and golf courses, access to municipally provided facilities is generally rationed by queuing rather than by prices. Failure to adopt a peak-load pricing policy in order to even out the demand over a day or a week has led to overinvestment in many local facilities. The provision at all times of reduced charges for children and students aggravates the problem.[157] Lower fares for specific groups might be justified if they were limited to off-peak hours—a policy that is frequently adopted by private facilities and one that approximates the use of a peak-load pricing structure.

Proposals for greater reliance on user fees to finance recreational facilities are unlikely to receive much support from local citizens who have become accustomed to the provision of these facilities at little cost to the individual user. Nevertheless, the subsidization implicit in the current approach to financing creates demands on local budgets that are difficult to justify, given the private characteristics of the services in question. The current charges generate insufficient revenue, encourage overinvestment in local public facilities, and are inequitable in their overall impact on the distribution of

---

[157] Bird and Slack, supra footnote 3, at 70-73.

income. Greater dependence on user charges is essential if these deficiencies are to be overcome, or at least partially overcome.

## Library Charges

The current structure of user fees employed by most local public libraries may be in need of reorganization. Local public libraries collect rental fees for certain materials, fines for overdue books, and membership fees from non-residents but they never charge local residents on a usage basis. Consequently, an extremely high percentage of funding for local public libraries comes out of general revenue.

### Evaluation

This high degree of subsidization may be warranted if significant and positive externalities arise from the existence of public libraries. Clearly, positive externalities do arise from the easy accessibility of library resources: a more educated society is better off than a less educated one. In addition, however, substantial private benefits accrue directly to the users of library services. For this reason, it may be difficult to justify the degree of general funding that libraries currently receive. A policy that involved a usage charge that approximated the private portion of the marginal cost of each visit, plus a subsidy from the local government to cover the remainder of the marginal cost, would lead to a level of library services closer to the optimal level and a better use of scarce local resources.

Failure to price local public library services on a usage basis may have unplanned and perhaps unwanted consequences. For example, failure to charge for local library usage means that both users and non-users share in the cost of the library system, yet high-income users generally outnumber low-income users. It is questionable whether this form of redistribution would be tolerated if it were direct and open.

## Solid Waste Collection and Disposal

In a recent survey of municipalities across Canada, 75 percent of the 327 responding municipalities indicated that they used property taxes alone in funding solid waste collection. A further 22 percent reported that they used charges to pay for the service, but in nearly all cases the charges were periodic flat rate charges. Only 29 municipalities, or 2.4 percent of the total, reported using prepaid tags—that is, a user fee—as a way of funding all or part of residential garbage collection costs. Only 3 municipalities used this system exclusively; the other 26 used it to charge for extra cans or bags above a specified limit.[158]

---

[158] James C. McDavid and K. Anthony Eder, *The Efficiency of Residential Solid Waste Collection Services in Canada: The National Survey Report* (Victoria, BC: University of Victoria, School of Public Administration, Local Government Institute, 1997), 15.

Large industrial and commercial enterprises generally employ private contractors to collect and dispose of their garbage. Most municipalities use tipping fees to fund some or all of the cost of landfill sites. Growing reluctance to raise property taxes in order to fund local services and difficulties in locating disposal sites have encouraged municipal officials to take a serious look at the possibility of employing user fees, generally in the form of a specific charge per bag or container, for collection and disposal.

## Evaluation

There are persuasive arguments in favour of imposing a charge per bag or container of garbage. It is possible to identify the users of waste collection services and to calculate the per unit costs of the service, just as it is possible to identify the users of water and to calculate the per unit cost of water provision. A charge that includes the full marginal social costs of collection and disposal is critical if one is to discourage the current overpackaging of many goods.[159] As well, correct prices will lead to more efficient use of local resources and provide incentives for individuals to minimize the amount of garbage they produce.[160]

Unlike the use of user fees for water, however, the use of user fees for waste collection may have negative spillover effects. For instance, some individuals may avoid the tax by throwing their refuse onto neighbouring properties or disposing of it in rural areas. The higher is the price, the greater these undesirable spillovers are likely to be. The tradeoff between an acceptable price and the avoidance of spillovers is at the root of the current experimentation with user fees. Because of concerns about spillovers, prices are likely to be less than the socially efficient price, yet the practice of imposing a user fee of some sort should be applauded. It will certainly lead to greater concern about the generation of garbage and encourage other attempts to improve efficiency in local service provision.

## Police Services

Police services, which include numerous functions, are financed almost entirely from general local revenues. The only services for which special charges are levied are those that involve the policing of special events. In fact, a few municipalities charge higher rates for these services at certain times of the year, such as Christmas and New Year.

---

[159] For a detailed discussion of proper pricing for solid waste disposal (landfill sites), see James J. McRae, *Efficient Production of Solid Waste Services by Municipal Governments*, Government and Competitiveness Project Discussion Paper no. 94-11 (Kingston, Ont.: Queen's University, School of Policy Studies, 1994).

[160] *Fair Taxation in a Changing World*, supra footnote 9, at 583-94.

*Evaluation*

To the extent that police services generate positive externalities—as indeed, most police services do—a case can be made for funding them out of general revenues. To the extent that police services have private-use characteristics, however, it would be more efficient and more fair to impose charges on the direct users of the services. The "privateness" of some police services is demonstrable. For instance, individuals and businesses can and do purchase protection services from private agencies. They can also purchase security systems and guard dogs. The fact that these activities are priced in the private sector suggests that it should be possible to price the provision of similar protection services by the public sector. Indeed, pricing might very well generate the revenue needed to finance a level of police services that is more nearly optimal than the current level.

The difficulty of approximating a "price-equals-marginal-social-cost" charge on an individual basis for police services with private-good characteristics is such that charges of this kind are unlikely to be implemented. One might argue, however, that all individuals who benefit from a certain service ought to pay a price that is the same for all members of that group. For example, special vehicle or operator licence fees levied at the local level, or a transfer to local governments of provincially collected gasoline-tax revenue or—a policy recently introduced in Ontario—revenue from fines for traffic offences, would help to cover part of the police costs associated with traffic control and safety.

Another measure would be to institute fines or charges for people who fail to lock their automobiles or their residential, commercial, or industrial properties. Failure to protect private property adequately encourages criminal behaviour and increases the cost of police protection. In fact, it has been suggested that special fees or charges be imposed on properties that require more than usual levels of protection.[161]

In short, provided that the administrative costs of imposing an expanded system of user charges for police services is not prohibitive, a strong case can be made for greater use of user charges in funding these services.

## Fire Services

Fire protection of local properties is a municipal responsibility that is financed from local revenues. A number of municipalities, however, charge neighbouring municipalities for fire assistance. Many also charge individuals or their insurance companies for dealing with road accidents.

---

[161] For more detail on the rationale behind this suggestion and a discussion of how it might be implemented, see Bird, supra footnote 4, at 129-33; and Bird and Tsiopoulos, supra footnote 4.

*Evaluation*

The issue is whether general property tax funding for fire protection is fair and efficient. Although the presence of positive externalities suggests that funding from general revenue is appropriate, the externalities tend to be reciprocal. Reciprocal externalities create a basis for charging every taxpayer full direct costs. There is no need for general-revenue funding of fire protection; instead, everyone should be required to buy fire protection.[162]

Prices for fire protection, as distinct from police protection, already exist through the extensive use of insurance policies. Fire insurance premiums can reflect both fire insurance experience and the risks associated with various structural types, taking into account the use of fire-resistant building materials and sprinkler systems. Factors that affect insurance risks also determine municipal expenditures for this service. Failure to vary the municipal price charged for fire protection on the basis of risk is almost certain to lead to an oversupply of fire-fighting equipment. Thus failure to impose varying prices reduces the incentive for the owners of risky properties to undertake actions designed to minimize their demand for fire protection and hence generates a demand for expenditures on fire protection that is greater than it would be if prices did vary. The practice of charging neighbouring municipalities for fire assistance and individuals for assistance in road accidents is an appropriate one, even though there is no indication that fire departments currently price these services correctly.

Because insurance premiums take property values, fire probability, and damage susceptibility into consideration, they could provide a basis for a municipal user fee. As long as the charge varies to reflect varying risks, a more efficient level of service should ensue.[163] Finally, the existence of a private market for fire insurance premiums suggests that the administrative costs of managing such a system should not be prohibitive.

## Summary

Local governments in Canada derive the vast majority of their revenues from three major sources—property taxes, user fees, and grants. Property taxes and user fees, however, are the only two sources over which local governments have any control. Grants are at the discretion of the province and are generally used to promote provincial objectives, which may not coincide with the objectives of local governments.

Property taxes, which include taxes on real property, special assessments, business taxes, and local improvement levies, represent the third-largest source of tax revenue in Canada. Since 1971, property taxes and user fees have increased in relative importance in every province, and this trend is likely to continue as provinces further reduce their grants to municipalities.

---

[162] Bird, supra footnote 4, at 137.

[163] Bird and Tsiopoulos, supra footnote 4, at 81.

Given the importance of property taxes and user fees as means of funding local public services, a number of issues should be addressed, not the least of which is the role that these revenue sources should play. In general, it is accepted that local governments should operate under the benefits-received model of financing, which is based on the principle of setting a per-unit fee or tax (price) that is equal to the marginal social cost of providing the last unit of the service consumed. Of course, there are sometimes efficiency reasons for deviating from this principle, such as when second-best problems or capacity constraints arise. User fees are a fair, efficient, and accountable means of financing if it is possible to identify individual beneficiaries of the service, allocate the service to those who are willing to pay, exclude non-users the service, and estimate the per-unit cost of provision. Property taxes are appropriate if they are used only to finance services whose benefits are enjoyed collectively by the residents of the local jurisdiction; that is where it is not possible to identify individual beneficiaries or to exclude individuals or properties from the service.

Current practice in setting property taxes and user fees, however, generally deviates from fairness, efficiency, and accountability. This, it must be emphasized, is the current practice; it has nothing to do with whether or not property taxes and user fees are appropriate revenue sources for local governments. Indeed, they are! Our point here is simply that both their design and their application could be and should be improved. In the case of the property tax, improvement implies the assessment of all properties, commercial, industrial, and residential, in a uniform manner; that is, assessed value should in every case be the same percentage of the assessment base. The choice of the assessment base is itself an issue: the base that minimizes transaction and transition costs and that could, with some modifications, meet the conditions for being efficient, fair, and accountable is market value. Most analysts of public sector policy and public sector administrators agree that market value is superior to either site-value assessment or unit assessment.

If different property types are to be taxed at different rates, this should be accomplished through the use of variable tax (mill) rates. The variation in rates should accommodate differences in the cost of servicing different properties according to property type or location. In this connection, there are solid analytical and empirical arguments in support of reversing the current tax discrimination against commercial and industrial properties. In every province, non-residential properties are currently taxed at higher rates than residential properties, yet the available evidence suggests that residential properties receive the majority of local benefits. Furthermore, if the property tax is a tax on capital, current tax rates on non-residential properties should be reduced. More closely aligning property taxes with services received would reduce the extent to which non-residential property taxes are exported (in the form of higher product prices) and, consequently, improve both the efficiency and the fairness of the tax. Additional improvements would be secured by eliminating the current practice of exempting certain properties from the tax base.

The most important misconception about the residential property tax is that it is extremely regressive. In fact, we do not really know whether it is regressive or not. The evidence is inconclusive. Some studies claim that the tax is mildly regressive, others that it is proportional or, possibly, progressive. This uncertainty has not, however, deterred provincial and local governments from introducing relief schemes of doubtful fairness and efficiency (property tax credits, tax deferrals, grants, exemptions, and reductions, cancellations, or refunds) to remove any regressivity that may exist.

Property taxes are used not only for funding municipal operating expenditures. Municipalities also impose special assessments and municipal bonusing and development charges on property for the purpose of funding capital projects. Under the benefits model, these taxes are especially appropriate where specific beneficiaries can be identified. Problems occasionally emerge in their application, however.

Recent concern over property tax increases in many municipalities has renewed interest in municipal access to local income, sales, fuel, and hotel and motel occupancy taxes. These taxes are generally viewed as supplementary and not as substitutes for property taxes. A local income tax, either one "piggybacked" onto the provincial income tax or one applied directly to local employment earnings (a payroll tax, for example), is likely to produce more revenue and to create fewer distortions and inequities than either a retail sales tax or a hotel and motel occupancy tax. A far less satisfactory alternative to the property tax is the poll tax: poll taxes would be difficult and costly to administer, and they would almost certainly be more regressive than property taxes. A fuel tax would be especially appropriate for funding municipal transportation and public transit.

User fees too would benefit from changes in their structure. Ultimately, the objective in setting correct prices is to establish a clear link between services received and prices paid. It should be relatively easy to establish this link in the case of services such as water and sewers, public transit, public recreation, libraries, and solid waste collection and disposal; the price structures for these services should take into consideration the cost differentials that arise from matters such as distance from source and peak-period use. It would be more difficult, but not impossible, to set user fees for certain services provided by municipal police and fire departments. Indeed, the employment of user fees in this context would almost certainly improve the allocation of municipal resources. In the case of services that provide collective benefits, such as roads, street lighting, and elementary and secondary schooling, user fees would not be appropriate. Local property taxes are a better alternative.

# 8

# Transfers to Individuals

## The Existing Transfer System

Governments do not use all of their tax revenues to purchase goods and services for the public sector. They disburse substantial amounts as transfer payments to individual members of society or to other levels of government.[1] This chapter discusses transfer payments to individuals. These transfers account for a large and growing proportion of government activity at all levels of government. Table 8.1 shows how transfers to individuals grew over the period 1926 to 1996. Table 8.2 shows the proportion of all transfer payments made by each level of government. Each level's share of total transfers has changed relatively little since the end of World War II. Slightly more than 60 percent of the transfers come from the federal government, almost 40 percent from the provinces, and a very small proportion from municipalities.

As the tables indicate, transfers to individuals have evolved over many years and after the war the federal government instituted programs to assist veterans. Limited municipal and provincial transfers were in effect before World War I. The first major federal initiative in the field, however, was the Old Age Assistance Act of 1927. Old age assistance was a federal-provincial shared-cost program that provided allowances to persons over 70 years of age on the basis of a means test. Since then, numerous federal, provincial, and municipal programs have been introduced, withdrawn, and altered as governments have come and gone or the direction of social policy has changed.

Transfer payments fulfil a number of functions. They may be intended simply to redistribute income in the economy, in which case they can be thought of as negative taxes. They may be intended as a form of insurance that the private insurance industry is unable to provide. They may be intended to provide assistance to particular needy groups of individuals in the economy. They may be intended to facilitate particular sorts of expenditures such as housing or health. Or they may be intended to achieve a combination of these ends. Some programs are administered federally, others provincially or municipally, still others jointly. This section will outline the various types of transfer schemes. Subsequent sections will consider the economic effects of different transfer schemes and the structural problems associated with these schemes.

---

[1] A transfer payment is a payment for which no good or service is received in return (that is, there is no quid pro quo). A survey of intergovernmental transfers may be found in Robin W. Boadway and Paul A.R. Hobson, *Intergovernmental Fiscal Relations in Canada*, Canadian Tax Paper no. 96 (Toronto: Canadian Tax Foundation, 1993).

**Table 8.1    Transfers to Individuals as a Percentage of Government
Disbursements, Selected Years 1926 to 1996**

|  | All levels of government | Federal government |
|---|---|---|
|  | *percent* | |
| 1926 ................. | 9.9 | 13.5 |
| 1930 ................. | 11.8 | 15.7 |
| 1935 ................. | 20.3 | 11.2 |
| 1940 ................. | 12.0 | 6.1 |
| 1945 ................. | 10.6 | 8.9 |
| 1950 ................. | 25.5 | 26.8 |
| 1955 ................. | 23.4 | 26.5 |
| 1960 ................. | 26.7 | 30.3 |
| 1965 ................. | 18.9 | 28.2 |
| 1970 ................. | 19.0 | 27.4 |
| 1975 ................. | 21.1 | 30.9 |
| 1980 ................. | 20.7 | 27.6 |
| 1985 ................. | 27.5 | 28.2 |
| 1990 ................. | 28.4 | 28.1 |
| 1995 ................. | 32.1 | 31.6 |
| 1996 ................. | 32.3 | 32.6 |

Sources: Statistics Canada, *National Income and Expenditure Accounts*, vol. 1, *The Annual Estimates 1926-1974*, catalogue no. 13-531; Statistics Canada, *National Income and Expenditure Accounts, 2nd Quarter, 1981*, catalogue no. 13-001; and Statistics Canada, *National Income and Expenditure Accounts, Quarterly Estimates, 4th Quarter*, 1992 and 1996, catalogue no. 13-001.

**Table 8.2    Distribution of Transfers to Individuals by
Level of Government, Selected Years 1926 to 1996**

|  | Federal | Provincial | Municipal | Total |
|---|---|---|---|---|
|  | *percent* | | | |
| 1926 ................. | 52.7 | 35.1 | 12.2 | 100.0 |
| 1930 ................. | 44.1 | 46.8 | 9.0 | 100.0 |
| 1935 ................. | 21.5 | 64.8 | 13.7 | 100.0 |
| 1940 ................. | 29.9 | 61.8 | 8.3 | 100.0 |
| 1945 ................. | 70.5 | 26.8 | 2.8 | 100.0 |
| 1950 ................. | 60.1 | 37.5 | 2.3 | 100.0 |
| 1955 ................. | 71.5 | 26.1 | 2.4 | 100.0 |
| 1960 ................. | 63.9 | 33.8 | 2.4 | 100.0 |
| 1965 ................. | 67.5 | 29.9 | 2.6 | 100.0 |
| 1970 ................. | 59.2 | 37.8 | 3.0 | 100.0 |
| 1975 ................. | 65.3 | 33.2 | 1.5 | 100.0 |
| 1980 ................. | 60.8 | 37.9 | 1.3 | 100.0 |
| 1985 ................. | 61.7 | 36.7 | 1.7 | 100.0 |
| 1990 ................. | 60.2 | 37.5 | 2.3 | 100.0 |
| 1995 ................. | 61.2 | 38.8 | [a] | 100.0 |
| 1996 ................. | 61.7 | 38.3 | [a] | 100.0 |

[a] Combined with the provincial total.

Sources: Same as table 8.1.

Transfers to individuals can take many forms. It may be convenient to classify them as follows: demogrants, guaranteed income, social insurance, and social assistance.

## Demogrants

A demogrant is a transfer of a given amount to all members of a particular group in the population. The most general form of a demogrant is a poll or head subsidy that provides an equal grant to all members of the population. Usually, however, demogrants apply to a specific category of persons, such as the aged or children. The important characteristic of demogrants is that their size is not related to any economic variable such as income or need. All persons in a given category receive the same amount. On the other hand, demogrants must sometimes be included as income for tax purposes, so the net-of-tax amount received can vary with income.

## Guaranteed Income

Under a guaranteed income scheme, the amount of transfer is related to the income of the recipient: the higher is the income, the lower is the amount received. As the name implies, a guaranteed income scheme ensures that the recipient's income does not fall below a guaranteed minimum. A person who earns no other income will receive the guaranteed minimum. As income rises, the amount of the transfer may fall. The ratio of the amount by which the transfer falls to the amount of increased income is called the *recapture rate*. If the recapture rate is 100 percent, any increase in income will be completely offset by reductions in transfers, so that earning income makes the individual no better off until his income exceeds the guaranteed minimum. A demogrant has a recapture rate of 0 percent. A recapture rate of 50 percent implies that for every dollar earned the transfer is reduced by 50 cents. In other words, the transfer is subject to an implicit tax of 50 percent. Guaranteed income schemes are also referred to as negative income tax programs.

Table 8.3 illustrates the effect of four different recapture rates on a guaranteed income of $9,000 per year. If the recapture rate is 100 percent, the individual receives transfers until his income reaches the guaranteed minimum. If the recapture rate is 50 percent, he receives transfers until his income reaches twice the guaranteed minimum. If it is 25 percent, the cutoff point is four times the guaranteed minimum. In general, the lower is the recapture rate, the higher is the income on which transfers will be paid. A lower recapture rate gives individuals a stronger incentive to undertake income-earning activities, since more of any increase in income is retained. On the other hand, the lower the recapture rate is, the more the government must pay to achieve a given guaranteed minimum income.

## Social Insurance

The purpose of social insurance schemes is to compensate persons for loss of their regular income either temporarily or permanently. The major causes

**Table 8.3   Guaranteed Income Schemes with a Guaranteed Minimum of $9,000 per Year and Various Recapture Rates**

| Individual or family income ($ per year) | Transfer payment ($ per year) at a recapture rate of | | | |
|---|---|---|---|---|
|  | 0 per cent | 25 percent | 50 percent | 100 percent |
| 0 | 9,000 | 9,000 | 9,000 | 9,000 |
| 3,000 | 9,000 | 8,250 | 7,500 | 6,000 |
| 6,000 | 9,000 | 7,500 | 6,000 | 3,000 |
| 9,000 | 9,000 | 6,750 | 4,500 | 0 |
| 12,000 | 9,000 | 6,000 | 3,000 | |
| 15,000 | 9,000 | 5,250 | 1,500 | |
| 18,000 | 9,000 | 4,500 | 0 | |
| 36,000 | 9,000 | 0 | | |

of loss of income are unemployment, disability (through employment or war), death of a family income-earner, and retirement; typically, a separate program is established for each cause. Social insurance might also be construed as including schemes that finance medical and hospital payments.

Social insurance programs exist because the private sector insurance industry is perceived as being unable to provide adequate coverage, perhaps because of the risk involved. For example, the private sector would not likely provide comprehensive employment insurance. Private pension plans do not have the characteristics of public ones, such as universality and portability over employment and provinces.

Unlike private insurance, most social insurance systems are not actuarially sound; that is, they include an element of subsidy. This is true of employment insurance and retirement insurance. Obviously, the private sector would not provide subsidized insurance plans. The question remains why social insurance plans should not be required to be actuarially sound—a point we shall discuss later in the chapter.

## Social Assistance

Finally, there are those transfer schemes whose purpose is to assist persons in need who have no recourse to other support programs. Thus the beneficiaries of social assistance include the disabled and other unemployables, widows, single parents, and, sometimes, low-income persons who are not eligible for other means of support. Social assistance payments are allocated on the basis of either need or means or both, and they are administered by local agencies whose function it is to determine the extent of need. Administration itself can be a costly function that requires the gathering of detailed information for each recipient.

## Federal Programs

The discussion here restricts itself to programs that provide pure transfers. It omits schemes whose primary purpose is to provide support for particular types of expenditures such as medical care or hospital insurance. The major income-security programs are the responsibility of the federal government and include the old age security (OAS) pension, the guaranteed income supplement (GIS), the spouse's allowance, the goods and services tax (GST) credit, and the child tax benefit.[2] The federal government is also responsible for the Canada Pension Plan (CPP) and the employment insurance (EI) program.

## The Old Age Security (OAS) Pension

Old age security payments are available to all persons over 65 or over who satisfy a residency requirement.[3] Table 8.4 shows the basic OAS pension payable for selected years from 1951 to 1998. These benefits are indexed for inflation, as determined by the consumer price index, on a quarterly basis. OAS benefits are taxable and therefore subject to full or partial recovery from high-income recipients. In 1998, the clawback was 15 percent of net individual income in excess of $53,215 to a maximum of the full benefits received. The clawback is deductible from taxable income.[4]

The OAS program does not operate on insurance principles. That is, pensioners' receipts are not "funded" by contributions that they have made during their working lives. Before 1972, OAS payments came out of an earmarked fund that was financed by special taxes on personal and corporate income and on sales. In 1972, however, these earmarked taxes were eliminated, and in 1975 the OAS fund was terminated, so that now OAS payments are pure transfers financed from general revenues. The implications of this arrangement will be discussed below.

## The Guaranteed Income Supplement (GIS)

The GIS is an income-tested supplement to the OAS payment to pensioners. As of January 1, 1998, the maximum GIS was $483.86 per month (or $5,806.32 per year) for a single person and $630.34 per month (or $7,564.08 per year) for a married couple (see table 8.4). The GIS operates as a negative income tax system with a 50 percent recapture rate: for every dollar of other family income earned, the GIS is reduced by 50 cents. In 1997, the GIS for a single person was completely eliminated when family income reached $11,612.64 per year. For a married couple, it was eliminated when family income reached $15,128.16. The GIS, like the OAS, is fully indexed to the inflation rate on a quarterly basis.

Because of the economies that presumably arise from living together, a married couple receives a supplement about 30 percent larger than the

---

[2] Karin Treff and David B. Perry, *Finances of the Nation 1998* (Toronto: Canadian Tax Foundation, 1998), 9:4.

[3] The residence requirement is that the recipient must have been resident in Canada for at least 10 years preceding application or have 3 years prior residence for each year out. Aggregate residence of 40 years after age 18 is also satisfactory. Those not satisfying these residence requirements are not eligible.

[4] Supra footnote 2, at 3:6.

**Table 8.4   Maximum Monthly Pension Under the Old Age Security
Act, Selected Years from Inception of the Program**

| Effective date | Basic pension (OAS) | Guaranteed income supplement (GIS) | | Maximum payment | |
|---|---|---|---|---|---|
| | | Single | Married couple | Single | Married couple |
| | | *dollars* | | | |
| January 1, 1952 ........ | 40.00 | — | — | 40.00 | — |
| January 1, 1967 ........ | 75.00 | 30.00 | — | 105.00 | — |
| April 1, 1974 .......... | 80.00 | 55.00 | 95.00 | 135.00 | 255.00 |
| January 1, 1975 ........ | 120.06 | 84.21 | 149.58 | 204.27 | 389.70 |
| January 1, 1980 ........ | 182.42 | 149.76 | 249.04 | 332.18 | 613.88 |
| January 1, 1985 ........ | 273.80 | 325.41 | 423.86 | 599.21 | 971.46 |
| January 1, 1986 ........ | 285.20 | 338.95 | 441.50 | 624.15 | 1,011.90 |
| January 1, 1987 ........ | 297.37 | 353.41 | 460.34 | 650.78 | 1,055.08 |
| January 1, 1988 ........ | 310.66 | 369.21 | 480.94 | 679.87 | 1,102.26 |
| January 1, 1989 ........ | 323.28 | 384.19 | 500.46 | 707.47 | 1,146.82 |
| January 1, 1990 ........ | 340.07 | 404.13 | 526.46 | 744.20 | 1,206.60 |
| January 1, 1991 ........ | 354.92 | 421.79 | 549.46 | 776.71 | 1,259.30 |
| January 1, 1992 ........ | 374.07 | 444.54 | 579.10 | 818.61 | 1,327.24 |
| January 1, 1993 ........ | 378.95 | 450.34 | 586.68 | 829.29 | 1,344.58 |
| January 1, 1994 ........ | 385.81 | 458.50 | 597.30 | 844.31 | 1,368.92 |
| January 1, 1995 ........ | 387.74 | 460.79 | 600.28 | 848.53 | 1,375.76 |
| January 1, 1996 ........ | 394.76 | 469.13 | 611.14 | 863.89 | 1,400.66 |
| January 1, 1997 ........ | 400.71 | 476.20 | 620.36 | 876.91 | 1,421.78 |
| January 1, 1998 ........ | 407.15 | 483.86 | 630.34 | 891.01 | 1,444.63 |

— not applicable.

Source: Karin Treff and David B. Perry, *Finances of the Nation 1998* (Toronto: Canadian Tax Foundation, 1998), 9:6, table 9.4.

supplement for a single person, rather than twice as large. As of January 1998, the maximum OAS and GIS payment for a married couple over 65 was $1,444.63 per month or $17,335.56 per year.

Several provinces provide supplements to OAS and GIS payments. Most provinces also provide pensioners with various services in kind, including old age homes and subsidies for expenditures such as housing, dental care, and medical expenses. In addition, Ontario, Manitoba, Saskatchewan, Alberta, British Columbia, the Northwest Territories, and the Yukon provide financial supplements to OAS/GIS recipients whose incomes fall below specific limits.

## The Spouse's Allowance

The spouse's allowance is an income-tested pension payment that is available to needy people between the ages of 60 and 64 whether or not they receive the guaranteed income supplement and whether their spouses are living or dead. As of April 1998, the maximum allowance was $722.32 per month for a spouse whose partner was living and $797.45 for a widowed spouse. The allowance is fully indexed on a quarterly basis, and it diminishes as family income grows. As of April 1, 1998, in the case of a couple in which one spouse was a pensioner, the allowance began to disappear when family income reached $21,696 for a couple (where one spouse was a non-pensioner) and $15,912 for a widow or widower aged 60 to 64.[5]

## The Canada Child Tax Benefit (CCTB)

The CCTB aims to fight child poverty and remove the financial disincentives for a family to leave social assistance for low-income employment.[6] The CCTB is composed of a basic benefit plus the national child benefit supplement. The basic annual benefit is $1,020 per child under 18, a supplement of $75 for the third and each additional child, and an additional supplement of $213 for each child under the age of 7. These amounts are reduced by 25 percent for any amount claimed for child care expenses on the income tax return.

The annual national child benefit supplement is $605 for one child, reduced by 12.1 percent of the amount of family net income in excess of $20,921; $1,010 for two children, reduced by 20.2 percent of family net income over $20,921; and $1,010 for the first two children plus $330 for each additional child, reduced by 26.8 percent of the amount of net family income over $20,921.

Benefits from provincial and territorial programs are combined with the CCTB into a single monthly payment, but provinces are allowed to vary the value of the child tax benefit, provided that the average benefit per child financed federally is unchanged. Two provinces vary the way in which federal payments are disbursed. In Quebec, payments under the federal child tax benefit program are based on both the age of the child and the number of children in the family. In Alberta, payments are based on the age of the children.[7]

## The Goods and Services Tax Credit

The federal sales tax credit, which is applied after the calculation of basic federal tax, provides relief from the GST for low-income families and individuals. In 1998, the credit provided a maximum of $199 per adult and $105 per dependent under 18. The credit was reduced by 5 percent of net income over $25,921 and disappeared when an individual's income exceeded $30,000 and a family's income exceeded $35,000. Single individuals were eligible for a supplementary credit equal to 2 percent of net income in excess of $6,456 to a maximum of $105.

---

[5] Ibid., at 9:7.

[6] For a listing of the major developments in tax and transfer benefits for children in Canada from 1918 to the introduction of the child tax benefit, see Jonathan R. Kesselman, "The Child Tax Benefit: Simple, Fair, Responsive?" (June 1993), 19 *Canadian Public Policy* 109-32, at 110.

[7] For more detail on provincial programs, see supra footnote 2, at 9:8-9.

## The Canada Pension Plan (CPP)

The CPP was introduced in 1966 to supplement the existing OAS scheme and private pension plans. It was phased in over a period of 10 years and hence was fully operational by 1975. At the same time, Quebec set up its own pension plan (the QPP) on basically the same principles as the CPP.

The CPP is in part a social insurance scheme, since the benefits paid are at least partially related to contributions. It is also in part a transfer program since, as we shall show below, it is not actuarially sound: an individual's contributions during his working years are not expected to cover exactly his expected benefits upon retirement. In the long run, the CPP incorporates transfers between generations—that is, from the working to the retired.

### Contributions

Contributions[8] to the CPP are compulsory for almost all employed and self-employed persons in Canada. Contributions are not required from persons under the age of 18 or over 70, pensioners, armed forces personnel, certain provincial government employees, casual or migratory workers, or certain other employees. The CPP is financed by what is basically a proportional payroll tax with a fixed exemption level and an upper limit. Table 8.5 shows how the figures for exempt earnings, yearly maximum pensionable earnings, and maximum contributions for employers and employees have changed since the program began. In 1998, the maximum contribution, for employees and employers alike, was $1,068.80 ($2,137.60 for the self-employed). A tax credit for these contributions is applicable against income tax liability.[9]

In December 1997, concern about the CPP's inability to generate sufficient revenues to fund future pension benefits led the federal government to legislate increases in the contributory rate. The rate will rise annually until 2003—from 6.0 percent of contributory earnings in 1997 to 9.9 percent—and remain steady thereafter. Initially, the higher rates will generate a surplus, and the government anticipates that the returns from investment of the surplus will keep the contributory rates lower in the long run than it would otherwise be.

### Benefits

#### Retirement Benefits

The CPP makes an earnings-related pension available to any contributor aged 60 years[10] or more. These benefits, however, are intended only to supplement existing pension arrangements, public and private. The benefits paid to

---

[8] Contributory rates are described in chapter 6.

[9] See the discussion in chapter 3.

[10] The normal age of eligibility is 65; however, reduced benefits are available as early as age 60 and increased pensions are available up to age 70.

**Table 8.5  Canada Pension Plan Monthly Contributions and Benefits, Selected Years from Inception of the Program**

| Effective date | Exempt earnings | Yearly maximum pensionable earnings | Maximum contributions, employers and employees[a] | Maximum monthly pension | | | |
|---|---|---|---|---|---|---|---|
| | | | | Retirement | Surviving spouse under 65 | Orphan[b] | Disability |
| | | | | *dollars* | | | |
| Jan. 1, 1966 | 600 | 5,000 | 79.20 | — | — | — | — |
| Jan. 1, 1970 | 600 | 5,300 | 84.60 | 43.33 | 67.16 | 26.53 | 92.88 |
| Jan. 1, 1975 | 700 | 7,400 | 120.60 | 122.50 | 88.31 | 37.27 | 139.35 |
| Jan. 1, 1980 | 1,300 | 13,100 | 212.40 | 244.44 | 148.92 | 57.25 | 240.58 |
| Jan. 1, 1985 | 2,300 | 23,400 | 379.80 | 435.42 | 250.84 | 87.56 | 414.13 |
| Jan. 1, 1990 | 2,800 | 28,900 | 574.20 | 577.08 | 324.37 | 107.96 | 709.52 |
| Jan. 1, 1991 | 3,000 | 30,500 | 632.50 | 604.86 | 396.96 | 113.14 | 743.61 |
| Jan. 1, 1992 | 3,200 | 32,200 | 696.00 | 636.11 | 358.24 | 154.70 | 783.89 |
| Jan. 1, 1993 | 3,300 | 33,400 | 752.50 | 667.36 | 372.11 | 257.48 | 812.85 |
| Jan. 1, 1994 | 3,400 | 34,400 | 806.00 | 694.44 | 384.59 | 160.47 | 839.09 |
| Jan. 1, 1995 | 3,400 | 34,900 | 850.50 | 713.19 | 392.24 | 161.27 | 854.74 |
| Jan. 1, 1996 | 3,500 | 35,400 | 893.20 | 727.08 | 399.70 | 164.17 | 870.92 |
| Jan. 1, 1997 | 3,500 | 35,800 | 944.78 | 736.81 | 405.25 | 166.63 | 883.10 |
| Jan. 1, 1998 | 3,500 | 36,900 | 1,068.80 | 744.79 | 410.70 | 169.80 | 895.36 |

[a] Since self-employed persons contribute as both employer and employee, their contributions are double the amount shown. [b] Reduced by one-half for each orphan in excess of four.

Sources: Statistical Bulletin, Canada Pension Plan; and Karin Treff and David B. Perry, *Finances of the Nation 1998* (Toronto: Canadian Tax Foundation, 1998), 9:16, table 9.10.

a person are related to the level of contributions and the length of time during which contributions have been made.

Table 8.5 shows the maximum CPP payments for selected years since the inception of the program. In 1998, the maximum monthly pension was $744.79. Pensions are indexed annually in line with the increase in the consumer price index. As the table shows, CPP retirement benefits are considerably higher than the benefits for a surviving spouse under 65 but lower than disability benefits.

## Survivors' Benefits[11]

In addition to ordinary retirement benefits, the CPP provides various benefits to surviving members of contributors' families— a situation that, of course, puts families at an advantage relative to single contributors. This situation is one reflection of the CPP's lack of actuarial fairness. Survivors' benefits include lump-sum death benefits, benefits to spouses, and benefits to orphans. For one's survivors to be eligible for these benefits, one must have contributed to the program for at least two years.

The death benefit is frozen at $2,500. Otherwise, the benefits described here are all indexed annually for inflation. Spouses of deceased contributors receive a survivor's pension if they are disabled, supporting dependent children, or over 34 years of age. In 1998, as table 8.5 shows, the maximum monthly survivor's pension was $410.70. On reaching age 65, the survivor receives a pension equal to 60 percent of the deceased's pension as indexed for inflation since his death. Surviving spouses who are not disabled or have no dependent children receive the full spousal benefit as outlined if they are over age 45; between ages 35 and 44, their benefits are proportionately reduced.

Orphans' benefits are paid to surviving dependent children of the deceased who are orphans, under 18 years of age, and unmarried. The age limit is extended to 25 for orphans who are still in school. The benefits are a straight allowance and were $169.80 per month in 1998.

## Disability Benefits

Contributors to the CPP are eligible to collect disability benefits if they become severely disabled before normal retirement age provided they have made contributions (on earnings over $3,500) in four of the six years before they become disabled. The maximum disability pension in 1998 was $895.36 per month. The pension is indexed annually on the basis of the consumer price index. Any dependent children of the disabled individual are eligible for the orphan's benefit, which is calculated as if the individual had died. Once the disabled individual reaches age 65, he receives the full retirement pension; the pension is calculated on the basis of his contributions up to the

---

time he became disabled and indexed for the increase in the consumer price index since that time.

## Financing the CPP

During the CPP's first two decades or so, contributions exceeded payments and the program generated an annual surplus. For the past decade, however, the situation has been reversed. Indeed, the aging of our population has caused a cash drain on the system sufficient to generate fears that the CPP will become extinct.[12] This concern has led to new federal legislation, effective on January 1, 1998, to ensure that the CPP remains viable as a public pension plan.[13] In particular, the legislation provides for an increase in the contributory rate each year until 2003, reductions in some benefits, new investment policies,[14] and reductions in administration costs.[15]

Although these changes appear to improve the CPP as a pension vehicle, the program still is not fully funded.[16] If it were, there would always be money in the pension fund out of which benefits could be paid. Under a fully funded plan, individuals' contributions over their working lives would, on average, fully finance their pensions. In other words, a fully funded plan would be actuarially sound in the sense that for each contributor, expected contributions plus interest on these contributions would equal expected benefits. The CPP falls short of actuarial soundness in this sense in four distinct ways. First, current recipients of CPP benefits are receiving more than they have contributed. In fact, any contributor who was over age 18 in 1966 will contribute for less than his full working life. Second, the plan bases benefit payments on average maximum pensionable earnings during the contributor's last five years of work, which will almost certainly be higher than the contributor's lifetime average earnings. Third, single individuals and individuals with families pay into the plan at the same rate, but the latter

---

[12] For a discussion of the crisis in public pensions in Canada, see "Public Pensions" (September 1995), 16 *Policy Options* (entire issue).

[13] For a discussion of these changes and alternatives, see James Pesando, "From Tax Grab to Retirement Saving: Privatizing the CPP Premium Hike" (June 1997), no. 93 *C.D. Howe Institute Commentary.*

[14] Funds in the Canada Pension Plan were previously invested in non-negotiable provincial bonds at concessionary rates (which may have induced the provinces to spend more). New funds are invested in a diversified portfolio of private investment securities and provincial bonds in order to increase the return (and eliminate cheap financing for the provinces).

[15] Other suggestions for reform have included raising the retirement age, eliminating the year's basic exemption ($3,500 of pensionable earnings), and eliminating the dropout provision. See Newman Lam, James Cutt, and Michael Prince, "The Canadian Pension Plan: Retrospect and Prospect," in Keith G. Banting and Robin Boadway, eds., *Reform of Retirement Income Policy: International and Canadian Perspectives* (Kingston, Ont.: Queen's University, School of Policy Studies, 1997), 105-34.

[16] The chief actuary estimated that the unfunded liability of the CPP was $556 billion at the end of 1995: Canada, *An Information Paper for Consultations on the Canada Pension Plan: Released by the Federal, Provincial and Territorial Governments* (Ottawa: Department of Finance, 1996).

receive benefits that the former do not. Finally, the plan does not require persons known to have a higher "risk" to contribute at a higher rate, as it would do if the plan were operated on insurance principles. All contributors pay at the same rate, regardless of the benefits they are expected to receive later on. To the extent that individuals can be categorized on the basis of life expectancy, pensionable earnings, retirement age, or any of the other variables that influence the relation between contributions and benefits, a pure insurance scheme would charge correspondingly different premiums.

As we noted above, the CPP is, in fact, a combination of an insurance plan and a transfer program. It is partially funded, but also partially financed from current revenues—that is, on a "pay-as-you-go" basis. It involves both a transfer from the working population to the retired population and a transfer from the working population to the families of contributors. In addition, some groups in the population pay more in contributions relative to the benefits they are expected to receive than other groups do.

Although the recent legislation has improved the future viability of the CPP, the plan retains its fundamentally ambiguous roles as a vehicle for both income support (redistribution)[17] and income replacement (pension).[18] The primary element of income support or redistribution in the plan is its provision of spousal and survivor benefits, disability benefits, and benefits to those who have temporarily left the work force in order to bear or rear children. The exemption from contributions of the first $3,500 of income is another distributional feature of the plan. Given the popularity of these supplementary benefits, it is not likely that the government will eliminate them. The question, then, is how they ought to be financed. The problem with the present approach, once again, is that it is not actuarially sound: those who are ineligible for the supplementary benefits subsidize those who are eligible. One alternative would be to fund the supplementary benefits under the CPP from general revenues and the purely earnings-related portion of the plan from contributions. Another would be to remove the redistributive elements from the CPP system and deal with them as part of an income-redistribution program.[19]

## Employment Insurance (EI)

Employment insurance, like the Canada Pension Plan, combines elements of insurance with elements of income transfer. The scheme's insurance aspect is fairly obvious: it provides income for persons who are unexpectedly out of work temporarily. EI is not a pure insurance scheme, however, since a person's contributions are not actuarially equal to the expected future employment benefits. The system makes no distinction on either the contri-

---

[17] See Ken Battle, "A New Old Age Pension," in *Reform of Retirement Income Policy*, supra footnote 15, 135-90.

[18] See Lam, Cutt, and Prince, supra footnote 15.

[19] Keith G. Banting and Robin Boadway, "Reforming Retirement Income Policy: The Issues," in *Reform of Retirement Income Policy*, supra footnote 15, 1-26, at 19-22.

butions side or the benefits side between persons in low-risk occupations and persons in risky occupations—that is, between those who are less likely and those who are more likely to claim benefits in the future. For example, EI treats salaried office workers in exactly the same manner as seasonal workers such as construction workers and fishers, even though the former are considerably less likely than the latter ever to receive EI benefits.

Employment insurance does not cover everyone. It excludes individuals who are not in the labour force and those who do not have a strong attachment to it, self-employed persons, and persons who have exhausted their benefit entitlements.

## Contributions

Employment insurance is financed jointly by the private sector and the federal government. The private sector's share derives from a proportional payroll tax on the employment earnings of each worker. Both employees and employers pay premiums,[20] and the employer's premium is 1.4 times that of the employee. In 1999, the employee's tax rate is 2.55 percent and the employer's tax rate 3.57 percent (1.4 times the employee's rate) of insurable earnings to a maximum of $39,000 annually. The 1999 maximum contribution's are $994.50 for an employee and $1,392.30 for an employer. Before 1998, contributions were calculated on weekly earnings up to a maximum limit ($845 per week in 1996 and 1997, and $780 in 1994). As of 1998, the weekly limits were removed, and the rate now applies to all earnings up to $39,000. Contribution rates and maximum amounts have fallen over the past few years,[21] primarily because the benefits have been reduced and because the program has become less expensive to operate.

## Benefits

### General Benefits

Employment insurance benefits vary with the length of the period over which the recipient has contributed, with the insurable earnings of the recipient while he contributed, and with the regional rate of unemployment. Claimants may receive benefits for 14 to 45 weeks. The benefit rate for most claimants is 55 percent of their average insured earnings, though for low-income recipients with dependants the rate can be as high as 65 percent.

---

[20] Contributory rates were also described in chapter 6.

[21] For example, in 1994, contribution rates for the employee and employer were 3.07 and 4.298 percent, respectively, of insurable earnings to a maximum of $780 per week; the 1996 rates were 2.95 and 4.13 percent of insurable earnings to a maximum of $845 per week; the 1997 rates were 2.9 percent for employees and 4.06 percent for employers up to maximum insurable earnings of $845 per week. The 1998 rates were 2.7 percent for employees and 3.78 percent for employers.

The length of the qualifying period has been a contentious issue, and it has changed several times since the program was introduced. Currently, claimants require a minimum of 910 hours of work to qualify for benefits. Claimants must wait 2 weeks before they can receive benefits, and they cannot receive benefits for more than 45 weeks in a 52-week period. Individuals who voluntarily leave their jobs or lose their jobs because of misconduct are not eligible for benefits. Finally, claimants who refuse suitable employment forgo 7 to 12 weeks of benefits, and their benefit rate is lowered to 50 percent of average insurable earnings.[22]

### Fishers' Benefits

Fishers are the only self-employed workers covered by the employment insurance program and they are covered for both seasonal and year-round employment.

### Special Benefits

Different rules apply to those on maternity, parental, adoption, and sickness leave.[23] The maximum special benefit entitlement is 30 weeks, but claimants who have 20 weeks of insurable employment are entitled to 15 weeks of sickness leave, 15 weeks of maternity leave, and 10 weeks of parental or adoption leave.[24]

### Financing EI

Table 8.6 shows the annual revenue generated in the employment insurance account, annual benefits paid from the account, and the annual surplus or deficit in the account for selected fiscal years from 1942 to 1996.[25] Since the mid-1990s, the account has generated a large and growing surplus,[26] a circumstance that has sparked controversy and led to demands from a number of associations and employer groups, some provincial politicians, and various policy analysts for further cuts in EI premiums. Not everyone supports these demands, however. Whether or not one believes that EI premiums should be reduced depends in part on one's view of the premiums' role. Those who argue that the premiums should be earmarked for EI benefits can make a case for reducing them. On the other hand, those who view EI as simply one tax in the mix of taxes can make a rather stronger case for not

---

[22] Supra footnote 2, at 9:1-3.

[23] Quebec has proposed a parental insurance plan that would pay workers 75 percent of their net income during maternity and parental leave.

[24] Supra footnote 2, at 9:3.

[25] For a discussion of financing the unemployment insurance program up to the early 1980s, see Jonathan R. Kesselman, *Financing Canadian Unemployment Insurance*, Canadian Tax Paper no. 73 (Toronto: Canadian Tax Foundation, 1983).

[26] It has been suggested that at the end of 1998 the EI account would have a surplus of $20 billion: Bruce Little, "Tax Cut Battles Loom," *The Globe and Mail*, June 1, 1998.

Table 8.6 **Employment Insurance Account for Selected Fiscal Years Ending March 31, 1942 to 1996**

| Year | Total revenue | Payment of benefits | Surplus or deficit (−) |
|------|---------------|---------------------|------------------------|
| | *millions of dollars* | | |
| 1942 . . . . . . . . . . . | 44 | — | 44 |
| 1950 . . . . . . . . . . . | 140 | 86 | 54 |
| 1960 . . . . . . . . . . . | 283 | 415 | −132 |
| 1970 . . . . . . . . . . . | 623 | 542 | 81 |
| 1975 . . . . . . . . . . . | 2,544 | 2,521 | 23 |
| 1980 . . . . . . . . . . . | 5,143 | 4,202 | 941 |
| 1985 . . . . . . . . . . . | 10,726 | 11,702 | −976 |
| 1990 . . . . . . . . . . . | 13,735 | 12,773 | 962 |
| 1993 . . . . . . . . . . . | 18,012 | 20,397 | −2,385 |
| 1994 . . . . . . . . . . . | 18,722 | 19,356 | −634 |
| 1995 . . . . . . . . . . . | 19,432 | 16,669 | 2,763 |
| 1996 . . . . . . . . . . . | 19,003 | 15,091 | 3,912 |

— not applicable.

[a] For the 15-month period ended March 31, 1997.

Sources: Public Accounts; and Karin Treff and David B. Perry, *Finances of the Nation 1998* (Toronto: Canadian Tax Foundation, 1998), 9:5, table 9.3.

reducing them.[27] They can point, for example, to the fact that social security taxes in Canada (EI and CPP) are low relative to the equivalent taxes levied by our major trading partners, whereas personal income taxes and property taxes in Canada are relatively high.

## Provincial and Local Programs

Provincial, and in some cases, local governments in Canada are responsible for social assistance or welfare programs.[28] These programs provide financial assistance to individuals and families whose resources are not sufficient to meet their needs and who have exhausted other avenues of support. Until recently, the Canada Assistance Plan (CAP),[29] which transferred federal funds to the provincial and territorial governments for the explicit purpose of funding social assistance, provided the basis for coordinating the various provincial and territorial public welfare programs. On April 1, 1996, the CAP was replaced by the Canada health and social transfer (CHST), a block transfer that the provinces can distribute between social assistance, health care, and post-secondary education at their discretion.[30]

---

[27] See chapter 6 for a discussion of this view.

[28] Each province and territory also has its own workers' compensation program. For a discussion of these programs see chapter 6.

[29] For a discussion of this program before 1996, see Karin Treff and Ted Cook, *Finances of the Nation 1995* (Toronto: Canadian Tax Foundation, 1995), 9:6-7.

[30] For a discussion of the impact of this change on net provincial revenues, see Tracy R. Snoddon, "The Impact of the CHST on Interprovincial Redistribution in Canada" (March 1998), 24 *Canadian Public Policy* 49-70.

The CHST has given the provinces more flexibility in determining their spending priorities and greater leeway in establishing welfare schemes than they had under the CAP. In particular, they are no longer required to use a "needs test" to determine eligibility for social assistance in order to qualify for federal contributions, although all of them appear to have retained a needs test.[31] The needs test is, in fact, a means test, which compares the budgetary requirements of the applicant and the applicant's dependants with the household's assets and income. Assistance is meant to cover basic requirements, including food, clothing, shelter, utilities, and other household and personal necessities. Applicants and recipients may be eligible for extra assistance (either in cash or in kind) in most provinces if they have special needs, such as medication, prosthetic devices, technical aids and equipment, special clothing, or dental care. Provinces are free to set their own benefit rates. The CHST provisions prohibit residency requirements, although some provinces have, on occasion, attempted to impose them. In addition to providing income supplements, provincial and local assistance programs may finance health care for the needy, child welfare agencies, work activity projects, homes for special care, social or subsidized housing, and a variety of other welfare services.

Most of the provinces assume full responsibility for funding and administering welfare programs. Nova Scotia, Ontario, and Manitoba share the funding and administration of welfare with their municipalities. Since welfare assistance programs are designed to make up the difference between need and the recipient's income, increases in income are usually offset by reductions in welfare assistance. Some provinces exempt the first few hundred dollars of annual income earned. Even so, the type of welfare scheme in place may create a disincentive to work (a point we discuss below). Furthermore, neither the CHST nor any of the other plans we discuss in this chapter are designed to serve the needs of the working poor, whose main source of protection is the minimum wage laws.

Table 8.7, which provides estimates of welfare income by type of household in 1996, gives some idea of the range and breadth of welfare coverage across the provinces and territories in Canada.[32] Since 1996, however, most of the provinces have initiated a number of welfare reforms. Thus most provinces have tightened the conditions for eligibility for welfare. As well, Ontario and British Columbia, to name two provinces, now require able-bodied welfare recipients to perform some community service in order to receive benefits. Newfoundland now takes parental financial circumstances into consideration in determining welfare eligibility for young people. New Brunswick has introduced a refundable tax credit for dependent children and a working-income

---

[31] The elimination of the needs test as a national standard cleared the way for the provinces and territories to impose work-for-welfare programs (and some have done so) and to disqualify certain groups from applying for welfare.

[32] For a detailed discussion of these estimates, see National Council of Welfare, *Welfare Incomes 1996* (Ottawa: Public Works and Government Services, 1997).

**Table 8.7   Estimated Welfare Income by Type of Household, 1996**

| | Basic social assistance | Additional benefits | Federal child tax benefit[a] | Provincial child benefits | GST credit[b] | Provincial tax credits | Total income |
|---|---|---|---|---|---|---|---|
| | | | *dollars* | | | | |
| **Newfoundland** | | | | | | | |
| Single employable | 2,502 | — | — | — | 199 | — | 2,701 |
| Disabled person | 6,810 | 1,500 | — | — | 236 | — | 8,546 |
| Single parent, one child | 11,262 | — | 1,233 | — | 494 | — | 12,989 |
| Couple, two children | 12,186 | — | 2,040 | — | 608 | — | 14,834 |
| **Prince Edward Island** | | | | | | | |
| Single employable | 5,245 | — | — | — | 206 | — | 5,451 |
| Disabled person | 7,956 | 1,092 | — | — | 247 | — | 9,295 |
| Single parent, one child | 10,242 | — | 1,233 | — | 483 | — | 11,958 |
| Couple, two children | 14,698 | 175 | 2,040 | — | 608 | — | 17,521 |
| **Nova Scotia** | | | | | | | |
| Single employable | 5,922 | — | — | — | 199 | — | 6,121 |
| Disabled person | 8,568 | — | — | — | 241 | — | 8,809 |
| Single parent, one child | 10,560 | — | 1,233 | — | 480 | — | 12,273 |
| Couple, two children | 13,602 | — | 2,040 | — | 608 | — | 16,250 |
| **New Brunswick** | | | | | | | |
| Single employable | 3,132 | — | — | — | 199 | — | 3,331 |
| Disabled person | 6,483 | — | — | — | 215 | — | 6,698 |
| Single parent, one child | 8,673 | 900 | 1,233 | — | 452 | — | 11,258 |
| Couple, two children | 9,711 | 1,000 | 2,040 | — | 608 | — | 13,359 |
| **Quebec** | | | | | | | |
| Single employable | 6,000 | — | — | — | 199 | — | 6,199 |
| Disabled person | 8,268 | — | — | — | 235 | — | 8,503 |
| Single parent, one child | 10,200 | 1,080 | 1,082 | 248 | 469 | — | 13,079 |
| Couple, two children | 12,000 | 1,219 | 1,972 | 305 | 608 | — | 16,104 |

(Table 8.7 is continued on the next page.)

## Table 8.7  Continued

| | Basic social assistance | Additional benefits | Federal child tax benefit[a] | Provincial child benefits | GST credit[b] | Provincial tax credits | Total income |
|---|---|---|---|---|---|---|---|
| | | | | *dollars* | | | |
| Ontario | | | | | | | |
| Single employable | 6,240 | — | — | — | 225 | 344 | 6,809 |
| Disabled person | 11,160 | — | — | — | 293 | 306 | 11,759 |
| Single parent, one child | 11,484 | 105 | 1,233 | — | 503 | 351 | 13,767 |
| Couple, two children | 14,568 | 407 | 2,040 | — | 608 | 453 | 18,076 |
| Manitoba | | | | | | | |
| Single employable | 5,539 | — | — | — | 199 | 531 | 6,269 |
| Disabled person | 7,157 | 840 | — | — | 230 | — | 8,227 |
| Single parent, one child | 9,636 | — | 1,233 | — | 462 | — | 11,331 |
| Couple, two children | 14,640 | — | 2,040 | — | 608 | 633 | 17,921 |
| Saskatchewan | | | | | | | |
| Single employable | 5,760 | — | — | — | 199 | — | 5,959 |
| Disabled person | 7,500 | 1,020 | — | — | 235 | — | 8,755 |
| Single parent, one child | 10,380 | — | 1,233 | — | 477 | — | 12,091 |
| Couple, two children | 14,643 | 160 | 2,040 | — | 608 | — | 17,451 |
| Alberta | | | | | | | |
| Single employable | 4,728 | — | — | — | 199 | — | 4,927 |
| Disabled person | 6,348 | 240 | — | — | 201 | — | 6,789 |
| Single parent, one child | 9,192 | — | 1,148 | — | 453 | — | 10,793 |
| Couple, two children | 14,472 | 150 | 2,137 | — | 608 | — | 17,367 |
| British Columbia | | | | | | | |
| Single employable | 6,046 | 35 | — | — | 201 | 50 | 6,232 |
| Disabled person | 9,252 | 35 | — | — | 255 | 50 | 9,592 |
| Single parent, one child | 11,166 | 698 | 1,233 | — | 503 | 100 | 13,700 |
| Couple, two children | 13,632 | 1,426 | 2,040 | — | 608 | 200 | 17,906 |

(Table 8.7 is concluded on the next page.)

**Table 8.7  Concluded**

| | Basic social assistance | Additional benefits | Federal child tax benefit[a] | Territorial child benefits | GST credit[b] | Territorial tax credits | Total income |
|---|---|---|---|---|---|---|---|
| | | | *dollars* | | | | |
| **Northwest Territories** | | | | | | | |
| Single employable ......... | 11,229 | — | — | — | 296 | — | 11,525 |
| Disabled person ........... | 11,529 | 1,500 | — | — | 304 | — | 13,333 |
| Single parent, one child ..... | 19,074 | — | 1,233 | — | 503 | — | 20,810 |
| Couple, two children ........ | 22,956 | — | 2,040 | — | 608 | — | 25,244 |
| **Yukon** | | | | | | | |
| Single employable ......... | 7,740 | 155 | — | — | 228 | — | 8,123 |
| Disabled person ........... | 7,740 | 1,655 | — | — | 251 | — | 9,646 |
| Single parent, one child ..... | 12,540 | 572 | 1,233 | — | 503 | — | 14,848 |
| Couple, two children ........ | 19,080 | 685 | 2,040 | — | 608 | — | 22,413 |

—  not applicable.

[a] The single-parent family with one young child was eligible for $1,233 ($1,020 as the basic child tax benefit and $213 as a supplement for each child under 7). The two-parent family with two children aged 10 and 15 was eligible for $2,040 ($1,020 for each child). Neither household received the $500 supplement for earned income, since it was assumed that all of each household's income came from welfare or other government sources. [b] The GST credit is paid in quarterly instalments. In 1996, adults and the first child in a single-parent family received maximum payments of $49.75 each every three months, and the maximum for each child was $26.25 every three months. The special GST supplement for single persons and single-parent families is included in the totals for the year.

Source: For a detailed discussion of the derivation of the other figures in this table, see National Council of Welfare, *Welfare Incomes 1996* (Ottawa: Public Works and Government Services, 1997).

supplement for low-income families; it has also increased the earnings exemption. Quebec has made a number of changes, including the introduction of a parental insurance plan and a new child allowance program.[33]

Some provinces also use refundable tax credits to provide assistance to low-income families or to seniors. The credits vary in design, but they all decrease as income—generally, family income—increases. Ontario offers refundable property tax and sales tax credits to offset a portion of property taxes and sales taxes; seniors get a separate property tax and sales tax credit. Until 1999, residents of Nova Scotia can obtain a refundable tax credit through a home-ownership plan. Quebec has the largest number of refundable tax credits—for child care expenses, adopted children, direct ascendents (parent or grandparent), property taxes, and sales taxes. Manitoba has a refundable cost-of-living tax credit and a property tax credit. British Columbia has a refundable sales tax credit.

## Evaluation of Transfer Programs

### Equity

The equity or fairness of government transfer programs is generally discussed in terms of their incidence on individuals across income groups. Incidence analysis attempts to determine which income groups benefit from a particular program and which income groups bear the costs of the program. Government transfer programs are generally intended to be progressive,[34] since they have been introduced with the express purpose of redistributing income to those in need. For example, OAS payments are clawed back from high-income earners; GIS goes to low-income individuals; the spouse's allowance is an income-tested pension payment; the child tax benefit decreases as family income rises; employment insurance payments go to the unemployed, who are concentrated at the low end of the income range; and provincial welfare programs are almost always based on family income.

Table 8.8 shows the percentage of household income attributable to government transfer payments by income decile and by province in 1992.[35] Not

---

[33] For a recent critical examination of the provincial welfare schemes, see National Council of Welfare, *Another Look at Welfare Reform* (Ottawa: Public Works and Government Services, 1997).

[34] Transfers are deemed to be progressive (regressive) if the amount received as a percentage of income falls (rises) as income rises.

[35] There are no recently published studies on the distributional pattern of government transfers across income groups. Two studies that are now out of date (because of numerous changes in programs and eligibility) but may be noted are J.E. Cloutier, *The Distribution of Benefits and Costs of Social Security in Canada 1971-1975*, Discussion Paper no. 108 (Ottawa: Economic Council of Canada, 1978); and David A. Dodge, "Impact of Tax, Transfer, and Expenditure Policies of Government on the Distribution of Personal Income in Canada" (March 1975), 21 *Review of Income and Wealth* 1-50.

## Table 8.8  Government Transfer Payments by Family as a Percentage of Family Income, 1992

| Decile | Newfound-land | Prince Edward Island | Nova Scotia | New Brunswick | Quebec | Ontario | Manitoba | Sas-katch-ewan | Alberta | British Columbia |
|---|---|---|---|---|---|---|---|---|---|---|
| First | 83.5 | 73.2 | 81.0 | 84.5 | 83.7 | 75.3 | 74.4 | 81.1 | 73.3 | 73.6 |
| Second | 78.5 | 64.9 | 73.1 | 67.5 | 66.1 | 63.4 | 60.8 | 68.5 | 62.3 | 63.8 |
| Third | 61.6 | 60.7 | 52.9 | 52.6 | 51.1 | 41.8 | 46.0 | 51.0 | 40.5 | 39.5 |
| Fourth | 46.6 | 33.7 | 34.9 | 39.9 | 28.3 | 23.8 | 31.5 | 32.0 | 17.9 | 33.9 |
| Fifth | 36.7 | 20.4 | 26.1 | 24.5 | 21.4 | 14.2 | 21.5 | 20.4 | 11.5 | 18.8 |
| Sixth | 28.6 | 20.8 | 17.2 | 18.4 | 15.4 | 11.2 | 17.2 | 18.1 | 10.2 | 13.1 |
| Seventh | 21.9 | 13.3 | 14.7 | 10.0 | 12.3 | 7.4 | 12.0 | 8.7 | 5.9 | 9.6 |
| Eighth | 12.6 | 8.9 | 12.2 | 7.6 | 8.3 | 6.3 | 8.6 | 6.9 | 4.6 | 5.4 |
| Ninth | 8.1 | 6.8 | 7.3 | 6.2 | 6.1 | 3.9 | 7.0 | 4.8 | 3.1 | 5.2 |
| Tenth | 11.1 | 4.9 | 2.5 | 3.0 | 3.4 | 2.8 | 2.8 | 3.2 | 1.6 | 4.7 |

Note: Government transfer payments include family allowances (existed in 1992), including the federal child tax credit, old age security/guaranteed income supplement, Canada/Quebec pension plan benefits, unemployment insurance, provincial social assistance and provincial income supplements, goods and services tax credits, provincial tax credits, federal sales tax credits, and other income from government sources.

Source: Calculated from date in the 1992 Statistics Canada, *Survey of Family Expenditures* (Ottawa: Statistics Canada, 1994).

surprisingly, the table indicates that in 1992 government transfers accounted for most family income in the lowest income deciles. In recent years, as we noted earlier, there have been changes in many of the transfer programs, and these changes have almost certainly produced a distribution of transfer payments that is even more progressive than the one shown in the table.

## Economic Effects

Transfer payments, like taxes, influence the allocation of resources, income distribution, and the stability of aggregate demand. The literature devotes a good deal of attention to the resource allocation effects of transfer programs, in particular their effects on labour supply and savings decisions. In recent years, as both the federal government and the provinces have altered their income transfer systems, the economic effects of transfers have become a matter of growing controversy. The following discussion considers some of the more important economic issues raised by the existing transfer schemes.

### Labour Supply

Transfer programs can influence labour supply in a wide variety of ways. Their effect depends on the tax rate implicit in the transfer, the amount transferred, and the ability of the recipient to vary hours worked or to either work or not work. The theoretical literature has concentrated on the effect of transfers on hours worked by an individual who is able to vary hours worked at will and on the decision to work or not to work either temporarily or permanently.

The following discussion of the effects of transfers on labour supply applies only to programs that transfer income to the working or potentially working population. It ignores, however, the effect on labour supply of how the transfer is financed, largely because there is really no solid empirical evidence on this topic.

### *Choice of Hours Worked*

Transfer programs, like income taxes, have two sorts of effects—income (or wealth) effects and substitution effects. The income effect of a given program is the change it causes in individuals' purchasing power or real income. In the case of transfer programs, of course, the change in purchasing power is positive. The substitution effect is the change that the program causes in the relative wage rate of labour, or equivalently, the change in the relative price of taking additional leisure in terms of income forgone.

Any transfer scheme that relates the amount transferred to the amount of income earned has a substitution effect. At one extreme is the guaranteed annual income program that reduces the guaranteed transfer payment by one dollar for each dollar of income earned. A scheme of this kind has an effective 100 percent recapture rate or tax rate; consequently, the net-of-transfer wage from working is zero until the guaranteed income level is reached.[36] In this case, the substitution effect is very strong—the relative price of taking leisure is zero. At the other extreme is the demogrant, whose size is the same regardless of income earned. A demogrant has a positive income effect but no substitution effect, since it does not change the wage rate. In between are schemes such as the negative income tax, which provides a guaranteed minimum income but has a recapture rate of less than 100 percent. A scheme of this kind does have a substitution effect, since the net-of-transfer wage rate received from working additional hours is positive but less than it would be in the absence of the tax.[37]

The effect of a transfer scheme on the number of hours a recipient chooses to work depends on the combined influence of the substitution and income effects. The substitution effect alone has an unambiguous effect on work effort: if the transfer program tends to decrease the net-of-transfer wage that would result from working more hours, there will be an incentive to substitute leisure for work at the margin. The greater is the fall in the net wage, the greater will be the disincentive to work. Given the substitution effect alone, therefore, one would expect that for a given amount of real income transferred a demogrant would result in more hours worked than would a negative income tax, and a negative income tax in more hours worked than a guaranteed annual income scheme with a 100 percent recapture rate.

The income effect of transfer programs, on the other hand, is ambiguous. One cannot say a priori whether, all other things being equal, an increase in real income would cause an individual to supply more or less labour. The usual presumption is that leisure is a normal good; consequently, increases in real income will be "spent" in part on leisure—that is, any increase in real income will induce a decrease in work effort. If this is so, then the income effect will supplement the substitution effect and any of the transfer programs mentioned above will tend to reduce hours worked—the more so the greater is the substitution effect.

Although it is not possible to avoid the income effect in transfer schemes (since their whole purpose is to transfer real income to low-income persons), suggestions have been made for transfer schemes that avoid the adverse substitution effect. One such scheme is a wage subsidy that subsidizes low-wage earners by increasing their wage rates above the market level. The subsidy rate could vary with wage rates.

---

[36] In the example in table 8.3, the aggregate income including transfer is $9,000 for any income earned up to $9,000.

[37] For example, in table 8.3, when the recapture rate is 25 percent, each $1,000 of additional earned income causes the individual's after-transfer income to rise by $750. Thus the after-transfer wage is effectively 75 percent of the market wage, so the price of taking additional leisure has been reduced.

It is worth comparing the labour supply effects of a negative income tax scheme and wage subsidy scheme. The general formula for the negative income tax is

$$T = t(Y-B),$$

where $Y$ is the individual's before-transfer income, $B$ is the breakeven level, $t$ is the marginal tax or recapture rate, and $T$ is the total tax paid by the individual. If $Y$ is less than $B$, $T$ is negative, which implies that the person is paying negative taxes or, in other words, receiving a subsidy.[38] We shall assume this to be the case. After-transfer income is given by

$$Y - T = tB + Y(1 - t).$$

This equation shows that under the scheme each individual obtains a guaranteed level of income, $tB$, plus a proportion $(1 - t)$ of all income earned. If the scheme's recapture rate is 100 percent ($t$ is 1), after-transfer income is $B$ regardless of the amount of before-transfer income earned. As $t$ falls, the greater is the increase in the individual's income from any increase in $Y$.

The wage subsidy scheme may be written as follows:

$$S = s(W_b - W),$$

where $W$ is the hourly wage rate, $W_b$ is some breakeven wage rate, above which the wage subsidy does not apply, $s$ is the subsidy rate, and $S$ is the subsidy per hour worked for an individual with wage $W$. Note that the subsidy increases as the wage rate declines, so more assistance is given to low-wage persons. In any case, the wage rate after subsidy is $W + S$.

Figure 8.1 illustrates the effects of the various transfer schemes on the choice between work and leisure. The diagram refers to a person of a particular wage level who obtains all of his income from employment. Line $A$ shows the combinations of leisure and income available to the individual in the absence of any transfers. As the individual takes more and more leisure (works less and less), his income falls. The slope of "budget line" $A$ is the wage rate or the price of leisure—the rate at which income falls as leisure rises. Budget line $B$ shows the effect of a guaranteed annual income scheme with a 100 percent recapture rate. The individual obtains the same income whether he works or not. There is no incentive at all to work, since the price of leisure is zero. Line $C$ represents the effect of a negative income tax scheme. The price of leisure, or slope of the budget line, is greater than zero but less than the price in the absence of the transfer.[39] The fact that line $C$ slopes less

[38] Notice that the payment of the subsidy is not without administration costs. In the absence of a negative income tax, only individuals with income above the exemption level need file income tax returns and pay taxes. Here, however, those below the exemption (or breakeven) level must file income tax returns in order to determine the amount of subsidy for which they qualify.

[39] If the wage rate is $w$, earned income $Y$ is $wH$ where $H$ is hours worked. Thus after-transfer income is given by $Y - T = tB + wH(1 - t)$. The price of leisure is $w(1 - t)$, the net-of-tax wage. It is the income lost per hour of additional leisure taken.

## Figure 8.1    Budget Lines Under Various Transfer Schemes

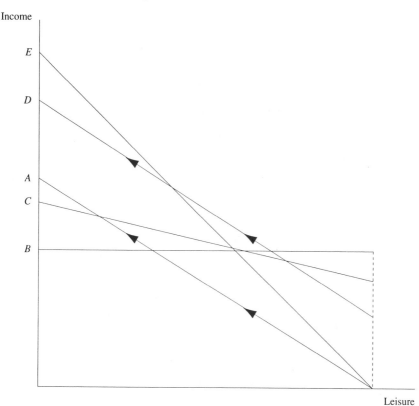

than line *A* but more than line *B* indicates that the negative income tax scheme has an adverse substitution effect but not as great as does the guaranteed annual income scheme. Budget line *D* shows the effect on the price of leisure of a demogrant scheme that gives the individual the same amount of transfer regardless of his income from employment. The individual's budget line has been shifted outward, so that its slope is the same as that of *A*, the market wage rate, and there is no substitution effect. Finally, line *E* is the budget line under a wage subsidy scheme. Its slope exceeds that of line *A*, indicating a higher wage rate or price of leisure. Thus the wage subsidy scheme provides an incentive to substitute work for leisure, in contrast to the other transfer schemes.

For any given amount of income transferred, individuals will work more under a wage subsidy scheme than under a negative income tax scheme. This is so because a negative income tax reduces the net wage from additional work (that is, reduces the price of leisure), whereas the wage subsidy scheme increases it. In other words, a negative income tax has an adverse substitution effect on work effort and a wage subsidy has a beneficial substitution effect.

A major difficulty with a wage subsidy scheme is that it is suitable for the working poor but does nothing for the non-working poor; hence a complementary scheme would be required for the latter. In addition, the costs of administering a wage subsidy scheme might be quite high, since the government would have to know individual wage rates, not just aggregate income earned. Also, if the supply of labour is fairly inelastic, as it appears to be in Canada (see chapter 6), or if the demand for labour by firms is elastic, the subsidy might end up being largely shifted back to firms in the form of lower wage rates paid. In that case, the greatest impact of a wage subsidy scheme might be an increase in employment of low-income workers. No government in Canada has ever instituted a scheme of this kind.

The above discussion is somewhat unrealistic since workers are typically unable, in the short run at least, to vary their hours worked. Changes in hours worked per employee occur at infrequent intervals and over long periods. Furthermore, once hours of work are established (for example, the seven-hour day), many individual workers are not free to depart from the norm. In most cases, workers will have a choice in the short run between working the prescribed work day and not working at all. Exceptions to this rule arise in the cases of part-time and overtime work and moonlighting.

## The Decision To Work or Not To Work

Transfer payments can influence the decisions of individuals to work or not to work in a number of different contexts. Perhaps the main distinction is between individuals who stop working temporarily and those who stop working permanently (through retirement, for example). In addition, transfer programs may induce some individuals to work when otherwise they would not. The following is a catalogue of the various ways in which transfer programs may affect the decision to work. It is worth emphasizing that the discussion does not include persons who are out of work through involuntary unemployment; that is, persons who would be willing to work at the going wage but cannot find a job. It is concerned only with the effect of transfers on the decision to work when the suppliers have a choice.

### 1) Transfer-induced permanent unemployment and retirement

To the extent that transfer schemes provide a minimum guaranteed level of income on a permanent basis (a negative income tax, for example, or a guaranteed annual income scheme), they may lead some individuals to choose not to work rather than to work if those are the only alternatives available. This may be especially true of low-income workers who face transfer schemes with high recapture rates (such as welfare programs with 100 percent rates of recapture). Of course, the higher their earned income is above the guaranteed minimum and the lower is the effective tax rate payable, the more likely they are to choose to work. Also, the apparent stigma attached to not working may offset the voluntary unemployment effect of transfer schemes.

A numerical example may help to illustrate the tendencies at work. Consider again the guaranteed income scheme of table 8.3. Suppose that an individual may choose either to work for an income of $6,000 or not to work at all. If the recapture rate is 100 percent, his net income will be $9,000 whether he works or not, so he perceives no financial advantage in working. If the recapture rate is 50 percent, his income is $12,000 when he works. The additional $3,000 that he obtains by working may or may not be sufficient to compensate him for his loss of leisure. The lower is the recapture rate, the greater will be his additional income from working, and the greater is the chance that he will work. The same principle applies if his income is above $9,000. The lower the recapture rate, the less will be his disincentive to work.

## 2) Participation rates

Closely related to this effect of transfer payments is their effect on the rate of participation in the labour force, especially by marginal workers or those who do not need to work in order to survive. For example, if a guaranteed annual income or negative income tax were made available to spouses regardless of family income, or to students, their participation rates would presumably decrease sharply.

On the other hand, other transfer schemes may increase participation in the labour force by some persons, at least temporarily. Schemes that have a minimum eligibility requirement and whose benefit payments exceed aggregate contributions during the eligibility period may have this effect. Thus, an employment insurance program with a short eligibility period might attract spouses and students into the work force temporarily. Similarly, spouses may enter the labour force in order to become eligible for CPP benefits. Persons who are marginally indifferent to working will be induced to work by the additional advantages that are to be gained through the transfer scheme. The shorter is the eligibility period, presumably, the greater will be the effect on participation rates.

## 3) Temporary unemployment and seasonality

A large proportion of unemployment is temporary in the sense that it refers to workers who are out of work for a short time and then return to the same job. These workers have some degree of attachment to a particular job, despite their knowledge that they may be subject to periodic bouts of temporary unemployment. Temporary unemployment may have either one of two causes. First, it may be induced by supply-side influences that affect the productivity of labour, such as seasonal fluctuations in the fishing, agriculture, and construction industries. These fluctuations are relatively predictable, and workers who enter these industries will take them into consideration when choosing a job. The other cause of temporary unemployment is fluctuation in demand: in industries where demand fluctuates, workers are laid off when demand is low. In this case, the exact duration and timing of the fluctuations will not be known, but workers who take employment of this kind may have a rough idea of the risk of being laid off.

In the absence of employment insurance (or other transfer schemes), workers would enter industries with fluctuating employment only if firms offered wages high enough to compensate for the possibility of temporary layoffs, and firms would have to offer these wages in order to attract workers. In other words, workers would select employment not solely on the basis of the going wage rate but on the basis of both the wage rate and the expected pattern of employment. Because the costs of changing jobs—moving, searching, and personal costs—are high for workers, and the costs of labour turnover—hiring, training, and termination costs—are high for firms, both have an interest in establishing a stable employment relationship in which laid-off workers return to the same firm. Economists have referred to the arrangement by which both the workers and the firm take into consideration the long-run implications of employment and wage strategies as an implicit contract.[40]

The presence of an employment insurance scheme is likely to have a significant impact on the employment terms of an implicit contract.[41] If insurance contributions are not directly related to the payment of benefits to the workers of a given firm—that is, if the contributions are not experience-rated[42]—the scheme will reduce the opportunity cost of laying off workers. Workers would willingly enter into an implicit contract that called for more frequent layoffs if they could collect employment insurance benefits, so firms would be less reluctant to lay them off in times of reduced production. In addition, firms would have an incentive to substitute layoffs for reduced work hours if workers could not collect employment insurance benefits on the latter basis. Thus, employment insurance is likely to increase both the rate of layoffs and the unemployment rate.

The incentive to lay off workers will be stronger the greater is the ratio of benefits to the going wage rate—that is, the wage replacement ratio. It will also be stronger the less contributions are related to the firm's layoff record. With these points in mind, Feldstein has argued that an unemployment insur-

---

[40] There is a voluminous literature on implicit labour contracts. The main original contributions are Martin Neil Baily, "Wages and Employment Under Uncertain Demand" (January 1974), 41 *Review of Economic Studies* 37-50; Costas Azariadis, "Implicit Contracts and Under-Employment Equilibria" (December 1975), 83 *Journal of Political Economy* 1183-1202; Donald F. Gordon, "A Neo-Classical Theory of Keynesian Unemployment" (December 1974), 12 *Economic Inquiry* 431-59; and Martin S. Feldstein, "Temporary Layoffs in the Theory of Unemployment" (October 1976), 84 *Journal of Political Economy* 937-57.

[41] Martin Neil Baily, "On the Theory of Layoffs and Unemployment" (July 1977), 45 *Econometrica* 1043-63; and Feldstein, supra footnote 40.

[42] For a discussion of the merits of experience rating, see Oliver Franke and Derek Hermanutz, "Employment Insurance: Returning to Insurance Principles" (Summer 1997), 5 *Canadian Business Economics* 61-72, at 68-70.

ance scheme should include the following two provisions:[43] First, unemployment insurance benefits should be taxable, which they have been in Canada since the tax reform of 1972; second, contributions should be experience-rated—that is, they should depend on a firm's past layoff and benefit-payment record. If full experience rating were in effect, a firm and its workers would achieve no mutual gain from an increase in the frequency of layoffs.

Quite apart from its effect on layoffs, the fact that employment insurance contributions are not experience-rated is likely to influence the allocation of workers over industries. In particular, it gives workers an incentive they would otherwise lack to enter industries with seasonal layoffs or in which the risk of layoffs owing to reduced demand is high, since in industries of either type expected contributions under EI will fall short of benefits. In short, one would expect more resources to be allocated to industries with fluctuating output in the presence of employment insurance than in its absence, unless the EI system incorporated some form of experience rating to temper this resource allocation effect.[44]

### 4) Frictional unemployment

Frictional unemployment refers to persons who are temporarily unemployed while they are changing jobs. One of the important costs of changing jobs (or of looking for a first job) is the income lost during the search for new employment. Employment insurance effectively reduces this cost and thus is likely to increase both the rate of job turnover and the average duration of the job search. Both of these effects may increase the unemployment rate, at least in the short run. In the long run, however, the increase in search time may actually reduce the unemployment rate. That is, it may increase the efficiency of labour markets by allowing workers to find more suitable employment and thus reduce their future turnover.

### 5) Retirement

The CPP and, to a lesser extent, other transfer schemes as well may influence the age of retirement whenever individuals have a choice in the matter. Pension benefits that include an element of transfer (as CPP benefits do for those who were already in the work force when the scheme was introduced), will increase the lifetime wealth of the individuals who receive them. This extra wealth may induce earlier retirement, since it reduces the amount of

---

[43] Martin Feldstein, "Unemployment Compensation: Adverse Incentives and Distributional Anomalies" (June 1974), 27 *National Tax Journal* 231-44.

[44] Full experience rating is equivalent to each firm's insuring its own workers. A natural question to ask here is, why should such a scheme be imposed? If it were beneficial to both firms and workers, it would be undertaken voluntarily by the firms. Part of the answer may lie in the fact that workers cannot be explicitly tied to one firm. A worker could leave a firm permanently after collecting insurance payments. Of course, there are other ways in which firms induce workers not to change firms, such as by providing non-vested pensions or training that is available only through employment in that firm.

time that the individuals have to work in order to provide comfortable pensions for themselves. One can think of this outcome as the "income effect" of public pensions. This effect, however, might instead work in the opposite direction. For example, if the lifetime return on contributions to a public pension is less than the return that the contributor could earn on capital markets, his lifetime wealth will be lower than it would have been in the absence of the scheme and the contributor may, accordingly, retire later rather than sooner.

The CPP also creates a strong substitution effect against working. Each additional year of working beyond eligibility for the CPP yields an increase in earned income against which the worker must set the loss of the pension income that he would have otherwise received. Since this loss is equivalent to an income tax up to the amount of the pension, it creates a strong disincentive to work. The disincentive will be mitigated to the extent that additional years of work increase the rate at which future pensions are paid. We shall discuss the effect of public pensions on retirement further below.

### 6) Empirical evidence on work effort

As we note above, economic theory predicts that both the income and the substitution effects of a negative income tax system would give low-income beneficiaries an incentive to reduce the number of hours they worked. US studies of the effect of various income maintenance experiments on hours worked by individuals have tended to confirm the disincentive to work in terms of both hours worked and participation in the labour force.[45] The only Canadian study on the extent to which a guaranteed income scheme might affect work response concludes that the labour supply response is much lower in Canada than comparable US studies show it to be in the United States.[46] In particular, the results indicate

> a labour supply response of 0.8 to 1.6 per cent for men compared to a combined response of 5 per cent from the U.S. experiments; a response

---

[45] For surveys of the US studies, see E. Cain and H.W. Watts, eds., *Income Maintenance and Labour Supply: Econometric Studies* (Chicago: Rand McNally, 1973); George F. Break, "The Incidence and Economic Effects of Taxation," in Alan S. Blinder et al., *The Economics of Public Finance* (Washington, DC: Brookings Institution, 1974), 119-237; and Jerry A. Hausman, *Taxes and Labor Supply*, Working Paper no. 1102 (Cambridge, Mass.: National Bureau of Economic Research, March 1983).

[46] Derek Hum and Wayne Simpson, *Income Maintenance, Work Effort, and the Canadian Mincome Experiment*, a study prepared for the Economic Council of Canada (Ottawa: Supply and Services, 1991). The experiment's design involved selecting participants (the aged, disabled, and institutionalized were included) randomly from three sites in Manitoba (Winnipeg, Dauphin, and a number of small rural communities) and assigning them to different negative income tax programs or, alternatively, to a control group. Participants were given monthly income payments for three years while the control group received nothing. All participants were interviewed three times yearly to obtain detailed information on their work effort. This experiment generated Canadian panel data on labour-supply behaviour in which households were assigned a variety of tax rates and income guarantees.

of 2.4 to 3 per cent for married women compared to 21 per cent in the United States; and a response of 3.8 to 5.3 per cent for single female heads compared to 13.2 per cent in the United States.[47]

The prediction from economic theory that guaranteed income schemes create a disincentive for people to work is one of the strongest arguments against these schemes. The Canadian results suggest that this concern may be overblown, and that in fact individuals and families are likely to be fairly insensitive to changes in the tax-transfer system facing them.

Although there has been a distinct scarcity in Canada of studies of the effect of income maintenance schemes on labour supply, there have been a number of Canadian studies of the effect of unemployment insurance on the unemployment rate. Most of them use econometric regression techniques to find the statistical relationship between the rate of unemployment and a characteristic of the UI scheme, such as the ratio of UI benefits to weekly wages. These studies have generally concluded that the generosity of the UI program was responsible for some unemployment, although there is no consensus on the precise amount that could be attributed to UI.[48] Several studies have also suggested that the generosity of the UI program relative to the comparable US program contributed to the fact that the unemployment rates in Canada were higher than those in the United States.[49]

An (un)employment insurance scheme should not necessarily be designed to minimize the unemployment rate, since it is an important component of a social safety network. It should not, however, create incentives for people to abuse the system. Indeed, concerns over the generosity of the UI program prompted a number of structural changes in the 1990s, the most significant of which were made in 1996. The program is now substantially less generous than it used to be in terms of both eligibility and benefits. The lack of experience rating, however, continues to produce distortions and biases in the program (see the discussion of this point in chapter 6).

## Savings and Investment

The impact of transfer programs on aggregate savings and investment depends primarily on the manner in which such programs impinge on house-

---

[47] Hum and Simpson, supra footnote 46, at xiv-xv.

[48] Shelly Phipps, "Does Unemployment Insurance Increase Unemployment?" (Spring 1993), 1 *Canadian Business Economics* 37-50, at 45 concludes "that the disincentives to the individual labour supply generated by the Canadian UI system are likely to be extremely small." Larger disincentives have been reported in David Andolfatto, Paul Gomme, and Paul Storer, "US Labour Market Policy and the Canada-US Unemployment Rate Gap" (February 1998), 24 *Canadian Public Policy* S210-32; and Michael Baker, Miles Corak, and Andrew Heisz, "The Labour Market Dynamics of Unemployment Rates in Canada and the United States" (February 1998), 24 *Canadian Public Policy* S72-89.

[49] See many of the articles in W. Craig Riddell and Andrew Sharpe, eds., "The Canada-US Unemployment Rate Gap" (February 1998), 24 supplement *Canadian Public Policy* (entire issue).

hold savings decisions.[50] In analyzing the effect of transfer programs on household savings, it is convenient to regard an individual's saving decision as being taken in a lifetime context. An individual can expect to receive a stream of earned income that begins at the end of his schooling period and, as a rule, rises until he retires. This stream of income, along with any inheritances the individual receives yields an amount of lifetime total wealth that the individual can allocate between consumption during his life and bequests to his heirs. To simplify matters here, we shall ignore both inheritances and bequests. A typical pattern of lifetime savings and consumption is as follows. In his early years, the individual's consumption is supported by his parents. Once he is self-supporting, he will at first spend more than his income; that is, he will borrow. During this period, he will acquire consumer durables such as housing. In his middle and later years of working life, he will earn more than he consumes. His saving will repay the debt accumulated earlier, and it also will provide a stock of wealth to be consumed during retirement. This "lifetime" model suggests that the chosen pattern of consumption and saving (or dissaving) depends upon three things: the lifetime wealth of the individual, the rate of interest, and the premium that the individual places on present consumption relative to future consumption (which economists call the rate of pure time preference). The lifetime wealth of an individual is the present value of his lifetime earnings. The greater is his lifetime wealth, the greater will be the level of consumption that he maintains over his lifetime. The rate of interest reflects the rate at which the individual can substitute future consumption for present consumption. The higher is the interest rate, all other things being equal, the lower will be the level of present consumption relative to future consumption. That is, the individual will save more (or dissave less) in earlier years in order to consume more in later years. This tendency will be offset somewhat, however, by the individual's rate of time preference. The greater is the premium that he places on present consumption relative to future consumption, the higher his present consumption will be relative to future consumption.

Government policies can affect both the lifetime wealth of an individual and the rate of interest on savings. Increases in lifetime wealth (or "permanent income") increase the individual's consumption over his lifetime as a whole. If the increase in wealth occurs in his early years, he will save more in order to finance higher consumption in later years. If, instead, he expects the increase in wealth to occur later in life, he will save less and consume more in his earlier years. Likewise, he will save more if interest rates rise and consume more if interest rates fall.

Transfer programs have their primary impact on the wealth of recipients rather than on the rate of return to savings. An increase in transfer receipts increases lifetime wealth, and this increase, in turn, increases lifetime consump-

---

[50] The government's role in this context is also important to the extent that it has discretion over the use of funds accumulated in public pension plans. The latter point is pursued later in this chapter.

tion. If transfers are received early in life, savings over the lifetime are likely to increase; if they are received later in life, savings are likely to decrease.

At the same time, however, the transfers will be financed by reductions in the wealth—through, say, taxes—of other members of the economy. The cost of tax-financed transfers will be borne mainly by individuals who are in the income-earning phase of their lives and will cause a corresponding fall in their lifetime consumption and saving. If the transfers are financed by government debt, some funds that might otherwise have gone to private investment will be diverted to financing the transfer.

Transfer schemes such as negative income taxes and welfare programs tend to increase income throughout the recipient's life. If these transfers are financed out of current tax revenues raised from the working population, no a priori prediction can be made about their effect on aggregate savings. The increase in the consumption and the wealth of the recipients will be offset more or less by decreases in the consumption and the wealth of the tax-paying population, but it is difficult to predict the effect of this shift on savings and hence on private investment. If the transfers are financed by government debt, they will to some extent replace private investment as a use of savings.

The impact on savings is likely to be greater in the case of the various public pension schemes (CPP, OAS, and GIS), which provide transfers to persons only after retirement. The impact of a general negative income tax scheme would be similar to the extent that it involved a net transfer to retired persons. Our consideration here of the impact of a public pension scheme on the savings pattern of a typical individual rests on an important assumption—that the individual regards the pension as being a binding commitment on the part of society to provide the currently expected level of benefits when he retires. Public pensions typically involve no explicit contract. Their provisions can be changed at the whim of the government in power. There is therefore no guarantee that an individual's current contributions will be "made good" when he retires. Of course, as matters stand now, pension benefits exceed current contributions, and it is in order to maintain the existing level of benefits that the federal government has recently increased the contributory rates for the CPP. Thus there would seem to be an implicit contract between generations that people can take as binding. The implications of the fact that it is not binding will be examined later.

Consider, then, an individual's savings response to a public pension scheme. Assume initially that the retirement age remains unchanged. If pensions are financed by taxes on earnings during the individual's working years, his after-tax earnings during his working life will fall, but his income during retirement will rise by the amount of the pension. If the scheme is actuarially fair, the present value of contributions will equal the present value of benefits and the individual's lifetime wealth will not change. Consequently, the individual will not wish to change his lifetime consumption pattern and public pension contributions will completely replace private savings for retirement. If the scheme is not actuarially fair, and benefits in retirement exceed contributions plus their interest, the individual will obtain an increase in lifetime wealth. He will want to increase his consumption over his lifetime and will therefore reduce his private saving by more than the amount of his pension contribution. Alternatively, if benefits fall short of contributions compounded by the going interest rate, lifetime wealth will fall and the individual will reduce his private savings by less than his pension contribution. In any case, one would expect public pensions to displace private saving for retirement to a great extent.

The impact of a public pension scheme on aggregate savings depends critically upon the manner in which the scheme is financed. If current pension payments are financed out of current taxes, pensions represent an ongoing transfer from current working generations to the currently retired. Current contributions come at the expense of private saving for retirement that would have gone to finance investment. Instead, the contributions go to current pensions of the retired, which are largely consumed. The aggregate savings of the economy might fall by as much as the pension amount. When the plan is being phased in, it will increase the lifetime wealth of individuals who are of working age or older, since they will receive more than they have contributed. If they save part of their windfall and pass it on to their heirs, the impact of the pension on savings will be partially offset. Once the plan is fully operational, however, current savings will be reduced,[51] unless measures are taken to offset this effect.

Similar arguments apply if the pension is financed currently by the issuance of debt. In this case, private savings will not necessarily fall, but investment will fall, since the debt issued to finance current pension payments—and hence the consumption of the retired—would otherwise have been used for investment.

The alternative to a pension scheme financed by current revenue or debt—a pay-as-you-go scheme—is the funded pension scheme. A scheme of this kind avoids the adverse effect on aggregate investment that characterizes the pay-as-you-go approach. Under a funded scheme, the representative individual contributes during his working life an amount that with the interest it accumulates is equal to what he is expected to receive during retirement. Each person's contribution goes into a fund that is then used to finance private (or public) investment. In this case, the public pension plan simply replaces private savings for retirement and aggregate savings do not necessarily decline. Furthermore, provided that the accumulated funds are put into the capital markets just as private savings for retirement would have been, private investment does not necessarily decline either. Thus, how a public pension plan affects investment depends on whether the plan is funded or not and, if it is funded, on how the fund is used. A plan that incorporates some transfer of income between generations will reduce aggregate savings and investment, whereas one that does not need not. In

---

[51] Banting and Boadway, supra footnote 19, at 15.

Canada, the CPP is partially funded, and the OAS and GIS operate on a pay-as-you-go basis.

One consideration that significantly tempers the adverse effect of unfunded pension schemes on savings is the fact that the age of retirement is variable. As we argued earlier, the existence of a pension plan encourages early retirement, since the opportunity cost of continuing to work after the age of eligibility under the plan includes the forgone pension earnings. This cost is offset only to the degree that extending one's working life increases the pension eventually attained. Individuals who retire early because the pension is available will save more during their working years than they would in the absence of the pension in order to maintain their consumption levels during their extended retirement. One cannot predict a priori whether the reduction in savings attributable to the substitution of public pensions for private saving will be greater than or less than the increase in savings attributable to the early retirement induced by the availability of the public pensions.

Two final effects of transfer schemes on an individual's lifetime decisions are worth noting. First, an individual decides not only on his retirement age and his lifetime savings and consumption profiles, but also on his "investment" in schooling or training before he begins working—that is, his investment in human capital. It has been argued that negative income tax schemes and the like, by reducing work effort, reduce the return from investment in human capital and, therefore, reduce the incentive to invest in it.[52] The evidence to support this proposition is scanty, however, and also there are other, perhaps more important, influences at work in the opposite direction. For one, education is heavily subsidized, so the private cost of investing in human capital is much lower than the social cost. Also, for structural, demographic, or other reasons, the rate of unemployment among youths under age 25 is much higher than the rate for the rest of the population. Since for these individuals the probability of getting a job is relatively low, the opportunity cost of taking further education in terms of expected forgone earnings is relatively low as well.

The existence of transfer schemes may also affect the extent to which individuals save in order to make bequests to their heirs as well as to provide for their own retirement. As we have said, an unfunded public pension scheme will tend to reduce the capital formation and net wealth of the economy. It has been argued that individuals may try to offset the ill effects on future generations of this reduction in wealth by increasing their bequests.[53]

---

[52] Samuel A. Rea Jr., "Investment in Human Capital Under a Negative Income Tax" (November 1977), 10 *Canadian Journal of Economics* 607-20.

[53] This point was made by Robert J. Barro, "Are Government Bonds Net Wealth?" (November-December 1974), 82 *Journal of Political Economy* 1095-1117. For a contrary view, see Martin Feldstein, "Social Security and Saving: The Extended Life Cycle Theory" (May 1976), 66 *The American Economic Review* 77-86.

Published evidence of the effect of public pensions on savings in Canada is sparse. A few studies in the 1970s found no evidence that the CPP/QPP had a negative effect on personal savings (many contributors to these public plans would not have saved in the absence of a pension)[54] and no evidence that the OAS or the CPP had a significant effect on aggregate savings.[55] Between the mid-1980s and the mid-1990s, the savings rate in Canada declined from 14.8 percent of personal income to 8.2 percent (table 3.21), whereas savings in the form of registered retirement savings plans (RRSPs) increased from 1.9 percent of personal income to 4.1 percent. Contributions to the CPP/QPP and RRSPs combined accounted for almost 20 percent of personal savings in 1984 and 66 percent of personal savings by 1995 (see table 3.21). The growth in both the absolute importance and the relative importance of RRSPs is not surprising, given the incentive to save in this way—individuals may deduct savings put into RRSPs from taxable income and pay income tax on the proceeds upon retirement. This is, in effect, a form of lifetime averaging in which both the contributions and the interest earned accumulate tax-free. In theory, one would expect the RRSP program to induce substantial amounts of retirement savings, and in practice, it apparently has.[56]

Further evidence on the extent to which tax-based savings incentives can be a powerful tool for promoting household and national savings appears in a study of the effects of cancelling the registered home ownership savings plan (RHOSP) in Canada.[57] The RHOSP was a tax-subsidized home owner-

---

[54] James Pesando and S.A. Rea Jr., *Public and Private Pensions in Canada: An Econometric Analysis* (Toronto: University of Toronto Press for the Ontario Economic Council, 1977).

[55] Phelim Boyle and John Murray, "Social Security Wealth and Private Saving in Canada" (August 1979), 12 *Canadian Journal of Economics* 456-68; Peter Wrage, *The Effects of the Growth of Private and Public Pension Plans on Saving and Investment in Canada*, Discussion Paper no. 174 (Ottawa: Economic Council of Canada, 1980); and Michael J. Daly and Peter Wrage, *The Impact of Canada's Old Age Security Program on Retirement Saving, Labour Supply and Retirement*, Discussion Paper no. 203 (Ottawa: Economic Council of Canada, 1981).

[56] John Burbidge, Deborah Fretz, and Michael R. Veall, "Canadian and U.S. Savings Rates and the Role of RRSPs" (mimeograph, McMaster University, Department of Economics, Hamilton, January 1998). These authors also argue that the differences between Canadian and US aggregate savings rates do not appear to be attributable to the registered retirement savings plan program in Canada. A similar argument has been made by John Sabelhaus, "Public Policy and Savings in the United States and Canada" (May 1997), 30 *Canadian Journal of Economics* 253-75. In particular, Sabelhaus argues that the higher savings rate in Canada vis-à-vis the United States in the 1970s and 1980s was not a consequence of the RRSP program but rather largely a consequence of relatively low provision of public and private pensions at higher income levels—US social security pays more to high-income retirees than does the Canadian public pension system.

[57] Gary V. Engelhardt, "Tax Subsidies and Household Saving: Evidence from Canada" (November 1996), 111 *Quarterly Journal of Economics* 1237-68. For a description and evaluation of the RHOSP, see Robin W. Boadway and Harry M. Kitchen, *Canadian Tax*

(The footnote is continued on the next page.)

ship savings plan which ran from 1974 to 1985. Its objective was to provide annual tax deductions (subject to limits) for first-time home buyers. The empirical results suggest that the subsidy had a substantial impact on saving: each dollar contributed to RHOSPs led to between 56 and 93 cents of new household savings and between 20 and 57 cents of new national savings.[58] Although much of the US evidence also suggests that tax-assisted savings plans lead to net additions to savings,[59] not everyone agrees. It has been argued, for example, that government tax-assisted savings programs affect only the allocation of savings and wealth and not their overall levels.[60]

## Administration Cost and Compliance

Concern about ongoing deficits and rising debt have driven governments at every level to reduce their costs. This effort has involved not only reductions in some government services, and increased restrictions on eligibility for benefits, but also efforts to reduce the costs of administering transfer programs. For example, the federal government has explicitly announced that one goal of reforms to the CPP is a lowering of administration costs. In particular, "by 2030, costs are to be reduced by just over 9 percent compared to what they otherwise would be by then."[61] Since child tax benefits and GST credits were launched, Revenue Canada has implemented a number of changes designed to improve the delivery and reduce the administrative costs of these programs.[62] Provincial and local governments have also undertaken initiatives to lower the costs of administering their social assistance programs.

Governments have also recently introduced or proposed changes in a number of transfer programs in order to control or reduce the risk of non-compliance with the terms of these programs through error, fraud, or abuse. Non-compliance is a serious concern, since it impairs a government's ability to fund social policy objectives and undermines the integrity and fairness of social programs. Although the eligibility requirements for EI payments and provincial social assistance programs have been tightened substantially over the past few years, serious concerns persist about the child tax benefit and

---

[57] Continued ...

*Policy*, 2d ed., Canadian Tax Paper no. 76 (Toronto: Canadian Tax Foundation, 1984), 76-78 and 83-84.

[58] Engelhardt, supra footnote 57, at 1261.

[59] James M. Poterba, Steven F. Venti, and David A. Wise, "How Retirement Savings Programs Increase Savings" (Fall 1996), 10 *Journal of Economic Perspectives* 91-112.

[60] Eric M. Engen, William G. Gale, and John Karl Scholz, "The Illusory Effects of Saving Incentives on Saving" (Fall 1996), 10 *Journal of Economic Perspectives* 113-38.

[61] Canada, Human Resources Development, *The Canada Pension Plan (CPP): Securing Its Future for All Canadians* (Ottawa: Human Resources Development, CPP Programs Division, September 25, 1997).

[62] For an indication of these changes, see Canada, *Report of the Auditor General of Canada to the House of Commons* (Ottawa: Public Works and Government Services, September 1996), chapter 19, at 19-21.

GST credit programs. In fact, the auditor general's 1996 report claimed that the existing control environment for these programs was inadequate for the purposes of limiting potential abuse, ensuring accountability, and achieving equity in the delivery of the $8 billion (annually) program. The report identified five areas in which fundamental checks and balances were lacking: (1) enrolling children for benefits; (2) accounting for deceased children on the benefit roll; (3) processing benefit applications that were incomplete or that contained inconsistent information; (4) reconfirming eligibility; and (5) maintaining source documents.[63]

The importance of implementing tighter controls over the GST credit and the child tax benefit may be apparent from the results of an audit of the Ottawa tax centre, which is just one of many. The auditor general's 1996 report estimated that overpayments under the two programs in 1995-96 amounted to between $5 and $6 million.[64] The report also suggested that because of the way in which GST credits are processed that program may be a greater source of error and abuse than the child tax benefit program. A GST credit applicant is required only to report the number of children claimed, whereas an applicant for the child tax benefit must provide basic information about each child. Moreover, the spouse of an applicant for the GST credit does not have to file a tax return in order for the applicant to receive benefits—the spouse's income is deemed to be what the applicant reports; if nothing is reported, Revenue Canada may assume that it is zero. Finally, the family member who receives the GST credit may vary from year to year, a circumstance that complicates the government's ability to track payments and to ensure that duplicate payments are not being made.[65] The child tax benefit, by contrast, generally goes to the same person every year.

## Issues

The main problem that confronts policy makers in designing an appropriate income transfer system is to ensure that a socially adequate amount of purchasing power is transferred to the needy without establishing unacceptable disincentives to work or to save. Over the past two decades, as we have noted, Canadian governments have attempted to remove many of the harmful disincentives and distortionary tendencies embodied in the income transfer system. Some important issues remain, however. In chapter 9, we shall discuss the broad question whether income redistribution should be handled through the tax system or through transfer programs. Here we shall consider several current issues of somewhat more limited scope.

---

[63] For a detailed discussion of why these are deemed to be areas of concern, see ibid., at 19-24 to 19-30.

[64] Ibid., at 19-29.

[65] Ibid., at 19-31.

## Should Canada Have a Negative Income Tax?

Twenty years ago, when suggestions were made for the introduction of a negative income tax, the political will and public approval necessary for this step were virtually non-existent.[66] Since then, however, government transfers in Canada have changed dramatically. Many programs have been redesigned so that they are similar, if not identical, to a negative income tax. Thus, the GIS and child tax benefit diminish as family income increases; the OAS is clawed back from high-income earners; the spouse's allowance is income tested; provincial welfare programs are generally related to family income; and refundable tax credits are based on family income. The question, then, is whether we should take the final step and adopt a comprehensive negative income tax system.

A negative income tax (NIT) system is a compromise between the demogrant, with its zero recapture rate, and schemes with 100 percent recapture rates. By selecting a recapture or tax rate between 0 and 100 percent, a NIT both maintains some incentive to work and economizes on payments by concentrating them on those who need them most. The main things to be decided in designing a NIT system are how comprehensive it should be and what the guaranteed minimum and the recapture rate should be.

The argument for replacing all transfer schemes with one all-encompassing scheme is that of administrative simplicity. A single scheme, consisting of a guaranteed minimum level and a given recapture rate on earned income applicable to all persons (or families), could be administered through the existing tax system. All persons below some exemption level would receive transfers (negative taxes), and all persons above the exemption level would pay taxes. Refunds and additional payments would be claimed once a year when tax forms were completed. This system would not be adequate, however, for persons who currently receive transfers, since the circumstances of many of these persons can change significantly from month to month. Consequently, the scheme would probably have to incorporate some system of monthly payments, and these payments would have to be revised in accordance with changes in individual circumstances and expected annual earnings. Otherwise, there could be either a significant overpayment that might be hard to recoup at the end of the tax year or an underpayment that might place the recipient in temporary financial difficulty. In short, the system would have to be flexible. Even so, it would almost certainly be less costly to administer than the existing transfer system.

The main apparent disadvantage of a universal NIT scheme is that the recapture rate and the guaranteed minimum are uniform for all recipients, instead of varying appropriately with the type of person or need in question. Ideally, a scheme designed to help the working poor would have a low re-

---

[66] See the discussion in Boadway and Kitchen, supra footnote 57, at 343-46.

capture rate (to minimize the disincentive to work) and a low guaranteed minimum (so that the program would not be too costly). This arrangement, however, would be inadequate for the unemployable, for whom a relatively high guaranteed minimum would be appropriate and the recapture rate largely irrelevant. Yet the high guaranteed minimum suitable for unemployables would make the scheme too expensive to operate for the working poor. For example, if the guaranteed minimum were, say, $9,000 and the recapture rate 33.33 percent, individuals with incomes of up to $27,000 would receive transfers.[67]

This problem would be relatively easy to solve by keeping the principle of NIT but abandoning the notion of applying the same rates to all. Just as the income tax system differentiates among persons according to family size, age, and other characteristics, so could a NIT system. The guaranteed minimum could be set at different rates for persons in different categories—the disabled, the aged, and so forth. One could also have different recapture rate structures for different persons and families (although this is not done in the income tax system). A NIT system integrated with the income tax system could replace the current transfer system—though obvious constitutional difficulties would arise if the federal government undertook the role of welfare-assistance provider in place of the provinces. The alternative would be for the provinces to incorporate the principle of negative income taxation in their welfare-assistance programs.

## Public Pensions and Government-Assisted Private Pensions

The governments of all of the countries in the OECD are involved in the provision of income for retirement. Most, like Canada, have an array of programs. The World Bank, in a landmark report on pension reform in developing countries, classifies public retirement income programs into three "pillars."[68] The first pillar is the system of payments to the elderly that is intended to be redistributive; that is, to provide a social safety net for the poor elderly. The appropriate program for this pillar, in the World Bank's view is one financed out of current tax revenues (that is, unfunded) and targeted to those most in need. The second pillar is a mandatory savings system intended to ensure that persons save enough in their working years to provide for themselves adequately in retirement. The World Bank argues that this pillar should be fully funded and privately managed to ensure both the long-term viability of the program and a good rate of return, comparable to what one would obtain on ordinary savings. This pillar, though privately managed, would have to be regulated to ensure that the pension funds were

---

[67] The formula for a NIT is $Y - T = tB + Y(1 - t)$. If $t = 1/3$, $Y$ = other income and the guaranteed minimum is $9,000, then $tB = \$9,000$, so $B = \$27,000$, the breakeven level of income.

[68] World Bank, *Averting the Old Age Crisis: Policies To Protect the Old and Promote Growth* (Washington, DC: World Bank and Oxford University Press, 1994).

run prudently and in a balanced manner. The third pillar would be a program that encouraged persons to save voluntarily for their own retirement and thereby make themselves less dependent on the public sector in retirement. In this case, the government's role would be limited to providing tax incentives for retirement savings, to the extent that encouragement was thought to be desirable. The third pillar would of course be fully private, and it would consist of either a self-managed individual pension or company pension according to the circumstances of the person involved. All three pillars could have elements of *insurance*, not only insurance against market risk by appropriate diversification, but also insurance against other risks such as disability, health expenses, and uncertainty about the length of life.

These three pillars reflect what economists have argued is the rationale for government intervention in the retirement income system. Three main arguments have been advanced for public sector involvement in retirement savings.[69] The first is the *redistributive argument*, and it has two dimensions. Redistribution to the elderly can be motivated by either intragenerational or intergenerational considerations. Intragenerational redistribution is called for because some households in any given age cohort have lower lifetime incomes than some of their contemporaries. They may be particularly poor in retirement because they had low incomes during their working years and were simply unable to accumulate enough savings to see them through retirement. In principle, one might use the standard tax-transfer system to address their needs, but as a rule governments maintain special programs of transfers to the elderly. A reason for this is that the elderly poor, unlike other low-income persons, are not in the labour force, so work incentives are not an issue.

Intergenerational redistribution might be called for if one generation is worse off than another generation. There may be "unlucky" cohorts that for some reason—war, depression, national disaster— are disadvantaged relative to those born earlier and later. The disadvantage may also arise from demographic shocks: the members of a particularly large cohort will have relatively poor labour-market prospects when they are young and both relatively low capital income and relatively few workers to support them once they retire. A temporary use of intergenerational transfers, such as unfunded public pensions, would smooth out per capita incomes across lucky and unlucky cohorts, a policy that is referred to as intergenerational risk sharing.[70]

Indeed, given that, historically, the trend of per capita incomes is upward, so that each future generation may well be better off than its predecessor, it might seem reasonable to make the transfers from younger to older persons permanent rather than temporary. But the case for such a policy is not as

---

[69] These arguments are discussed in more detail in *Reform of Retirement Income Policy*, supra footnote 15.

[70] The temporary use of deficit financing of public expenditures would achieve a similar result. Indeed, that is why debt financing is an important way to finance wars: it spreads the financial cost across several generations.

sound as it might appear to be at first glance. For one thing, in view of the current degradation of the environment and the fact that the earth's resources are finite, it is by no means guaranteed that each new generation will be better off than the one before. For another, a permanent system of unfunded pensions might have the adverse effect on savings, and hence on investment and the creation of wealth, that we mentioned earlier in this chapter. What is more important, however, a permanently unfunded pension scheme would not make all current generations better off. As we noted earlier, the primary beneficiaries of an unfunded system are those who are alive during the transition to the system. Even when the system is entirely in place, it will make all succeeding cohorts worse off than they would be in the absence of the scheme as long as the rate of interest in the economy exceeds the rate of growth. The reason is simply that an unfunded public pension provides an implicit rate of return equal to the rate of growth of the economy—the transfers that one receives from the next generation of workers will exceed one's own contributions by the rate of growth of the economy. If the contributions had instead been saved, they would have yielded the rate of return given by the market interest rate.

Thus the argument for intergenerational transfers really applies only to their temporary use in order to provide social insurance for relatively unlucky cohorts. There is a fundamental obstacle, however, to their use for any purpose—the fact that only a far-sighted government would implement them. Many observers would argue that governments, however well-meaning they might be, tend by their nature to have limited time horizons. They are elected to serve the current constituency and are unable therefore to engage in intergenerational risk-sharing arrangements. Some might go further and suggest that governments are prone to passing on current liabilities to future generations. If this is so, it would be unwise to expect them to implement sensible long-term intergenerational policies. Instead, policies should be put in place to deter them from exploiting future generations.

The second argument for government assistance to retirement income is the *lack of savings argument*. Many households do not save adequately for their own retirement.[71] This failure may be the result of simple myopia or irrationality. Or it may be that these households have reckoned (perhaps quite rationally, if unconsciously) that if they do not provide for their own retirement, governments will do it for them. Indeed, this seems to be a fair presumption. Governments face what is referred to as the "Samaritan's dilemma": they find it difficult to commit themselves to a policy of forcing households to provide for their own retirement by refusing to help those that have not done so. In the end, inevitably, they come to the rescue. This consideration seems to be the basis for the policy of mandatory saving for retirement that many OECD countries have implemented.

---

[71] This was documented some time ago in the classic article by Peter Diamond, "A Framework for Social Security Analysis" (1977), 8 *Journal of Public Economics* 275-98.

The final argument for government intervention in the retirement income system, the *savings-rate* argument, refers specifically to government assistance to retirement savings. This argument is simply that it is desirable, for a number of reasons, to increase the savings rate. A higher savings rate makes persons more self-sufficient and less reliant on government in retirement. It also leads to a higher level of investment, which may itself bring benefits to society at large. For example, investment may create benefits in the form of new knowledge or improvements in human capital that are not appropriated entirely by those who have undertaken the investment. As well, the provision of a tax advantage for retirement saving can be justified by an appeal to the arguments that we discussed in chapter 2 for using consumption rather than income as the tax base. To fully shelter savings for retirement is essentially equivalent to accepting consumption as the appropriate base for personal taxation.

These three arguments translate directly into the World Bank's three pillars. The redistributive argument yields the first pillar, the lack of savings argument the second pillar, and the savings-rate argument the third pillar. The system of pensions and transfers to the elderly in Canada has elements of all three pillars. The OAS/GIS transfers correspond to the first pillar: they are funded out of general revenues and are to some extent targeted to the needy.

The CPP/QPP system of public pensions corresponds to the Word Bank's second pillar. It is essentially a form of mandatory savings, but one that is strikingly different from the World Bank's ideal. For one thing, it is largely unfunded, which implies that it is an intergenerational transfer. As such, it is largely of benefit to those who contributed to it while it was being phased in and whose benefits, consequently, outweigh their contributions. The system as it is currently constituted has accumulated unfunded liabilities—$556 billion in 1995—of the same order of magnitude as the national debt.[72] Given the current demographic realities, contribution rates would have to rise to 14.2 percent by 2030 in order to maintain the current benefit structure for retirees. Another problem with the system is that it is publicly managed and does not yield market rates of return. The CPP is fully invested in provincial debt at concessionary rates, hardly either a good investment portfolio or a sensible incentive for the provinces. The proposed reforms of the CPP would address both of these issues. They would increase the contribution rate to 12.2 percent over a six- to eight-year period in order to transform the system into a funded one (or, under another option, increase contribution rates to 10.9 percent and reduce benefits by 10 percent). And they would adopt a system of financial management of the funds that would invest them in private markets rather than earmark them for provincial debt. This change too would contribute to the system's funding. Of course, there would be gainers and losers, and that is the essence of the political debate. The gainers would

---

[72] This is well documented in *An Information Paper for Consultations on the Canada Pension Plan*, supra footnote 16.

be the next generation of workers, whose contribution rates would be lower, and the losers would be those currently in the work force, who would face higher contribution rates. Thus, future generations would be made better off at the expense of the current ones, a tradeoff that essentially involves weighing the benefits to one generation against the costs to the other.

The third pillar is the system of RPPs and RRSPs, which afford a tax incentive to income earners to save more for retirement on their own account. These plans shelter the income on the accumulated savings in a way that is very similar to treating it on an expenditure-tax basis. Contributions are deductible from income for tax purposes, and they are allowed to accumulate tax-free. They are only taxed when taken out of the plan. This arrangement differs in several ways, however, from full-fledged expenditure-tax treatment of income. There is a limit to the amount that an individual can contribute in any one year. In the case of RPPs, funds cannot be withdrawn to finance consumption except at retirement. Once the contributor reaches a certain age, he must convert the registered funds into an annuity or otherwise take them out over a fixed period, whereupon they become taxable whether they are used for consumption or not. Critics who support the notion of expenditure-based personal taxation argue that there should be no limits on either contributions or the time stream of removals of funds from registered plans. Detractors argue that sheltering savings for retirement from taxation tends to help most those in the higher income-tax brackets. They suggest that funds accumulating in such plans should be at least partially taxed, as they are in some OECD countries, such as Australia. Again, we discussed the case for expenditure rather than income as a personal tax base at length in chapter 2.

## Should the Employment Insurance Program Be Based on Insurance Principles or Should It Be a Form of Income Redistribution?

The current employment insurance program has several "objectives as part of a larger social security framework: prevention of poverty, redistribution of income, stabilization of the economy and facilitation of labour market adjustment."[73] In essence, these objectives reduce to two: the provision of insurance for those who become unexpectedly unemployed and the provision of income to meet other distributional goals.[74] It has been argued, however, that in trying to achieve both goals the current system has achieved neither particularly well.[75] As an income distribution program, it is poorly targeted

---

[73] Canada, Human Resources Development, *From Unemployment Insurance to Employment Insurance: A Supplementary Paper* (Ottawa: Supply and Services, 1994).

[74] For a discussion of the assumptions and rationales behind these two divergent views of the purpose of the unemployment insurance system, see Miles Corak, "Unemployment Insurance, Work Disincentives, and the Canadian Labour Market: An Overview," in Christopher Green, Fred Lazar, Miles Corak, and Dominique M. Gross, *Unemployment Insurance: How To Make It Work* (Toronto: C.D. Howe Institute, 1994), 86-159.

[75] Franke and Hermanutz, supra footnote 42.

and does not always reach those in need. For example, a study of UI recipients in Newfoundland in 1992 found that the UI program transferred considerable sums of money to families that had no need whatsoever and did not give money to the families most in need.[76] A study based on 1986 data for all of Canada found that the UI program had a mildly progressive incidence pattern.[77] It has been argued that this progressivity, though desirable, is small relative to the overall size of the program; thus, the EI program may not be an efficient program for redistributing income.[78]

As an insurance program, EI is inefficient because there is considerable cross-subsidization across industries, firms, and regions.[79] This cross-subsidization exists because premiums are not experience rated; that is, they are not based on the risk of unemployment.[80] Although experience rating would improve the efficiency and equity of the program by internalizing the costs of unemployment, it has been criticized on the ground that it would establish "a two-tier benefits system [that] goes against the basic principles of our social security system, of which UI remains an integral part."[81] The point has been made, moreover, that individuals become unemployed involuntarily: an experience-rated system would penalize those who are most vulnerable to unemployment[82] and increase unemployment during recessions by weakening the automatic stabilization role of the EI program.[83] These concerns, however, are also concerns of those who advocate experience rating and moving the EI program toward one based on insurance principles. Income distribution should not be covered through the EI program. It would be more appropriately handled and targeted at truly needy families if it were delivered through existing but enhanced government transfer programs.[84] Indeed, a logical extension of this strategy would be to convert all government transfer

---

[76] Doug May and A. Hollett, *The Rock in a Hard Place: Atlantic Canada and the UI Trap* (Toronto: C.D. Howe Institute, 1995).

[77] G.C. Ruggeri, D. Van Wart, and R. Howard, *The Government as Robin Hood: Exploring the Myth* (Kingston, Ont.: Queen's University, School of Policy Studies, and the Caledon Institute of Social Policy, 1996).

[78] Franke and Hermanutz, supra footnote 42, at 65.

[79] For an indication of the interregional, interindustry, and interfirm cross-subsidization, see Miles Corak and Wendy Pyper, *Workers, Firms and Unemployment Insurance*, Statistics Canada catalogue no. 73-505E.

[80] For a discussion of experience rating, see chapter 6.

[81] Mario Seccareccia, "The Case Against a Two-Tier Benefits System for Canada's Unemployed" (Winter 1995), 3 *Canadian Business Economics* 53-61, at 53.

[82] Ibid., at 60.

[83] H. Bougrine and M. Seccareccia, *Unemployment Compensation and Unemployment: An Analysis of the Aggregate Demand-Side Effects for Postwar Canada*, Working Paper no. 9419E (Ottawa: University of Ottawa, Department of Economics, 1994).

[84] Thomas J. Courchene, *Social Canada in the Millennium: Reform Imperatives and Restructuring Principles* (Toronto: C.D. Howe Institute, 1994); Alice Nakamura, John Cragg, and Kathleen Sayers, "The Case for Disentangling the Insurance and Income Assistance Roles of Unemployment Insurance" (Fall 1994), 3 *Canadian Business Economics* 46-53; and Franke and Hermanutz, supra footnote 42.

programs, at least at the federal level, into one comprehensive guaranteed or negative income tax program.

## Provincial Social Assistance Programs: Workfare Versus Welfare

In 1996, Ontario became the first government in Canada to introduce a workfare program. The newly implemented Ontario Works Act replaced the former General Welfare Assistance Act and the Family Benefits Act. Under this new program, it is intended that able-bodied individuals receiving social assistance will earn their welfare by participating in community placement or retraining programs that will lead to jobs. Community projects require participants to work for an average of 17 hours per week on projects organized by municipalities and community groups.

Social welfare policy in Canada involves striking a balance between providing adequate support for those with low incomes and maintaining incentives for individuals to earn their own incomes. It is the question of incentives, then, that is at the heart of the analytical debate.[85] For those who believe that welfare creates a decline in the work ethic (that is, individuals become dependent on welfare and not interested in employment), voluntary programs will not work and compulsory workfare is the answer. Indeed, there is evidence to support the view that the longer one stays on welfare the less likely one is to find employment.[86] For those who believe that welfare recipients are willing to work but lack the required skills, voluntary programs designed to upgrade the skills are what is required (the "skills deficiency" hypothesis).[87]

At the moment, there is no conclusive evidence that workfare is or is not an effective way of moving individuals into the permanent work force. On the one hand, if it forces welfare recipients to maintain touch with the labour market, it may prevent a deterioration in their human capital and facilitate their move from welfare to work.[88] On the other hand, evidence from the United States (where workfare has been in place for some time) suggests that government-sponsored welfare-to-work programs generally do not achieve their objectives.[89]

---

[85] The Canadian public's reaction to workfare versus welfare may be noted from a Gallop poll in the fall of 1994, in which 86 percent of respondents favoured making people on welfare go to work.

[86] Organisation for Economic Co-operation and Development, *OECD Economic Surveys: Canada* (Paris: OECD, 1994).

[87] Adil Sayeed, "Workfare: An Overview of the Issues" (May 1995), 16 *Policy Options* 3-5, at 4.

[88] Marc T. Law, Howard I. Markowitz, and Fazil Mihlar, "The Harris Government: A Mid-Term Review" (1997), supplement *Fraser Forum* 1-50, at 19.

[89] Dan Bloom, *After AFDC: Welfare-to-Work Choices and Challenges for States* (New York: Manpower Demonstration Research Corporation, 1997); and Fazil Mihlar and M. Danielle Smith, *Government-Sponsored Training Programs: Failure in the United States, Lessons for Canada*, Fraser Forum Critical Issues Bulletin (Vancouver: Fraser Institute, 1997).

Given the lack of empirical evidence in support of workfare programs, and given the lack of incentives in many of the current provincial welfare programs, it would make sense to replace provincial welfare systems with a negative income tax system. This strategy would increase the incentives for welfare recipients to find employment and therefore might help to break the pattern of extended and even intergenerational dependency that seems to characterize the current welfare system.[90]

---

[90] US evidence suggests that children raised in families receiving welfare are three times more likely to be on welfare when they become adults than children whose parents do not receive welfare. See Anne Hill and June O'Neil, *Underclass Behaviour in the US: Measurement and Analysis of Determinants* (New York: City University of Baruch College, 1990).

# 9

# Issues in Tax Reform

## Introduction

The Canadian tax system has evolved considerably in recent years, largely as a result of several sources of exogenous pressure. Some of the change has been induced by the rapid globalization of product and capital markets, a process that the free trade agreement in North America and the formation of the World Trade Organization have institutionalized. Meanwhile, rapid technological change and rapid growth in developing countries, especially in Asia and Latin America, have put enormous competitive pressure on Canadian producers. In these circumstances, streamlining the Canadian tax system to make the economy more competitive and taxes less intrusive in economic decision making has become an important concern—one that distinguishes the recent tax policy agenda in Canada from that of an earlier era, when the dominant concern was the protection of selected domestic industries. At the same time, budgetary pressures resulting from the exponential growth of public sector debt during the 1980s have induced Canadian governments to rationalize the tax-transfer system. Finally, rapid growth of provincial expenditures in the areas of health, education, and welfare and increased reliance by the provinces on their own revenue sources have forced the federal government and the provinces to consider reforms in the way in which the federal and provincial tax systems interact.

As we pointed out in previous chapters, the federal government has in recent years implemented major reforms in the individual and corporate income tax systems and in the general sales tax system. The intention of these reforms, which have been followed to varying degrees by the provinces, was to rationalize the entire tax system by broadening bases and reducing rates, and more generally to make the tax system more neutral and less intrusive on private sector economic decisions. We shall begin with a summary of the main government initiatives in tax reform in recent years and then discuss some tax reform issues that governments may or should deal with in the future.

## Major Tax Reforms of the 1980s and 1990s

Again, there have been major reforms of two of the three broad tax bases—the income tax base and the general sales tax base. Although payroll taxation, the third broad tax base, has not undergone the same general overhaul, there have also been some reform initiatives there as well. This section outlines the accomplishments of tax reform to date and the prospects for future reform for each of the major tax bases.

## Income Taxation

The federal government implemented a major reform of the personal and corporate income tax system in 1987, the first since the 1971 reform in the wake of the Carter report. The 1987 reform aimed at making the system simpler, more efficient, and more fair by broadening the income bases, reducing many tax preferences, and simplifying the rate structures. In the case of the personal income tax system, the base broadening applied mainly to capital income. The reforms eliminated a $1,000 annual deduction for interest income, increased the proportion of capital gains subject to tax from one-half to three-quarters, and reduced the dividend tax credit. Several deductions and exemptions were converted into credits, including the standard exemptions for persons, spouses, dependants, age, and disability and the deductions for expenditures such as charitable contributions, medical and dental expenses, and political contributions. The credits had the same value for all taxpayers (at least those in a tax-paying position), whereas the value of deductions had been higher for taxpayers in the higher tax brackets than for those in the lower brackets. Consequently, the substitution of credits for deductions increased the effective progressivity of the system. The rate structure was simplified from 10 brackets to 3, a change that resulted in a nominal top marginal rate, including the average provincial rate, of about 44 percent. In practice, however, the top rate has been much higher, owing to frequent use of surtaxes by both the federal government and the provinces. Since 1987, further reforms have increased the amount of capital income that is subject to tax by eliminating a lifetime exemption for a limited amount of capital gains and some tax advantages that applied to family trusts.

Apart from the 1987 reforms, three other developments in personal income taxation are worth noting. The first concerns the tax treatment of savings for retirement. Three main forms of retirement savings are eligible for tax sheltering—registered retirement savings plans (RRSPs), defined benefit registered pension plans (RPPs), and money purchase RPPs. One of the intentions of Canadian tax policy has been to rationalize the retirement savings system so that the three forms of savings are treated comparably by the tax system. This would mean allowing taxpayers to increase their contributions to RRSPs and money purchase RPPs, and indeed a program of gradually increasing the limits on contributions to these plans was introduced in 1991. In 1996, however, the federal government's efforts to reduce the deficit led it to reduce the contribution limit for RRSPs and money purchase RPPs. This limit will remain in effect until at least 2002. Thus the system has yet to be fully rationalized as originally proposed. One can shelter more savings for retirement from tax in defined benefit RPPs than in money purchase RPPs, and more in the latter than in RRSPs.

The second development in the area of personal taxation is the innovation of using refundable tax credits—the goods and services tax (GST) credit and the child tax benefit—to deliver transfers to the needy. These are significant initiatives; they represent the first major attempt to use the tax system to deliver transfers—that is, as a negative income tax system. The reform bases the credits not on individual income, as the tax system does, but on family income and family size. Refundable credits based on family income were also a feature of the proposed seniors benefit, a transfer to the elderly that would have replaced the existing old age security and guaranteed income supplement programs and thus completed the gradual transition from universal transfers for the elderly to targeted transfers. The seniors benefit was shelved in 1998 in response to considerable opposition from seniors themselves. There is at present a joint federal-provincial initiative in progress to replace part of the component of provincial welfare payments directed at families with children by an enlarged child tax benefit that would be available to the working and non-working poor alike. In principle, there is no reason why other existing tax credits could not be made refundable in the same way. We shall return to this subject later in the chapter.

The third development is a recent flurry of initiatives by the provinces to reduce their personal income tax rates. In 1996, British Columbia, Ontario, and Nova Scotia reduced their basic personal income rates and Alberta announced that it would consider tax reductions. Ontario's income tax reduction was to be particularly dramatic: the tax rate was to fall by 30 percent, from 56 percent of basic federal tax in 1995 to 40.5 percent in 1999. At the same time, however, the province imposed a new "health levy" in the form of a progressive high-income surtax that largely offset the tax rate reduction for high-income taxpayers. British Columbia's more modest income tax rate reduction (from 52.5 percent of basic federal tax to 50.5 percent) was accompanied by an increased surtax on higher incomes, so in this case too the effective tax rate on high-income taxpayers was little changed. As long as the provinces continue to balance their budgets or even realize surpluses, the impetus for income tax rate reductions is likely to remain high. This may also be true at the federal level.

The corporate tax reform of 1987, like the personal tax reform, aimed at base broadening and rate reduction. The reform eliminated, among other tax preferences, the 50 percent straightline accelerated capital cost allowance on machinery and equipment and the general investment tax credit, applicable to all investment, of 7 percent. This change accompanied a significant decline in the standard federal corporate income tax rate, from 36 to 28 percent. Provincial corporate tax rates for most provinces range from 14 to 17 percent—except in Quebec, where the rate is 8.9 percent. In an attempt to attract capital to the province, Quebec deliberately reduced its corporate tax rate and made up the lost revenue by increasing its payroll and capital taxes, which are deductible against federal corporate taxes. If one omits Quebec, the combined federal-provincial corporate tax rate is comparable to the top personal tax rate. Like the top personal tax rate, however, the corporate tax rate is increased by a federal surtax, in this case one of 4 percent.

The corporate income tax reform reduced the differential treatment of different industries and types of investment, but as we saw in chapter 4 several sources of preferential treatment remain. Income from manufacturing and processing in Canada is taxed at a preferential rate federally and in most provinces. The same is true of income from small businesses. Investment tax credits are available in regions of high unemployment and for research and development (R & D) expenditures. For some types of capital expenditures, moreover, writeoffs are significantly higher than actual costs. Thus rapid writeoffs are available for machinery and equipment and for exploration and development expenditures in the resource industries, and firms may treat expenditures on many types of intangible assets as current costs. The corporate tax also favours investment in machinery and equipment and the acquisition of intangible assets over investment in longer-lived assets such as buildings and land and over investment in inventories. As the Mintz committee pointed out, the corporate tax system favours resource industries and manufacturing over trade, services, and other tertiary industries. This state of affairs makes little sense, given that the latter sectors account for an increasing share of economic activity and include some of the most innovative and dynamic industries in the economy. Of course, in the case of investment in matters such as R & D and training, one can make an argument for preferential treatment on the basis of externalities. In the case of the resource industries and manufacturing and processing, however, the argument for preferential treatment is less obvious.

Two further aspects of corporate taxation have so far escaped reform but may be candidates for reform in the future. One is the tax treatment of different sources of finance. The Canadian income tax system makes it more costly for firms to finance investments by new equity issues than to finance them by debt or retained earnings. This is so because interest deductibility favours debt finance, and preferential taxation of accrued capital gains favours retained earnings. New equity issues tend to be more costly because of the relatively less favourable taxation of dividends. As a consequence, firms that tend to rely heavily on new equity, such as small, innovative, growing firms, are at a disadvantage relative to larger and more mature firms, which find it easier to borrow or have sufficient internal financing.

The other matter is the tax treatment of firms in a loss position. The tax system effectively discriminates against these firms by treating negative tax liabilities differently from positive tax liabilities. Firms in a loss position tend to be small, growing firms or firms engaged in risky enterprises—that is, firms that find it relatively difficult to obtain outside financing. This state of affairs can retard the economy, since small, new firms are often important innovators and job creators. The 1997 federal budget reported that businesses with fewer than 50 employees had generated between 70 and 80 percent of the new jobs in Canada over the previous three years. There are ways to address the discrimination that new firms in a loss position face under the current tax system, such as by introducing refundability provisions or allowing flowthrough share financing, which is allowed in the oil and gas and mining industries. Policy makers (and policy advisers, such as the Mintz committee) have embraced refundability in the personal tax but are reluctant to extend it to the corporate tax. Nevertheless, refundability of negative tax liabilities (or some equivalent) would seem to be the only way to remedy the problem created by the present tax treatment of firms that are in a loss position.

## Sales Taxation

The replacement in 1991 of the federal manufacturers' sales tax by the GST was a much more substantial reform than the 1987 reform of the income tax system, since it involved a complete change in the sales tax base, rate structure, and method of administration. As we noted in chapters 1 and 5, the GST is a value-added tax whose base includes almost all consumption goods and services. Though the tax has been politically controversial, it has many of the features of an ideal indirect tax. Its base is very broad. Its multistage form ensures that traded products are treated fairly on both domestic and international markets and prevents the cascading of taxes on business inputs and the taxation of investment goods. Moreover, the fact that the GST was accompanied by a system of refundable GST credits for low-income households ensured that the change from the old tax to the new was not only revenue-neutral but also approximately distribution-neutral. Although several political parties have vowed to eliminate the GST and replace its lost revenues from some unexplained alternative source, it is probably here to stay.

Even those who defend the GST, however, do not as a rule regard it as being perfect. Those who stress efficiency argue that its base should be broadened further by removing its preferential treatment of food, residential rents, housing, and the municipal, university, schools, and hospital (MUSH) sector. Those who are concerned about equity argue that more necessity goods should be exempt. But these are reservations that can apply to any major tax. By and large, it is recognized that a broadly based value-added tax has significant advantages as an efficient revenue source in the wider tax system.

The main issues in the sales tax field involve not the GST itself, but its provincial counterparts. Five provinces maintain retail sales taxes (RSTs) that have relatively narrow bases and that suffer from the problems associated with single-stage taxes, especially the inability to treat domestic and foreign products on a par and the unavoidable taxing of some business inputs. There are various ways of addressing this problem. One is to eliminate provincial sales taxes and make up the revenue from other broadly based taxes. It is not clear that this is an optimal solution, however, especially if the chosen alternative is the income tax. Increased reliance on provincial income taxes would put considerable pressure on the tax collection agreements and threaten the harmonization of the income taxes. Moreover, increasing tax liabilities for higher-income persons would exacerbate an already existing "brain-drain" problem.

Another way to address the problems posed by RSTs would be for the five provinces that levy them to join the harmonized sales tax (HST) system. The HST, as we mentioned earlier, is an augmented version of the GST that applies in New Brunswick, Newfoundland, and Nova Scotia. The federal government applies a tax rate of 15 percent on transactions in these provinces rather than the 7 percent that it applies elsewhere in Canada under the GST.

The difference of 8 percentage points is then turned over to the three provinces in proportion to the final consumption expenditures in each province. There are problems with this option from the provinces' perspective, the main one being that it requires them to abide by both a common base and common rate level and rate structure—in essence, to sacrifice tax policy independence for the sake of harmonization. The non-participating provinces, especially the larger ones such as Ontario and British Columbia, have been reluctant to join what is in effect a revenue-sharing system in which they would have input only through a federal-provincial consultative body, the Tax Policy Review Committee, which reviews all proposals for change to the HST.

A third alternative would be for the provinces to retain their own separate single-stage taxes but broaden the bases of these taxes to make them conform with the GST base. Since retailers already collect the GST, this solution would not involve any increase in compliance costs. It would combine the advantages a broader base with those of provincial independence in the sales-tax policy area. Its disadvantage is that it would not capture the full benefits of value-added taxation, in particular the ability to ensure that business inputs and exports are fully relieved of sales tax through the crediting mechanism of value-added taxation.

Finally, the provinces could establish their own VATs alongside the federal GST, as Quebec has already done. The main issue here is the administrative feasibility of dealing with cross-border transactions in a federation where no border controls exist to collect taxes on imports. Quebec's system operates on the principle of self-assessment. A firm that sells to a purchaser outside of the province need not collect Quebec sales tax (QST) (but must collect GST). A firm that purchases inputs outside of the province does not pay the QST on its purchases, but when it sells a product that uses the untaxed input tax is collected on the sale and there is no input tax credit. In this way, the tax eventually gets collected on imported inputs. (Of course, as in the case of an RST, consumers are supposed to pay taxes on products imported from other provinces.) This system, though still in its infancy, seems to work reasonably well.[1] It could presumably be extended to other provinces. Of course, as more provinces adopted their own VATs, each perhaps with its own base and rate structure, the complexity of the system would increase and so would the compliance costs faced by firms. If the problem of administrative costs could be overcome, this system of dual VATs seems from an economic point of view to be the best of the available alternatives.

## Payroll Taxation

The third broadly based mode of taxation is payroll taxation. In this case, there is less to report in terms of reforms accomplished than in terms of

---

[1] The case for the dual VAT system is outlined in Richard M. Bird and Pierre-Pascal Gendron, "Dual VATs and Cross-Border Trade: Two Problems, One Solution?" (July 1998), 5 *International Tax and Public Finance* 429-42.

reforms still on the agenda. Currently, the only payroll taxes at the federal level are earmarked taxes for the funding of employment insurance (EI) and the Canada Pension Plan (CPP). Payroll taxes at the provincial level are also nominally for the support of social programs but in practice are highly fungible, since apart from workers' compensation contributions they do not constitute the main source of financing for any particular program. There is a good case for funding CPP out of payroll taxes if one views the program as one of forced saving by employees. Given recent reforms of the CPP that are intended to move the system toward full funding, the earmarking of payroll taxes and crediting them to particular individuals makes good sense. Nonetheless, in terms of the tax mix, CPP (and QPP in Quebec) contributions ought to be regarded as payroll taxes: they are compulsory levies on the payrolls of Canadian firms.

The theoretical case for earmarking is perhaps not as strong for EI contributions as it is for CPP contributions, at least given the current structure of the program. EI is not a true insurance program, since premiums under the program bear no close relation to benefits. Instead, the structure of benefits is determined independently of premiums and is based on redistributive as well as insurance objectives. Some industries benefit systematically at the expense of other industries, and some groups of workers benefit at the expense of other workers. It might well be asked why payroll taxation should be used to fund a program that is essentially redistributive in nature. Nonetheless, the funding of EI by an earmarked payroll tax is likely to continue. This arrangement does at least make it easy for the public to identify the costs of the program. It also allows for the possibility of incorporating insurance elements, such experience rating, into the program in the future.

Given the EI program as it stands, the main concern is to set rates high enough to ensure that the program is funded over time—that surpluses in years of low unemployment will cover deficits in years of high unemployment. In the past, there has been a tendency not to build up a large enough surplus to cover contingencies during recessions, with the consequence that the government has had to increase EI rates precisely when they are most burdensome. In recent years, of course, the problem has been exacerbated by the unexpected tenacity of high unemployment rates. The lesson is that the government should be prudent in determining how large a surplus to retain in the EI account and cautious about lowering EI contribution rates.

Is there some scope for expanding reliance on payroll taxation as a source of general revenues, apart from its use for CPP and EI? Payroll taxation has grown fairly rapidly over the past three decades. A recent study for Statistics Canada has calculated "effective payroll tax rates" for Canada annually between 1961 and 1993.[2] These rates are defined as the ratio of federal and provincial payroll tax revenues (unemployment insurance premiums, public

---

[2] See Z. Lin, G. Picot, and C.M. Beach, *The Evolution of Payroll Taxes in Canada: 1961-1993*, Research Paper no. 90 (Ottawa: Analytical Studies Branch, Statistics Canada, 1996).

pension contributions, workers' compensation premiums, and health and education levies) to total payrolls (wages, salaries, overtime compensation, vacation pay, performance bonuses, and fringe benefits, except for employers' pension contributions). The effective payroll tax rate rose from 2.1 percent in 1961 to 4 percent in 1970 to 5.5 percent in 1980 to 11.6 percent in 1993. Yet payroll tax rates in Canada are low compared with those in other countries in the Organisation for Economic Co-operation and Development (OECD), including the United States. There may well be further scope for increased reliance on payroll taxes.

As we have mentioned, payroll taxes have many desirable features. They are broadly based and efficient taxes with relatively low collection and compliance costs. Moreover, they are attractive taxes for use by the provinces. Because they are relatively easy to administer, the need to harmonize them across provinces is not as great as the need to harmonize sales and income taxes. The mobility of labour, of course, may limit the provinces' scope for setting their payroll tax rates independently of their neighbours. On the other hand, it may give them scope for engaging in socially unproductive tax competition in order to attract skilled workers and businesses. But it is not obvious that the problem is greater in this case than it is in the case of other broad tax bases: ultimately, both income taxes and sales taxes are largely taxes on residents' labour incomes as well.

## The Macro Dimension

In the recent past, the overriding imperative of fiscal policy has been to halt the accumulation of public debt by cutting the budget deficit. In order to avoid increasing the ratio of taxes to gross domestic product (GDP), the federal government has chosen to reduce its deficit by cutting expenditures rather than by increasing tax rates. Nevertheless, because of the elasticity of the tax base, especially the elasticity arising from bracket creep, tax revenues have increased more rapidly than GDP. Most of the initial expenditure cuts were either reductions in transfers to the provinces or reductions in program spending outside of the main categories of transfers to persons (that is, EI and transfers to the elderly). Subsequent announced reforms of EI and transfers to the elderly were aimed at rationalizing these programs, though in the latter case the reforms have been set aside. The reductions in transfers to the provinces have in turn forced the provinces to balance their own budgets. For the most part, they too have chosen to cut expenditures rather than to increase tax rates. The large spending categories such as health, education, and welfare have all borne a share of the reductions. The provinces have also cut their transfers to municipalities, with the result that municipalities too have had to practise budgetary restraint. The municipalities have followed the higher levels of government in cutting expenditures to the extent possible, but some have been obliged to increase their revenues as well. Much of the additional revenue has come from new user fees of various sorts, but property taxes have not been left untouched.

The final result of this sequence of responses to fiscal pressure has been a reduction in and a rationalization of expenditures at all levels of government. The federal government and the provinces been able to hold the line on tax rate increases. Only the municipalities have had some difficulty in keeping tax rates from rising, thereby exacerbating Canada's position as a country with relatively high property tax rates. Although income tax rates have held steady, income tax revenues have risen more rapidly than GDP. This is so largely because in the absence of full indexation bracket creep has pushed more and more income into higher tax brackets and into increased liability for surtaxes—an effect that has contributed significantly to deficit reduction but increased the burden of taxes, especially on middle- and upper-income earners.

For the near future, the only major tax increase in sight is a proposed increase in the contribution rate to the contributory public pension, the CPP. Its purpose is to enhance the funding of the system. The compulsory nature of CPP contributions makes them equivalent to a payroll tax in terms of their economic effects. EI premiums, another compulsory payroll levy, may fall in the coming years if the unemployment rate moves to a lower plateau and the EI fund continues to be in a surplus position.

## Outstanding Issues in Tax Reform

As a result of the reform initiatives of the past decade, the tax system is better placed than it was before to meet the needs of the new economy, one that is characterized by increased competitiveness, leaner governments, and a high degree of decentralization of fiscal responsibility. But tax reform is an ongoing process. Circumstances change, and so do policy objectives, and it is impossible to predict with any certainty what objectives will emerge in the coming years. Nevertheless, it is possible, on the basis of our account of individual taxes and their economic effects, to identify a number of issues (some of which represent unfinished business) that may reach the policy agenda in the reasonably near future. The following discussion summarizes the potential issues that seem to us to be important, though not necessarily important in the order of their presentation here.

## The Allocation of Tax Powers

Canada's decentralized tax system is a strength. The provinces and their municipalities have exclusive legislative responsibility for delivering some of the most important public services available to citizens, including all health, education, and welfare services. At the same time, as we have seen, they have substantial taxing authority. By most measures, in fact, Canada is among the most decentralized federations in the world—it is much more decentralized than, say, Australia or the United States. The states that make up these federations have fewer expenditure responsibilities than do the provinces of Canada. In Australia, welfare is in the domain of the federal government; in the United States, the federal government delivers many health programs and, until recently, was responsible for welfare as well. Perhaps more to the point, the US and Australian states occupy far less tax room than the Canadian provinces do. In Canada, the provinces share all of the major broadly based taxes (income, sales, and payroll taxes) with the federal government and also obtain substantial revenues from taxes on resources and property, bases that they alone use.

The allocation of taxes in the Canadian federation has evolved largely without explicit planning, and there may be little that policy makers can do to change it. The provinces and the federal government both have more or less unfettered access to all tax bases, so any deliberate effort to reallocate taxes would require an unprecedented degree of federal-provincial cooperation. Nevertheless, it is worth asking from an economic perspective whether the present allocation of tax powers is appropriate, if only to establish a benchmark for future federal tax policy.

The tax allocation problem has two dimensions, the assignment of taxes to each level of government and the division of the tax room.

## Tax Assignment

The economic arguments for assigning various taxes to each level of government are well developed in the literature on fiscal federalism,[3] and there is widespread agreement on general principles. The criteria for determining which types of taxes ought to be available to lower levels of government are the same as those that economists use in judging economic policies more generally—efficiency, equity, and administrative simplicity. These criteria take on particular forms in a federal context.

The efficiency issues relevant to the decision about which taxes to decentralize concern the efficiency with which goods, services, and factors of production are allocated across provinces; that is, the efficiency of the internal economic union. Provincial taxes can distort the internal economic union in at least three ways. First, a misallocation of resources in the federation may arise if different provinces impose different taxes on products and factors that are traded across provinces. Second, provinces may use their tax systems to attract desirable products and factors and repel less desirable ones. In the end, this "beggar-thy-neighbour" strategy will be partially self-defeating and will result in an inefficient set of provincial tax rates. Third, if tax capacity (the size of tax bases) varies across the provinces, the ability to finance a given level of public goods and services will vary as well. This variation can lead to fiscally induced migration and hence inefficiency: persons and businesses will base their locational choices partially on fiscal

---

[3] For a statement of general principles, see Charles E. McLure Jr., ed., *Tax Assignment in Federal Countries* (Canberra: Australian National University Press, 1983) and Robin W. Boadway, "Tax Assignment in the Canadian Federation," in Neil A. Warren, ed., *The Future of Australian Federalism* (Sydney: Australian Tax Foundation, 1997), 61-90.

considerations rather than production costs, with the result that too many of them will choose lower-tax jurisdictions. In summary, decentralization is relatively undesirable in the case of taxes whose bases are mobile across provinces or distributed unevenly across provinces, although the federal government can mitigate the latter problem by providing transfers to compensate for differences in provincial tax capacities.

The role of equity in the assignment of taxes is somewhat more controversial. Observers may differ not only about the importance of equity relative to efficiency, but also about which level of government should be responsible for redistributive policy. A common view, one associated with so-called normative public economists, is that redistribution is a legitimate role of government and that the federal government should have ultimate responsibility for it. Obviously, the argument that government should assume a redistributive role rests on a value judgment. But that governments do assume this role can hardly be disputed. Indeed, one can argue that a very high proportion of what government does on the expenditure side of its budget reflects redistributive concerns.

The question of which level of government should ultimately be responsible for redistribution requires another value judgment. Thus the argument for assigning the responsibility for redistributive policy to the federal government is based on the assumption that all of the citizens of a nation should be given equal weight regardless of where they reside. This assumption implies that reasonably uniform standards of vertical and horizontal equity ought to apply nationwide. The decentralization of taxing responsibilities to the provinces can obstruct the goal of nationwide equity in several ways. For one thing, provinces may adopt different degrees of redistribution and hence different standards of vertical equity. For another, if provinces have redistributive taxes at their disposal, they may use them strategically and compete away redistribution in what is called a "race to the bottom." (Race-to-the-bottom policies are to equity what beggar-thy-neighbour policies are to efficiency.) Finally, provinces' abilities to redistribute will differ if the sizes of their tax bases differ: higher-income provinces can achieve a given amount of redistribution by using tax rates lower than those that lower-income provinces have to use to achieve the same outcome. The result is fiscal inequity—otherwise similar individuals end up paying different taxes in different provinces. These equity considerations suggest that tax bases that are important for redistribution or that are distributed unevenly across provinces should not be decentralized. Taxes that are closer to being benefit taxes are better candidates for decentralization.

Finally, the costs of administration and compliance may increase if tax bases are decentralized. Different provinces will typically choose different structures for a given type of tax, unless formal harmonization measures are in place, and this variation across provinces will increase the compliance costs of taxpayers who operate in more than one jurisdiction. Under some taxes, indeed, cross-border transactions may give rise to both high compliance costs and substantial opportunities for avoiding tax. Thus taxes on bases that may apply to taxpayers who operate in more than one jurisdiction are not good candidates for decentralization.

Given these considerations, one can judge the suitability for use by the provinces of each of the various tax types. Broadly based consumption taxes that are levied on a destination basis would seem to be good candidates for use by the provinces, since their base is relatively immobile; that is, the base is roughly equivalent to the labour income of residents, and residents themselves are relatively immobile. Moreover, consumption taxation is not an important tax instrument for redistributive purposes. Consumption taxation at the provincial level, however, is not without its difficulties. The destination basis of a consumption tax might be costly to enforce if cross-border shopping is easy. More important, the single-stage RSTs that most provinces use at present are less efficient than a multistage VAT, which permits the proper crediting of business inputs and treats domestic goods on a par with foreign goods. The administration of a VAT system at the provincial level, however, would involve keeping track of cross-border transactions for crediting purposes, and this would be difficult if each province operated its own VAT system with its own rate structure. Thus, if one wants to obtain the advantages of VAT taxation, the decentralization of the sales tax to the provinces becomes problematic. We shall consider below the possibility of overcoming the problem by adopting a system of tax harmonization among the provinces and between the provinces and the federal government.

Specific excise taxes are also good candidates for decentralization, but there are difficulties here as well. Again, cross-border shopping can be a problem. These taxes apply mostly to goods with low elasticities of demand, so they tend to be regressive. The issue of tax spillovers between jurisdictions arises when the provinces and the federal government co-occupy the same excise tax fields; we shall consider this issue below.

If the provinces have significant revenue-raising responsibilities, it is highly desirable that more than one broadly based tax be available to them. One of the most obvious candidates is payroll taxation. Its base, labour income, is not very mobile across borders. If it is applied on a broad base, it is an efficient mode of taxation. In fact, most economic analysis suggests that it is much less distorting than income taxation. It is not important for redistributive purposes. Finally, it is relatively easy to administer, since a high proportion of its revenues can be collected through payroll deductions. It is surprising, in fact, that general payroll taxation is not more popular with Canadian governments than it is. One likely reason for this relative unpopularity is the public perception of payroll taxation as "a tax on jobs." As we argued in chapter 6, however, this perception is illusionary. In a general sense, the effects on the economy of a tax on labour should be similar to those of a tax on consumption. Indeed, virtually any broadly based tax will overlap considerably with a tax on labour income, given the importance of labour income as a share of national income.

Personal income taxation is less suitable for use at the provincial level than is payroll taxation, despite the fact that their bases overlap to some extent. Personal income taxation is an important component of redistributive policy: to the extent that redistribution is a national objective, it is more appropriate for personal income tax policy to be a federal responsibility. The personal income tax base, assuming that it encompasses all forms of income, includes the income of unincorporated businesses. Given the mobility of capital, this inclusion violates one of the criteria for decentralization. Moreover, collection and compliance may be difficult under a provincial income tax, especially in the case of personal capital income. In particular, capital income that is earned outside the province may be difficult to account for. In Canada, many of these problems are overcome by the use of a harmonized federal-provincial income tax system.

Corporate taxation is an even less appropriate candidate for decentralization to the provinces. Corporate income is highly mobile among jurisdictions, so provincial governments might be tempted to use corporate taxation to influence the location of corporations. Because corporations may operate in more than one province and can move funds freely from one province to another, the compliance and collection costs of a provincial corporate tax are likely to be high. There is, however, another consideration. One of the functions of the corporate tax, perhaps the most important, is to act as a withholding device for personal income tax—that is, to tax at source income that would otherwise escape taxation or that would be taxed only at a later date, when funds are taken out of the corporation. This being the case, the corporate tax should be integrated with the personal tax, and this is presumably most easily done if the personal and corporate taxes are collected by the same level of government. Arguments similar to those against decentralizing corporate taxes apply to the decentralization of capital taxes, whose base is also mobile, at least in the long run.

In the case of the taxation of natural resources, the tax-assignment criteria give conflicting advice. On the one hand, resources are essentially immobile, so provincial taxation of them cannot cause the base to move to another jurisdiction (although, of course, the capital needed to develop resources is highly mobile). On the other hand, resource endowments may be very unevenly distributed, with the result that the ability to raise revenue from resources varies widely from province to province. These considerations suggest that resource bases whose distribution among the provinces is relatively even should be decentralized, whereas those whose distribution is highly uneven should remain federal. However, even the revenues from unevenly distributed resources can be decentralized without sacrificing fiscal efficiency and equity if the federal government provides transfers to the provinces that seek to undo the effects of the uneven distribution. Whether this solution is sustainable politically when the distribution of resources across provinces is highly uneven is another question.

Like resource taxes, property taxes are suitable for decentralization to lower levels of government, including municipalities. As in the case of resource taxation, it would be desirable to have a system of federal transfers that equalized tax capacities across jurisdictions—in this case, both across provinces and within them.

Perhaps the least suitable taxes for decentralization to the provinces are personal taxes on wealth or the transfer of wealth (such as inheritance and bequest taxes). The bases for these taxes are mobile, and in any case the main purpose of them is to redistribute wealth among households. On the other hand, user fees and licences are good provincial and local revenue sources. Because they are in effect benefit taxes, they do not give rise to efficiency or equity concerns. However, they are also unlikely to raise large sums of revenue.

The actual set of tax responsibilities that will be decentralized to the provinces depends on the amount of revenues that have to be raised, which in turn depends upon how decentralized expenditure responsibilities are. For highly decentralized federations such as Canada, where the provinces have to raise almost as much own-source revenue as the federal government raises, it is inevitable that the tax bases assigned to the two levels of government should overlap somewhat. This sharing of tax bases has the advantage that it makes possible the joint administration of the taxes levied by the two jurisdictions, which reduces collection and compliance costs. Nor is this arrangement inconsistent with the retention by each level of government of the right to set its own tax rates. The disadvantage of joint administration is rather that it requires all jurisdictions to abide by the same base. This loss of tax policy independence may not be acceptable to either level of government.

If the tax-base sharing occurs in the absence of a single tax administration, there will be no saving of costs. In fact, if taxpayers have to deal with two tax administrations, compliance costs might be significantly higher than they would be if the tax base were not shared, since each administration might apply a different set of rules. In this case, it might be preferable if the two levels of government did not occupy the same tax base or, at least, tacitly accepted similar definitions of that base (as the US federal government and many of the states apparently do).

Another problem is the effect of tax-base sharing on the *marginal cost of public funds* (MCPF); that is, the marginal cost to the economy of raising an additional dollar of tax revenues. This cost is typically greater than unity, since an additional dollar of tax revenues, in addition to transferring a dollar's worth of resources from the private sector, causes a marginal deadweight loss. In other words, an increase in the tax rate reduces the tax base and thus causes a loss of revenue. The more elastic the tax base is, the greater is the revenue loss. If a provincial government increases its tax rate, the federal government bears part of the cost of the resulting reduction in the base in the form of reduced revenues. The provincial government, however, has no incentive to take this loss of federal revenue into account in choosing its tax rate and may therefore set its tax rate too high. The implications for tax assignment of this effect, which is called a *vertical tax externality*,[4] are not

---

[4] The consequences of this and other fiscal externalities are summarized in Bev Dahlby, "Fiscal Externalities and the Design of Intergovernmental Grants" (July 1996), 3 *International*
(The footnote is continued on the next page.)

obvious. All broadly based taxes have large overlaps, so vertical tax externalities will arise from provincial use, exclusive or shared, of any broad base.

As we have mentioned, it is not clear that it would be easy to change the assignment of taxes in the Canadian federation. If they were to be changed, however, the changes would presumably take into account at least some aspects of the present assignment of taxes that are at variance with the principles that we outlined above. Four examples stand out of taxes that, for economic reasons, probably should not be decentralized. The first is the corporate tax, which is potentially a source of significant distortions among provinces. The second is capital taxation, a form of taxation that all of the provinces use. The third is wealth transfer taxation, such as taxes on inheritances. Indeed, the demise of inheritance taxes in Canada is a textbook example of how interjurisdictional tax competition can result in the competing away of what many observers would regard as being a suitable component of the tax mix. The final example is rather more controversial, and that is resource taxation. The major resources—oil and gas and certain minerals—are distributed very unevenly among the provinces. Economic arguments suggest that the public's share of the rents from these resources ought to accrue to the federal government, but for constitutional, historical, and political reasons this outcome is not an option at present. The same arguments, however, also support the notion of an effective system of equalization to account for the uneven allocation of resources among provinces.

## The Division of Tax Room

Although very little might be done to change the assignment of taxes or, indeed, to reduce the decentralization of revenue-raising responsibilities to the provinces, it is possible nonetheless to limit the deleterious economic effects of decentralization. This possibility arises if the federal government occupies enough of the tax room for a given tax base to induce harmonization of that base. By the same token, if formal harmonization agreements already exist, as they do for the income taxes and, to a more limited extent, the GST, then the larger is the federal government's share of the relevant tax room, the greater is the chance that the tax harmonization scheme will be maintained. It is, of course, impossible to say how much of the tax room for a given tax the federal government must occupy in order to have sufficient influence to accomplish the harmonization of that tax. Some would even argue that harmonization is possible without the connivance of the federal government: the provinces could agree to a scheme of harmonization among themselves. Unfortunately, there are no precedents for an agreement of this kind and no assurance that it would be viable.

---

[4] Continued ...

*Tax and Public Finance* 397-412. Its consequences for federal-provincial tax setting is studied in Robin Boadway and Michael Keen, "Efficiency and the Optimal Direction of Federal-State Transfers" (May 1996), 3 *International Tax and Public Finance* 137-55.

Given the extent to which the tax system as a whole is decentralized, the federal government cannot be dominant in all of the major tax fields. In deciding on its own tax mix, therefore, the federal government must decide which, if any, of the major tax bases it should strive to dominate. Let us take each of the three broadly based taxes in turn.

In the case of the income tax, the claims of efficiency, equity, and administrative simplicity alike make harmonization an important policy objective. The mobility of business income and of highly skilled persons suggests that efficiency objectives would be compromised if the provincial income tax systems varied significantly from province to province. Similarly, since the income tax is the main tax instrument for pursuing national redistributive objectives, vertical and horizontal equity might be violated if provinces used their access to the income tax to pursue their own redistributive policies or, more to the point, to compete away redistribution. Finally, since any income tax is inherently complex, considerable administrative simplicity is gained if both levels of government use the same income tax base, and the gain is even greater if taxpayers have to deal with only one tax collection authority. These considerations make a strong case for federal dominance of the income tax field.

The payroll tax, in contrast, is an ideal tax for decentralization to the provincial level. It applies only to wage income, which is significantly less mobile than capital or business income. It is very simple to collect and enforce, and compliance is not a problem. It is also a relatively efficient tax and one that is not used for redistributive purposes. Moreover, it is not nearly as important to harmonize a payroll taxation as it is to harmonize the income tax. These considerations suggest that there is no need for the federal government to maintain a dominant share of the payroll tax field. Indeed, it might be argued that the federal government should encourage the provinces to make much more use of general payroll taxation than they do now. It could provide encouragement not only by making more payroll tax room available to the provinces, but also by maintaining the provisions that allow the deduction of provincial payroll taxes from federal income tax liabilities.

General sales taxes present much more difficult choices. On the one hand, it is very tempting to argue that the federal government should reduce its reliance on other taxes in favour of greater reliance on the GST. The GST is, after all, a highly efficient tax, and one with great potential as a revenue raiser. Moreover, Canada makes less use of general sales taxes than most other OECD countries (although not less use than the United States). On the other hand, greater federal reliance on the GST would come mainly at the expense of federal income tax room and thus would jeopardize the harmonization of the income tax. In return, it might be argued, the substitution of general sales tax room for income tax room would make it easier for the federal government to achieve harmonization of the sales tax field, which in itself is a useful objective. Given the current views of the provinces, however, this argument is less than compelling. The large provinces are very unlikely to agree to the harmonized sales tax arrangement that the federal government has with three of the Atlantic provinces, since it would essentially take general sales tax policy out of their hands.

A feasible alternative is harmonization of the sort achieved by Quebec through its QST, which is independent of the federal GST but harmonized with it. It remains to be seen how well the QST performs, but even if the use of a tax of this kind by one province turns out to be administratively viable, its use by several provinces at once would probably result in a great deal of administrative complexity. In any case, since the QST system leaves Quebec with significant discretion to deviate from the federal GST structure, it is not clear that further harmonization of the sales tax field depends on federal domination of the field. Indeed, both the provincial HST rates and the QST rate exceed the federal GST rate, and this circumstance has not prevented harmonization from proceeding. One is left, therefore, with the tentative conclusion that it is much more important that the federal government retain a dominant share of the income tax room than it is that it try to capture more sales tax room.

Of course, if sales tax harmonization is possible without federal dominance of the field, why not income tax harmonization as well? The difficulty here is that the provinces might very well prove unwilling to abide by income tax harmonization measures, such as the tax collection agreements, if the federal share of the income tax room should continue to erode. Some provinces have already questioned the relevance of these agreements and contemplated withdrawing from them. In addition, the provinces have resorted increasingly to the use under the tax collection agreements of province-specific credits and other measures that appear to violate the spirit of the agreements, and the federal government seems not to be able to resist them. It is reasonable enough that provinces should be more willing to harmonize their sales taxes with the federal sales tax than to retain the current harmonization of income taxes. Income taxation, after all, is a more powerful instrument for the purpose of attracting desirable factors of production and engaging in tax competition.

## The Income Tax Collection Agreements

Recent developments have brought to the fore the problem of maintaining the integrity of the tax collection agreements for the personal and corporate income taxes, instruments of harmonization that have served us extremely well over most of the post-war period. As the provinces occupy more and more of the income tax room, they quite naturally demand more and more say in formulating tax policy. The current system of agreements leaves relatively little scope for the making of independent income tax policy by the participating provinces. Evidence of the strains on the system abound. The provinces have requested and the federal government has granted a growing number of province-specific credits under the collection agreements for both the personal income tax and the corporate income tax. These credits include venture capital tax credits, tax credits for resource industries, investment tax credits, and tax holidays. Even the principle of a common base and rate structure has been violated: the federal government has permitted some provinces, under the collection agreements, to apply a flat tax to net income. Some of these measures not only change the effective progressivity of the provinces' tax systems but also have potentially adverse implications for the efficiency of internal markets. Apart from the growing use of credits and other special measures, various provinces have expressed open dissatisfaction with the current system and have considered leaving it.

It is partly in response to this dissatisfaction that the federal government has worked out with the provinces a proposal that would allow them more say in their personal income tax systems without jeopardizing the harmonization of the base that the existing tax collection agreements achieve. This agreement is based on a report prepared by the Federal-Provincial Committee on Taxation and released in 1998.[5]

According to the agreement, provinces may choose at any time to move from the current system to one in which they would be allowed to select, within limits, their own rate structures and non-refundable tax credits, which the federal government would administer alongside its own rate structure and credits. This change would transform the personal income tax from a "tax on tax" to a "tax on income." To be more specific, provinces that adopted this option would have to continue to abide by the federal definition of taxable income but would be able to apply to this taxable income base their own tax brackets and rates, including a zero-rate bracket for persons with very low incomes. The provinces would also be able to maintain their surtaxes and low-income tax reductions, but provinces that levy flat taxes would have to fold them into the new rate structure; of course, a province's chosen rate structure could itself be very flat, with as few brackets as the province chose. Provincial non-refundable tax credits would be based on a set of gross credits multiplied by the lowest non-zero provincial tax rate. The set of credits would include all of the federal credits that existed in 1997 and any additional, unique provincial credits. The value of any provincial credit that mimicked a federal credit could not be less than the lesser of the 1997 value of the corresponding federal credit and its current value. Thus provinces would be limited in the extent to which they could reduce the value of these non-refundable tax credits. No restriction of this kind would apply to additional provincial credits, except that it must be possible for Revenue Canada to administer them.

This system would obviously give provinces considerable flexibility in using the provincial income tax system to achieve provincial tax policy objectives, especially objectives with a redistributive dimension. Moreover, it should relieve some of the provinces' dissatisfaction with the current

---

[5] Federal-Provincial Committee on Taxation, "Tax on Income," report prepared for presentation to ministers of finance, October 1998.

system, which manifests itself in threats to withdraw from the agreements or attempts to achieve provincial tax policy objectives through the use of special credits, exemptions, deductions, and the like. The danger is that the provinces will use their enlarged freedom to choose rate structures to engage in self-defeating rate-structure competition in order to attract higher-income residents at the expense of lower-income ones.

## The Tax Mix

All countries use a mix of broadly based taxes—income taxes, consumption or sales taxes, and wage or payroll taxes. As we showed in chapter 1, however, the tax mix can vary considerably from country to country. There is no widely accepted definition of the optimal mix of taxes, and in any case the three main broad tax bases overlap considerably. The presumption is that the use of a mix of taxes ensures that the tax rate on any one base is not excessive and thus minimizes avoidance and evasion and reduces the visibility of the tax.

In spite of the considerable overlap among the three major bases, however, they are by no means identical. Income taxes are taxes on wages and capital income. A mix of income and payroll taxes ensures that capital income is taxed less heavily than wage income, a result that most economists would suggest is appropriate. Similarly, consumption and payroll taxes overlap considerably, at least in present-value terms: the present value of lifetime consumption is equal to the present value of lifetime labour earnings plus net bequests. The taxation of consumption through a sales tax, therefore, is a way of getting at consumption that is financed out of inherited wealth rather than out of earnings, and perhaps also consumption that is financed out of income that has evaded or avoided taxes.

Most other OECD countries rely less on income and property taxation than Canada does and more on sales and payroll taxation. An exception is the United States, where income taxes are also a substantial component of the tax mix. However, since overall tax levels are much lower in the United States than they are in Canada, income tax rates are lower there as well. The implication is that Canada makes relatively heavy use of progressive taxation, with the consequence that the more mobile skilled segment of the labour force is taxed more heavily than its counterparts elsewhere. Given this consequence, there may be a case for substituting sales and payroll taxes for income taxes. Any concern about the redistributive consequences of the new tax mix for low-income persons could be addressed through appropriate changes in the system of refundable tax credits delivered through the income tax system.

## Instruments of Redistribution

Two institutions exist for redistributing from the better-off to the less well-off—the income-based tax-transfer system and the needs-based welfare system. The former system is largely determined by the federal government, whereas the latter is exclusively provincial. Of course, a considerable amount of redistribution is also achieved by means other than income-based or needs-based transfers. Many public services take the form of in-kind transfers that serve redistributive goals. Obvious examples are the education system, the health care system, and welfare services.

What is perhaps surprising about Canada's system of redistribution is the fact that it makes relatively little use of the tax system as a means of delivering transfers, despite widespread support for negative income taxation among policy specialists. Indeed, until recently, all of the federal government's transfer programs (such as old age security, the guaranteed income supplement, and family allowances) were delivered outside the tax system and made relatively little use of income testing. Instead, they were largely demogrants, reflections of the principle of universality that dominated the post-war welfare state. The idea of targeting transfers has recently become much more fashionable, in part no doubt because of the imperatives of budget discipline.

An important recent innovation in the federal tax system has been the use of refundable tax credits—the GST credit and the child tax benefit. Refundable tax credits have the potential to convert the income tax system into a proper tax-transfer system. They take advantage of the principle of self-reporting, which keeps their administrative costs low (but also creates the possibility of errors, intentional or otherwise). In addition, it is possible to make them conditional on criteria, including family income and various demographic indicators, that can be monitored through the income tax system. Against these advantages, however, must be set the fact that transfers delivered through the tax system have a limited ability to respond to changes in a recipient's circumstances over a short period. As well, they cannot be based on indicators of need that are too detailed for the income tax system to pick up, such as expenditures of various types or housing requirements. Thus they are best suited to assist those whose incomes are low over long periods.

These shortcomings reinforce the need to complement transfers delivered through the tax system with transfers delivered by social agencies, which have the ability to monitor applicants ex ante to determine who is in need and how much they need. Social workers can target assistance to those most in need on the basis of criteria more general than income or observable demographic characteristics, and they can respond quickly to changes in circumstances. They can also monitor the job-search activities of applicants.

In the end, a balance must be struck between transfers delivered through the tax system and those delivered through the welfare system. Ideally, the two systems would be coordinated. The difficulty is that they are the creatures of two different levels of government. Nevertheless, some co-ordination is desirable to ensure that the structure of marginal tax rates provides proper incentives to work and to save. It has been alleged, for example, that the welfare system has excessively high clawback rates for transfers to poor individuals who earn income. Similarly, a major objection to the federal government's proposed—but subsequently abandoned—seniors benefit was that it imposed high implicit tax rates on savings for retirement. It is obviously important to avoid high implicit marginal tax rates in circumstances of this kind. It may even be desirable that marginal income tax rates at the lower end of the income scale be negative; that is, that there be some positive inducement for low-income individuals to increase their labour supply. The case for wage subsidies for low-income persons who receive transfers is now well established in the literature.[6] In addition to inducing low-skilled persons to enter the labour force, wage subsidies help to offset the substantial implicit tax rate on labour supply of the sales and payroll tax systems, and to reduce the involuntary unemployment induced by firms that offer high wages in order to encourage their workers to be productive (the so-called efficiency-wage concept).

## Targeting Criteria for Transfers to the Poor

The strategy of using refundable tax credits to deliver transfers to the poor was innovative not only in its use of the income tax system as a redistributive mechanism, but also in its choice of criteria for eligibility for those transfers. As we noted in chapter 3, the credits are based not on individual income as defined by the income tax system but on both family income and the number and age of children. The welfare system too uses notions of need that are somewhat divorced from standard income measures, such as expenditure requirements. This raises the issue of the appropriate criteria to be used in targeting transfers to the poor.

The traditional view might be that the transfer side of the tax system should be treated symmetrically with the tax side, and that consequently some notion of comprehensive income should be used to determine the size of transfers. Recent literature on the targeting of transfers, however, has argued that income may not be an adequate basis for targeting transfers to the poor.[7] For one thing, income as conventionally measured may not be a good indicator of individual (or household) well-being. Different households have different preferences and needs, and targeting transfers on the basis of factors that reflect these preferences and needs would improve the effectiveness of transfer policies. Factors that may be relevant include household size and composition, disability, location, and employment status. More accurate targeting could improve the cost-effectiveness of transfer programs: the more successful a given program is in targeting those in need, the lower will be the cost to the treasury of delivering a given level of support to the poor.

[6] For example, see the discussion in Michael Keen, "Peculiar Institutions: A British Perspective on Tax Policy in the United States" (December 1997), 50 *National Tax Journal* 779-802.

[7] See Dominique van de Walle and Kimberley Nead, eds., *Public Spending and the Poor: Theory and Evidence* (Baltimore: Johns Hopkins Press for the World Bank, 1995).

There is another, somewhat more subtle reason, one that the literature on optimal redistribution has emphasized, why targeting transfers on the basis of observable individual characteristics other than income might improve the efficiency of the redistributive mechanism.[8] The argument is that income, in addition to being a very imperfect indicator of individual well-being, is at least in part determined by individuals themselves. If the tax-transfer system redistributes according to income, persons who are capable of earning a relatively high income will be tempted to masquerade as low-productivity persons by earning a low income and thus obtain transfers intended for low-income persons. In these circumstances, the use of indicators other than income might discourage mimicking behaviour of this kind and allow the system of redistribution to be more effective in getting funds to those that need them most. Of course, the precise way in which transfers should be targeted is very much a matter of ongoing debate.

## Competitiveness and Taxes

We have stressed the fact that the world economy is increasingly open and interdependent. Our producers face ever-tougher competition in domestic markets for goods and services and enjoy ever-greater opportunities to exploit large-scale international markets. Capital and businesses are becoming increasingly mobile. Even labour, especially highly skilled labour, can move among countries more readily than it could in the past. In particular, the free trade agreement with the United States has increased the opportunities for the more desirable workers in both countries to relocate. All of these factors make it mandatory to ensure that our tax system facilitates the ability of Canadians to compete.

Competitiveness does not imply that all firms should succeed, or that we be good at all lines of business. Instead, the Canadian economy should focus on the activities in which it has a comparative advantage in the international economy. Comparative advantage is best determined by the price mechanism: activities that are successful on the basis of market prices alone are those that have a comparative advantage. A competitive tax system is therefore one that is neutral with respect to market decisions, except to the extent that market prices clearly do not reflect social benefits and costs. Apparent externalities that cause market prices to diverge from social benefits and costs include environmental externalities and the externalities of knowledge that arise from investment in R & D and human capital. Apart from correcting for externalities of this kind, the tax system should not systematically favour some activities over others and to the extent possible, given other objectives, should not provide incentives for mobile factors and businesses to leave the country.

---

[8] For a further discussion of this point, see Robin Boadway, "Public Economics and the Theory of Public Policy" (November 1997), 30 *Canadian Journal of Economics* 753-72.

These considerations favour a tax system whose primary taxes are as broadly based as possible and have uniform rates. The Canadian tax system falls short of this description in a number of respects. It is well documented, for example, that the Canadian business tax system discriminates against service and tertiary industries, and in favour of manufacturing and resource industries.[9] This bias is a result of several features of the system, including a preferential tax rate for manufacturing and processing activities, depreciation rates that are sometimes excessive, rapid writeoffs for capital expenditures in the resource industries, and selective investment tax credits.

The present tax system also discriminates implicitly against small, growing firms and those that involve themselves in risky activities. The discrimination arises largely from the fact that firms in a loss position are treated asymmetrically relative to firms in a tax-paying position. The system also makes it more difficult for smaller firms to compete by affording preferential treatment to retained earnings as a source of financing: larger firms have access to more internal financing than smaller firms do.

The level of taxes is another source of competitive disadvantage. Canada's high business tax rates may lead firms to locate outside of Canada rather than in Canada. They may also erode the Canadian tax base by inducing multi-national firms to shift their incomes abroad by means of various tax-planning devices (such as debt financing and transfer pricing).

Canada's high personal tax rates, especially for persons at the upper end of the income scale, may make Canada less attractive than other countries to highly skilled workers and professionals. Not only will these persons prefer to reside abroad, but the firms that hire them will also be induced to locate abroad. Of course, this conclusion assumes that the high taxes are not fully offset by a high level of public services to the same mobile persons, but it seems likely that the assumption is a valid one.

All of these factors constrain governments' ability to implement their own policies. If tax rates in the United States are significantly lower than tax rates in Canada, that circumstance in itself may be enough to discourage firms from starting or expanding operations in Canada. Canadian policy makers cannot ignore this possibility in deciding on the level of tax rates in Canada.

## Growth and Productivity

One of the main concerns that faces policy makers today is the slowdown in productivity growth over the past two decades. Governments that long relied on income growth as a source of additional tax revenues are now faced with the more painful prospect of funding new initiatives from higher tax rates.

---

[9] This point is fully documented in Canada, *Report of the Technical Committee on Business Taxation* (Ottawa: Department of Finance, April 1998). The recommendations of this committee, which have been set out in chapter 4, are largely based on making the tax system as neutral as possible for competitive reasons.

As the population ages and ever-fewer working persons are called on to support the demands of an ever-larger retirement population, the imperative to encourage growth becomes more apparent. Per-capita income growth arises from a variety of sources. Investment increases the ratio of capital to labour, and this "capital deepening" will cause wages to rise. An increase in investment, however, is likely to be no more than a temporary source of productivity growth. Permanent growth requires improvements in technology, including both cost-reducing new processes and the discovery of new products. It is important, therefore, that the tax system be favourable to investment that promotes technological progress.

This investment can take several forms. Investment in R & D, obviously, may lead to new knowledge that in turn leads to technological progress. Investment in physical capital too may lead to improvements in productivity. New capital embodies the latest techniques of production, and it also provides opportunities for management and workers to gain experience and knowhow on the job. Investment in human capital too improves the skills of workers and professionals.

For some investments in these categories, the market will provide an appropriate reward. Firms that invest more will enjoy higher productivity and earn more profits. But other investments will yield productivity increases whose benefits do not accrue to the investors alone. Secondary benefits are especially likely to arise if the productivity gain results from new knowledge that other firms can readily appropriate. In these circumstances, it may enhance efficiency to provide incentives to investment through the tax system.

It is difficult, however, to know when secondary benefits are present. By their very nature, they are not priced by the market. Moreover, there are always some winners and some losers, and even the market does not know which investments will fall into which category. Consequently, it is also difficult to target tax incentives to the right sorts of investments. One could argue, accordingly, that incentives to invest should be broadly based and available to all investment—or, at least, that the tax system should not discourage any investment.

Again, there are three forms of investment that the tax system should take particular pains not to discourage—investment in physical capital, investment in R & D, and investment in human capital. By and large, the tax system treats the latter two liberally. Investment in R & D benefits from both a rapid writeoff and the scientific research and experimental development (SR & ED) tax credit, which we discussed in chapter 4. As the Mintz committee pointed out, Canadian tax incentives for R & D are among the most generous in the world—so generous that the committee recommended reducing them.

Investment in human capital too is treated well. Although the tax system does not provide any explicit incentives for investment in human capital, firms in a tax-paying position can effectively write it off immediately. Quite apart from the tax incentives, firms benefit from the enhancement of human capital provided by a subsidized education system. Whether the tax incentives and the subsidies are sufficient to compensate for the externalities that arise from investment in human capital is, of course, difficult to know for certain, but the incentives are probably as generous as it is reasonable for them to be in the absence of more information.

Investment in physical capital is not treated nearly as well as investment in R & D or human capital. Indeed, the marginal tax rates on investment in physical capital are especially high in the service and high-tech sectors—the very sectors that are most likely to achieve technological innovations. The problem is aggravated by the fact that the tax system's failure to allow full loss offsetting discriminates against risky ventures. Innovation, of course, is risky virtually by definition.

## The Taxation of Capital Income

The extent to which capital income should be taxed is one of the most contentious issues in tax policy. On the one hand, capital income apparently accrues disproportionately to higher-income persons, so failure to tax it seems to be inequitable—all the more so to the extent that capital income is obtained from inherited wealth. On the other hand, if the bulk of inherited wealth is passed on to the next generation, taxing the capital income that it generates may result in double taxation. As to capital income earned from ordinary savings, it simply reflects a person's level of earnings. If the earnings are taxed progressively, it is not clear that the capital income has to be taxed as well. If the tax system needs to be more progressive, it might be better to make the rate structure applicable to earnings more progressive and, if necessary, to tax transfers of wealth separately—a point we shall discuss later.

A tax base that excludes capital income has a number of advantages in its own right. For one thing, it does not discourage saving, including saving for retirement, and there may be good reasons to increase the level of savings in the economy. More savings provide more finance for investment, which may be beneficial for employment and growth of the economy. As well, the more that persons save for their own retirement the less dependent they will be on the public purse later in life. Equity arguments too may favour exempting capital income, or sheltering savings from taxation. Tax systems that exempt capital income, or that allow taxpayers to shelter savings from income taxation through registered savings plans, are equivalent (in present-value terms) to taxes based on consumption. Many would argue that consumption is a more equitable basis for taxation than is income. As we discussed in chapter 2, the argument is summarized in the notion that consumption, not income, is what determines a person's well-being. Alternatively, as Kaldor put it in his seminal book *The Expenditure Tax*, it is better to tax persons on what they take out of the social pot (their consumption) than on what they put into it (their income).[10] It is important to recognize that adopting consumption as a tax base need not detract from vertical equity.

---

[10] Nicholas Kaldor, *An Expenditure Tax* (London: Allen & Unwin, 1955).

The rate structure that one applies to a personal consumption base can be as progressive as one wants it to be.

There are also administrative advantages to sheltering capital income from taxation. These advantages stem from the fact that it is virtually impossible to include capital income properly in the tax base. Some forms of capital income are very difficult to measure, including imputed rent on consumer durables such as housing, the return on human capital investment, accrued capital gains, and capital income from unincorporated businesses. The difficulty of taxing capital income is even more pronounced in an open economy, in which assets can be shifted across borders at will. In fact, if one also takes sheltered retirement savings (RPPs and RRSPs) into account, the proportion of capital income that the tax base excludes at present is so substantial that the personal tax is closer to being an expenditure tax than it is to being a comprehensive income tax.

There are also "second-best" arguments for relieving capital income of some taxation at the personal level. Elsewhere in the tax system there are taxes that impinge indirectly on capital or its income. Property taxes levied at the provincial/municipal level are effectively taxes on some forms of capital. The corporate income tax is in part a tax on capital in the corporation, at least to the extent that corporate tax payments are not fully integrated with personal taxes.

The literature on optimal taxation reinforces all of these arguments by suggesting that a fully optimal tax system that takes efficiency and equity into account would apply much lower tax rates to capital income than to labour income. Indeed, the tax rate on capital income would not even necessarily be positive rather than negative.[11]

These arguments have led many tax policy experts to advocate moving to a fully fledged consumption-based personal tax system. As we noted in chapter 2, this advocacy includes influential reports from the US Treasury, the Meade committee in the United Kingdom, and both the Economic Council of Canada and the Macdonald royal commission in Canada. No country has as yet abandoned the income tax for a consumption tax, but most countries do have various ways of sheltering capital income from taxation, such as retirement savings schemes, heavy reliance on consumption and payroll taxes, and exemptions of various forms of capital income. Given the importance of the national savings rate, the issue of the taxation of capital income will no doubt remain on the policy agenda.

## Wealth Taxation

Wealth taxation may be defined broadly or narrowly. In its broadest context, it may include taxes on the ownership of assets (an annual net wealth tax on

---

[11] This literature is summarized in Robin Boadway and David Wildasin, "Taxation and Savings: A Survey" (August 1994), 15 *Fiscal Studies* 19-63.

the value of all property, including the value of human capital; a paid-up capital tax on the net worth of businesses; and property taxes), taxes on transfers (death and gift taxes and transfer taxes, primarily those that apply to land transactions), and taxes on purchases (excise tax on capital goods, for example).[12] The term "wealth tax," however, usually refers only to the first two categories. For the purposes of the discussion here, wealth taxation refers to a wealth transfer tax or an annual wealth tax.

Although Canada does have taxes that are levied indirectly on wealth itself (property taxes and corporate capital taxes), it is one of the few OECD countries that does not currently have a wealth tax that is levied directly on individuals, such as a wealth transfer tax[13] or an annual wealth tax[14] (it does, however, tax the deemed realization of accrued gains on capital assets at death). This has not always been the case, however.[15] In 1972, the federal government vacated the gift and estate tax fields,[16] leaving it to the provinces to decide whether they wanted to impose their own taxes on these two revenue sources. Initially, all of the provinces except Alberta adopted succession duties and gift taxes; by the mid-1980s, however, every government in Canada had dropped them. Their termination resulted from a number of factors, including the relatively small sums of revenue generated, high administrative and compliance (enforcement) costs, and tax competition among the provinces—once one province had eliminated them, other provinces followed.

## A Wealth Transfer Tax

A wealth transfer tax may be an estate tax, an inheritance tax or succession duty, an accessions tax, or a gift tax.[17] An estate tax is levied on total wealth

---

[12] For a description of these taxes, see Jack M. Mintz, "The Role of Wealth Taxation in the Overall Tax System" (September 1991), 17 *Canadian Public Policy* 248-63, at 250-51.

[13] Probate fees do exist, but they do not apply to gifts or to several types of property transferred at death, such as pensions, life insurance, and jointly owned property. They are levied on the value of property that is transmitted under a will. In most provinces, the maximum rate varies between $3 and $7 per $1,000. In Ontario and British Columbia, however, the rates on estate assets in excess of $50,000 are $15 and $14, respectively. In Alberta, the probate fee is capped at $6,000 once the estate reaches $1,000,000. In Quebec, a flat nominal charge applies to holograph wills and wills made in the presence of witnesses. It is not necessary in Quebec to probate notarial wills. Some observers have argued that a probate fee is a wealth transfer tax, but it is more appropriately characterized as a user fee to cover the cost of processing wills.

[14] Organisation for Economic Co-operation and Development, *Revenue Statistics of OECD Member Countries, 1965-1996* (Paris: OECD, 1997); and Richard M. Bird, "The Taxation of Personal Wealth in International Perspective" (September 1991), 17 *Canadian Public Policy* 322-34.

[15] For a historical discussion of personal wealth taxation in Canada, see Roger S. Smith, *Personal Wealth Taxation: Canadian Tax Policy in a Historical and an International Setting*, Canadian Tax Paper no. 97 (Toronto: Canadian Tax Foundation, 1993), chapter 6.

[16] For a discussion of why the federal government abolished these taxes, see Ontario, *Fair Taxation in a Changing World: Report of the Ontario Fair Tax Commission* (Toronto: University of Toronto Press in cooperation with the Ontario Fair Tax Commission, 1993), 361-63.

[17] *Report of the Technical Committee on Business Taxation*, supra footnote 9, at A.4.

transferred at death; it generally provides a basic exemption and has a rate structure that varies with the size of the estate. Inheritance taxes or succession duties are paid by the beneficiary. An accessions tax is imposed on the recipient of gifts and bequests at a rate that is generally determined by the amount received from all sources on a lifetime basis. A gift tax, based on the transfer of wealth during the life of a donor, usually complements a death tax; its function is to prevent taxpayers from escaping tax by disposing of assets before death.

There are four important arguments in favour of a wealth transfer tax. The strongest is based on equity:[18] a wealth transfer tax enhances the overall progressivity of the tax system and ensures that it is based on ability to pay. In Canada, even a wealth transfer tax applied at a fixed rate would be progressive, since the ratio of wealth to income tends to increase as income rises. For example, it has been estimated that the richest 2 percent of the population in Canada holds 30 percent of the wealth.[19]

The second argument is that a wealth tax will ensure that at least some tax is collected from taxpayers who have avoided personal income taxes.

Third, by treating gifts and bequests as a form of consumption expenditure by the donor and not permitting the donor to deduct them from income, a tax on gifts and inheritances may assist in achieving a comprehensive income tax base. To accommodate the concern that income or wealth transferred from one spouse to another may not, in reality, increase the ability of the recipient to command goods and services, these transfers should be exempt from tax. Similarly, income passed to other family members should be taxed only in part; specifically, the portion of income on which the tax is paid should vary inversely with the "closeness" of the donor to the recipient. This treatment taxes the family unit rather than the individual, an approach that has been suggested for all forms of income and transfers (see chapters 2, 3, and 8) if the objective is to achieve more equity in the overall tax system.

Finally, wealth transfer taxes are believed to have relatively little effect on the savings decisions of taxpayers during their active years and therefore little effect on overall economic activity. Consequently, they may be more efficient than most other taxes.

Critics of wealth transfer taxes advance five main arguments.[20] The first is that wealth taxes may force taxpayers who are income-poor but asset-rich to

---

[18] For strong arguments and recommendations in favour of a wealth transfer tax for Ontario, see *Fair Taxation in a Changing World*, supra footnote 16, at chapter 19.

[19] James B. Davies, "The Distributive Effects of Wealth Taxes" (September 1991), 17 *Canadian Public Policy* 279-308.

[20] The strongest and most recent criticisms of a wealth tax appear in *Report of the Technical Committee on Business Taxation*, supra footnote 9, at A.4 to A.7.

dispose of assets in order to pay the tax. This is similar to the argument that property taxes may force individuals to sell their property in order to pay the property tax—an argument that has been countered by the introduction in some provinces of tax-deferral schemes, tax relief, or reverse mortgages.

The second argument is that the taxation of wealth involves unfair double taxation—assets subject to taxation under a wealth tax were purchased with accumulated savings that have already been taxed under an income tax. This argument has some shortcomings, however. First, if a wealth tax collects taxes from individuals who would otherwise not pay income taxes, then double taxation does not exist. Even if it is argued that double taxation exists, however, it is possible to question the merit of the argument that wealth taxation is unfair. The income tax is levied on the donor, whereas the wealth tax is levied on recipients. As well, to the extent that wealth increases one's ability to pay, its taxation does not represent double taxation, since a wealth transfer tax is directed at the additional taxable capacity associated with wealth. Finally, to argue that a tax on wealth constitutes double taxation may have no more validity than arguing that a tax on sales or a tax on property constitutes double taxation—one pays the income tax and, subsequently, sales and property taxes.[21]

The third argument is that the administration and compliance costs of a wealth tax could be high, since it would be necessary to introduce anti-avoidance provisions in order to counter the sophisticated tax-planning techniques that the tax would undoubtedly invoke.[22] In addition to being costly to administer, a wealth tax would likely generate relatively small sums of revenue. Few countries raise more than about 0.5 percent of GDP from wealth transfer taxes.[23]

Fourth, a wealth tax is not needed, since Canada already has deemed realization of capital assets at death; that is, any increase in the value of property held by a deceased person is subject (with some deferrals) to income tax in his final personal income tax return. Very few countries with wealth transfer taxes also have deemed realization. Indeed, the introduction of a wealth transfer tax in Canada when deemed realization exists would lead to double taxation and create pressure to relax the income tax rules for deemed realization at death.[24]

Finally, provincial experience with wealth transfer taxes suggests that the only effective tax would be one at the federal level. Otherwise, collection costs would be high and capital would move from province to province to avoid the tax (the federal government would face the same problem at the international

---

[21] *Fair Taxation in a Changing World*, supra footnote 16, at 370.

[22] Robert D. Brown, "A Primer on the Implementation of Wealth Taxes" (September 1991), 17 *Canadian Public Policy* 335-50, at 348-49.

[23] *Revenue Statistics in OECD Member Countries*, supra footnote 14.

[24] *Report of the Technical Committee on Business Taxation*, supra footnote 9, at A.5.

level). A federal tax, however, would not be practicable unless the provinces agreed to it—an unlikely outcome given Canada's recent record in federal-provincial cooperation.

## An Annual Net Wealth Tax

An annual net wealth tax is based on the net wealth of a taxpayer, measured annually. Although net wealth taxes are not used as extensively as wealth transfer taxes, they are used in some OECD countries.[25] Typically, these taxes are levied on a relatively broad base—namely, the total value of each household's worldwide assets less the total value of its worldwide liabilities and the total value of its exempt assets. Exempt assets generally include pensions, household and personal effects, life insurance, modest personal savings, works of art, and scientific and historical collections. The net value of owner-occupied homes is usually included in the tax base, but special valuation rules apply to agricultural land and small businesses.

The chief argument in favour of an annual net wealth tax is the same as that for a wealth transfer tax—that it would increase the fairness of the tax system. Proponents have argued that it is fairer than income taxation as a way of distributing the tax burden, since it requires those with substantial assets that are not producing immediate revenues to pay current taxes. It has also been argued that since the tax is based on net wealth rather than the income from wealth it does less to distort economic behaviour than an income tax does and is therefore more efficient. Finally, proponents have suggested that a wealth tax is more difficult to evade than an income tax—a feature that may be especially important for a tax system in less-developed countries.

Critics, on the other hand, argue that the taxation of certain forms of savings under the current Canadian income tax system already constitutes a form of personal wealth taxation and that to tax these savings further under a wealth tax would constitute double taxation. The value of certain other assets is also already subject to tax; for example, property taxes that exceed the value of services provided (see chapter 7) and capital taxes paid on corporate capital (see chapter 4) may be deemed to be forms of wealth taxation. The critics also argue that an annual net wealth tax would reduce the return on savings; constitute an additional burden on assets acquired from savings, and thus possibly discourage Canadians from saving for retirement, education, and so on; be expensive to administer; provide incentives for taxpayers to create ingenious schemes to avoid the tax; and generate relatively small amounts of revenue.[26]

## Should Canada Implement Wealth Taxation?

There is no clear answer to this question. In 1993, the Ontario Fair Tax Commission concluded that Ontario should introduce a wealth transfer tax; in

---

[25] *Revenue Statistics of OECD Member Countries*, supra footnote 14.

[26] *Report of the Technical Committee on Business Taxation*, supra footnote 9, at A.6 to A.7.

1998, the Technical Committee on Business Taxation argued against any additional form of wealth tax for Canada. The difference in opinion is largely attributable to the fact that the commission and the committee assigned different weights to the arguments for and against a wealth tax that we outlined above. In any case, there has been no groundswell of public support for a wealth tax and no political party appears to be offering wealth taxation as a serious alternative or supplement to existing taxes.[27]

If a decision were reached to implement a wealth tax, however, a consensus would likely emerge in favour of a wealth transfer tax (a conclusion reached by the Ontario Fair Tax Commission). The annual taxation of some savings and the existence of property and capital taxes mean that Canada already has some of the ingredients of an annual wealth tax. To stretch these taxes any further would almost certainly foster considerable taxpayer resistance. One can, however, make a serious and solid case for a wealth transfer tax. In spite of some administrative problems and the difficulty of implementing the tax in a way that would minimize taxpayer avoidance, a wealth transfer tax might produce a more equitable distribution of income without creating substantial economic distortion. Of course, if a wealth transfer tax were implemented, it would be necessary to re-evaluate the current policy of deeming realization of capital gains on a taxpayer's death, since this policy serves as a partial tax on the transfer of asset wealth at death.

## Indexing for Inflation

In addition to concerns about the personal tax base and the level of tax rates, there are concerns about the way in which income is measured in times of inflation. Rising price levels distort the intent of the tax system in a number of ways.

In the case of personal income taxation, three problems stand out. First, nominal capital income received may overstate the real return to capital. In the case of interest income, inflation will reduce the real value of the underlying asset on which interest is paid. Part of the nominal interest payment will simply offset the decline in the real value of the asset and not add anything to the purchasing power of households. Since the tax system does not account for this implicit decline in wealth, the tax base overstates true interest income. On the other hand, since share values presumably rise with inflation, this problem does not arise in the case of dividends, which are the return paid on shares. However, the nominal capital gains on shares will overstate the shares' value, and capital gains are not indexed for inflation, so the overstatement of value is not addressed in this case either. It is true that only three-quarters of capital gains are subject to taxation, but this arrangement may be more of a form of integration for corporate taxes withheld than a means of compensation for inflation. At least, that is how the Mintz committee viewed the three-quarters inclusion.

---

[27] Smith, supra footnote 15, at chapter 7.

The second problem at the personal tax level concerns the rate structure, which includes both the set of credits and the tax brackets. In the absence of indexation, increases in nominal income will increase the proportion of personal income that falls into a higher tax bracket and reduce the value of personal tax credits. The result will be an increase in taxes proportionately greater than the increase in nominal income. The Canadian tax system takes partial account of this problem by increasing both the level of credits and the boundaries of the tax brackets by the amount by which the increase in the consumer price index exceeds 3 percent. The effect of this absence of full indexation is bracket creep, which surreptitiously increases the average tax rate and generates more revenue for the government.

Partial indexation also applies to the transfers offered by the federal government through the tax system, the refundable tax credits, with the result that their value erodes over time. In 1986, an attempt by the federal government to shift from full to partial indexing of OAS/GIS payments met considerable political resistance and was abandoned. Critics have argued, however, that the continuing partial indexation of refundable tax credits amounts to "social policy by stealth"[28] and is highly regressive.

The absence of indexation also plagues the corporate tax system and the system of business taxation generally. Like capital income received by individuals, capital income received by corporations is not indexed—interest income and capital gains are taxed on a nominal basis. What is perhaps more important, however, interest costs are deductible on a nominal basis, an arrangement that overstates the true cost of interest financing. This policy provides a tax incentive for debt financing in times of inflation. Against this one must set the fact that indexation does not apply to other deductions for capital costs, including capital cost allowances on depreciable capital and writeoffs for inventory usage. Capital cost allowances are based on historic cost, which understates the cost of replacing the capital when it has reached the end of its useful life. Writeoffs for inventory are based on first-in-first-out (FIFO) accounting, which again understates the replacement cost. The net result of these two offsetting effects of inflation depends on the circumstances of each corporation—its reliance on debt financing, the amount of inventory it uses, and the age structure of its capital. Studies of how inflation affects the aggregate METRs of corporations suggest that on average inflation has relatively little effect on most forms of capital; the principle exception is inventories. Nevertheless, the effect on some firms may be significant.

The relatively low rates of inflation in recent years have blunted the effects of the absence of full indexing. Moreover, the revenue gains from bracket creep have been welcomed during a period in which governments have been primarily concerned with fighting budget deficits. As that era

---

[28] The term is attributable to Grattan Gray, "Social Policy by Stealth" (March 1990), 11 *Policy Options* 17-29. Grattan Gray was a pseudonym for Ken Battle, who now presides over the Caledon Institute for Social Policy.

passes, however, concern with the hidden effects of inflation on the tax system will likely surface again.

## Environmental Taxation

Environmental taxes are often recommended, and occasionally implemented, as a means of limiting production and consumption activities that would otherwise harm the environment. In the absence of any form of taxation or regulation, overproduction or overconsumption of the activity arises because the cost of the externality—the harm to the environment—is not captured in the pricing decision. The overproduction or overconsumption leads to a welfare or deadweight loss and a lower level of economic well-being than would otherwise exist.[29] One way to remove or reduce the deadweight loss is to implement a tax whose rate is equal to the marginal cost of the externality, which is the difference between the private marginal cost of production and the social marginal cost of production (private production costs plus the cost of the externality) at the allocatively efficient level of output.[30] If the tax rate is successfully matched with the marginal cost of the externality, the cost or price per unit of output rises, the level of output falls, the deadweight loss is reduced or eliminated, and society is better off. In practice, however, the social costs of pollution and other forms of environmental degradation are very difficult to quantify. Consequently, most current environmental taxes are based on a mix of factors, including environmental concerns, revenue objectives, and political considerations.

Governments at all levels in Canada have introduced taxes, tax provisions, and fees that are intended to control environmental problems. Thus the federal government and the provinces have introduced special writeoffs under the corporate income tax for investments in matters such as renewable energy and energy conservation, energy efficiency, water and air pollution control, and wetland rehabilitation. In addition, federal and provincial fuel taxes (see chapter 5) might be viewed as environmental taxes, although they were never introduced under this rationale and have never been based on any assessment of the cost of environmental damage. Provincial governments have also introduced vehicle efficiency taxes and excise duties on heavy vehicles, special tire taxes, and taxes on lead acid batteries, beverage containers, disposable diapers, and other commodities.[31] The intent is to discourage consumption of these pollution-generating items, although the revenue goes into the general fund. Municipal governments are making greater use of charges and taxes as means of minimizing environmental

---

[29] For a more detailed discussion of welfare, deadweight, or efficiency losses, see chapter 2.

[30] For a discussion of taxes and other market-based incentives that put an explicit price on pollution (subsidies, marketable emission permits, and deposit-refunds), see Nancy Olewiler, *Pricing and the Environment*, Discussion Paper Prepared for the Government and Competitiveness Project no. 93-22 (Kingston, Ont.: Queen's University, School of Policy Studies, 1993).

[31] *Report of the Technical Committee on Business Taxation*, supra footnote 9, at 9.1.

problems. Thus many municipalities have revised their user fees for water and sewerage and introduced fees for solid waste collection and disposal with environmental considerations in mind (see chapter 7).

In setting environmental taxes and charges, governments in Canada have not as a rule given priority to efficiency considerations. Yet it is important that environmental taxes or charges be designed to vary with the amount of emissions or environmental damage that a given activity creates. Otherwise, they will produce incentives to shift to untaxed or undertaxed forms of emissions and activities and lead to a misallocation of society's resources.

A recent report has recommended that the federal government replace its fuel excise tax (currently 10 cents per litre for gasoline and 4 cents per litre for diesel) with more broadly based environmental taxes.[32] The report notes that the existing fuel tax adversely affects the part of the transportation sector that competes with operators in the United States, who face lower excise-type taxes, and generally adds to the costs of Canadian businesses. It argues that a more appropriate base for the tax would be all major energy sources, including oil, natural gas, coal, biofuels, and electricity. Further, tax rates should reflect the environmental damage associated with energy sources. Similar recommendations have been made in connection with provincial environmental taxes and municipal water, sewer, and solid waste charges in Ontario.[33]

## Taxes Versus User Fees

Growing concern about tax burdens and about the quality (if not the quantity) of public services has led many citizens and policy analysts and a growing number of politicians to argue for greater reliance by governments on user fees or charges. Currently in Canada, revenues from the sale of goods and services (which are generally regarded as being user fees) account for about 4.5 percent of total federal government revenues, almost 3 percent of provincial and territorial own-source revenues, and more than 26 percent of municipal own-source revenues.[34] As these data suggest, user fees are most appropriate at the municipal level of government, since it is the level that provides most of the services that can be easily and properly priced (water, sewerage, recreation, public transit, and so on).

Although responses to the question "how far should user fees or charges be extended?" may vary, the choice between user fees and taxes should be based, in part at least, on the use of the revenues collected. If the purpose of the revenues is to fund public services, then the appropriate answer may be different from the answer that would be appropriate if their purpose were to stabilize economic activity, redistribute income, or expand economic growth.

---

[32] Ibid., at chapter 9.

[33] *Fair Taxation in a Changing World*, supra footnote 16, at chapters 25 and 26.

[34] Calculated from data from the Public Institutions Division of Statistics Canada.

In the case of public services, user fees are most appropriate for financing all or part of the cost of services whose specific beneficiaries can be identified, services that can be allocated to those who are willing to pay and whose non-users can be excluded from payment, and services whose per-unit costs it is possible to estimate. In financing services that provide benefits of a collective nature—benefits that cannot be allocated to specific individuals or properties—governments should rely on taxation. They should also use tax revenues when the object is to redistribute income, stabilize economic activity, or fund economic growth.

Where user fees are employed, there is a greater likelihood that society's resources will be allocated in an efficient, fair, and accountable manner. Allocative efficiency, fairness, and accountability are best achieved if the fee, charge, price, or tax per unit of output equals the extra cost of the last unit of output consumed (marginal cost-pricing). Setting the price, fee, or tax equal to the marginal cost (or a modification of it) has all the advantages of private sector pricing. It is efficient because it rations output to those who are willing to pay for the service and because it indicates to suppliers (governments or their delivery agents) the quantity and quality of output desired. It is fair because those who benefit from the service pay for it. It is accountable because the user is aware of the cost of the service and can judge whether the fee or charge warrants its consumption.[35]

## Profit-Insensitive Taxes

Profit-insensitive taxes are taxes paid by businesses that are unrelated to the profitability of the business. Examples in Canada include the capital taxes and payroll taxes levied by the federal government and the provinces and the property taxes levied by local governments. Recent growth in the revenue yield of these taxes has generated considerable criticism in the business community, but it is their impact on the allocation of society's resources that is potentially more serious and that must be addressed.[36] A tax is allocatively efficient if the tax rate equals the extra cost of the last unit of public service consumed, or if the tax captures all or some of the economic rent generated by the producing unit, or if the tax can be passed on without causing any change in economic behaviour. Resources will not be allocated efficiently, however, if there is no correlation between the tax and public service provision, or if the tax does not capture economic rents, or if it causes individuals to alter their behaviour.

The questions that surfaces, then, is, to what extent are profit-insensitive taxes in Canada distortionary or allocatively inefficient? Since there is no evidence that profit-insensitive taxes capture any economic rent, the issue is whether they are related to the cost of public services consumed or whether

---

[35] For a more detailed discussion of user fees, see chapter 5.

[36] *Report of the Technical Committee on Business Taxation*, supra footnote 9, at chapter 2.

they affect economic behaviour in some distorting way. Although the payroll taxes levied by the federal government and the provinces are not related to the cost of public services consumed, this does not mean that they are distortionary. Most studies suggest that in the longer run payroll taxes on employers are largely shifted to employees. This circumstance should mitigate their longer-run impact on the cost of hiring, and make them relatively neutral in their impact on economic behaviour. In the short run, however, because of economic lags in adjusting to the tax, employers may bear part of it. As well, payroll taxes may exacerbate the impact of existing rigidities in the labour market (such as unions), and they may have a disproportionate impact on low-wage employment.[37] To the extent that payroll taxes drive up labour costs, Canada's competitive position is weakened and employment opportunities are reduced. In addition, high labour costs may cause businesses to substitute machinery and equipment for labour in the production process.

Capital taxes are levied by both the federal government and the provinces. Provincial capital taxes and the portion of the federal capital tax that cannot be offset by federal corporate income taxes (see chapter 4) effectively represent a fixed cost to business—a cost that is neither related to public services consumed nor likely to be passed on without distorting economic behaviour. Similarly, there is some evidence that non-residential property taxes (discussed in chapter 7) exceed the cost of the municipal services consumed by the non-residential sector.[38] Once again, this is a fixed cost that businesses must pay and that may very well distort economic behaviour.

Profit-insensitive taxes that lead to overtaxation of businesses result in less economic activity, lower output, fewer jobs, and a less competitive business environment. Canadian governments should seriously consider replacing profit-insensitive taxes with taxes that are more neutral or less distorting. Profit-based taxes and taxes such as the GST encourage a more efficient use of resources, improve the prospects for economic growth and job creation, and lead to greater competitiveness internationally. The last consideration is particularly important, given Canada's heavy reliance on exports and resources and its exposure to unstable world prices.

---

[37] See the discussion in chapter 6.

[38] Harry M. Kitchen and Enid Slack, *Business Property Taxation*, Discussion Paper Prepared for the Government and Competitiveness Project no. 93-24 (Kingston, Ont.: Queen's University, School of Policy Studies, 1993), 19-30.

# Index

Abbott, Michael, on payroll tax, 330
Accessions tax, wealth transfer tax, 485-88
Administration and compliance
   commodity taxes, 294
   comprehensive tax base, difficulties,
     95-96
   consumption taxes, 97-98
   costs, 84-86
   decentralization, effect on, 469-70
   payroll taxes, 337-38
   personal income taxes, 151-52
   transfer programs, 447-48
Allocation of tax, 468-75
Alternative minimum tax (AMT), 141-42

Ballentine, J. Gregory, on property tax,
   357-58
Basic federal tax, calculation of, 13, 125-26,
   128-29, 131, 133-39
Beach, Charles, on payroll tax, 329, 330
Beggar-thy-neighbour policies, interprovin-
   cial competition, 31-32, 174, 261, 468, 269
Benefit principle, 86-88
Bischoff, Charles W., on effect of corporate
   tax, 229
Boadway, Robin, on incidence analysis, 218,
   224, 234
Bracket creep, 6, 105, 167, 490
Browning, Edgar K., on tax burden, 69
Bruce, Neil, on effect of corporate tax, 234
Business income, 121
Business tax, 26, 272-78

Caisses populaires, deductions, 194
Canada Assistance Plan (CAP), 425-26, 430
Canada health and social transfer (CHST),
   21-22, 425-26, 430
Canada Pension Plan (CPP)
   contributions, 131, 318, 418
   coverage, 317
   disability benefits, 420-21
   financing of, 421-22
   pension reform, 453
   retirement, effect on, 439-40
   retirement benefits, 418, 420
   savings, effect on, 83, 446-47
   survivors' benefits, 420
Canadian child tax benefit (CCTB), 417

Canadian-controlled private corporations
   (CCPCs), 16, 180, 199-200
Capital, mobility, 3, 27-28
Capital accumulation, 83-84
Capital cost allowance (CCA)
   acceleration of, 182
   calculation of, 184
   categories of assets, 184-85
   deductions for, 183-88
   eligibility, 185
   imputed costs, lack of, 250-53
   ineligible purchase, 186
   manufacturing, 188
   mining, 187
   obligation to claim, 186
   oil and gas, 187-88
   patents and licences, 186
   R & D, 187
   recapture, 186-87
   rentals, 186
   service lives, 186
Capital expenses, 105-6, 181
Capital gains
   charities, 153
   comprehensive income base, 91
   defined, 153
   economic growth, 155-56
   illusory, effect of inflation, 103-4
   indexation, 155
   individual corporation, benefits of, 208-9
   joint ownership, 156
   locked-in effect, 156
   outline, 153-54
   preferential tax treatment, 154
   taxable, by income group, 154
Capital income, 48
   distortions, 75-76
   inflation indexation, 85, 103-4, 489, 490
   intercorporate flowthrough, 261-62
   international, Mintz committee recom-
     mendations, 276-77
   preferential treatment, 42-43
   rent on owner-occupied housing, 148-49
   rental income from real property, 104
   tax reform issue, 483-84
Capital investment, tax reform issue, 482-83
Capital taxes, as supplements to corporate
   income taxes, 18, 203-4